# YOCKEY: A FASCIST ODYSSEY

KERRY BOLTON

# YOCKEY

## A FASCIST ODYSSEY

ARKTOS
LONDON 2018

Printed in the United Kingdom.

| | |
|---|---|
| **ISBN** | 978-1-912079-15-5 (Paperback)<br>978-1-912079-12-4 (Hardback)<br>978-1-912079-14-8 (Ebook) |
| **EDITING** | Sam Richardson<br>John Bruce Leonard<br>Charles Lyons |
| **COVER AND LAYOUT** | Tor Westman |

www.arktos.com

# Table of Contents

# Foreword

*by Dr Tomislav Sunic*

An experienced reader can tell a well-written scholarly book by first checking the author's style and then the size and the quality of his footnotes. There is no lack of either in Kerry Bolton's prose; neither in the book's bibliographic substance, nor in Bolton's very readable style. This is the first time an exhaustive work on the prominent Euro-American fascist activist and philosopher, Francis Parker Yockey, is being offered to a wider readership in the English-speaking world. Naturally, for a starter, a big question that comes to mind immediately is: 'What's the point of reading Bolton's thick book and how relevant is Yockey's anti-communism and anti-liberalism in dealing with the ongoing decay of the multicultural West, which is currently subject to an open invasion of non-European masses?' Since Bolton often uses the German word *Zeitgeist* in his description of the dominant political ideas of Yockey's times, a neophyte might likewise wonder if and how Yockey's political prognoses are being validated by the dominant political ideas of our time. For many nationalist old-timers, both in Europe and America, Yockey is a household name that is indispensable in studying the intellectual developments of cultural fascism. Yet for many young identitarians today, regardless of whether they identify as alt-right, new right or traditionalist, the name Yockey, along with his magnum opus *Imperium*, may sound a bit outdated. Several years ago, when Bolton started writing this book, he was aware that Yockey, with all his literary baggage and worldwide acquaintances, would today become more timely than ever before. The successors to Yockey's Bolshevik arch-enemies have replaced their erstwhile iconography of the cosmopolitan and borderless proletariat with a new liberal imagery of mixed-raced and stateless pederasts accompanied by masses of non-European migrants. Yockey's enemies are alive and thriving, irrespective of their change in ideological color.

As far as the composition of the book is concerned, Bolton provides a wide historical-literary framework in which Yockey serves as a springboard, or better yet as a major sidekick, for a better understanding of similar and like-minded authors and political protagonists of his times. In the following pages, Bolton first goes into the clarification of political concepts and their semantic distortions that have been orchestrated by the victorious communist and liberal elites over the past 70 years. While using Yockey as a guide, Bolton sheds additional light on the values of the modern system that keeps rewriting the intellectual history of the West as it best fits its mercantile and rootless agenda. 'A System that once produced Shakespeare but now produces sitcom scriptwriters; that once birthed Beethoven and Mozart but now lauds Lady Gaga.' This process of cultural degeneration did not, however, start with Lady Gaga or the recent welcoming calls to millions of non-White migrants. It has its roots in the eighteenth century Enlightenment and its political offshoots in America and France. The secular religion of human rights subsequently gave birth to communism and then to its modern ersatz, multiculturalism. The following chapters also explain how the reception of Yockey's work varied among different European and American identitarians, with some calling Yockey 'anti-American' and others praising him to the heavens.

Yockey's own criticism of 'Americanism' and the 'money-based Puritan culture of WASP America, where Jews ... could buy their influence' must have played a role after the Second World War in his registering on the FBI's radar. His critical remarks about the American Jews and their role in the media, the combination of which we call today in a coded language 'fake news', earned him a great deal of intellectual respect among prominent European nationalist scholars who had traditionally looked down upon America as a stray-away and uncultured Jew-run entity. Yockey's openly pro-German stance, especially when serving as a young attorney at the Wiesbaden show trials in 1946, must have been seen as an additional irritating detail for the American ruling class and several Jews on the bench. His openly pro-European, anti-communist and anti-liberal attitudes may be compared today with the views of some segments of the American alt-right, who are walking in Yockey's footsteps unawares, realizing that petty nationalist inter-White squabbles, tribal infighting amidst traditionalists, racialists, right-wing Catholics, Protestants and pagans, are outdated and need to go away.

One name that repeatedly springs up in Bolton's pages is Oswald Spengler. Indeed, the whole of Yockey's work must be seen as a sequel to Spengler's *The Decline of the West,* where he radically rejects the money-obsessed capitalist West and its beacon, America. It is to the merit of Bolton that he does not just drop the names of dozens of American and European authors, scholars and activists, some of whom were close friends and acquaintances of Yockey, but instead tries to explain the context or background behind each person, organization and political concept under consideration. This is important insofar as Bolton's reader will come across numerous terms like 'ethical socialism' or 'Prussian socialism', with which Yockey is often associated, and whose historical meaning needs to be further explained to younger readers. Bolton's pages are literally teeming with quotes and citations, particularly in the realm of modern historiography and legal studies, especially in the chapters where Bolton examines the myth of the so-called freedom-loving West. The post-Second World War mass shootings of thousands of German POWs and mass rapes of German women were not just part of a well-recorded folklore among Soviet soldiers in vanquished Germany but also a customary, albeit well-hidden, escapade of many British and American soldiers 'showing the extent of the torture regime against Germans after the war'. Nowadays, we may all fake concern for victims of mass purges and communist killing fields in Eastern Europe in late 1945. However, one does not need to speculate much about those who served as role models to East European communists. After the Second World War, communist prosecutors and henchmen in Eastern Europe were only copying in a more brutal way the techniques of their former war allies. Well, the chickens have finally come home to roost. The new Brussels — guided liberal governance in Eastern Europe is largely staffed by former communist apparatchiks, or to put it more precisely, by the rebranded progeny of former communist cut-throats — with the full blessing of the 'free West'.

Yockey was a multilayered and multifarious character bursting with intellectual curiosity, which is highlighted in Bolton's subsequent descriptions dealing with Yockey's numerous peregrinations across Europe and his contacts with prominent post-fascist literati and aspiring nationalist leaders — at least those who had managed to evade the Allied rope. Ironically, the Western and American liberal world-improvers, at the beginning of the Cold War, were willy-nilly obliged to later tap into the expertise of their former foes. Yockey, as Bolton chronicles, was on good terms with numerous post-fascist figureheads — such as Giorgio Almirante, once a high-ranking politician in the late Mussolini government, who at the beginning of the Cold War played an important role in regrouping Italian nationalists. Yockey also nurtured ties with Sir Oswald Mosley, the former leader of the British Union of Fascists, as well as with the short-lived post-Second World War political party, the Socialist Reich Party of Germany, which had regrouped a large number of former National-Socialist members and former SS officers. Again, we need to revisit the famed notion of the *Zeitgeist*, the spirit of the time, which when Yockey was alive was very diffuse and liquid on all fronts: on the one hand staged trials and constant surveillance of former Nazi 'killers' were running full steam in the Eastern and Western jurisprudence; on the other, the Western occupying forces, headed by the American world-improvers, were getting ready for a full-scale military conflict against their former ally, the communist Soviet Union. Hence, the reason they needed to rely on the expertise of their former fascist foes. It is often forgotten that at the start of the Cold War, the occupying American authorities in Germany were reliant upon former German SS operatives, just as the build-up of the early *Bundeswehr* would have been nearly impossible without the prior consent of some former Wehrmacht officers. One may raise an additional philosophical question, which certainly crossed Yockey's mind when he had landed in prison in 1960: 'What would have happened if the Soviets and the Americans had entered into the military conflict by the early 1950s?' It is not hard to guess that Yockey himself would have played an additional historical role in America and Europe, and that his book *Imperium* would have likely shaped a new form of the *Zeitgeist* in students' curricula.

The following pages read like a lengthy, detailed police report on hundreds of unknown or forgotten individuals who nevertheless played an important role in determining Yockey's fate and who also had an enormous impact on political developments in Europe and America. Bolton also tackles the unavoidable theme of American Jews portrayed by Yockey and his fellow travellers as far more dangerous than Soviet Jews. Besides having archival value, this book is an important tool in studying the ongoing practice of criminalizing and pathologizing political opponents by the false use of the worn-out word 'fascism'. This word, which has now totally lost its original meaning, has become a means to silence political opponents and prevent serious scholarly inquiry. If the liberal-minded President of the United States, Donald Trump, or the liberal German Chancellor, Angela Merkel, are denounced by their detractors as 'fascists', then one must also give full credit to Yockey for trying to restore the true and original meaning of this word.

Dr Tomislav Sunic
Zagreb, Croatia
October 13, 2017

Francis Parker Yockey,

Notre Dame Year Book, 1941.

# Introduction

As one of Francis Parker Yockey's closest colleagues, John Anthony Gannon, stated, one does not just 'read' *Imperium* or even fully comprehend its philosophy on the rationalistic level; one intuits Yockey's thought. *Imperium* appeals to a different faculty of perception in a manner that books like *Das Kapital* or *The Wealth of Nations* never could. The closest parallel is the immediate connection one might feel with the *Bible*, *Koran* or *Bhagavad Gita*. *Imperium* is an act of Faith and Yockey wrote it for that Faith, which cannot be comprehended through the 'wisdom of this world' alone, in St. Paul's words, but which requires rather a feeling for the ebb and flow of History. It is a Faith for which Yockey died. Because it is one of *feeling with the blood*, it lies outside the ken of the liberal intelligentsia, political pundits and those who can only weigh and measure in all things.

This is why Yockey was rejected even by much of the 'Right' that can only weigh and measure, particularly in regard to 'race'. Ironically, while his most vehement critics were the Hitlerites of the Anglophone world, it was German veterans who were quick to appreciate Yockey. His philosophy is based on a German rather than an English worldview, the former being metaphysical, the latter materialistic or mercantile. Referring to a worldview as 'German' or 'English' indicates the time and space from which that worldview was given birth, not necessarily the nationality of the person expressing the new world-feeling. As Spengler pointed out, there are Germans who are imbued with the worldview of the English (those whom he and Yockey called the *Michel* element) and British such as Carlyle who embody the 'German' or, as Spengler put it, 'Prussian' spirit of the new epoch. Fortunately, there were some on the 'Right' in the Anglophone world who saw the fundamental value of Yockey's added perception in thinking—his *Cultural Vitalism*.

Yockey commences where Spengler stopped. To Spengler's cultural morphology, or the organic lifecycles of High Cultures, Yockey explained the factors of *Culture-distortion*, *Culture-retardation* and *Culture-parasitism*. This added faculty in perception enables us to see how pathologies work within the cultural organism and what antibodies are required to form a resistance, enabling the High Culture to proceed with its organic lifespan. Whatever else of Yockeyan thought might become historically passé, *Cultural Vitalism* will remain valid for the foreseeable future, or at least as long as there exists a culture-bearing stratum capable of discernment.

Moreover, while Spengler ended his final work, *The Hour of Decision*, with a clarion call for Western resistance, Yockey provided the fighting creed for Western resurgence, enlisting Spengler's morphology in active resistance against the forces of cultural pathology.

'Fascism' is referred to herein. The word is problematic because it has been ill-defined by academics at best. However, Yockey had no problem with the word. His close American colleague H Keith Thompson referred to himself in a series of articles as an 'American Fascist'. The European Liberation Front newsletter *Frontfighter* often used the word *Fascist* self-descriptively. If one wants a definition of Fascism then perhaps the obvious place to look would be original sources such as *The Doctrine of Fascism* by Mussolini and Giovanni Gentile, or insightful post-war assessments by those directly involved, such as Maurice Bardèche. Certainly, nothing is to be gained, other than sheer entertainment, from those who define 'Fascism' as anything and everything from General Pinochet to Donald Trump. Fortunately, in recent decades there have been some credible attempts by orthodox academics to define a 'generic Fascism' and the Israreli scholar Zeev Sternhell[1] and the Oxford scholar Roger Griffin are among the most worthwhile.[2]

Fascism was an answer to cultural crisis and moral decline. Fascism reasserted that the nation is an organic social unit, not a collection of individualities following separate ego-interests, whether in the form of the atomistic-individualism of Liberalism or the class-conflict of Marxism. This commonality of interests within a territory forms a 'people' and the unifying

1 Zeev Sternhell, *The Birth of Fascist Ideology* (Princeton University Press, 1994).

2 Roger Griffin, *Fascism* (Oxford University Press, 1995).

mechanism of that people is the State. The place of this people-nation-state in History will depend on geographic locality and the vicinity and types of other people-nation-states.

Fascism arose as an answer to the crisis of decline in nations after the cataclysm of World War I. Because of the universality of the crisis within Western Civilization, Fascism took on universal aspects despite its nationalism. Mussolini looked to the twentieth century as 'the Fascist century'. Certain idealists within the Fascist movements saw a new Europe emerging that would be united by an Idea and a Faith but would not be subjected to any one nation. The Waffen SS, with its foreign legions that came to outnumber the Germans in its ranks, was seen by many as a new European order in embryo. However, within Fascism there remained the counter-force of nineteenth-century national-chauvinism. Fascism was defeated by the combination of Eastern hordes mechanised with Western technics. Oswald Spengler had warned of this prospect in *The Hour of Decision*.

Many of those who survived the mass lynchings, 'denazification' and starvation of occupied Europe in the aftermath of World War II saw that the error of Fascism was that it had too often remained 'national' rather than pan-European. Europe stood prostrate between two non-Western powers, the USA and the USSR. It was debatable for many after the war as to which of these posed the greater menace. New movements soon emerged to fight for a united Europe. Into this milieu stepped a young American lawyer named Yockey, ostensibly as part of the anti-European occupation forces, imbued with the European spirit and with an Idea for the post-war era. Some saw him as an upstart — but nobody could deny his brilliance.

Yockey saw in Fascism a 'provisional' form of the embryonic Western Imperium. Indeed, he regarded the word 'Imperialist' as more aptly describing what was required to set a derailed Western Civilization back on the path of its destiny. This was not the imperialism of the nineteenth century, nor of any one particular colonial power, let alone the neo-imperialism of the USA, but the imperialism of Western Civilization as an organic unity. From Spengler, Yockey adopted the morphology of culture lifecycles. However, Yockey added an invaluable factor to this, that of *Cultural Vitalism*. This describes how a culture-organism can be infected with pathologies like any other organism.

Spengler had stated that a Civilization declines when at an advanced state of life it becomes thoroughly imbued with money-thinking. Then all values and arts can be bought and sold like commodities. This process describes the stage when a Civilization is opened to corruption. Yockey proceeded from this premise and added *Cultural Vitalism* to explain the manner by which pathogens are able to enter late-stage Civilization through *Culture-distortion*, *Culture-retardation* and *Culture-parasitism*.

Without succumbing to dogmatism, we can for the moment say that these laws of culture morphology and culture pathology will remain as valid as the laws of physics for as long as there are High Cultures and humanity is not reduced to a nebulous mass of *Fellaheen* primitives on a global scale. The 'evidence' is here for all who have eyes to see, all who are able to sense that there is something fundamentally wrong with a Civilization that once produced Shakespeare but now produces sitcom scriptwriters; that once birthed Beethoven and Mozart but now lauds Lady Gaga; whose culture-bearing stratum, which once patronized Leonardo, has been replaced by art dealers and Saatchis peddling Jeff Koon or Ofili. All of these symptoms of Culture pathology are excused or applauded in the name of 'progress'. What Spengler and Yockey showed is that none of this is 'progress'; it is a mere reversion towards decay over thousands of years, of the same type that afflicted prior Civilizations. If a Greek, Roman, Egyptian, Hindu, Arab or Chinese was time-transported from the era of decline of his respective Civilization into our own, he would see ours as remarkably familiar and might proffer an unheeded warning.

In 1998, I made an effort to write a biography of Yockey with the limited resources of the time and included some hitherto unpublished MSS and some newspaper articles on Yockey's capture and death.[3] This was a year prior to the publication of Kevin Coogan's *Dreamer of the Day*.[4] Since that time there have been new, *de lux* editions of *Imperium* and *The Proclamation of London* published by Wermod & Wermod, under the direction of Alex Kurtagic, who

3 K. R. Bolton, *Varange: The Life and Thoughts of Francis Parker Yockey* (Kapiti, New Zealand: Renaissance Press, 1998).

4 Kevin Coogan, *Dreamer of the Day: Francis Parker Yockey and the Postwar Fascist International* (Brooklyn: Automedia, 1999).

also provided hitherto unpublished family background on Yockey.[5] I had the honour of writing the introduction to the Wermod edition of *Imperium.*

But why the need for another biography on Yockey, given Coogan's exhaustive research? I hope that the reader will soon find that this biography and Coogan's are very different. Firstly, I have endeavoured to place Yockey's life and thought in historical, political and social contexts. Secondly, I have added much material to the basic facts. This is a book that should have been written by Keith Stimely, who spent much of the 1980s interviewing Yockey's old friends and colleagues, collating a large corpus of material. Tragically, his early death robbed him of the opportunity to start work on the biography itself. Since that time, important sources and people have passed away, including John Anthony Gannon, who did much to tell the Yockey story to Stimely, and Elsa Dewette and Peter Huxley-Blythe. Moreover, the extensive archives of DTK, the publisher of *Yockey: Four Essays* and of the Yockeyan magazine *TRUD* during the 1970s, were sunk by Hurricane Katrina. His insights have been of much help. Thanks to another veteran activist, Martin Kerr, for facilitating the communication.

5 Francis Parker Yockey, *The Proclamation of London of the European Liberation Front* (Shamley Green, UK: The Palingenesis Project, Wermod & Wermod Publishing Group, 2012), introduction by Dr Michael O'Meara. Francis Parker Yockey, *Imperium: The Philosophy of History and Politics* (Shamley Green, UK: The Palingenesis Project, Wermod & Wermod Publishing Group, 2013), introduction by K. R. Bolton.

# Acknowledgements

I was fortunate to have been in contact during the 1990s with Yockey's American colleague, H Keith Thompson, now deceased. Thanks to Dr Christian Bouchet for his advice on the influence of Yockey in France and on the pan-European revolutionary Jean Thiriart. Johnny and Suzanne von Pfügl, son and daughter-in-law of Baroness Alice von Pfügl, provided memories of the woman who funded the first edition of *Imperium*. Tim Turner of Biffers Books provided photocopies of rare pamphlets written by Yockey and his German-American father-figure Frederick Weiss. Thanks to Gerhard Lauck, an interpreter of Yockeyan thought at a young age, for the copy of his interesting essay. Acknowledgements to Dr Michael O'Meara for his insights into Yockeyan thought in various published essays. Thanks to Kyle Bristow for his efforts in tracking down official files and records; to Dominik for the important *Der Weg* material, to Vance for Yockey's 1941 Notre Dame Yearbook photo.

My thanks also to Jeff Wallder of the Friends of Oswald Mosley for facilitating access to the articles by Raven Thomson on 'social pathology' and a Yockey article from the first issue of *Union*. To Ken Hoop for his memories on the American nationalist movement. To Keith Thompson of Steven Books for the Weiss pamphlet on Einstein. To Margot for her research on the Yockey family tree. To Linton Hall for copies of letters from H Keith Thompson and for a rare essay on constitutional law by Yockey. To the Cadbury Research Library: Special Collections, University of Birmingham, for permission to use archives from the Oswald Mosley collection; to Sartor for his suggestions on the draft MS; to Dr Tomislav Sunic; and to John Bruce Leonard, Sam Richardson and Charles Lyons of Arktos Media for their colossal editorial work.

Enduring appreciation must be given to the late Keith Stimely,[1] whom I never knew, but who laid the foundations for Yockeyan studies, and to Yockey's faithful friend and comrade, John Anthony Gannon, who provided so much for that research, kept for posterity in the Stimely collection at the University of Oregon.

1 For a biography on Stimely and links to his articles as chief editor of the *Journal for Historical Review*, see: http://codoh.com/library/authors/2333/.

# 'An Exceptionally Brilliant Student'

Even the mainstream press expressed puzzlement that the bail of $50,000 for passport fraud was so high. The headlines ran: '3 passports jail mystery visitor here: secrecy in arrest, high bail on US fraud charge'; 'Mystery surrounds man seized with fake passports'; 'Sister visits mystery man'; and then more ominously, 'Both sides favour Yockey mind test'; 'New charges fly in passport probe'; and finally, 'Mystery man suicide'; 'Passport mystery man kills himself'; 'Neo-Nazi's jail, death poses new mystery'; 'Find passport mystery man dead in jail'. Then there were headlines on another mystery man, 'Holocaust survivor' Alex Scharf, who had suddenly disappeared after Yockey's arrest: 'New link to Yockey sought in Israel.' The surprise of the sensationalist media soon subsided into lurid accounts of this globetrotting, intense man as a mastermind of an international Fascist revival who had long been sought by the FBI. After initial interest in Scharf and the question of Yockey's suicide, the whole matter was suddenly dropped from public view.

A legend was born, however, at least among Right-wing fringes around the world. That legend has grown and Yockey, a controversial figure even among the 'extreme Right', now has a far larger audience than he did during his lifetime, as is often the case for 'artists'.

If one's psychological disposition affects one's politics — and there is much reason to believe that political behaviour is no less shaped by psychology than any other behaviour[1] — then it can be said that Yockey was raised in a milieu that predisposed him towards the Right. This does not mean that his parents

1 See K. R. Bolton, *The Psychotic Left: From Jacobin France to the Occupy Movement* (London: Black House Publishing, 2013).

were Right-wingers who imbued him with proto-fascist ideas. It means that Yockey stood out early as a child prodigy and an individual of independence and depth of thought. With such characteristics, what would he become other than a Fascist, when academic conformity even then demanded a Leftist orientation under the New Deal regime, and when social turmoil delineated extremes of Left and Right throughout the world. As Dr Michael O'Meara pointed out, Yockey, being of Irish-Catholic descent, was part of a recognisable minority that had still not fully assimilated into the dominant, money-based Puritan culture of WASP America — in which Jews, on the other hand, could buy their influence.[2] Catholicism was also a significant factor in Fascism, both in the USA and throughout the world. Many Fascist movements and states were specifically Catholic, so much so that the name 'clerical fascism' has been attached to them: Dollfuss' Austria, Salazar's Portugal, Franco's Spain, Pétain's France, Adrian Arcand's National Unity Party in Canada and Father Charles Coughlin's National Union of Social Justice, right on Yockey's doorstep. The hierarchical nature of the Catholic Church, its historical animosity towards Jews as 'Christ-killers', and in particular its opposition to usury and call for a new social system that would eschew the twin materialist doctrines of socialism and capitalism,[3] spawned many political movements which aimed to implement 'Catholic social doctrine'. Perhaps most importantly, the Church was unique in having a conception of 'Europe' and the 'West' as an organic unity. It was also the source of Yockey's higher education, at the Catholic universities of Georgetown and Notre Dame.

***

The Yockeys are of German and Irish-English descent. They came from Bayern, the region of south-east Germany. Jacky derives from the Swiss Jacggi, originating in or near the western Swiss villages of Gsteig and Teutorsoey, from the mid-sixteenth century, evolving to Jaegky, and then to Jacky. The

2 M O'Meara, 'Introduction', *The Proclamation of London of the European Liberation Front* ([1949] Shamley Green: Wermod & Wermod, 2012).

3 In particular the papal encyclicals: Pope Leo XIII, *Rerum Novarum: Rights and Duties of Capital and Labour* (1891); and Pius XI, *Quadragesimo Anno* (1930).

name became Yockey with their arrival to the USA. In the German and Swiss German languages, the pronunciation of Jaegky and Jacky is Yockey.

Francis Parker Yockey was born in Chicago on September 18, 1917, to Louis Francis (b. 1883) and Rose Ellen (Nellie) Foley (b. 1881). He was the youngest of four children, including Vinette,[4] James[5] and Alice Louise.[6]

Louis' parents were Valentin Jacky (b. 1828, Bayern) and Eleanor Thompson (b. 1845, Ireland, d. 1935, Chicago). Valentin Jacky's parents were Johann Jacob Jacky (1787–1847, Bayern), and Maria Catherine Kern (1792–1847, Bayern).

Nellie's parents were James Foley (b. 1844, New York) and Lavina Parker (b. 1848, New York). Lavina Parker's parents were Miles Parker (b. 1820 New York, d. 1893, Michigan) and Susan McLaughlin (b. Ireland, 1816, d. Michigan 1900).

Nellie Yockey was a graduate of the College of Music, Michigan,[7] and was described as 'an avid piano player'.[8]

Louis Yockey was a graduate of Kent College of Law, Chicago. He was a representative of the American Radiator Company in France and Belgium. It is ironic that while Francis was born in the USA, after the family's relocation in 1915, Vinette and James were born in Europe. In 1932, the Yockey family moved from Chicago to Ludington, Michigan, where Louis worked for the State Auditor General's Department.[9] Louis lost his money during the stock market crash in the same period that Francis had an automobile accident in which the tendons in his hand were cut, thwarting his ambition to be a concert pianist.[10] In July 1936, Louis died in a road accident.[11]

Years later in 1948, when the FBI checked the family background for Yockey's application as a legal analyst with a war crimes tribunal in Germany,

4 Vinette Yockey 1910–1992 (m. William Coyne, 1915–2009).

5 James Yockey 1911–1989.

6 Alice Yockey 1915–2011 (m. Spurlock).

7 FBI security report, July 8, 1952, p. 8, file no. 105–8229 — 1.

8 FBI report, October 14, 1952, p. 3; file no. 105–8229 — 1.

9 FBI security information, August 6, 1952, p. 1; file no. 105–8229 — 1.

10 August 28, 1959, ibid., p. 16, file no. 105–8229 — 3.

11 Alex Kurtagic, Appendix to Francis Parker Yockey, *Imperium*, op. cit., p. 811. Kurtagic provides much background information on the Yockey family in this appendix.

he was remembered by former students at Ludington as 'an exceptionally brilliant student'.[12] All members of the Yockey family had been 'highly regarded' by the community and had been considered 'loyal' Americans during the war. According to a family friend, speaking to the FBI in 1948, the Yockey family 'entertained considerably and had a wide circle of acquaintances'.[13]

Intriguingly, in 1942 the FBI investigated Yockey over his acquaintance with Herbert Hans Haupt, one of four Germans who had landed at Long Island, New York, from a German submarine. This was to be part of a two-year operation sabotaging defence industries. Another group had landed in Florida. By June 27, all eight had been arrested and soon after six were sentenced to death. Haupt was one of two would-be saboteurs who had gone to Chicago.[14] The conclusion of the FBI investigation was that the Yockeys had been innocently acquainted with the Haupt family and were 'not un-American'.[15]

Much later, it was noted that Francis Yockey had 'sponsored pro-Nazi meetings in Chicago in early 1940'. His association with Haupt might have had significance.[16] Yockey had been a friend of Haupt before the latter left the USA for Germany to be trained as a saboteur.[17] The initial assumption seems to have been that the connection between the Yockey family and Haupt was innocent because there had been a relationship between Haupt and Yockey's sister, Alice. She had known Haupt before he visited Mexico.[18] It was also later noted that Haupt had attended a meeting of the Keep America Out of the War Committee, in Chicago in 1940.[19] It seems that Alice was also inclined towards the 'Right', or was at least interested in the burgeoning anti-war movement.

---

12 Loyalty of Government Employees, Detroit, Michigan, June 29, 1948, FBI file CG 100–25647, p. 1.

13 Loyalty of Government Employees, ibid., (Administrative page, p. 2).

14 'George John Dasch and the Nazi Saboteurs', Famous Cases and Criminals, FBI, http://www.fbi.gov/about-us/history/famous-cases/nazi-saboteurs.

15 Loyalty of Government Employees, op. cit., p. 2.

16 FBI office memorandum, Chicago, April 27, 1954, p. 13.

17 CIA director to FBI director J Edgar Hoover, January 5, 1952, FBI Yockey file 105–8229 — 1.

18 FBI memorandum, January 2, 1952, January 5, 1952, ibid.

19 FBI report, May 20, 1954, p. 4; file no. 105–8229 Section 2.

Certainly, in later years, Alice and Vinette never wavered in their commitment to their brother.

Yockey's first political lecture seems to have been at a meeting of the Silver Legion near Chicago in 1939.[20] The Silver Shirts were a uniformed movement of considerable size, founded in 1933 by journalist, novelist and ex-Hollywood scriptwriter William Dudley Pelley. He had been shocked by the horrors of Bolshevism while serving as a consular courier during the Russian Civil War, in which the number of Jews involved was conspicuous and widely commented on at the time in military and diplomatic circles. The Great Depression awoke him to the horrors of international finance, also noted for its Jewish bankers. Along with dozens of others, who led the fight to keep the USA out of war in Europe, Pelley was charged under the 1917 Sedition Law in 1942 and sentenced to 15 years' jail. The only two witnesses permitted to testify in his defence were aviation hero Colonel Charles Lindbergh and Congressman Jacob Thorkelson, both leaders of the America First movement. Three months later, he was sent to Washington to again stand trial with 29 others for 'sedition', this time under the Smith Act of 1940. After eight months the charges against all defendants were dismissed. Though he had the same evidence and charges brought against him as the other 29, Pelley nonetheless was incarcerated until 1950 under the original sedition charge.[21] Yockey maintained a particular regard for Pelley and praised him when it was least opportune to do so: when serving in the army. Stationed at Fort Custer with the Red Cross in 1951, Yockey's praise of Pelley and the Silver Shirts was duly noted.[22]

Yockey also associated with activists of the German-American Bund.[23] The Bund was a uniformed, pro-Hitler organisation of notable strength,

20 CIA director to FBI director J Edgar Hoover, January 5, 1952, FBI Yockey file 105-8229 — 1.

21 'William Dudley Pelley', biography prepared by the Pelley family," http://toto.lib.unca.edu/findingaids/mss/pelley_william/pelley_biography/pelley_family_biography.htm.

22 FBI Memorandum, January 8, 1952, 105–8229 — 1.

23 Director, CIA, to FBI director J Edgar Hoover, January 5, 1952, FBI Yockey file 105–8229 — 1.

representing Americans of German descent.[24] Yockey worked with the Bund in Miami, Florida, during 1939.[25] He toured the radical Right and Fascist circuit under the name Francis Parker, lecturing on legal matters while a law student, and working at the Arcade Cafeteria, Chicago — a hang-out for local Bund leaders.

Yockey made an impression as an orator among the America First milieu. A report of the time states that Mrs Lois de Lafayette Washburn of the National Liberty Party recommended Yockey for the party leadership.[26] Paradoxically, it was remarked by Yockey's leading post-war colleague in England, Anthony John Gannon, that Yockey was not an orator and left public speaking for the European Liberation Front to others. Perhaps Yockey did not feel an American accent expounding European unity to Englishmen would be entirely appropriate. As will be seen, Yockey's speaking talents were likely to have been notable.

Yockey had also been associated with the movement around Newton Jenkins in 1938.[27] Jenkins was a leader of the Keep America Out of the War Committee and the America First Committee.[28] Jenkins, a lawyer describing himself as a 'Progressive Republican', had, like Father Charles Coughlin, originally supported Roosevelt's New Deal. He could have gained a position in the

24 Director, CIA, to FBI director J Edgar Hoover, op. cit., January 5, 1952.
The Bund was founded in 1936 by Fritz Kuhn. He had fought in World War I and was awarded the Iron Cross, migrating to the USA during the Weimar era. The Bund grew mainly from the Friends of New Germany, and co-operated with other organisations such as the Ku Klux Klan, Silver Legion, Italian Fascists, and exiled Russian Fascists. After being interned in the USA during the war, Kuhn was deported to Germany, where he spent five years in and out of prison on the more than bizarre charge of being a 'war criminal', despite his internment in the USA for the duration of the war. He died in 1951. See Susan Canedy, *America's Nazis: A History of the German American Bund* (Manlo Park, California: Markgraf Publications Group, 1990).

25 FBI report, July 28, 1959, p. 2; file no. 105–8229 — 3.

26 FBI security report, July 98, 1952, p. 12, FBI Yockey file 105–8229 — 1; citing Raymond J Healy, 'I did Hitler's dirty work in Chicago', *Chicago Daily Times*, September 22, 1940. Healy was a member of the Khaki Shirts and the National Socialist Workers Party, considering himself an American 'Hitler'. He turned against National Socialism because of the Hitler-Stalin Pact. Mrs Washburn was a defendant at the Sedition trials.

27 FBI report, May 20, 1954, p. 1; file no. 105–8229 Section 2.

28 FBI report, May 20, 1954, ibid., p. 2.

Roosevelt Administration but turned against Roosevelt and, like Coughlin, saw the 'progressive' president as a frontman for banking interests and the Jewish-dominated 'Brains Trust'. Jenkins ran for the Chicago mayoralty in 1935 under the banner of the newly formed Third Party and published a journal called *American Nationalism* in which he wrote that America needs someone like Hitler to stir it from lethargy.[29] The aim was to promote a 'militant nationalist' organisation.[30] Jenkins attended many Bund meetings and was highly regarded among Bundists, in turn calling the Bund 'a fine, patriotic American organization' and its leader, Fritz Kuhn, 'a real American'. Jenkins spoke at the July 4, 1937 national rally of the Bund in New York, where he stated that he was 'thoroughly familiar with your high ideals'. He hoped to unite some 125 nationalist organisations under his Third Party banner with Fritz Kuhn as one of the primary leaders. The movement would be formed around the American National Political Action Clubs. Jenkins had his law and party offices in Chicago and it was there that Yockey began serving a political apprenticeship.

Chicago was also a centre of activity for the Christian Front, the militant branch of Father Coughlin's movement, whose predominately Irish-American lads sold *Social Justice* on the streets while fighting off attacks from Jews and Communists. It was in this widely read newspaper that Yockey had his first political article published.

Yockey was billed to give a talk to a meeting of Coughlinites, Silver Shirts and Bundists in 1939, several months after his *Social Justice* article, under the name of Francis Parker.[31] This was to be a protest meeting on behalf of five Silver Shirts charged with breaking the windows of a Jewish department store.[32] The handbill proclaimed 'Protest Defense Mass Meeting ... Help Free Imprisoned Patriots ... Five Followers of Rev. Father Charles Coughlin, Jailed

---

29 *House of Representatives Investigation of Un-American Propaganda Activities*, Vol. 2, 1938, p. 1209.

30 See William Mueller, 'Fascist Union US Nazi Goal', *Sunday Times*, Chicago, Vol. 9, No. 7, September 12, 1937; pp. 1, 3, 18, 19, 20, 22, 23, 30, 31.

31 Rendered 'Frances' on the advertising poster for the meeting.

32 'Two Silvershirts Confess Brick Hurling Plot', *Daily Times*, Chicago, October 25, 1939, p. 16.

in Goldblatt Frameup'. The handbill claimed that the Coughlinites had been 'savagely and brutally beaten into signing a "confession" that they destroyed Goldblatt's Dept Store Property'. One, Mr Heppner, 'had suffered a broken eardrum and many body bruises'. 'Jews are persecuting Christians.' The meeting of December 12, 1939, was organised by the 'Friends of Rev Father Charles Coughlin' (Chicago Post No. 49). The 'prominent speakers' comprised: Rev Burton Hastings of Detroit; Father Sullivan of New York; Thomas Gust of Albany; Raymond Joseph Healy of New York and Miami, author, writer, lecturer and editor; and Frances [sic] Parker of the University of Virginia, 'noted intern'l [sic] law authority'.[33]

Those involved in the charges of damaging the Goldblatt shop, one of whom (Homer Mertz) was sentenced to seven years' jail,[34] had their bonds posted by William Wernecke, who owned a farm and worked as a property broker. Wernecke was a mainstay of Fascist activity in the Chicago area, being former secretary of the Chicago branch of the German-American Bund and head of its stormtroop corps, associated with the Silver Shirts, Knights of the White Camelia (a Klan-type organisation), White Shirts, Gentile Workers Party of America, and chairman of the Joint Committee of Patriotic Organizations.[35] He also worked with Newton Jenkins' organisation.[36] Wernecke had organised and funded the meeting of the 'Friends of Rev Father Charles Coughlin'.[37] Allegations of paramilitary training, stockpiles of dynamite and cavalry practice at the Wernecke farm are shown by the FBI to have been inventions of the media — typical journalistic hysteria about an alleged 'Fifth Column'.[38]

33 Handbill in the William Wernecke file, FBI, 65–582–152. Although a student of international law at the time, Yockey did not attend the University of Virginia. The meeting does not appear to have eventuated.

34 W. S. Devereaux, 'Re: William Werneke [sic]', FBI Chicago office, 61–8118–1, February 14, 1940, p. 3.

35 Wernecke file, FBI, 65–582–152, September 13, 1939.

36 'Excerpts from Reports', Wernecke file, FBI, 65–582–152.

37 Statement of Frank E Northcutt, Collector of Inland Revenue, August 20, 1940, Wernecke file, FBI, 65–582–152.

38 See for example W. S. Devereaux, FBI Chicago office, teletype message, August 26, 1940; Wernecke file, 65–582–152. Also: Thomas E Kennedy, Sheriff, Lake County, Waukegan, to Devereaux, Chicago FBI office, September 13, 1940, Wernecke file, ibid.

Herbert Haupt, the young German-American executed as a saboteur, was also a friend of Wernecke and claimed that they shared a tenancy in a farm.[39] However, a strange incident arose as the result of the Wernecke/Yockey association: In 1941, the Chicago office of the FBI received an anonymous phone call from an associate of Wernecke's, claiming that Marcella Misavice, 21, was being 'detained against her will' by Yockey's brother-in-law and sister, William and Vinette Coyne. Police enquiries with Vinette determined that Misavice had lived with Wernecke and his mother for five years as a domestic servant at the Wernecke farm but that she had 'run away', claiming that Wernecke had 'molested her'. Misavice and the Coynes were asked to call at the Summerdale Police Station to give any additional information on Wernecke. The Coynes, Misavice and Yockey's sister Alice[40] were interviewed at length on November 15. Misavice had been staying with the Coynes for about a month, while Wernecke had been trying to locate her and force her to return. The Coynes stated that Wernecke had been 'bothering them' about the return of Misavice. Wernecke phoned William Coyne's employer on November 19, claiming to be an FBI agent. On November 22, Wernecke visited FBI Special Agent William E Helme, denying the accusations against him and making allegations against the Coynes, which Helme regarded as 'all obviously of an untrue nature'. Helme strongly cautioned Wernecke against making untrue statements and against impersonating a Federal officer. Helme did not believe that Wernecke would desist from his actions.[41] It seems however that the primary reason for the feud between the Coynes and Alice Yockey on the one side and Wernecke on the other was that 'Francis Yockey was the person who had won Miss Misevich's [sic] affections away from Wernecke', according to Wernecke's lawyer, Herbert M Wetzel.[42]

---

'Trojan Horsemen Melt away as FBI Investigates Fifth Column in County', *The Waukegan Post*, June 11, 1940, in Warneke FBI file 65–582–152.

39 J. J. Fisher, FBI Special Agent, 'Memorandum for the File', September 27, 1940, ibid.

40 Alice Yockey and Herbert Haupt double-dated with Wernecke and Misavice. E. D. Dixon, Memo for SAC, Re: W. B. Wernecke 7/2/42, p. 3; ibid.

41 William B Helme, 'Memo for File 65–582', Chicago Illinois, December 3, 1941, ibid.

42 J Edgar Hoover, 'Memorandum for Mr L. M. C. Smith, Chief, Special Defense Unit', August 20, 1941, p. 99.

Wernecke stated in 1942 that he believed Haupt, dating Yockey's sister Alice, was 'also very friendly' with Yockey.[43] According to William Pinsley, Chicago head of the Anti-Defamation League's 'fact-finding' department, Wernecke believed Yockey had helped Federal authorities in his 1943 prosecution under the Selective Services Act. Yockey was certainly livid with Wernecke's antics against family members in regard to the Misavice feud. In 1955, Pinsley also informed the FBI that William and Vinette Coyne had moved from California to Massachusetts, an indication of the close scrutiny this Zionist spy network maintained on the entire Yockey family.

Oddly, after Wernecke was eventually inducted into the army (first having served a term in jail and being fined $10,000 for draft dodging) Misavice, who had been left in charge of the Wernecke farm and eleven pieces of property, requested he be given three weeks' furlough to assist her in straightening out the property matters.[44]

Considering the attention that the FBI had turned on Wernecke before and during the war, and his friendship with the would-be saboteur Haupt,

---

43 E. D. Dixon, Memo for SAC, Re: W. B. Wernecke 7/2/42, p. 3; ibid.

44 Although sentenced to five years' jail, there are contradictory comments as to whether he actually served any time or if he rather was inducted into the army in December 1943, at a camp used for inducting those under sentence. William Bernard Wernecke, FBI file 61–8118, November 9, 1945, Chicago file 65–582; and 61–8118, March 4, 1946. Wernecke's Army record was so good that he had been assigned to Military Intelligence. FBI Office Memorandum of G. C. Callan to A Rosen, 'William Bernard Wernecke, Selective Service', May 5, 1945; although he had been 'one of the most subversive German-American Bundists brought to our attention', ibid., May 26, 1945. In 1955 Wernecke founded the Nationalist Conservative Party. He had contact with the new generation of post-war Fascist luminaries such as Matt Koehl, DeWest Hooker, J. B. Stoner and Eustace Mullins. Wernecke was actively involved in animal welfare, and added a plank to his party platform demanding strict laws against animal abuse. (Nationalist Conservative Party, 'Humane Plank'). (It was a question that had been enacted most assiduously in the pioneering animal welfare policy of National Socialist Germany.) The famous bombing of a synagogue in Atlanta, Georgia, and others, in 1958, brought new intensive FBI scrutiny on Wernecke et al. 'William B Wernecke, Internal Security—X (Racial Matters)', FBI Office Memorandum, Chicago 65–582, December 31, 1958; 'William B Werencke Bombing Matters', Chicago 65–582, august 25, 1959. FBI attention on Wernecke only stopped with his death in 1965. 'William Bernard Wernecke, Potential Bombing suspect', Chicago 65–582, May 28, 1965.

it is strange or inept that the FBI regarded the close associations between Wernecke, Yockey, his two sisters and brother-in-law as of little consequence. Yockey's going AWOL from the Army to travel to Mexico also seems to have been of no great interest to the Army or FBI. Rather, when the FBI was collating material on Wernecke and re-examining the matter of Misavice, it was reported that the Coynes had given refuge to Misavice at the request of Alice Yocki [sic], a nurse at St Francis Hospital, Evanston. Michael Ahern, a Lieutenant at the Chicago Police Department, stated that after Wernecke and his mother had failed to take Misavice from the Coyne residence, they had gone to her parents and claimed that the Coynes were holding her against her will as a prostitute. Lt Ahern remarked that 'the Coyne family is actually a high-class respectable family, Mr Coyne, who is now an ensign in the US Navy, being a chemical engineer, and Mrs Coyne having formerly been a nurse, like her sister, Miss Yocki [sic]'. Lt Ahern sought to reach a peaceful accord by calling into his office the Misavice family, the Coynes, Alice Yockey, Wernecke and his mother, Martha, and the lawyers of the Coynes, Misavices, and Werneckes. This ended in a 'near riot', with the lawyers exchanging abuse.[45]

***

Yockey's article, 'The Tragedy of Youth', in Father Coughlin's magazine *Social Justice*, addressed the moral decay imposed on young Americans by a corrupt system, and the forces that were pushing them to war. The article was subtitled: 'Their Generation, Now Unemployed, Must Fight the War then Become Slaves in Red State that Follows.' Yockey wrote that youth is the primary target of the forces of subversion and that it is from youth that resistance must come. He stated that 'alien' influences, through their control of entertainment and the press, pour out a constant stream of propaganda aimed at 'complete spiritual power over the minds of young Americans'.[46] This took the form of 'exhibitionist dancing', 'a perverted and insane pictorial art' and 'jungle music',

45 Statement by Lt Ahern to FBI Special Agent D. F. McMahon, August 3, 1942; R. P. Kramer, FBI Memorandum to L. D. Ladd; 'Associates in the George Dasch et al Sabotage Case', July 30, 1942, pp. 54–55.

46 Francis Parker Yockey, 'The Tragedy of Youth', *Social Justice*, August 21, 1939, p. 7.

which are the norm for American adolescence. For the more serious, thinking youth, they have been targeted by internationalist, class war propaganda. There has been 'spiritual regimentation' of the young in Leftist-controlled academia, 'by the preachers of Roosevelt-Leftism'.

> The tragedy of this conscription of American youth under the banners of atheism, class-war and social degeneration is just this: *that the continuance of the economic and spiritual distress of the youth is an integral part of the revolutionary program of the same Communist forces which have seduced and indoctrinated them.*[47]

Quoting the French Communist leader, Maurice Thorez, Yockey, like other anti-New Dealers, saw the Roosevelt Administration as the US application of the Communist party's 'popular front' strategy as a prelude to revolution, which had recently reduced Spain to civil war. This impending 'bloodbath Communist dictatorship', paved by New Deal socialism, cannot succeed if the population is productive and prosperous. As with the other opponents of the New Deal, Yockey regarded the Roosevelt policies as driving the USA to bankruptcy and ruin while making most of the population dependent on the Government. These state-dependent workers were seen as the coming draftees of a 'Left Army' of labour unions, relief workers, 'organized Negroes', teachers 'and the greater part of youth'. These widespread concerns might seem highly paranoid. However, it was the way matters had proceeded in Spain and, as cited by Yockey, Thorez had outlined precisely that strategy for the Popular Front Government in France. We have seen in our own day Allende's Chile — with its Popular Front Government — proceed along the same lines until aborted by the Pinochet coup. Yockey wrote:

> The tragedy for youth lies in this, that every condition for the success of the Communist scheme is created at the expense of youth, and every tactic employed in actualizing it makes the position of youth more desperate and more nearly hopeless.[48]

47 Francis Parker Yockey, 'The Tragedy of Youth', ibid.

48 Francis Parker Yockey, 'The Tragedy of Youth', ibid.

The revolutionists did not want conditions to improve. A primary means of impoverishment was 'the burden that the ever growing national debt imposes', which was 'almost solely a burden on the youth'. The choice being offered was either Red dictatorship or enslavement to debt. Added to this was the feeling of uncertainty brought by constant talk of war. The prospect was that they would soon be drafted to fight in Asia and Europe, '*unless a powerful Christian nationalism arises to cast out the alien-thinking minority in Washington*'. A war would give the Roosevelt Administration not only the chance to 'avenge wrongs done to it by those foreign governments which have liquidated class war within their nations' but also 'to defeat by their repressive war-dictatorship the incipient movement among the people against radicalism and in favor of a Christian nationalist government'. Yockey concluded: 'Youth of America — *Awake!* It's *your* problem and *your* task. You are the special victim if they win.'[49]

In 'Tragedy of Youth', Yockey had identified himself as a 'Christian nationalist' with a keen analytical mind in seeing the broad picture of events. He had declared himself in favour of Italy and Germany. Interestingly, he recognised the crucial role of debt-finance in enslaving a nation. The question of debt and the international bankers was the *raison d'être* of Father Coughlin's National Union for Social Justice. Coughlin, once he realised that Roosevelt had no intention of throwing out the 'money changers' and was, rather, in league with them, established the National Union to campaign for state credit and the elimination of usury. It was pure Catholic social doctrine and part of the Church's traditional role in condemning usury.[50] However, the Church hierarchy was persuaded by Roosevelt to shut Coughlin down, while in April 1942

49 Francis Parker Yockey, 'The Tragedy of Youth', ibid.

50 Point 6 of the 16 point NUSJ programme stated: 'Abolition of private banking, and institution of a central government bank'. Point 7 demanded the control of the value of money by central government. The Federal Reserve Bank, like other central banks that were being formed around the world, gave the appearance of being a state bank, but such banks are run by international financiers. The Federal Reserve Bank was based on the blueprint of Paul Warburg, a scion of the Warburg banking dynasty. Germany, Italy and Japan broke free of the international financial system and operated on state credit and barter. While the Axis states flourished in the midst of a world depression, Roosevelt's acclaimed New Deal, which tried to ape the success of the Italian corporatist

*Social Justice* was charged under the violation of the Espionage Act and barred from the mails. Being an obedient servant of the Church, Coughlin returned to the obscurity of his parish and so was silenced one of the most dynamic forces in American history.

Yockey showed that he was acutely aware of the cultural degeneration being fostered by Hollywood and New York, and that youth were succumbing to the cycle of decadence in art, dancing and 'jungle music', which had become the 'spiritual norm'. Yockey returned to these issues in *Imperium* in 1948 and *The Proclamation of London* in 1949, where he explained them as symptoms of Culture-distortion.

Although 'Tragedy of Youth' seems to have been Yockey's first published political essay, he had written 'The Philosophy of Constitutional Law' as a student paper while at Georgetown University School of Foreign Service in 1936. It is evident that at 19, Yockey was imbued with the thinking of Oswald Spengler. In 'The Philosophy of Constitutional Law', Yockey applies Spengler's morphology on the organic cycles of Culture to analyse 'constitutional law' as part of that cyclic process in the life of nations:

> The kind of law is dependent directly and completely on the kind of lawgiver, and therewith on the society in which he has matured—whether primitive or cultured, whether feudal or cosmopolitan, aristocratically or democratically ordered, industrial, agricultural, whether Russian, Western, Chinese, Indian, Egyptian, or Classical. A nation is as much a legal unit as it is a political or economic unit. In the law of a people its world-outlook finds pure and clear expression (there are outstanding exceptions but in these cases the alien-ness of the law dominated the legal picture), and eventually the law was either spiritually transformed (Roman law by the Arabian Culture), or became the object of a violent political abrogation (Roman law by Germany in 1935).[51]

Each nation has its own legal outlook, as an expression of its soul and how it relates to the *Zeitgeist* of an epoch of history: 'It is apparent that every nation

economy, got nowhere and the USA only achieved recovery through war production. See K. R. Bolton, *The Banking Swindle* (London: Black House Publishing, 2013).

51 Yockey, 'The Philosophy of Constitutional Law', (1) Georgetown University School of Foreign Service, 1936, unpublished MS.

has its own distinctive living constitution, the expression of the national soul. The memory of this national soul is what we call tradition.'[52]

Hence, from the Spenglerian viewpoint of the epoch in which he lived, Yockey could see a decisive world conflict approaching, what Spengler called the 'conflict between money and blood',[53] represented by the Democratic and the Fascist powers respectively; two conflicting outlooks, the first embedded in the previous century and based on money thinking, the second a revolt against the capitalist ethos with an 'ethical socialism' that transcended money-thinking entirely, including that of Marxism. However, the Democracies were of historical necessity obliged to take on the mantle of absolutist, authoritarian politics because of the total-war character of the epochal struggle for world mastery. Hence, the money-powers behind Democracy, whose chief power is the USA, could only win against the Axis revolt by assuming the outward expressions necessitated by this era of absolute politics and the struggle for world-power. The situation pertains today with the USA and its allies marching behind the banner of 'Democracy' but extending world power through military means while, as in the aftermath of World War II, killing off the defeated leaders with the use of laws invented for the Nuremberg Trials. American world democracy is as Absolutist as Fascism but works in the service of Money, as did Communism.

Yockey's university days were varied but successful, spanning diplomacy, medicine, and law. He attended the University of Michigan, Pre-Medical (1934–1935), University of Chicago (1936), Georgetown University Foreign Service School (September 1936 to June 1938), University of Arizona Law School (1938–1939), Northwestern University Law School (1938 to 1939), De Paul Law School (September 1939 to June 1940), and Notre Dame University Law School, where he obtained his law degree *cum laude* on June 1, 1941.[54]

---

52 Ibid., (V), 'Morphology of constitutions; actual source of constitutional law'.

53 Oswald Spengler, *The Decline of The West* ([1926] London: George Allen and Unwin, 1971), Vol. II, pp. 506–507.

54 FBI security report, July 8 1952, p. 6, file no. 105–8229 — 1.

## 1940—Life as an Art

In 1940, while a student at Notre Dame University, Yockey wrote an essay that already explicates all of the essentials of his philosophy, 'Life as an Art'.[55] Here, he refers to his vision of a 'Western Empire', his 'Idea of Imperium', and shows the two dominant influences from this time as being Spengler and Friedrich Nietzsche.

The latter's concept of the 'higher man' forms the basis of Yockey's rejection of equality in favour of a resurgence of hierarchy; the concept of the will-to-power and that of an over-riding self-discipline. He applies these Nietzschean themes to the concept of the 'Mission', which emerges as an involuntary compulsion welling up from whatever set of complexes within the 'higher man'. This is an inner imperative to follow a life's path that is no more to be subjected to rationalizing, intellectualizing and analyses than the instinctual impulsion of a bird of prey acting on his nature. Of 'higher' and 'lower' men, Yockey wrote, reminiscent of Nietzsche in *Thus Spoke Zarathustra*:

> Higher men and lower men—the few called to rule and the masses born in order that the higher men may actualize a grander destiny—differ in spirituality so much that they cannot be comprehended otherwise than as two different species. In all reverence it can be said that the lower men rely on God and the higher men on themselves. This basic natural hierarchy is the fundament upon which rests all practical philosophy of human nature. It must therefore be definitively set forth.
>
> THERE ARE TWO SPECIES OF MEN AS DIFFERENT IN SPIRITUALITY AS LIONS AND LAMBS. THEIR WHOLE MANNER OF EXPERIENCING LIFE, OF NOURISHING THEMSELVES IN THE STRUGGLE OF LIFE, OF FIGHTING THE BATTLE OF LIFE, OF SOLVING INWARDLY THE PROBLEMS WHICH LIFE PRESENTS, THE RESULTING PICTURES OF LIFE ALL ARE TOTALLY DIFFERENT.[56]

The 'art' of the life of higher man is not aesthetic, as in prior centuries, but is of a martial nature. When Yockey stated that Western Civilization has exhausted its aesthetic possibilities and its art must now focus on other tasks,

55 Yockey, 'Life as an Art', South Bend, Indiana, December, 1940; unpublished MS.

56 Yockey, ibid.

he was drawing from Spengler. Spengler foresaw the emergence of *Caesars* who, after the overthrow of the rule of Money in the epochal crisis of Western Civilization, would triumph in a battle of wills: blood versus money.[57] By 'blood', Spengler means the instinctual-intuitive rhythm of Life contra that of the counting-house that dominates the senile epoch of a Civilization. Authority overthrows Plutocracy. Like much of Spengler and Yockey, it is a hard pill to swallow: realising that the West has nothing more to say aesthetically. However, so far one would be hard-pressed to show that Spengler and Yockey are wrong. Those who are of aesthetic sensibility cannot do much more than appreciate the great Western music, painting and literature of past centuries. Anything 'new' of High Culture has so far necessarily shown itself to be at best derivative of what was begun centuries ago. Yockey writes of this:

> But the present form of our world-knowledge leaves no doubt that the Western Soul has in this field closed its cycle of development, and that the future field of development of this soul is not in religion, philosophy, art and science, but in the field of technical, economic, and political activity. The WESTERN SOUL HAS BECOME FINALLY EXTROVERTED. It has entered the last stage.[58]

The task that Yockey gave these Spenglerian Caesars, or Nietzsche's 'higher men', was to create a new Empire of the West that would fulfil creative possibilities in a new direction. As Yockey mentioned, a forerunner of these possibilities was Napoleonic Europe, an era ushered by a 'higher man', a new *Caesar*, who not only negated the doctrines of the French Revolution by imposing a return to authority and hierarchy but also sought to shape a united Europe. National Socialist Germany had sought to regenerate Western aesthetics and could do no better — nor worse — than to re-create the best of both the monumental Classical Tradition and the Gothic. Here, one sees the possibilities of an aesthetic renaissance within the context of the Yockeyan martial state, regardless of the sneers of modernist art critics.[59] However, as if to prove the contention of Yockey and Spengler that the West had fulfilled its

---

57 Oswald Spengler, *The Decline of The West*, op. cit., Volume II, p. 507.

58 Yockey, 'Life as an Art', op. cit.

59 F Spotts, *Hitler & the Power of Aesthetics* (London: Random House, 2002). J Petropoulos, *The Faustian Bargain: The Art World in Nazi Germany* (London: Penguin Books, 2000).

aesthetic possibilities (insofar as great *new* art forms would not be forthcoming), it is notable that this artistic flowering in Germany was derivative from the best of bygone ages. This is evidenced by the Third Reich's monumental neo-Classical sculptures of Arno Breker or the neo-Classical architecture of Albert Speer.

'Life as an Art' parallels Spengler. Spengler had written, for example:

> And herein, I think, all the philosophers of the newest age are open to a serious criticism. What they do not possess is real understanding in actual life. Not one of them has intervened effectively, either in higher politics, in the development of modern technics, in matters of communication, in economics, or in any other *big* actuality, with a single act or a single compelling idea.[60]

The final sentence of *The Decline of The West* states what Yockey expressed in his essay, that the 'mission' of the 'higher man' is not something that is realised by intellectual processes but something that is already within, something that instinctively impels the 'higher man'—the new 'Caesars'—to act in accordance with historical necessity: 'And a task that historic necessity has set will be accomplished with the individual or against him.'[61]

For 'higher men', there is no option other than to unfold one's inner being and act according to historical necessity:

> This it is that distinguishes the higher natures—they have reverence for themselves; their own souls contain in them something precious which must be brought to fulfilment, for the higher natures have some of the attributes of superpersonal souls. Like history in its fulfilment laying waste human resources, denying and frustrating human wishes, reaching deep into private life to chasten souls with tragedy, the higher men deny and subordinate their own emotions, sacrifice their private lives, and all because *there is something more important to them than all this: the mission.* In the conduct of his life, the higher man does not employ reason any more than history itself employs reason. There is no REASON for the cycle of the generations, for the universal life cycle of birth, growth, fulfilment, decline and death, for the human life span of 70 years, the

60 Oswald Spengler, op. cit., Vol. I, p. 42.

61 Ibid., Vol. 2, p. 507.

> culture's of 1,000 years, the nation's of 300. Instinct is the sure guide of the higher man, and unconscious decision is his surest method of accomplishment. …[62]

Yockey quotes the American Ralph Waldo Emerson:

> "I shun father and mother and wife and brother when my genius calls me." This sentence describes every higher man. His genius—genius means *creative force*—or, using the word honorifically instead of descriptively, it means *great creative force*—is his hallmark …
>
> It deprives him of all contentment, and happiness until the mission is accomplished. But creative force—this will remain forever incomprehensible to those, far more than 99% of humanity—who cannot see deeply into the soul of Culture-man—IS AT BOTTOM ARTISTIC. In the deeps the will-to-power merges with the aesthetic instinct. In the brief moment of satisfaction which follows the completion of a work—a novel, a building, a suspension bridge, a symphony, a victorious battle, the soul of a higher man feels an intense and profound aesthetic satisfaction in the form of self-reverence and a feeling of union with the essence of Being.[63]

Here we glimpse why Yockey, who revered marriage and family, and loved his children, could not settle into a stable family life himself: the man described by those who knew him best as an 'artist' was impelled to fulfil a 'mission'; that was his nature, which had to unfold if he was true to himself. His relations with people could often be judged harshly but this is true also of many artists and geniuses.

It is in this essay that Yockey also names what he regards as the religion most apt for our time: *skepsis* and the ethos of 'discipline'. Of the former, he explains that it is not the nineteenth century skepticism of the rationalists, materialists and atheists. To the contrary, it is skepticism in regard to the ability of intellectualism to understand anything of life.

> Napoleon heralded the man of the future, Nietzsche described his nature, Spengler has announced his imminent arrival.[64]

---

62 Yockey, 'Life as an Art', op. cit.

63 Ibid.

64 Ibid.

> Skepsis and Discipline! Just as the skepsis of the coming age is a new and deeper skepsis, so is the discipline. It is the discipline of self, first of all. The ideal of self-discipline will be realized of course only by the higher man, just as in Gothic times, the ones to realize the dominant idea of the time were the saints, the higher men, the bearer of the mission in those days. But the idea of self-discipline nevertheless is dominant, and it will attract with irresistible power the leading men of the coming time. But the discipline will only start with the self, it will continue into the field of the training of the young, the organization of the economic life, the form of the State. Above all, it will bring back the eternal ideas of political organization, the monarch — call him dictator or president, he will return, and the hereditary idea is too strong in our Western blood not to break out once our rationalism is finally buried. Education, law, technics, armies and fleets, all will be governed by discipline, all will be at the service of the State.[65]

This discipline and service to authority was what Spengler called 'Prussian Socialism'.[66] Yockey called it 'ethical socialism' in *Imperium* and *The Proclamation*. Yockey continued his explanation of both this state-duty and the previous Spenglerian theme of the 'art' of the new epoch being that of high statecraft in the service of 'Western Empire':

> They will be in the service of the State rather than the service of the Church, rationalism, "humanity", universal equality, the proletariat, or something else, simply because the new idea is completely externalised. It has no religion, no art, no Golden Age of literature, no Utopia, to bring forth. It contains the germs of no Renaissance, no Flemish school of painting, no Spanish drama, no German metaphysics, no English economic imperialism, no French chauvinism and militarism. *It will be the complete actualization of the Idea of Power.* In his Cultural biography, Western man has pursued at successive times eternal salvation, Truth, beauty, knowledge, and has even sought to enthrone Reason. There is left for him the externalised pursuits of technics, the military art, political imperialism, and state organization. The same intensity that developed the arts of oil painting and the fugue, that wrested from Nature her secrets, that proclaimed the universal rule of Liberty and Equality, will now turn to write the history of the planet in terms of Western Empire.[67]

---

65 Ibid.

66 Spengler, *Prussianism and Socialism*, 1919.

67 Yockey, 'Life as an Art'.

Within this 1940 essay are all the primary themes that Yockey elaborated on in *Imperium* eight years later.

***

Yockey attended Loyola University, Chicago, in 1942, where it was recalled to the FBI in 1948 that he was 'radically minded' and 'continuously stirring up discord'. At Michigan University, he had been described as 'pro-Communist' during his first year (1934) and 'got into trouble' for playing the 'Internationale' on the piano at a party at the home of a University dean. However, Yockey was soon known as a 'Nazi'.[68] He was in later life notorious for alienating even his admirers by what seemed to be a compulsion to play *l'enfant terrible*. This is more likely to explain Yockey's behaviour than a flirtation, however brief, with Communism.

On October 4, 1941, he was admitted to practise at the Circuit Court, Mason County, Michigan, where he specialised in torts and insurance.[69]

On May 20, 1942, Yockey enlisted in the US Army, 43rd Infantry Division, at Kalamazoo, Michigan. However, he went AWOL from September 21 to November 22, 1942. He gave himself up to the Army in November 1942 and by feigning 'mental incompetence' was given an 'honorable discharge'[70] on July 13, 1943.[71] Yockey had travelled to Mexico at this time to contact 'Hans, the German sailor boy' and to 'enquire about transportation to Spain from San Antonio or Mexico'. Yockey was using the alias Torquemada and signed into the Saint Anthony Hotel in San Antonio under the name George Patterson.[72] Yockey later alluded to 'espionage' work for the Germans during World War II, to the Italian artist and Fascist, Edigio Boschi. By 1943, he had already been put on a list of 'disloyal' and 'subversive' persons by 'another government

68 FBI office memorandum, December 16, 1954, p. 1; 105–8229 — 2.

69 Harold Rubenstein, FBI, August 8, ibid., p. 4, 105–8229 — 2, 1952.

70 Final Statement of Yockey, Francis P US-16084518, discharged Milledgeville, Ga., January 15, 1943.

71 CIA to FBI, 105–8229 — 2, January 5, 1952.

72 FBI memorandum, July 21, 1952, file no. 105–8229 — 1.

agency'.[73] On July 6, 1943, Yockey married Alice MacFarlane, with whom he had two daughters in Germany, separating in 1946.[74]

Yockey was to recall, when in custody in 1960, that he had 'snowed' an army psychiatrist 'into believing he was a psychopath'.[75] In 1945, Yockey remarked to a female friend that he had been 'almost shot for treason when in the US Army',[76] presumably due to his mysterious 'desertion' in 1942.

In 1948, the FBI were considering taking Yockey before a Loyalty Board hearing and had sought out former acquaintances, mostly in the Office of Price Administration. Although several remembered that Yockey had made some pro-Hitler and anti-Semitic remarks, the FBI could not come up with anything substantial against him.[77]

---

73 CIA to FBI, op. cit.

74 FBI report, August 7, 1954, p. 5, file no. 105–8229 — 2.

75 FBI memo, file no. SF 105–1769, June 13, 1960.

76 FBI report, August 7, 1954, p. 10, file no. 105–8229 — 2.

77 Ibid.

# War Crimes Investigator

From January to December 1946, Yockey was employed by the US War Department in Germany. He also managed to spend some time in Zurich, Switzerland, in 1946,[1] where he studied at the *Institut Minerva*.[2]

After obtaining his law degree in 1941, Yockey worked for the law firm of Thompson and Lannin at Mount Vernon, Illinois, until 1942. He was elected to the Detroit Bar Association in May 1944. From February to September 1943, he had a private law practice in Detroit. From September 1943 to December 1944 he was an Assistant Prosecuting Attorney on the staff of Wayne County, Michigan public prosecutor.[3] During 1944, he was living in Ludington with his wife, Alice MacFarlane, and was an attorney with the firm of Dykoma, Jones and Whoat.[4] He had passed the Illinois and Michigan State Bar Examinations 'without difficulty due to his outstanding brilliance', according to an informant who had known Yockey since childhood.[5] He worked as a 'rent attorney' with the office of the housing expediter at the Office of Price Administration in Detroit during January to November 1945, where he had been noted as having pro-German sympathies.[6] An employee at OPA recalled in 1948, in a statement to the FBI, that he had heard Yockey talk of Germany fighting for the unity of Europe and speaking of Jewish influence.

Another informant who had known Yockey since 1939 or 1940 stated to the FBI that he had been eager to go with the US occupation in Germany and

1 FBI report September 26, 1952, p. 4; 105–8229 — 1.

2 FBI report, August 7, 1954, p. 5; 105–8229 — 2.

3 Loyalty of Government Employees, ibid., p. 8.

4 Harold Rubenstein, FBI, August 8, 1952, p. 12, 105–8229 — 1.

5 Harold Rubenstein, FBI, August 8, 1952, p. 2, 105–8229 — 1.

6 Loyalty of Government Employees, op. cit., p. 3, 105–8229 — 1.

to help organise 'a new Germany', by which he clearly did not mean a new Germany of the liberal variety. A CIA report notes that in 1948 an informant had told the agency Yockey, as a 'review attorney' for the war crimes tribunal, 'had created an unfavourable impression in Germany when interceding on behalf of German war criminals who had been sentenced to death'.[7]

Reaching Germany in January 1946, Yockey was assigned to the 7708 War Crimes Group at Wiesbaden, Frankfurt, as a civilian employee of the US War Department. This unit investigated 'lower-level accused war criminals'. Yockey served as a post-trial review attorney evaluating petitions for clemency. As usual, he does not seem to have been particularly discreet, playing German anthems on a piano at his quarters. According to DTK, such was 'the Yockey magic' that 'one day he strikes up a conversation with a local German and by late afternoon a piano is being hoisted into his quarters!'[8]

His motives were several: to obtain documents that could be used in future defence cases, to run interference with the commission by offering objective analyses rather than vengeful propaganda and to live in devastated Germany for the purpose of contacting the post-war resistance.

According to Yockey's closest English friend and comrade, Anthony Gannon, Yockey 'often spoke of his experiences as a member of the War Crimes Group'. Yockey's 'investigative manner of cross-examination of the so-called "Nazi victims" usually went something like this: In which concentration camp were you held? Reply: In Belsen (or some other fabled place). What kind of camp was it? Reply: An extermination camp. How come YOU were not exterminated? End of scene!!!'[9]

At the time, at Wiesbaden, Dr Weit, a bank director, advised the Occupation authorities that an American named 'Francis Jockey' was 'spreading Nationalist-Bolshevist propaganda in the US zone'. Yockey was contacting ex-Wehrmacht and ex-Nazi officers and was attempting to find a German translator for his 'anti-capitalistic and anti-Semitic book'; *Imperium*, which Dr Weit had read and described as being based on the theories of Spengler

7 DTK to Bolton, April 25, 2014.

8 DTK to Bolton, ibid.

9 Anthony Gannon to Keith Stimely, February 15, 1981, Stimely Collection, University of Oregon.

and Nietzsche. Another informant at Wiesbaden stated that Yockey attempted to recruit him into an 'underground "resistance" movement' and that he was particularly looking for young ex-Wehrmacht officers who 'would "stand up" against the occupation authorities'. This informant stated he had translated a pamphlet by Yockey, 'Why the Americans did not go to Berlin', which aimed to 'expose the Jewish-Communistic-Capitalistic influences that were directing American military policy'.[10]

Was Yockey advocating an accommodation with the USSR even at this time? It seems unlikely that Dr Weit would have referred to Yockey as a 'Nationalist-Bolshevist' unless recalling the pre-war movement led by Ernst Niekisch, who survived the war and the Nazis and taught in Soviet Germany. Indeed, Niekisch had founded a periodical, *Widerstand*, in 1926 to campaign among the Right for an alliance between Germany and the USSR. The 'National-Bolshevists' had been a factor on the Right in Weimar Germany that advocated an alliance with the USSR against the liberal-democratic plutocratic powers. Even among the anti-Communist conservative politicians, diplomats and military officers, such an alliance had significant support.[11]

Yockey and Spengler did not recognise Russians as 'Western'. Spengler pointed out in a speech to Essen industrialists in 1922 that Russia was still a young race with a crusading, mystical outlook that the West had not known since the Gothic era. The veneer of alien Bolshevism could not repress this racial mystique. Spengler foresaw a 'new culture' that would emerge between Europe and East Asia, represented by the peasantry as the 'true Russian people'. He stated that the USSR was being exploited as a 'colony' by 'foreign business interests' and that since Russia and Germany have the same enemy, the 'financial interest-groups of the Allied nations', German foreign policy could be directed to mutual benefit towards Russia. Grand politics was needed to seize the opportunity. He told his audience of industrialists that commerce needed to be harnessed to politics.[12]

---

10 FBI Memorandum, December 18, 1951, 105–8229 — 1.

11 K. R. Bolton, 'Junger and National Bolshevism' in *Junger: Thoughts and Perspectives*, Vol. 11, ed. Troy Southgate (London: Black Front Press, 2012).

12 Spengler, 'The Two Faces of Russia and Germany's Eastern Problems', Rhenish-Westphalian Business Convention, Essen, February 14, 1922; published in Spengler,

***

Yockey reached Germany in time to participate in the establishment of the 7708 War Crimes Group, under the command of Colonel Clio E Straight, an Iowa lawyer and businessman who had worked in the US Army Judge Advocates Office during the war.[13] The purpose of these US Army courts, as distinct from the four-power tribunals, was to investigate alleged war crimes committed against American personnel. From April 1945 to December 1947 these war crimes groups undertook 222 trials. The army set up an independent reviewing authority, supposedly to provide a 'fair trial for the defendants'.[14] As is evident from Yockey's experiences, it resulted in no such thing.

The head of the post-trial section was Samuel Sonenfield, whose name could only have confirmed Yockey's suspicions as to the character of the Nuremberg judicial regime. This US army group was responsible for the infamous trial of the Malmedy Massacre defendants, from May 16 to July 16, 1946; that is, during Yockey's employment. The defendants had been accused of shooting American soldiers who had surrendered during the Battle of the Bulge in Belgium. The US Army later investigated the methods of extracting confessions, after a process set in motion by German nationalists who managed to bring the matter to the attention of American politicians. A dissertation on the US War Crimes Group, although favourable towards the war crimes process, nonetheless states of the defendants that:

> Most were locked in the dungeon of Schwaebisch Hall for months where they were refused clean clothing or the ability to take a bath. After taking the German prisoners from their dank cells, American interrogators roughly interviewed them and coerced confessions and sworn statements from each using psychological torture, threats and physical violence. Though the SS men were veterans of some of the bitterest fighting in history, most of them were young and did not have the education or experience to withstand the pressure of the investigators.[15]

---

*Politsche Schriften* (Munich, 1932).

13 FBI Memorandum, December 18, 1951, op. cit., p. 140.

14 FBI Memorandum, ibid., p. 134.

15 Reynolds and Mueller, 'Review, US vs. Altfuldisch, et al',1-2, Office of the Judge Advocate, *Complete List of War Crimes Case Trials*, 49-53; cited by Wesley Vincent Hilton, 'The

Willis M Everett, appointed by the US Army as chief defence counsel, was uneasy about the number of Jews who were involved in the war crimes process. James J Weingartner writes of this:

> Other factors entered into Everett's refusal to accept the outcome of the Malmedy trial. While not a racist, he shared with many contemporaries a suspicion of Jews as a clannish subculture with views and interests not entirely in harmony with the best interests of the countries of which they were citizens. This manifested itself in a distrustful attitude towards the Jewish principals in the Malmedy investigation and trial, particularly the law member of the court, Colonel Rosenfeld, in the assumption that Germans, SS men at that, could not have received just treatment at their hands. In a nutshell, Everett believed that confessions had been extorted and then legitimated in court by a collusive system which had been weighted against his clients from the beginning.[16]

Everett also regarded the alleged crimes of the Waffen SS youngsters in the heat of battle as having their counterpart in the US Army. Everett recalled talking with General Josiah Dalbey, president to the Malmedy court, at the officer's club in Dachau. Dalbey stated that the sentencing of the seventy-three defendants had been the most difficult undertaking he had ever encountered because he knew that American soldiers had been guilty of similar offences. Dalbey agreed with Everett that the case should not have come to trial. The review officer of the Malmedy case, Maximillian Koessler, after the trial, pushed for a speedy review. He referred to convictions, including death and life sentences, as being secured on vague and contradictory testimony and to interrogation methods that included the use of hoods, false eyewitnesses and mock trials. Clio Straight was displeased with Koessler's reviews (although he could not adequately articulate his reasons) and they were rejected.[17]

Hence, Yockey was not the only review case officer who was rebuked for not rubber stamping court judgements. Nor was his contention that the war crimes trials were *Talmudic* vengeance at odds with the observations of

---

Blackest Canvas: US Army Courts and the Trials of War Criminals in Post World War II Europe', PhD Dissertation, Texas Tech University, December 2003, p. 138.

16 James J Weingartner, *Crossroads of Death: the Story of the Malmedy Massacre and Trial*, (Berkley: University of California Press, 1979), p. 169.

17 Ibid., pp. 170–172.

others involved with the trials. Everett took the matter to the US Supreme Court, despite the Army refusing to provide him with the court transcripts of Malmedy. The Justices however ruled that they did not have jurisdiction over Army trials.[18]

German and American nationalists, along with sundry liberals expressing disquiet about the vengeance being wreaked upon Germany, took the matter up with Senator Joseph McCarthy, a member of the US Senate Judiciary Committee, pressing him for an enquiry.[19] The Secretary of the Army, Kenneth C Royall, established a tribunal headed by Gordon Simpson of the Texas Supreme Court, Leroy van Roden, Pennsylvania judge, and Lieutenant Colonel Charles W Lawrence of the US Army.[20] The Simpson Commission recommended the commutation of all death sentences of the Malmedy defendants.[21] While the Simpson Commission report was 'bland', van Roden returned to the USA fully endorsing the allegations that interrogators had subjected the defendants to beatings, including 'blows to the genitals', threats of hanging during interrogations and refusal of drinking water.[22] Colonel Strong, head of the War Crimes Group at Wiesbaden, testifying before the Senate investigation, was critical of the prejudiced manner of Colonel A. H. Rosenfeld, the 'law member' of the court trying the Malmedy defendants, and stated that the prosecution team had obstructed and threatened witnesses.[23] Rosenfeld 'had wielded great power, interpreting the law and making frequent procedural rulings for a bench whose members were combat soldiers inexpert in such matters. Rosenfeld had not allowed the defence to challenge the credibility of prosecution witnesses'.[24]

The most prominent of the interrogators at Schwaebisch Hall was William R Perl, a Prague-born Jewish lawyer from Austria, who had been active with Zionist emigration programmes. He was attached to the War Crimes Branch

18 Ibid., p. 187.

19 Ibid., p. 199.

20 Ibid., p. 190.

21 Ibid., p. 193.

22 Ibid., p. 194.

23 Ibid., p. 209.

24 Ibid., p. 225.

of the US Army in 1945. When incessantly questioned by Senator McCarthy, Perl 'exploded' that there was so much 'noise' about 'one or two Germans getting slapped'.[25]

This was the situation in which Yockey had placed himself as a review officer for the War Crimes Group at Wiesbaden. The Malmedy case, as recent disclosures show, was typical of the war crimes procedures. A 'secret torture prison' was operated at Bad Nenndorf in north-west Germany by the Combined Services Detailed Interrogation Centre (CSDIC), a division of the British War Office. The centre of the township was emptied of people and surrounded with barbed wire. At night the villagers could hear the screams of the prisoners. Most of the interrogators were 'German-Jewish refugees'. The warders were the 'most unruly' elements of the British Army, who could be expected to resort most readily to violence.[26]

> The Foreign Office briefed Clement Attlee, the prime minister, that "the guards had apparently been instructed to carry out physical assaults on certain prisoners with the object of reducing them to a state of physical collapse and of making them more amenable to interrogation".[27]

Another 'secret center' was operated in London where German POWs could be held and tortured in England without the knowledge of the Red Cross. In 2005, at the request of *The Guardian* newspaper, documents were declassified showing the extent of the torture regime against Germans after the war. The documents refer to 'living skeletons', tortured, beaten and exposed to extreme cold. The prisoners expanded from members of the Nazi party and the SS to anyone who had succeeded under the Third Reich. They even included Germans who had escaped from the Russian zone and offered to spy for the British. They were tortured—one dying—to determine whether they were sincere. A former diplomat incarcerated at Bad Nenndorf was there simply

---

25 Ibid., pp. 218–219.

26 Ian Cobain, 'Britain's Secret Torture Chamber: The Interrogation Centre that Turned Prisoners into Living Skeletons', *The Guardian*, December 17, 2005, http://www.theguardian.com/uk/2005/dec/17/secondworldwar.topstories3?guni=Article:in%20body%20link.

27 Ian Cobain, ibid.

because he knew too much about the interrogation techniques, while another was there for eight months due to a clerical error. Apart from physical brutalities, threats to kill a prisoner's wife and children were accepted techniques of interrogation. An anti-Nazi who had spent two years in Gestapo custody stated he had never experienced such brutality as he had at Bad Nendorf.[28]

***

Yockey was noted for his 'absenteeism'. He spent much of his time searching for German veterans and urging resistance to the Occupation. On December 27, 1946 Yockey was fired for 'abandonment of position'. Willis Carto, in his 'Introduction' to the Noontide Press edition of *Imperium*, states that when Yockey was called before Sonenfield, he was told: 'We don't want this type of report. This has entirely the wrong slant. You'll have to rewrite these reports to conform to the official viewpoint.' Yockey responded that he was 'a lawyer, not a journalist. You'll have to write your own propaganda'.[29]

Despite his pro-German record, his wartime and post-war AWOL and absenteeism from the Army, and his disruptive activity in Germany, in 1951 Yockey was still with the Army, at Fort Custer and Fort Hood, albeit employed by the American Red Cross.[30] At Fort Custer, he was again remembered as being 'disruptive' and 'radical minded' and as having praised Pelley and the pre-war Silver Shirts.[31] He was assigned with the 2nd Armored Division and returned to Germany on July 15, 1951, stationed at the Rhine Military Post and at the Headquarters of the 7th Army, as liaison officer for the Red Cross. He resigned from the American Red Cross on October 24, 1951,[32] having stated to a colleague his dissatisfaction with his position.[33] A colleague recalled to the FBI that Yockey had condemned the US State Department as being infiltrated by 'Commies' and that he could easily pick out a Communist. He also expressed his pro-German sympathies. He was described as 'an exceptionally

28 Ibid.

29 W. Carto, 'Introduction', *Imperium* (Sausalito, California, Noontide Press, 1962), xi-xii.

30 CIA to FBI, op. cit., January 5, 1952.

31 FBI Memorandum, January 8, 1952, 105–8229 — 1.

32 FBI security information sheet, July 3, 1952, 105–8229 — 1.

33 FBI security report, July 8, 1952, p. 11, 105–8229 — 1.

intelligent person' who, despite his cantankerous nature, 'has the ability to be affable and pleasant and when it is his desire, makes a favorable impression'. It was opined that Yockey had joined the Red Cross for the sole purpose of getting back to Germany.[34]

***

The Germany among whose ruins Yockey wandered, seeking out the persecuted and the condemned, was that of the Morgenthau Plan which aimed to reduce Germany to a dismembered pastoral territory with a decimated population that would eventually become extinct. Many American soldiers did not like what they found among the Jewish Displaced Persons, a US Army periodical commenting:

> The new GIs found it difficult to understand and like people who pushed, screamed, clawed for food, smelled bad, who couldn't and didn't want to obey orders, who sat with dull faces and vacant, staring eyes in a cell, or concentration camp barrack, or within a primitive cave, and refused to come out at their command.[35]

Those traits were widely perceived, even among the highly cultured and assimilated German-Jews before the war, to be inherent in large numbers of the Eastern Jewish population. These Eastern Jews had been regarded with loathing or embarrassment by noble German Jews such as Walther Rathenau, foreign minister in Weimar Germany, who wrote: 'You rarely find a middle course between wheedling subservience and vile arrogance.'[36]

General George Patton, initially the commander organising the Displaced Persons, running the Ohrdruf camp, was at first appalled by the conditions in which he had found the inmates. However, he soon implemented a pass system that applied only to Jews at the camp and maintained a barbed wire fence. Rabbi Judah Nadich, General Dwight Eisenhower's adviser, told Eisenhower

34 FBI security report, ibid.

35 Anton Gill, *The Journey Back from Hell: An Oral History: Conversations with Concentration Camp Survivors* (New York: William Morrow, 1988), p. 41; quoting *Army Talk*, no. 151, November 30, 1946.

36 Walter Rathenau, 'Hear, O Israel!', *Zukunft*, no. 18, March 16, 1897.

of this and Patton was ordered to remove the wire and the passes, but the good rabbi informed Eisenhower that this had not been done. Nadich recalled:

> Eisenhower ordered General Patton to report to him the following morning at 8 o'clock, which meant an overnight ride for General Patton from Munich, and I was later told by General W Smith (General Eisenhower's chief of staff) that Eisenhower said to Patton … "George, why don't you do something for these Jews?" And General Patton replied, "Why the hell should I?" To which General Eisenhower got very angry and burst out with the words, "Godammit, if for no other reason but because I ordered you to". A short time later General Patton was removed as commander of the 3rd Army.[37]

It was Eisenhower who oversaw the herding of German POWs into large, fenced paddocks, without shelter. The prisoners were placed on starvation rations. Around 750,000 of these POWs died of disease and starvation as a consequence. Of the 630,000 prisoners that France took from the Americans as forced labourers, 250,000 died from starvation and mistreatment. Any civilians who approached the fences with food for the prisoners were shot. This was therefore a deliberate policy of mass starvation, quite different from the food situation that the German concentration camps faced during the closing months of the war, when Allied bombing of railroads ensured that supplies could not reach the camps. The deaths at the American-run camps were obscured in the statistical columns as 'other losses'.[38]

Patton remarked of the Eastern Jewish DPs that:

> These people do not understand toilets and refuse to use them except as repositories for tin cans, garbage, and refuse... They decline, where practicable, to use latrines, preferring to relieve themselves on the floor… Where, although room existed, the Jews were crowded together to an appalling extent, and in practically every room there was a pile of garbage in one corner which was also used as a latrine. The Jews were only forced to desist from their nastiness and clean up the mess by the threat of the butt ends of rifles. Of course, I know the expression

37 Rabbi Judah Nadich (Interviewee) and Lilly Singer (Interviewer). *Oral History Transcript. Fred Roberts Crawford — Witness to the Holocaust Project Files, September 24, 1981*, Atlanta, Georgia, Special Collections, Woodruff Library, Emory University, p. 8.

38 James Bacque, *Other Losses* (Toronto: Stoddard Publishing, 1989).

> "lost tribes of Israel" applied to the tribes which disappeared — not to the tribe of Judah from which the current sons of bitches are descended. However, it is my personal opinion that this too is a lost tribe — lost to all decency.[39]

Ordered by Eisenhower to attend a synagogue service, Patton wrote:

> This happened to be the feast of Yom Kippur, so they were all collected in a large, wooden building, which they called a synagogue. It behoved General Eisenhower to make a speech to them. We entered the synagogue, which was packed with the greatest stinking bunch of humanity I have ever seen. When we got about halfway up, the head rabbi, who was dressed in a fur hat similar to that worn by Henry VIII of England and in a surplice heavily embroidered and very filthy, came down and met the General … The smell was so terrible that I almost fainted and actually about three hours later lost my lunch as the result of remembering it.[40]

Following an order that German houses, such as they remained after the Allied carpet bombing of civilian areas, be forcibly requisitioned for DPs, Patton wrote of the vengeance being wreaked against Germany as a 'Semitic' policy inaugurated by US Treasury Secretary Henry Morgenthau Jr, and perennial presidential adviser and international banker Bernard Baruch:

> Evidently the virus started by Morgenthau and Baruch of a Semitic revenge against all Germans is still working. Harrison (a US State Department official) and his associates indicate that they feel German civilians should be removed from houses for the purpose of housing Displaced Persons. There are two errors in this assumption. First, when we remove an individual German we punish an individual German, while the punishment is not intended for the individual but for the race.
>
> Furthermore, it is against my Anglo-Saxon conscience to remove a person from a house, which is a punishment, without due process of law. In the second place, Harrison and his ilk believe that the Displaced Person is a human being, which he is not, and this applies particularly to the Jews, who are lower than animals.[41]

---

39 George Patton, diary entry May 20, 1945. See Martin Blumenson, *The Patton Papers 1940–1945* (Da Capo Press, 2009).

40 Patton, diary entry September 17, 1945.

41 Ibid.

Patton wrote on several occasions that the Allied policy in Germany, including the blowing up of factories, and sending POWs to work as slave labour, was 'Semitic'. In his diary, he recorded:

> Today we received orders ... in which we were told to give the Jews special accommodations. If for Jews, why not Catholics, Mormons, etc? ... We are also turning over to the French several hundred thousand prisoners of war to be used as slave labor in France. It is amusing to recall that we fought the Revolution in defense of the rights of man and the Civil War to abolish slavery and have now gone back on both principles.[42]

After visiting Berlin, Patton wrote to his wife:

> Berlin gave me the blues. We have destroyed what could have been a good race, and we are about to replace them with Mongolian savages. And all Europe will be communist. It's said that for the first week after they took it (Berlin), all women who ran were shot and those who did not were raped. I could have taken it (instead of the Soviets) had I been allowed.[43]

Patton wrote of the Jewish agitation for vengeance:

> There is a very apparent Semitic influence in the press. They are trying to do two things: first, implement communism, and second, see that all businessmen of German ancestry and non-Jewish antecedents are thrown out of their jobs.
>
> They have utterly lost the Anglo-Saxon conception of justice and feel that a man can be kicked out because somebody else says he is a Nazi. They were evidently quite shocked when I told them I would kick nobody out without the successful proof of guilt before a court of law ...
>
> Another point which the press harped on was the fact that we were doing too much for the Germans to the detriment of the DPs, most of whom are Jews. I could not give the answer to that one, because the answer is that, in my opinion and that of most nonpolitical officers, it is vitally necessary for us to build

---

42 Patton, diary entry September 14, 1945.

43 Patton, July 21, 1945.

> Germany up now as a buffer state against Russia. In fact, I am afraid we have waited too long.[44]

Eisenhower 'kicked Patton upstairs' as commander of the Fifteenth Army. Patton wrote to his wife that he was pleased to be out of the former post as he had been 'a sort of executioner to the best race in Europe'.[45]

When the US press attacked Patton for being 'soft on Nazis' he wrote to Major General James B Harbord, who had returned to the USA, of the 'communist and Semitic elements' that had been smearing not only him but other straight military men who did not condone the unchivalrous policy of *Talmudic* vengeance. He regarded it as a deliberate plan to alienate the officers from the enlisted men because the 'communist' and 'Semitic elements' feared the role of the Army now that Germany had been defeated. What they feared, Patton makes plain, was the political influence of 11,000,000 veterans and their votes. Patton wrote to Harbord that he intended to start 'an all-out offensive' against this subversion once he returned to the USA.[46]

Patton, after having had his Cadillac hit by an army truck on his way to Mannheim, had recovered in hospital and was due to be released when he died. Recently discovered papers of OSS[47] assassin Douglas Bazata, and his confession during an interview, reveal that Patton was killed due to his opposition to post-war policy towards Germany. After the crash, Bazata shot Patton with a 'low velocity projectile', which broke his neck. The Soviet secret police, NKVD, were then permitted to poison him in hospital. Bazata had been told by OSS chief Bill Donovan that Patton was 'destroying everything the Allies had done'. Patton's Third Army had been prevented from taking either Berlin or Prague.[48]

Canadian journalist James Bacque, who exposed the mass starvation of German POWs under US control, also documented the deaths of 9,000,000 Germans after the war as the result of post-war policies under the 'Morgenthau

44 Patton, September 22, 1945.

45 September 29, 1945.

46 Patton to Harbord, October 22, 1945.

47 Predecessor to the CIA.

48 Robert Wilcox, *Target Patton: The Plot to Assassinate General George S Patton* (Regnery History, 2010).

Plan'. This genocide was carried out until 1950 and included over 2,000,000 deaths of ethnic Germans expelled from their ancestral homes in Eastern Europe on a death march to Germany.[49]

It was into this situation that Yockey played German anthems on a piano, tried to assist alleged war criminals and sought out German veterans to resist the Occupation.

Professor Deborah Lipstadt, who denies that the Morgenthau Plan was ever enacted, has Yockey responsible for having 'laid out the essential elements of holocaust denial'. Lipstadt seems to have coined the term 'holocaust denial',[50] a worthless expression in terms of scholarship. Lipstadt spends several pages discussing *Imperium*, Yockey and his posthumous American publisher, Willis Carto. She seems not even to have read *Imperium* or any other primary sources on these subjects. She quotes from a secondary source part of what Yockey writes in *Imperium* about the atrocity propaganda against Germany.[51] The complete passage from *Imperium* reads:

> This propaganda announced that 6,000,000 members of the Jewish Culture-Nation-State-Church-People-Race had been killed in European camps, as well as an indeterminate number of other people. The propaganda was on a worldwide scale, and was of a mendacity that was perhaps adapted to a uniformized mass, but was simply disgusting to discriminating Europeans. The propaganda was technically quite complete. "Photographs" were supplied in millions of copies. Thousands of the people who had been killed published accounts of their experiences in these camps. Hundreds of thousands more made fortunes in post-war black-markets. "Gas-chambers" that did not exist were photographed, and a "gasmobile" was invented to titillate the mechanically-minded.[52]

Alex Kurtagic, publisher of the Wermod edition of *Imperium*, concurs in a way with Lipstadt in stating that Yockey, having written of this six million propaganda circa 1947–1948 would be 'one of the earliest Holocaust revisionists, along with Harry Elmer Barnes. He predates Paul Rassinier, whose book,

49 James Bacque, *Crimes and Mercies: The Fate of German Civilians Under Allied Occupation 1944–1950* (London: Little Brown and Co., 1997).

50 Deborah Lipstadt, *Denying the Holocaust* (London: Penguin Books, 1993).

51 Deborah Lipstadt, ibid., p. 148.

52 Yockey, *Imperium*, Wermod ed., op. cit., p. 669.

*The Drama of the European Jews*, was not published until 1964, and David Hoggan, whose *The Myth of the Six Million*, was not published until 1969 (although it was written in 1960)'.[53]

While Lipstadt et al insist that Yockey was writing as an 'American Hitler'[54] (sic), he was in fact writing as an eyewitness who had access to legal documents, heard witness testimony and questioned accusers. Yockey absconded with much documentation after leaving his job at Wiesbaden.

Yockey pointed out in *Imperium* that, hitherto, enemies within the same High Culture would accord each other honour. In a chapter on 'The Terror' imposed on Europe after World War II, Yockey opens by quoting Frederick the Great in 1764 that 'it is a weakness, in fact a stinginess of heart, not to speak well of one's enemies, and not to pay them the honour they deserve'. The defeated who belonged to the same culture, i.e. Western Christendom, were shown 'generosity and respect' by the former foe once the power is gained, the object is reached and the matter is settled. Malice towards a defeated foe over an extended period was not the norm.[55] With World War II, however, this was a fight to annihilation between two different culture-souls: the Jewish and the Western, as total as the war between Rome and Carthage. It was therefore necessary to more than militarily or politically and economically defeat the Western culture-soul represented by Germany, Italy and their allies, but to annihilate it. Yockey wrote of this:

> Since this is so, Culture-distortion proceeded to wage a European Terror after the War, when there was no longer any political struggle whatever going on in the Western Civilization.

---

53 Alex Kurtagic, *Imperium*, ibid., note 473. The others mentioned, Barnes, Rassinier and Hoggan, were recognised scholars. Professor Rassinier, an ex-communist, a Socialist, and a leader of the French Resistance, decorated after the war and elected to the National Assembly, had been interned at Dora and Buchenwald camps. He had been struck by the claims after the war that there had been 'gassings' at these camps, and investigated the same allegations about other camps, including those in the East, such as Auschwitz, concluding that all such claims were bogus. See: Paul Rassinier, *Debunking the Genocide Myth* (Torrance: Institute for Historical Review, 1978).

54 Lipstadt, op. cit., p. 147.

55 Yockey, *Imperium*, Wermod ed., op. cit., p. 745.

> The history of the "war crimes" program shows its nature. Its foundations were laid in the anti-European propaganda with which America was deluged from 1933 onward. The propaganda itself showed that extra-Cultural influences were at work, since it rejected the comity of nations and political honor. The leaders of Europe were represented as common criminals and sexual perverts, and through this vile propaganda, the idea was spread that these leaders could and should be killed. Gradually the thesis was widened and the twentieth century Idea of Ethical Socialism was equated with evil itself, and the populations in its service were described as suffering from mass-insanity, and in need of "re-education" by America.[56]

'The Nuremberg spectacle' was evidence of the 'irreconcilability of two Culture-souls, and of the abysmal depth to which Culture-disease can descend'.[57] Indeed, one might say that the code of the post-war occupation of Europe was that of the Old Testament and the *Talmud*, where the Israelites are commanded to exterminate their enemies and destroy every vestige of their memory. This was the aim of the Morgenthau Plan, put into effect for five years, until a rebuilding of Germany in the face of the USSR was unavoidable.

The French self-described 'fascist' intellectual Maurice Bardèche had published his *Nuremberg or the Promised Land* in the same year (1948) that *Imperium* was published. In 1950, Bardèche published *Nuremberg II ou les Faux-Monnayeurs* (*Nuremberg II or The Counterfeiters*).[58] At the time, Bardèche represented several French groups as their delegate to the European Social Movement, which included Mosley's Union Movement and others from Sweden, Germany and Italy. Yockey had read *Nuremberg or the Promised Land*, probably in German translation, and had contacted Bardèche under his *nom de plume*, Ulick Varange. He sent Bardèche 'a certain number of extremely valuable documents coming from archives of which he had knowledge and which were intended for the headquarters of General McCloy, concerning the requests for clemency for a certain number of the persons condemned by the international military tribunal'. Bardèche states: 'I made use of that documentation in the second book that I did on the Nuremberg trial under

---

56 Ibid., pp. 748–749.

57 Ibid., p. 753.

58 M Bardèche *Nuremberg II ou les Faux-Monnayeurs* (Les Sept Couleurs, 1950).

the title *Nuremberg II ou les Faux-Monnayeurs*'. Yockey also sent Bardèche a copy of *Imperium*.[59] Of the 'war crimes' trials Bardèche, like Yockey, discerned something decidedly alien, despite the façade of Western legal trappings. For Bardèche, the proceedings had no more legitimacy than the 'justice' meted out to defeated chiefs by an African tribal potentate:

> For this modern machinery, as one knows, had the result of resurrecting a jurisprudence like that of Negro tribes. The victorious king is set on his throne and has his witchdoctors called in: then, in the presence of warriors sitting on their heels, someone cuts the throats of the vanquished chiefs. We start to suspect that all the rest is a bit of comedy, and the public, after eighteen months, is no longer taken in by this kind of play-acting. The chiefs have their throats cut because they were vanquished; the atrocities with which one reproaches them, well, no just man can avoid saying to himself that the commanders of the Allied armies could be reproached with atrocities just as serious: the phosphorus bombs well counterbalance the concentration camps. An American court which condemns Göring to death has no more authority, in the eyes of men, than would a German court which presumed to condemn Roosevelt. A court which creates the law after being seated on its bench brings us back to the beginning of history.[60]

## Colonel Knöchlein's Case

The documents obtained by Yockey were used to aid the defence of Lieutenant-General Otto Ohlendorf, commander of the anti-partisan *Einsatzgruppe* in the Ukraine. Yockey also assisted with the defence of Lieutenant Colonel Fritz Knöchlein, commander of the 2nd Totenkopf unit, who was hanged in 1949 for his alleged responsibility for the shooting of British POWs at Dunkirk in 1940. Knöchlein claimed that he had been tortured in detention at the 'London Cage' while under the jurisdiction of Lieutenant Colonel Alexander Scotland, who dismissed the allegation as 'lame'. Knöchlein was beaten when he complained to Colonel Scotland. We now know that the 'London Cage' was used as a torture centre run by MI19, a section of the War Office responsible

59 Bardèche to Stimely, 'Note on F. P. Yockey', 1982.

60 Bardèche, *Nuremberg or the Promised Land*, p. 14, http://www.vho.org/aaargh/fran/livres7/BARDECHEnureng.pdf.

for extracting information from POWs. About 1,000 were induced to sign 'confessions'.[61]

Gannon states that when Yockey reached England after his stint in Germany, 'he continued to work for the freeing of "war criminals", knowing at first-hand how these unfortunates had been framed-up. This was at the time of his collaboration with OM [Oswald Mosley], and it is to the credit of OM that he was not afraid to publicly support the ending of this ritual-execution of prisoners of war. Senator Joe McCarthy was involved with this work, having made visits to Germany with parties from Congress, and FPY was in touch with him'.[62]

While Guy Chesham, one of those who worked with Gannon and Yockey in the initial stages of Sir Oswald Mosley's Union Movement, castigated Mosley for supposed failure to oppose the 'war crimes trials',[63] Gannon alludes to this not being the case. Mosley had written of such issues already in 1947, in his first post-war book, *The Alternative*, prior to the formation of the Union Movement. Having mentioned the incidences of atrocities committed by British, American, French, Russian and other soldiers during World War II, he was surely among the first to raise the question of whether deaths in the German concentration camps were largely the result of 'Allied bombing and consequent epidemics'. Mosley stated that atrocities by anyone on any magnitude could not be excused on moral grounds, so the only question was one of 'mitigation'. What concerned Mosley in regard to the hypocrisy of the 'war crimes' trials and propaganda directed against Germans and others, was that 'it strangles the soul of Europe'.

> The wounds of Europe must be healed before the work of construction can begin. They bear wounds of the spirit, and they are kept open by these animosities and memories of atavistic savagery. These old wounds have no interest to the

---

61 Ian Cobain, 'Secrets of the London Cage', *The Guardian*, November 12, 2005, http://www.theguardian.com/uk/2005/nov/12/secondworldwar.world.

62 Gannon memoir, op. cit.

63 Guy Chesham, 'A Memorandum of Disassociation' August 31, 1949, p. 5, University of Birmingham, Oswald Mosley papers, OMD 8/4/1/1.

> creative mind, but they impede our work. That is why we ask Europe not to look back, but to stride forward.[64]

Yockey took up the Knöchlein case as what must have been one of his first activities in England. Gannon recalled:

> When in England, Yockey remained quite busy. He continued to distribute *Imperium* by every avenue open to him, presenting copies to the Library of the House of Commons, Library of the US Congress, and to the principal universities. In addition, he took a keen interest in the so-called "war crimes" industry and in the case of a certain Colonel Knöchlein, in particular. This German officer was being held on a "war crimes" charge by the British authorities, and Yockey and many others believed that he was the innocent victim of a false charge. Yockey worked with might and main with the Labour Member of Parliament, Reginald Paget Q.C. (now Lord Paget) and Captain Liddell Hart to save him, but all in vain and, in due course, Colonel Knöchlein was executed.[65]

The charge against Knöchlein read:

> The accused Fritz Knöchlein, a German national, in the charge of the Hamburg Garrison Unit, pursuant to Regulation 4 of the Regulations for the Trial of War Criminals, is charged with committing a war crime in that he in the vicinity of Paradis, Pas-de-Calais, France, on or about 27 May 1940, in violation of the laws and usages of war, was concerned in the killing of about ninety prisoners-of-war, members of The Royal Norfolk Regiment and other British Units.[66]

Dr Uhde, Knöchlein's defence attorney, stated that the accused had not been present at the shooting of the British soldiers, who had used illegal dumdum bullets on the Germans[67] and had misused a flag of truce.

---

64 Oswald Mosley, 'Atrocities', *The Alternative* (Mosley Publications, 1947). Available from: Black House Publishing, http://www.blackhousepublishing.com/oswald-mosley/the-alternative.

65 Gannon memoir, op. cit.

66 See 'British Military and Criminal History 1900–1999', http://www.stephen-stratford.co.uk/pooleys_revenge.htm.

67 The British army were the first to use dumdum bullets during the nineteenth century and the Germans were the first to protest their use as inhumane, resulting in their ban

Paget maintained a strident opposition to the 'war crimes trials'. He was a mainstay of the Constitutional Research Group. Founded in 1941, this informal group of prominent individuals, with Lord Sempill as president, opposed American and other un-British encroachments on British interests. Among its supporters were ex-Cabinet minister Lord Maurice Hankey, Captain Liddell Hart, Major General J. F. C. Fuller; William Inge, Dean of St Paul's Cathedral, and others. Paget was defence counsel for Field Marshall Erich von Manstein and wrote *Manstein, His Campaigns and Trial* (1951).[68] Given Yockey's association with Liddell Hart, Fuller and Paget, one might surmise that he worked with the Constitutional Research Group but nothing definite seems known of this.

In reply to criticism by Guy Chesham, mentioned by Chesham in his vitriolic response to Mosley, the latter stated that public support from him for Knöchlein would only harm the German's case;[69] surely a reasonable assumption from someone who was himself still treated as a pariah. However, Gannon mentions that Mosley and Union Movement General Secretary Raven Thomson did try to assist Knöchlein.[70] Although Paget successfully defended General Erich von Manstein on 'war crimes' charges, he was unsuccessful with Knöchlein, who was hanged in January 1949.

When the commander of 'The Cage', Alexander Scotland, intended to publish his memoirs in 1950 he was threatened with prosecution under the Official Secrets Act and Special Branch raided his retirement home. Cobain comments:

> An assessment by MI5 pointed out that Scotland had detailed repeated breaches of the Geneva Convention, with his admissions that prisoners had been forced to kneel while being beaten about the head; forced to stand to attention for up

---

in warfare by the Hague Convention in 1899. That was a time, however, when there remained vestiges of chivalry that were finally extinguished by World War II.

68 Graham Macklin, *Very Deeply Dyed in Black* (New York: St. Martin's Press, 2007), pp. 126–127.

69 Guy Chesham, 'Memorandum of Disassociation', op. cit.

70 Anthony Gannon to Keith Stimely, February 15, 1981; Stimely collection, University of Oregon.

> to 26 hours; threatened with execution; or threatened with "an unnecessary operation".[71]

Scotland's memoirs were published in 1957,[72] after much had been expunged. Regarding Knöchlein, Cobain found in the National Archives 'a long and detailed letter of complaint from one SS captain [sic], Fritz Knöchlein, who describes his treatment after being taken to The Cage in October 1946'.

> Knöchlein alleges that because he was "unable to make the desired confession" he was stripped, given only a pair of pyjama trousers, deprived of sleep for four days and nights, and starved.
>
> The guards kicked him each time he passed, he alleges, while his interrogators boasted that they were "much better" than the "Gestapo in Alexanderplatz". After being forced to perform rigorous exercises until he collapsed, he says he was compelled to walk in a tight circle for four hours. On complaining to Scotland that he was being kicked even "by ordinary soldiers without a rank", Knöchlein alleges that he was doused in cold water, pushed down stairs and beaten with a cudgel. Later, he says, he was forced to stand beside a large gas stove with all its rings lit before being confined in a shower, which sprayed extremely cold water from the sides as well as from above. Finally, the SS man says, he and another prisoner were taken into the gardens behind the mansions, where they were forced to run in circles while carrying heavy logs.
>
> "Since these tortures were the consequences of my personal complaint, any further complaint would have been senseless," Knöchlein wrote. "One of the guards who had a somewhat humane feeling advised me not to make any more complaints, otherwise things would turn worse for me". Other prisoners, he alleged, were beaten until they begged to be killed, while some were told that they could be made to disappear.[73]

While the War Office took the allegations seriously, they considered that an investigation would delay Knöchlein's execution. After 'The Cage' had been mistakenly identified to the Red Cross and its cover exposed, with a Red Cross representative unsuccessfully trying several times to inspect the

71 Ian Cobain, op. cit..

72 A. P. Scotland, *The Cage* (London: Evans, 1957).

73 Ian Cobain, op. cit.

houses, its work was moved to internment camps in Germany, where conditions were even worse. A 27-year-old German journalist who had been held by the Gestapo said that his treatment as an inmate at a British internment camp was far worse.[74]

74 Ian Cobain, ibid.

# 'The Philosopher'

It was stated in an FBI report that Yockey had become a convert to 'European Authoritarian Nationalism' when he went to Europe as a 'review attorney' with a war crimes review board. The hearsay originated from a smear against Yockey by Natinform, a pro-American, anti-Soviet group. However, at 23, with the writing of the essay 'Life as an Art', the premises of Yockey's ideas were already all present.

Yockey regarded National Socialist Germany and Fascist Italy as 'provisional forms' of the European resurgence. Spengler saw in Fascist Italy such a provisional form of the future European resurgence, concluding in his last book, *The Hour of Decision*:

> At this point advancing history towers high over economic distress and internal political ideals. The elemental forces of life are themselves entering the fight, which is for all or nothing. The prefiguration of Caesarism will soon become clearer, more conscious and more unconcealed. The masks will fall completely from the age of the parliamentary interlude. All attempts to gather up the content of the future into parties will soon be forgotten. The Fascist formations of this decade will pass into new, unforeseeable forms, and even present-day nationalism will disappear. There remains as a formative power only the warlike, "Prussian" spirit—everywhere and not in Germany alone. Destiny, once compacted in meaningful forms and great traditions, will now proceed to make history in terms of formless individual powers. Caesar's legions are returning to consciousness.
>
> Here, possibly even in our own century, the ultimate decisions are waiting for their man. In presence of these the little aims and notions of our current politics

> sink to nothing. He whose sword compels victory here will be lord of the world. The dice are there ready for this stupendous game. *Who dares to throw them?*[1]

Spengler's final thoughts had influenced Yockey's essay 'Life as an Art' and had an enduring influence on his philosophy and deeds. Spengler wrote of 'the elemental forces of life' and the destiny that was grabbed by new Caesars, or what Yockey called in Nietzschean terms 'higher men'. The theme of both is that democratic ideals, petty politics and economic thinking will give way to titanic struggles for world supremacy. That indeed did take place in the form of the 'total war' of annihilation fought between the Axis and the plutocracies in alliance with the USSR. The combination of the latter was such as to swamp the provisional forms of the new Caesarism and abort the historical epoch of Western imperium. Yockey foresaw that while fighting in the name of 'democracy', the Allied states were compelled to adopt totalitarian methods. Democracies cannot win wars, nor overcome even economic crises.

The Western Imperium was aborted by another imperium, anti-Western and headed by the USA in the name of the 'West', which in the era of mediocrity promotes its own 'Caesar' in the form of the US Presidency as the 'leader of the Western world'. Although this is a historical travesty, it is one that remains today the primary factor in world politics.

However, the Spengler/Yockey schema looks at the History of a Civilization in terms of centuries and of epochs. The victory against the 'provisional forms' of the Western Imperium is a supreme, epoch-changing example of Culture-distortion. After the war Europe did unite, albeit around the nexus of trade, but it nonetheless attests to European unity being the overshadowing theme of this epoch that even anti-Western forces have been obliged to bow to it. The European Union and the US Presidency are sickly, fetid reflections of Western Imperium and Caesarism respectively, hideously distorted beyond recognition by culture pathogens. 'The sword that compels victory' was picked up from amidst the ruins of a millennium of Europe's High Culture — reduced to rubble within a few years, courtesy of Bomber Command — and placed upon the banner of the European Liberation Front by Yockey in 1948.

***

1 Spengler, *The Hour of Decision* (New York: Alfred A Knopf, 1933), pp. 229–230.

Yockey's Spenglerian inspiration, when he entered the post-war milieu of European resistance, revived a pre-war conflict between Spengler and Hitlerism. It prevented National Socialists, particularly in the Anglosphere, from appreciating the epochal importance of Yockey's concept of *Cultural Vitalism*. Spengler held that 'race' is formed by landscape and moulded by history. 'Race' to the Spenglerian is a spiritual-cultural metaphysical phenomenon that does not relate to callipers and skull measurements. This zoological interpretation of 'race' belongs to nineteenth century materialism, the callipers of the zoologist being the counterpart to the weights and measures scales of the merchant.

The American scholar, Professor Revilo P Oliver, wrote of Spengler in regard to Yockey:

> The great modern philosopher of history is, of course, Oswald Spengler, whose *Decline of the West* formulated the problem in terms so clear and universal that everything written on the subject since 1918 has perforce had to be a commentary on Spengler — an attempt to extend, modify, or refute his magisterial synthesis.[2]

Dr Oliver wrote of Yockey:

> Francis Parker Yockey proudly proclaimed himself the disciple of the man to whom he often refers as simply The Philosopher, and it is true that at least a general understanding of Spengler's historionomy is taken for granted in the pages of Yockey's major work [*Imperium*]. But the young American had his own method and reached conclusions of his own. We must recognize in him a powerful and original mind.[3]

Adapting Spengler's cyclical outlook on the life and death of civilizations, Yockey's primary advancement of Spenglerian thought is *Cultural Vitalism* with the concepts of *Culture-parasitism*, *Culture-distortion* and *Culture-retardation*.[4]

---

2 Revilo P Oliver, 'The Shadow of Empire: Francis Parker Yockey After Twenty Years', *The American Mercury*, June 1966. Online at: http://www.revilo-oliver.com/news/1966/06/the-shadow-of-empire-francis-parker-yockey-after-twenty-years/.

3 Oliver, ibid.

4 Yockey, *Imperium*, Wermod edition, 'Cultural Vitalism', pp. 317–553.

Keith Stimely summed up Spengler's premises for *The Decline of The West*, after a lengthy exposition:[5]

> Human history is the cyclical record of the rise and fall of unrelated High Cultures. These Cultures are in reality super life-forms, that is, they are organic in nature, and like all organisms must pass through the phases of birth-life-death. Though separate entities in themselves, all High Cultures experience parallel development, and events and phases in any one find their corresponding events and phases in the others. It is possible from the vantage point of the twentieth century to glean from the past the meaning of cyclic history, and thus to predict the decline and fall of the West.[6]

Stimely pointed out that although Spenglerianism sees Western Civilization as being in its cycle of decline and approaching death, the West still has a mission to fulfil:

> Spengler, as the title of his work suggests, saw the West as doomed to the same eventual extinction that all the other High Cultures had faced. The West, he said, was now in the middle of its "civilization" phase, which had begun, roughly, with Napoleon. The coming of the Caesars (of which Napoleon was only a foreshadowing) was perhaps only decades away. Yet Spengler did not counsel any kind of sighing resignation to fate, or blithe acceptance of coming defeat and death. In a later essay, *Pessimism?* (1922), he wrote that the men of the West must still be men, and do all they could to realize the immense possibilities still open to them. Above all, they must embrace the one absolute imperative: The destruction of Money and democracy, especially in the field of politics, that grand and all-encompassing field of endeavor.[7]

It was to fulfil this mission that Yockey wrote *Imperium* and formed the European Liberation Front in the aftermath World War II. Yockey affirmed that this 'mission' was the total unity and supremacy of Western Civilization. His added perception of *Cultural Vitalism* shows that during the culture crisis

---

5 Oswald Spengler, *The Decline of The West*, ([Vol. I, 1918; Vol. II, 1922] London: George Allen and Unwin, 1959).

6 Keith Stimely, 'Oswald Spengler: An Introduction to His Life and Ideas', *Journal of Historical Review*, Vol. 17, March–April, 1998, no. 2.

7 Ibid.

of Western Civilization, at a phase where the role of money predominates, the 'culture distorter', in the case of the West, represented by the Jewish nation, is able to rise to the top through its historic acumen in trade and finance. In Yockey's development of Spengler's organic approach to history, it is innate to the Jewish character to play this role, the Jews being formed through centuries of ghetto life and commerce. It was when the liberal revolts against tradition, fomented in the name of 'the people' — or 'liberty, equality, fraternity', as the French revolutionaries put it — overthrew the traditional hierarchy that the ghettos were thrown open and the Jews rose to the top of a trade-based society.

***

When *The Decline of The West* was published after World War I, to the defeated Germans the tome put their predicament into world-historical context and offered a vision for the future of Western Civilization as a unified cultural organism. So with such promise, a second, revised edition of *The Decline of The West,* Volume One, was published in 1922, soon followed by the second volume, 'Perspectives of World-History'. *The Decline* was an immediate success and despite the academic critics, Spengler became a national figure, talked about in influential circles.

## Pessimism?

Despite the criticism of 'pessimism' or 'fatalism' that continues to be levelled at Spengler, he did not see this in his historical morphology. It could be said that because all mortals are destined to die, one might as well give up without living whatever life's course one might unfold. So it is with cultures.

Spengler had addressed the misunderstanding of 'pessimism' as early as 1921 when he replied to those who saw his outlook as a prophesy of 'dreadful catastrophe', writing of *The Decline of The West*: 'My title does not imply catastrophe. Perhaps we could eliminate the "pessimism" without altering the real sense of the title if we were to substitute for "decline" the word "fulfilment"...'[8]

8 Spengler, 'Pessimism?' *Preussische Jahrbücher*, CLXXXIV, 1921.

## German Socialism

In 1919, Spengler gave a speech entitled *Prussianism and Socialism*, which was published as a pamphlet under that title. This extolled the Prussian ethos of duty to the State as the true form of anti-capitalist 'socialism', not only Prussian but required for a universal Western resurgence. This Prussian ethical socialism or what we might call *Duty*, Spengler contrasted with Marxian 'socialism', which is nothing other than a mirror image of English economics, aiming to replace one ownership class with another, while maintaining the same nineteenth century *Zeitgeist* of money-thinking.

*Prussianism and Socialism* examined a number of issues that were explained in the final chapters of the second volume of *The Decline of The West* several years later. *Prussianism and Socialism*, like other published speeches such as *The Political Duties of German Youth* and *Reconstruction of the German Reich* (both 1924), and Spengler's final book, *The Hour of Decision* (1934), are intended as a practical philosophy to inspire new thinking and prompt action in the political realm, addressed to youth, workers, aristocrats and industrialists. Spengler explained that socialism was not Marxism and that socialism was the same as the 'spirit of Old Prussia'.[9]

In the same vein, among the final paragraphs of Volume II of *The Decline of The West*, Spengler concludes with an impassioned appeal. He calls for The West to overthrow the dictature of Money. Spengler defined 'Capitalism' as the 'money-powers' that see politics and laws as nothing other than the means for personal acquisition. 'Prussian Socialism' is 'the will to call into life a mighty politico — economic order that transcends all class interests'.[10]

***

Spengler's final essay was an answer to a question on world peace put to well-known individuals such as Eleanor Roosevelt and Mahatma Gandhi, by the Hearst magazine, *International-Cosmopolitan*, published in January 1936. Spengler began by stating that the question can only be answered by someone who knows history and the enduring characteristics of humanity. 'There is a

9 Spengler, *Prussianism and Socialism*, 1919.

10 Spengler, *The Decline of The West*, op. cit., Vol. II, p. 506.

vast difference, which most people will never comprehend, between viewing future history as it will be and viewing it as one might like it to be… Peace is a desire, war a fact; and history had never paid heed to human desires and ideals.'[11]

Spengler explained history in Nietzschean terms as a will-to-power among all healthy life forms, which take economic, social, political and military shape between individuals, classes, peoples and nations. Violence is always the ultimate recourse. 'Talk of world peace today is heard only among the white peoples, and not among the much more numerous colored races. This is a perilous state of affairs.' When individuals talk of peace their pleas are meaningless but when entire peoples become pacifistic 'it is a symptom of senility'.[12]

> Strong and unspent races are not pacifistic. To adopt such a position is to abandon the future, for the pacifist ideal is a static, terminal condition that is contrary to the basic facts of existence. Should the white peoples ever succumb to pacifism they will inevitably fall to the colored world, just as Rome succumbed to the Teutons.[13]

***

This extended discourse on Spengler is necessary because Yockey was the apostle of Spengler. Spengler had offered *The Decline of The West* to a defeated Germany and more broadly to a devastated West in the face of the rise of Bolshevism and of the 'coloured world', which he addressed more specifically in *The Hour of Decision*.[14] Yockey offered *Imperium* to a defeated Europe, which had suffered an even more epochal collapse than that of 1918. Both stated that the West is passing through a cycle of decay from which it can emerge through force of Will as a unified Empire, as other civilizations had done over the millennia. Both offered 'The West' a mission that was yet to be fulfilled, amidst the ruins of 1918 and then of 1945.

---

11 Spengler, 'Is World Peace Possible?', *Cosmopolitan*, January 1936.

12 Ibid.

13 Ibid.

14 Spengler, *The Hour of Decision* ([1934] New York: Alfred A Knopf, 1962), 'The Coloured World-Revolution', pp. 204–230.

Spengler and Yockey are both condemned as having a 'pessimistic' outlook; fatalistic in the old Germanic sense of the end of the West in a type of technical *Ragnarok*, vanquished by the mechanised forces of a plutocratic Loki and an unleashed communist and Asiatic Fenrir, devouring civilization. However, the great lesson of *Ragnarok* is that the Gods knew their fate and embraced it as their destiny. They knew that from the cataclysm something new would emerge, a new Earth and even new Gods. Spengler and Yockey were prophets of this cycle that is more accurately termed 'fulfilment', as Spengler was to state, while the prophets of the post-Western civilization are undoubtedly now emerging, perhaps in Russia, whose civilization remains young and unfulfilled.

Yockey addressed the matter of so-called 'pessimism' in *Imperium*, referring specifically to how *The Decline of the West* had been greeted by the 'day-before-yesterday thinkers with a cry of "Pessimism"'. 'By this word it was apparently thought possible to conjure away the spirit of the coming age, and summon to new life the dead spirit of an age that had passed away.' To those who do not see History organically, they seek to do whatever they like with the 'Past'. However, 'facts are not pessimistic or optimistic, sane or insane.'[15]

Those whose historical thinking is based on a 'progressive' view of History as a type of Darwinian evolution from primitive to modern, without end, feel affronted by the notion that their own outlook is not 'new' or 'modern'. It is merely analogous to the thinking of a certain type that manifests in a specific historical cycle in all Civilizations. Their type has been seen and heard throughout the course of Civilizations rising and falling over thousands of years. As Spengler showed, there is nothing 'new' or 'progressive' in today's feminism, population control, liberalism, equality, debt-finance and Marxism. It has all been done and said for millennia by cultural pathogens in human form, whom Yockey called 'Culture-distorters', 'Culture-retarders' and 'Culture-parasites'. That is why Spengler was attacked so indignantly and is now largely forgotten: because his fact-history causes discomfort to those who think they are offering something grandly 'new' and laudable.

This optimism among the highest intellectual circles, industrialists, scientists, diplomats and politicians, was cogently expressed by nineteenth

---

15 Yockey, *Imperium*, Wermod ed., 'Pessimism', pp. 71–72.

century Darwinian biologist A. R. Wallace, in a book aptly titled *The Wonderful Century* (1898), indicating the conceit of the 'late' Westerner for the unparalleled supremacy of his technics:

> Not only is our century superior to any that have gone before it but … it may be best compared with the whole preceding historical period. It must therefore be held to constitute the beginning of a new era of human progress. … We men of the nineteenth century have not been slow to praise it. The wise and the foolish, the learned and the unlearned, the poet and the pressman, the rich and the poor, alike swell the chorus of admiration for the marvellous inventions and discoveries of our own age, and especially for those innumerable applications of science which now form part of our daily life, and which remind us every hour of our immense superiority over our comparatively ignorant forefathers.[16]

This promise of a gleeful universal paradise wrought by science and enshrined by democracy and universal human rights is the outlook common to capitalism and Marxism alike, because both see History as a march in a straight line rather than as that of waxing and waning tides. It is this utopianism that impels wars for notions such as 'human rights' and the parliamentary democracy that must be imposed to ensure the happiness of a Historically meaningless 'humanity'. The assumed benefits of this 'progress' must be brought to every Amazon Indian, Hottentot and New Guinean head-hunter that Western technics can reach. It is a warped religious duty, a form of *messianism.*

Yockey cites Spengler as saying that the title of his epochal book *The Decline of the West* was chosen in 1911 as a counter to the wildly optimistic feelings that technology and Darwinism were encouraging, when in fact Spengler could foresee an age of wars of annihilation. This again affronted those who saw the coming of a utopia brought about by peaceful world trade. Then when Germany and The West in general were sunken in pessimism after World War I, Spengler sought to counter that pessimism with a message that there is yet a mission of the West to fulfil and defeated Germany would be an important part of that destiny.[17] Above both optimism and pessimism,

---

16 Asa Briggs (ed.), *The Nineteenth Century: The Contradictions of Progress* (New York: Bonanza Books, 1985), p. 29.

17 Yockey, *Imperium*, Wermod ed., op. cit., p. 79.

Spengler and Yockey counselled realism and stated that the new *Zeitgeist* was one of Heroism; the mission was that of building the Empire of the West. The ethos of the new epoch states that 'it is preferable to die on its feet than live on its knees'.[18]

## Other Influences

Anthony Gannon recalled the extent of Yockey's commitment to Spengler:

> He travelled with a general and a particular collection of personal items; the general, contained in a large cabin trunk which usually preceded his arrival and, sometimes, remained for a time after his departure; the particular always stayed with him. In the latter were copies of *Decline of the West*, *Man and Technics*, *Hour of Decision*, and *Prussianism and Socialism* by Oswald Spengler, and, of course, *Imperium* and the *Proclamation of London*. Yockey was, by far, the best informed student of Spengler I have ever known, and I doubt if his equal could be found, in this respect, anywhere in the world. He did *not* seek to outdo Spengler, or to become a rival as did Toynbee; instead he honestly and willingly acknowledged the greatness of the Master and his work, which he used to make his situation-estimations.[19]

Gannon recalled other influences on Yockey: Nietzsche, Hegel, Goethe and Edmund Burke. He was 'derisive' of British historian Arnold Toynbee, who had formulated his own cyclic theory of history in his multi-volumed *Study of History*.[20] While the presence of Burke in Yockey's writings does not loom large, he is mentioned in *Imperium* along with Goethe, Hegel, Schopenhauer, Metternich, Wellington, Carlyle, and Nietzsche, as those of the culture-bearing or leadership strata of a civilization who opposed the ruinous character

---

18 Ibid., p. 83.

19 Gannon memoir on Yockey.

20 Arnold Toynbee, *A Study of History* (Oxford University Press, 1935). First published in 1934 under the auspices of the Royal Institute of International Affairs, of which Toynbee was director of studies, there are certain similarities with Spengler, such as the comparative study of civilizations, their primarily spiritual foundations, their 'rhythm' of rise and fall, and the universal outreach in the later stages. Stimely asked Gannon about Yockey's views on Toynbee on the assumption that there would be much in common. Stimely to Gannon, January 11, 1981, question 3.

of democracy.[21] However, Yockey points out that democracy is a necessary part of a civilization's cyclic process, albeit in the epoch of senility. It is easy to misunderstand Yockey and Spengler if one does not appreciate the historical-dialectics at work: that to state something is an inevitable part of culture-destiny is not the same as applauding it, any more than to say that one is going to grow old and die is to offer a moral judgement but merely to state a fact.

## Schmitt and Haushofer

This is of added interest insofar as it has been suggested recently that Yockey plagiarised the German legal and constitutional scholar Dr Carl Schmitt, a conservative who had an influence on National Socialist jurisprudence. Dr Michael O'Meara, one of the most perceptive of present-day Yockey critics, states that Yockey 'synthesised the historical philosophy of Oswald Spengler, the political theory of Carl Schmitt, and, to a lesser extent, the geopolitics of General Haushofer'; 'offering an understanding of the world that sought to bestow not just historical, but political and geostrategic authority on the idea of a European Imperium'.[22] Further, O'Meara thinks that Yockey was one of the first Americans to not only recognise but to develop Schmitt's ideas.[23]

Schmitt held that politics is a reflection of the 'friend/enemy' dichotomy and the basis for the development of kinship and, by extension, tribe, nation, state and ethnos. It relates to how one sees oneself in relation to 'the other'. Preparedness for war or law in regard to 'the other' is therefore a stark reality beyond moralising. This 'friend/enemy' dichotomy is evident in *Imperium*, and is a primary means of delineating the unity of Western civilization vis-à-vis 'the other', or the 'outer enemy', as Yockey called the 'Jewish-American symbiosis'.

The primary proponent of the idea that Yockey 'plagiarised' Schmitt is Sebastion Linderhof, the 'pen name of an American political scientist'.[24]

---

21 Yockey, *Imperium* Wermod ed., op. cit., pp. 327–328.

22 Michael O'Meara, Introduction, *The Proclamation of London of the European Liberation Front* (Shamley Green: Wermod & Wermod, 2012 [1949]), viii.

23 Michael O'Meara, ibid., p. l.

24 Sebastion Linderhof, 'Concealed Influence: Francis Parker Yockey's Plagiarism of Carl Schmitt', *The Occidental Quarterly*, Vol. 10, No. 4, Winter 2010–2011; http://toqonline.

Linderhof comments that it 'is doubtless unfortunate that a man of such brilliance and passionate devotion to the cause of European survival and flourishing plagiarised another man's work, and that he plagiarised so extensively'.[25] Moreover, Linderhof states that he does not know the reason why Yockey would want to pass off Schmitt's ideas as his own, by not acknowledging him while he fully acknowledged Spengler.[26]

The primary similarities are between 'The Twentieth Century Political Outlook', in *Imperium*,[27] and Schmitt's *The Concept of the Political* (1927).[28]

Linderhof, an evident enthusiast for Schmitt, using his Yockey paper primarily to introduce Anglophone readers to the German philosopher rather than to besmirch Yockey, points out: 'Nonetheless, [Yockey] often made interesting use of Schmitt's ideas and theories, frequently employing and applying them in ways never pursued by Schmitt himself'.[29] Further: 'Despite its plagiarism, *Imperium* is a profound and noble book and retains its place in the small pantheon of significant works advancing the movement for European survival and freedom.'[30]

There cannot really be any suggestion that Yockey would 'plagiarise' Schmitt for dubious purposes. Yockey freely acknowledged the sources of his ideas. He cited many philosophers throughout *Imperium*. Of intriguing interest is that, according to someone familiar with the Schmitt library, the beleaguered scholar held a copy of *Imperium*.[31] This invites the question as to whether Yockey and Schmitt were in personal communication.

Karl Haushofer (1869–1946), founder of the Institute of Geopolitics at Munich University, and editor of the *Zeitschrift für Geopolitik* ('Journal of

com/archives/v1on4/TOQv1on4Linderhof.pdf.

25 Sebastion Linderhof, ibid., pp. 19–20.

26 Sebastion Linderhof, ibid., p. 35, note 41.

27 Yockey, *Imperium* op. cit., pp. 163–314.

28 Sebastion Linderhof, op. cit., pp. 37–58.

29 Sebastion Linderhof, ibid., p. 58.

30 Sebastion Linderhof, ibid., p. 61.

31 Communication with the author, October 2014.

Geopolitics') is regarded as the founder of the German school of *Geopolitik*.[32] An adviser to the NSDAP and the Third Reich, Professor Haushofer, while commonly held accountable for the Reich's expansionist policies was, rather, an avid advocate of a Russo-German alliance against the plutocratic democracies. Influenced by the 'Heartland Theory' of the British geopolitical theorist MacKinder, he regarded Russia as the 'heartland' for a new geopolitical bloc. Haushofer's geopolitics postulates that cultural rather than military or economic considerations should determine the character of a state's territorial expansion and that small states are a historical regression and too small to maintain autonomy. They should be superseded by larger autarchic geopolitical blocs. Zoological conceptions of 'race' are not of primary importance.[33] Haushofer was an avid advocate of the Nippo-German alliance. Although acquitted of 'war crimes', he and his Jewish wife committed suicide. Haushofer has an enduring influence in particular via the present-day Russian geopolitical theorist Dr Alexander Dugin,[34] who is the leading advocate of that 'Eurasian' bloc which was being advocated as the ultimate aim for German policy by Haushofer.

Haushofer, like Schmitt, was a major influence on Yockey, who acknowledges the importance of Haushofer both near the beginning and the end of *Imperium*. Stating that life is a battle between the young and the old, the old and the new, Haushofer is one of those who represent the Future but who were overwhelmed by the past; Copernicus burned as a heretic, or Haushofer, driven to suicide.[35] In crediting Haushofer with the foundation of the Geopolitics of the new era, Yockey wrote:

> Geopolitics, as developed before this time, was not founded on the twentieth century view of history and politics, but on tacit materialistic ideas left over from the nineteenth century. The researches of this science have, however, permanent

32 Much nonsense has been written about Haushofer as a high adept of the occult, and 'Hitler's occult mentor'. Professor Nicholas Goodrick-Clarke examines such claims in *Black Sun* (New York University Press, 2002), pp. 1154–117.

33 George W White, *Nation, State and Territory: Vol. 1: Origins, Evolutions and Relationships* (Maryland: Rowman and Littlefield Publishers, 2007), pp. 232–233.

34 Dugin, 'The Fourth Political Theory', http://4pt.su/.

35 Yockey, *Imperium*, Wermod edition, op. cit., p. 48.

> value, and its assertion of large-space thinking was an historically essential development. The name of Haushofer will remain honored in Western thought. The future of geopolitics will be a readaptation of the whole structure to the fundamental spiritual orientation of the world — the division between the West and its colonies on the one hand, and the outer forces on the other.[36]

Why then did Yockey 'honour' Haushofer yet not mention Schmitt? Linderhof suggests that Yockey assumed his 'plagiarism' would not be realised because Schmitt had not been translated into English. It suggests intellectual dishonesty on the part of Yockey, despite the regard Linderhof maintains for him. However, Yockey did not write solely for the Anglophone world. He had written *Der Feind Europas* in German and had published it in Germany as the third volume of *Imperium*. He was especially eager to introduce *Imperium* to the German political and military 'elite'. Indeed, *Imperium* was enthusiastically received by the émigré group around *Der Weg* in Argentina, and by major figures in Germany involved with the burgeoning Socialist Reich Party and the important German veterans' association, *Bruderschaft*. Germans would readily recognise Schmitt's ideas in *Imperium*, regardless of them being read in English. Indeed, Kevin Coogan makes the point that Yockey knew his readers would recognise Schmitt's ideas. Coogan also states that Thomas Francis[37] suggests that Yockey did not cite Schmitt precisely because of the difficulties with the Occupation authorities.[38] However, Linderhof rejects the first notion and does not mention the second.

Of the myriad of influences that Yockey freely acknowledges in *Imperium*, all but Schmitt were dead. Schmitt refused to bow to the de-Nazification inquisitors. In April 1945, after being questioned for several hours by the Russian authorities, Schmitt was allowed to return to his home and was left in peace by the Soviets. In November, however, the Americans raided his home, arrested him and seized his library of 5,000 volumes at the instigation of Karl Loewenstein, one of the Jewish returnees formulating and implementing American occupation policies. The aim was to try Schmitt, one of

36 Ibid., p. 704.

37 Thomas Francis translated Yockey's *Der Feind Europas* and edited the American Yockeyan journal *TRUD* during the 1970s.

38 Kevin Coogan, *Dreamer of the Day*, p. 80.

the foremost legal experts of the time, as a 'war criminal'. The case against him was prepared by Loewenstein. Loewenstein was encouraged by Kurt Grossman, executive assistant of the World Jewish Congress and a friend of Nuremberg prosecutor Robert Kempner, who interrogated Schmitt in jail. Loewenstein and Grossman tried to influence American opinion through the hack journalist Walter Winchell. At the instigation of Loewenstein, Schmitt was interned for a year at various camps.[39] Although a case could not proceed, Schmitt was made *persona non grata* in Germany, just like other leading intellectuals, such as Martin Heidegger.

Given that Schmitt was being harassed and that Walter Winchell, Loewenstein and the World Jewish Congress were pushing his persecution publicly in the USA, it seems sensible that Yockey refrained from citing Schmitt in *Imperium* precisely at the time that he was undergoing these ordeals.

39 Joseph W Bendersky, 'Carl Schmitt's Path to Nuremberg: A Sixty-Year Reassessment', *Telos*, no. 139, Summer 2007, pp. 6–43, http://nazbol.net/library/authors/Uncategorized/ebooksclub.org__Telos__A_Quarterly_Journal_of_Radical_Thought_vol_139.pdf.

# *Imperium*

In 1947, Yockey travelled to Brittas Bay, Ireland, to isolate himself and write *Imperium*, his *magnum opus*. He stated to Gannon that he chose Brittas Bay as 'the most "Western part of Europe"' for its seclusion and 'he had a woman somewhere in the background' (so the seclusion was not absolute). He bashed out the manuscript in six months on a typewriter he called his 'devil-machine', demonstrating his efficiency as a typist.[1]

*Imperium* appeared in early 1948, under the imprint Westropa Press, with funding from Baroness Alice von Pflügl. Westropa Press was registered under the name of John Anthony Gannon, Yockey's closest British colleague.[2] 'Brock, a semi-crook printer, who had done work for Oswald Mosley' printed volume one; Brooks & Dale printed the second volume.[3]

*Imperium* developed the themes that Yockey had already been formulating while a university student in 1940 and as far back as 1936. Yockey's notion of 'Culture pathology' continues where Spengler ends, explaining that culture is an organism and that like every organism it is vulnerable to disease. There are three forms of Culture pathology:

- Culture-Parasitism
- Culture-Distortion
- Culture-Retardation[4]

---

1 Gannon to Stimely, November 24, 1981.

2 Gannon to Stimely, July 13, 1980.

3 Gannon to Stimely, November 24, 1981.

4 Ulick Varange (Yockey), *Imperium*, Wermod ed., op. cit., 'Cultural Vitalism: (B) Cultural Pathology', pp. 465–553.

An un-acculturated foreign body in the cultural organism will represent what is regarded as a pathogen, with an innate tendency to destroy or distort the host organism. The cells of the culture organism are attacked like a cancer attacks the cells of a body. This is the deeper meaning of problems such as Third World immigration and the influence the 'Jewish Culture-State-Nation-People-Race'.

In 'Life as Art', Yockey had introduced the Nietzschean concept of 'higher men', which repudiates Marxist and democratic notions of equality and of the role of the masses in shaping history. In conceiving history in terms of Heroic Vitalism,[5] the hero is impelled to follow a predetermined destiny, dictated by an innate nature that reflects not so much genes as spirit. One such figure, looming large on the world stage, was Napoleon — who was the harbinger of a new era and indeed the champion of a united Europe. Carlyle, the exponent of the Hero as the shaper of History, is among the philosophers whom Yockey listed as belonging to the 'organic side'.[6]

In 1940 Yockey had written of the 'Western soul' and its destiny, of the Resurgence of Authority, whether in the form of a monarch or a dictator, and of the 'Actualization of the Idea of Power'. What remains in the present Historical context is for the West 'to write the history of the planet in terms of Western Empire'. Yockey believed, like Spengler, that the possibilities of Western aesthetics had been fulfilled.[7] The tasks that remain are of a martial character. Spengler and Yockey, unfortunately, seem to have been broadly correct: compared to the Medieval, Baroque and Classical periods of Western art, what can be said today of the West in terms of 'High Culture'? As Yockey would point out, behind the scenes as promoters, directors, scriptwriters, publishers and editors are largely those of the Jewish-People-Nation-Culture-Race, who have an innate urge to change a host society according to a temperament forged over centuries. This is what Yockey called 'Culture-distortion'.

There is no point in moralising about such matters any more than one becomes morally indignant at a pathogen in a living organism. Nor is there any point to moralising about Jews. Any foreign body with influence in a host organism is going to act as a distorting influence in some manner, whether

---

5 Thomas Carlyle, *On Heroes, Hero Worship, and the Heroic in History* (1840).

6 Yockey, *Imperium*, Wermod ed., op. cit., pp. 18–22.

7 Yockey, 'Life as an Art', op. cit.

they be Jewish scriptwriters or British Missionaries to Africa. The question is that of perspective as to how one identifies for or against the culture organism into which one is born. Of course, for the most part, the masses of a culture are indifferent and inert until they are led to a consciousness of their identity, which is the role of the 'Hero' in History and the 'cultural-bearing stratum'. There are whites aplenty who not only reject but also actively oppose Western culture and are what Yockey called the 'inner enemy'. They assist Culture-distortion through their acquiescence and are found mostly among the political and commercial classes.

Already in 1940 Yockey wrote of what he saw as his life's mission, to formulate an idea that was to result eight years later in the publication of *Imperium*. With *Imperium* he undertook to correct what Spengler had seen as lacking in philosophers:

> And herein, I think, all the philosophers of the newest age are open to a serious criticism. What they do not possess is real understanding in actual life. Not one of them has intervened effectively, either in higher politics, in the development of modern technics, in matters of communication, in economics, or in any other *big* actuality, with a single act or a single compelling idea.[8]

This was Spengler's intention for his final work, *The Hour of Decision*, in calling for a revitalised West and warning of the 'coloured world revolution' that was being led by Bolshevism but seeing in Italian Fascism the harbinger of coming legions. With *Imperium,* Yockey had combined and elaborated on both the culture morphology of Spengler and the warning of impending, epochal conflict in his first and last books respectively. To this, Yockey added 'Culture pathology'.

The importance of Spengler's Culture *morphology* is that it explains *how* and *when* social, cultural, economic and political conditions arise at a certain cycle of a High Culture, which permit alien elements to enter the culture organism — something that would not be permitted in healthy circumstances. Using the analogy of pathology, we might say that a young, healthy organism has the immunity to resist disease and lives life vigorously, whereas in old age that immunity has broken down and is susceptible to illness. The sick

8 Oswald Spengler, *The Decline…*, op. cit., Vol. 1, p. 42.

organism can be brought back to health by surgery, antibiotics and a regimen of fitness. Spengler provided the method of diagnosis; Yockey expanded it and added the remedy.

The message of Yockey in this large tome, *Imperium*, is really that simple — and also that profound.

## Culture-Distortion

For Western Civilization, Yockey identified the 'Culture distorter' as being of Jewish temperament. This was to be understood in a spiritual and cultural sense, of a people welded over centuries through the force of History, rather than in terms of genetics. Hence, someone of 'non-Jewish' parentage might be thoroughly imbued with the Jewish outlook while someone born a 'Jew' might be in accord with the Western culture stream.

Marx and Freud represent two archetypal examples of the 'Culture distorter'. The idea is best explained by going to a respected Jewish source, Howard Sachar, who wrote that the primary motivation of pioneer Freudians was:

> …the unconscious desire of Jews to unmask the respectability of the European society which closed them out. There was no more effective way of doing this than by dredging up from the human psyche… sordid and infantile sexual aberrations… Even Jews who were not psychiatrists must have taken pleasure in the feat of social equalisation performed by Freud's "new thinking". The B'nai B'rith Lodge of Vienna, for example, delighted in listening to Freud air his theories …[9]

The same situation pertains to the Jewish promotion of Marxism, 'modernism' in the arts or the promotion of pornography: revenge lust against an alien culture organism, whether consciously or unconsciously. Yockey examined in separate chapters Darwinism, Marxism and Freudianism as products of nineteenth century materialism and rationalism that had 'contributed greatly to lead Europe into its present abyss'.[10]

What Yockey saw in occupied Germany was a deliberate, enforced policy to destroy Western Culture in the heartland of Europe. The US occupation

9 H Sachar, *The Course of Modern Jewish History* (Vintage Books, 1991), pp. 400–401.

10 Yockey, *Imperium*, Wermod ed., op, cit., p. 94.

forces brought Germany Culture-distortion as part of the 're-education' process. The classical composer John Borstlap comments on this:

> The country that suffered the most from the postwar modernist revolution was Germany. Its musical tradition was considered contaminated by the annexation of the nazis, especially romanticism was seen as a pool of evil and bad taste, and Wagner — the former icon of "Aryan" culture and its antisemitism — became the symbol of everything that was wrong with tonality, expression and the so-called "humanist tradition" in music. Postwar new music had to symbolize the birth of a new Germany, a country fully integrated into western democracy, and joining western modernity of which the USA were the leaders. In music, modernism became the flagship of German modernity, but a flagship that had left its original harbor for a sea where audiences did not want to follow. While new modernist music was supported and funded by the institutions, the central performance culture was restored as a museum culture, where the "dangerous" masterpieces of the past could be enjoyed as objects behind the glass of history, and thus reasonably "safe".[11]

This imposition of Culture-distortion was not a temporary policy — like the starvation programme of the Morgenthau Plan — to punish Germany. The purpose was to destroy Western culture first in Germany and then throughout Europe. What has been called the 'Cultural Cold War'[12] was undertaken firstly to crush the Western cultural revival that had taken place under German auspices and secondly to counter the USSR with what Stalin called 'rootless cosmopolitanism'.[13] The Soviet bloc succumbed after decades from what are lauded as the 'colour revolutions'.[14] There are still generations of youth to contaminate. The US State Department sponsors hip-hop festivals and tours to show off the wonders of 'American culture', as it sponsored jazz

---

11 J Borstlap, *The Classical Revolution* (New York: The Scarecrow Press, 2013).

12 Frances Stonor Saunders, *Cultural Cold War: The CIA and the World of Arts and Letters* (New York: The New Press, 1999).

13 K. R. Bolton, *Stalin: The Enduring Legacy* (London: Black House Publishing, 2012), pp. 28–54.

14 K. R. Bolton, *Revolution from Above* (London: Arktos Media Ltd., 2011), pp. 227–244. See also: Bolton, Václav Havel: The 'Inner enemy', *Counter-Currents*, December 27, 2011, http://www.counter-currents.com/2011/12/vaclav-havel-the-inner-enemy/.

and abstract expressionism during the Cold War. The State Department calls the present-day programme 'Hip-Hop Diplomacy'.[15]

Jewish influence, according to the laws of culture morphology, is ultimately not a *cause* but a *symptom*, the cause being the primacy of economics in what Spengler called the 'Winter' cycle of a civilization.[16] Brooks Adams has explained the cycles concomitant with the role of money in *The Law of Civilization and Decay* and, although neither Spengler nor Yockey mention him, reading Adams is rewarding.[17] When money rules — that is, *plutocracy* — it measures the value of all things and defines the citizen in terms of property relations. Politics becomes nothing more than the calculations of the Counting House, whether on a local, national or global scale. None of this is Jewish *per se* but the doctrines of rationalism, democracy, pluralism and English Free Trade, as expressions of the *Zeitgeist* of a Late Cycle, allow entry of the 'Other' into the culture organism where he was hitherto denied. Yockey writes of this in *Imperium*:

> The more materialistic the Culture became, the more it approached the Jew and the greater was his advantage. The West gradually abandoned its exclusiveness but he retained his, invisible to the West.[18]

> This movement toward Materialism was a movement toward the Culture-distorter in the sense that it made his entry into Western affairs possible. When men were counted, naturally he too was included …[19]

The victory of money-thinking and the replacement of the aristocratic and other traditional ruling and culture-bearing strata by merchants and bankers, ushered in by the democratic revolutions, also brought about the entry of Jews into positions of control. This is the difference between alien groups that act as Culture-parasites and those that become empowered to act as

15 Bolton, *Babel Inc.* (London: Black House Publishing, 2013,), pp. 179–212.

16 Oswald Spengler, *The Decline of The West* (London : George Allen & Unwin, 1971), Vol. II, pp. 469–507.

17 Brooks Adams (1896), *The Law of Civilization and Decay*. http://www.archive.org/details/lawcivilizationooadamgoog.

18 Yockey, *Imperium*, Wermod ed., op. cit., p. 533.

19 Ibid., p. 551.

Culture-distorters. While the French Revolution of 1789 was epochal in destroying the vestiges of the Western traditional social order, as the harbinger of both labour-socialism and capitalism, the Reformation, Calvinism and the English Puritan Revolution had already sown the seeds of disintegration. Yockey refers to this process leading up to the 1789 Revolution when he states that:

> The Reformation was a schism in the whole soul of the West. In it appeared as a symbol of the coming triumph of materialism the system of Calvinism. Calvin taught the sanctity of economic activity; he sanctioned usury; he interpreted wealth as a sign of Election to salvation. This spirit was abroad; Henry VIII legalized usury in England in 1545. The old Western doctrine of the sinfulness of usury was rejected. This represented liberation for the Jew, accessibility to power, even if disguised, invisible power.[20]

Class-war socialism and capitalism go hand-in-hand, because labour-socialism seeks to expropriate rather than replace the capitalist ethos, and states to the workingman that he too can become the master of money.[21] As Spengler put it:

> There is no proletarian, not even a communist, movement that has not operated in the interests of money, in the direction indicated by money, and for the time being permitted by money—and that, without the idealist amongst its leaders having the slightest suspicion of the fact.[22]

At the juncture of the old and the new epoch, two conceptions of state organisation arose, both called 'Socialism'. One reflected the materialism of the nineteenth century, the other the coming epoch, where 'money is overthrown only by blood',[23] as Spengler put it on the final page of *The Decline of the West*. Spengler countered the economic model of socialism perfected by Marx in

---

20 Ibid., p. 531.

21 Yockey discusses this in the chapter, 'Culture distortion arising from parasitic activity', *Imperium*, ibid., pp. 523–553.

22 Spengler, *The Decline of The West*, op. cit., Vol. II, p. 464, note 1.

23 Ibid., p. 507.

England with the idea of 'Prussian Socialism',[24] which posits the state idea of duty in contrast to the democratic-rationalist-Marxian idea of 'the Rights of Man and the Citizen', as the Jacobins put it. Yockey referred to this new-era socialism as *Ethical Socialism*, 'the superpersonal Idea… as the form of the next Western age', that had arisen during World War I, when Germany—albeit unconsciously[25]—was fighting against the lingering age of capitalism represented by England.

Prussia-Germany was the power embodying the next epoch, the actualisation of ethical socialism, as England had been the harbinger of the old *Zeitgeist*. Thus the inner development of the West tended towards a contest between these two powers, England and Germany. World War I, although in appearance a contest between two old nationalisms, was on a deeper level a contest between two conflicting Ideas: ethical socialism and capitalism.[26] It was the prelude to what Spengler said would be the 'conflict between money and blood'.

The fullest manifestation of this conflict between ethical socialism and capitalism was World War II.[27] The plutocracies, with the manpower of a mechanized horde from the East, the 'Barbarian', in an epochal, earth-shattering display of Culture-retardation, maintained the nineteenth century money *Zeitgeist* into the twentieth century. The West self-destructed as an example of a refusal to give up the 'Past' because the status quo served both the Culture-distorter and the inner enemy or traitor who profits from his sycophancy. Yockey stated that every new idea in a culture is opposed but that until the 'horrible outbreak of culture-sickness in the twentieth century', referring to World War II, 'the opposition to the creative had never attained to a totality that can only be adequately described as maniacal'.[28] Yockey referred to 'ethical socialism' again in *The Enemy of Europe*, describing one of the primary

24 Oswald Spengler (1919), *Prussian and Socialism.*

25 As distinct from the *conscious* fight for Ethical Socialism represented by National Socialist Germany and Fascist Italy.

26 Yockey, *Imperium*, op. cit., 'The World Situation: The First World War', pp. 705–712.

27 Yockey remarks that the struggle was more precisely between Socialism and chaos. Yockey, *Imperium*, ibid., 'The Second World War', p. 715.

28 Ibid., p. 519.

aspects of World War II as a conflict between capitalism and socialism, the old worldview versus the new worldview of the West, represented by England and Germany respectively.[29] In some random private notes circa the early 1950s, Yockey referred to 'Prussian socialism' as '*spiritual* socialism, not, like the American variety, psychological. In Prussia, socialism is a value, a conscious ethic, an ideal, an organisation-form, a means of accomplishment. In America it is unconscious, an inhibition, a negation, an inability to be individual, thus a denial of the human in man and an assertion of the herding animal in man.'[30] One might more readily identify 'ethical socialism', at least in practice, as the 'organic' or 'corporate' state.

29 Yockey, *The Enemy of Europe* (Liberty Bell ed.), pp. 25, 29, 42

30 Yockey, 'Thoughts Personal and Superpersonal', typewritten notes, n.d.

# The Race Question

The primacy of the spirit and the 'race soul' saw Yockey, controversially among the right, repudiating what he regarded as concepts of 'race' belonging to the age of materialism. When everything was measured and quantified, races were classified on the basis of skeletal structure and physiology, without regard for the spiritual qualities that make history. In this he drew again from Spengler.[1] For the new historical conception of 'race', 'Materialistic means shallow as applied to living things, for with all Life, *the spirit is primary*, and the material is the mere vehicle for spiritual expression.'[2] Hence:

> Race is *not* group anatomy;
> Race is *not* independent of the soil;
> Race is *not* independent of Spirit and History;
> Races are *not* classifiable, except on an arbitrary basis;
>
> Race is *not* a rigid, permanent, collective characterisation of human beings, which remains always the same throughout history.[3]
>
> The twentieth century outlook, based on facts and not on the preconceptions of physics and mechanics, sees Race as *fluid*, gliding with History over the fixed skeletal form determined by the soil.[4]

---

1 Spengler, *The Decline of The West*, Vol. II, Chapter V, 'Cities and Peoples', '(B) Peoples, Races, Tongues', p. 155; Chapter VI, '(C) Primitives, Culture-Peoples, Fellaheen', pp. 159–186.

2 Yockey, *Imperium*, op. cit., 'Cultural Vitalism', '(A) Cultural Health', 'Race, People, Nation, State', p. 353.

3 Ibid., p. 363.

4 Ibid.

When describing how one individual might be imbued with the new *Zeitgeist*, while another is imbued with the old, in determining who now belongs to the Western culture organism, Yockey stated in *The Enemy of Europe* that 'of importance only is the spirit that permeates [one's] inner life'.[5]

> Europe's churchills and toynbees[6] prove that it is possible for Americans to be born and raised in Europe. The example of Mussolini shows that an ethical Prussian can be born and raised in Romagna, and the examples of Ezra Pound, William Joyce, Robert Best, Douglas Chandler[7] and others show that Europeans can be born and raised in America… The race one feels is everything, the anatomic-geographic group to which one belongs means nothing.[8]

## 'Vertical Race' and 'Horizontal Race'

The two types of race theory according to Yockey are 'horizontal race' and 'vertical race'.[9] The first is the race of the 'spirit', culture and soul, expounded by the German Idealists, Herder, Goethe, Fichte, et al. The second is biological and materialistic, measured and tabulated, influenced by Darwin and introduced to Germany by Haeckel. Ironically, the Hitlerites largely adopted the English school rather than the German.

This most contentious of Yockey's theories among the Right is a by-product of Yockey's total rejection of materialism. Biological race theory is analogous to the counting house mentality of English nineteenth century economics, from which both capitalism and Marxism emerge. The nineteenth-century English *Zeitgeist* that continues to prevail over much of the world is based on the quantitative rather than the qualitative. Hence, in politics it is headcounting and is called democracy, in economics it is a matter of statistics, in race it was cephalic indices; although any form of racial differentiation now

---

5 Yockey, *The Enemy of Europe* (West Virginia: Liberty Bell Publications, 1981), p. 43.

6 Yockey used lower case when referring to the names of those whom he regarded as 'inner traitors' to the West.

7 Each of these individuals from Allied states broadcasted for Germany or Italy during World War II.

8 Yockey, *The Enemy of Europe* (West Virginia: Liberty Bell Publications, 1981), pp. 43–44.

9 Yockey, *Imperium*, Wermod ed., op. cit., p. 383.

intrudes upon democratic head-counting of the post-1945 world that heralds a nebulous concept called the 'human race'.

Yockey contended that for the new era, race means 'a horizontal differentiation of men'. The materialism of the nineteenth century regarded race as a 'vertical differentiation of men', as part of the 'will-to-systemise', augmented by the political phenomenon of nationalism, which has divided the Western peoples.[10] For Yockey *'History' creates 'Race'*, as distinct from the determinism of other race theorists, which states that *race creates history*. Within this framework, it is 'men of race' who 'create the deeds of History'.[11] We see here that Yockey's *Cultural Vitalism* embraces the *Heroic Vitalism* of Carlyle. Contrary again to nineteenth-century racism, Yockey pointed out that 'strong minorities' who form races welcome racial outsiders, and weld them into a 'race' with a common destiny. Alluding to National Socialist Germany, Yockey said that the adoption of narrow definitions of race was a 'grotesquerie'. What matters to a cultural 'unit' that has a 'mission' is the 'strength of will' that others can bring to it. Race purity is 'sheer materialism'. 'Race is the material of history, not the reverse'. While race purity might be satisfying 'aesthetically', like the 'Nordic' ideal claimed to have been the obsession of Hitlerism, what matters is the 'Mission' that defines a 'race'.[12] What gives meaning to 'race' is the pursuit of its historic destiny.[13]

The 'subjective meaning of race' explains that 'the man who, after associating with Jews, reading their literature, and adopting their viewpoint, actually becomes a Jew in the fullest sense of the word. It is not necessary that he have "Jewish blood". The converse is known: many Jews have adopted Western feelings and rhythms, and have thereby acquired Western race.'[14]

An irony of History is that among the most genuinely Westernised Jews were those in Germany who were vociferous in rejecting both Zionism and Marxism, and were conspicuous among frontline soldiers during World

10 Ibid.

11 Ibid., p. 384.

12 Ibid., p. 385.

13 Ibid., p. 386.

14 Ibid., 'Subjective Meaning of Race', p. 379.

War I, such veterans forming the League of Nationalist German Jews.[15] The Menuhin family is a famous example of Jews who have contributed positively to Western High Culture.[16]

Spengler defined race as 'a character of duration' shaped by the landscape. 'Tribes, septs, clans, families — all these are designations for the fact of a blood which circles, carried on by procreation, in a narrow or a wide landscape.'[17] Yockey stated that 'purity' of race is 'directed to *feeling*, and not to anatomical derivation.'[18] However, total alienness of physique or culture such as that existing between White and Negro will generally prevent interbreeding; 'an extreme case of race-difference preventing assimilation.'[19]

This racial instinct that impels those who 'have race',[20] who think with blood and not money, is undermined during the Late (Spengler's 'Winter') epoch of a civilization, where even the instinct for procreation — the continuity of one's family line — becomes questionable and is determined by economics. It is one of the primary symptoms of decay that can be readily observed today as evidence for the efficacy of Spengler's historical morphology and Yockey's Cultural Vitalism. Yockey said of this, 'Decadent means moving toward extinction...'[21]

---

15 K. R. Bolton, 'German-Nationalist Jews During the Weimar and Early Third Reich Eras', *Journal of Inconvenient History*, http://inconvenienthistory.com/archive/2013/volume_5/number_3/german_nationalist_jews.php.

16 Gerhard Menuhin was removed as chairman of the German branch of the Yehudi Menuhin Foundation in 2005 for his outspoken Nationalist views, stating in an interview with *Deutsche Stimme*, newspaper of the 'far right' National Democratic Party, that Germany was being morally blackmailed. He was also a columnist for the 'far right' newspaper *National Zeitung*. His grandfather, Moshe, had been the newspaper's arts editor and wrote *The Decadence of Judaism in Our Time*. Gerhard's father, Lord Yehudi Menuhin, had played charity concerts to support the plight of German expellees from Eastern Europe after World War II.

17 Spengler, *The Decline of The West*, Vol. II, Chapter V, 'Cities and Peoples', '(B) Peoples, Races, Tongues', p. 113.

18 Yockey, *Imperium*, op. cit., 'Race and Polity', p. 390.

19 Ibid., p. 399.

20 Ibid., 'Subjective Meaning of Race', ibid., p. 378.

21 Ibid., p. 378.

> The great symbol of this in the Western Civilization is everything suggested by the name Hollywood. The message of Hollywood is the *total* significance of sexual love as an end in itself—the erotic without consequences. The sexual love of two grains of sand, two rootless individuals, not the primeval sexual love looking to the continuity of Life, the family of many children... The instinct of decadence takes many forms in this realm: dissolution of marriage by divorce laws, attempts to discard... the laws against abortion...[22]

The primacy of spirit over matter in Yockey's philosophical schema, as with Spengler's, was a rejection of the nineteenth century zoology and Darwinism that had been applied to race, especially in England, where the economic and materialistic *Zeitgeist* was most pronounced. Ironically, those who favoured the aping of Hitler most closely in outer form maintained those aspects of Hitlerism most in accord with this English *Zeitgeist*, rather than the new spirit embodied in German thought. Hitlerist race theory was an attempted synthesis of English Darwinism and German idealism. Yockey however called it 'grotesque'.

In particular, Yockey's detractors condemn him for being so foolish as to state, like Spengler, that landscape forms race. Yockey wrote of this:

> The succession of human generations, related by blood, have the clear tendency to remain fixed in a landscape. Nomadic tribes wander within larger, but equally definite, bounds. Within this landscape the forms of plant and animal life have local characteristics, different from transplantations of the same strains and stocks in other landscapes.
>
> The anthropological landscape ... uncovered a mathematically presentable fact which affords a good starting point to show the influence of the soil. It was discovered for any given inhabited area of the world there was an average cephalic index of the population. More important, it was learned, through measurements on immigrants to America from every part of Europe, and then on their children born in America, that this cephalic index adheres to the soil, and immediately makes itself manifest in the new generation. Thus longheaded Jews from Sicily, and short-headed ones from Germany, produced offspring with the same average head measurement, the specifically American one.[23]

22 Ibid., p. 380.

23 Ibid., 'Race, People, Nation, State', p. 355.

Yockey then wrote that similar studies found that bodily size and span of growth were reaching what we might here call an 'American type' even among such disparate groups as Indians, Negroes and Whites.[24] Yockey explained:

> From these and other facts, both comparatively new and of ancient observation, it is apparent that the landscape exerts an influence on the human stocks within its bounds as well as on the plant and animal life. The technic of this influence is beyond our ken. The source of it we do know. It is the cosmic unity of the totality of things, a unity which shows itself in the rhythmic and cyclic movement of Nature. Man does not stand out of this unity, but is submerged in it...[25]

This unity with and shaping by a universal soul, which permeates everything in a pantheistic manner, was a major factor in German Idealism and was even accepted by Darwin's primary German apologist Haeckel.

Racial activists seized upon this as a heresy akin to Liberalism and Communism. Even someone as erudite as Dr Revilo P Oliver, in a critical tribute to Spengler, wrote:

> For all practical purposes, Spengler ignores hereditary and racial differences. He even uses the word "race" to represent a qualitative difference between members of what we should call the same race, and he denies that that difference is to any significant extent caused by heredity. He regards biological races as plastic and mutable, even in their physical characteristics, under the influence of geographical factors (including the soil, which is said to affect the physical organism through food) and of what Spengler terms "a mysterious cosmic force" that has nothing to do with biology. The only real unity is cultural, that is, the fundamental ideas and beliefs shared by the peoples who form a civilization. Thus Spengler, who makes those ideas subject to quasi-biological growth and decay, oddly rejects as insignificant the findings of biological science concerning living organisms.[26]

Yockey did not however discount the occurrence of races that were so disparate that differences in physique and culture generally prevent widespread

---

24 Ibid.

25 Ibid., p. 356.

26 Revilo P Oliver, 'Spengler: Criticism and Tribute', *Journal of Historical Review*, Vol. 17, No. 2 (March–April 1998), pp. 10–13.

mating. Yockey referred to the 'striving of a race towards its own physical type' being 'one of the great facts with which one cannot tamper by trying to substitute ideals of amalgamation with types totally alien, as Liberalism and Communism tried to do during the Reign of Rationalism.'[27] It is History that however gives race 'form.'[28]

Racial activists and theorists immediately recognised that in regard to the influence of landscape on skull formation and other 'racial' traits, Yockey had accepted the findings of Franz Boas, a Jewish socialist with pro-communist sympathies. Boas is credited with founding cultural anthropology, with its Leftist political agenda of denying 'race'. What Yockey was referring to was the passage in *The Decline of the West* which more than any other makes Spengler and Yockey anathema to many racial activists. Spengler stated that where men migrate they settle to become another 'race' by the impress of the new land. He cited Gould and Baxter as showing that Whites of all types were becoming, after subsequent generations, the same average size of body and growth rates. 'Boas has shown that the American-born children of long-headed Sicilian and short-headed German-Jews at once conform to the same head-type.'[29]

Spengler was sceptical as to the amount of history that can be deduced from the fossil of a jaw-bone or an arm bone. He stated that what mattered was to discern the meaning not of the 'bone of the face, but its mien'. He regarded 'the science of the Darwinian age' as 'glib' and 'mechanistic'. Reading history from this is to read a corpse rather than the living being. It does not take into account 'the power of the land over the blood', 'secrets that cannot be inspected and measured, but only livingly experienced and felt from eye to eye'. Spengler saw the weakness of racial taxonomy in the failure of scientists to agree on criteria, whether skull shape, nose shape, or hair texture.[30] More important than skull form is reading the 'flesh, the look, the play of feature'.[31] The contention has recently been highlighted by the perplexity

27 Yockey, op. cit., p. 361.

28 Ibid., p. 362.

29 Spengler, *The Decline…*, op. cit., Vol. II, 'Peoples, Races, Tongues', p. 119.

30 Ibid., Vol. II, p. 125.

31 Ibid., p. 129.

among physical anthropologists caused by the skull of Kennewick Man. He was first thought to be Caucasoid, until after years of measuring it has been decided that he is a mixture of Ainu and proto-Polynesian,[32] although it has still not definitively been decided whether Ainu are 'Europid'.[33] Ethiopians are taxonomically 'Europid'[34] (that is, they can be measured as such with calipers), so perhaps they can be accorded a place in 'white pride' movements?

One might therefore discern more about the race from studying the portraiture of its great artists, rather than with the use of calipers on skulls. A racial type can be best interpreted from its archictecture, art, religion, science, diplomacy, warfare, number-system and other culture forms.

As for the unforgivable sin committed by Yockey and Spengler in citing the studies of Boas and others who claimed that landscape modifies racial physiology, more recent reassessments contend that Boas was mainly correct after all. Gravlee et al state in terms reminiscent of Spengler and Yockey:

> As Boas hypothesized, our results show that children born in the US environment are markedly less similar to their parents in terms of head form than foreign-born children are to theirs. This finding thus corroborates Boas's overarching conclusion that the cephalic index is sensitive to environmental influences and, therefore, does not serve as a valid marker of racial phylogeny.[35]

Gravlee et al state that their use of analytic methods not available to Boas 'provide stronger support for Boas's conclusion'. Boas and generations of cultural anthropologists influenced by him, such as Ashley-Montagu and in turn his proteges, were Leftists of mainly Jewish descent who had an ideological stake in repudiating the role of genetics on human behaviour and race formation. However, Yockey and Spengler sought to redefine 'race' in terms

---

32 Joseph F Powell and Jerome C Rose, 'Report on the Osteological Assessment of the "Kennewick Man" Skeleton', http://www.nps.gov/archeology/kennewick/powell_rose.htm.

33 John R Baker lists Ainu as 'Europid'. Baker, *Race* (London: Oxford University Press, 1974), 'Table of Races and Subraces', p, 625.

34 Ibid.

35 Clarence C Gravlee, H Russell, Bernard William, R Leonard, 'Heredity, Environment, and Cranial Form: A Reanalysis of Boas's Immigrant Data', *American Anthropologist,* Vol. 105, No. 1, March 2003, pp. 125—138.

more profound than calipers and measurements, by offering an all-embracing Idea that completely repudiated the counting and measuring mentality of the nineteenth century which dominated economics, politics, art and science.

*Phenotypic plasticity* also accounts for the change of bodily form even at the molecular level, including the 'remodeling' of the brain by external stimuli.[36]

Johann Gottlieb Fichte, who was regarded as the father of German nationalism, described the metaphysical approach of German Idealism in the formation of races, peoples, nations and states. He delivered a series of addresses that delineated the German national revolution as distinct from the French. Fichte even alluded to the incoming of aliens resulting in what Yockey a century later called Cultural Vitalism. Here, Fichte referred to culture 'confusion' (analogous to Yockey's Culture-retardation) and 'violently disturbing the even progress of culture' (Yockey's Culture-distortion). Fichte referred also to the spiritual bond that forms a 'people' and hence its territorial unit, the 'nation'. The German concept of *volk* means much more than the English word 'people'; when Yockey used 'people' he did so in the sense of *volk*. Fichte likewise rejected any notion of cosmopolitanism and internationalism as a travesty against divine laws acting upon man. He can readily be seen as a precursor of Spengler and Yockey, the latter alluding to Fichte as a philosopher on the organic side of Western civilization.[37] Spengler referred to Fichte as establishing a basis for the 'Prussian (and now European) conception of State-Socialism'[38] (Yockey's 'Ethical Socialism'). Fichte stated:

> Only in the invisible qualities of nations, which are hidden from their own eyes — qualities as the means whereby these nations remain in touch with the source of original life — only therein is to be found the guarantee of their present and future worth, virtue and merit. If these qualities are dulled by admixture and worn away by friction, the flatness that results will bring about a separation from spiritual nature, and this in its turn will cause all men to be fused together in their uniform and collective destruction.[39]

---

36 Kathryn Phillips, 'Phenotype Plasticity', *The Journal of Experimental Biology*, June 15, 2006, pp. 1–3.

37 Yockey, *Imperium*, Wermod ed., op. cit., pp. 285, 288.

38 Spengler, *The Decline of The West*, op. cit., Vol. I, p. 362.

39 Johann Fichte, 'To the German Nation', 1806.

Carl Jung, who developed a German School of Psychology, even as there is a German School of Political Economy (Friedrich List) and a German School of Cultural Morphology (Spengler), writing of his visit to the USA, noted this metaphysical impress on race:

> In 1909 I paid my first short visit to the United States... I remember, when walking through the streets of Buffalo, I came across hundreds of workmen leaving a factory. The naïve European traveller I was then could not help remarking to his American companion: "I really had no idea there was such an amazing amount of Indian blood in your people." "What," said he, "Indian blood? I bet there is not one drop of it in this whole crowd." I replied: "But don't you see their faces? They are more Indian than European." Whereupon I was informed that probably most of these workmen were of Irish, Scottish, and German extraction without a trace of Indian blood in their veins. I was puzzled and half incredulous. Subsequently I learned to see how ridiculous my hypothesis had been. Nevertheless, the impression of facial similarity remained and later years only enhanced it. As Professor Boas maintains, there are even measurable anatomical changes in many American immigrants, changes which are already noticeable in the second generation.
>
> To a keen European eye there is an indefinable yet undeniable something in the whole makeup of the born American that distinguishes him from the born European.
>
> Man can be assimilated by a country. There is an x and a y in the air and in the soil of a country, which slowly permeate and assimilate him to the type of the aboriginal inhabitant, even to the point of slightly remodelling his physical features.
>
> The foreign country somehow gets under the skin of those born in it. Certain very primitive tribes are convinced that it is not possible to usurp foreign territory, because the children born there would inherit the wrong ancestor spirits who dwell in the trees, the rocks, and the water of that country. There seems to be some subtle truth in this primitive intuition. That would mean that the spirit of the Indian gets at the American from within and without. Indeed, there is often an astonishing likeness in the cast of the American face to that of the Red Indian.

The external assimilation to the peculiarities of a country is a thing one could almost expect. There is nothing astonishing in it. But the external similarity is feeble in comparison with the less visible but all the more intense influence on the mind. It is just as though the mind were an infinitely more sensitive and suggestible medium than the body. It is probable that long before the body reacts the mind has already undergone considerable changes, changes that are not obvious to the individual himself or to his immediate circle, but only to an outsider. Thus I would not expect the average American, who has not lived for some years in Europe, to realize how different his mental attitude is from the European's, just as I would not expect the average European to be able to discern his difference from the American. That is the reason why so many things that are really characteristic of a country seem to be merely odd or ridiculous: the condition from which they arise are either not known or not understood. They wouldn't be odd or ridiculous if one could feel the local atmosphere to which they belong and which makes them perfectly comprehensible and logical.

Almost every great country has [what] one might call its genius or spiritus loci. Sometimes you can catch it in a formula, sometimes it is more elusive, yet nonetheless it is indescribably present as a sort of atmosphere that permeates everything. ... In a well-defined civilization with a solid historical background, such as for instance the French, you can easily discover the keynote of the French espirit: it is "a glorie", a most marked prestige psychology in its noblest as well as its most ridiculous forms.

The old European inheritance looks rather pale beside these vigorous primitive influences. Have you ever compared the skyline of New York or any great American city with that of a pueblo like Taos? And did you see how the houses pile up to towers towards the centre? Without conscious imitation the American unconsciously fills out the spectral outline of the Red Man's mind and temperament.

There is nothing miraculous about this. It has always been so: the conqueror overcomes the old inhabitants in the body but succumbs to his spirit. Rome at the zenith of her power contained within her walls all the mystery cults of the East; yet the spirit of the humblest among them, a Jewish mystery society, transformed the greatest of all cities from top to bottom. The conqueror gets the

> wrong ancestor spirits, the primitives would say: I like this picturesque way of putting it. It is pithy and expresses every conceivable implication.[40]

While German Idealism, through Johann Gottfried von Herder (1744–1893), gave Western philosophy the notion of *Zeitgeist*, or the 'Spirit of the Age', and *Volksgeist* or 'spirit of a people', Jung refers here to the 'spirit of a loci'. Since that time the Jewish Culture, antiquated and fossilised, has given a pervasive Jewish countenance to American culture, in addition to Negroid rhythm and Indian nomadicism, from which has emerged an American culture that is a thoroughly muddled stew which Israel Zangwill celebrated in his play 'The Melting Pot'. Of this, Jung also observed:

> Another thing that struck me was the great influence of the Negro, a psychological influence naturally, not due to the mixing of blood. … The peculiar walk with loose joints, or the swinging of the hips so frequently observed in Americans, also comes from the Negro. American music draws its main inspiration from the Negro, and so does the dance.[41]

The USA has thus an inner primitivity behind the façade of Western technics. The American GI presented a childish picture to the European and still does to Muslims who suffer his occupation. Jung writes further:

> [T]he American presents a strange picture: a European with Negro behaviour and an Indian soul. He shares the fate of all usurpers of foreign soil. Certain Australian primitives assert that one cannot conquer foreign soil, because in it there dwell strange ancestor-spirits who reincarnate themselves in the new-born. There is a great psychological truth in this. The foreign land assimilates its conqueror. But unlike the Latin conquerors of Central and South America, the North Americans preserved their European standards with the most rigid puritanism, though they could not prevent the souls of their Indian foes from becoming theirs. Everywhere the virgin earth causes at least the unconscious of the conqueror to sink to the level of its indigenous inhabitants.[42]

---

40 C. G. Jung, *The Complications of American Psychology* (Originally titled 'Your Negroid and Indian Behavior'), 1930.

41 C. G. Jung, 'Mind and Earth', 1931.

42 Ibid.

However, for Yockey, an American, America remained part of the European 'mother-culture', whose destiny will hopefully be decided by another 'civil war'.[43] He marked 1915, the year of the founding of the second Ku Klux Klan, as the start of the 'second American Revolution'[44] and concluded by stating that:

> When the American National Revolution takes political form, its inspiration will come from the same ultimate source as the European Revolution of 1933. Therefore what is written here is also for the true America, even though the effective America of the moment, and of the immediate future, is a hostile America, an America of willing, mass-mind tools in the service of the Culture-distorting political and total enemy of the Western Civilization.[45]

Yockey and Spengler did not repudiate or confuse 'race', they explicated and freed it from the sterility of prior centuries, as part of their *total* rejection of the *Zeitgeist* of rationalism and materialism.

## Race Theory in the Third Reich

Ironically, the Third Reich was not as dogmatic as many of its post-war Anglophone admirers. German National Socialism was conflicted between its roots in the German Idealism of Fichte and others, and English materialism, introduced through Darwinism. The sociologist Dr A James Gregor, who became an authority on Fascist ideology,[46] pointed to several distinct trends in National Socialist race theory.[47] He quotes Third Reich philosopher Alfred Rosenberg as stating, in *The Myth of the Twentieth Century*, that 'nothing would be more superficial than to measure a man's worth by his physical

43 Yockey, *Imperium*, Wermod ed., op. cit., 'America', p. 698.

44 Ibid., p. 694.

45 Ibid., p. 698.

46 See for example his *The Fascist Persuasion in Radical Politics* (Princeton, N.J.: Princeton University Press, 1974); *Interpretations of Fascism* (Morristown, N. J.: Transaction Publishers, 1974); *Young Mussolini and the Intellectual Origins of Fascism* (Berkeley: University of California Press, 1979).

47 A. James Gregor, 'National Socialism and Race', *The European*, (Sanctuary Press, London) Vol. XI, pp. 273–291. No. 5, July, 1958.

appearance (with a centimetre rule and cephalic indices). A far more accurate measure of worth is conduct'.[48] Rosenberg's outlook in this regard is the same as that of Spengler's and Yockey's, although Spengler became *persona non grata* in the Third Reich.[49] However, despite major misgivings and intellectual rivalry, and condemnation by the National Socialist press, Rosenberg called Spengler's *Decline of the West* 'great and good', because it broke 'like a hail storm, cracked and rotten branches, and fertilised the longing fruitless earth', even if in 'error'. As is often the case, here too Spengler's supposed 'fatalism' is the major bugbear.[50]

While Hitler used the term 'Aryan' throughout *Mein Kampf*, he did not identify a specific sub-race.[51] 'Nordicism' did not become pronounced until after the National Socialist ascent to government, starting with Professor Hans Gunther's race theories. Theories of the Nordic as the sole repositor of civilization then became predominant.[52] A reaction to this Nordicism was present among National Socialist scientists by 1938. Ludwig Clauss, Fischer and Lenz were stating that the greatest historical figures — Socrates, Michelangelo, Goethe, Beethoven — were manifestly 'of mixed race' and that the purest of Nordic peoples did not evidence High Culture until 'stimulated by the bastard peoples from the Mediterranean'.[53] As early as 1933, seven months after assuming government, Hitler stated that 'we do not conclude from a man's physical type his ability, but rather from his achievements his

48 Alfred Rosenberg, *The Myth of the Twentieth Century* (Munich, 1930), cited by Gregor, ibid., p. 275.

49 Although not before being condemned by the National Socialist press for his final book *The Hour of Decision* in which the new regime is briefly mentioned in unflattering terms, while Fascist Italy is accorded a measured optimism. Ironically, one of the critics was Goebbels' deputy, Johannes von Leers, who criticised Spengler's thoughts on the 'coloured world revolution' as sowing distrust against 'Germany's natural ally, Japan'. The regime would, however, have preferred to co-opt Spengler to its side. See Bolton, 'Spengler: A Philosopher for all Seasons', in *Spengler: Thoughts and Perspectives Vol. X*, Troy Southgate (ed.) (London: Black Front Press, 2012), pp. 46–49.

50 Rosenberg, *The Myth of the Twentieth Century* (Torrance, California, The Noontide Press, 1982,), p. 247.

51 Gregor, op. cit., p. 275.

52 Gregor, pp. 275–278.

53 Cited by Gregor, ibid., p. 281.

race'.[54] By 1935 this had become the predominant trend in race theory. A major textbook stated, 'the men who bear the qualities of heroism, strength of will, a readiness to sacrifice and faith, have played a decisive role in deciding Germany's destiny, and they shall continue to do so even if they are not all tall, blond or blue-eyed'.[55] Richard Eichenauer even stated that 'men of extremely mixed race' have 'more powerfully grasped' the National Socialist ethos than the 'predominantly Nordic'.[56]

Gregor, at the time a Mosley supporter, concluded his article in *The European* by stating that this race theory that had been embryonically developing in the Third Reich, 'as yet half formulated and ill-expressed', is something 'with which our time must contend', in forming a philosophy that 'bears within itself the promise of Nietzsche's Good European'.

---

54 Cited by Gregor, ibid., p. 283.

55 Thieme, *Vererbung, Rasse, Volk* (Leipzig: Teubner, 1935), p. 41, cited by Gregor, ibid., p. 283.

56 Richard Eichenauer, *Die Rasse als Lebensgessetz in Geschichte und Gesittung* ('The Breed as a Living Law in Civilization and History: a Signpost for German Youth') (Leipzig: Teubner, 1934), p. 136; cited by Gregor, ibid., p. 285.

# With Mosley

Having sought out veterans in Germany who were re-forming a political opposition, Yockey proceeded to England in 1947 with the aim of meeting Mosley. Alexander Raven Thomson, the primary intellectual interpreter of Mosleyism, introduced him to John Anthony Gannon. Gannon set up one of the many groups of BUF veterans that sprang up immediately after the war, the Imperial Defence League, to prepare the way for the re-establishment of a Mosley organisation. He had joined the BUF in 1935, at the age of 14. He became Assistant District Leader (Propaganda) in Manchester, and a regional speaker. In June 1940, he was detained for six months under Regulation 18B, along with hundreds of other Britons opposed to the war, mostly BUF supporters. Gannon was introduced to Yockey in 1947 in Paddington, London, at the bookshop of the Union for British Freedom, run by Raven Thomson.[1]

Many were cautious about Yockey, including Gannon, because there had been 'a constant stream of agents provocateur from the US ADL[2] seeking to identify and entrap "English neo-Nazis", and some of these creatures had been successful in ruining those who had trusted them'. 'Having been subjected to the liquidation procedures of their counterparts within England, constantly, I was less inclined to confide in any of them. For all I knew at the time, FPY could have been, and some said that he was, one of the ADL hatchet-men.'[3]

Gannon next saw Yockey at the founding conference of Union Movement, where Gannon was one of the speakers calling on Mosley to lead a new movement. He saw Yockey the same evening at the house of a supporter in

1 Gannon to Stimely, July 13, 1980.

2 Anti-Defamation League of B'nai B'rith, an omnipresent information gathering Zionist organisation operating in the USA since 1913. The ADL will be considered further.

3 Gannon to Stimely, July 13, 1980, op. cit.

Kensington, and was impressed. However, 'the first real, meaningful contact' with Yockey was via Guy Chesham, who ran a Mosley front-club at Oxford University. Chesham was the closet contact Yockey had in England up until then.[4]

During the 1980s, Gannon wrote of his time working with Yockey:

> I first met FPY—Yockey to all and sundry—in the autumn of 1947 at the London bookshop headquarters of the Union for British Freedom, this being one of the regional organizations preparing for the return of Sir Oswald Mosley to active politics. Yockey was introduced to me by A Raven Thomson—pre-War Director of Policy in the British Union of Fascists—with the comment that I would find him an interesting companion.
>
> Yockey's American accent prompted me to ask him what he was doing in London. This was not an idle question for, at that time, London had many visitors from the USA seeking to make contact with groups deemed to be neo-fascist. Most of them were agents of the Anti-Defamation League of B'nai B'rith, and their purpose was to identify the leaders of such groups so that they could be given "the treatment"—repressed, put-down, evaporated! Of course, their general approach was that of the American "sympathizer" to the Cause but, sooner or later, it would be suggested that names and addresses should be exchanged so that contact could be maintained. Many of those who acceded to this request lived to regret it; they became the objects of unwelcome attention by hostile groups in their own localities, had their businesses undermined, or lost their employment.
>
> At the outset, it was obvious that Yockey did NOT follow this pattern—no request was made for name and address exchange—and in the ensuing conversation he told me that he had come to Europe to meet others in the service of the Idea, in particular, Sir Oswald Mosley, before writing a book. His intellectual gifts were very evident, as was his utter sincerity.
>
> We spoke together for a long time in complete agreement on what had happened to Europe and what needed to be done to restore its position, ending only when it became time for me to leave for the railway station to take my train for Manchester. It was agreed that we would meet again in the natural course of events, but no precise arrangement was made.

---

4 Gannon to Stimely, ibid.

> As I prepared to leave, I was approached by another man with an American accent, whom I had noticed in a general sort of way whilst speaking with Yockey, because he seemed to be taking some interest in our conversation. He asked if I was leaving, and I replied that I was bound for Euston station; to which he at once rejoined that he was also going in that direction, and that it would be a good idea to share a taxi together, to which I agreed. Once inside the taxi, my new acquaintance enquired if I knew Yockey, and I replied that I had met him for the first time that evening. He then warned me against having anything further to do with Yockey, stating that he was sure that Yockey was working for the FBI and the ADL. There then followed the routine request for my name and address so that we could keep in touch, which I declined on the grounds that I was going abroad for an indefinite period. By this time we had arrived at Euston, and I left Yockey's accuser with the certain conviction that *he* was an agent of the ADL, and that his denunciation of Yockey confirmed the latter's bona fides as one of us.
>
> My next news of Yockey came from a mutual friend, Guy Chesham, who was at that time acting as Sir Oswald Mosley's personal assistant. It seemed that Yockey had enquired of Chesham if he knew me, and that he had enjoyed our London meeting and would like to see me again.[5]

At the time Yockey was working on *Imperium* in Ireland, Mosley published his post-war manifesto for Europe-a-Nation, *The Alternative*. Mosley's opening lines are as a man 'without a party' whose aim is to promote 'the European Idea'. There is much similarity in the European Idea between Yockey and Mosley, Mosley referring to two world wars that had 'divided and conquered Europe'. 'Those who fought are in the position of the conquered whatever their country.' A lesson that Mosley never forgot, and reiterated in his autobiography in 1968,[6] was that while the Fascist movements were accused of serving the interests of a foreign country, i.e. Germany and/or Italy, the tragedy was that they 'had been too nationalistic even to mould the minds of men in a new sense of European kinship and solidarity which might have avoided disaster by universal consent'. 'Our creed was brought to the dust because the Fascist

---

5 Anthony Gannon, 'Francis Parker Yockey, 1917–1960: A Remembrance of the Author of Imperium', ca. 1980s; Stimely archives, Oregon State University.

6 Mosley, *My Life*, 1968 (London: Black House Publishing, 2014).

outlook in each land was too National.'[7] Mosley proceeded with a basically Spenglerian analysis of 'Mob and Money', or communism and international finance. Like Spengler, he saw the two as allied. He also regarded communism as 'Asian', firstly because it was 'invented by a Jew' and secondly because it had only thrived in Russia. 'Communism is the answer of the East, not the West...' He added in regard to the banality of relating communism with fascism that

> Fascism was the answer of the West and communism was the answer of the East; the first was conceived by Europeans; the latter by an Oriental. ... Between these two creeds lay a vast gulf which divides West from East.[8]

Again in Spenglerian mode, Mosley stated that 'Mob and Money thrive together in chaos'.[9] Like Spengler, Mosley recognised a dichotomy between the English and the German characters. Germany upheld the traditional European ethos. Puritanism from the seventeenth century had caused the breach of England's custody of European high culture. Since then, England provided the home soil of an economic *Zeitgeist*.[10] That is why, as Spengler stated, there is a difference between 'Prussian Socialism' and the class-war 'Socialism' of Marx that sprang up in England. Mosley, like Spengler and Yockey, saw the political conflict as ultimately spiritual, in repudiating the 'Materialist conception of History';[11] the 'conflict between money and blood', as Spengler put it in the concluding passages of *The Decline of the West*. 'The higher European is the final enemy of both Finance and Communism because he can neither be bought nor frightened.'[12] Given the tremendous spiritual forces of Europe, Mosley asked why communism and finance defeated Western civilization in the world war. He answered that the division of Europe through petty-nationalism caused the defeat.[13] Mosley concluded by foreseeing resurgent Germans

7 Mosley, *The Alternative* (Wiltshire: Mosley Publications, 1947), 'The Extension of Patriotism', p. 9.

8 Ibid., 'Communism and Fascism', p. 80.

9 Ibid., 'The Failure of Britain and Europe', p. 21.

10 Ibid., p. 33.

11 Ibid., 'Communism and Fascism', p. 83.

12 Ibid., 'Mob, Money, and the Division of Europe', p. 93.

13 Ibid., p. 93.

in their historical role as the bulwark of Europe, because 'no power on earth will keep them apart or hold them down'.[14]

When Yockey returned to England in 1948 with his completed manuscript for *Imperium*, he contacted Major-General J. F. C. Fuller, tank warfare specialist, military historian and Mosley's BUF military affairs adviser;[15] and Captain Basil Liddell Hart, also a noted military historian and strategist,[16] both of whom would later endorse *Imperium*.[17]

Yockey was at the founding conference of the Union Movement at Wilfred Street School hall, on February 7 and 8, 1948, attended by 250 delegates from 51 groups. The call was for a 'union of the West' in the face of the 'Russian communist menace' to world peace.[18] The policy points of the Union Movement would have been agreeable to Yockey, namely:

1. To secure the Union of the European Peoples.
2. To resist the menace of International Communism and International Finance.
3. To win the consent and enthusiasm of the people for a new way of life.
4. To win power in Britain by the vote of the people.
5. To abolish the Party game and thus to create a system of united national action.
6. To develop Africa as an estate of the European which can solve the economic problem of our continent.

---

14 Ibid., 'Character of the German People', p. 139.

15 Fuller somehow avoided 18B detention, despite other prominent figures such as Captain A. H. M. Ramsay, Tory Member of Parliament and founder of The Right Club, and Admiral Sir Barry Domville, former head of Naval Intelligence, and founder of 'The Link', devoted to Anglo-German friendship, being imprisoned.

16 Hart was among the prominent individuals who were members of the January Club, founded to support the BUF. Stephen Dorril, *Black Shirt*, op. cit., p. 258.

17 Stephen Dorril, *Black Shirt*, ibid., p. 571.

18 Raven Thomson, 'Mosley Speech to Conference', *Union*, No. 1, February 1948.

7. To abolish the values and influence of class which rest on hereditary wealth and impede the new life of the nation.
8. To provide continuing security in creative service of the people for the man who has built his own means of livelihood, and desires his children to follow after him in hereditary science, art, craft, profession or business.
9. To assert the right and will of the whole British people above every faction and thus to enable all to earn what they are worth, with full security in sickness and old age.
10. To create a new sense of service and a new morality in the State.[19]

In the Union Movement points, there is the 'ethical socialism', the organic state and the union of Europe that the European Liberation Front was to express in its 12-point policy. Gannon writes of this time:

> 1948 was a year of constant activity. Union Movement, led by Sir Oswald Mosley, had been founded, and *Imperium* had been written by Yockey under the pen-name Ulick Varange, printed, and published. This pen-name was symbolic of the extremities of Europe as seen by Yockey; Ulick was an Irish name indicating the western boundary, whilst the Varange were nomadic tribesmen operating on the eastern fringes of Europe. By now, my contact with Yockey and Chesham was intense, and we met as often as possible in London, maintaining contact by correspondence at other times.
>
> Meantime, things were not going well in the relationship between Sir Oswald Mosley and Yockey. At first this had proceeded smoothly, with Sir Oswald finding Yockey a stimulating, talented, and interesting companion. This changed with the appearance of *Imperium* and, according to Yockey, with his offer to Sir Oswald of *Imperium* as a gift to bring out under his own name, and as his own work. I accept, without reservation, that Yockey was completely sincere in this gesture of astonishing generosity. He had reasoned that Sir Oswald was a man of action, with a well-established international reputation, and further political ambitions yet to be actualized, but without the immediate opportunity to find the considerable time required to conceive and write such a work himself. Certainly, Yockey was not trying to patronize Sir Oswald, or to upstage him.

19 'Objects of Union Movement', *Union*, No. 1, February, 1948.

> In the event, Sir Oswald declined Yockey's offer, and their relationship ended soon afterwards in some contumely. It must be said that those familiar with Sir Oswald's own style of thinking and writing might have found it difficult to believe that *Imperium* was his own work and, thus, he could hardly be expected to accept Yockey's offer in the spirit in which it had been made. Nonetheless, as an alternative, and in recognition of the outstanding merit of *Imperium*, he could have sponsored the publication of the book.[20]

The first issue of the new Mosley movement newspaper, *Union*, featured articles by Guy Chesham[21] and Yockey. Yockey wrote on the organic law of epochs in civilizations and how the 'old' must inevitably make way for the 'new' despite resistance. The past era was that of 'democracy' and 'materialism', of money and party politics. No conservative reaction could prevent it. Now the new epoch was a resurgence of authority, of which fascism and National Socialism had been provisional forms. The military defeat of these provisional forms by the old forces of democracy and money would be no more enduring than the defeat of Napoleon by the forces of conservatism in the previous epoch. 'History has its own logic' and the old cannot forever hold back the new. Democracy was the Idea of the 'Spirit of the Age' from the nineteenth century but the Resurgence of Authority would be the Idea for the new *Zeitgeist*. Yockey wrote:

> It is not surprising that men resisted this Idea, for the New is always established only over the blind and sterile opposition of the Old. For two great reasons, the forces of the old idea fight the New Idea. First: the leading minds do not become the servants of the Old Order, for these ideas are claimed by the New Idea, the Idea of the Future. Thus the Old Order simply does not understand the Spirit of the Age. Second: this Old Order has material interests in the perpetuation of the existing forms of organization, which by their existence work for its purposes.

1848, the year of the democratic bourgeoisie revolutions throughout Europe, and the year of *The Communist Manifesto*, is superseded by 1948, when *Imperium* appeared and the European Liberation Front was born as the vanguard of the new *Zeitgeist*. No material force, not communism or international

20 Gannon memoir on Yockey, op. cit.

21 'G. C.', 'What Price Western Union?', *Union*, op. cit.

finance, and their puppet governments, can withstand the imperative of the Age, 'the mystical force of its Destiny'. Alluding to Spengler's theme, Yockey asked: 'Is a mighty Civilization to be strangled in this fashion? Is the Blood of the Western Civilization to be turned into Money?'

> The Spirit of the Age says: NO! This Spirit claims the best men of the Western Civilization all over the world, and imbues them with the mission of the Resurgence of Authority, and the destruction of that finance-capitalism which today covers up its operations of Death and Chaos with the outworn catchword of Democracy. … Against Money, we pit the Spirit of Heroism; against their compulsion-propaganda, our Discipline; against their cynicism, our Faith; against the reactionary rule of their unclean parties, our Leader on the path to the Future, Oswald Mosley.[22]

Here we see a major theme of Yockey's as-yet-unpublished *Imperium* manuscript. Like Karl Marx explaining the historical inevitability of communism, Yockey drew on Hegel to show the historical inevitability of Western Empire. As we know, there were 'right-wing' Hegelians and 'left-wing' Hegelians, Marx being among the most prominent of the latter. Yockey listed Hegel as one of the philosophers to develop an 'organic' theory of history, along with Goethe, Spengler, Carlyle, Nietzsche, et al. 'The Destiny-Idea is the central motive of organic thinking,' Yockey wrote in *Imperium*.[23] To Marx's 'dialectical materialism' as a 'scientific' analysis of history, Yockey countered with what the German Idealists called the *Zeitgeist*, or 'spirit of the age'. To the Hegelian dialectic, Yockey added Spengler's historical morphology and the *Heroic Vitalism* of Carlyle, to show that the historical dialectic is unfolded not by proletarian masses impelled by their stomachs but by heroic individuals with a sense of destiny. The instrument of that destiny Yockey hoped would be Mosley and the Union Movement.

Yockey was given a paid position in the Union Movement's European Contact Section as a liaison officer with overseas groups, working with Guy Chesham, a fellow lawyer and an Oxford graduate who was impressed with the scholarly Yockey. Mosley held Chesham in much regard.

---

22 'FPY', '1848–1948 Years of Decision', *Union*, No. 1, 1948.

23 Yockey, *Imperium*, Wermod ed., op. cit., pp. 16–19.

Considering the importance Mosley attached to cultivating contacts with European movements as a prelude to united Europe, the position was one of significance. Through this position, Yockey contacted Dr Alfred Franke-Gricksch, the German adviser to the Union Movement. Through Franke-Gricksch, Yockey established contact with the *Bruderschaft*.[24] The *Bruderschaft* was founded by former Third Reich officers to aid their comrades and promote the union of Europe. Franke-Gricksch had been head of the Personnel Section of the SS Reich Security Head Office, although he had been on the Strasser wing of the party, leaving the NSDAP in 1930. Indeed, he was a close colleague of Otto Strasser when the latter formed the anti-Hitler League of Revolutionary National Socialists, following him to exile in Prague. However, he returned to Germany in 1934, having broken with Strasser. It was suggested that he had been a spy for the NSDAP. It was certainly odd that he was able to secure a position in the SS if he had been a Strasserite. In this position, he was in charge of preparing a post-war plan for European unity that had been outlined in 1944 by Dr Franz Six of the German Foreign Country and Scientific Institute.[25]

Franke-Gricksch advocated the organic, corporatist state. He called on the youth of all European states to build a united Europe.[26] The *Bruderschaft* was intended as an elite brotherhood that would assume authority in Germany when the democratic system failed. Although many of the members supported a belligerent attitude towards the USSR, others did not. Ex-Wehrmacht General Helmut Beck-Broichsitter, *Bruderschaft* organiser, affirmed: 'Just because we are not militarists and not nationalists, we must not be available for mercenary or student assistant service as soldiers for east or west. We are for a Europe in which Germany is equally strong. An independent Europe is the best guarantee of peace.'[27] However, Franke-Gricksch and Beck-Broichsitter soon diverged towards pro-Soviet and pro-US lines respectively. General

---

24 FBI report, August 7, 1954, p. 11, 105–8229 — 2.

25 Franz A Six, *Europa und der Welt* (Berlin: Junker and Dünnhaupt, 1944).

26 'Bruderschaft', *Der Spiegel*, February 3, 1950.

27 'Bruderschaft', *Der Spiegel*, ibid.

Vincenz Müller, former vice chairman of the NDPD,[28] invited Franke-Gricksch to the DDR to discuss German unification.

Franke-Gricksch saw a new worldwide conflict emerging between Asia and the West. Spengler had foreseen this in 1934, in *The Hour of Decision*. However, Spengler regarded the USSR as the leader of a 'coloured world revolution' behind the banner of Bolshevism. Franke-Gricksch believed that the USSR would realise its interests on the white side.[29] This indeed occurred 15 to 20 years later with the Sino-Soviet split and the border conflicts between Russia and China.[30] Franke-Gricksch had however apparently overplayed his hand and was arrested in the DDR, sent to Moscow and executed as a war criminal. The verdict was overturned by Russia in 1995.

***

Yockey considered Mosley, with his charisma, recognition and comparatively large following, the logical choice as leader to implement the doctrine of *Imperium*. He had even offered to assign authorship of *Imperium* to Mosley. It is one of several significant indicators of Yockey's lack of egotism or narcissism that he was ever willing to take a back seat in service to the idea. However, Yockey's focus on Jewish 'Culture-distortion' and his opinion that the USA represented a deeper threat to Western civilization than the USSR, put him at odds with Mosley. Mosley had stated in *The European Situation* that under the USSR, European freedom would be 'killed', while under the USA freedom can still exist 'and even grow. That is the basic difference which must determine the question of attitude'.[31]

---

28 The National Democratic Party of Germany, not to be confused with its 'extreme Right' namesake in the Federal Republic, was organised on the insistence of Stalin to mobilise veterans and ex-Reich officials in support of the DDR. The party continued to play a significant role in the DDR until German unification. See K. R. Bolton, 'Stalin's German Nationalist Party', *Journal of Inconvenient History*, Vol. 6, No. 1, 2014, http://inconvenienthistory.com/archive/2014/volume_6/number_1/stalins_german_nationalist_party.php.

29 'Fehler', *Der Spiegel*, February 28, 1951.

30 See K. R. Bolton, *Geopolitics of the Indo-Pacific: Emerging Conflicts, New Alliances* (London: Black House Publishing, 2013), pp. 7–19.

31 Cited by Dorril, *Black Shirt*, op. cit., p. 574.

Mosley had (it is widely assumed) barely glanced at *Imperium*, although he had recognised Yockey's brilliance to the point of inviting Yockey as a guest to his home at Crowood, Wiltshire. According to Diana Mosley, her husband put any material on Yockey in his 'crackpot' file.[32] However, Desmond Stewart, the novelist, journalist and Arabist, who edited *The European* after Raven Thomson's death, 'effusively remembered "the very entertaining dinner party with Yockey", which he had attended with Mosley in 1948'.[33]

Raven Thomson regarded *Imperium* as full of 'Spenglerian pessimism' and as 'unnecessarily offensive to America'.[34] However, it seems that Thomson was sufficiently influenced by *Imperium* to develop his own theory of 'social pathology' based on Yockey's Cultural Vitalism.[35] Gannon stated Yockey had read Thomson's *magnum opus*, the semi-Spenglerian *Civilization as Divine Superman*, and

> knew Raven Thomson well, liked him as a man, but regarded him as an unconditional-Mosleyite. In truth, I can say that RT was both a good fascist and an intelligent, capable, kindly man — didactic, in type. I knew him for more than twenty years, first as Director of Policy in the British Union of Fascists, later as one of the leaders of the post-war UBF (Union for British Freedom, one of the pre-Union Movement groupings that merged to form UM). His kindly nature was often taken as a weakness, particularly by Yockey, who affected to despise such feelings.[36]

***

The issue of Russia was the catalyst for the break, with Yockey claiming that Mosley was a 'lackey' of the USA and of Churchill, while Mosley regarded him as obsessively anti-American and 'soft' on the USSR. The Mosleyites continued to evoke the menace to Europe from the Asian steppes to the extent of

32 Dorril, *Black Shirt*, ibid., p. 575.

33 G. Macklin, *Very Deeply Dyed in Black*, p. 91.

34 Dorril, *Black Shirt*, ibid., p. 575.

35 See below on Thomson's theory of 'social pathology'.

36 Gannon to Stimely, November 24, 1981. The word 'affected' should be noted. As will be seen, Yockey affected much of his persona depending on the nature of those with whom he was dealing.

conceding that American protection of Europe was still needed until Europe united on her own terms and was rid of both extra-European powers. The imminent danger to the West was from a Russia with the atomic bomb. Hence, the lead article by Mosley comprising most of the first issue of the *Mosley News Letter* in 1946 stated that the most immediate urgencies were (1) 'to secure the inspection of Soviet Russia to ensure that atomic weapons will not be produced there in secret' and (2) 'to prevent the kidnapping or cajoling of German scientists and technicians to provide Russia with the technical abilities which she lacks'.[37]

Mosley referred to the 'Soviet Government' as being the only factor preventing a 'proposed universal inspection by an international authority to inhibit the production of weapons, which may bring World Civilization to an early and irremediable disaster'. Mosley described the Americans as having 'extraordinary magnanimity' in offering to eliminate their atomic arsenal and subject themselves to an international inspection authority if other nations would do the same. Mosley found Russia's reasoning extraordinary:

> The attitude of Russia was that inspection would infringe on her national sovereignty! So the wheel has come full circle and the Communist Party, which prated for generations about "World Brotherhood", now obstructs peace and progress by means of the oldest slogan of that "obsolete Imperialism" which it was pledged to destroy. No peace for you, comrades, rasps the "third international". No security from fear for the "workers of the world". Far more important is the National Dignity and Sovereign Rights of Holy Russia.[38]

Mosley referred to Russia 'clinging to the veto' that would render impotent any proposed action of nations against her. He stated that the USSR had undermined a prime element of Communist propaganda and must therefore regard the atomic bomb as more important than the position of their Communist apparatus throughout the world.[39] While the USA had no business inter-

37 Oswald Mosley, 'Menace of Russian Communism and the necessity to prevent it developing and using the Atom bomb for World Conquest', *Mosley News Letter* (Wiltshire) No. 1, November 15, 1946, p. 1.

38 Oswald Mosley, ibid., p. 2.

39 Oswald Mosley, ibid., p. 3.

fering in a European quarrel during World War II, with the Atomic era US intervention was now necessary. Mosley also pointed out that the Russian offer for German scientists to live and work in the USSR was more realistic than the US occupation policy of relegating these experts to the trash heap. Mosley commented that the 'Slav' was unable to achieve technically without the aid of Western scientists and technicians. He ended his article with a call for a common front between Europe and America against the USSR and the menace of atomic obliteration, which supersedes all other issues.[40]

Much of what Mosley wrote was actually in agreement with what Yockey was to write several years later. The difference however was one of perspective. Yockey would point out that the USSR had changed. What Mosley was referring to was the so-called 'Baruch Plan' for the 'internationalisation of atomic energy' under a United Nations authority, informally named after its public protagonist, international Jewish banker and so-called 'elder statesman' of the USA Bernard Baruch, Churchill's close friend. The USSR saw this as a manoeuvre to place atomic energy under US control. Mosley, in referring to Russia's insistence that they retain a 'veto', is alluding to Russia's scuttling of another US idea that would have rendered the UN General Assembly a world parliament, in which the USA could have easily bought a majority of votes. The USSR insisted instead that authority be vested in the UN Security Council and that member states have the power to veto any decision. With hindsight, the reader is invited to contemplate what the world would be like with a UNO armed with atomic weaponry and the power to act against sovereign states by a majority vote in the General Assembly.[41] This was US one-worldism. That was the immediate post-war issue. Stalin scuttled this and Yockey realised it.

Mosley referred to the 'third international' and to the fact that the Russian assertion of national sovereignty could be made use of in a propaganda offensive against the world communist apparatus. However, Stalin shut down the Third International in 1943 and had already eliminated most of the 'Old Bolsheviks', the veterans of the 1917 Revolution. When the leaders of the

40 Oswald Mosley, ibid., p. 5.

41 On the Baruch Plan, the USSR and the UNO see Bolton, *Stalin: The Enduring Legacy* (London: Black House, 2012), pp. 125–139.

German and other communist parties sought refuge in the USSR from fascism, most were promptly liquidated.[42]

Both Mosley and Yockey held that Slavs relied on Western technics. However, the spectre of Mongol and Slavic hordes conquering Europe was of more concern to Mosley than to Yockey, who saw the American occupation with its 'coca cola army' as he called it, Jewish interrogators and the culture-disease of New York and Hollywood as more destructive to the Western culture-soul than Russian occupation. One might also conclude that while Mosley sought to play the American card against Russia in the interests of Europe, Yockey sought to play the Russian card. Both tactics had their protagonists among German Rightists and veterans.

42 On the destruction of the international communist movement by Stalin see Bolton, *Stalin: The Enduring Legacy*, ibid., pp. 3–9.

# 'An Act of Faith'

## European Liberation Front

After this breach with Mosley, there were sufficient supporters of Yockey to form their own movement. At a meeting in the London home of Baroness Alice von Pflügl, Yockey condemned Union Movement as a tool of US foreign policy.

An FBI report cites an informer who stated that at the founding meeting, Yockey urged the formation of a partisan underground in West Germany that would align with the USSR in ousting the US-led occupying powers. He allegedly announced that if those involved accepted his ideas, a group would be formed that would be part of a worldwide movement working to establish 'real National Socialism'. At first, Jews would not be targeted but an anti-US newspaper was proposed for agitation purposes against the occupation of Europe.[1]

Peter J Huxley-Blythe, fishing for information that the FBI had on Yockey in 1961, cited the FBI information it had reported a decade earlier on the founding meeting of the ELF. He claimed 'Yockey praised Soviet policy in Germany and in particular the so-called Army of Seydlitz and von Paulus'.[2]

---

1 FBI report, August 7, 1954, op. cit., p. 12.

2 Peter J Huxley-Blythe to FBI, October 2, 1961, p. 2, 105–8229—3. FBI director J Edgar Hoover declined to give Huxley-Blythe information, commenting that it was against FBI policy, noting in a letter to the legal attaché in London that Huxley-Blythe is an Englishmen who was seeking information in return for information that was already known to the FBI. Hoover commented that Huxley-Blythe had been a member of the Northern League, an international movement promoting pan-Nordic unity. Hoover note to Legal Attaché, London, October 12, 1961; 105–8229—3.

> He then asked those present to help him organize secret partisan bands of neo-Nazis in Western Germany; bands which would collaborate with the Soviet military authorities against the Western occupation powers.
>
> The Baroness then interrupted and told everyone present that the new National Socialist Europe would be created by help from the East, i.e. from the Soviet Union; that the USSR would drive the Western Allies out of Europe and found the new Nazi Imperium. "Our liberation will come from the East," she said as she finished her passionate plea for help.
>
> Yockey continued that if those present would agree to help him they would be initiated into a vast worldwide secret organization working to establish an Authoritarian State ("the real National Socialism").
>
> He claimed this organization is already millions strong and that he was the representative of the leader whose name he could not divulge.[3]
>
> Outlining the future programme Yockey said "to start with" he did not contemplate the use of anti-Jewish propaganda. First he wanted to found a sensational newspaper specialising in anti-American propaganda.[4]

While Anthony Gannon objected to Stimely decades later that Yockey did not suggest any such strategy, and that it was Huxley-Blythe making false claims, on the other hand the outlook does seem in line with what Yockey was already writing in *Frontline* at least as early as 1951, as will be seen below.

This upstart, impatient American was nonetheless quickly able to attract a following around him that included some of Mosley's best men. Among those who joined him from Union Movement were Guy Chesham, Peter J Huxley-Blythe and Gannon. Gannon gives the founding membership of the Front as precisely 148.[5] Given that the number of Union Movement active members

---

3 If Yockey, or someone claiming to represent him, made this claim he could have been referring to the *Bruderschaft* in Germany and other organisations around the world, including the émigrés around *Der Weg* in Argentina. This network has been referred to as *Die Spinne* and *ODESSA*. In correspondence I had with H Keith Thompson, who was US agent for *Der Weg*, he referred to individuals such as Johannes von Leers and Otto Remer as constituting a 'higher authority'. They were moreover impressed by Yockey.

4 Peter J Huxley-Blythe to FBI, October 2, 1961, p. 2.

5 Gannon to Stimely, November 24, 1981.

was, according to MI5, at the time 1,200,[6] the departure of 148 members was a more significant split than one might suppose. Moreover, most of the leadership cadre of UM in the North and North West of England joined Gannon and Yockey.[7]

During 1939–1940, Chesham was British Union District Leader for the Combined Universities, although not one of the hundreds of BUF members detained during the war.[8] He was assigned to manage Euphorion Books, established shortly after the war to prepare the way for Mosley's return.[9] His 'Memorandum of Disassociation' from Union Movement is particularly vitriolic towards Mosley. Chesham rather quickly concluded that Union Movement was a failure, as indicated between what he called the 'wild enthusiasm' of the first UM conference and the 'stunned apathy' of the second. He put membership at 2,000 to 3,000 and he regarded these of the lowest calibre.[10] Again, harsh, at least given that some of those who remained committed to Mosley included Demsond Stuart and Henry Williamson. Chesham was also sceptical about Mosley's insistence that UM would assume authority in a crisis situation and regarded that as a rationalisation for failure. He regarded UM as devoid of ideology and compromising with the enemies of Europe.[11]

Chesham seems to have intended to focus on overseas organisational efforts with the UM as a home base. However, Chesham did not regard the UM leadership as capable of impressing those across Europe. He referred to a broadsheet intended by Mosley for Germans, *Deutsches Flugblatt*, which he stated had appalled Germans when shown the proofs. Chesham challenged Mosley that he had promised the Germans this newspaper would not be circulated in Germany. When Chesham had complained that *Deutsches Flugblatt* had gone to Germany, he states that Mosley claimed 'blandly' that 'a few must have leaked through from South America', although *Union* was

6 G. Macklin, op. cit., p. 59.

7 Gannon to Stimely, April 20, 1982.

8 Jeffrey Wallder to Bolton, November 5, 2014.

9 G. Macklin, *Very Deeply Dyed in Black: Oswald Mosley and the Resurrection of British Fascism* (London: I B Tauras, 2007), 91.

10 Guy Chesham, 'A Memorandum of Disassociation', August 31, 1949, p. 1.

11 Ibid., p. 2.

advertising *Deutsches Flugblatt* for dispatch to Germany.[12] From Jewish media accounts of the time, it seems that the British occupation zone had banned *Deutsches Flugblatt* before copies had reached there but that it had been sent to members of UM who were serving in the occupation forces.[13] The two-page broadsheet was published mainly to advertise the German edition of Mosley's book *The Alternative*. One contention of Chesham was the danger to Germans being sent such material through the mails.

Chesham's dispute with Mosley on Russia soon appears. In a subsection of the memorandum, entitled 'The 1948 War Scare', Chesham described Mosley's 'unreal attitude towards the Washington war hoax'. He referred to a memorandum that had been addressed to Mosley the previous year, which Mosley had considered 'childish' but which Chesham regarded as 'a masterly exposition of the power aspect of the international situation'; Mosley had rejected it as a 'highly personalised policy of romanticist Mongol-hating—a policy which has resulted in your present impotent dissolution'.[14] Chesham criticised Mosley for a 'pro-American deviation' which was 'indistinguishable from that of the volunteer lackeys of America'. He maintained the line that was becoming increasingly widespread among European nationalists—that in any conflict between the USSR and USA, which represented a conflict between 'barbarism and decadence', Europe must remain neutral. He accused Mosley of wanting to be seen as the leader who could unite ex-Fascists in a conflict with the USSR.[15]

Chesham considered that Mosley had not done enough to help the victims of the 'war crimes trials' and criticised him for having refused to print an article in *Union* entitled 'Carnival of Murder'.[16] In common with Yockey, he believed that Mosley was pandering to Churchill,[17] 'this European traitor', 'as nauseating' as Mosley's 'synthesis of two great creeds of Fascism and

---

12 Ibid., pp. 2–3,

13 'Mosley's German language propaganda sheet did not reach Germany before ban imposed', Jewish Telegraphic Agency, August 8, 1948.

14 Guy Chesham, 'A Memorandum of Disassociation', op. cit., p. 3.

15 Ibid., p. 7.

16 Ibid., p. 5.

17 Ibid., p. 6.

Democracy'.[18] Chesham arrived at *Imperium* in section 5 of his 'memorandum'; '*Imperium*-Phobia'. He stated:

> At first I took the excessive resentment of this book and its author on the part of your entourage as the routine manifestation of pygmy jealousy habitually evinced by the caucus upon the impact of a superior intellect, and I thought that my own association with F. P. Yockey was resented on the usual grounds, namely, that no two persons of political intelligence must be allowed to meet in the group.
>
> It soon became clear however that a deeper hatred was entertained. This significant book was not even reviewed by you, contrary to your promise; paper was not provided to the author, contrary to your promise, and in spite of the fact that you were using up political paper to publish politically useless aesthetic works. Moreover, the character of the author was assailed with a bitterness and fury of the order usually reserved for the heroic William Joyce.[19]
>
> It was therefore necessary to listen to your explaining at tedious length why you could not review the book. These reasons were in inverse proportion to the force of the attacks on the author. A philosophical quibble on some difference between Goebbels and Spengler was, I recollect, your official excuse. How ironical that your group should set itself up as the keeper of the National Socialist conscience! It has no point of contact whatsoever with the Nazi movement, spiritual, ideological, organisational, traditional or cultural. It is not decent for people to take the names of Spengler and Goebbels in vain: the former, were he alive today, would be declared a war criminal, the Jews aver. The latter would have banned the anti-Nazi scribblings of *Union* in their entirety and have made short shrift of your own pretentiousness at the present time.[20]

While Chesham writes of the historical irony in reference to Spengler and Goebbels, it is also an irony that the European Liberation Front formed by

---

18 Ibid.

19 William Joyce, dubbed 'Lord Haw Haw' by BBC propaganda for his services to German radio during World War II, had been an official of the British Union of Fascists but had broken with Mosley to form the National Socialist League. He was hanged after the war for 'treason'. See: William Joyce, *Twilight Over England* (London: Black House Publishing, 2013), with an introduction by K. R. Bolton.

20 Guy Chesham, 'A Memorandum of Disassociation', op. cit., p. 7.

Yockey, Chesham, Gannon and other disaffected members of UM upheld the racial, philosophical and political heresies of Spengler that had caused him to become *persona non grata* during the one year that he lived under the National Socialist regime. The National Socialists, including Goebbels, attempted to cultivate Spengler without success. Spengler's main support within the NSDAP came from Gregor Strasser, who attempted to recruit Spengler to the party in 1925, and his brother Otto, whose Black Front broke with the NSDAP, and whose own doctrines were heavily influenced by Strasser. Such contacts might have put Spengler into deep trouble with the regime, had he lived longer.[21] Chesham continues:

> It was left to your factotum Thompson[22] [sic], in a further burst of his alarming candour, to suggest to me that *Imperium* aroused your blind fury because he himself had, quite unwittingly, aroused your personal jealousy of the author.
>
> Yet I feel the cause lies deeper. With this book you acquired a heaven sent opportunity to supply your group with a granite-like ideology. It is true that your treatment of the author under-lined your well-known inability to tolerate men of intellect and imagination about you, but it was your failure to adopt the ideology of the book which displayed the full extent of your retreat from real politics into the cloudcuckooland of your purely social-economic activity and your incredible delusions of grandeur. You hated *Imperium* because it was a summons to action, because it demanded a shattering of illusion and a manly facing of political facts.
>
> Take note: the acceptance of *Imperium* among political and intellectual circles at home and abroad is now a political fact.[23]

The tenor of Chesham's critique of Mosley suggests the fairly typical character of a disillusioned devotee; perhaps overly vitriolic. On the other hand,

---

21 See: K. R. Bolton, 'Spengler: A Philosopher for All Seasons', in Troy Southgate (ed.) *Spengler: Thoughts and Perspectives*, Vol. Ten (London: Black Front Press, 2012), pp. 15–24.

22 Alexander Raven Thomson, Britain's leading philosophical exponent of the corporate state, was editor of the BUF's *Action* before the war, and the UM's *Union*.

23 Guy Chesham, 'A Memorandum of Disassociation', op. cit., p. 8.

Chesham remained committed to European liberation and union, and to Yockey's philosophy even after the two had their own falling-out.

Chesham concluded:

> All that matters today is the creation of a real movement in the Island. The only legitimate political task is the ridding of Europe from all Anti-Western influences. For Englishmen, this means the destruction of the inner American in these Islands. To this task, to this real activity, I dedicate myself: those who would speak with me will find me among the Frontfighters of Island Liberation and of European Imperium.[24]

Chesham's closing words were '*Was Mich Nicht Umbringt, Macht Mich Staerker…*', Nietzsche's famous axiom in *Twilight of the Idols*, 'What does not destroy me makes me stronger', and the final words of Yockey in *Imperium*.

Gannon stated of the situation:

> Yockey departed from Sir Oswald's movement and Guy Chesham and I went with him, joined soon afterwards by a number of others; it was our intention to establish a new organization devoted to the liberation of Europe, concerning which I will have more to say later.
>
> Our immediate task was to distribute *Imperium* — as well and as widely as our resources would permit. From a house in Park Square West, on the edge of London's Regent Park,[25] went a steady stream of copies of *Imperium* to those in the service of the Idea in other European lands, in South Africa, Canada, USA, South America. If *Imperium* had been received with hostility in Britain by those expected to welcome it, this was not the case elsewhere. The reaction to *Imperium* from abroad was overwhelmingly enthusiastic and approving, and messages of support and praise were received from — to mention but a few — Germany: General Otto Remer, Heinz Knöke (famous Luftwaffe ace), Hans-Ulrich Rudel (*the* Stuka pilot), all associated with the Socialist Reich Party, and Karl Heinz Priester[26] of the European Social Movement; Italy: Giorgio

24 Ibid., p. 9.

25 Baroness Alice von Pflügl's residence.

26 Head of propaganda for the Hitler Youth prior to serving as an officer in the Waffen SS, he was a frequent writer for the post-war, pan-European journal *Nation Europa*, promoting European unity, and worked with Mosley and Oswald Pirow. He established his own revisionist publishing house, Verlag Karl-Heinz Priester. A founder

Almirante (Movimento Sociale Italiano), Marchese Patrizi,[27] Julius Evola, and Principessa Pignatelli of the Women's Social Movement; France: Maurice Bardèche, René Binet, Claude-Marie Dagon,[28] Louis Girard[29]; Portugal: Dr Francisco dos Santos; Switzerland: M. G. A. Amaudruz; Canada: Adrien Arcand; South Africa: Oswald Pirow (former Minister and founder of the New Order Party), Ray Rudman,[30] Johan Schoeman;[31] Argentina: Emilio Gutierrez Herrero (Union Cívica Nacionalista).[32]

Whereas, in England, despite the reaction of the former leaders of British fascism, such notables as Major General J. F. C. Fuller and Captain Basil Liddell Hart wrote glowing tributes in praise of *Imperium*. *Imperium* had been launched

---

of the European Social Movement (headed by the Swedish Fascist Engdahl, Maurice Bardèche, and MSI representative Fabio Lonciari) and leader of its German affiliate, Deutsch-Soziale Bewegung, he became a leader of the National Democratic Party (NPD) established after the prohibition of the Socialist Reich Party.

27 The Patrizi Naro Montoro are a very eminent Italian noble family. The Marchesse Patrizi had been Special Economic Attaché at the Italian Embassy in London just prior to World War II.

28 Dagon worked with René Binet on his newspaper *La Sentinelle*.

29 Louis Girard was a Swiss Fascist and a founder, with fellow Swiss Amaudruz, of the New European Order, which had split from the European Social Movement in 1951 to follow a more biological worldview.

30 Rudman was leader of an Afrikaner National Socialist movement, 'Boerneasie'.

31 Schoeman wrote many pamphlets, including 'Hear the Other Side: The Afrikaner Side and the German Side' (1945); 'A Request to the British Field Marshal to Let the British King Visit the Graveyards of the British Belsen Camps in South Africa' (1947); 'Warning, and Smuts Damns British Imperialism, Being Two Essays' (1948); 'Goering's Last Letter to Winston Churchill' (1949); 'Small Essays on Big Subjects' (1952); 'Die Krisis in Suid-Afrika' (1952); 'Whose is the Hidden Hand' (1961); 'Eichmann is Not Guilty' (1962), etc. Schoeman was decribed by a Jewish source as 'an incorrigible pamphleteer, an ardent admirer of Hitler and a self-confessed anti-Semite'. The SA Jewish Board of Deputies unsuccessfully tried to get Schoeman's material banned by the South African authorities. South African Jewish Board of Deputies, Annual Report, April 1958 to August 1960, p. 17.

32 Emilio Gutierrez Herrero had been invited by Perón to the post of Minister of Posts and Telegraph, but rejected the offer, regarding Perón as not being a genuine 'Fascist'. Gannon to Stimely, November 24, 1981. Herrero fell foul of the Peronist regime thereafter.

on a tide of great success, and Yockey felt greatly encouraged thereby; in time, he met most of those who had supported his great work.[33]

Gannon described the founding of the European Liberation Front:

> It was now time to establish the new organization, and Yockey put forward the words European and Liberation for incorporation in the title, whilst Guy Chesham and I thought the word Front should be included; thus, the name European Liberation Front came into being, it being argued and accepted that it would be difficult for any opponent to attack the liberation of Europe as an objective.
>
> To the best of my knowledge, we were the first organization in the world to use the words Liberation Front in its title. Since then the use of these two words have spread throughout the world in the titles of other political groupings to an astonishing degree. We had, like most of our kind, no money and few resources except for our own enthusiasm and contacts. Several centres of activity were set up in Britain, and most of those abroad who had welcomed *Imperium* agreed to work with us.
>
> A monthly bulletin was produced under the name of *Frontfighter* in a duplicated format, all that we could afford, but at least [it was] a medium of regular contact with our supporters. Public meetings were held, and new members recruited to the Cause. However, the most important project was the writing of the *Proclamation of London* by Yockey. He had long had the idea that, to coincide with the centenary of the publication of the *Communist Manifesto* of 1848, we should issue a European manifesto setting out the situation for the "masses", and calling for action to liberate Europe from its occupation by the Extra-European forces of the USA and USSR. In spite of very limited funds being available, the *Proclamation of London* was printed, in Manchester, by two Anarchist brothers who were personal friends of mine, knew my own political position and respected it, and genuinely believed in the rights of others to publish their case for public consideration. The front cover of the *Proclamation* was printed in a bright red colour, with a panel in white carrying the title in black lettering — the Imperial colors, as used on the dust-jacket of *Imperium*. On the back cover was printed the Program of the European Liberation Front, a radical program to say the least, which Yockey, Chesham, and I had put together one afternoon. Over

33 Gannon memoir, op. cit.

> the Program flew the ELF flag, a red flag, with white center circle carrying the black sword symbol of Liberation. It was all quite impressive and, like *Imperium,* very well received by our comrades at home and abroad.
>
> It must be clearly understood that the founding of the European Liberation Front was an act of faith in the future and destiny of the European Imperium; this act was made without illusions as to the likely outcome in the measurable future. The foundation of mass movements with a prospect of popular success requires enormous financial backing over a long period of time, and we had no expectations of that kind. Of course, at times of supreme crisis in the affairs of nations different rules apply and finance is less important. In 1948, no such crisis existed, nor was one in prospect. Britain and the rest of Europe had sustained grievous damage resulting from the recent war; full employment was a fact for the masses, maximum production was required from industry for every kind of item, the populations were weary from the prolonged bloodletting and years of wartime destruction; their desire was only for peace and material improvement — to be left alone. We had envisaged these conditions and outlooks and knew that the chance of success for a new mass party was remote, as the experience of others — even without our radical position — confirmed on every side. Knowing this did not discourage us; it was our task to erect signposts, to produce situation-estimations showing what had happened to Europe, and *why* it had happened, and what was required to liberate Europe. Within our strictly limited resources we could not do more. Destiny would decide the outcome.
>
> In time, Yockey quarrelled with Guy Chesham on a matter of no great importance, and certainly not on a matter of ideology, and Guy withdrew from our number. This was a great loss in every way, and one for which Yockey was mainly to blame, as I told him at the time. However, I was not prepared to abandon Yockey over such an issue, and the magnitude of his contribution in terms of thinking and writing redeemed this regrettable, but petty incident.[34]

It is notable that Gannon remarks on the realistic perception of the world situation by Yockey and his leading associates, as Yockey has been regarded by others (e.g. Bardèche and Binet in France) as unrealistic in terms of what could be accomplished to 'liberate Europe'. On the other hand, as Gannon notes, despite his frenetic lifestyle, Yockey was not prone to depression or

34 Ibid.

bi-polarity. Perhaps stoicism with a lively sense of humour, tempered by a sharpened sense of honour and dignity, could describe Yockey. Yet there was also an underlying faith that History would redeem Europe, perhaps not for centuries hence, Gannon writing: 'Of the future he had no doubt. It would be the fulfilment of the Destiny of the Western High Culture — the Rebirth of Religion, the Resurgence of Authority, the Age of Caesarism and of Unlimited Imperialism.'[35]

Of course, Yockey knew that few people would read *Imperium*, Gannon adding that 'fewer read and FEEL it', but contented himself that the few who did would be sufficient to carry the message forward. 'FPY had a greater regard for INSTINCTIVE acceptance than for mere intellectual comprehension.' He and his colleagues 'all FELT Imperium'.[36]

Gannon stated also of the ELF that it was founded:

> ...to mark a symbolic turning point in the final period of the Western Imperium, providing the philosophical basis, milestone, and finger-posts for those who came after. We, FPY, Chesham and myself, were realists, and we realised that there was NO chance of a mass-movement succeeding in the prevailing political/economic situation of that time, or of the near or mid-term future. You must remember that the 'Fifties and 'Sixties were periods of full employment and constantly advancing social prosperity in England, and in the rest of Europe. In that situation it was absurd to believe that a movement such as ours could advance with mass support — unless, a huge supply of money could be pumped into the operation. This was as likely as rain in Northern Chile! There was also the unremitting war waged against all of our breed by the Culture Distorters and their hirelings, most of us being wiped out, financially, in the process. It was our aim to create an elite nucleus in each of the lands of the Western Imperium, to accept THE BOOK, and its situation-estimation as the basis for future action whenever possible, and to maintain contact in the interim. That is why FPY travelled endlessly within the IMPERIUM, and outside of it in search of gold to finance the future. None of this can be sneered at, in retrospect, as Marx was never the source of practical revolution in his own lifetime, whatever the wishful thinking embroiderers of history may claim. In fact, it can be claimed in utter

35 Ibid.

36 Gannon to Stimely, February 15, 1982.

> truth that the task facing us was of immensely greater difficulty than that facing Marxists in the nineteenth and twentieth centuries.[37]

Yockey was looking across centuries rather than a few years or even decades. The immediate aim was achievable; the creation of a nucleus imbued with a new doctrine. Gannon continues:

> We had the idea of founding an Order, secret of necessity, of the Elite of our Idea within the Imperium which would work to secure the adherence of highly-placed people in all Western lands, knowing that all revolutions are made from above and not below. This was, also, a task that FPY set himself on his weary, miserable journeys throughout the Imperium. How far he succeeded, I cannot say. That he deserved to do so, I can! My own position in the ELF in England was not, formally, created in other parts of the Imperium, but I feel sure that the basis was made by FPY in Italy, and possibly in Germany. FPY had no organisational position of command, nor did he seek such. He recognised that his work lay in writing The Book and in establishing its acceptance, in which he succeeded completely, with the Elite of the Imperium. Of course, he was sometimes depressed and frustrated, but he never despaired of the final outcome, nor do I. FPY and I never conversed in bravado style, nor did I ever find him a moaner or a subject of self-pity. Realism in our relationship forever prevented either rapturous exultation or abject misery at tomorrow's prospects. For us, tomorrow might be one hundred years hence, but it would CERTIAINLY BE! … FPY could always have deserted the Idea, concentrated on money-grubbing with great success — as I could also — but NEVER, ever considered such TREASON![38]

With funding from Baroness von Pflügl, 1,000 copies of *Imperium*'s first volume were printed and 200 of the second volume.[39] A 32-page distillation of the ideas of *Imperium* was published in 1949 as the *Proclamation of London of the European Liberation Front*, and a newsletter, *Frontfighter*, was established. Although *Frontfighter* named Peter Huxley-Blythe as the editor, the publication was under the direction of Anthony Gannon.[40]

---

37 Gannon to Stimely, ibid.

38 Gannon to Stimely, ibid.

39 S. Dorril, op. cit., p. 576.

40 Gannon to Stimely, July 13, 1980.

## Action Programme

Despite the elitist character of *Imperium*, the European Liberation Front was not a mere intellectual dilettantism. The impression has been left that the Front was nothing other than a publishing enterprise.[41] However, in the summer of 1950 the ELF started public meetings in the town squares of the North, North-West, North-East and North-Midlands of England. The first public meeting for 1951 was held at Preston Market Square, Lancashire, on Sunday, June 3. Speakers were L. F. Simmons, director of organisation; Frontleader, Anthony Gannon, and Thomas Davies, director of propaganda. Preston was regarded as having the greatest potential for the ELF, with audiences reported as being large and enthusiastic. The town was described as the potential 'Lower Saxony' for the ELF, a reference to the centre of strength for the Socialist Reich Party. There was even an aim of standing Front candidates in the Preston municipal elections.[42] Public meetings by the Front continued in 1952 on the market squares of the 'principal towns of the North and North Midlands'. These were 'highly successful'.[43] Gannon reports that the ELF had many public meetings in the North and Midlands of England, where 850 members were recruited.[44] How this squares with Gannon's statement that *Frontfighter's* maximum circulation was 500[45] is not known, although Gannon cannot be assumed in any way as having been dishonest in his reminiscences. Rivalry between the Front and Union Movement was bitter. Gannon states that the ELF frequently held outdoor meetings around the same venues as those of UM, especially those of Jeffrey Hamm, a very effective speaker. Gannon claims that the ELF often drew crowds away from Hamm, which must have been a considerable achievement. Gannon was a practised speaker from a young age, with his

41 Carto, 'Introduction', *Imperium*, Noontide Press, ed., op. cit., xiii, where Carto states that other than Yockey getting 'beaten up outside Hyde Park nothing much happened'.

42 Thomas Davies, Director of Propaganda, 'Are YOU doing enough?', *Frontfighter*, No. 13, June 1951, pp. 3–4.

43 Thomas Davies, 'Front Public Meetings', *Frontfighter*, No. 23, April 1952, p. 3. Thomas Davies, 'Front Public Meetings', *Frontfighter*, No. 7, November 1950, p. 3.

44 Gannon to Stimely, July 13, 1980.

45 Gannon to Stimely, November 24, 1981.

time in the pre-war BUF. What is certain is that Manchester was an area of focus for both the ELF and UM.

Gannon described one of the ELF meetings, with his particular dislike of Jeffrey Hamm:

> The venue, Market Place Derby, on a summer evening, one Sunday in the early Fifties … The Market Place is a large square, a traditional venue for political meetings, not requiring special Police permission for such. Huxley-Blythe opened up our meeting from our portable ELF rostrum at one end of the square, whereas the Hamm [sic] was dilating to some 20 people some 10 yards away from a UM soap-box. Hamm departed from his "theme" to attack Blythe, myself and the ELF Whereupon, I took over from Blythe, launched into the counter-attack, describing the Hamm as the "only unrationed ham in England" … and in a few minutes our crowd of some 40 people were joined by Hamm's 20, followed quickly by others passing by who were attracted by the "sound and fury"; the result was that Hamm was left addressing the "birds", and he then gave up and joined the crowd around the ELF rostrum … I held outdoor meetings for the ELF on market places all over the North West and West/East Midlands in the period of activity; we could not afford to pay for meeting halls …[46]

## Italian Alliance

One of the earliest outreaches by the ELF to Europe was in Italy. Already, in 1949 Yockey met with N Neri, a pseudonym for someone apparently well-connected in the Movimento Sociale Italiano (MSI), who was heading the European League. An 'Italo-English Convention' united the ELF and the League with the aim of moving the Front's headquarters to Rome. The statement reads:

> I
>
> From today, the European League assumes the name European Liberation Front. The direction of the European Liberation Front is assumed by the direction of the European League. The headquarters of the ELF is established in the city of Rome. U Varange and N Neri mutually pledge themselves to realise at once the integration of the two organisms.

46 Gannon to Stimely, April 20, 1982.

II

The ELF operates on the European plane, creating and co-ordinating mass-movements. Europe is understood to comprise the area from the Urals to the Atlantic, from the Mediterranean to the Arctic.

III

The ELF considers itself in all things the weapon of the Fascist struggle.

IV

The strategical objective is the integral realisation of Fascism in Europe and in the world. The tactical objective is the liberation of Europe from military, political, economic subjugation by extra-European forces, from Jewry, Masonry, Liberalism, Bolshevism, Capitalism, Parliamentarianism, and Individualism.

V

In view of the possibility of orienting world-opinion by means of a manifesto expressing the beliefs of the elite which fights against all manifestations of materialism, and which, simultaneously, answers modern problems, social, political and economic, individual and collective, therefore such a manifesto must be elaborated in collaboration with the elite of the Fascist movements, and must be discussed and approved by an international convention to be held in 1950.

VI

The present ITALO-ENGLISH CONVENTION, stipulated in Rome on 21 November, 1949, in the Italian language, in two copies, was signed by U Varange for the ELF, and by N Neri for the EL.

| for the | for the |
|---|---|
| European Liberation Front | European League |
| U Varange (signed) | N Neri (signed)[47] |

It seems from this statement that Yockey was willing for Neri to assume leadership of the ELF. What happened to these plans is not known, although Yockey

47 Varange, Neri, 'Italo-English Convention', Rome, 1949, Archives Canada, MG30-D91, finding no. 1293, Vol. 4, file no. 1.

was back in Italy in 1951 organising the foreign delegates to an international convention organised by a Fascist/Catholic aid society. With mention of co-ordinating 'mass movements' in a worldwide 'Fascist struggle', the objectives seem unrealistic. Yet in 1949 this was not the case. The MSI had been formed in 1946, mainly by veterans of the Italian Social Republic (Republic of Salò). Giorgio Almirante, a high Salò official in the department of propaganda, who endorsed *Imperium*, led the MSI for decades. During the 1948 elections the MSI gained six seats in the Chamber of Deputies.[48] In Germany the Socialist Reich Party, formed in October 1949, soon had a membership of 10,000 and gained 11% of the vote in Lower Saxony in 1951.[49]

## Peter J Huxley-Blythe

Huxley-Blythe edited the monthly newsletter *Frontfighter*, until issue 10, in March 1951, when he was recalled to naval duty as a member of the Royal Fleet Reserve. He had enlisted in the Royal Navy in 1939, serving throughout World War II in the Battle of the Atlantic, in the Mediterranean and in the Far East. He related in his remembrance of Yockey in 2005 that they had met in 1948 'at the second large meeting of the newly launched Union Movement'.

> The first time I met Yockey was when I was introduced to him by Anthony (Tony) Gannon from Manchester, England. Tony had a long history in British fascism. As a boy he had joined the BUF in 1935 and as he got older he became an important fascist speaker in the north of England. He had been arrested, like Mosley, in June 1940, and held without trial for six months. After the war he founded the Imperial Defence League, one of numerous Mosley-oriented organizations that eventually merged into Union Movement.[50]

Huxley-Blythe writes of Yockey's ideas being shaped by his experiences in the aftermath of World War II, of the Morgenthau Plan, the travesties and tortures undertaken to secure the execution of German war veterans, the actions

48 R Eatwell, *Fascism: A History* (London: Vintage Books, 1996), p. 198.

49 R Eatwell, ibid., p. 220.

50 Peter J Huxley-Blythe, 'Inside the Mind of Ulick Varange', *The Barnes Review*, May/June 2005, p. 20.

of 'Jewish brigades' in murdering Germans after the war, and of the terrorism undertaken by the Stern and Irgun gangs against the British in Palestine.[51]

Huxley-Blythe's own experiences were different. Having served in the war, he was motivated by the jingo-patriotism of 'my country, right or wrong', even though he was vocal in stating that Britain was fighting the wrong side. While serving at a shore base in Ceylon, he found a copy of Count Richard Nikolaus von Coudenhove-Kalergi's book *Pan-Europa*.[52] The Third Reich accurately regarded this Pan-Europe movement as being under Masonic influence and the cosmopolitan vision of Europe being propounded by Coudenhove-Kalergi was very different from the 'Fascist' vision. Coudenhove-Kalergi wrote in 1925 in his book *Practical Idealism*:

> The Mankind of the future will be a racial mongrel. Today's races and castes will fall before the increasing overcoming of space, time, and prejudice. The Eurasian Negroid race of the future, outwardly similar to the ancient Egyptians, will replace the multiplicity of Folks through a multiplicity of personalities.[53]

The movement was banned under the Third Reich and Coudenhove-Kalergi fled Europe. Nevertheless, Huxley-Blythe became 'an English-European and have remained so ever since'.[54] It was an odd source of inspiration for a 'European Fascist'. Coudenhove-Kalergi, of Austro-Hungarian and Japanese descent, was a Freemason, backed by Rothschilds and Warburgs.[55] He continues to be lauded as the father of the European Union.

---

51 Peter J Huxley-Blythe, ibid., pp. 20–22.

52 Richard Nikolaus von Coudenhove-Kalergi, *Pan-Europa* (Vienna: Paneuropa Verlag, 1923).

53 Cited in the National Socialist expose on Freemasonry: Dieter Schwarz, *Freemasonry: Ideology, Organisation, and Policy* (1938), chapter 3. Online: http://der-stuermer.org/freemasonryen.htm.

54 Peter J Huxley-Blythe, op. cit., p. 22.

55 Coudenhove-Kalergi wrote in *Pan Europe* that he received initial funding from Max Warburg after being recommended by Baron Louis Rothschild. He travelled to the USA with the assistance of Felix and Paul Warburg. See: K. R. Bolton, 'Introduction' to Hillarie Belloc, *Europe and the Faith* (London: Black House Publishing, 2012). For the Freemasonic involvement see Bolton, ibid., pp. 29–32.

Huxley-Blythe, on leaving the Navy in 1947, joined Union Movement and became a speaker around Britain. He became disillusioned with Mosley 'having discovered he was not the same man he had been before the war'. He thought that Mosley's 'fire had gone out' and if so, Mosley should not try to lead a European political movement. Another factor was Mosley's support for the continued domination and occupation of Europe by the Washington regime. He also saw Mosley as 'apologising for pre-war Fascism' instead of building upon it.[56] These were the same conclusions that had been made by Gannon and Chesham, although it is odd that Huxley-Blythe criticised Mosley as 'pro-American', given that he soon joined Natinform, which condemned Yockey and anyone else critical of the USA as a 'Red agent'.

Huxley-Blythe left UM in 1949 and tried to form the League of National Ex-Servicemen, intended to include veterans from all states. It seemed like a plausible aim. There were many BUF members who had served in the armed forces, and many especially Waffen SS veterans who were pan-European. He attempted to organise a congress in Ireland — a sensible choice given her wartime neutrality. Huxley-Blythe contacted Gannon, who had appraised him of the split from UM He met Yockey at Gannon's home in Manchester and joined the ELF.

Huxley-Blythe could not accept that the USSR had undergone a fundamental change and was no longer Kosher. He also believed that there would be a groundswell of American nationalism that would overthrow the Washington regime and would 'free the world from communism'.[57] Hence, he departed from Yockey and joined with vehemently anti-Yockey factions. While publishing his anti-Communist newsletter *World Survey*, he focused on counter-revolutionary activities among Russian émigrés, primarily with the 'Russian Revolutionary Forces'. This brought him into factional dispute

56 Peter J Huxley-Blythe, op. cit.

57 Peter J Huxley-Blythe, ibid., p. 24.

with George Knupffer.[58] Both regarded the other as a Stalinist *agent provocateur* among Russian émigrés.[59]

## Baroness Alice von Pflügl

Baroness Alice von Pflügl merits more attention than being vaguely remarked upon as the 'mysterious'[60] pro-Soviet financier of *Imperium*. The initial support she gave to Yockey in the publishing of *Imperium* and the creation of the European Liberation Front is significant. She was the daughter of Gustav Alexander, son of a cotton merchant, of English and German origins, who was living outside Manchester on a large property cared for by 20 gardeners. Her mother was Helene Ziane, a Belgian. Gustav and Helene were married in Belgium and moved to England. Alice was one of three children.[61]

After graduating from the prestigious Slade School of Fine Art, London, she left for Munich circa 1931. Like Unity Mitford, she was a rebellious spirit, and 'quite a challenge to her family'. Fluent in French and German, she mixed well with all nationalities, was a socialite and keen sportswoman, being particularly adept at skiing.[62]

---

58 Knupffer, head of the Russian Supreme Monarchist Council, whatever his failings according to Huxley-Blythe, had an exceptional understanding of the character of the banking system, and the need for banking reform. He deserves credit at least for his excellent book *The Struggle for World Power* (London: Plain-Speaker Publishing Co., 1971) where he includes a 'Party of the Right' political programme based on banking reform (pp. 210–211). Knupffer's political programme is reprinted in Bolton, *The Banking Swindle* (London: Black House Publishing 2013), pp. 153–154. Huxley-Blythe is remembered in political circles primarily as the author of *The East Came West* ([1964] Caldwell, Idaho: The Caxton Printers, 1968), detailing the forced repatriation by the USA and Britain of anti-Soviet Russian and Cossack refugees back to the USSR. Online: http://www.scribd.com/doc/112880781/East-Came-West-The-Peter-J-Huxley-Blythe#scribd.

59 Peter J Huxley-Blythe, *World Survey*, Lancashire, Vol. 3, No., 1, 'A fuhrer without a following', May/June 1958. The issue is devoted to the feud between Knupffer and Huxley-Blythe, reflecting the feuds among Russian émigrés. Arcand collection, Archives Canada. This was the final issue of *World Survey*, which was then incorporated into Roger Pearson's journal *The Northlander*.

60 Dorril, *Black Shirt*, op. cit., p. 574.

61 Johnny and Suzanne von Pflügl to Bolton, June 7, 2014.

62 Ibid.

Alice had been drawn to Munich as the centre of the National Socialist movement. It was here that she met a young Austrian, Leopold von Pflügl. Leopold, an engineer from Linz, was the son of Egon von Pflügl, diplomat and Under Secretary of State for Austro-Hungary until the outbreak of World War I. Leopold served in the Afrika Corps. A brother, Wolfgang, was confined to a Soviet concentration camp for 12 years.[63] Leopold and Alice were married in Vienna in 1932. Circa 1938, Alice's father, Gustav, went to Austria to persuade her to return to England, as he believed war was imminent. With her first son, Peter, she agreed to return, although during the war she had hoped to work as a nurse at the Russian Front.

In Britain, the family suffered from wartime hysteria and Peter was harassed at school to the extent that this outgoing boy became introverted.[64] Second son Johnny was born in March, 1940; the same year she was detained under Regulation 18B. One day, Peter came home to an empty house and was told that his mother had been interned. The two brothers lived with an aunt and uncle who farmed Churchill's estate at Chequers.[65] Alice was confined to Holloway Prison, where Lady Diana Mosley was interned, although they never met. She was soon moved to the Isle of Man, where she was confined until the end of the war, and was told that if the Germans invaded she would be shot. Johnny von Pflügl recalls: 'In the camp she was very self-sufficient and it probably made her stronger.' He states that his mother was 'very much against the last war, and was definitely Right-wing and at all times said what she thought!'[66]

After the war, she and her sons moved to Park Square West, near Regents Park, London. 'It was a huge house' and 'her ex-gaoler at the Isle of Man became her housekeeper', a Danish woman who stayed with them for years.[67] This would seem to attest to Alice's character as a really *noble* woman. Gannon also refers to a manservant, who was a '"Vichy" Frenchman'.[68]

---

63 Ibid.

64 Suzanne von Pflügl to Bolton, June 21, 2014.

65 Ibid.

66 Johnny and Suzanne von Pflügl to Bolton, June 7, 2014.

67 Ibid.

68 Gannon to Stimely, November 24, 1981.

Johnny recalls of Yockey that he was 'much admired' by his mother. However, after a falling out with Yockey, she moved to France, where she took a studio at St Paul de Vence, while her aunt, the artist Juliette Cambier, kept a studio at the next village, and served as an inspiration for Alice's creativity. In 1957 she moved to Florence, then to Rome the following year, where she was 'very involved in the Italian cultural scene'.[69] She established a close friendship with Caresse Crosby, the patron of the arts and literati,[70] when living in Italy, offering to assist Crosby in her work amidst the 'frightful chaos' of the era.[71]

The Baroness remained committed to a united Europe. She also remained a devout Catholic, attended Mass every week, and had tried to resist the divorce from Leopold in 1949. She was a 'tough' character, 'talented, creative and outspoken'. 'I guess life made her that and she actually did not care what people thought of her, or so she said! She was very kind and generous, loyal, very sensitive too, underneath, and a very caring mother. She died of cancer in the UK in 1971'.[72]

## Guy Chesham

Gannon claims that von Pflügl started Ostropa Press to spread the message that revival would come from the East.[73] If this is correct, nothing seems to have remained of Ostropa Press and the Baroness seems to have committed herself mainly to artistic pursuits. However, it seems that Guy Chesham mooted the pro-Soviet plan for a European underground against the USA at a meeting held without Yockey at Chesham's London residence in July 1950. Chesham had broken with Yockey because of the latter's opinion that Chesham allowed himself to be pressured by his wife, towards whom Yockey

69 Johnny and Suzanne von Pflügl, June 7, 2014.

70 Crosby, with her second husband, Harry Crosby, established Black Sun Press, and published Hemingway, Archibald McLeish, Anais Nin, Henry Miller, James Joyce, Ezra Pound, D. H. Lawrence, et al. Alice became a frequent guest at Crosby's artist colony at the castle Rocca Sinibalda. Caresse Crosby Papers 1912–1970, Southern Illinois University Special Collections Research Center, Box 63, Folder 7.

71 Alice von Pflügl to Caresse Crosby, January 31, 1969.

72 Johnny and Suzanne von Pflügl, op. cit., June 7, 2014.

73 Gannon to Keith Stimely, July 13, 1980.

was not well disposed. British Nationalist stalwart John Bean was to recall that Chesham 'was always at pains to point out to me that it was essential to look after our economic affairs and the unemployed were no use to the movement whatsoever'.[74] To someone like Yockey, who did not put any personal considerations before the Idea, such an attitude would have been seen as self-interested rather than practical.

Despite Gannon's lifelong admiration, he regarded Yockey as being at fault for the break with Chesham, who had been a mainstay of the Front. However, the personal break with Yockey did not dampen Chesham's enthusiasm for Yockey's ideas. In 1953, he was involved in organising the National Front Movement. The NFM was founded by ex-Navy Commander Andrew Fountaine, a Norfolk landowner. He had fought an impressive campaign for the Conservative Party in the Labour stronghold of Chorley, Lancashire, in 1950 but was expelled from the party for his nationalist views. Fountaine spent the rest of his life as a mainstay of British nationalism in organisations such as the National Labour Party and the later National Front, founded in 1967. Although the NFM had a policy of 'all out support for empire development', it was also against any commitment with the USA. Chesham edited the Movement's journal, *Outrider*. Despite the British imperial focus of the Movement, *Outrider* included quotes from Yockey and passages from *Imperium*.[75]

## The Proclamation of London

*The Proclamation of London of the European Liberation Front* was published in 1949 as a distillation of the essential points of *Imperium*. As Michael O'Meara writes in his introduction to a recent edition, *The Proclamation* 'distilled *Imperium's* 619-page argument into a 32-page pamphlet'.[76]

Gannon stated that with Westropa Press being registered as a business in his name, *The Proclamation*, like *Imperium*, was printed in Manchester

74 John Bean, *Many Shades of Black* (London: New Millennium, 1999), p. 95.

75 J. Bean, op. cit., p. 94.

76 Michael O'Meara, Introduction, Yockey, *The Proclamation of London of the European Liberation Front* (Shamley Green, UK: The Palingenesis Project, Wermod & Wermod, 2012), xiii.

by 'personal friends' of Gannon's 'in the face of enormous difficulties'.[77] The Westropa edition of *The Proclamation* ran to 10,000 copies. The intention had been to publish this in 1948 as the answer to the manifesto of the Culture-distorter a century after *The Communist Manifesto*. This was not achieved until the following year but was backdated for symbolic purposes.[78]

That *The Proclamation* was intended as Western Civilization's answer to Marx's *Communist Manifesto*, like *Imperium* vis-à-vis Marx's *Das Kapital*, is apparent from the opening line: 'Throughout all Europe there is stirring today a great superpersonal Idea, the Idea of the Imperium of Europe, the permanent and perfect union of the peoples and nations of Europe'.[79] Marx and Engels had opened their sterile economic screed with: 'A spectre is haunting Europe — the spectre of Communism.'[80] Where Marx heralded Europe's convulsion by economic wars based on class conflict, Yockey posited a united Europe, transcending classes and subordinating economics. Yockey wrote: 'What is the imperative of Marx: get rich at the expense of the rich. Marx understood greed, therefore he made the whole world and its history into a sticky mass of greed. To Marx, the world is a huge money-bag; to Freud it is a dung-heap; to Darwin a zoo.'[81]

While Marx saw the clash of classes as the means of Western civilization's downfall, what Spengler had foreseen is a revolt against The West expressed as a 'coloured-world revolution' and class war, both behind the banner of communism. Spengler stated that in such a crisis there would be a reaction

---

77 Gannon to Lewis Brandon (a.k.a. David McCaldon, Director of Noontide Press), April 2, 1980. Gannon had given an original edition of *The Proclamation* to Noontide Press to prompt its republication. (Gannon is unlikely to have known that it had been kept in print by American Nazi Party founder-member Rev James K Warner via his Sons of Liberty Books. This was a long-running 'Christian Identity' enterprise that published a large quantity of archival material from the 'Right', with a focus on anti-Semitic materials). McCaldon was in fact, at least after his falling out with Willis Carto and departure from the IHR, dismissive of Yockey, referring to *Imperium* as a handy door-stop.

78 Gannon to Stimely, July 13, 1980.

79 Yockey, *The Proclamation*, Wermod ed., ibid., p. 3.

80 Karl Marx and Frederick Engels, *The Communist Manifesto* (Moscow: Progress Publishers, 1975), p. 40.

81 Yockey, 'XXth Century Metaphysics', unpublished notes, n.d. Unpublished MS.

against democracy, liberalism and economic supremacy, and new Caesars would emerge to militaristically meet the challenge. He saw fascism as a sign of this resurgence. However, the challenge had been faced by Europe and was crushed by what Yockey identified as 'outer' and 'inner' enemies.[82] The Imperium had been aborted; quantity swamped quality. This Idea, the union of Europe, 'embodies in itself the entire content of the future, for unless this Idea is fulfilled, there will be no European future'.[83] Against this idea of the future stood the old forces — which had combined in the world war — 'the old powers of reaction, finance-capitalism, class-war, and Bolshevism'.[84]

*The Proclamation* 'is addressed to the entire Western civilization: to the colonies planted all over the world, and to the heart and soul of the West, the Mother-soil and Father-culture of Europe'.[85] It is of interest here that Yockey departs from Spengler in a significant detail. Spengler held that when Germans, Englishmen, Dutch, Spanish, et al departed from their homelands to far-flung colonies they did so not as part of a nationality but as individuals settling in new land where they form into new nationalities or 'races'. Hence, those who had left Poland, Germany, England, Italy, Ireland, etc. to live in the USA have become a new people, 'Americans'. Spengler wrote:

> A race does not migrate. Men migrate, and their successive generations are born on ever-changing landscapes, but the landscape exercises a secret force upon the plant-nature in them, and eventually the race-expression is completely transformed by the extinction of the old and the appearance of a new one. Englishmen and Germans did not migrate to America, but human begins migrated thither as Englishmen and Germans, and their descendants are there as Americans...[86]

Yet Yockey insisted that these former colonies of the defunct European empires were still 'cultural colonies' of Western civilization. He referred to the 'true Americans' and even the Russians, whom he often related to the outer barbarian, as having 'wide and deep strata which inwardly belong to the

82 Yockey, *The Proclamation*, Wermod ed., op. cit., p. 3.

83 Ibid., p. 3.

84 Ibid., p. 4.

85 Ibid., p. 4.

86 Spengler, *The Decline*, op. cit., Vol. II, p. 119.

Western civilization and who look to the sacred soil of Europe as to their origin, their inspiration and their spiritual home. To these also, this proclamation is addressed'.[87]

The first section of *The Proclamation* addresses the question as to whether Western civilization can even be an organic unity, considering the fratricidal wars that had devastated Europe, not least of which were the two World Wars. Here, Yockey points to the common ethos of Western culture that had transcended the differences for a millennium:

> From its very birth-cry in the Crusades, the Western culture had one state, with the emperor at its head, one Church and religion, Gothic Christianity, with an authoritarian Pope, one race, one nation, and one people, which felt itself, and was recognised by all outer forces, to be distinct and unitary. There was a universal style, Gothic, which inspired and informed all art from the crafts to the cathedrals. There was one ethical code for the Culture-bearing stratum, Western chivalry, founded on a purely Western feeling of honour. There was a universal language, Latin, and a universal law, Roman law. Even in the very adoption of older, non-Western things, the West was unitary. It made such things into an expression of its proper soul, and it universalized them. More important than anything else, this culture felt itself to be a power-unit against all outer forces, whether barbarians like the Slavs, Turks and Mongols, or civilized like the Moors, Jews and Saracens. Embryonic national differences existed even then within the West, but these differences were not felt as contrasts, and could not possibly become at that time the focus of a power struggle. ... The outer forces recognised as well this inner unity of the West. To Islam, all Westerners whatever were lumped together as Franks, *giaours*.[88, 89]

A *People* is formed by its self-perception, the way it perceives others, and the way it is perceived by others. This 'we-feeling' is heightened if it comes into conflict with outsiders. Germanic tribes had, prior to the West's high culture, united against Roman invasion. European nationalities had united in the Crusades and other wars against what Yockey called the 'outer enemy'. Conflicts between Pope and Emperor, and between nations, were

---

87 Yockey, *The Proclamation*, op. cit., p. 4.

88 Giaour, offensive word used by Turks to describe non-Muslims, especially Christians.

89 Yockey, *The Proclamation*, ibid., pp. 9–10.

subordinated to the conflict with the 'outer enemy'. An attack on Europe was met with a united response from the nations. The 'first political expression of Europe was in the Crusades'.[90]

The Renaissance, Reformation and Counter-Reformation began the process of organic disintegration of Western civilization, as religious contentions became political. Petty statism arose and from here large-scale wars between Western states. However, the process of disunity even then was limited by the acknowledgement that defeating an enemy was not the same as annihilating him. These wars were conflicts for power between dynasties, distinct in character from the total wars against the outer enemies — one example being the devastation wrought during the Hussite Wars of the fifteenth century, where the Czech followers of heretic John Hus rampaged over Germany for 16 years. Yockey calls it the forerunner of Bolshevism, 'the spirit of negation and destruction' of everything Western.[91]

'The Age of Materialism' arose as the 'inner aspects' of Western Culture receded before the 'outer', culminating in the cultural crisis of the French Revolution of 1789.[92] These 'inner' and 'outer' possibilities of a High Culture are the differences between what Spengler called the *Culture* epochs and those of a *Civilization*. A High Culture is dominated by aesthetics; a civilization by technics. The first by 'blood' (family dynasties), the second by 'money' (plutocrats), the first by faith, the second by materialism. The architecture becomes utilitarian. Wars are fought for trade. Great art and music are no longer created. The men of destiny within the Late Civilization epoch — such as Napoleon, Hitler, and Mussolini — must work within that context. Spengler contended that the aesthetic possibilities have already been exhausted and the new possibilities are restricted to power politics and technics.[93] The man of destiny in a Late Civilization is faced with the task of 'breaking the dictature of money'.[94] This is the great task that remains for a civilization. It is therefore far from 'pessimism'. The Hitlerites that bewail this as 'pessimism' might just

90 Yockey, *The Proclamation*, ibid., p. 11.

91 Yockey, *The Proclamation*, ibid., pp. 13–14.

92 Yockey, *The Proclamation*, ibid., p. 14.

93 Spengler, *The Decline of The West*, op. cit., Vol. II, 'The Machine', pp. 499–507.

94 Spengler, *The Decline of The West*, ibid., pp. 506–507.

as well say that Hitler's 'Thousand-Year Reich' was pessimistic because it was to be of a limited duration. Even the *Holy Bible* alludes to the reign of Christ lasting a thousand years, after which Satan is unleashed from the Pit again.[95] Yet we are assured that this is not 'pessimism' but the playing out of a great and hopeful divine plan.

Yockey states of the French Revolution that it fundamentally transformed the thinking of the West:

> This total revolution marked the victory of democracy over aristocracy, parliamentarianism over the State, mass over quality, Reason over Faith, equality ideals over organic hierarchy, of Money over Blood, of liberalism, pluralism, free capitalism, and criticism over the organic forces of Tradition, State, and Authority, and in one word, of Civilization over Culture. Rationalism and materialism were the common denominators of all the new ideas which rose in revolt against the old order of faith, State, economy, society, war and politics. Metaphysics was to be a matter of weighing and measuring; government was to be a matter of counting noses; economy was to be entirely reduced to money-trading; the structure of society was to be a reflux of money; international relations of war and politics were to be the apotheosis of national egoism, with utter disregard of the great, inclusive, Cultural unity, of which the nations are mere separate manifestations.[96]

Yockey held out hope, not pessimism, stating that even amid the ruins of Europe after the war and the lynching of its leadership stratum, a 'Gothic youth' that retained its pride and its unity was extant. He stated that Europe was at a 'second great turning point of the maturity of Culture'.[97] There is nothing 'eternal' about parliamentarianism, democracy and finance-capital.[98]

Now we are reminded on a daily basis, that 'parliamentary-democracy' justified by the 'global war on terrorism', is the ultimate in political perfection. This 'optimism' is the same as that of the Darwinists who assured all — from merchant to workhouse denizen — that nineteenth century Industrial Briton was the highest form of human evolution and everyone can look forward to

---

95 *Revelation* 20: 7-10.

96 Yockey, *The Proclamation*, op. cit., pp. 14–15.

97 Ibid., p. 15.

98 Ibid., p. 16.

perpetual sunshine in the never-ending march of 'progress'. We continue to be assured that the hope of humanity lies in every New Guinea and Amazon bush native being accorded the benefits of parliament and free trade. No effort should be spared, even if war is required, in bringing the joys of consumerism and parliament to every corner of the world.

The democratic revolts of the mid-nineteenth century could not ultimately be suppressed because they were working within the *Zeitgeist* of the epoch and brought the merchant class to power with Jews on their coattails. The new *Zeitgeist*, Yockey contended, returns Authority and Faith. Those who resist this new *Zeitgeist* are agents of the past, just as those who resisted the liberal-democratic-bourgeois revolts of the nineteenth century were attempting to maintain the past *Zeitgeist*. This past includes both the liberal-capitalist-communist epoch but also the attempts by the 'Right' to return petty-statism. 'Petty-statism' Yockey condemned as 'suicidal'. The *Zeitgeist* of the epoch is 'the Idea of the monolithic Culture-State-Nation-Race-People of Europe and the prelude to the greatest task of all: the expression of the absolute Western will to unlimited political Imperialism'.[99]

In Section II of *The Proclamation*, entitled 'The Chaos of the Present', Yockey charges liberalism, democracy, communism and materialism, all deriving from the same *Zeitgeist*, and therefore having the same character, with injuring the body and thwarting the destiny of Europe. 'Class-War', brought to the Western Cultural organism through Jacobinism, Freemasonry and Republicanism, 'fought all signs of rank'. This was made possible by weaknesses in the ruling strata, first in France.[100] Indeed, if one reads the works on the French Revolution by historians such as Nesta Webster, it is evident that the levelling ideals of 'liberty, equality, fraternity' that emanated from the Masonic lodges of the Grand Orient de France had infected the ruling circles, which were charmed by the depraved and diseased lawyers and charlatans who spread the revolutionary doctrines. The Duc d'Orleans — Grand Master of the Grand Orient — lavished his money to fund the revolution to buy the dregs of Mersailles.[101]

---

99 Ibid.

100 Ibid., Part II: 1, p. 22.

101 Nesta H Webster, *The French Revolution* (1919, 1969), and subsequent editions.

The liberal-democratic revolutions throughout Europe during the mid-nineteenth century brought the triumph of commerce. The democratic ideal of counting heads is analogous to the capitalist ideal of counting money. Marxism, so far from transcending this, systemises both into a single ideology. Both are based on weighing in the balance, regardless of quality. Yockey pointed out that the liberal revolutionaries had only replaced aristocrats with plutocrats. Now there arose class-war between economic groups in a grab for goods. Yockey explained that while bourgeois and proletariat fought against each other for scraps, the finance-capitalist maintained his dominance as the 'unseen and unknown master'. The productive forces of capital and labour were pitted against each other while the parasitic forces of finance-capital stand in the background, manipulating markets and ultimately determining the prices, profits and conditions of work, for which entrepreneurs are blamed.[102] As Spengler had pointed out in *Prussianism and Socialism*, *The Hour of Decision* and *The Decline of The West*, the worker's associations and labour-socialism, arising in reaction to cut-throat capitalism, placed the 'labour movement' on the side of the finance-capitalists against the industrialists. Yockey reiterates this. Like Spengler, Yockey states that the trade union and the strike weapon were entirely capitalistic. The class war merely reduced the labour class to attempting to supplant the entrepreneurial class. In nineteenth-century socialism, there was nothing that transcends capitalism. With the strike, instead of manipulating the supply of goods or the supply or money, the labour-leader sought to manipulate the supply of labour. 'The labour-leader now becomes the third member of the snarling capitalist trinity.'[103]

Into this situation, the Jew appeared. His rise within the Western cultural organism was enabled by the victory of materialism as the new *Zeitgeist*. People were now regarded not by their birth and faith but by how they acted as traders and workers. Their differences in outlook meant that under liberalism and commerce, Jews became an integral element of commercial society, whereas previously they had been regarded as alien in every sense.[104] They came as members of a Culture that had already exhausted its possibilities in

102 Yockey, *The Proclamation*, op. cit., p. 23.

103 Ibid., p. 24.

104 Ibid., Part II: 2, 'The Emergence of the Jew', p. 24.

centuries past, 'already completed and rigidified' by the time that the West's Gothic high culture began.[105] Yockey was not alone in this observation. Arnold Toynbee, although a liberal and a universalist, similarly described the Jews as 'fossils' of the Syriac civilization[106] (what Spengler called the 'Magian'). This is not unique to the Jews and Toynbee states that the Parsees, for example, also a 'fossil remnant' of the Syriac civilization, have played an analogous role in Hindu society.[107]

The barriers were broken down by the use of Freemasonry and the Illuminati,[108] spreading revolutionary doctrines from which both liberal-capitalism and Marxism proceeded. Bernard Lazare, a nineteenth century apologist for Jewry, mentions that there were Jews around Adam Weishaupt, the founder of the Illuminati, and that the 'Jew of Portuguese origin', Martinez de Pasquales, 'established numerous groups of Illuminati in France'.[109] The mystical lodges of Martinez de Pasquales and the rationalist and atheist lodges of the Grand Orient de France worked in tandem, states Lazare. If Jews became prominent in the secret societies, it was not because they were the founders but because 'the doctrines of these secret societies agreed so well with their own'.[110] Of the epochal liberal revolutions that swept Europe in 1848, 'the Jews were the most active, the most zealous of missionaries'.[111] Their contribution to 'present-day socialism' 'still is very great', while they are also 'found among the representatives of contemporary industrial and financial capitalism… Rothschild is the antithesis of Marx and Lasalle; the struggle for money finds its counterpart in the struggle against money, and the world-wide outlook

105 Ibid., p. 26.

106 Arnold Toynbee, *Study of History*, abridged ed. (London: Oxford University Press, 1954), p. 22.

107 Ibid., p. 135.

108 Yockey, *The Proclamation*, op. cit., p. 28.

109 Bernard Lazare, *Antisemitism: Its History and Causes* ([1894] London: Britons Publishing Co., 1967), p. 152.

110 Ibid., p. 154.

111 Ibid., p. 155.

of the stock-speculator finds its answer in the international proletarian and revolutionary movement'.[112]

Liberalism provided the battering ram for the Jews to enter public life in Western civilization. Thanks to the revolts against the traditional order, the Jewish speculator and money-changer became dominant over Europe. The Jews, by their own option, however, remained 'a closed organism inside an open one'. Later in the nineteenth century, Jews were able to enter the USA without the burden of that Tradition which they sought to destroy in Europe, because a cultural colony cannot have the same 'spiritual profundity and continuity of the Mother-soil of the Culture'. This culminated in 1933 with the assumption to the presidency of Franklin D Roosevelt.[113]

The German Idealists, at first joining the liberal revolts of the mid-nineteenth century, soon recognised their Jacobin character as alien to the German spirit. The German ghettos were opened by the liberal revolts, as they had been by the French Revolution, and an alien spirit was let loose over Europe. Richard Wagner, who had joined the liberal revolt in Dresden, became among the most vociferous and influential of the German Idealists to reject the Jacobin influence in the German revolution, writing:

> I have no hesitation about styling the subsequent revolutions in Germany entirely un-German. "Democracy" in Germany is purely a translated thing. It exists merely in the "Press" and what this German Press is, one must find out for oneself. But untowardly enough, this translated Franco-Judaico-German Democracy could really borrow a handle, a pretext and deceptive cloak, from the misprised and maltreated spirit of the German Folk. To secure a following among the people, "Democracy" aped a German mien; and "*Deutschthum*", "German spirit", "German honesty", "German freedom", "German morals", became catchwords disgusting no one more than him who had true German

112 Ibid.

113 Yockey, *The Proclamation*, op. cit., p. 30.
Roosevelt's chief legal aide and speechwriter, Samuel Rosenman, played a primary role in the establishment of the 'war crimes trials'. Rosenman was the first White House Legal Counsel. Other key Roosevelt advisers included Supreme Court Justice Felix Frankfurter, noted for both his Bolshevik and his Zionist sympathies; Supreme Court Justice Louis Brandeis and Roosevelt's chief economic adviser James Warburg, of the international banking dynasty.

> culture, who had to stand in sorrow and watch the singular comedy of agitators from a non-German people pleading for him without letting their client so much as get a word in edgewise. The astounding unsuccessfulness of the so loud-mouthed movement of 1848 is easily explained by the curious circumstance that the genuine German found himself; and found his name, so suddenly represented by a race of men quite alien to him.[114]

The German revolution underwent a profound change in rejecting Jacobin origins and Jewish input. German Idealism seeded the foundation of the new *Zeitgeist*, against the English mercantilism of the old epoch. Among its spokesmen were Herder, Goethe, Fichte, and later Wagner and Nietzsche. They spoke not just to Germany but to the entire West.

## Culture Pathology

In *The Proclamation*, Yockey succinctly explained the meaning of Culture Pathology, which manifests as Culture-parasitism, Culture-distortion, Culture-retardation.

The presence of a 'Culture-alien' causes 'culture-disease' that occurs when groups 'which do not share the same Culture' are in contact. When one group does not belong to the Culture, as with the Blacks in South Africa and in Brazil, the result within the dominant culture is 'simply Culture-parasitism. The disease condition displaces Culture-members and has a slowly sterilising effect on the Culture-body'.[115]

A more pathological condition arises when the Culture-alien is able to intervene in the 'public and spiritual life of the host, for then he must of his own inner necessity distort the life of the host, warping its proper tendencies to make them serviceable to his alien needs'. 'This is Culture-distortion and in Western civilization this is the role of the Jewish Culture-State-Nation-Race-People.'[116]

'The domestic elements', those born into the host culture and acquiring influence, wish to retain the 'outmoded ideas and methods of the Past'. That is, they want to continue the *Zeitgeist* of a prior epoch and to oppose the 'creative

114 Richard Wagner, 'What is German', 1876.

115 Yockey, *The Proclamation*, op. cit., pp. 30–31.

116 Ibid., p. 31.

spirit' and destiny, or what Yockey called the 'mission' of a culture. These are the 'forces of Culture-retardation'. They are the political and business leaders who place themselves at the disposal of the Culture-distorter, the 'rejects of higher history that offer themselves to the forces of negation and destruction'. In attempting to resist the forces of destiny, they will ally with forces that would bring about their destruction.[117]

The victory of rationalism, materialism, atheism, Jacobinism, democracy and liberalism resulted in communism as 'their most intransigent product'.[118]

Communism represented the most forceful weapon for 'Social Degeneration'. The Jews, who championed communism and class-war among the Gentile states, the result of which was disintegration, advocated the closest unity among their own people. We might here consider the role played by Moses Hess in formulating both communism and Zionism, before Marx and Herzl respectively. Moses Hess advocated Communist world revolution among the Gentiles while seeking to rally Jews to their racial cause. Professor Shlomo Avineri of Hebrew University, Jerusalem, alludes to this dual policy, stating that a Jew remains a Jew regardless of his religion, because Judaism is a matter of nationality. 'It is for this reason that Hess argued that modern rationalism — and secularism — may pose a danger to Christianity but not to Judaism. If Judaism would have been a religion, it would be doomed to disintegrate under the impact of the Enlightenment, just like Christianity. But because Judaism is also a national culture, and not a mere religion of personal salvation, it has, paradoxically, a future which Christianity does not possess.' Hence, Moses Hess as a communist and a Jew could state that religions will disappear but the Jews will remain.[119] It is such a self-assurance that has permitted Jews to retain their Jewishness while being the most rabid advocates of world socialist revolution and many other forms of Culture-distortion. However, Christianity did until the Reformation represent something other than personal salvation insofar as it was synonymous with Western civilization and to be a Christian meant to be a part of the Western cultural organ-

117 Ibid., pp. 31–32.

118 Ibid., p. 32.

119 Shlomo Avineri, *Moses Hess: Prophet of Communism and Zionism* (New York: New York University Press, 1985), p. 181.

ism. Professor Revilo P Oliver, despite being an atheist, tried to impress this on American Christians before turning his back on them in frustration.[120] It was the debasement of Church doctrines that has made Christianity into another secular, cosmopolitan creed aligned with all things anti-Western to the point of embracing its own destruction.

'The degradation of the social life did not merely happen, it was planned, deliberately fostered and spread…' The prominence gained by the Culture-distorter in mass entertainment, news media and education has provided the means for 'social degeneration'. From Hollywood, the Culture-distorter 'spews out an endless series of perverted films to debase and degenerate the youth of Europe, as he has so largely succeeded in doing with the youth of America'. The literature the Culture-distorter purveys has the same 'message of destruction of healthy individual instincts, of normal familial and sexual life, of disintegration of the social organism into a heap of wandering, colliding, grains of human sand'. The message of Hollywood 'is the total significance of the isolated individual, stateless and rootless, outside of society and family, whose life is simply, the pursuit of money and erotic pleasure'.[121] 'Divorce replaced marriage, abortion replaced birth, the home requires a purely commercial *raison d'être*, the family becomes the battleground of individual strife for personal advantage.' Feminism is a significant product of this process.[122] 'From the standpoint of race' the outcome is the 'dying out of racial instincts', replaced by 'money-madness and erotomania'. This was formulated a century previously by Marx as a plan aimed at the destruction of nationalism, family and marriage,[123] the foundations of Western civilization. 'America is their programme in process of actualization.'[124]

Marx had indeed written clearly in *The Communist Manifesto* that all the foundations of Western civilization were merely products of bourgeois

---

120 Revilo P Oliver, *Christianity and the Survival of the West* (Cape Canaveral: Howard Allen Enterprises, 1973).

121 Yockey, *The Proclamation*, ibid., II: 3, 'Social Degeneration', p. 33.

122 Yockey, *The Proclamation*, ibid., II: 3, 'Social Degeneration', p. 34.

123 Yockey, *The Proclamation*, ibid., p. 35.

124 Ibid.

economics and would be replaced by a rootless proletariat, the socialisation of children and the elimination of family.[125]

Today it seems superfluous to even document the manner by which Western civilization has succumbed to this Culture-distortion of Hollywood and the breakdown of marriage and family. Culture-distortion is even flagrantly appraised by US strategists such as Colonel Ralph Peters[126] as the means by which America extends and maintains control over the world with a permanent *kulturkampf.*

It is significant, in so far as Yockey is charged with 'pessimism', that he *did not* regard this Culture-pathology as inevitable:

> But let there be no mistake: there is nothing inevitable about this Culture-disease. As long as the Culture-organism retains its traditions, its racial instincts, its will-to-power, and its natural exclusiveness and resistance to everything culturally alien, this result cannot be.[127]

Yockey gives as examples of resistance to this Culture-pathology the 1944 revolt in Quebec among conscripts, who took up arms and refused to be sent to fight in Europe; the Boer resistance; and the mass movement of 'isolationists' who opposed the USA's entry into World War II. Yockey, himself involved in this 'America First' opposition to US involvement in the war, points to this as an example of the healthy bond that continues to exist among large numbers of Americans to the Western 'Mother-Organism'. The so-called 'isolationism' is a desire to isolate from the 'foul treason against Europe which was hatched and directed in Washington'. Hence, the mission of the European Liberation Front exists in the USA as well, and in all the 'colonies' of Western civilization. The struggle for liberation embraces Western civilization as an organic unity and not merely an aggregate of separate nation states.[128]

---

125 Marx and Engels, *The Communist Manifesto*, op. cit., 'Proletarians and Communists', inter alia.

126 Ralph Peters, 'Constant Conflict', *Parameters*, US Army War College, Summer, 1997, pp. 4–14; http://ssi.armywarcollege.edu/pubs/parameters/Articles/97summer/peters.htm.

127 Yockey, *The Proclamation*, op. cit., p. 36.

128 Ibid., p. 37.

The result has been the 'destruction of the political unity of Europe' with wars of annihilation in the service of export markets and the Culture-distorter, where until the nineteenth century wars had been of a limited dynastic character within Europe. Nations based on dynasties had been replaced by nations based on money since the French Revolution. Until 1914 the 'Concert of Europe' had maintained a feeling of *Europe* as an identifiable concept. Increasingly, jingoism shattered Europe into conflicting nationalities based mainly on linguistics and economics.[129] The nations forming during the nineteenth century were the results of the 1789 and 1848 liberal-democratic revolutions — paradoxically from the perspective of the 'Right' that most zealously upholds this 'nationalist' legacy today. It is strange to see French Nationalists invoke the Jacobin 'Marseillaise' and the Tricolour flag, and uphold the Republican ideals of the Grand Orient; also to see American Nationalists regard as sacred texts the Liberal-Masonic-Deist US Constitution and Bill of Rights. We should recall however, that the German Idealists, Herder, Hegel, Fichte, Richard Wagner, et al, responded to this Jacobin-liberal-democratic civic-nationalism with a *volk* nationalism that placed Germany as the custodian of the new *Zeitgeist* for the twentieth century and beyond. Even National Socialism did not completely escape the *Zeitgeist* of the past, with its uneasy attempt to accommodate Darwinism and chauvinism. Spengler had announced the new *Zeitgeist* to Germany and The West after World War I but the new *Zeitgeist* was only partially accepted by the Hilterites. Yockey announced the new *Zeitgeist* again after the catastrophe of World War II.

Yockey cited the chivalric treatment that was still being accorded to the defeated in the late nineteenth century, such as that given to the French Emperor by Bismarck after the Franco-Prussian War. The Western unity that could still be summoned vis-à-vis the *outsider* was manifested in 1900 during the Boxer Rebellion, during which European states together with America joined forces under a German Field-Marshal.[130] It was what Yockey calls 'vertical nationalism' that led to the final break-up of the traditional order of Europe with World War I. However, the cataclysm of the World War

129 Ibid., p. 43.

130 Ibid., p. 44.

heralded the beginning of a new epoch in Western civilization[131] and the death of the materialism of the past several centuries. Whereas English materialism and technics had represented the *Zeitgeist* of the prior century, it was in Germany that the manifestations of the new *Zeitgeist* arose in sharpest form: ethical socialism and the creative force of the state as distinct from free-trade economics. In Germany and Fascist Italy, society was again looked upon as an organic entity and not as fractured against itself. This was what Yockey called the 'provisional form of the restoration of Europe to health, and the new ethos was gradually embraced by other countries in Europe, besides Italy and Germany.[132] The Waffen SS represented united Europe in embryo and Operation Barbarossa a Crusade of the West not seen since the Crusades to Jerusalem. The World War which was unleashed against Western civilization was one of annihilation, a total war such as can only be fought between two completely irreconcilable foes. Europe, left to itself, would have united and proceeded towards its destiny. The mass mobilisation of two outer forces, the USA and the USSR, intervened. Europe was shattered into parliamentary entities and 'European humanity' was treated 'as an entry in a ledger' of the USA. The occupation by the outer enemies of the USSR and USA were abetted by the 'inner traitors'.

Another result of this disintegration of Europe was the emasculation of its 'World-Empire', of the rule over most of the world by the European powers. The coloured world had seen Europeans fight themselves to destruction in two world wars. The USA had already intervened. In particular, one of the primary Culture-distorters, Jacob Schiff of Kuhn, Loeb & Co., Wall Street, assured Russia's defeat by Japan in 1905, by advancing loans to Japan, for which he was honoured by the Emperor.[133] Not only had Russia been weakened by the war but the coloured world had seen that a 'white' state could be defeated. Moreover, Schiff funded the revolutionary movement. American journalist George Kennan, by his own account, had been provided with funds from Schiff

131 Ibid., pp. 44–45.

132 Ibid., p. 46.

133 Cyrus Adler, 'Jacob Henry Schiff: A Biographical Sketch', American Jewish Year Book, pp. 26–29, American Jewish Congress, http://ajcarchives.org/AJC_DATA/Files/1921_1922_3_SpecialArticles.pdf.

to propagandise 52,000 Russian POWs in Japan, and turn them into revolutionary cadres.[134] Russia had been 'lost' to the West through Bolshevism, and was, as Spengler had predicted in *The Hour of Decision*, leading a 'coloured world revolution' while on the other hand promoting internal social disintegration in the 'white world' through its use of class-war — which was also noted by Yockey.[135]

Yockey observed that Russia had been a Western state until the overthrow of its Western-oriented ruling strata by the Asiatic elements in tandem with Jewish money and Jewish intellect, but that the Western elements had yet to be re-awakened.[136]

World War II was the answer of the Culture-retarder and the Culture-distorter to a resurgent Europe. Italy's invasion of Abyssinia was the first manifestation of the West's resurgence and destiny towards Empire. The Civil War in Spain was the prelude for the World War against Western resurgence. Only 'outer forces' could have brought about such a war, as Europeans had no enthusiasm for undertaking a war of destruction against their own culture and Mother-soil.[137] One might recall here the lacklustre opposition put up by Europeans to their incorporation into the Reich sphere of influence, despite the conflated legends about the 'resistance'. The numbers of volunteers to the Waffen SS foreign legions from all of Europe are indicative. Even in the 'Protectorate of Bohemia', the Czechs could not be prevailed upon to resist German occupation, and Reinhard Heydrich was assassinated by commandos from Britain to try and undermine the goodwill that existed between Czechs and Germans.[138] The difference between the constructive peace with

134 Robert Cowley, 'A Year in Hell', in Oliver Jensen (ed.) *America and Russia: A Century and a Half of Diplomatic Encounters* (New York: Simon and Schuster, 1962), pp. 92–121. Kennan at a meeting of the Friends of Russian Freedom in New York, celebrating the February revolution, credited Schiff as funding the revolutionary movement, according to a report in *The New York Times*, March 24, 1917, pp. 1–2.

135 Ibid., p. 51.

136 Ibid., II: C, 'The Destruction of Europe's World Empire', op. cit., p. 53.

137 Ibid., pp. 54–55.

138 An extraordinarily objective writer on the Waffen SS states of this: 'It is worth also mentioning here, however, in the Balkan context, that Heydrich was assassinated in Prague *not* because of repressive measures against the Czech population, but because he began

Japan and the total destruction sought against Germany after the war is noted by Yockey as indicating a different outlook vis-à-vis the two states.[139] What was the crucial difference? Both Japan and Germany had rebelled against the international financial and trade system. The difference would seem to be that Germany dealt with Jews not only in finance and politics but also in their role as Cultural arbiters. Yockey had seen the results while working at Wiesbaden. The occupiers 'sought to engraft on the Culture of Europe, the device of the scaffold'. The chivalric traditions of Europe were shredded and were replaced by the Mosaic code of the Old Testament.[140]

The third and final section of *The Proclamation* expresses 'The Mission of the Liberation Front'. The identities of both the 'inner' and the 'outer' enemies of Europe have been established and their plans and methods exposed. These 'outer enemies', centred in New York, Moscow and Tel Aviv, are 'the arbiters of Europe'. Europe was even then being redefined as a reservoir of manpower for the US military because the wartime alliance with Moscow had become unstuck; as a 'loan-market for the European financier' and a 'beggar colony watching for crumbs from the table of rich America', 'Europe as a museum' for visiting colonials, as a 'moribund collection of petty states', as 'an economic mad-house' of trade and class-wars, as 'a backward population waiting for reeducation by the American world-clown and the sadistic Jew', as a 'Black Mass of scaffolds'.[141] The 'sacred soil of the Western Culture' is now occupied by Mongols, Negroes, Jews and Senegalese. 'This is democratic Europe, liberal Europe'.[142]

Europe is now inundated with alien migrants and their descendants who are regarded as equal to 'Europeans' — legally — as Germans, Danes, French, Swedes, English, Italians or Spaniards. The USA was subsequently obliged to force a measure of 'European unity' on their own terms in the face of the refusal of the USSR to play along with the USA's attempt to build a United

restoring — albeit in a limited fashion — civil liberties which the British government saw as a threat to the budding resistance movement.' Bruce Quarrie, *Hitler's Samurai: The Waffen-SS in Action* (Wellingborough: Patrick Stephens, 1084), p. 30.

139 Yockey, *The Proclamation*, op. cit., p. 56.

140 Ibid., p. 57.

141 Yockey, *The Proclamation*, ibid., III: 'The Mission of the Liberation Front', pp. 61–62.

142 Ibid., p. 62.

Nations world state — a breach in the wartime alliance that Yockey noted in later essays. The 'European Union' is however an abortion of the European Idea. It is merely a consolidation of Europe's petty states, meant to better serve the 'inner traitors' and 'outer enemies' while allowing the USA to pose as the 'leader of the Western world'. But its only leadership can be as the pied piper of Western oblivion.

Yockey's message however is optimistic, despite being saddled with charges of Spenglerian 'pessimism'. 'These conditions are only external, material. The soul of Europe cannot be occupied, ruled, or dominated by Culture-aliens.' Only materialists would think otherwise. Power is a reflection of 'inner qualities' and the outer enemies do not have such qualities. They lack a superpersonal soul, a sense of world-mission and destiny.[143]

For Yockey, the victor will ultimately be he who represents an 'Inner Imperative', an Imperative which must arise as an organic process and not as part of an artificial construct. Men are impelled by History. They are in the service of a Mission, in accord with the Spirit of the Age. The inner enemy serves the past *Zeitgeist*. The European Liberation Front, the vanguard of those serving this Mission and Imperative of the Age, had two 'great tasks':

1. The complete expulsion of everything alien from the soul and from the soil of Europe, the cleansing of the European soul of the dross of nineteenth century materialism and rationalism with its money-worship, liberal-democracy, social degeneration, parliamentarianism, class-war, feminism, vertical nationalism, finance-capitalism, petty statism, chauvinism, the Bolshevism of Moscow and Washington, the ethical syphilis of Hollywood, and the spiritual leprosy of New York;
2. The construction of the Imperium of Europe and the actualizing of the divinely-emanated European will to unlimited political Imperialism.[144]

---

143 Ibid.

144 Ibid., p. 63.

Replacing 'Culture-disease' will be 'the pristine ethical values of Europe: Authority, Faith, Discipline, Duty, Order, Hierarchy, Fertility, Will-to-Power'.[145]

*The Proclamation* 'is thus a Declaration of War'. The Liberation Front represents Europe's Destiny. The ELF was carrying forward History and hence could not be defeated by mere material forces. The 'Jewish-American forces' would be thrown out and the Asiatic armies of Moscow thrown back into the remoteness of Asia. In this battle all Europeans would unite:

> Race now means, in Europe, the duality of having honour and pride;
> People means the we-feeling of all Europeans;
> Nation now means the organism of Europe Itself.[146]

Yockey states something of the way this new Europe would be organised when he refers to English, German, French, Italian and Spanish being 'mere place-names and linguistic variations' while such local cultures would nonetheless possess 'a perfect autonomy in the European Imperium'.[147] With the passing of the old 'vertical nationalism', that is to say the walls that had separated the nations of Europe into squabbling states, one would expect a multiplicity of local cultures to be reasserted, such as the Flemish, Catalans, Tyroleans, et al. Hence, when Evolian traditionalists and present-day American Nationalists, who often now advocate 'ethno-states' for all races of the world, are suspicious of a Yockeyan centralised Europe, they are mistaken. A united Europe along Yockeyan lines would replace the artificial states based on nineteenth century liberal-democratic ideas (states such as Belgium, where the Flemish are subjugated) with ethnic autonomy within the Western Imperium.

Yockey alludes to a theme that became increasingly pronounced in his thinking: that Europe would not be conned into fighting a war between the USA and the USSR ostensibly to save Europe from Bolshevism.[148] Indeed, he regarded Soviet occupation of half of Europe as a material occupation and therefore a surface phenomenon of limited harm. In contrast, 'the ethical

145 Ibid., pp. 63–64.

146 Ibid., p. 64.

147 Ibid.

148 Ibid., p. 65.

syphilis of Hollywood and the spiritual leprosy of New York' rots the soul of the Western cultural organism and is the real danger to Western Civilization.

Yockey evoked the vision of the Gothic epoch in appealing to the liberation, unity and empire of Europe as a vision not of 'human will,' but as 'a direct emanation of God.' He often refers to such ideas as 'old' but 'eternally young'. Again, the message is one of optimism. Yockey appeals to the same spirit as that of the Crusader knights, to which every European belongs so long as he is not a traitor. When the liberation is achieved is historically irrelevant, but it is assured, as Europe's will is unbroken, 'our resolution stronger than ever'. What awaits is 'a millennium of European history, of joy and sacrifice, of heroism and nobility...' when the European banner is unfurled 'from Galway to Memelland and from North Cape to Gibraltar'.[149]

## Elsa Dewette (Darciel)

What is not generally acknowledged is that with *The Proclamation,* Yockey had a co-author — the famous paragon of Flemish modern and folkish dance, Elsa Dewette, whose professional name was Darciel. In December 1980, Gannon met Elsa Dewette for the first time. 'She claims to have collaborated with Y in the writing of *Proclamation*, and that he was in her company for the total period of its creation.' Gannon stated that Dewette was 'not a poseur' so he could not understand why she had made the claim, as he was convinced Yockey had not collaborated with anyone else in any writing other than the 12-point ELF programme.[150]

Yockey and Dewette met in Belgium in 1949. While it has been remarked that Yockey had 'a woman in every port', with Dewette there was a meeting of souls. Although the two were soon parted, Dewette held Yockey's memory dear until the end of her long life in 1998. Just prior to his death in 1960, Yockey, who knew that he would not survive his capture one way or another, wrote a farewell to Dewette.[151] Although she had not heard from Yockey since 1954, three weeks before his death she received a long letter from him, from

149 Ibid., pp. 68–69.

150 Gannon to Stimely, March 1, 1981.

151 Ibid.

San Francisco, saying goodbye. She had not realised that it was a premonition of death[152] and she only learned of his demise by chance, after a friend had seen a reference to Yockey's fate in the German edition of *Imperium* in a bookshop in June 1980.[153]

Flanders was an obvious choice for those seeking support for the European Liberation Front. While the young, charismatic Rexist leader Leon Degrelle and his division of Francophone Walloons served in the Waffen SS with epic heroism on the Eastern Front, the Dutch-speaking Flemish were also notably supportive of the Germans. Prior to the war, Flanders had its Fascist and folk-nationalist movements, such as the Flemish National Union (VNV), Union of Netherlandish National Solidarity, German-Flemish Working Community and the Flemish Nationalist Workers Party. Some sought an independent Flanders, while others sought union with the Netherlands or with the German Reich. During the Occupation, all parties merged with the VNV, resulting in a membership of 100,000.

Militarily, the Waffen SS Legion *Flandern* had over a thousand men serving on the Eastern Front, a thousand with the SS Division *Wiking* and another thousand with the Volunteer Regiment *Nordwest*.[154] Both the Flemish and their folk cousins, the Dutch, contributed more volunteers to the Waffen SS, proportionately, than any other Western European people. Like the Walloons under Degrelle, they were among the most battle hardened of the Waffen SS.[155]

Flemish culture was encouraged under German occupation and Elsa Dewette played a notable role in that Flemish renewal. Born in Ghent in 1903, she was the granddaughter of Edward Blaes, conductor and composer, and remembered the family discussing Nietzsche, Wagner and Heine when she was a child. During World War I, the family had moved to London, where she studied the arts and chemistry. However, after seeing a performance by Isadora Ducan, it was dance that Else dedicated herself to. In 1930, she established the Elsa Darciel School of Eurythmy, d'Arcielle being the name of

---

152 Ibid.

153 Ibid.

154 Richard Landwehr, 'The European Volunteer Movement in World War II', *The Journal for Historical Review*, Vol. 2, No. 1, Spring 1981.

155 Jonathan Trigg, *Hitler's Flemish Legions* (Gloucestershire: The History Press, 2007).

a great aunt. Elsa became internationally recognised as the creator of a new form of dance, *eurythmy*.

The Flemish cultural festival of 1942, organised by the National Cultural Association, around the theme 'Dutch Art in the Middle Ages', featured the ballet of Elsa Darciel.[156] During this era, she formulated her doctrine on Flemish dance along folkish lines.

Elsa's father, an admirer of Hitler, was accused of 'collaboration' during the German occupation. He had been on cordial terms with a high-ranking German officer and this would have been sufficient to condemn him. Elsa was interrogated by the police and departed to the USA to avoid further persecution. Returning to Belgium, where her dancing career nonetheless flourished, she met Yockey in 1949 while staying at the house of a Flemish painter. Elsa's father had asked her to go to the house to translate for Yockey and the painter. Yockey, penniless as he often was, accompanied Elsa to her home and the two discussed *Imperium*. They travelled to Bavaria and he proposed to her, undaunted by still being married. Although the relationship was brief, they remained devoted to the memories for the rest of their lives.[157]

How plausible is it that Elsa Dewette co-authored *The Proclamation*? Gannon states it is not plausible because Yockey did not co-author works other than the 12-point ELF programme with Guy Chesham. However, in this Gannon is mistaken. We know that Yockey co-authored letters and articles with H Keith Thompson and Frederick Weiss. 'The World in Flames', Yockey's final essay, was written jointly with Thompson. Gannon states that he did not know why Dewette would falsely claim to have co-authored *The Proclamation*. He also states that she would have had the intellectual acumen.[158] In 1941, during the German occupation, she had written an important essay on Flemish dance. She referred to the era as one of 'Sturm and Drang' and of 're-evaluation of all values', citing Nietzsche. In this, the Flemish must play their part, determining also the role they will play 'in the next order'. The

---

156 Herman van de Vijver, *België in de Tweede Wereldoorlog*, Part 8: "The cultural life during the occupation" (Kapellen: DNB/Uitgeverij Peckmans, 1990), p. 22.

157 Dr Piet Tommissen, 'Elsa Darciel en Francis Parker Yockey: De Vlaamse danslegende', *Mededelingen 137*, April 30, 2009.

158 Gannon to Stimely, op. cit.

Flemish, despite centuries of 'serfdom' under foreign rule, will emerge with their 'soul', their 'mystical gifts and juices bubbling life' to have something valuable to offer the next order. Her concept of dance 'eurythmy' makes this an expression of the *psychophysiologische*, 'partly with the personal nature, partly with the characteristics of nation and race'. Dewette claimed that the dominance of materialism and rationalism had made the arts, and perhaps dance most of all, lack inward meaning, whereas art is the 'interpretation of the spiritual' and the artist a conduit of the divine.[159]

It is evident that Dewette was committed to a European new order and, deploring the dominance of rationalism and materialism over spiritual, racial and national values, would readily identify with Yockey's ideas and be willing and able to assist him with *The Proclamation*. It could well have been a token of Yockey's appreciation for Dewette that he suggested such a collaboration. As her 1941 treatise shows, she already had the same worldview as Yockey.

## Political Programme of the ELF

After *The Proclamation of London*, a further distillation was made in a 12-point programme. This was drafted by Yockey, Guy Chesham and Anthony Gannon. They took as their model the 24-point programme of the NSDAP.[160]

The Liberation Front fights for nothing less than the following:—

1. Liberation of Britain and of Europe from the regime of the inner-Traitor and the outer-Enemy.
2. Integration of liberated Britain into one sovereign European People-Nation-State.
3. Immediate expulsion of all Jews and other parasitic aliens from the Soil of Europe.
4. Establishment of the Organic State.

159 Elsa Darciel, 'Naar Een Vlaamsche Danskunst' (Brussels: *The Phalanx*, February 1941), pp. 5–32.

160 Gannon to Stimely, op. cit.

5. Cleansing of the Soul of Europe from the ethical syphilis of Hollywood and the Marxist Bolshevism of Moscow.
6. Recognition of the fundamental significance of the Family and Motherhood, and the real protection of the spiritual and material welfare of both.
7. Recognition of the Youth as the Vanguard of To-morrow, and thus its systematic training, without exception, including the provision of educational facilities to each youth according to his ability, regardless of his social and economic status.
8. Affirmation of the Duty to Work and the abolition of all unearned income.
9. Immediate ending of the suicidal Export-War and the smashing of the Tyranny of interest.
10. Abolition of Poverty.
11. Intensive development of the soil of the Homeland and the Colonies overseas, along with the rationalisation of Industry, to secure the existence of the People and raise its standard of life.
12. Since the LIBERATION FRONT is the only force within Britain which is an integral part of the EUROPEAN LIBERATION FRONT therefore, the LIBERATION FRONT is opposed to all other parties within Britain.

YOUR PLACE IS IN THE FRONT!

MARCH WITH US![161]

The programme is of added interest for its allusion to the practical measures entailed by 'Ethical Socialism'. Point Four, 'the Organic State', is the logical expression of the nation as a social organism. Another name for the 'organic state' is the 'Corporate State'. Like many common political terms, 'corporatism' is frequently inadequately defined, often referring to connections between large business corporations and government. The corporatist — organic — state is

161 The programme was included at the back of the original edition of *The Proclamation*.

based on the living organism. An organism is composed of organs, each with its own function but contributing to the functioning of the whole. Hence, a corporatist state is one that brings into a unitary accord all elements of the nation. The most commonly known form of corporatist organisation was the Medieval Guild. In ancient Rome, these Guilds were known as corporations, hence the derivation of the word Corporatism, from the Latin root *corpus* (plural: *corpora*), meaning 'body'. In post-feudal or 'modern' times, the Classical and Medieval corporation was revived in the corporate states of Fascist Italy, the 'New State' of Salazar's Portugal, Vargas's Brazil, Dollfuss's Austria, and many others.[162]

National Socialist Germany developed an Organic State through the Labour Front, which included all sectors of production, and the Reich Food Estate in the agricultural realm. The Marxist will tiresomely retort that this was a means of enslaving labour to those business interests that he imagines controlled the Reich. What the organic state really achieved was to root out class-war as a social pathology. Karl Marx, foreseeing that this would negate the historical dialectic of class struggle, raged with special vehemence against nineteenth century efforts to revive the Guilds, which he condemned as 'reactionism'.[163]

Harlow J Henneman, Professor of Political Science at the University of Michigan, described the National Socialist organic state as he understood it:

> The basic unit in the new German industrial order is the *Betriebsgemeinschaft*, the "works-community", which is to be thought of as a cell in a larger organism, the *Volksgemeinschaft*. Each *Betriebsgemeinschaft* is not complete if one part of the cell is missing. According to National-Socialist theory, the works-community is a place of employment which includes the owner or employer, or someone acting as his representative, and workers, united in the performance of productive functions under the guidance of the state.[164]

---

162 K. R. Bolton, 'Corporatism as a Perennial Method of Traditional Social Organisation', *Aristokratia* (Manticore Press, 2014), Vol. II, pp. 40–61.

163 Marx, *The Communist Manifesto*, op. cit., p. 46.

164 Harlow J Henneman, 'Labor Relations in National-Socialist Germany', *Michigan Alumnus Quarterly Review*, December 10, 1938.

For the *corporati* of Classical Rome and the Guilds of Medieval Europe, economics was *not* the primary motive. Fascism and National Socialism attempted to resurrect that ethos in modern labour and social relations. That these efforts have been obscured by Leftist propaganda claiming that the organic state aimed at enslaving the working-class is another example of how the Left (whose own doctrine is a singular failure in whatever form) plays the lackey to its supposed capitalist enemy.

Both in the pagan Classical world and the Christian Western Medieval world, craftsmen and artisans regarded their calling as emanating from Divinity. One modern economist who nicely captures the spirit of the Medieval era, writing of Nuremberg, states that Medieval man saw himself not as an isolated unit but as 'part of a larger organism'.[165] Bliss writes that to the Nuremberger (or Medieval man), 'competition is the death of trade, the subverter of freedom, above all, the destroyer of quality'.[166]

The French Revolution eliminated the vestiges of the traditional organic state with the Chapelier Law of 1791, when the Guilds or *corporations*, as they were called in France, were suppressed. Henceforth, Western man became an atomised production and consumption unit, which the socialism of the 'Left' does nothing to transcend.

As Marx noted with outrage, there were efforts, especially in German reactions against the Liberal doctrines of the French Revolution, to restore an organic social order. Adam Müller (1779–1829), the most important of the Romanticist political theorists, upheld Medieval Germany as an ideal based on spiritual rather than commercial principles, which unified the 'members of the body politic'.[167] Müller regarded the family as the microcosm of the organic state.[168] The influential philosopher George W. F. Hegel was also a

165 W. D. P. Bliss, *New Encyclopaedia of Social Reform* (New York: Funk and Wagnalls, 1908), p. 545; cited in Bolton's 'Introduction' to Hillarie Belloc's *Europe and the Faith* (London: Black House Publishing, 2012), p. 10.

166 Bliss, ibid., p. 545.

167 Donald A Swan, 'The Ideological Background to the German Corporate Tradition', *Journal of Social, Political and Economic Studies*, Washington, Vol. 32, No. 2, Summer 2013, p. 156.

168 Müller, Adam, *Die Elemente der Staatskunst*, 1808–1809, Vol. I, Part 2., (Vienna: Wila), p. 33; cited by Swan, ibid., p. 156.

corporatist theorist, holding that the Estates mediated between government and people through the corporations.[169] Karl Marlo (1810–1865) was one of the earliest proponents of a vocational — 'social' — parliament and was spokesman for the handicraft workers' movement (1848–1849), advocating a return of the Guilds,[170] in an example of what Marx attacked as 'reactionism'. The Catholic Social Movement, led by Wilhelm Emmanuel Baron von Ketteler (1811–1877), Bishop of Mainz, arose during the 1870s as an alternative to Marxism, advocating corporations as the basic units of labour organisation.[171] Franz Hitz (1851–1921), an adherent of Bishop Ketteler, advocated a corporative Chamber of Estates to supplement parliament.[172] Adolf Stoecker, a 'monarchical socialist', Lutheran minister and leader of the Christian-Social Workers' Party, advocated a familial bond within enterprises — ideas which would influence the corporatism of the Third Reich.[173]

The Catholic Church was a significant proponent of the organic state, particularly when faced with Capitalism and Socialism, which the Church regarded as equally materialistic and atheistic. The Catholic social doctrine that was reiterated from the late nineteenth century was the heir to Classical Rome. As Thomas Aquinas expressed it: 'As the part and the whole are in a certain sense identical, so that which belongs to the whole in a sense belongs to the part.'[174] The Church sought to address the tumults of both the French Revolution and the Industrial Revolution. Several Papal Encyclicals were important for developing political alternatives to both liberal-capitalism and socialism, particularly Leo XIII's *Rerum Novarum: Rights and Duties Capital and Labour*, 1891; and Pius XI's *Social Order: Quadragesimo Anno*, 1931. These inspired numerous Catholic-oriented 'Fascist' movements across the world following World War I. Father Charles Coughlin's Social Justice movement, where Yockey began his activism, was one of these.

---

169 Swan, op. cit., pp. 158–159.

170 Ibid., p. 161.

171 Ibid., pp. 166–167.

172 Ibid., pp. 168–169.

173 Ibid., p. 172.

174 Aquinas, Thomas, *Summa theologiae*, IIa–IIae, q. lxi, are. l, ad 2m.

Other points in the Front's programme — the welfare of motherhood and family, the training of youth regardless of class, 'affirmation of the Duty to Work and the abolition of all unearned income', abolition of debt-finance, an *autarchic*[175] European bloc repudiating export-driven economics and the 'abolition of poverty' — are all aspects of the Organic State.

This organic polity had been explained in *Imperium* as a political law. 'The Organic Laws of Sovereignty and Totality' refer to all 'political units', Yockey had written. 'Totality' refers to both *issues* and *persons* within the organism. Any issue is subject to political considerations and every person is part of the organism. If the political unit is not true to these organic laws, then it is 'faced with sickness and death'.[176] This pathology includes anything that divides the group, such as class-war or a ruling stratum that does not serve the organism. Therefore, if the organism is to remain healthy, authority must be maintained over all aspects of its life. Yockey points out however that this need not imply state interference in every aspect of life, as it does in communism; it means simply that every component of the organism will perform its duty for the totality.[177] Hence the 'Total State', before any mention of which the liberal-democrats and capitalists stand outraged but trembling. This is the meaning of Spengler and Yockey's 'socialism'. Yockey proceeds in this vein to explain the pathology of the 'pluralistic state' and of democracy with its money values that buy group interests and form factions and conflicting classes.[178]

---

175 *Autarchy* or economic self-sufficiency, as distinct from reliance on the global struggle for export markets, which was a major Allied war aim in both world wars (as per the Fourteen Points and the Atlantic Charter), was a factor of the German Economic School of F List, as distinct from English Free Trade Economics. After the war Mosley, Yockey and others argued that a united Europe would have a sufficiently large internal market to enable *autarchy*. The Common Market, EEC and present European Union instead embarked on the US-imposed policy of what is today called globalisation, as a precondition for Marshall Aid after World War II.

176 Yockey, *Imperium*, Wermod ed., op. cit., 'The Laws of Totality and Sovereignty', p. 197.

177 Ibid., p. 198.

178 Ibid., pp. 203–219.

## *Frontfighter*

*Frontfighter* was the monthly newsletter on ELF activities and ideology. Although Peter J Huxley-Blythe was listed as the first editor until his recall to naval duties in 1951, Gannon states that he was primarily responsible for it. Starting with issue number 11, L. F. Simmons, a motor mechanic, was listed as editor.[179] The ELF took their date from the practice of Fascist Italy, starting from the assumption to power in the year of the Fascist March on Rome in 1922. Hence 1951, for example, was XXIX E.F. ('Era Fascista'). *Frontfighter* was by-lined 'Voice of the European Liberation Front in Great Britain', and was published by Westropa Press, London. Circulation of *Frontfighter* reached 500, including, and perhaps mostly going to, supporters outside Britain. It ran through late 1949 to August 1954. *Frontfighter* was printed on a rotary duplicator, 'worked to death' by Len Simmons and his wife or by Gannon and his wife, at one or other of their homes.[180]

Although Huxley-Blythe, rather oddly, had been attracted to the idea of European unity by reading the internationalist Freemason Count Coudenhove-Kalergi, he was not fooled by the European Common Market. So far from being the prelude to Imperium, Huxley-Blythe wrote of the new European zealots, who had instigated the war to crush a European union, that they were 'agents of the Jewish-White House-Wall St clique'. These were the 'Inner Traitors' that were climbing on board 'the band wagon of the New Age'. However, the Spirit of the Age demands the eradication, not the elevation, of 'the International Jewish Money Power' and the creation of the 'ORGANIC STATE', without which European union is an illusion. Europe was looking for a standard that would 'recapture the greatness of the Fascist Revolutions of 1922 and 1933', that would achieve Imperium over the ruins of the 'Jewish War of Hate'. Imperium 'is the logical conclusion of the NEW ORDER envisaged and worked for by Hitler and Mussolini'. It was fitting that the ELF had adopted as its symbol 'the SWORD of LIBERATION' and had taken upon itself the 'invincible mantle' of the 'HEROES'.[181]

---

179 *Frontfighter*. No. 11, April 1951.

180 Gannon to Stimely, November 24, 1981.

181 P. J. Huxley-Blythe, 'The Strasbourg Farce', *Frontfighter*, No. 7, November 1950, p. 1.

Gannon pointed to the success of the Movimento Sociale Italiano as the rebirth of the spirit of Mussolini, despite efforts by the Italian state, at the behest of Washington, to have the party banned.[182] There remained a bitterness towards the Mosley movement. On the other hand, despite antagonism with veteran fascist Arnold Leese, Gannon expressed solidarity when Leese was being prosecuted for libel against the chief of police; Gannon was sure that he would 'conduct himself like a man and like a Fascist'. Messages of support for the ELF were received from Raymond K Rudman, South African National Socialist, and O. E. Kellerman of the Universal Civic Union, also in South Africa.[183] There was a particular camaraderie between the ELF and the Union Cívica Nacionalista headed by Emilio Gutierrez Herrero, who had been harassed and exiled by the Peronist Government, prompting a critique of Peronism by Gannon.[184] It had been assumed by many that Perón was following a course close to Fascism but Gannon was sceptical, alluding to comments in the Jewish press about the existence of pro-Peronist Jewish associations.[185]

Gannon returned to his grievance with Mosley, taking up three of the four pages in the March 1951 issue of *Frontfighter* with ridicule of Mosley's move to Ireland, which had left the UM primarily to A Raven Thomson. Gannon saw this as a retreat, regardless of how UM justified it, and as reflecting the failure of Mosley as a post-war leader.[186]

On the sixth anniversary of the 'foul murder' of Mussolini, Gannon wrote of him as the 'European Hero and Martyr'. Fascism as an idea had reached over the whole Earth and would be the dominant creed of the twentieth century. The wartime defeat was a 'temporary setback'. Whatever is 'organic', whatever reflects the Spirit of the Age, although it might be attacked by parasites,

182 A Gannon, 'The Spirit of Mussolini', ibid., pp. 2–3.

183 'Our Differences with Arnold Leese', and 'The Mosley Group', ibid., p. 4.

184 A Gannon, 'Argentine Enigma?', *Frontfighter*, No. 11, April 1951, p. 2.

185 Ibid. It should be pointed out, however, that the Jewish Peronista association, OIA was established in direct conflict with the mainstream Jewish DAIA. Perón was fully aware of the Jewish, Zionist, Communist, Masonic and capitalist offensive against him. See: K. R. Bolton, *Perón and Peronism* (London: Black House Publishing, 2014), pp. 289–298.

186 A Gannon, '"Fuhrer" in Search of a Following', *Frontfighter*, No. 10, February/March 1951, pp. 2–4.

distorted, stunted and retarded, will reassert its life-course and there will yet be 'the full flowering of the European Imperium'. This Imperium would be 'hierarchical, monolithic, heroic, Fascist' and 'nourished by the blood and sacrifices' of the 'countless legionnaires of Europe' under the 'Sword-banner' of the ELF.[187] With this sense of historic mission, and of representing the new *Zeitgeist*, the ELF could be confident of victory, even if that victory must come a century hence.

187 A Gannon, 'Mussolini the Immortal!', *Frontfighter*, No. 11, April 1951, p. 1.

# Reaction

Chesham had written to Mosley that *Imperium* had already been accepted among advanced political thinkers,[1] and indeed *Imperium* did appeal to advanced thinkers. Through Gannon, Yockey had visited two military strategists and historians: Major Gen J. F. C. Fuller, recognised as father of modern tank warfare, who had been Mosley's military adviser in the British Union of Fascists; and Captain Basil Liddell Hart, official British military historian of World War I, who had been involved in the pro-Mosley milieu before the war.[2] Both gave *Imperium* enthusiastic endorsements. Fuller called *Imperium* the most prophetic book since Spengler's *Decline of The West*. Liddell Hart referred to it as 'a work of genius'. Gannon states that Yockey met Fuller and Hart in person and 'emerged well from such meetings'.[3]

*Imperium* was endorsed by German air ace Hans-Ulrich Rudel; by Giorgio Almirante, veteran of Mussolini's Salò Republic and leader of the post-war Italian Social Movement (MSI); and by Princess Maria Pignatelli Cerchiara, wartime Fascist heroine and founder of a post-war Fascist aid society. Maurice Bardèche, the French Fascist intellectual, translated *Imperium*. Accolades came from Mosley's colleague, Oswald Pirow, who had served as South Africa's Minister of Defence, Justice and Commerce. Major General Otto Remer and world war air ace Heinz Knöke, both leaders of the Socialist Reichspartei, also endorsed *Imperium*. Emilio Gutierrez Herrera, the Secretary-General of the Argentine movement Union Cívica Nacionalista, who had been offered

1 Chesham to Mosley.

2 Stephen Dorril, op. cit., p. 310.

3 Anthony Gannon to Keith Stimely, September 7, 1908, Stimely Archives, op. cit.

a position in the Perón regime but declined it, endorsed *Imperium*.[4] When Herrera ran into trouble with the Argentine authorities, he was lauded by Gannon as sharing a 'common ideology' with the European Liberation Front.[5] Adrian Arcand, the popular pre-war Quebec fascist leader, met Yockey in 1951 and promoted him among the Francophone intelligentsia as the pre-eminent philosopher of the 'Right' who had given 'the next two hundred years the new political gospel'. Arcand a decade later wrote to Yockey's American colleague H Keith Thompson that he knew 'from the first reading [of *Imperium*] that it was THE book'.[6]

## Julius Evola

In rejecting the Mosleyite conception of 'Europe-a-Nation' as a materialistic concept, Baron Julius Evola — the Italian philosopher who has in recent years received increasing interest — alluded to Yockey (Varange) in *Men Among the Ruins*[7] as he explained his own concept of an 'organic European Empire'. In 1951, Evola reviewed *Imperium* in the Italian journal *Europa Nazione* and in response, *Frontfighter* referred to him as 'Italy's greatest living authoritarian philosopher'.[8] Evola, a World War I veteran, was an occultist and a traditionalist who gave critical support to the Fascist regime but was dubious about its mass character, seeing elements of democracy therein. He was nonetheless a supporter of the corporate, organic state as the Traditional means of social

---

4 Gannon to Stimely, July 13, 1980.

5 Anthony Gannon, 'Argentine Enigma?', *Frontfighter*, No 11, April 1951, p. 2.
Emilio Gutierrez was a veteran nationalist, having founded Union Cívica Nacionalista in 1942, with the axiom: 'Sovereignty, national recovery and social justice.' There would seem to be a kinship with Peronist Justicialism but UCN presented its own list of candidates in the 1946 elections. In 1955, the year of Perón's overthrow, the UCN entered into alliance with the newly formed militant Grupo Tacuara de la Juventud Nacionalista. The two movements, under the name of the UCN ran in the 1962 elections. Gannon moved to South America in 1955 and he met Perón just prior to the President's overthrow.

6 Arcand to Thompson, July 16, 1961.

7 J Evola (1972) *Men Among the Ruins: Post-War Reflections of a Radical Traditionalist* (Vermont: Inner Traditions International, 2002), p. 276.

8 *Frontfighter*, No 11, April 1951, p. 4.

organisation.[9] His doctrine was 'Hermetic', that is he believed the terrestrial was a manifestation of the metaphysical, including politics and economics, and that 'normal' (i.e. traditional) societies were organised hierarchically and were connected to the cosmic order by priest-kings. Evola was therefore a 'fascist' insofar as fascism included aspects of this traditional order. Evola saw European unity being formed through an inevitable need, by the threat of non-European blocs and interests, including the USA and the USSR. However, he stated that little was understood of the 'inner form' of Europe. What was being created was moreover a federal Europe rather than an organic unity, which could only proceed from a 'creative force'. Evola referred to *Imperium* as 'a significant work' for use as a 'starting point' in considering the problems of European unity.[10]

Evola had introduced and translated Spengler's *Decline of The West* into Italian but, while applauding Spengler's repudiation of the linear-Darwinian ascent of civilizations, stated that Spengler lacked an understanding of the metaphysical and transcendent qualities of history. Evola wrote from a theosophical viewpoint, seeing civilizations as emanating from a common metaphysical source. Hence, he rejected Spengler's view of separate and distinct civilizations each with their own morphologies.[11] Evola described Yockey's Spenglerian approach to the cycles of a high culture and Yockey's call for a resurgence of authority. He then described Yockey's theory of 'culture pathology'. Here, Europe must eliminate its traitors and agents of culture pathology. Europe can then unite from an 'inner imperative' and not through federations, customs unions and other economic measures. In the third phase the West must expand territorially towards the East.[12] Evola thought that Yockey had not grasped the full implications of Western Imperium. Where Yockey is seen as advocating the elimination of nations in forming a European nation, Evola states that nations must not be eliminated but must become or-

---

9 J Evola, *Men Among the Ruins* (Rochester, Vermont: Inner Traditions International 2002), 'Economy and Politics — Corporations — Unity of Work', pp. 224–234.

10 J Evola, 'On the Spiritual and Structural Prerequisites for European Unity', *Europa Nazione*, Vol. 1, No. 1, 1951, pp. 48–54; reprinted as the 'Afterword' for *Imperium*, Wermod ed., pp. 781–797.

11 J Evola, *The Path of Cinnabar* (London: Arktos, 2010), pp. 202–205.

12 J Evola, op. cit., 'On the Spiritual and Structural Prerequisites for European Unity'.

ganic cells of the European super-organism, overseen by a supra-national authority. It would be a hierarchical ordering of nations.[13] Evola had overlooked Yockey's statement that a united Europe would maintain national cultures and not impose a type of European melting pot. This was more explicit in *The Proclamation of London*, as mentioned previously.[14] Evola also criticises Yockey, like Spengler, for basing the resurgence of authority on ideas that are part of the decadent epoch of civilization, rather than harking back to Evola's ideal of Medievalism. Evola believed that a united Europe must be based on a supra-national spiritual authority, like the priestly and royal castes that in traditional societies form a nexus between the earthly and the divine, in which society is seen as a reflection of the metaphysical.[15]

Evola had become a sage for a young generation of Italian neo-fascist revolutionaries who looked upon themselves as a type of *kshatriya,* or spiritual warrior caste, battling the forces of cosmic decay. Yockey wrote from hard facts and with an urgency as Europe faced physical and cultural destruction. Evola believed that nothing can be done politically in this epoch other than to 'ride the tiger',[16] that is, for an elite to preserve traditional ideas, perhaps as a secret order, so that another traditional civilization might arise after the collapse of the old. Nonetheless, Evola had given *Imperium* serious discussion, for which the European Liberation Front was grateful.

## The Britons, Arnold Leese, et al

Apart from the followers of Mosley, there was a survival of more orthodox National Socialists after World War II around Arnold S Leese, a veterinary surgeon who made his name during World War I as an expert on camel diseases, which was an important issue in the war. Leese had been leader of the pre-war Imperial Fascist League (IFL), which had expounded 'racial Fascism' and adopted as its symbol the swastika in the centre of the Union

---

13 Ibid.

14 Yockey, *The Proclamation*, op, cit., p. 64.

15 J Evola, *Revolt Against the Modern World* (Rochester: Inner Traditions, 1995).

16 J Evola, *Ride the Tiger* (Rochester: Inner Traditions, 2003).

Jack.[17] Hence, although banking reformer Arthur Kitson had mentored Leese in 1926,[18] his concentration on the 'Jewish issue' prevented the development of an IFL ideology. It was Kitson, who joined the IFL, who introduced Leese to the 'Jewish Menace'.[19] Leese and a colleague, who were impressed by the efficiency of Mussolini's new Italy, had stood successfully as independent 'Fascist' candidates for Stamford borough in 1924.[20] When former junior Labour minister Sir Oswald Mosley called for the unity of Fascists in 1932 and founded the British Union of Fascists, Leese was one of the few who rejected the call. Leese maintained that Mosley's was 'Kosher Fascism'.[21] Mosley proceeded to develop both a detailed philosophical creed and a fighting organisation.

Kitson, a successful inventor and businessmen, whose pioneering work on financial reform has been overshadowed by Major C. H. Douglas' *Social Credit*, introduced Leese to The Britons Society, founded by Captain Henry H Beamish[22] in 1919.[23] The Britons focused on publishing and lectures, their views being quite typical of the Conservative British middle and upper-class distaste for the crassness of Jewish business and social habits — meaning the 'new rich'. It was a reactive type of snobbery towards those of lesser birth but greater money by those of greater birth but lesser money; but it was a healthy, instinctive defence-mechanism against social pathology nonetheless,

17 The original symbol, displayed on the masthead of the IFL newspaper, *The Fascist*, was the *fasces*. This was replaced by the swastika the same year *The Fascist* was founded; 1929. The by-line was 'the organ of Racial Fascism'. Nonetheless, Leese maintained his policy was one of putting the British Empire first, and he believed that Mosley was willing to concede too much to Fascist Italy and Germany.

18 See Arnold S Leese, *Out of Step: Events in the Two Lives of an Anti-Jewish Camel Doctor* (1946, reprinted by Sons of Liberty, Hollywood, California, n.d.), p. 48.

19 Ibid., p. 50.

20 Ibid., p. 49.

21 Ibid., p. 52.

22 Ibid., p. 50.

23 G. C. Lebzelter, *Political Anti-Semitism in England 1918–1939* (London: The Macmillan Press, 1978), p. 49. Beamish met Mussolini in Rome in 1923 and Hitler in Munich. He addressed a Hitlerite meeting on January 18, translated by Dietrich Eckart, which was received enthusiastically, although in 1918 he had stood for parliament on an anti-German platform. (Lebzelter, pp. 50–51). In 1922, The Britons had already started reprinting publications from the German National Socialist party. (Ibid., p. 64).

until economic destitution forced many old families to marry into Jewish-American wealth. Ironically, The Britons started at a time when German imperialism and Jewish interests were considered among these Conservative quarters to be working in alliance ('The Hidden Hand') against the British Empire.[24] One oft-mentioned example of this German and Jewish collusion was the support given by the German General Staff, German-Jewish banker Max Warburg and Marxist millionaire arms dealer Israel Helphand (a.k.a. Parvus) for the transportation of Lenin and his entourage on a sealed train to Russia in 1917.[25]

With the founding of the IFL, leading members of The Britons joined Leese, including Beamish, who served as a vice president of the IFL,[26] Kitson, Anthony Gittens and some ex-military notables such as Brigadier-General R. B. D. Blakeney.[27]

Leese, Mosley and The Britons all emerged from World War II to continue their activities.[28]

One might expect that there would have been much in common between Leese, The Britons and Yockey. In fact, there was far less common ground than between Yockey and Mosley. Anthony Gittens served as secretary to The

24 One leading journal started by Beamish in 1920 was called *The Hidden Hand or Jewry Ueber Alles*, and was as much opposed to 'the Hun' as the Jew.

25 For this accusation from 'anti-Semitic' British Conservatives see Nesta H Webster, *Boche and Bolshevik* (New York: The Beckwith Co., 1923). Mrs Webster was highly regarded as an historian by Winston Churchill, Lord Kitchener and other British luminaries. She was invited to lecture on Bolshevism to the British Secret Service, these lectures forming the basis of her book *World Revolution*. Mrs Webster was a council member of the British Fascisti, the first British Fascist group, and was one of the primary writers for The Britons.

26 Richard Thurlow, *Fascism in Britain* (Oxford: Basil Blackwell, 1987), p. 70.

27 G. C. Lebzelter, op. cit., p. 76.

28 Another major factor was the 'Empire Loyalists' around A. K. Chesterton, a pre-war official of the BUF who, however, did not accept Mosley's post-war vision of European union. The League of Empire Loyalists (LEL) throughout the 1950s flamboyantly protested against imperial scuttle and American usurpation of British world influence. Chesterton's journal, *Candour*, continues to be published. The LEL joined with several other groups in 1967 to found the National Front with Chesterton as the first chairman.

Britons from 1949 to 1973 and both he and Leese reacted vehemently against Yockey. Gittens wrote of the 'Varangeites' and of *Imperium*:

> When the late pioneer anti-Jew fighter Henry H Beamish founded The Britons in 1918 it was not to criticise but to help those who had similar ideas but who preferred to work on their own. When however the ideas behind a Group or Book are based on a fundamentally wrong premise and the sponsors are anonymous, it is our duty to warn all Jew-wise patriots.
>
> Such is the case when the book "Imperium" (2 vols. 12/6 each Westropa Press) written by an American lawyer of unknown origin with the alias "Ulick Varange" who claims to interpret the "Soul of Europe" to the Europeans. Based on the inflated philosopher Oswald Spengler, "Imperium" gives long paraphrases of Spengler's eulogies on the "will to power", but is aimed at a new public.
>
> Spengler preaches Prussian domination of a type gratifying to those elements in Germany whose egoism and narrow class feeling was worked up to prevent race consciousness among the Aryan population. Varange's philosophy attempts to adapt Spengler to present day politics — to build up a spurious "aristocracy" irrespective of race or creed. Even here Spengler pointed the way in his later works on the "stupendous game" for world power.
>
> Varange's Hollywood version is a "mammoth" creed intended to appeal to those who feel frustrated in the genuine and very necessary efforts to cleanse their own countries of the present corrupt system. "Imperium" accentuates Spengler's arrogant, ignorant and fatuous rejection of racial truths. Just as World Jewry found a useful and possibly unexpected ally in Spengler, Varange would today be most useful to World Jewry by condemning the racialist movement as "materialistic" and false, and by opening the way for an arrogant "aristocracy" of mixed blood.
>
> Spengler clung to his theories obstinately in face of all the scientific discoveries of such men as the English Galton, the Americans Grant and Stoddard, the Germans Günther, Bauer, Fischer and Lenz, the Frenchman Gobineau; and the Law of the Augstinian monk, Gregor Mendel. Varange following in the footsteps of the discredited Spengler resurrects his crazy ideas in order to destroy nationalism and create a Super State stretching from the Urals to Europe. Already there are Varangeites who tell us that "the soil of Europe will change the shape of a man's skull" (and presumably his brains!) and others who mistake Military Band

> records worked by some Jew from a Moscow Radio station for the "march past of anti-Jewish storm troops"!
>
> Our advice to patriots is therefore — not to accept this unknown "Imperium" on its face value but to apply a simple test: — Any project in Europe should be judged according to the policy of: "One-People, Many Nations."[29]

Gittens was an expert on subversive movements and had infiltrated, for the British Secret Service, communist groups at the time of the General Strike in 1926. He had been a researcher for Nesta H Webster, whose books *Secret Societies and Subversive Movements*, *The French Revolution* and *World Revolution* became seminal classics of the genre at a time when it was possible to discuss the Jewish issue in influential circles.

However, Gittens was a diehard conservative with Hitlerite leanings and, like the group around Leese, was motivated by the Jewish issue. Like most of the Right in England and in the USA, he could not see the bigger picture presented by Yockey, who was drawing on a European legacy, heralding the new *Zeitgeist*. It was the conflict between two epochs; the old and the new. Much of the right was and remains stuck in the prior *Zeitgeist*.

Gittens did not understand Spengler and Yockey's observation that the new *Zeitgeist* for the twentieth century and beyond would change focus from nineteenth century English economics to German *ethos*. He assumed superficially that Spengler and Yockey were referring to German or Prussian supremacy, whereas Spengler in *The Hour of Decision*, no less than Yockey, called for white world unity. An Englishman, Frenchman or American, if attuned to the new *Zeitgeist*, could have the 'Prussian' ethos regardless of skull length.

Gannon later said of Leese:

> I am sure that Yockey never met Arnold Leese. Leese detested FPY without ever having known him.
>
> For Leese, vertical race was everything; for FPY horizontal race was the deciding issue. Perhaps, Leese was too old and too rigid in his thinking to ever be

29 Anthony Gittens, 'An unknown authority', *Free Britain*, London, no. 69, July 23, 1950, p. 2.

> expected to grasp such a new approach to race. After all, he was born in the nineteenth century, which for FPY was, almost, a total disqualification for a true understanding of his thinking. Anyway, Leese abused FPY in his propaganda and accused him of being all sorts of mongrel, even a Yaqui Indian [...] To which FPY replied in *Frontfighter* citing Leese as "Leese or Louse". Guy Chehsam and I once met two of Leese's collaborators to see if any kind of co-operation were possible but it was not.[30] It puzzles me to observe that FPY is now so widely acclaimed by vertical race merchants and it occurs to me that they have accepted *Imperium* without having read it, and FPY without ever having known him. FPY, and I, never did indulge in fratricide with our old-fashioned "comrades" but merely defended our position when under attack. We both regarded vertical race as having significance and value, for aesthetic reasons and others, but also KNEW that only horizontal race could explain the situation. After all, if every blue-eyed blonde was a friend, and every dark-eyed brunette an enemy—how simple life would be. Life is otherwise, and all history proves it![31]

The issue of *Free Britain* came out the same time as Leese's *Gothic Ripples*, where the grandfather of British National Socialism denounced Yockey in the same terms. Leese entitled his anti-Yockeyan article 'Lysenkoism Comes to Town'.[32] This was a reference to the Soviet biologist T. D. Lysenko,[33] who declared that characteristics acquired through changes wrought by the environment on an organism would be inherited by the next generation. Critics saw Franz Boas' theories as being analogous to those of Lysenko and as having similar Marxist motives.[34]

Leese called *Imperium* 'the 'doctrinal basis' of a 'world propaganda drive'. Identifying Varange as Yockey or 'Jockel', a US lawyer 'of unknown mixed races and equally unknown past', Leese stated that Yockey was being funded

---

30 One of Leese's collaborators was A. F. X. Baron, who worked with Natinform, another vehemently anti-Yockey entity, based on Cold War anti-Soviet rhetoric.

31 Gannon to Stimely, September 7, 1980.

32 Arnold S Leese, 'Lysenkoism comes to town', *Gothic Ripples*, No. 66, July 15, 1950, Guildford, Surrey.

33 Zhores A Medvedev, *The Rise and Fall of T. D. Lysenko* (New York: Anchor Books, 1971).

34 Gary Bullert, 'Franz Boas as Citizen-Scientist: Gramscian-Marxist Influence on American Anthropology', *Journal of Social, Political and Economic Studies*, Washington, Vol. 34, No. 2, Summer 2009, pp. 208–243.

'by Mrs Alice von Pflügl, who is reported to have a Jewish grandfather'. The possibility of the Baroness having a Jewish grandfather would have meant for Leese et al that Yockey was being financed by the Jews to disrupt the right. Leese had always been dismissive of Mosley, referring to the BUF as 'kosher fascism'.[35] Furthermore, Alice von Pflügl was reported to be 'a von Paulus devotee favouring an Eastern Zone mentality'. Here again was an association between Jews and the USSR, as von Paulus was the German General who had gone over to the USSR when a POW during World War II. Leese stated that 'the European Liberation Front, as the drive is called in Britain, dallies with the Jew Menace as Mosley did to attract Nationalists but the main object is the Jewish one of a European Superstate'.

It could be contended that anyone who sought to achieve anything other than being rid of Jews was 'dallying with the Jew Menace'. After World War II, Leese subtitled his newsletter *Gothic Ripples* 'an occasional report on the Jewish question issued for the Jew-wise by Arnold Leese's Anti-Jewish Information Bureau'.

Leese wrote that 'the ridiculous doctrine, which is the foundation of *Imperium*, draws largely on the discredited anti-racial philosopher Spengler resembling the theories of Soviet Prof Lysenko. Spengler always sought to belittle racial science and to discredit National Socialism earning the gratitude of World Jewry'.[36] How Spengler received the gratitude of World Jewry is not explained. Leese claimed that it was symptomatic of Spengler's anti-racism that in *Prussianism and Socialism* he praised the sound political instincts of the Jew Disraeli as prime minister.[37] In Spengler's last book, *The Hour of Decision*, he alludes in passing to Disraeli as among those conservative prime ministers who served as a defensive reaction against the renunciation of the state by Liberalism.[38] It seems predictable that Leese should dismiss Spengler with a quip on a Jew, Disraeli, without finding any other significance in Spengler. Leese concluded: 'That this Lysenkoism should deceive any that understand race or the spelling of the word JEW is tragic. "What does it mat-

35 Leese, *Out of Step: Events in the Two Lives of an Anti-Jewish Camel-Doctor* (ca. 1946), 52.

36 Leese, *Gothic Ripples*, op. cit.

37 Ibid.

38 Spengler, *The Hour of Decision* ([1934] New York: Alfred A Knopf, 1963), 118.

ter?" say Lysenkoists, "if the Russians overrun Europe since they will absorb Culture?" — Aryan, get your Gun!'[39]

What Yockey rejected as outmoded and divisive was what he called 'vertical race'; precisely what Leese was promoting in dividing Europeans into sub-races: Nordic, Mediterranean, Dinaric, Alpine and East Baltic. Only the Nordic has created civilization, wrote Leese, concluding; 'Can the Nordics recover Europe? That is in the laps of the Gods. But through no other channel can Europe itself recover.'[40]

The fourth issue of *Frontfighter* was devoted to answering the attacks of Gittens and Leese. The newsletter's editor, P. J. Huxley-Blythe, described these attacks as 'loathsome', stating that they opened with a letter to him by Leese. 'He gave me the poisoned ivy and I threw it back in his face,' he wrote, adding: 'Lying attacks made on any one member of the FRONT is an attack on the entire FRONT. That is our order-code.'[41] It is unfortunate that Huxley-Blythe was to parrot some of those 'loathsome lies' shortly thereafter when he became the British representative of Natinform, although, as will be seen at the conclusion of this biography, many years later he returned to Yockey in a fulsome tribute.

Frontleader Anthony Gannon opened with characteristic candour: 'Arnold Leese is an old heel. He should be knitting socks instead of spending his senility lying about and smearing men whose boots he isn't fit to black, and in smearing organisations in which he would not be accepted as an office janitor.' Gannon noted the similarity and timing of Gittens' attack on Varange in *Free Britain*. Gannon stated that Leese had written to him accepting that the ELF 'is sincerely anti-Jewish and that he cannot accuse us of pulling-our-punches against the Jews; then he writes to my Editor saying that the FRONT is part of the Jew Plan'. He went on: 'He writes to me saying that there will be no fratricidal strife between the FRONT and him; and then he smears the FRONT with lying insinuations in the *Ripples*.'[42]

---

39 Leese, *Gothic Ripples*, ibid.

40 Leese, *Racial Inequality in Europe* (ca. 1950).

41 P. J. Huxley-Blythe, "Attention!," *Frontfighter*, No. 4, August 1950, p. 1.

42 A. Gannon, "There's no fool like an old fool," ibid., 1.

In answering Leese's main criticism that Yockey's attitude towards 'race' is Lysenkoism, Gannon replied: 'Lysenko is a materialist like Leese. He does not believe in the human soul.' He said 'The FRONT rejects materialism *in toto*', whether coming from Lysenko or Leese. 'It believes in the supremacy of the spirit. When we talk about environment we refer to spiritual environment. For example the spiritual ghetto which the Jew carries everywhere within him and which makes Jews even in Eskimoland. The Jew, like Blacks and Asiatics, is a TOTAL CULTURAL ALIEN. We state that very many Gentile traitors with fair-hair, blue-eyes and long heads who have been subjected to a Jewish environment, spiritually, behave exactly like Jews.' For practical purposes, 'and we are REALISTS always, these types must be considered as Jews … That is what we term HORIZONTAL RACE — total race'. The Jews could only have reached their present power with the help of such Gentiles as are 'in many cases more Jewish than the Jews'. Gannon stated that Leese had never read Spengler or *Imperium* and even if he did, he would never understand. Gannon stated that Spengler in his final book, *The Hour of Decision,* hoped that National Socialism would be up to the tasks required. Gannon wrote that had Spengler lived, Jews have said he would have been treated like the Nazis at Nuremberg. Perhaps so, given the suspicion and sanctions by the post-1945 Occupation against anyone of even conservative tendencies, such as the eminent jurist Carl Schmitt. Gannon saw *Imperium* as the rightful inheritor of the National Socialist legacy. He pointed out that Yockey had dedicated *Imperium* to 'the Hero of the Second World War', Hitler. 'Leese and his ilk should stick to works containing words of not more than one syllable — that way they will not overtax their microscopic brains.' 'This flea-bitten, nasty old buzzard did not know what a Jew was until he was heading on for 50 years of age. He is not quick to see the obvious, you will admit.' Alluding to his own early membership of the British Union of Fascists, Gannon said: 'I was fighting Jews at the age of 13 years. I have dedicate my life to this fight — not my retirement like Leese.'[43]

Of Gittins (sic) or 'The Git', like 'his master' Leese, Gannon wrote that he could not read *Imperium* or Spengler.

---

43 Ibid.

> I remember having a conversation with this poor fellow in a railway tea-room. I tried to talk to him about real things and, in particular, about Spengler. He tried to pretend to me that he had read Spengler then. Every word he spoke proved that to be a lie. Being a kind-hearted fellow I did not try to show-him-up, but he knew that I knew that he had never read Spengler in his entire life.[44]

Yockey's response to Leese was characteristic of the contempt he had for 'leaders' who did not match his intellect but sought to ridicule ideas they could not understand. He wrote:

> A curious tirade by a certain leese[45] has been drawn to my attention. His name comes back to my mind as the author of a letter, in my possession, in which he says that he could not read *Imperium*, the book which he is attempting to attack despite a total lack of comprehension of its thesis. He widens the attack and brings in Oswald Spengler, the greatest European thinker of the twentieth century. Strangely, he tries to make Spengler into an agent of the Jew, although the American Jewish press in 1945 repeatedly said that if Spengler were alive they would try him as a War Criminal.[46]

Yockey pointed out that 'to leese the idea of Europe constituted as one Culture-State-Nation-People-Race is also a Jew idea'. However, 'this was the great leading idea of Adolf Hitler, and is the Destiny of the Western Culture'. 'Thus, in the "logic" of leese, Adolf Hitler becomes an agent of the Jew, as well as Spengler and Mussolini'. Yockey compared Leese's smears with 'the New York Jew Walter Winchell'.[47]

> Both are evil-minded slinking snakes who think that they have achieved something when they unearth some trivial fact of a personal nature. Thus, leese crows like a cock on a dung-hill when he discovers my passport name, a name known to everyone with whom I am well acquainted. This he chooses to call my "real" name, although a pen-name is just as real as any other. The determining thing about a name is whether one can be proud of it or ashamed of it. The name leese

44 Ibid., 2.

45 Yockey often gave lower case to the first letters of names of those he held in contempt, such as churchill, et al.

46 Ulick Varange, 'Varange Speaks!', *Frontfighter,* op. cit., 3-4.

47 Winchell, the well-known muck-raker of American journalism.

> can only be ashamed of it, for he has made it synonymous with the lowest king of prurient Jew obsession.[48]

Leese had never 'fought the Jew *politically*, never has he struck a blow for White European Civilization—while others fought the Jew he sat on the side, interrupting constantly to say: that one's great-great-grandfather was a Jew—that one has a Jewish mistress, and other idiocies'.[49]

Leese, quite typically, regarded Yockey as being of 'mixed race' and Yockey's dark hair would probably have been enough to count him as non-Nordic, to which Yockey replied: 'My race is perfectly clear and definite, whereas the race of leese is a matter of grave doubt.' Leese had 'never been known to espouse any positive cause or idea, but has contented himself with shadow-boxing with his beloved Jews'. When a man 'devotes himself to a negation' he 'turns into a carbon copy' of what he is resisting.

> If there were no Jews in the world, Leese would lose his reason for existence. He has now been driven into the arms of Hollywood Bolshevism, and is angry because FRONT rejects Washington and Hollywood along with Moscow.[50]

> Whenever anyone announces and formulates an Idea which expresses the Spirit of the Age, an Idea which cuts across all older classifications and theories, he may expect the petty-raceless dim-wits from the day-before-yesterday, survivals from the previous century, will fail to understand, and will greet with great hatred that to which they are not equal. However, none of that alters our course. The Liberation Front will continue to resist the Judaization of the West, and to fight for the sacred soil of Europe from Jew, Russia and America.[51]

Several years later, Leese was still condemning the European Liberation Movement (sic) because of the influence Yockey was having on some sections of the American Right. Yockey's essay on the 'Prague Treason Trial' was first published in the *NRP Bulletin* and the venerable American nationalist magazine *Women's Voice* reprinted it on January 29, 1953. Leese suspected

48 Ulick Varange, 'Varange Speaks!', op. cit.

49 Ibid.

50 Ibid.

51 Ibid.

that sinister forces were funding the Front and that those involved 'look like Dagoes and Wops' who would integrate Britain into 'a Europe composed of similar Dagoes and Wops, and to "play off" Russia against America'. Leese harkened back to *Frontfighter* issue 4, which contained the Front's reply to Leese's smears.[52] Leese's quips about Italians and Spaniards, among the forefront of the European vanguard both during and after the war, were the result of precisely the kind of 'vertical race' theories that Yockey rejected.

Yockey wrote to Canadian fascist leader Adrian Arcand in regard to the attacks by Gerald L. K. Smith, Leese, et al that he was *not* won over to the 'Prussian Idea' because National Socialist Germany was anti-Semitic; that he was 'not first an anti-semite, but am anti-semitic only because they are frustrating our Western Destiny, but they are not the only group, and NOT THE MOST POWERFUL GROUP doing that. Our worst enemy is the inner enemy, the liberal-capitalist-democrat, for it is he alone who enables the Jew to enjoy his present power'.[53]

The crux of the matter is to defeat what Spengler referred to as the power of 'Money'. The only Idea opposing capitalism is not the 'socialism' of the Marxian-democratic-proletarian type, which merely sought to expropriate capitalism, but 'Prussian socialism'. By rejecting or not understanding Yockey or Spengler, Leese and Smith lacked historical perspective.

In reply to Arcand on obtaining publicity for *Imperium*, Yockey commented that he had attempted this by sending copies to prominent enemies. This had failed and he was now focusing on sending *Imperium* only to those who already had the 'instinct' to appreciate it. 'It will give them a firm foundation, and make them more articulate.'[54] Gannon had also written of those with the 'instinct' to appreciate *Imperium*. It is something that the reader will or will not comprehend on the basis of personal experience.

Despite the repudiation by Mosley, Leese and Gittens, *Imperium* sold between 1,000 and 1,500 copies, mostly in Britain,[55] which is to say most of the

52 Arnold Leese, 'Colleagues', *Gothic Ripples*, No. 98, March 12, 1953, p. 3.

53 Varange to Arcand, November 21, 1950, Arcand collection, Archives Canada, Vol. 1, File no. 1.

54 Varange to Arcand, November 21, 1950, ibid.

55 FBI report, February 20, 1956, p. 10, file no. 105–2889 — 2.

copies that were published — a considerable achievement for a fringe of the fringe operating a few years after the war.

However, Gannon states that the financial situation with the Front did not improve, nor the personal fortunes of its leading members.

> Chesham and Yockey quarrelled over Chesham's lack of resolve, in FPY's opinion, in resisting the threats of Mrs Chesham to depart the domestic scene! We lost contact with Guy, and I never heard of him, or from him since. In FPY's thinking, Chesham had gone soft and proven worthless. As he had a wife and two children to support, I took a kinder opinion of Guy; after all, I had the same situation myself, but stood by FPY, who had been abandoned by almost every other.[56]

Gannon left England for South America in October 1954, 'much against FPY's entreatments', and heard nothing further until Yockey's death.[57]

Huxley-Blythe pursued his own course with those opposed to Yockey. In 1954, he helped form the Nationalist Information Bureau (Natinform) from 1954 to 1958, publishing *Natinform World Survey*. He worked with Gittens and the Britons Publishing Society, with A. F. X. Baron, and with Colin Jordan, Leese's heir, and founder of the British National Socialist Movement. *World Survey* was incorporated into *Northern World*, the well-produced journal of the Northern League. That in turn was incorporated into Willis Carto's journal *Western Destiny* in the USA, which was merged with *The American Mercury*, the literary magazine, when it was purchased by Carto.

The up-and-coming Rightist movement in Britain was not however to be Mosley's or Jordan's but the National Front, reaching its high point in the 1970s as Britain's fourth largest party. However, the NF was adamantly opposed to Mosley's 'Europe-a-Nation', let alone Yockey's 'Imperium', and was based on the reformation of the British Commonwealth of White Dominions into an autarchic power-bloc independent of both the USA and the USSR. Its ideological mentor was A. K. Chesterton. Gannon related that many of the

56 Gannon to Stimely, July 13, 1980.

57 Gannon to Stimely, ibid.

early NF leaders knew Yockey and 'hated him', 'making fun of his name and speculating as to his origins, Jew or Yaqui Indian'.[58]

## *Der Weg*

Johannes von Leers, in reviewing *Imperium* for *Der Weg*, was effusive in his praise. Citing British military historian Captain Liddel Hart in referring to *Imperium* as 'a work of a genius' and Major General J. F. C. Fuller's view of it as 'perhaps the most prophetic book since Spengler's *Demise of The West*', he said *Imperium* 'is indeed a bright spot to help in the darkness of our day.' Von Leers referred to the foreign volunteers of the Waffen SS as a model for the future of European unity and lamented the conquest of Europe by the 'barbarians' (Russia) and by 'senseless democracy' (USA). He believed that *Imperium* could inspire 'the next big European revolution'. He urged that it be published in all the languages of the West, as being 'more important than all the books published by the "Left" in the world — because it's ours and it shows where the march must go'.[59]

In the same issue, von Leers, writing under the *nom de plume* of Felix Schwarzenborn, concluded a review of Julius Evola's *Orientamenti*[60] with a recommendation for the European Liberation Front. Evola's conception of united Europe was of decentralised, federated states. He opposed centralised nation-state conceptions, including those of the German Reich. The model of a new Europe was the international volunteer divisions of the Waffen SS. Western Imperium would be maintained around the axis of an imperial chivalric order. Von Leers concluded his review of Evola with reference to Yockey:

> That these things are in the air, in other counties, is shown by a small, mimeographed magazine from England, *Frontfighter* (even large movements have once

58 Gannon to Stimely, July 13, 1980, op. cit.

59 J. von Leers, 'Ulick Varange: Imperium', *Der Weg*, Buenos Aires, Argentina, pp. 662–663, Vol. 5, No. 9, 1951.

60 Julius Evola, 'Orientamenti' (Guidelines), *Imperium*, Rome 1950. This *Imperium* was an Italian neo-Fascist magazine. The essay was developed in Evola's books such as *Men Among the Ruins*. Evola's essay can be found at: http://www.renatus.it/files/evola_julius_orientamenti.pdf.

> started with mimeograph) which openly pronounce: "After the years of the great dying on the Jewish war of hatred, Europe looked out for an Idea that could free it again from the foreign yoke of outer control of Europe, and to absorb the splendour of the Fascist revolutions of 1922 and 1933. Europe has not waited in vain. From the ruins came the idea of the Imperium. This idea is the logical result of the new order, for which Hitler and Mussolini worked ... The mantel of Heroes is now fallen on our shoulders and it is the cloak of invincibility. Let the jackals of Strasbourg enjoy their little hour. Their slogans and exhortations will freeze on their pale lips, before they close. Only the rigidity of death awaits them. Strasbourg will only bring about plans for Ju-SA colonial rule. The future belongs to European Imperium..."
>
> No matter how small this group may be (European Liberation Front, Mr P. J. Huxley-Blythe, London WC 1, Westropa-Press)—it is significant that slowly certain ideas prevail: the Elite, Empire Europaeum, and that we come out of mourning for the dead to the knowledge of the task and the tremendous possibilities. It's not over yet![61]

If there were differences between Yockeyan and Evolian conceptions of European Imperium,[62] they were minor in the grander scheme of things and more likely assumed than actual.

Although Yockey had failed with Mosley and with Gerald L. K. Smith, this was surely compensated for many times over by enthusiastic endorsements from Johannes von Leers and Otto Remer, direct links with the Third Reich; and with veterans from Mussolini's Salò Republic. Remer and von Leers were part of what H Keith Thompson called the 'higher authority', ominously named *Die Spinne* by sensationalist journalists, who saw their web spreading over Latin America and the Arab states. *Der Weg* ('The Way'), which was described as the 'official publication' of *Die Spinne*, said that they had 'an underground army of more than 200,000 fanatic recruits'.[63] Published by Dürer

---

61 Felix Schwarzenborn, 'Imperium Europaeum', *Der Weg* Vol. 5, No. 9, 19951, pp. 646–647. (Translation by Bolton).

62 See J Evola, 'On the Spiritual and Structural Prerequisites for European Unity', *Europa Nazione*, Vol. 1, No. 1, 1951, pp. 48–54; reprinted in Yockey, *Imperium*, Wermod ed., op. cit., pp. 781–797. Despite the differences Evola comments that Varange 'is certainly worth following'. (p. 786).

63 Paul Meskil, *Hitler's Heirs* (Pyramid Books, 1961), p. 9.

Verlag, Buenos Aires, and run by Eberhard Fritsch, the magazine was edited by Johannes von Leers, who also wrote as Felix Schwarzenborn, according to a CIA report.[64] Dr von Leers, a multi-linguist, had been a specialist on Jewish affairs in the Goebbels ministry. He was opposed to racism entering foreign policy considerations during the Third Reich and hence was a keen supporter of the alliance with Japan, Japanese being among the languages in which he was fluent. He persuaded the Third Reich *not* to apply its racial laws restricting civic rights to any race other than Jews. Hence, it is an irony that National Socialist Germany had fewer race laws than many states of the USA and Africans could live freely in Germany.[65]

An admirer of Islam since before the war, von Leers moved to Egypt with the support of the Grand Mufti of Jerusalem, Amin al Husseini. The Grand Mufti had aligned with the Axis during the war, after meeting Hitler in Berlin on November 28, 1941.[66] Von Leers, converting to Islam with the name Omar Amin, assumed a leading role in Egyptian President Nasser's information department,[67] where Yockey had previously worked. In 1933, von Leers wrote an article urging the humane resettlement of Jews from Europe. While recognising the need for a zionistic resettlement into a Jewish homeland, he was even then resolutely opposed to a Jewish state in Palestine,[68] writing:

> Palestine is unable to absorb the coming Jewish masses since it cannot support them, nor is it the right location. Furthermore, England has to consider both the native Arabic population and the world-wide Islamic community, which makes it impossible to settle even a reasonably significant part of the Jewish masses there.
>
> Only a barbarian standing outside of the last great divine manifestation of world history would propose a general anti-Semitic battle aimed at the extermination

64 'The recent books by Werner Naumann and Johannes von Leers', Central Intelligence Agency, report from Frankfurt, August 7, 1953, EGF-271.

65 See: V. K. Clark, *The Controversy of Black Nazis II* (Vera Icona Publishers, 2012.

66 'Adolf Hitler and the Grand Mufti of Jerusalem', official transcript of meeting, November 28, 1941, World Future Fund, http://www.worldfuturefund.org/wffmaster/Reading/Total/hitler.mufti.htm.

67 See: Martin Lee, *The Beast Reawakens* (London: Little Brown and Co., 1997), pp. 121–154.

68 Which was also opposed by Hitler. See Hitler/Mufti transcript, op. cit.

> of this people. The goal of the highly developed peoples is not to promote hatred where there is a decent way to solve the problem.[69]

Von Leers envisaged a homeland in Africa or South America, large enough to support Jews productively, while those states from which they emigrated would provide vocational training, particularly in agriculture.[70] His aim was to end the perennial phenomenon of the 'Wandering Jew'.

While editing *Der Weg* in Argentina, von Leers continued to promote Yockey's ideas. Several months prior to reviewing *Imperium*, *Der Weg* ran Yockey's article from *Frontfighter*, 'America's Two Ways of Waging War', where Varange had stated that for Europe the Cold War is 'as interesting as a tribal war between two negro clans in the Sudan'.[71] In 1952 von Leers, as Schwarzenborn, wrote that alleged anti-Semitism in the USSR was a myth, reiterating the Jewish character of Bolshevism and the 1917 Revolution. He stated that the Stalinist purges during the 1930s were internal power struggles that had not broken Jewish control, citing the continuing well-placed position of Jews in the Soviet bureaucracy and economy and the disproportionate number of Jewish Soviet spies in the USA. What was required was not a world revolution based on communistic class struggle but a world revolution against the Jewish ruling class.[72] However, early the following year *Der Weg* ran Yockey's seminal article, 'What is behind the hanging of eleven Jews in Prague?' under the title 'Stalin und die Juden', acknowledging Frederick Weiss's Le Blanc Publications as the source.[73]

---

69 J von Leers, 'The End of Jewish Migration', Das Ende der jüdischen Wanderung (1933), pp. 229–231, http://research.calvin.edu/german-propaganda-archive/gercke.htm.

70 The idea of a Jewish homeland somewhere other than Palestine was not unusual. Jewish colonisation societies considered Cyprus, Australia, Uganda, Argentina, and other places. See: Rabbi Berel Wein, "The Jewish Homeland," http://www.rabbiwein.com/blog/the-jewish-homeland-661.html. Poland in 1937 and Germany in 1940 proposed Madagascar. See: https://www.youtube.com/watch?v=46pwZyTC3yg.

71 U Varange, 'Zwei Wege der Kriegführung Amerikas', *Der Weg*, Vol. 5, No. 7, 1951, pp. 481–482.

72 Felix Schwarzenborn (von Leers), 'Wird Bolschewismus judenfeindlich? (Will Bolshevism become hostile to Jews?)', *Der Weg*, Vol. 6, no. 7, 1952, pp. 4980–495.

73 'Stalin und die Juden', *Der Weg*, Vol. 7, No. 2, 1953, pp. 115–118.

# The Meaning of Europe

> One of the great plans was the re-uniting, the concentration of those same geographical nations which have been separated and parcelled out by revolution and policy. There are in Europe, dispersed, it is true, upwards of thirty millions of French, fifteen millions of Spaniards, fifteen millions of Italians, and thirty millions of Germans; and it was my intention to incorporate these people each into one nation. It would have been a noble thing to have advanced into posterity with such a train, and attended by the blessings of future ages.
>
> — Napoleon[1]

Does Europe even exist as the possibility of a unitary Nation-People-State? Or is such a 'Europe' only a utopian wish of defeated Fascists who saw the folly of an excessive pre-War nationalism; or conversely as an economic ideal of international business interests who see 'European Union' as a means of diminishing world trade barriers? Can 'European Union' be more than a convenient tool for US foreign policy, expanding the scope of NATO? Or does Europe, as the 'Mother-soil' of Western Civilization, have a mythos, history and therefore a potential destiny that has been thwarted?

The consciousness of being 'European' has a long tradition vis-à-vis the 'outer enemy'. A 'people' is a psychological 'we-feeling' that does not arise until one recognises being different from others. Yockey pointed out that the Western culture became conscious of itself in its battles against Slavs, Moors, Mongols and Turks. He stated that the Western culture had been a 'spiritual

1 Napoleon Bonaparte, quoted by Count de las Cases, *Memoirs of the Life, Exile, and Conversations of the Emperor Napoleon* (London: Henry Colburn, 1836), Vol. 4, pp. 104–108; quoted by Hans Kohn, *Nationalism: Its Meaning and History* (New York: Van Nostrand Reinhold Co., 1965), p. 126.

unit' from the beginning and its 'birth-cry' was the Crusades, with one state with the Emperor at its head; one Church and faith, 'Gothic Christianity'; one ethos, chivalry; a common style, 'Gothic'; a universal language, Latin; and a universal law, Roman.[2] The Western culture was preserved as a unit 'vis-à-vis the Barbarian' down to the middle of the eighteenth century.[3]

In describing the Battle of Poitiers against the Arabs in AD 732, the *Chronicle of Isidore* of Spain refers to the Christian armies of Charles Martel as the 'Europeans'. The contemporary chroniclers name the empire of Charlemagne (AD 768-814) as 'Europe'. In 755, the priest Cathwulf praised Charlemagne as chosen by God and ruling over 'the glory of the empire of Europe'.[4] In 799 Angilbert, Charlemagne's son-in-law and Court poet, described the Emperor as 'the father of Europe'—*Rex, pater Europae*.[5] The 'Kingdom of Charles' was called 'Europa' in the *Annals of Fuld*. Alcuin (735-804), master of the palace school, theologian and Court rhetorician, called this 'the continent of faith'. The Franco-British Catholic writer Hilaire Belloc said in similar terms: 'Europe is the faith and the faith is Europe.' Belloc explained:

> In the next period [after Rome]—the Dark Ages—the Catholic proceeds to see Europe saved against a universal attack of the Mohammedan, the Hun, the Scandinavian: he notes that the fierceness of the attack was such that anything save something divinely instituted would have broken down. The Mohammedan came within three days' march of Tours, the Mongol was seen from the walls of Tournus on the Sâone: right in France. The Scandinavian savage poured into the mouths of all the rivers of Gaul, and almost overwhelmed the whole island of Britain. There was nothing left of Europe but a central core. Nevertheless Europe survived.
>
> In the refloresence which followed that dark time—in the Middle Ages—the Catholic notes not hypotheses but documents and facts; he sees the Parliaments arising not from some imaginary "Teutonic" root—a figment of the

---

2 Yockey, *The Proclamation of London*, Wermod ed., op. cit., p. 9.

3 Yockey, *Imperium*, op. cit., p. 769.

4 Denis de Rougemont, *The Idea of Europe* (New York: Macmillan Co., 1966), p. 46.

5 Angilbert, *Monumenta germ.Poet.Carol. I*, 368. Quoted by Denis de Rougemont, *ibid.*, p. 46.

> academies — but from the very real and present great monastic orders, in Spain, in Britain, in Gaul — never outside the old limits of Christendom. He sees the Gothic architecture spring high, spontaneous and autochthonic, first in the territory of Paris and thence spread outwards in a ring to the Scotch Highlands and to the Rhine. He sees the new Universities, a product of the soul of Europe, reawakened — he sees the marvellous new civilization of the Middle Ages rising as a transformation of the old Roman society, a transformation wholly from within, and motivated by the Faith.[6]

Yockey wrote that 'the decisive turning point' for the West represented by the French Revolution in 1789 'was prepared for by centuries of slow changes'.[7] Of these we might cite the most obvious: The Reformation started the process not only of a fractured Europe but of the victory of Money over nobility, then the reign of Henry VIII, the English Puritan Revolution, the 1789 French Revolution, and the liberal national revolutions across Europe during the mid-nineteenth century. Belloc traced the process of Western disintegration as far back as Philip the Fair of France who, during the fourteenth century, challenged both the temporal power of the Holy Empire and the spiritual power of Pope Boniface VIII. This, states Belloc, was the first manifestation of the 'sovereign rights' which resulted in the disintegration of the spiritual-cultural-political unity of Europe. The Age of Discovery leading to the colonial empires placed the focus on the Atlantic and to trade rivalry between states. The Reformation undermined the spiritual unity, while the instigators such as Luther and Calvin did not speak of Europe.[8] The Protestants sought to replace the Holy Empire and the Papacy with federated states[9], ultimately giving rise to what is familiar in our own times as schemes for federated and regional combines in the interests of trade and other economic factors.

Yockey stated that Calvin taught the 'sanctity of economic activity' and 'sanctioned usury' which had been anathema for Western Christendom and regarded with hatred as the occupation of Jews. Henry VIII legalised usury

---

6 Hillarie Belloc (1920), *Europe and the Faith* (London: Black House Publishing), p. 52.

7 Yockey, *Imperium*, Wermod ed., op. cit., p. 531.

8 Denis de Rougemont, op.cit., p. 76.

9 Ibid., p. 90.

in England in 1545. Puritanism continued the process.[10] Indeed, the way was opened for Jews to rise to positions such as to render them Culture-distorters when money rather than land became power. In seeking readmittance of the Jews to England,[11] following the Puritan Revolution and under the reign of Oliver Cromwell, Rabbi Menasseh ben Israel, leader of the Jews of Amsterdam, then the money capital of the world, wrote to the Lord Protector in 1655. He asserted that economics is the basis of human activity in an assertion that foreshadows both Marx and the free-trade philosophers by two centuries: 'Profit is a most powerful motive, and which all the World prefers before all other things...'[12] It also gives sanctity to money-making as a religious duty that inspired the Calvinists and Puritans. His appeal is to profit and he starts from the belief that there is nothing higher. While Jewish apologists have claimed that Jews were forced into commerce because every other profession was denied to them, Menasseh states:

> It is a thing confirmed, that merchandising is, as it were, the proper profession of the Nation of the Jews... God... hath given his people, as it were, a natural instinct, by which they might not only gain what is necessary for their need, but that they should also thrive in Riches and possessions, whereby they should not only become gracious to their Princes and Lords, but that they should be invited by others to come and dwell in their Lands.[13]

Menassah wrote that dispersion of the Jews throughout the world (the Diaspora) is actually an advantage for it allows the Jews to build up an international network, which means that they can grant credit among each other in far-flung regions and act as international negotiators. They also have a common language, which unites them across national, cultural and linguistic boundaries, thus making them the focus for the development of international capitalism.

---

10 Yockey, *Imperium*, Wermod ed., op. cit., p. 531.

11 The Jews had been expelled from England in 1290.

12 Menasseh ben Israel, 'To His Highness the Lord Protector of the Commonwealth of England, Scotland and Ireland, How Profitable the Nation of the Jews Are', reproduced in *The Jew in the Modern World—A Documentary History*, ed. Paul R Mendes-Flohr and Jehuda Reinharz (Oxford University Press, 1980), pp. 9–12.

13 Menasseh ben Israel, ibid.

> Now in this dispersion our Forefathers flying from the Spanish Inquisitor, some of them came to Holland, others got into Italy, and others into Asia, and so easily they credit one another, and by that means they draw the Negotiation wherever they are ...[14]

Menasseh cites the Turkish Empire as the main centre of World Jewry at the time, and boasts of the Jewish control of the empire's finances, as well as their influence as advisers:

> ...[W]here some of them live in great estate, even in the Court of the Grand Turk at Constantinople, by reason there is no Viceroy, or Governor or Pasha, which hath not a Jew to manage his affairs, and to take care for his estate: Hence it cometh that in short time they grow up to be Lords of great revenues, and they most frequently bend the minds of the Great ones to most weighty affairs in government.[15]

The rabbi wrote of a similar situation existing in Germany and then goes on to speak of Poland, in which 'the whole of Negotiation is in the hand of the Jews, the rest of the Christians are either all Noble-men, or rustics and kept as slaves'. The situation was the same in Italy.[16]

The situation pertained throughout Europe, evidently Monarchical England having been one of the last to succumb in its Puritan revolution. Britain was soon lumbered with a National Debt held by the privately owned Bank of England, which was based on the Amsterdam model.[17]

The Puritan sanctification of moneymaking as a religious duty was the foundation of the USA and has shaped the American mentality with a secularised *messianic* mission to convert the world in its image. Yockey mentions this as 'the American universalizing of ideology' turning into 'messianism' — 'the idea that America must save the world'.[18] With the sanctification of moneymaking, it was a short distance to the triumph of rationalism and materialism

14 Ibid.

15 Ibid.

16 Ibid.

17 K. R. Bolton, *The Banking Swindle* (London: Black House Publishing, 2013), pp. 24–26.

18 Yockey, *Imperium*, op. cit., p. 573.

over Christendom, marked by the French Revolution and the assumption to power of the bourgeoisie.

The national revolutions throughout mid-nineteenth century Europe were inspired by republican and liberal ideals which sought to destroy the principalities and dynasties of Europe. At that time, nationalism was a revolutionary ideal. German nationalism however was divorced from the French by Fichte, Wagner et al, who redefined nation-peoples-states as having a spiritual meaning and a *volkish* basis. They sowed the seeds of the *Zeitgeist* of the new epoch. Spirit and race confronted economics. Although appropriated by German nationalists, Nietzsche looked to Europe as the next development beyond petty-statism and loathed German nationalism:

> Thanks to the morbid estrangement which the lunacy of nationality has produced and continues to produce between the peoples of Europe, thanks likewise to the short-sighted and hasty-handed politicians who are with its aid on top today and have not the slightest notion to what extent the politics of disintegration they pursue must necessarily be only an interlude — thanks to all this, and to much else that is altogether unmentionable today, the most unambiguous signs are now being overlooked, or arbitrarily and lyingly misinterpreted, which declare that Europe wants to become one. In all the more profound and comprehensive men of this century the general tendency of the mysterious working of their souls has really been to prepare the way to this new synthesis and to anticipate experimentally the European of the future.[19]

Nietzsche then mentions as those who foreshadow the European of the future Napoleon, Goethe, Beethoven and Richard Wagner who, even when they identified themselves as nationalists, or 'patriots for the Fatherland', were merely 'taking a rest from themselves'. 'They are related, fundamentally related, in all the heights and depths of their needs: it is Europe, the one Europe, whose soul forces its way longingly up and out through their manifold and impetuous art — whither? Into a new light? Towards a new sun?'[20]

Here, we see in Nietzsche the foreshadowing of Spengler and Yockey in identifying the *Zeitgeist* that impels great figures to act in a certain way,

---

19 Friedrich Nietzsche, *Beyond Good and Evil* (Penguin Books 1984), Section 256, pp. 169–170.

20 Friedrich Nietzsche, *Beyond Good and Evil,* ibid., p. 170.

regardless of their conscious temperaments. Even German ultra-nationalists such as Wagner, being attuned to the coming epoch, were harbingers of European unity.

The 'good European' was embodied in Goethe, whom Nietzsche referred to as 'not a German event but a European one'.[21] It was Goethe's rendering of the legend of Doctor Faustus that gave Spengler the very term 'Faustian'[22] to describe the uniquely 'Faustian soul' of Western man,[23] reaching always for the infinite and reflected in the West's art, architecture, music, technics, exploration, mathematics and physics, etc. Spengler defined the 'Faustian soul' of Western man as being symbolised by 'pure and limitless space'. It is what distinguishes Western High Culture and civilization not only from the Levantine (Arabian and Jewish) and Chinese but even from other white cultures such as the Graeco-Roman (Classical), Indo-Aryan and Russian.

In politics, the Faustian imperative takes the form of 'Prussian State-Socialism' which Spengler stated was not merely 'Prussian' but 'European', described by Fichte as the 'Right to Work', which in the new epoch of Western civilization Spengler stated would be the '*Duty* to Work'.[24] This is precisely the phrase we find in point 8 of the programme of the European Liberation Front, expressing Yockey's 'Ethical Socialism'. What makes it 'Faustian' or uniquely Western as distinct from the Jewish messianic and English utilitarian 'Socialism' most commonly known as Marxism is the 'organic concept of the Deed that leads to the concept of work as commonly understood, the civilised form of the Faustian effecting the insistent tendency to give to life the most active forms imaginable'; 'the higher Ethos which values deeds only', as distinct from the 'moral programs' of the socialist movement', which 'remain mere words'.[25]

---

21 F Nietzsche, *Twilight of the Idols* (Penguin Books, 1985), 'Expeditions of an Untimely Man', p. 79. Goethe is not merely German, but a 'European event', as are Schopenhauer, Hegel and Heine.

22 J. W. von Goethe, *Faust*.

23 Surprisingly, Yockey does not use the term 'Faustian'.

24 Spengler, *The Decline of The West*, op. cit., Vol. I, p. 362.

25 Spengler, ibid.

It is to Goethe and Nietzsche that Spengler owes 'practically everything', as he stated in the introduction to *The Decline*.[26] While the Hitlerite National Socialists rejected Spengler as an apostle of a Ragnarokian[27] fate and of a race theory that did not accord with their English Darwinism, there were unavoidable similarities between the two, especially in terms of Ethical Socialism. The similarities were unavoidable because both Spengler's Faustianism and National Socialism emerged under the influence of the same *Zeitgeist* and in reaction against European decay. It was actually the anti-Hitler 'revolutionary National Socialists', Otto and Gregor Strasser, who were closer to Spengler and to Yockey in outlook, being influenced directly by Spengler's thinking.[28] One is tempted to see much more kinship between Yockey and Strasser than Yockey and Hitler, and Yockey, as a Spenglerian, might have also found himself *persona non grata* in the Third Reich. However, Yockey did always maintain, despite dedicating *Imperium* to 'the Hero' of World War II,[29] that National Socialism was only a 'provisional form' of the new Europe.

The Third Reich struggled with an internal dichotomy of elements from both old and new epochs. Paradoxically, the old, which often held supremacy in Reich thinking and policy, was of a more English than German origin. Hence, Darwinism contended with the attitudes towards 'race' of German idealism, and petty-statism and chauvinism contended with pan-Europa, most acutely in differences between the old military caste and the new caste of the Waffen SS. Among the pan-Europeanists was Robert Ley who, as leader of the Labour Front, was responsible in large part for the implementation of the Ethical Socialism of the new era. Writing of Europe, Dr Ley stated:

---

26 Spengler, ibid., xiv.

27 Norse *Ragnarok*, German *Gotterdammerung*, 'The Twilight of the Gods', in which the Gods face their doom, knowing their fate is predetermined but also that after the destruction of both antagonists in the final great battle, a new world with new Gods will arise, born from the sole surviving God, Baldr.

28 See Bolton, 'Spengler: A Philosopher for all Seasons' in Troy Southgate, ed. *Spengler: Thoughts & Perspectives Vol. X* (London: Black Front Press, 2012), pp. 15–24. Gregor was eliminated during the Night of the Long Knives in 1934; his brother Otto lived in exile until after the war.

29 Yockey, *Imperium*, Wermod ed., op. cit., v.

> It is clear that it will take time for our part of the earth to grow together. A civil war that has lasted a thousand years cannot be overcome in a year. Nonetheless, the increase in cooperative work between the European peoples has greatly increased in recent years. The struggle against Bolshevism will drive them even closer together. Jewish Bolshevism is at the gates, and must be fought, whatever the cost. This common defensive battle teaches peoples to appreciate each other, and the Jew on the enemy side, with his Jewish stupidity and arrogance, does the rest of what has to be done. Here we can only say: *We are happy that our enemies have their Jews.* What all the eloquence on European cooperation has not achieved, the Jew in his blindness will quickly hammer into the European peoples the knowledge *that they must stand together in their battle against Bolshevism and in their battle against the Anglo-barbarians, that they share a common struggle against Judah.* Our allies and their brave soldiers, the European legions of the Norwegians, Danes, Dutch, Flemish, Walloons, the many millions of Europeans hard at work in Germany, all these are proof that Europe has awakened, and is beginning to find a European community in the midst of hard sacrifices and suffering, in the midst of incendiary and explosive bombs.
>
> Charlemagne, Prince Eugen, Frederick the Great, Napoleon Bonaparte and Victor Hugo all wanted a united Europe, and fought for it. As Napoleon Bonaparte sat in St Helena, miserable and demoralized, he wrote the following prophetic words: "I failed. I was not strong enough to unify Europe. But someone will come after me who will raise my banner once more, and finish my work, and then no one will speak of England any longer, but rather one will speak of a Napoleon."
>
> These prophetic words of Napoleon Bonaparte, England's sworn enemy, are now being fulfilled. European unity is being forged now that the Jew has been driven from it. Under the leadership of its Führer Adolf Hitler, Germany will carry the banner of this ancient, yet ever young, part of the earth. *At the end of this war, Germany will win and Europe will be united!*[30]

Here Ley expressed the new outlook of united Europe, not German supremacy. He saw united Europe in embryo in the hundreds of thousands of volunteers who came from all over Europe to work in Germany and of the hundreds of thousands who volunteered for the Waffen SS. He saw the battle

30 Robert Ley, *Pesthauch der Welt* (Dresden: Franz Müller Verlag, 1944).

against what Yockey called the 'outer barbarian' and the Culture-distorter as a unifying factor for Europe in adversity and the imperative towards European unity as deriving from ancient sources, though it remains ever-youthful, the means by which, in a Spenglerian sense, spring comes again even though winter must be endured.

Not since the Crusades, 'the birth-cry' of a united West,[31] had Western Civilization manifested such unity of purpose as in the Foreign Legions of the Waffen SS. Most recruits came from outside Germany and they were motivated by the new European idea. Some, such as the Flemish, saw the possibility of a greater freedom for their folk and culture within a united Europe, rather than within the artificial states, such as Belgium, which had been imposed — no less than Latvians or Estonians under the Soviet Empire, now independent states in which those Waffen SS divisions are still honoured.

Leon Degrelle, leader of the pre-war Rexists, a mass movement among the Francophones of Belgium, and volunteer for the Waffen SS in its fight on the Eastern Front, was one of those veterans who remained true to the European Idea after the war. Degrelle had risen from Private to General; he had been wounded on numerous occasions and awarded the Ritterkreuz, the Oak-Leaves, the Gold German Cross and numerous other decorations for outstanding valour under enemy fire. One of the last to fight on the Eastern Front, he flew 1,500 miles across Europe under constant fire, toward Spain, where he crash-landed on the beach of San Sebastian, receiving critical wounds. He remained in exile in Spain for the remainder of his long life. In the early 1980s, he wrote of the European idealism:

> For the European SS the Europe of petty jealousies, jingoism, border disputes, economic rivalries was of no interest. It was too petty and demeaning; that Europe was no longer valid for them. At the same time the European SS, as much as they admired Hitler and the German people, did not want to become Germans. They were men of their own people and Europe was the gathering of the various people of Europe. European unity was to be achieved through harmony, not domination of one over the others.

31 Yockey, *The Proclamation of London*, op. cit., p. 9.

> I discussed these issues at length with both Hitler and Himmler. Hitler like all men of genius had outgrown the national stage. Napoleon was first a Corsican, then a Frenchman, then a European and then a singularly universal man. Likewise Hitler had been an Austrian, then a German, then a greater German, then Germanic, then he had seen and grasped the magnitude of building Europe.[32]

Richard Landwehr, one of the foremost authorities on the foreign legions of the Waffen SS, wrote of their nationalities:

> The final tally sheet for the European Volunteer Movement ran roughly as follows (*Waffen-SS* only):
>
> *Western Europe*: 162,000 volunteers, ranging from about 55,000 in Holland to 80 from Liechtenstein. Out of this total about 50,000 were killed or missing. Included in this figure would be 16,000 Dutchmen and 11,500 Belgians.
>
> *Baltic States and Soviet Nationalities*: About 250,000 soldiers. Casualties and post-war losses through forced repatriation and execution were enormous.
>
> *Balkan and Slavics*: About 100,000. Considerable losses. Ethnic Germans not from Germany: About 300,000.
>
> *Germans from the Reich*: 400,000. For the Germans and ethnic Germans, losses in killed and missing were about one-third.[33]

However, the foreign legions of the Waffen SS do not tell the whole story of Europe's fight. For example, 18,104 Spaniards volunteered to serve on the Eastern Front in 1941 and formed the 'Blue Division' of the Wehrmacht. Hitler noted that they were among the toughest of soldiers. The Legion of French Volunteers (LVF) comprised 6,000 selected from 13,000 volunteers and were also noted for their toughness.[34]

---

32 Leon Degrelle, 'Epic: The Story of the Waffen SS', *The Journal of Historical Review*, Winter 1982-83, Vol. 3, No. 4.

33 Richard Landwehr, 'The European Volunteer Movement in World War II', *The Journal of Historical Review*, Spring 1982 Vol. 2, 1.

34 See Carlos Jurado, *Foreign Volunteers of the Wehrmacht 1941-45* (Osprey Publishing, 1983).

It was among the remnants of these veterans that Yockey, Mosley and others sought to continue the struggle for European unity amidst a Europe devastated by aerial fire-bombings, mass rape, lynching and enforced mass starvation. Mosley recalled:

> At any earlier stage young Germans fresh from the army, and particularly from the SS regiments, were passionately European and entirely supported my advanced European ideas. I had heard form many of them long before I was free to travel, and had an insight into what they were then thinking which is perhaps almost unique.[35]

Yockey said of them:

> Hundreds of thousands of French, Walloon, Flemish, Dutch, Danish and Norwegian soldiers returned home after years of battle against Asiatic Russia and found themselves accused of "treason" and condemned to death or sentenced to years of imprisonment in concentration camps. (In Belgium alone, the Americans incarcerated 400,000 from a population of 8 million). For under the *Neuordnung* of the Washington regime, the struggle of Europeans for the survival and power of Europe was designated "treason".[36]

Among these war veterans were Hans-Ulrich Rudel, the German air ace, whose memoirs, *Stuka Pilot*, were published by Mosley's Euphorion publishing house with a foreword by Britain's air ace, Douglas Bader—both men having the distinction of a missing leg thanks to their military action.[37] These were the veterans that Yockey had also sought out, since the immediate aftermath of the war, when he was in Germany, ostensibly as a researcher for the 'war crimes' office at Wiesbaden.

---

35 Oswald Mosley, *My Life* ([1968] London: Black House Publishing, 2014), p. 465.

36 Yockey, *The Enemy of Europe* (Reedy, West Virginia: Liberty Bell Publications, 1981), p. 37.

37 Oswald Mosley, op. cit.

# Of Yearning Onward, Upward & Away[1]

Since 1951, the US State Department had been trying to 'pick up' Yockey's passport, due to his 'pro-Fascist' activities, 'but his exact whereabouts' over the past several years had not been known, FBI director J Edgar Hoover wrote to the director of Naval Intelligence in mid 1955. By the time of his capture in 1960, Yockey had garnered an impressive array of pseudonyms: Francis Downey, Franz, Frank Healy, Francis Jockey, Francis Parker, Edward Max Price, Edward Briceman, Ulick Varange, Franz Ludwig Yorck, Frank Yockey, Francis P Yokey, Richard Allen and others. The FBI was confused and wondered whether Yockey was also another enigmatic American named Maynard Nelson, or 'The Patriot who was writing inflammatory segregationist propaganda for the Southern states', or an elderly German named Frederick C. F. Weiss.[2]

Yockey's worldwide contacts were mainly via Gannon and later through Frederick Weiss. Yockey visited the contacts Gannon established throughout Europe. Certainly, their work in the European Contact Section of the Union Movement would have been important for this. Gannon wrote that through him, Yockey met the leaders of the MSI in Italy and was funded by Princess Pignatelli, a 'heroic noblewoman of Naples, devoted to the Duce, and who had tried to save his life'. He also introduced Yockey to the Italian artist and Fascist veteran Egidio Boschi. Other contacts were established through Gannon in Germany, Belgium, France and Austria. 'Also through me he visited Gerald

1 Johann Wolfgang von Goethe, *Faust: A Tragedy*, Scene XXIII.

2 FBI report, August 28, 1959, file no. 105–8229—3.

L. K. Smith of the Christian Nationalist Crusade in the US, but this was not a great success', as Yockey felt that the money at Smith's disposal 'was not being used to finance a world-revival of neo-fascism'. He was in turn 'resented' by Smith 'as an upstart'.[3]

## Gerald L. K. Smith

The attention of the FBI after the war was first drawn to Yockey when he addressed two meetings of Gerald L. K. Smith's Christian Nationalist Party in June 1950, in St Louis.[4] Yockey had sought out the Christian Nationalist Party, which had been founded there in 1947, on his return from Europe in 1949. According to an FBI report, Yockey called at the office there, expressing interest in Smith's magazine *The Cross and the Flag*.[5] However, the contact was not as informal as the FBI report implies. Anthony Gannon had put Yockey in contact with the Smith organisation, as he had with others.[6] Yockey met Smith at Gannon's request. Gannon states that at first they co-operated, the European Liberation Front and *The Proclamation of London* were mentioned favourably in Smith's magazine *The Cross and the Flag*, and Smith helped Yockey financially. Later, Smith 'took a dislike to Y and advised his followers to put him on the "drop-dead" list. I could never decide whether this was just another case of Y's being unable to sustain a relationship with "leader" types, or another case of intellectual jealousy'.[7] However, the letters between Gannon, Yockey and Arcand reveal details that Gannon must have forgotten three decades later.

Smith started his career as a pastor and became an aide to Huey P Long, Louisiana Senator and Governor. Smith was organiser of Long's populist 'Share the Wealth' campaign, which became a nationwide movement that threatened the Roosevelt regime and the whole system of oligarchy.[8] Long

3 Gannon to Stimely, July 13, 1980.

4 FBI report, July 7, 1960, p. 62, 105–8229—3.

5 FBI report, July 7, 1960, p. 71, 105–8229—3.

6 Gannon to Stimely, July 13, 1980.

7 Gannon to Stimely, March 1, 1981.

8 On Huey Long and Smith see: G. L. K. Smith, 'Huey P Long: A Summary of Greatness, Political Genius', American Martyr, 1975, http://www.thecrossandflag.com/smith_and_long.html.

was assassinated in Smith's presence in 1935, in the foyer of the Louisiana State Capitol Building, by Dr Carl Weise.[9] It is possible that the assassination was at the instigation of the Roosevelt political machine, as Long was likely to have been elected to the presidency in 1936. Smith, who delivered the oration at Long's funeral, the biggest in US history with an attendance of 250,000,[10] attempted to keep the Long organisation functioning, but it was captured by a Jewish political manipulator, Seymour Weiss.[11] Smith joined forces with Father Charles Coughlin and was associated with Charles Lindbergh, Congressman Clare E Hoffmann and other notable figures in the America First movement. Described by H. L. Mencken as the greatest American orator of all time, Smith was also condemned as America's leading 'anti-Semite' while nonetheless being able to win over even former opponent Senator Jack B Tenney, who became an avid supporter.[12]

In 1942, Smith founded the Christian Nationalist Crusade (which the FBI report erroneously refers to as the 'Christian Democrats') and *The Cross and the Flag*. Unlike much of the Right, Smith had considerable resources. At Eureka Springs, Arkansas, he built a 20-metre-high statue, 'Christ of the Ozarks', staged an annual 'Passion Play' and built a replica of ancient Jerusalem, in the expectation that one day there would not be much left of the Christian holy places in Israel.[13] The FBI referred to no 'identifiable information' concerning the 'Christian Democrats', perhaps because they had the name wrong.[14] This might have been remedied had they consulted their files on Gerald L. K. Smith.[15]

---

9 G. L. K. Smith, *Besieged Patriot* (Eureka Springs: Christian Nationalist Crusade, 1978), pp. 120–121, 126.

10 G. L. K. Smith, ibid., pp. 121–125.
See also: http://thecrossandflag.com/.

11 Gerald L. K. Smith, 'Long', Section 5, 'The Second Louisiana Purchase', http://www.thecrossandflag.com/smith_and_long.html#here.

12 See Gerald L. K. Smith, *Besieged Patriot* (Eureka Springs, Arkansas: Christian Nationalist Crusade, 1978).

13 'The Great Passion Play', http://www.greatpassionplay.org/christ-of-the-ozarks.html.

14 FBI report, February 20, 1956, p. 8, file no. 105–8229 — 2.

15 'Gerald L. K. Smith', FBI file # 62–43818.

Yockey worked with the Smith organisation for several months. He spoke at a meeting of the Christian Nationalist Party on June 13, 1950, where other speakers included Don Lohbeck, party candidate for Congress of the 11th Missouri Congressional District, who chaired the meeting, and John W Hamilton, Senate candidate for Missouri. Yockey's talk was on the activities of the political underground in France, Germany, England and Belgium.[16] Yockey spoke on the injustice of the war crimes trials.[17]

He spoke at another meeting on June 29, where he was billed as representing the European Liberation Front, speaking on the subject, 'Is Europe Dead?', according to a Christian Nationalist Party flyer advertising the event. He condemned the war crimes trials during which 'thousands of White Christian Germans' had been convicted before being tried. John W Hamilton followed the theme by stating that Americans should be more concerned at the fate of the Germans than of Koreans.[18] This indicates a more unorthodox approach to politics by Hamilton. Hamilton, publisher of the long-running *White Sentinel* and head of the National Citizens' Protective Association (a relatively influential pro-segregationist lobby founded in 1951) was friends with Yockey.[19]

Yockey had great hopes for Smith as the 'leader' of the 'Idea'. He had the money, the resources and a following that had carried over from the pre-war days.

Gannon and the Canadian fascist leader Arcand had noted Smith's ideological simplicity, Gannon commenting that Smith et al 'are fascists' but wished to avoid the smears. Gannon referred to American politics as 'notoriously immature'.[20] The 'Ten Principles of Christian Nationalism' upon which the Christian Nationalist Party and Christian Nationalist Crusade were founded included: 'Safeguard American liberty against the menace of bureaucratic

16 FBI Memorandum, July 13, 1960, 105–8229—3.

17 FBI Memorandum, July 13, 1960, 105–8229—3.

18 FBI Memorandum, July 13, 1960, p. 2, 105–8229—3.

19 Douglas T Kaye to Bolton, April 13, 2014.

20 Gannon to Arcand, March 6, 1950, Arcand collection, Archives Canada, vol. 1, file no. 1.

fascism.'[21] Gannon commented to Arcand that the Christian Nationalist ideology (indeed, that of much of the American 'Right' to the present day) is hopeless in its terminology; 'it is the terminology of the Enemy, and only propagates the ideas of the Enemy — Jewish "Gestapo", "Bureaucratic Fascism", etc. Why not "Jewish GPU or NKVD", "Bureaucratic Socialism or communism", etc?'[22] Gannon quoted Smith's late mentor, Huey Long, saying 'when Fascism comes to America we will call it Democracy'. Gannon noted the factionalism that had plagued American nationalists before the war, which had prevented them from really challenging 'the arch-Devil' Roosevelt. He had requested that Smith stock *Imperium* and *The Proclamation*.[23] Gannon commented that Yockey was in the USA and hoping to contact Smith.[24]

Several months later, writing to Arcand, Yockey stated that he had spoken at the Christian Nationalist convention in Los Angeles and could see why Arcand 'did not feel any urge to go'. The American nationalist movement in that form and under that leadership was 'devoid of a future'. Yockey seemed to have had briefly a good working accord with Don Lohbeck, head of the Christian Nationalist Party. They were planning a 'World News Service' but this and other publishing activities were not politics: 'At most they are useful adjuncts to politics.'[25] Here, we get an insight into Yockey's thinking on what constitutes action. Willis Carto suggested that the combination of philosopher and man of action is a rarity and Yockey was perhaps no exception.[26] However, Yockey, unlike many of the 'Right' the world over, past and present, was fully aware that writing and publishing were not of themselves politics. Militant, hierarchical organisation, overt and covert, was required. Yockey did not eschew speaking to the masses and street-level agitation. The ELF was intended as an 'Order' guiding mass movements, as indicated by the 'Italo-English convention'.

---

21 Gerald L. K. Smith, 'Foreword', *Besieged Patriot* (Eureka Springs, Christian Nationalist Crusade, 1978), p. 10.

22 Gannon to Arcand, November 6, 1950, p. 3; Arcand collection, Archives Canada, vol. 1, file no. 1.

23 Gannon to Arcand, March 6, 1950, op. cit.

24 Gannon to Arcand, March 30, 1950, Archives Canada.

25 Yockey to Arcand, July 18, 1950, p. 1, Archives Canada.

26 Willis Carto, 'Introduction', *Imperium* (Sausalito: Noontide Press, 1969), xiii.

Yockey met Smith and his wife Elna with Lohbeck at lunch, where Smith said he had not read *Imperium* or *The Proclamation*. As with the Mosley debacle, it must have been a bitter blow, not to Yockey's ego but to his hopes for the 'Idea'. Lohbeck told him that Smith 'reads nothing'. Yockey wrote to Arcand that he had given Smith a short memorandum

> … outlining the offer which I was bringing to him to form a supra-national, supra-continental white Imperialist organization, with him as leader, setting forth the advantages to his organization and to mine. He was to be leader and was to furnish financial assistance to the European organizations for the immediate future, until the people come out of hiding and a large enough effort can be made to attract the attention of all Europe in spite of the conspiracy of silence on the part of the press.[27]

Yockey said that Smith did not even care to discuss the proposals with him, 'for reasons unknown'. Realistically, Smith would not have had an iota of understanding for Yockey's doctrines and objectives, any more than Arnold Leese. This is not to disparage Smith; he, like Leese, was working on another level. What is surprising is that at the Christian Nationalist convention, despite the ungracious introduction by Smith to Yockey, it was Yockey, and no other, who received a standing ovation from the plain-thinking, old-time Christians. Yockey stated that when Smith introduced him to speak at the convention, Smith claimed he did not know what Yockey was going to say and that they had only just met. Gannon stated to Arcand that Yockey had been invited to speak at the Christian Nationalist Party convention at Los Angeles at the party's expense. The 'pompous, disassociating remarks' with which Smith introduced Yockey, stating that they had just met and that he did not know what Yockey was going to say, were lies. 'Smith had been provided a draft of V's speech through Lohbeck.' Nonetheless, Yockey's speech was the success of the convention.[28]

The first part of Yockey's speech was on the brutality of the American occupation regime in Europe and how the American flag and uniform had

---

27 Yockey to Arcand, July 18, 1950, ibid.

28 Gannon to Arcand, November 6, 1950, Arcand collection, Archives Canada, vol. 1, file no. 1.

become the hated symbols of Jewry to Europeans. The second part of the speech was on 'the glorious past of the true American type' and that this must rise again. The third part welded the interests of the 'true America' and the 'true Europe' in the fight for liberation from 'jewry, democracy, class-war, finance-capitalism, social degeneration, liberalism and the ethical syphilis of Hollywood'. Yockey concluded with a call for America not to fight any war other than against Jewish domination 'and the demand for unlimited white Imperialism, the natural and organic way of living of the white race, the spirit of the Teutonic knights and of the Vikings'. Of the approximately 30 speakers, only Yockey received a spontaneous standing ovation.[29]

Smith responded with an attack on Yockey, saying that Americans love democracy and he would not unite with Yockey in fighting Jewry or defending Western civilization. The focus of the convention was on religion.[30] Smith refused to allow Yockey to display the ELF flag,[31] which Yockey had made especially for the occasion and of which he was particularly proud; it was subsequently stolen there.

Another particularly annoying individual associated with Smith, was Ernest F Elmhurst. He was indicted by a grand jury for sedition in 1944, along with other Nationalists who tried to keep the USA out of the war, including Pelley. In 1938, Pelley had introduced and published Elmhurst's book, *The World Hoax*, a series of biographies on mostly Jewish Bolsheviks.[32] Elmhurst was associated with many organisations prior to World War II and was a guest at the international congress of the National Socialist news agency, World Service, in Germany in 1937.

When Yockey had met Elmhurst, the latter had spoken with the political seriousness of a 'European' as contrasted to an 'American'. Elmhurst regarded Smith as a charlatan and said that Smith would not be interested in Yockey's proposals for co-operation as they included a financial commitment without a 'threefold return'. However, on the last day of the Christian Nationalist

29 Varange to Arcand, July 28, 1950, p. 1, Arcand collection, Archives Canada, vol. 1, file no. 1.

30 Varange to Arcand, July 28, 1950, ibid.

31 Varange to Arcand, July 28, 1950, ibid., p. 2.

32 E. F. Elmhurst, *The World Hoax* (Asheville, N.C.: Pelley Publishers, 1938).

convention he told Smith and Lohbeck that Yockey was an impostor and 'not the creator of *Imperium*'. This undermined Yockey's good working relationship with Lohbeck, whose Christian Nationalist Party was interested in serious politics and who 'had a streak of European consciousness in him'. Yockey regarded Elmhurst as having a 'suspicion-mania', as he had warned Yockey he considered others at the convention to be 'agents of the enemy'. Yockey understood this 'morbid suspicion' as Elmhurst had 'suffered long and hard persecution', and living in New York believed that Jews were constantly trying to poison him.[33]

Yockey considered Smith's beliefs to be sincere, but not his actions. He thought firstly of his own comfort and that of his wife, in Yockey's view, and 'lacks entirely what we call in Europe the heroic world-outlook'. Smith had told the convention audience he did not live in St Louis because there had been a plot to kill him and therefore his mother would not be able to visit him, nor would he and Mrs Smith be able to live in 'peace and quiet'. The final four minutes of Smith's speech were devoted to his digestive system and his not needing laxatives. Smith's information service was sound but there was no political potential.[34]

Lohbeck, on the other hand, was quite different and had come under the influence of *Imperium* such as Smith never could 'because the intellectual basis is not there'. Yockey had persuaded Lohbeck to carry the fight onto the streets of St Louis and leave the safety of the convention halls. Although Gannon stated that Yockey did not speak in England, the assumption that Yockey was an uninspiring speaker is incorrect. While still a college student, as we have seen, he was regarded as an effective speaker among American Nationalists. He spoke in Italy and he spoke at the Smith convention to a standing ovation. While in the USA in 1950 he also spoke at Pershing Square, in the centre of Los Angeles — usually the speaking abode of Communists. With 'Kurts of New York', they spoke on 'Communism, Jews and the Korean war'. Yockey's speaking style must have been impressive to hold a street audience. Jews 'and their *guks* who tried to intervene were silenced by the audience'. *Guk* was the word Yockey used to describe anyone not of the white race

33 Varange to Arcand, July 28, 1950, op. cit., p. 2.

34 Varange to Arcand, July 28, 1950, ibid.

or Western civilization; the Yockeyan equivalent of the Jews' word for Gentile: *goy*. It was the word used by American soldiers to designate all Koreans, north and south. Yockey intended the word to be widely used in all languages.[35]

'Kurts of New York' was likely to be C Daniel Kurts, leader of the Queens, New York section of Father Coughlin's Christian Front before the war. Kurts attempted to revive the Christian Front immediately after the war, holding an open-air meeting in New York in October 1945, which included Elmhurst and German-American activist Kurt Mertig.[36]

Elmhurst and Smith wrote disparaging letters about Yockey to Gannon. Gannon commented to Arcand that the letters made him feel 'positively ill'. While Gannon was not surprised at the attitude of Leese, who would jeopardise any person or cause for the sake of a personal whim or dislike, he was disappointed with Smith's reaction. Like Leese, however, Smith did not have the intellectual acumen, according to Gannon. By European standards, his ideas were 'childish and crude — a composite of chauvinism, economic liberalism and individualism, the whole being varnished over with a coat of anti-Jewism'. Gannon and Yockey, conversely, saw Arcand as a 'European Fascist' and not as a North American. He had understood and, more importantly, 'felt' *Imperium* from the start.[37] Indeed, Arcand had come from the French milieu of Quebec and was steeped in Franco-Catholicism. Like Yockey, he was a man of depth and very much a man of action, having inspired a mass movement before the war and still boasting a significant following. His programme of 'National Corporatism' was a detailed exposition of Canadian fas-

---

35 Varange to Arcand, July 28, 1950, ibid.
The now widely-used word *gook*, employed by American troops in Vietnam, is perhaps derived from *guk*, which was also used by Americans in the Philippines as far back as 1920.

36 *American Jewish Year Book 1946-47* (New York: American Jewish Committee), pp. 179–180. Elmhurst and Mertig were jailed for 6 months in 1946 for having distributed anti-Semitic material (on Jewish ritual murder) at the meeting. Mertig, head of the pre- and post-war Citizens' Protective League, campaigning for German-American rights and the alleviation of conditions in post-war Germany, founded the long-running National Renaissance Party in 1949, with which Yockey was briefly associated.

37 Gannon to Arcand, November 6, 1950, p. 2, Arcand collection, Archives Canada, vol. 1, file no. 1.

cism with a Catholic inspiration. It is little wonder that between Arcand and Yockey there was not the discord or clash of egos that often plagued Yockey's work with others of lesser character.

If matters seemed to be promising with Lohbeck, who was, like Yockey, a classical pianist, this was short-lived. Lohbeck promised to advertise *Imperium* and *The Proclamation* in *The Cross and The Flag*, of which he was editor. He would use the money from sales to print and distribute an American edition of *Imperium*. Lohbeck also promised to help with cheap printing of *Frontfighter* and ELF leaflets and posters. This came to nothing. Elmhurst had spoken to Yockey at length and stated that Lohbeck and Smith were 'fortune-hunters and charlatans', then went to Smith and Lohbeck claiming this was what Yockey had said about them. Despite, or because of, the success of Yockey's speech at the convention, it was totally ignored in *The Cross and the Flag*, the contents of which Gannon regarded as less than 'baby-stuff'.[38]

In 1953, Lohbeck was replaced as editor of *The Cross and The Flag*. Just a few months after Yockey's death in 1960, Lohbeck was the target of a State investigation into his background. He had been appointed by New Mexico governor John Burroughs as chairman of the governor's advisory committee on atomic affairs. Bizarrely, it was Lohbeck's former colleague, Kenneth Goff,[39] head of the Soldiers of the Cross and a close associate of Smith's, who publicly raised Lohbeck's background and threatened to petition for a grand jury investigation unless Lohbeck was removed.[40] Such was the milieu in which Yockey had attempted to work in 1950.

## Senator Joseph McCarthy

Yockey 'approved' of senators Robert Taft, an old-time American isolationist, and Joseph McCarthy, 'with the usual reservations'. He regarded McCarthy

38 Gannon to Arcand, November 6, 1950, p. 2, vol. 1, file no. 1, Arcand collection, archives Canada.

39 Goff and Lohbeck had been arrested and each fined $100 in 1947 for placing placards outside the Russian embassy in Washington D.C.

40 'Oliver Kenneth Goff, Correlation summary', FBI HQ Main file no. 62–80382, September 1, 1964, p. 39.

as a 'shoot-to-kill' politician.[41] Although after the war Yockey had given up hope of an 'American Nationalist revolution', many of the radical Right saw McCarthy as a figure around which an American nationalist revival might occur. McCarthy, even before his famous Senate investigations into communist and Soviet subversion and espionage, had made a name among nationalists for his forceful criticism of American-run war crimes trials in Germany in 1949. As an anti-communist crusader, McCarthy's name was appropriated by James Madole, who formed a front in 1954, 'Patriots for McCarthy', for the 'neo-Nazi' National Renaissance Party.[42]

In 1952, McCarthy's office requested that Yockey write a speech for the Senator. Yockey stated of this:

> I called on Patterson[43] who arranged an appointment for me with Senator McCarthy for Saturday P.M. He wanted me to write a speech for him, based on a whole batch, a huge corpus of material, to have it ready by Monday. There are still several things to settle with him but it looks as though I have a job. Really quite unbelievable that it should be this particular job.[44]

Gannon is definite that Yockey and McCarthy met.[45] The association between Yockey and McCarthy drew the attention of the FBI but the bureau considered the speech Yockey wrote, 'America's Two Ways of Waging War',[46] to be the work of McCarthy and did not know the precise character of the association. This seems indicative of the inept character of the FBI in these matters: the FBI wondered whether Yockey was actually Weiss and sundry other very unlikely individuals but could not discern that the McCarthy speech is replete with Yockey's style. Although McCarthy did not deliver the speech, its theme of 'non-win' wars was taken up by the American conservative movement, par-

41 Gannon to Stimely, November 24, 1981.

42 'National Renaissance Party', FBI report, NY 105–6112, November 5, 1954, p. 7.

43 Perry Patterson, legal counsel to the conservative-orientated *Washington Times Herald* and a friend of Yockey's from law school days. (For the latter, Stimely to Gannon, February 28, 1982).

44 Yockey letter, February 5, 1952, cited by Stimely to Gannon, 'More Questions on Francis Parker Yockey', # 10, ca. December 1981.

45 Gannon to Stimely, March 31, 1982.

46 Yockey, 'America's Two Ways of Waging War', February 1952.

ticularly by The John Birch Society and similar organisations, and became a major talking point in subsequent decades. It was a theme that McCarthy had just addressed in his book on US Secretary of Defense George C Marshall, based on a 60,000 word speech delivered in 1951.[47] Perhaps the large corpus of material at McCarthy's office from which Yockey was to draft the speech was from this book?

The speech refers to the US rulers, the 'inner enemy', 'leading America to a defeat' in the Korean war. 'America's two ways of waging war' were the total war unleashed against the Third Reich, compared with the compromise in fighting communism in Korea, and in 'the Chinese war'. In contrast to US aims in World War II, the US administration spoke of merely containing communism to the North and of preventing its escalation further a field. He alludes to the sacking of General Douglas MacArthur, another *cause celebre* of the right, for his opposition to Washington's 'no-win' policy. Yockey stated that such a 'no-win' war is being fought under the direction of the United Nations Organisation and under the UN flag; which has remained a major concern of the American conservative Right.

Halfway through the speech, Yockey reverted to simplified philosophical concepts, in stating:

> Fellow Americans, God made this world as it is and in its ever-recurring forms we dimly perceive his divine plan. World-history, in which America is now caught up, involved for its very life in the tempest of events, is the history of NATIONS. The units of history are NATIONS. Those individuals who lead those nations owe their primary duty to that nation whose destiny God has placed temporarily in their hand. It is not allowed to a ruler to sacrifice his people on the battlefield to abstract aims like United Nations of some kind or other, like humanitarian principles of one kind or another; it is the duty of every government of every form to serve the national interests, and no government has the right to expend one single soldier for any other purpose.

Yockey ended with a characteristic reference to Western civilization and the 'divine plan', and his idiosyncratic use of lower case when citing the name of Secretary of State Dean Acheson:

---

47 Joseph R McCarthy, *America's Retreat from Victory: The Story of George Cartlett Marshall* ([1951] Boston: Western Islands, 1965).

> It is not a part of the divine plan that a great superpersonal force working for order and creativeness in the world, like the Western Civilization, is to be overcome by an onslaught of barbarians against an America weakened by corruption and betrayed by a horde of achesons.

The USA would assume its place in the world as the leader of Western Civilization and defeat the outer and inner enemies. Of course, by that time Yockey considered that the USA was the enemy of Western Civilization and conversely to the theme of the speech preferred Soviet occupation of Europe to American. However, McCarthy represented the resurgence of healthy forces and perhaps these could coalesce around the Senator's anti-Communist crusade. It was a means to an end. However, McCarthy was soon destroyed by the 'inner enemy'; not by 'Communists' or 'Soviet agents' but by those representing the wealthiest and most powerful interests led by the likes of international banker Herbert Lehman in the Senate, *The Washington Post*, Anti-Defamation League, Goldman Sachs banker Sidney Weinberg's Business Advisory Council, et al.[48]

Gannon states that Yockey had a 'considerable relationship' with McCarthy 'and found him to be well-informed on the Culture-distorters issue'. He also had 'some considerable respect' for the abilities of Richard Nixon, regarding Nixon's role in exposing State Department eminence Alger Hiss as a Soviet agent (albeit one who seemed to have most of his mentors in the upper echelons of Washington). Yockey felt that the 'Culture-distorters' would never forgive Nixon for ending the meteoric career of Hiss, 'which they never did'.[49]

---

48 K. R. Bolton, 'Joe McCarthy's Real Enemies', *The Occidental Quarterly*, Vol. 10, No. 4, Winter 2010–2011, pp. 75–102; http://toqonline.com/archives/v10n4/TOQv10n4Bolton.pdf.

49 Gannon to Stimely, February 15, 1982.
Despite the pervasive presence of Henry Kissinger, Nixon probably shaped his attitude on Jews at an early stage of his political career, when they were conspicuous among Soviet agents and in the Communist Party. However, by the time he was President and working for US-Soviet détente, Jews had become vociferously anti-Soviet, especially in agitation for increased Jewish emigration from the USSR to the USA and Israel. Nixon commented to Kissinger, with the latter taking the role of a fawning Court Jew, that if Jews sabotaged his efforts he would publicly expose them: 'Let me say, Henry, it's gonna be the worst thing that happened to Jews in American history. I won't mind one goddamn but to have a little anti-Semitism if it's on that issue. They put the Jewish interest above

## Maurice Bardèche

Maurice Bardèche, the post-war apologist for wartime 'collaboration' during the German occupation of France and exponent of 'Fascist socialism' and European unity, met Yockey in 1950. Yockey had read Bardèche's pioneering book critiquing the Nuremberg trials and had sent Bardèche *Imperium*. In his novel *Suzanne in the Slums*, Bardèche makes light of Yockey as an odd American trying to recruit for a vague plan of European liberation. Bardèche described Yockey as someone who drank too much coffee, had a bladder problem and was overly opinionated and humourless. Bardèche had only met Yockey once. Yockey seems to have left those he met with widely divergent opinions as to his character but usually they were favourable. Those who knew him well attest to his great sense of humour, although he often became mischievous to his own detriment.

Bardèche later regretted not having given Yockey the credit he deserved; the result of not really knowing him. Bardèche, whose brother-in-law and literary colleague, Robert Brasillach,[50] had been executed for 'collaboration' with the Germans, seemed impatient with people. In this respect, Yockey and Bardèche were very much alike. Bardèche relates that he sent those who irritated him on to others. He wrote of Yockey:

> One of these was the original Ulick Varange that I repent of having spoken with in lightness, in *Suzanne in the Slums*, while I did not know his tragic destiny. He was an American in his thirties called Yockey, who had worked as librarian of the public prosecutor at the Nuremberg trials.[51] He came to see me because

---

America's interest and it's about goddamn time that the Jew in America realizes he's an American first and a Jew second.' Nixon to Kissinger, Oval Office tapes, April 19, 1973. Of Nixon aide Leonard Garment: 'Goddamn his Jewish soul!' On appointments: 'No Jews. We are adamant when I say no Jews.' June 14, 1973, speaking to presidential counsellor Anne Armstrong. See: Elspeth Reeve, 'Some newly uncovered Nixon comments on the subjects of Jews and Black people', August 21, 2013; http://www.thewire.com/politics/2013/08/some-new-comments-richard-nixon-subject-jews-and-blacks/68595/.

50 Bardèche and Brasillach co-authored *The History of Cinema*, published in 1935, which long remained a seminal work on the subject.

51 Bardèche had misunderstood Yockey's role as a researcher with the Wiesbaden war crimes commission. Brasillach was executed for 'collaborationism'. Bardèche, although suspected and briefly jailed, had remained aloof from politics during the war, and had

> of my book on the [Nuremberg] trial.[52] He knew many things, too many things and forwarded me the documents prepared by the defense for use by Ohlendorf and several other defendants. These documents gave a different version than the charge. He had written a book in two volumes entitled *Imperium* that appeared in London in 1948. This testament was both a critical ideology of the twentieth century and a statement of what the author called Cultural Vitalism. The book quite fitted the ideas that I developed in my book on the Nuremberg trials by giving them more scope and unity and I had found [*Imperium*] so remarkable that I had even started a translation. Yockey had not found a publisher in France. Neither had he found political collaborators for the kind of world organization he wanted. He returned to the United States. [...] I do not know the vicissitudes of the hunt for him and his persecution. I only know that Yockey's enemies made him out to be insane to shut him up. He committed suicide, they say...[53]

In 1982, Bardèche provided Keith Stimely with a detailed memoir on Yockey, whom he first met in the winter of 1950/1951, when representing several French groups on the presidium of the European Social Movement. Yockey, as Ulick Varange, had entered into correspondence with Bardèche in connection with the latter's first book on the Nuremberg trials. He had sent Bardèche,

> a certain number of extremely valuable documents coming from archives of which he had had knowledge and which were intended for the headquarters of General McCloy, concerning the requests for clemency for a certain number of persons condemned by the International Military Tribunal. I made use of that documentation in the second book that I did on the Nuremberg Trial under the title *Nuremberg II or the Counterfeiters*.[54]

---

his sentence commuted by President Coty, although he was barred from the teaching profession. After the war he avidly condemned the crimes perpetrated by the Allies and the 'Liberators' and upheld Fascism until his death in 1998. He was a co-founder with Mosley and others of the European Social Movement in 1951. In 1952 he founded the journal *Défense de l'Occident*, and established a publishing house, Les Sept Couleurs.

52 Maurice Bardèche, *Nuremberg or the Promised Land* (Paris: Les Sept Cpouleus, 1948. Online: http://vho.org/aaargh/fran/livres7/BARDECHEnureng.pdf.

53 Maurice Bardèche, *Souvenirs* (Editions du Pilon, 2007), p. 208.

54 Bardèche to Stimely, 'Note sur F. P. Yockey', 1982.

> At the same time Varange had sent me his book entitled *Imperium* which interested me a great deal and to such a point that I began the translation of it which is still in my files.
>
> At the time of his visit to Paris Varange did not at any time mention to me that he himself had founded a European movement under the title European Liberation Front. He simply asked me to put him in contact with the most important nationalist groups in France and it was at that time that I put him in contact with René Binet who led a small, very active movement.[55]

The meeting took place between Yockey and Binet[56] at Bardèche's home, which he relates in his novel *Suzanne in the Slums*. Bardèche regarded Yockey's brilliance to be handicapped by an unrealistic expectation of an impending liberation of Europe, a 'utopian' outlook that Bardèche said was shared by others present at that meeting; in particular by Binet, who was also said to be difficult to work with. Bardèche states that the discussion between Yockey and Binet was 'passionate and violent', neither were open to compromise, and Bardèche stayed out of trying to arbitrate.[57] What the disagreement was is not stated.

What can be seen in Bardèche's first book on Nuremberg, which he concludes with a call for the unity of Europe and a rejection of both Sovietism and American democracy, is a great deal of similarity between his thoughts and Yockey's. Like Yockey, Bardèche did not believe that the Germans, having been condemned to near-extinction, should suddenly fall in line behind the USA to oppose the USSR in the name of 'democracy':

> And today even those who wrote this verdict turn toward German youth: "Germans, good Germans," they say to them, "don't you like the cause of Freedom? Aren't you ready to defend the world with us against Bolshevik

55 Bardèche to Stimely, 'Note sur F. P. Yockey', ibid.

56 René Binet (1913–1957) had started in politics as a Communist and was soon arrested when the Germans occupied France. He converted to National Socialism and served with the French SS Charlemagne Division during the war. He founded *Combattant européen* in 1946 and other journals and organisations. In 1951 he accompanied Bardèche to Malmö, Sweden, and participated in founding the European Social Movement. However, he soon broke from this to establish the European New Order, intended to be more radical in its racial outlook, with Gaston-Armand Armaudruz of Zurich, who continues to publish *Courrier du Continent* as the 'bulletin du Nouvel Ordre Européen'.

57 Bardèche to Stimely, 'Note sur F. P. Yockey', op. cit.

barbarity? Germans, young Germans, would you not look good on long Sherman tanks, like dark gods of combat?" … It is necessary to know what one wants. We will not fight for clouds. Nor will the Germans apparently. The antidote for Bolshevism has borne a name in history. Let us cease to pronounce this name with fear and to look at this flag with horror. … We are sure to be submerged if a powerful architecture does not make of the European peninsula an impregnable citadel, a kind of Gibraltar for the white race of the Occident. … We must address ourselves to the new Germany and be trustworthy and honest in doing so. Our first task is to give up this falsification of history which we intend to impose. It is not true that Germany is responsible for this war: the responsibility of the warmongers in England and France is at least as heavy as the responsibility of Hitler. It is not true that the National-Socialist Party was a criminal conspiracy: it was a party of militants similar to other parties of militants in power, it was obliged to resort to force to defend its work and its effectiveness, as in dramatic circumstances all parties do which believe themselves to be in charge of the future of a great mission. It is not true that the Germans were "monsters": the nations which did not hesitate to buy their victory with the lives of 2,650,000 German civilians, that is, with 2,650,000 lives of German workmen, old men, women and children, do not have the right to direct this reproach at them. A dishonest investigation and a gigantic propaganda campaign have been able to deceive our consciences for a while. But the day will come when these same enemies of Germany may find it in their interest to restore the facts… Let us not forget that what we have destroyed and condemned was, not only for the Germans but also for millions of men throughout the Occident, the only durable solution to the dilemma of the modern world, the only manner of escaping capitalist slavery without accepting Soviet slavery. … Because the danger of war lies not in the existence of States which are powerful and differently polarized like the United States and Soviet Russia; it lies on the contrary in the existence of weak zones open to competition between these two great powers, or, in other words, the danger of war increases with the possibilities of interference; war will be caused by agents from abroad who work among us. If, on the contrary, an Occidental block could be established, living by its own means as rigidly closed to American influence as to Communist influence, this neutral block, this impermeable citadel would be a factor for peace and perhaps for interaction. …[58]

58 Bardèche, *Nuremberg or the Promised Land*, op. cit., pp. 82–84.

## Princess Maria Pignatelli

Meeting Maurice Bardèche and René Binet in France, Yockey proceeded to Italy, again through the contacts of Gannon, and with the funding of a remarkable fascist woman, Princess Maria Pignatelli.[59]

In October 1951, Yockey was in Naples, writing in a letter that he was 'organizing the foreign part of a fascist convention to be held 25–28 October'.[60] This 'Fascist convention' was organised by the Movimento Italiano Femminile Fede e Famiglia (Italian Women's Movement of Faith and Family, MIF). Monsignor Silverio Mattei and Princess Maria Pignatelli di Cerchiara di Calabria had founded this on October 28, 1946 — the anniversary of the Fascist March on Rome. The aims of MIF were to assist political prisoners after World War II morally, materially and legally. Gift packs were provided to prisoners and fugitives and volunteers were assisted, particularly with travel to Latin America, and often with Vatican help. Assistance was also given to find employment or secure the reinstatement of positions to Fascist veterans.

For the first several years, the MIF operated clandestinely. Then on January 1, 1948, a magazine was established, *Donne d'Italia* ('Women of Italy'), which opened its columns to writers and journalists who had remained loyal to Fascism.

Although the MIF is considered the women's auxiliary of the Movimento Sociale Italiano (MSI), which was founded in December 1946 by ex-officials of the Salò Republic (Italian Social Republic), a formal relationship between the two did not exist until 1952. The Salò Republic was established in 1943 after Mussolini's daring rescue by German paratroopers commanded by Otto Skorzeny. It was in the last two years of the war that Mussolini's redoubt pursued an uncompromising programme of fascism, including what Norling calls 'Fascism's unstoppable march towards Europeism'. The radicalised ideologues of the Salò Republic saw the chauvinism of the past as an error that had driven Europe to the abyss. Norling states that the Salò Republic was the first European state to include 'Europeism' in its governing programme, the foundation of which was the 'Verona Manifesto' of November 15, 1943. The

59 Gannon to Stimely, July 13, 1980, op. cit.

60 FBI report, August 7, 1954, p. 12, file no. 105–8229 — 2.

8th point of the manifesto referred to a foreign policy that takes account of 'the setting up of a European community, federating all nations' that are fighting against plutocracy and capitalism. The programme also called for a joint colonial policy in Africa.[61] In 1944, The Salò Republic's ministry of foreign affairs drafted a plan for a 'European Social Republics Union'.[62] Mussolini, during his last great public appearance in Milan on December 16, 1944, stated that 'each nation should join the European community as a well defined entity, to prevent that community from sinking into socialist internationalism or vegetate in the generic and equivocal cosmopolitanism of a Jewish and Masonic brand'.[63]

The MSI, in the radical spirit of the Salò Republic, declared: 'There are three solutions — Russia, the United States or the MSI.'[64] With such a legacy, Yockey's ideas would fall on ground more fertile — the very Mother-soil of Europe — than that of Britain or the USA.

Princess Pignatelli had been a Fascist partisan operating behind enemy lines when the Fascist redoubt of the Salò Republic had been established in 1943. She led a female squad within the Servizi Speciali, the 'Silver She-Wolves'. This was formed by girls younger than 18 on the naïve assumption that they would not be executed if captured. However, some died under torture.[65] The Princess's husband, Valerio Pignatelli, headed the Guardie ai Labari, organized to undertake guerrilla warfare in whatever parts of Italy were under Allied occupation.[66] His wife, helped by priests and monks, made an arduous journey to reach German lines with plans to kidnap the philosopher Croce, in reprisal for the murder of Fascist philosopher Giovanni Gentile. Although captured she escaped,[67] otherwise execution would have been a likely outcome.

---

61 Erik Norling, *Revolutionary Fascism* (Lisbon: Finis Mundi Press, 2011), pp. 69–70.

62 Norling, ibid., p. 70.

63 Norling, ibid., p. 71.

64 Roger Eatwell, *Fascism: A History* (London: Vintage, 1996), p. 199.

65 See 'The Fascist Social Republic of Italy', Axis History Forum, http://forum.axishistory.com/viewtopic.php?t=46245.

66 Perry Biddiscombe, *The SS Hunter Battalions: The Hidden History of the Nazi Resistance Movement* (Gloucesterhire: The History Press, 2006), 'Italia Liberata/Italia Invada'.

67 Perry Biddiscombe, ibid.

The MIF attached importance to the cultivation of relations with groups of the Nationalist Right throughout the world and this was significant both for securing contacts to assist Italian fugitives and because the MIF was committed to a worldwide 'Fascist' resurgence. Yockey's responsibility for liaising with such groups worldwide in the organisation of the MIF's 1951 congress was significant.

At an 'unofficial level' there had been the 'weaving of a network of political relations with right-wing movements in many countries (Argentina, Brazil, Paraguay, but also Egypt, Lebanon, West Germany, Sweden)'. Princess Pignatelli in particular had maintained contacts with affiliates of the European Social Movement and its leaders, including veteran Swedish Fascist Per Engdahl, and the movement's German representative, Karl-Heinz Priester. Contacts with Franco's Spain were also frequent.[68]

## Egidio Boschi

In November 1951, it was reported with some urgency that Yockey was in Canada.[69] However, authorities could not determine when or if he had left, or whether he had returned to the USA.[70]

He had travelled to Canada with the artist Professor Egidio Boschi.[71] Yockey had met Boschi at the congress of the Movimento Italiano Femminile in Naples and Boschi regarded *Imperium* as his 'bible'.[72] Gannon states that he arranged for Yockey to meet Boschi, 'a veteran of the March on Rome, who had lived for 30 years in Argentina and Chile, playing an active role in the national fascist movements there',[73] and a 'close comrade' of Argentine

---

68 M. Eleanora Landini, 'Between Politics and Assistance: The "Black Aid" of the Italian Women's Movement, 1946–1956', Ph.D. thesis, Italy. 10.

69 FBI radiogram, 'urgent', November 28, 1951, file 105–8229 — 1.

70 FBI telegram, 'urgent', November 25, 1951, file 105–8229 — 1.

71 FBI telegram, 'urgent', November 25, 1951, ibid.

72 FBI report, September 26, 1952, p. 3;

73 Gannon to Stimely, July 13, 1980.

Fascist Gutierrez Herrera.[74] Indeed, Boschi seems to have joined the ELF, as indicated by his signing letters with the Front's salutation 'Front Hail!'.[75]

Although Yockey was not wanted by the FBI at this stage, there was a flurry of memoranda between the FBI, CIA and State Department, the latter wanting to detain Yockey for the purpose of confiscating his passport. The FBI was generally a step or two behind Yockey even when he visited the USA.[76] Yockey's sister, Vinette, had been visited in Chicago by Miles E Briggs, an agent of the US State Department. She had been 'very uncooperative', stated that her bother was 'out of town' and would not furnish details.[77]

Yockey's association with Boschi in Canada was of particular interest to the US. On March 24, 1952, Boschi had gone to the US Consulate in Montreal to obtain a non-immigrant visa but had been refused on the grounds that his admission 'would be prejudicial to the interests of the United States'.[78] In 1951, a conversation had been overheard and reported to the FBI regarding Boschi. The Consul General of the USA, in Montreal, Canada, conveyed the following to the FBI, showing that the noted artist had been a spy for the Axis in Chile during World War II:

> On November 7, 1951 _____ overheard a conversation between two men, later learned to be the two mentioned above [Yockey and Boschi]. The gist of the conversation was that they had been spies for the Nazis and Fascists during World War II. Mr Boschi stated that he was an artist and that during the war he had a rooming house in Santiago de Chile and certain connections on the waterfront. These connections directed American Naval Captains to his rooming house when they sought information as to where they could be entertained; that from information he obtained from women he introduced to them, he was able to learn the departure dates of their respective ships; that he would then wire this intelligence to German submarines and boasted he had supplied information resulting in the sinking of 12 British and American ships. They were familiar with all events of the war and were on intimate terms with high-ranking Nazis

74 Gannon to Stimely, November 24, 1981.

75 Boschi to Arcand, October 8, 1951, Arcand collection, Archives Canada, MG30 D-91, finding no. 1293, vol. 1, file no. 9.

76 FBI memorandum, March 21, 1952, in Yockey FBI file 105–8229 — 1.

77 FBI memorandum, March 24, 1952, FBI file CG 100–25647.

78 Glenn H Bethel, FBI Liaison Office, Ottawa, Canada, April 7, 1952; FBI file CG 100–25647.

> and Fascists, mentioning many names, events and places in connection with their espionage activities. They were in Montreal for the purpose of opening a *Fourth Front* magazine and mentioned a contact that they were here to make with a person later ascertained to be Adrian Arcand, a well-known Canadian Fascist. They mentioned that they were both wanted by the authorities but did not worry as long as they were in Canada where they knew they would be safe due to the inefficiency and stupidity of the Canadian intelligence service, and that they were free to avoid American Customs and Immigration regulations due to the stupidity of members of these two services... Mr Boschi mentioned to Mr Yockey that it was a pleasure to meet a high ranking member of the party and they made frequent mention of an underground movement...[79]

As later recalled by Adrian Arcand, a certain amount of this conversation was for the men's own amusement, as they knew that the secret service was eavesdropping.

The memorandum concluded that shortly later, Boschi and Yockey went to the Consul General to obtain visas. Boschi had travelled to Italy, France, Switzerland and England, and intended to stay with Yockey in Chicago.[80]

Boschi was renowned for painting landscapes on pinheads with the use of a single hair plucked from the back of his hand and attached to a match-stick. He practised yoga, which he had studied for many years in India, to enable the steadiness required for the work. Having lived in Argentina for 20 years he had painted a portrait of Argentine pro-Fascist president General Juan Perón[81] and planned to present it to him. The pinhead paintings were exhibited under microscopic lenses and he gained a position as instructor of miniature painting at the celebrated Belle Arti Academy in Turin. In 1958, he was exhibiting in many capitals throughout the world, including Washington, with acclaim[82] and presumably his fascist associations had been overlooked by the US State Department by that time.

---

79 FBI memorandum August 15, 1952, 105–8229 — 1.

80 FBU memorandum August 15, 1952, 105–8229 — 1.

81 See K. R. Bolton, *Perón and Perónism* (London: Black House Publishing, 2014).

82 'Pinhead Painter', *The Independent Record*, Montana, August 24, 1958, p. 12.

## Adrian Arcand

Yockey sought out Adrian Arcand, the world-renowned Franco-Canadian 'Fascist' who, even after the war, was achieving significant electoral results. Arcand had been a journalist of note in Quebec but had been removed from *La Press* by the publisher for attempting to organise a union. In 1929, he had been hired by writer and publisher Joseph Menard, who aimed to establish a nationalist movement in Quebec. Arcand was given editorship of *Le Goglu*, which was both nationalist and anti-capitalist. Menard founded two other journals in 1930, the Sunday *Miroir* and *Le Chameau*.[83] Around these a movement formed, *Ordre Patriotique des Goglus*, with a Fascist orientation,[84] like the fascist 'leagues' that had been forming in France since the 1920s. The *Ordre* reached 50,000 members with a strong interest among Montreal's 22,000 Italians.[85] By 1932, Arcand was writing supportively of Hitler as a fighter against international Jewish banking.[86] As always, Arcand, a devout Catholic, saw the struggle as being between Jewish materialism — whether communist or capitalist — and the teachings of Christ. It was an attitude that was widespread among Catholics throughout the world and incorporated Catholic social doctrine as the means of fighting this materialist hydra. In the USA, Father Coughlin translated this into a mass movement with Fascist inclinations.

In 1934, with support from Quebecois Catholic associations, the National Social Christian Party was formed under Arcand's leadership and this had a Corporatist programme.[87] Although there was much focus on the Jewish issue, unlike Leese's Imperial Fascist League this was not to the detriment of developing a coherent and detailed ideology called 'National Corporatism'. Arcand's radicalism did not deter Conservatives from trying to recruit him as an effective publicist who could regenerate the party. In 1936, Arcand was also an important figure in supporting of a newly formed Conservative party in

83 Lita-Rose Betcherman, *The Swastika and the Maple Leaf* (Ontario: Fitzhenry & Whiteside Ltd., 1975), p. 5.

84 Lita-Rose Betcherman, ibid., p. 6.

85 Lita-Rose Betcherman, ibid., p. 7.

86 Lita-Rose Betcherman, ibid., pp. 20–21.

87 Lita-Rose Betcherman, ibid., p. 38.

Quebec, Union Nationale, and he edited *L'Illusration Nouvelle*, a daily tabloid supporting the party.[88] The party's leader, Maurice Duplessis, became premier that year and Arcand's influence expanded accordingly.[89]

The National Social Christian Party continued under Arcand's leadership and became increasingly militant, with a paramilitary blueshirt organisation.[90] In 1938, at a congress of several thousand in Kingston, Ontario, the main nationalist parties merged under Arcand's leadership, with the name National Unity Party.[91] Despite the war-mongering against Germany that was already proceeding in 1938, Anglophone Canadians supported diplomacy or non-intervention, while Francophone Canadians were solidly against Canadian involvement in a war.[92] It was a phenomenon that Yockey was to remark upon as a sign of culture-health among Quebecois.[93] While the rest of Canada was inundated with war hysteria, in Quebec the NUP remained a large movement.[94] Although the Government ordered the NUP disbanded in September 1939, when Canada entered the war, hundreds of members in Quebec continued to meet in Church halls, thanks to the efforts of a priest, while smaller meetings were held privately in other parts of Canada.[95] Prompted by the internment of Mosley and his comrades in Britain, in March 1940 the RCMP detained Arcand and his aides, although the number only amounted to 11,[96] in contrast to the 1,000 Mosleyites and others detained in Britain. The 11 were detained after a two-day hearing. Arcand was not released until July 1945. In reduced circumstances, living in the little town of Lanorai, Montreal, Arcand continued to receive support from his old friend, Premier Duplessis, who provided him with translating and editing work.[97] The NUP continued into the 1970s, briefly surviving Arcand, who died in 1967. Despite

---

88 Lita-Rose Betcherman, ibid., p. 85.

89 Lita-Rose Betcherman, ibid., p. 86.

90 Lita-Rose Betcherman, ibid., p. 89.

91 Lita-Rose Betcherman, ibid., p. 119.

92 Lita-Rose Betcherman, ibid., p. 128.

93 Yockey, *The Proclamation of London*, Wermod ed., op. cit., p. 36.

94 Lita-Rose Betcherman, op. cit., p. 142.

95 Lita-Rose Betcherman, ibid., p. 145.

96 Lita-Rose Betcherman, ibid.

97 Lita-Rose Betcherman, ibid., p. 146.

his post-war hardships, Arcand ran in the federal elections in 1949, for the riding of Richelieu-Verchères, as NUP candidate, coming in second with 29% (5,590 votes)[98] and second again 1953 in Berthier-Maskinongé-delanaudière with 39.75% (7,496 votes) as a 'Nationalist'.[99]

Arcand's admiration for Yockey as a person and as a Thinker was unequivocal and enduring. Boschi and Yockey stayed with Arcand for several days at Lanorai. Arcand described Yockey as a 'wholehearted Gothic' who went to the village church with Arcand and played Bach fugues on the piano at Arcand's house.[100] Through Gannon, Arcand was among the first of the ELF overseas contacts. Already having read *Imperium*, Arcand had apparently been sent what was likely a draft of *The Proclamation of London* in 1949 and had an influence on it. Gannon writes to Arcand thanking him for his 'helpful and constructive criticism of *The Proclamation*'. Apparently, Arcand believed *The Proclamation* could be interpreted as anti-American per se and considered there should be a clearer distinction between 'the REAL American and the Jewish Regime'. Whatever Arcand's suggestions were, Gannon writes that they had been adopted.[101]

Indeed, Arcand was one of the few 'movement' individuals to whom Yockey gave fulsome respect and with whom he had a lasting friendship. Writing to Arcand from Bruxelles in 1951, Yockey said:

> You must never think that any suggestion you make to me would ever possibly be received in the wrong spirit. As I value them highly, and hope you will always feel free to tell me anything you wish to, but that you will continue to do so from time to time.

Both were influenced by Oswald Spengler. In 1963, Arcand wrote to long-serving Portuguese President Oliveira Salazar, congratulating him on his

98 Canadian Parliament, 'History of Federal Ridings since 1869', http://www.parl.gc.ca/About/Parliament/FederalRidingsHistory/hfer.asp?Include=Y&Language=E&rid=608&Search=Det.

99 Ibid., Berthier-Maskinongé-delanaudière, 1953.

100 Arcand to H Keith Thompson, June 30, 1960.

101 Gannon to Arcand, December 12, 1949, Arcand collection, Archives Canada, finding no. 1293, MG30 D-91, Vol. 1, file no. 1.

determination to maintain the Portuguese empire when most of the other European empires, exhausted by war[102] and pressured by the USA, were heading towards imperial scuttle. For Arcand, according to the organic cycles of History expounded by Spengler, the destiny of Western civilization was that of imperialism. He wrote to Salazar that 'the history of all civilizations teaches us that, once a high culture has reached its point of maturity, the organic law controlling it requires it to project its knowledge, benefiting everyone around the world'.[103] This is Yockey's Western Imperialism tempered with Arcand's paternalistic attitude towards colonial races based on the Catholicism that was the foundation of his outlook.

Arcand had written to H Keith Thompson, Yockey's American colleague, after being informed of Yockey's death in 1960: 'The news gave me quite a shock, though I knew that our friend had to be careful at all times. He was precious — or dangerous! — for his brains, and his opus was a real masterpiece...'[104] Several weeks later Arcand wrote of what an honour it had been that Yockey had stayed at his home in Lanorai for 'a whole week'. Arcand wrote later of first meeting Yockey at the Windsor Hotel, Montreal. He alluded to how they were aware that Yockey was under surveillance from the FBI and Canadian Intelligence. Arcand had been tipped off by the desk clerk, an Arcand supporter, that a tape recorder had been installed in the adjoining room, 'so we had the fun of our lives in giving the FBI and Canadian Intelligence improvised messages in most loud talk about the Zionists being masters of our mutual governments, FBI, RCMP and what not'.[105]

It was further reported that Boschi and Yockey, while affirming their commitment to Fascism, stated that they would work for the USSR but would not on any account ever serve the USA or England. Yockey remarked that he had travelled widely in Germany, Italy and Switzerland. He had been wanted by the military police in Germany but had evaded them, had returned to the USA, where he expected to be detained, but had entered without difficulty. He had been married in Germany to a German girl but had divorced. Yockey was

102 Portugal, like Spain, had remained neutral.

103 Quoted by Nadeau Jean-Francois, *The Canadian Führer: The Life of Adrien Arcand*, p. 275.

104 Arcand to H Keith Thompson, June 30, 1960.

105 Arcand to Thompson, July 16, 1961.

also well acquainted with German officials and ex-officials, including Franz von Papen.[106]

## US Return

In August 1952, Yockey was back in the USA under the name Francis Downey, exhibiting Boschi's landscape paintings on pin-heads, through May and June, at the Million Dollar Pier, Atlantic City, New Jersey. The remarkable exhibition had however failed to make money, although it had been successful at the Festival of Britain the previous year. The owner of the Million Dollar Pier had remarked to the FBI that his dealings with Yockey were 'completely amicable' and that he 'is a gentleman in every respect' and a man of 'intelligence and education'. Yockey had in June eloped with a married woman, to whom he had been introduced several years earlier. She was enthused about his political ideas, which she described to her parents in a telephone conversation as 'definitely not Communistic but just the "opposite"'.[107] The proprietor of the Lyric Hotel, Atlantic City, where the 'Downeys' stayed during May and June, regarded them as 'a wonderful couple'.[108]

While the FBI maintained an avid interest in Yockey's whereabouts they had no grounds for arresting him. A report concludes that Yockey was under investigation as a result of his pro-Nazi and Fascist sympathies and activities.[109] In particular, it was reported that from an early time Yockey had seemed to adopt a pro-Soviet attitude on account of an overriding opposition to the USA. It was the State Department that was at the time eager to speak to Yockey and to confiscate his passport. A State Department agent by the name of Balikoff had located Yockey in New York but he again avoided capture.[110] It was noted that since April 1952, when the FBI began to search for Yockey, 29 reports had been prepared about him but only the offices in Chicago and New York had provided 'definite leads'.[111]

106 FBI memorandum August 5, 1952, 105–8229 -1.

107 FBI report, August 20, 1952, p. 2, 105–8229 -1.

108 FBI report, August 8, 1952, p. 5; 105–8229 -1.

109 J. M. Fitzgerald, FBI office memorandum, April 4, 1954; file no. 105–8229 — 2.

110 FBI office memorandum, September 30, 1952, p. 2; 105–8229 -1.

111 FBI report, April 22, 1954, April 4, 1954; file no. 105–8229 — 2.

Yockey travelled to New York in June 1952, under the name Francis Parker, and attempted to set up the Boschi exhibition at Coney Island. Despite Boschi's acclaim, Yockey's promotional efforts on the artist's behalf were not successful. When Yockey was captured in California in 1960, he still had a Boschi pin valued at $5,000, noted by the FBI in their inventory.

## Egypt, USA, Germany

In 1953, Yockey was in Cairo writing anti-Zionist material.[112] He was employed by the Egyptian information ministry and had met Nasser, leader of the Free Officers' coup of July 1952 that had ousted King Farouk, and deputy to General Muhammmad Naguib, first president of Egypt. The new Egypt, like Perón's Argentina, was a primary destination for ex-officials and war veterans of the Third Reich, who worked there as propagandists and military and security advisers. Otto Skorzeny, the famed rescuer of Mussolini, was a key adviser to Naguib, although the president was relatively favourable towards Jews. Skorzeny promptly brought in other veterans of the Third Reich, such as SS General Wilhelm Farmbacher; Panzer General Oskar Munzel; Leopold Gleim, former chief of Hitler's personal guard and Gestapo security chief of German-occupied Poland; and Joachim Daemling, former chief of the Gestapo in Dusseldorf.[113]

It seems likely that Yockey went to Egypt in 1953 because that year the Ministry of National Guidance, the propaganda ministry of the new regime, was established. The Ministry was a major point of employment for ex-officials of the Reich propaganda ministry, particularly experts on the Jewish question, who set up a division on Jewish issues within the Egyptian ministry. Indeed, Hans Appler (Sakah Chaffar), who had been an official in Goebbels' Ministry, became Egyptian Minister of Information in 1956. Many of these Germans converted to Islam, the most notable being Dr Johannes von Leers, although he did not reach Egypt until several years after Yockey's departure.

In June 1954 Yockey, under the name 'Richard Allen', had re-married and was playing piano at the cocktail lounge of the Gilded Cage Bar in Monterey,

112 FBI report, August 7, 1954, p. 15, 105–8229 — 2.

113 G Infield, *Skorzeny: Hitler's Commando* (New York: St. Martin's Press, 1981), pp. 207–208.

California, and teaching piano. He also used the name 'Edward Parker'.[114] Yockey was apparently ill during this time and underweight, although he insisted on taking a daily swim regardless of the weather. He spent much of his time playing the piano and teaching his wife and her daughter. However, as his health improved he felt impelled to depart and left on October 1, 1954.[115] He returned to Europe with 'a French girl'.[116]

In 1955, Yockey was back in Germany, reportedly receiving money from his German mentor in the USA, Frederick Weiss. Around this time, he was using the name Edward Max Price and wearing horn-rimmed glasses.[117] The FBI went to extraordinary lengths in trying to determine whether Price was Yockey and his sisters were questioned at length. Yockey's brother-in-law, Lieutenant Commander Coyne, was particularly vulnerable because of his position in the Navy as an 'acting executive officer' and a former Security Officer with the United States Naval Post-Graduate School at Monterey.[118] Nonetheless, Coyne admitted to having sidestepped the FBI's questioning as much as possible, including questioning on the identity of Edward Max Price, whom he had to admit was known to him as someone to whom his sister-in-law Alice Spurlock had sent money in Germany. Coyne himself had purchased the money orders in amounts of $500 and $700. William Coyne defiantly retorted that he did not feel obliged to tell the FBI about his sister-in-law's dealings with 'Price'.[119] The FBI reported that Coyne had been 'completely evasive' apart from admitting the purchase of foreign remittance payable to 'Price'. Coyne is also described by the FBI as having talked at great length about his belief that Yockey had done nothing wrong, of Yockey's 'brilliance', of his being 'misunderstood' and the jealousy against him.[120]

Alice Spurlock became also of much interest to the FBI as they tried to prove that she had witnessed Yockey's application for a passport in Monterey,

---

114 FBI report, August 28, 1959, file no. 105–8229—3.

115 FBI report, June 14, 1960, file no. 105–8229—3.

116 FBI report, August 28, 1959, ibid., p. 5.

117 FBI office memorandum, January 14, 1955, p. 1, op. cit.

118 FBI report, May 3, 1955, file no. 105–8229—2.

119 FBI report, April 1, 1955, p. 8, ibid.

120 Ibid., p. 9.

under the name of Edward Max Price. However, laboratory tests could not determine whether Spurlock's signature was the same as that on the application.[121] This puzzle expended a large amount of FBI energy.

The FBI prepared reports on Lieutenant Commander Coyne's uncooperative attitude.[122] He was stated to have knowingly withheld important information on Yockey and the statements on Coyne were being prepared should the FBI want to furnish information to the Navy.[123] In July 1955, the Director of Naval Intelligence contacted FBI director J Edgar Hoover in regard to investigating Lieutenant Commander Coyne but Hoover replied that such an investigation was the responsibility of the Navy.[124] Hoover asked for any pertinent information that the Naval investigation might obtain from Coyne.

Attempts to locate Yockey in Germany failed.[125] During 1953 to 1955, Yockey assumed the name Franz Ludwig Yorck and was a staff member of the magazines *Quick* and *Weltbild*.[126] A German identification card for *Quick*, naming 'Yorch' as a 'staff member', was among the items found in Yockey's bag on his arrest in 1960.[127] *Quick* (1948–1992) was the first German magazine allowed to be published after World War II under the Occupation authorities. Traudl Junge, Hitler's secretary, worked for much of the magazine's existence as secretary for the chief of the editorial staff.

On March 18, 1955 the US State Department 'circularized all diplomatic and consular posts concerning Edward Max Price', 'with instructions to take up and hold his passport'. The Embassy in Paris advised that 'Price' had been in Paris in December 1954 and the Consulate in Stuttgart stated that 'Price' had been somewhere in Germany in April 1955. On June 13, 1956 the US State Department 'communicated to all diplomatic and consular posts throughout the world regarding the whereabouts' and activities of Edward Max Price.[128]

---

121 FBI office memorandum, October 13, 1955, p. 3; file no. 105–8229 — 2.

122 FBI report, April 27, 1955, p. 2, ibid.

123 FBI office memorandum, May 3, 1955, p. 1, ibid.

124 Hoover to Naval Intelligence July 11, 1955, file no. 105–8229 — 2.

125 Philip O'Brien, FBI liaison representative, Heidelberg, to J Edgar Hoover, FBI office memorandum, August 5, 1955, file no. 105–8229 — 2.

126 FBI memorandum, September 8, 1960, 105–8229 — 3.

127 FBI report, September 6, 1960, p. 27, 105–8229 — 3.

128 FBI report, June 27, 1956, p. 1; file no. file no. 105–8229 — 2.

To complicate matters, 'Price' assumed a new alias and a new passport as 'Edward Max Briceman'.[129] During 1954 to 1956, 'Briceman' travelled around Germany, France, England, Belgium and Austria.[130]

In mid-1958, Yockey was reported to have been living in Los Angeles, attempting to raise funds to publish another book, and had already been in the USA 'for some time'.[131] Between mid-1955 and mid-1958, Yockey went right off the FBI's radar. He moved to Reno, Nevada, in November 1958, using the name 'Jack Peter Forest', with 'Joan Forest' stated to be his wife.[132] During enquiries extending into 1959, there was added confusion as to whether Yockey's German mentor, Frederick C. F. Weiss, was in fact Yockey, but it was concluded that this was not the case since Weiss was considerably older.[133] There was also an enquiry as to whether Yockey was actually Don Bell, publisher of *Bell Reports*, but in 1959, on comparing photographs, this was disproven.[134] In late 1959, Yockey was in San Francisco under the name 'Harry F Shannon' with 'Pat Lagerstrom'. In February to March 1960, he was residing in New Orleans as 'Richard Hatch', with 'Pat Hatch'.[135] It was as 'Richard Hatch' that the FBI finally caught up with Yockey in California several months later.

At this time, circa March 1959, the FBI was also wondering whether Yockey was an anonymous identity called 'The Patriot'.[136] It seems that despite the proliferation of 'Rightists' involved with what the FBI labelled on their files as 'racial matters', anything that was reasonably articulate was suspected of being produced by Yockey. Yockey was regarded as 'a logical suspect in this case', 'this case' apparently being the distribution of leaflets on Jews and Negroes. This is indicative of the high state of paranoia that seems to have existed at the time in regard to dissent against the racial integration agenda of the US Government. This was a time when the Ku Klux Klan, the National States

129 FBI Airtel, August 6, 1960, p. 3, file no. 105–8229—3.

130 FBI memorandum, September 8, 1960, p. 2, 105–8229—3.

131 FBI office memorandum, June 24, 1958, file no. 105–8229—3.

132 FBI report, July 7, 1960, p. D, 105–8229—3.

133 FBI report, June 4, 1959, file no. 105–8229—3.

134 Report of FBI Special Agent John W Toedt, May 20, 1960, p. 2; file no. 105–8229—3.

135 Wayne K Welch, FBI Special Agent, July 7, 1960, 105–8229—3.

136 FBI Chicago Office to J Edgar Hoover, 'The Patriot, racial matters', March 5, 1959, FBI file no. SF 105–1769.

Rights Party and Rockwell's American Nazi Party were militantly active, along with a large number of proliferating conservative, anti-communist groups, such as The John Birch Society, which the Anti-Defamation League and the American Jewish Congress regarded as incipient Fascists. Although Madole's National Renaissance Party, according to the FBI, had only a handful of members, the Bureau expended a lot of time and energy tracking its activities as indicated by the files accumulated on the NRP over several decades. This was also a time when there had been bombings of synagogues in several southern states. The FBI launched an entire programme for undermining the racial right, called COINTELPRO (Counter Intelligence Program), specialising in factionalising the 'Right' by rumour-mongering.

Amid this environment of high anxiety, with White and Black rioting and desegregation imposed by armed force, 'The Patriot' appeared somewhat like Yockey, cast as a fascist Scarlet Pimpernell. Yockey was regarded as a 'logical suspect' because:

1. In the leaflet entitled "Dear Fellow American", paragraph 1, the writer of this leaflet claims to have had four years in college. College graduates in the "hate field" are very few. YOCKEY is a graduate of Notre Dame Law School.

2. The leaflet entitled "Newsletter", paragraph 5, line 4, states in part, "I know personally in Germany several Jews…" YOCKEY has spent considerable time in Germany in recent years.

3. This material, which is very well written, is very similar to YOCKEY's intellectual type writings.[137]

Yockey was said to have returned to the USA in late 1957 but efforts to locate him had been unsuccessful. The FBI now sought to interview him in regard to being 'The Patriot', along with 'other matters'.[138] Hence the hunt for 'The Patriot' became part of the bundle of FBI files on Yockey.

137 FBI Chicago Office to J Edgar Hoover, 'The Patriot, racial matters', March 5, 1959, pp. 1–2; FBI file no. SF 105–1769.

138 FBI Chicago Office to J Edgar Hoover, ibid., 'The Patriot, racial matters', March 5, 1959, p. 3.

The investigation was also involved with the hearsay that an underground organisation was emerging to resist Federally enforced desegregation. 'The Patriot' had written for the *Georgia Tribune* and was being published by 'Time for Truth Press, Inc.' of Palm Beach, Florida. The investigation also took in the National States Rights Party, a relatively successful segregationist party;[139] the Christian Educational Association, publishers of *Common Sense*, which was being promoted by a mysterious so-called 'instant organization';[140] and Gerald L. K. Smith's Christian Nationalist Crusade. The FBI investigation covered the USA but was focused on the Southern states and with connecting Yockey to the 'instant organization'.[141] The Federal authorities were particularly nervous about anti-desegregation activities in Little Rock, Arkansas, and Mississippi, where the Ku Klux Klan and other segregationists had mobilized.[142]

The 'instant organization' claimed credit for the mass resistance against school desegregation at Little Rock and stated that it would spread the resistance to other states, stating that 'the Battle of Little Rock is merely a tiny foretaste of the hell which is to follow in ever-increasing doses'.[143] An unknown individual, although not definitively identified as 'The Patriot' and/or Yockey, was said to be organizing cells of around eight members around the Southern states and collecting personal information on prominent Jewish families. The individual was well dressed, appeared to have money and was not interested in collecting fees for a formal organization.[144]

The elusive 'instant group' called for racial purity, opposed racial intermarriage, referred to the 'physiological inferiority of Jews and Negroes' and advocated 'an autocratic and aristocratic kingdom'.[145] Had anyone at the FBI

---

139 FBI memorandum, April 15, 1959, ibid., marked 'Subject: Francis Parker Yockey', FBI file no. SF 105–1769, 'cover page C'.

140 FBI memorandum, April 15, 1959, ibid., 'cover page D'.

141 FBI memorandum, April 15, 1959, ibid., 'cover page E'.

142 FBI memorandum, April 15, 1959, ibid., 'cover page G'.

143 FBI memorandum to OSI Georgia and South Carolina, 'Unknown subject, aka "The Patriot"', March 17, 1959, p. 2; FBI file no. SF 105–1769.

144 FBI report 'Unknown subject aka "The Patriot"', Mach 17, 1959, p. 13; cited in the FBI file on Yockey, SF 105–1769.

145 FBI memorandum to OSI Georgia and South Carolina, 'Unknown subject, aka "The Patriot"', March 17, 1959; FBI file no. SF 105–1769.

bothered to read *Imperium*, they would have seen that the themes expressed by 'The Patriot' were not those of Yockey. In particular one 'Patriot' missive entitled 'The Creation of Man'[146] was replete with Biblical citations and referred 'to a Darwinian survival of the fittest'. Neither Biblical quotations nor Darwinism form parts of Yockey's philosophy. 'The Patriot' turned the 'Almighty' into a cosmic initiator of *lex talionis*.

It seems that the only criteria for regarding Yockey as a 'logical suspect' was that 'The Patriot' wrote in an articulate manner and claimed to have attended college for four years. Contrary to what the FBI assumed, there were many college-educated writers and organisers in the American 'Right' at the time, including De West Hooker, graduate of Cornell; Weiss, Sorbonne; John Kasper, Columbia; Matthias Koehl, University of Wisconsin; Karl Allen, Harvard; and H Keith Thompson, Yale to mention some of the most radical.

However, it seems plausible that 'The Patriot' was influenced by Yockey. He wrote of 'elites' and 'aristocracy', drew on history and in particular cited theatrical productions of New York and Hollywood as 'The Jewish Centers of our Country, demoralizing our people'.[147] The reference suggests Yockey's concept of 'Culture Distortion' and his references to 'the ethical syphilis of Hollywood, and the spiritual leprosy of New York'.[148]

Whatever the relationship between 'The Patriot' and Yockey, if any, all FBI offices were instructed to 'intensify their investigation aggressively and continuously to develop and cover all leads that will ultimately lead to the location of Yockey'.[149] A further memorandum noted that investigations over a six-year period had failed to 'definitely locate the subject'.[150]

## Cuba

Circa 1959, Yockey had made contact with staff at *Bohemia* magazine in Havana, Cuba. On June 15, 1960, at San Francisco County Jail, Yockey by

146 'The Patriot', 'The Creation of Man', cited by the FBI as 'Unknown subject aka "The Patriot"', Mach 17, 1959, pp. 6–13; cited in the FBI file on Yockey, SF 105–1769.

147 FBI report 'Unknown Subject aka "The Patriot"', Mach 17, 1959, p. 13; cited in the FBI file on Yockey, SF 105–1769.

148 Yockey, *The Proclamation of London*, Wermod ed., p. 63.

149 FBI office memorandum, June 5, 1960; FBI file on Yockey SF 105–1769.

150 FBI office memorandum, June 11, 1959, SF 105–1769.

coincidence saw someone who was awaiting prison transfer, whom he had met at Miami early in 1960 and who intended travelling to Havana. Yockey asked if he would give an address in Havana to 'Emanuel', who worked at the editorial office of *Bohemia*, and ask that it be passed along to someone named Alford, who would know what to do. Yockey told the inmate, who was only serving a 90-day sentence, that if the message could be given he would be looked after in Havana. The inmate stated that when they met in Miami, Yockey was accompanied by Emanuel and a woman named Shena Dietz. Yockey asked him to contact Dietz at *El Mundo* newspaper concerning financial help.[151] The FBI was not able to determine the identities of these Cubans.

*Bohemia* during the 1950s focused on political writing. It seems plausible that Yockey was paid as a journalist, such a magazine providing scope for his opposition to US foreign policy. If he had worked for Czech intelligence as a courier, as has been suggested, the Cubans might have trusted him. When jailed in June 1960, Yockey told a fellow inmate, Jack Fambrough, an American Negro claiming to be a Cuban and with whom Yockey was planning an escape, that they could go to Cuba. Yockey said he had been there three or four months previously and that he was 'well connected with the Castro regime'.[152]

Even more enigmatic about this Cuban connection was Yockey establishing contact with the new regime for reasons other than journalistic. DTK states:

> I remember Papa Weiss suggesting that "our boy" (as he referred to Yockey) was offering assistance to the new regime, especially for the building of submarines! Even then I thought it was a bit over the top. Submarines? How could Yockey arrange for expertise in such a project? Yockey the broker of post-World War II German talent? Admiral Dönitz was recently released from Spandau and hundreds of former U-Boat personnel were still in contact and maintained strong circles of comradeship. Keith Thompson had a degree in naval architecture and as publicity agent for the Admiral in the USA was of course very close to all matters *Kriegsmarine*. Perhaps something was afoot, or afloat?[153]

151 FBI memorandum, July 7, 1960, p. 3, 1960, 105–8229—3.

152 FBI report, June 20, 1960, p. 2; 105–8229—3.

153 DTK to Bolton, January 30, 2015.

How plausible is it that the icon of thousands of shuffling, bearded youths throughout the world, proclaiming the glories of the Cuban Revolution, would contemplate any association with a 'Nazi'? Indeed, two SS veterans were recruited to train the Cuban military. A recent media report states:

> Bodo Hechelhammer, historical investigations director at German foreign intelligence agency Bundesnachrichtendienst (BND) said: "Evidently, the Cuban revolutionary army did not fear contagion from personal links to Nazism, so long as it served its objectives."[154]

In 1962, four SS veterans were invited to go to Cuba and two accepted. Documents also show that the Castro regime purchased 4,000 pistols through the mediation of Otto Remer and Ernest Wilhelm Springer.[155] It is notable that Remer was Yockey's closest contact in Germany immediately after World War II and had a particularly close association with H Keith Thompson. Moreover, Springer had been a Member of Parliament of Lower Saxony for the Socialist Reich Party and had gone to Syria with Remer in 1952, where they were involved in arms trading with other veterans. It is likely that Yockey had also known Springer shortly after the war, via his connections with the SRP.

DTK recalls further:

> One day I drove Herr Weiss on errands. We stopped at a very nice suburb of NY City and visited an ancient architect, one of America's top dogs. The home was furnished in early techno-baroque, part Weimar and part Italian Industrial Expressionism, a museum. In the study was the prototype of the Weiss invention, a pneumatic artillery shell-filling machine, which of course greatly improved safety in the manufacture of such ordnance. It looked like an espresso machine. How & why it was transported there, I don't know. Later, there was fairly open discussion about Y's attempt to bring submarine technology to Cuba, to Castro. The architect was supposedly "in" on this deal. What ever happened to any such best laid plans of... if indeed anything viable existed beyond comradely discussions is speculation. Y's demise cut everything off. Something was in the air. Herr Weiss supposedly held patents on the shell-filling pump and

154 Lee Moran, 'How Castro recruited former members of the Nazi SS to train troops during Cuban missile crisis', *Daily Mail*, October 15, 2012, http://www.dailymail.co.uk/news/article-2217980/How-Castro-recruited-members-Nazi-SS-train-troops-Cuban-Missile-Crisis.html#ixzz3UovrETy2.

155 Ibid.

> received monies from some blind source, perhaps from Germany, perhaps from Switzerland or Austria... perhaps from the Norodny Bank in Paris? Weiss, Y and the architect were in league to promote something, but exactly what, how and when are questions?[156]

Was this the explosive secret to which the US State Department cryptically referred when Yockey was captured?

Yockey had also spent an unspecified period of time in Argentina, from what he told an inmate at an Oakland jail on June 6, 1960.[157] Although nothing of this seems to have been known until after Yockey's death, it is certainly plausible that he travelled to Argentina, presumably sometime during the Juan Perón era, prior to the coup that ousted Perón in 1955.

Maynard Nelson was another enigmatic individual whom the FBI thought might be Yockey. In April 1960, just a few months prior to Yockey's coincidental capture, photographs of Nelson and Yockey were compared and it was decided that Yockey was not Nelson.[158] As a youth, Nelson had undergone considerable harassment by the FBI and was made to take a psychiatric exmaination, and pushed to what appears to have been a nervous breakdown over his activities with his Democratic Nationalist Party. He was considered however to have potential to be 'rehabilitated'. Nelson formed the Realpolitical Institute in 1954, whose officers included many of the luminaries of the racist Right, such as Eustace Mullins; George Lincoln Rockwell's heir as American fuehrer, Matt Koehl; and National Renaissance Party leader James H Madole. Nelson had been a member of the American Committee for the Advancement of Western Culture established by H Keith Thompson.[159] In 1955, Nelson had also visited one of Yockey's primary mentors, Frederick C. F. Weiss, to promote the Institute.[160]

---

156 DTK to Bolton, March 31, 2015.

157 FBI report, June 14, 1960, 105–8229 — 3.

158 Report of FBI Special Agent John W Toedt, May 20, 1960, p. 3; file no. 105–8229 — 3.

159 FBI Chicago office, 'Maynard Orlando Nelson', 'Racial matters', December 18, 1958, CG 105–5587.

160 Ibid., p. 6.

# Yockey's German Mentor

In Frederick Charles Ferdinand Weiss, Yockey had a patron of remarkably similar thinking. It was not merely that both shared pro-Hitler sympathies. Hitlerism is not particularly apparent in Weiss's thinking. Rather, Yockey had found in Weiss a fellow Spenglerian with the same outlook on post-war events. The influence of the German conservative historian-philosopher Oswald Spengler, not himself a Hitlerite, on both Weiss and Yockey is apparent. Like Spengler, Weiss and Yockey did not view 'race' as primarily a subject to be analysed with callipers, weights and measures but as unfolding through historical forces. They also viewed the occupation of Germany by the USA as more destructive to the culture of Europe than occupation by the USSR. Consequently, Yockey and Weiss were out of step with much of the Soviet-obsessed American radical Right.

Weiss was born on July 31, 1885, at Pforzheim, Germany.[1] He served in the German Army for a year from October 1905. Moving to the USA, during 1909 to 1914 Weiss earned a significant income as a financial mediator for the Northern Pacific Railway and was involved with patents and many businesses around New Jersey. He returned to Germany in 1914, just prior to the outbreak of war.[2]

Serving as a First Lieutenant,[3] he was wounded four times at the front and was highly decorated.[4] After the war, the French jailed him for 11 months for

---

1 'Animist Party', FBI New York office, File no. 105-1064, December 22, 1947. 'Frederick Charles Ferdinand Weiss', p. 3.

2 Marie Weiss letter to J Edgard Hoover, June 16, 1969, FBI file no. 105-23413.

3 FBI file no. 105-2413-26, October 22, 1954.

4 Dan Burros, *The Free American*, No. 3, p. 3, New York, December 1964. Burros regarded Weiss as a friend, admired Yockey, but was at odds with H Keith Thompson. Trying to

having executed villagers who harboured a partisan who garrotted a German paymaster.[5] He returned to the USA in 1930 and was interned as an 'immigration internee' from August to December 1942, due to irregularities with his entry. He made a living reselling business properties in New York.[6]

His wife, Marie Urbas, was born in Landshut, Bavaria.[7] She had been a 'Red spotter' at the railways for the *Freikorps* during the Spartacist revolt, informing the nationalist para-military of the movements of the Communists.[8]

Weiss was not a naturalised citizen and had to be circumspect as to his activities. He largely operated for several years through James Madole's National Renaissance Party (NRP), founded in 1949 as an overtly 'fascist' organization with Weiss providing most of the funding. The NRP served as the main vehicle for the distribution of Weiss's writings.

Weiss did however establish his own publishing project, Le Blanc Publications, in conjunction with H Keith Thompson, who edited articles from Weiss's imperfect English, mixed with good Latin and French. Together, this triumvirate of Yockey, Weiss and Thompson was able to establish a significant presence in the radical Right with their unorthodox views on race and the USSR, extending their ideas to the anti-communist newspaper *Common Sense.*

Something of Weiss's activities and thinking can be deduced from the following poem, originally written in German on orange cards for circulation in occupied Germany in 1951:

> To the New Deal Lacqueys
> When, from the Diet, there flows a steady

---

out-Nazi the Nazis, Burros shot himself when he was exposed in *The New York Times* in 1965 as a Bar Mitzvah'd Jew. Given that a distant cousin, Robert Burros, retained a rank within the National Renaissance Party after also being exposed as of Jewish descent, Dan, as usual, probably went too far. George Lincoln Rockwell, founder of the American Nazi Party, whose organization Burros had quit for its 'moderation', commented on the anti-Jewish self-hatred of Burros which extended to him advocating genocide. Rockwell ended his article with the quip: 'It killed him.' Rockwell, *The Rockwell Report*, Arlington Virginia, October–November 1965.

5 Dan Burros, ibid.

6 'Animist Party', FBI New York office, File no. 105–1064, December 22, 1947, p. 1.

7 DTK to Bolton, July 9 2014.

8 Dan Burros, *The Free American*, op. cit.

Whining about guilt and penance,
Forever you, in shameless squabbles,
Impale yourselves for New Deal favors,
If judgment flees your empty nugget (literally: soft pears)
Secluded, tired men, you all:
Your kiss on the hind part of "Jew Deal"
Is only bliss for "David's Star".
F.C.F.W.
New York, August '51[9]

Weiss began propagandising soon after World War II. In 1946, he published the booklet *Quo Vadis America*. The following year he published *Germania Delenda Est?*[10] under his Le Blanc imprint, Le Blanc being the French rendering of his name Weiss, meaning 'White'. Weiss had chosen the title from the Roman destruction of Carthage, '*Delenda est Carthago*' ('Carthage is destroyed'). Throughout the essay, Weiss refers to US Secretary of the Treasury Henry Morgenthau Jr as 'Morgenthau-Cato' whose name was given to a 'plan' to dismember and depopulate Germany, Cato the Elder being the foremost proponent for the destruction of Carthage during the Punic War of the second century B.C.

The themes are Spenglerian and so is the terminology, with references to the 'hour of decision', the title of Spengler's last book, and to the cyclic phases of a culture that Spengler used, Weiss referring to the pioneers having reached the New World in 'the spring-time of our Culture'. He warned against the class-war revolution and the revolt of the coloured world, led by Bolshevism, major themes of *The Hour of Decision*. Weiss appealed to whatever remnant of an 'Elite' might still exist in the USA, which has been replaced by an 'international Intelligentsia' that does not know anything of the creative imperative of a 'Nation'. Because of the actions of the USA, Germany, the one nation in Europe with the will to resist the rise of the East, had been destroyed. Weiss posed the question as to whether the USA, again in terms of Spengler's cultural morphology, had already grown old? He asked whether 'Uncle Sam' no

9 Translated at FBI New York office, September 1951. FBI file, F. C. F. Weiss, N.Y. 105–3100.

10 'Animist Party', FBI New York office, File no. 105–1064, December 22, 1947. 'Frederick Charles Ferdinand Weiss', pp. 3–4.

longer recalls, in his senility, the contribution of Germany to the flowering of Western culture, in Mozart, Beethoven, Kepler, Planck, Duerer, et al, and that instead Germany will be crushed by the vengeance-lust of Henry Morgenthau Jr and his tribe directing policy toward Germany. Gemanophobia had also 'killed the pride and self-respect' of German-Americans, a major element in the building of the USA, thereby undermining the USA's own foundations.[11]

Proceeding to the main body of *Germania Delenda Est?,* Weiss began with a characteristic Spenglerian concept:

> The German people like any other "people", are a unit of the soul. The great events of history in Central Europe, or anywhere else, were not really achieved by peoples; the events themselves created the peoples. Every act alters the soul of the doer. That which distinguishes the people from the population is always the inwardly lived experience in "we". The deeper this feeling is, the stronger is the *vis vitae* of the people… Though it is often justifiable to align peoples with races, "race" in this connection must not be interpreted in the present-day Darwinian sense of the word.[12]

The Spenglerian concept of landscape moulding a people was described by Weiss:

> A race has roots. Race and landscape belong together. Where a plant takes root, there it dies also. A race does not migrate. Men migrate, and their successive generations are born in ever-changing landscapes; but the landscape exercises a secret force upon the plant-nature in them, and eventually the race-expression is completely transformed by the extinction of the old and the appearance of a new one.[13]

From what we have seen already about Yockey and Spengler, with Weiss and Yockey there was a meeting of the minds that seems to be total. They were writing on the same themes at the same time, in the immediate aftermath of World War II. With ideas and the terminology so similar, one might at first think Yockey was heavily influenced by Weiss. But as we have seen, Yockey

---

11 X. Y. Z. (Frederick Charles F Weiss), *Germania Delenda Est?* (New York: Le Blanc, 1947), Preface.

12 Weiss, ibid., p. 1.

13 Weiss, ibid.

was developing these Spenglerian themes and his literary style when he was still at university, prior to the war.

In the process of forming nations and peoples, Weiss stated that Englishmen and Germans did not migrate to America but 'human beings migrated as Englishmen and Germans, and their descendants there are Americans whose specific character was born in the spiritual upheavals of 1775 and, above all, 1861-5'. Americans had thus become a 'people in the true sense of the word'.[14] Weiss was citing Spengler very closely.[15]

It is the 'felt harmony of a Destiny' that stirs people to enthusiasm; 'neither unity of speech nor physical descent were ever decisive'. It was the 'Kaiser idea', not 'blood purity', that welded 'the disjunct primitives of Charlemagne's time into the German nation'. Now, at this 'Hour of Decision', the White nations could no longer afford to battle against each other. What now had to emerge was not the destruction of Germany at the prompting of the Morgenthau clique, petty statism or United Nations one-worldism but the march of the united White peoples in an *Imperium mundi*, 'if they intend to have any future'.[16]

What is remarkable is this exactitude of convergence of ideas between Yockey and Weiss, even considering that both were Spenglerians. Yockey was secluded at Brittas Bay, Ireland, writing *Imperium* at the time that Weiss was writing *Germania Delenda Est?* and both were referring to a Western *imperium.*

Not Germany, stated Weiss, but the entire coloured world, guided by 'an international consensus', is the arch-enemy. Those of the coloured world are not pacifists and they laugh at the peace utopias of the 'world improvers'. They take up the sword when the white man puts it down.[17] Again, this is precisely the theme of Spengler's *Hour of Decision.*

The West's imperialism had been taken over by book keepers and materialists and had hence ceased to reflect high policy. Class war replaces high policy. Germany had sought to free herself from this financial grip and now

---

14 Weiss, ibid.

15 Spengler, *The Decline*, op. cit., Vol. II, p. 119.

16 Weiss, *Germania…*, op. cit., pp. 2–3.

17 Weiss, ibid., p. 3.

lay prostrate at the mercy of the Morgenthau clique. But with Germany gone, so is Europe's frontier against Asia.

> Is the position of the imperium of white nations not yet precarious enough? With our white brothers scattered all over the globe the Yellow-Brown-Black menace under a Red leadership lurks within the field of the power of the white races, not to speak of the Red Fifth Column within every white country. What good are A-bombs if the enemy is already within the fortress?[18]

It was the West that lost the war when coloured races from around the world were transplanted onto European soil in the war between white nations. But now with a war between East and West, 'who dares to believe that Germany ever was or ever will be our Archenemy?' Every material and spiritual resource had to be rallied against a 'global Coloured World Revolution'. Among the best that can be rallied are the 75,000,000 Germans.[19] The Germans had always welcomed an infusion of new blood from vigorous neighbouring races, to the extent that Germans are no longer predominately Nordic. However, now the 'international Intelligentsia' expects the Germans to be bastardised with 'the blood of our allies from the Asiatic steppes and from the Senegal jungle; if it is not sucked out before by our economic cannibalism'; after the mass rapes perpetrated against German women[20] and the millions sent to

---

18 Weiss, ibid., p. 4.

19 Weiss, ibid., p. 7.

20 See Professor Austin J App, *Ravishing the Women of Conquered Europe* (1946). The Soviet Army, however, was not alone in this mass rape and German women were not the only victims.

An American serviceman wrote to *Time* magazine, November 12, 1945: 'Many a sane American family would recoil in horror if they knew how "Our Boys" conduct themselves, with such complete callousness in human relationships over here.' An army sergeant wrote: 'Our own Army and the British Army... have done their share of looting and raping... This offensive attitude among our troops is not at all general, but the percentage is large enough to have given our Army a pretty black name, and we too are considered an army of rapists.'

According to testimony given in the United States Senate on July 17, 1945, when the colonial French troops under Eisenhower's command, presumably mostly Africans, entered Stuttgart, they herded German women into the subways and raped some two thousand of them. In Stuttgart alone, troops under Eisenhower's command raped more

Siberia. However, from this programme of extermination of the German people, 'the German Ghost HAS risen already' and will take revenge. The 70,000 German scientists delivered by the Morgenthau clique to the USSR will take their revenge under the command of Russia.[21]

With the hour of decision vis-à-vis East and West, could the USA, Weiss asked, continue to 'kill the pride and self-respect of our German-American element by castigating the German people as criminals?' Can Americans at the behest of the Morgenthau clique continue to demand the destruction of the ancestral homeland of many of America's best citizens, who have had a major influence on the shaping of the American character? The arrogance of the 'international clique' had however caused a reaction and in the USSR 'Marxian bolshevism' had been replaced by another form. The destruction of Germany, the historic bulwark of Europe against the Eastern steppes, means the destruction of Western culture. Such a lack of will also means that the Western culture has become too decrepit to find a political elite that would undertake what needs to be done to ensure the survival of Western culture.[22]

Weiss was advocating the reversal of the Morgenthau Plan towards Germany by the use of the Soviet bogeyman as an 'outer enemy' that might unite Europe to face the danger of barbarian hordes from the Russian steppes. Ironically, the Soviet bogeyman was also soon being used by the USA to try to scare Europeans to unite under US terms and indeed the Morgenthau Plan *was* reversed, in favour of rebuilding Germany as the USA's front line against the Soviet bloc. Given the new circumstances, the position of Weiss and Yockey became one of opposition to the USA to the extent that they were accused of being pro-Soviet. Such agitation was regarded with concern by the USA, as there was a major element in Germany, led by the 'neo-Nazi' Socialist Reich Party, that demanded neutrality during the Cold War. Germany had fought the USSR with devastating consequences, in its own interests. German patriots did not wish to do so again for US interests. Besides which, by playing

---

women in one week than troops under German command raped in all of France for four entire years.

21 Weiss, *Germania*, op. cit., p. 11.

22 Weiss, ibid., pp. 16–17.

one side off against another, concessions could be wrung from the occupying powers.

The connection between the Soviet bloc and Rightists in Germany and the USA was the subject of a feature by Edmond Taylor in *The Reporter* in 1954. Weiss gets an early introduction there, where one of his articles praising Soviet opposition to Jewish influences is cited. Taylor cites Bonn authorities as stating that Weiss 'is an important relay point in the international fascist network'. Weiss's contacts included Dr Werner Naumann, formerly an official at the Goebbels ministry, arrested in 1953 on charges of conspiring to overthrow the government; Naumann's associate Dr Ernst Achenbach, who had succeeded in infiltrating the Free Democratic Party; the air ace Hans-Ulrich Rudel, at the time an adviser to the Perón government, and according to Bonn a liaison with Werhrmach veterans working in East Germany. The article noted that Weiss had increasingly focused on Jewish interests rather than the USSR as being the prime enemy. Without naming the article, Taylor cites Yockey's essay on the 'Prague Treason Trial', published in the *National Renaissance Bulletin*, as an example of Weiss's pro-Soviet orientation. Taylor regarded a Rightist-Soviet nexus as being Soviet-inspired and a significant menace. He claimed that there had been overtures from Dr Fritz Dorls, leader of the banned Socialist Reich Party, for assistance from the Communist Party, to help with the clandestine publishing of rightist material, but the Communists had exposed the approach. In 1951 Dorls had met leaders of what Taylor calls 'East German nazi groups controlled by the Communists'.[23] This was presumably the National Democratic Party of Germany (NDPD), set up in Soviet Germany to mobilise nationalists for the Soviet cause.[24] Although Dorls was removed as leader of the SRP due to these exposures, the party,

---

23 Edmond Taylor, 'Germany: Where Fascism and Communism Meet', *The Reporter*, New York, April 13, 1954.

24 K. R. Bolton, 'Stalin's German-Nationalist Party', *Inconvenient History*, Vol. 6, No. 1, 2014, http://inconvenienthistory.com/archive/2014/volume_6/number_1/stalins_german_nationalist_party.php.
The NDPD was founded in 1948, the same year that East Germany announced the end of 'denazification', while the American-occupied West zealously continued the genocidal Morgenthau Plan. The NDPD continued throughout the entire existence of the DDR, and its leaders held prominent roles in government and the military.

under the leadership of Major General Otto Remer, continued to advocate a 'neutralist' line in the Cold War.

In 1954, Kurt Nippe of Brooklyn sent the FBI a detailed report on Weiss and his wife's trip to Germany and Sweden, where she met Einar Åberg, who had world notoriety among Jewish organisations as an anti-Semitic pamphleteer. Nippe stated that he had been told by Weiss 'underlings' that large amounts of money were being obtained from what he suspected was a Soviet source. Mr Nippe told the FBI that he expected this to be 'thoroughly investigated'. He also opined that Mrs Weiss might have received money in Sweden from 'Moscow' and wanted her investigated when she returned to the USA. Nippe stated that he was informed Moscow spends $10,000,000 to $200,000,000 annually in West Germany 'for propaganda purposes' and that 'Weiss is said to be trying to get his share of that'. Nippe said that Mrs Weiss's trip to Europe was to get money: 'We know that. And in all probability it will be Russian money.' Nippe provided three sources for information of Weiss and his 'agitation' in 'turning more and more' towards the Soviets.[25] The FBI response was to interview Nippe. It was noted that Nippe had himself been investigated by the FBI from 1941 to 1943.[26] The symbiotic relationship of the German nationalist revival with the Soviet bloc was of considerable concern for the American authorities. It was subsequently noted that Weiss was in contact with the *Schwarz-Weiss-Rot* (Black-White-Red) organisation in Germany, which advocated neutrality and 'is opposed to the European Defense Committee and to the strong alignment of Germay with the Western Allies'.[27]

A report shortly after comments that Weiss, who was distributing 'anti-Semitic literature rather widely' was reportedly advocating a pro-Soviet direction for Germany.[28] The same month, the FBI reported that Weiss was funding the Deutsche Reichspartei via the *Buerger-Zeitung*, organ of the

---

25 Kurt Nippe letter to J Edgar Hoover, June 29, 1954; FBI file no. 105–23413.

26 J Edgar Hoover, July 6, 1954, FBI file no. 105–23413-19.

27 FBI file no. 105–23413-24, August 31, 1954.

28 Director FBI 100–411706, July 14, 1954.

German-American Citizens League, edited by Arthur Koegel — who was described by an FBI informant as a 'dyed in the wool Nazi sympathizer'.[29]

In August 1954, the FBI noted that Weiss was in contact with H Keith Thompson at his father's printing company, Cooper Forms. It was noted that Thompson 'formerly was a leader in national socialism in New York City'.[30] He subsequently arranged for Weiss's printing at the firm.

Weiss stated that he had first heard of Yockey after receiving some of his writings from England in 1952. They met in Fall that year in New York City and he introduced Yockey to H Keith Thompson. Thompson was having trouble registering as a 'foreign agent', a mandatory registration for him as the American representative for the Socialist Reich Party. Weiss thought Yockey might be of assistance because of his being a lawyer. Weiss stated that Yockey left the USA aboard the SS United States in January 1953. He said Yockey left openly and there was no indication that he was violating any laws or that he was wanted by any Government agency. Weiss believed Yockey had gone to Germany to have his new book translated into German.[31] This 'new book' was *The Enemy of Europe*. Weiss commented that the German translation had been 'a very poor job'.

Yockey returned to the USA in February 1954. The views of Yockey on Russia were of particular interest to the FBI but Weiss denied that he had ever heard or read pro-Russian views from Yockey.[32] However, a 1955 report mentions that a 'reliable' informant claimed in 1953 that Weiss had been contacted early that year by two 'Russkys' wanting him to 'continue writing propaganda in the US' against Germany's alliance with the Western allies.[33] In 1953, an informant told the FBI he regarded pro-Russian pamphlets being published under Weiss's name as having been written by Yockey. The informant opined that Yockey 'may have connections with the Soviets' and it may be that Yockey put Weiss in contact with the Russians. It was claimed a Polish diplomat

29 Lloyd O Bogstad, Chicago FBI office, July 14, 1954, FBI file no. 105–2313-20.

30 Edward A Brandt, New York, august 31, 1954; FBI file no. 105–23413-24.

31 Edward A Brandt, FBI file no. 105–23413-26; October 22, 1954.

32 Ibid.

33 FBI Office Memorandum, File no. 105–23413-31; September 14, 1955.

named Hans Borczinski had visited Weiss several times. Weiss thought the USSR might be more 'eager to have a united Germany' than the USA.[34]

How close Weiss's thinking was to Yockey's on such matters is shown in his alleged comments, according to an FBI informant, that 'Europe will still be Europe' under Russian domination 'but that Europe would be lost under American domination. He stated that America is nothing but the homeland of international Jewry'.[35] This is precisely the theme of Yockey in *The Enemy of Europe* and various essays. Interestingly, Weiss commented that he had financially supported racial agitators such as James Madole to split the USA.[36]

In 1952, an FBI report noted that Gannon had posted Yockey the Mosleyite newspaper *Union*, French and Italian literature, the German-Argentine magazine *Der Weg* and German language leaflets. The latter included a poem, 'Das Lied Vom Braven Komrad', with a cartoon of anti-Semitic character, lampooning Eisenhower, Adenauer and the United Nations Organization, published by Weiss's imprint Le Blanc.[37]

Not only were the views of Yockey and Weiss close but articles in Weiss's name were written by Yockey. An FBI informant[38] stated in 1953 that from late 1952, Weiss claimed he was in contact with Soviet Russian agents, and a pro-Soviet attitude in Weiss's writings for the NRP *Bulletin* began to appear at this time. The informant stated that some of Weiss's articles were composed by Yockey, who was then in Europe. It was noted by some nationalists that

---

34 Edward A Brandt, FBI file no. 105–2413-7; December 7, 1953.

35 Edward A Brandt, FBI file no. 105–23413-9; March 29, 1954.

36 Ibid.

37 FBI report, October 14, 1952, p. 5; file no. 105–8229 — 1.

38 The informant, of 'unknown reliability', was in fact H Keith Thompson, who seems to have played a game of giving the FBI information of mixed reliability while including information on ADL machinations. For example, Thompson stated that Sandy Griffith, a very active ADL agent within the Right, using the name Alfred Sheffer, had provided funds for National Socialist groups, the ADL motivation being to use flamboyant organisations such as the NRP to keep the Jewish money flowing in to Zionist causes. See FBI Office Memorandum, New York Office, April 2, 1954, 105–6112.

Yockey took the 'extraordinary view that it would be better for Europe to be dominated by Russia rather than America'.[39]

***

Weiss's farm provided a safe house for Yockey on his visits back to the USA, despite the Anti-Defamation League of B'nai B'rith (ADL) having established 'anti-Nazi journalist' Sanford (Sandy) Griffith, described in an FBI report as having a 'known unsavory background',[40] in a residence down the road from Weiss. DTK states of this:

> The ADL had Griffith purchase a property near Weiss just to maintain surveillance! There was a great deal happening at the Weiss farm. Assorted screwballs dropped in as well as many VIP types. Of course Yockey resided there whenever he could get to the eastern coast and gain transportation to Mt. Hope, N.Y., which still is quite rural. The ADL and the Federal police were drooling with interest over Y's meanderings and contacts, as we all know, and spared no expense of time or dollars to pursue him.[41]

This proximity between Weiss and an ADL agent led to some extraordinary allegations about Weiss working with the ADL. DTK, who knew the Weisses well in later years, remarks that because the Weiss farm was up Shawangunk Road, a private dirt road, the usual surveillance techniques were not possible. Hence, the ADL provided Griffith with a nearby property.

---

39 'National Renaissance Party', FBI New York, November 17,1953, NY 105-6112, p. 4.

40 'Sanford Griffith — Security Matter', FBI report, February 29, 1944. Griffith was reported in 1944 as being employed by the ADL, spying on 'anti-Semites', operating through his own agency, 'Market Analysts'. FBI report, May 10, 1944, file no. 65-4098. The same report (p. 3) states that Griffith had also been employed by the American Jewish Committee. Griffith was also used by Jewish organisations to relay information to the famous muck-raking journalist Drew Pearson, who later smeared Yockey and Thompson. Ibid. In 1954 the FBI noted that Griffith's organisation Research Survey, Inc., 'continues to receive funds from the Anti-Defamation League'. 'Sanford Griffith — Registration Act', August 9, 1954, NY 97-1284. Griffith was now also collecting information on the Arab League for the ADL. In 1954 Griffith travelled to Europe for the ADL to investigate German contacts of the National Renaissance Party. (Ibid., p. 5).

41 DTK to Bolton, April 25, 2014.

> No they were not friends, co-conspirators, golf partners… no, they didn't invite each other over for dinner. Weiss gave Griffith a wide berth. Marie Weiss wouldn't speak to him or wave hello. There was a German family directly across the road from the Weiss house, and they, too, had nothing but suspicion and dislike for Griffith. Alas, the moronic rightwing gained knowledge of this unusual lookout post and made a mountain out of a molehill. What was Herr Weiss supposed to do? Lock up his home and move out? He was just a bit more careful about things.[42]

Indeed, the FBI reported that Griffith had bought a property in 1956 'about a mile away from Frederick Weiss', who was currently visiting Europe, 'in connection with his work for the ADL', and 'is known to be an agent for the Anti-Defamation League, NYC'. The FBI ascertained that Griffith's business telephone was also that of the ADL in New York City.[43]

DTK states that when Yockey was staying at the Weiss farm 'he often had to retreat to a nearby cistern under a nearby barn'. 'A friendly police chief in the town would get wind of the FBI in the area and place a call to the Weiss home. The code phrase was: I've seen the Fuller Brush Man[44] in town today. The Feds would arrive, apply pressure, scout about and depart. At the all-clear, FPY would emerge from the cistern and breathe a sigh of relief.'[45]

The Weisses were father and mother figures to Yockey. Marie Weiss nicknamed Yockey 'Muggele', 'in cheery southern Bavarian dialect, referring to facial planes of a refined and distinctive type'. Marie has been referred to as an insufferable nut. DTK writes of her that 'unkind persons of my generation who knew of her thought she was a rustic kook and worse. She was not. Coogan[46] tosses in some of this tripe when describing life in the Weiss circle'.[47] DTK recalls Marie's love of animals and her communion with them, to the

---

42 DTK to Bolton, May 19, 2014.

43 'Sanford Griffith — Registration Act', FBI New York, May 24, 1957, NY 97-1284; and June 5, 1957.

44 A reference to door-to-door salesmen.

45 DTK to Bolton, May 19, 2014.

46 Kevin Coogan, *Dreamer of the Day: Francis Parker Yockey and the Postwar Fascist International* (Brooklyn: Automedia, 1999).

47 DTK to Bolton, May 20, 2014.

extent of her removing wasp nests to glass jars and keeping them in the Weiss dining room for the winter. She was dedicated to both her husband and to Yockey.[48]

DTK states that Weiss died in March 1968, recalling, 'What a giant! What a brain!' Weiss, who had briefly known Ho Chi Minh in France during the 1920s, warned in the early 1960s of the impending Vietnam War.[49] As the extant writings of Weiss show, in the booklets on Russia for example, he was an incomparable theorist in both *realpolitik* and *geopolitik*.

One of the most vehement critics of Weiss was the Cornell University educated De West Hooker, scion of a wealthy family. Hooker established the Nationalist Youth League and the US Nationalist Party in New York, and vied with Madole for members. DTK states that when he was a guest of Hooker in Milan, Italy, in 1966, Hooker had mentioned that 'he had met Yockey several times and was impressed by his knowledge'.[50] However, Hooker was a close friend of George Lincoln Rockwell, founder of the American Nazi Party. 'Unfortunately, the two [Rockwell and De West Hooker] shared much mid-1950's Cold War thinking... Hooker said Yockey was "playing a very dangerous game with the Reds"'.

Indeed, De West Hooker had been a mentor to Rockwell, who acknowledged him as a major influence in his autobiography *This Time the World*.[51] DTK states further:

> Additionally, he delivered a barracks humor aside about Y's relentless libido: "Yockey would screw a snake if he knew how to hold on to it long enough." Also, Hooker was a dedicated foe of Weiss. Hooker circulated newsletters claiming that Weiss was a dedicated agent of the International Communist Conspiracy, that he was educated in Paris, and that that was a basis for his internationalist/Red outlook, etc., etc. All this from an educated man, a graduate of the elite

48 DTK to Bolton, July 9, 2014.

49 DTK to Bolton, May 20, 2014.

50 DTK to Bolton, April 25, 2014.

51 George Lincoln Rockwell, *This Time the World* (1963), 'Acknowledgements'. Rockwell states that West Hooker first taught him 'to know the cunning and evil ways of the enemy'.

> Cornell University, New York. Then there was the easily answered question of Sanford (Sandy) Griffith living down the road from the Weiss farm.[52]

In 1954, Weiss, under his Le Blanc imprint and in association with James Madole of the National Renaissance Party, published a pamphlet entitled 'Oswald Spengler, The American Jewish Committee and Russia', which the FBI reported to have a 'pro-Russian slant'.[53] The pamphlet, signed 'X.Y.Z.', like many of Weiss's pamphlets, which were often joint efforts between Weiss, Yockey and H Keith Thompson, was opined to perhaps have been at least partly written by Yockey. It was stated that Yockey, under the alias of Frank Healy, was writing 'a great deal' of Weiss's material.[54] This matter was raised again in 1959, when an FBI report alludes to an informant stating that Weiss continued to have Yockey writing for him. It was stated that both Yockey and the well-known 'anti-Semitic' publicist Eustace Mullins were utilised by Weiss for his publications. Weiss preferred Yockey, whom he regarded as a 'genius' because Mullins had 'emotional complications' which made it difficult to keep him 'on track'. However, Yockey was 'elusive'.[55] Weiss had been sent an enigmatic letter from the West Coast purporting to be from a 'German-American', however Weiss recognised Yockey's style. He was enthused at the prospect of regaining contact with Yockey after what would have been years of absence.

## *Hang on and Pray*: A Spenglerian Critique of Toynbee

*Hang on and Pray* is likely to be one of the notable collaborations between Weiss and Yockey as 'X.Y.Z.' It is plausible that *Hang on and Pray* was written by Yockey from a draft by Weiss and this was probably published in 1956.[56] As

52 DTK to Bolton, April 25, 2014.

53 FBI report, August 4, 1954, p. 3; file no. 105–8229 — 2.

54 FBI report, August 4, 1954, p. 4; file no. 105–8229 — 2.

55 FBI Chicago office, 'Eustace Clarence Mullins Jr, Racial Matters', October 16, 1959, SAC Chicago (105–1152).

56 Three libraries in the USA hold copies: University of California, Riverside; Abilene Christian University, Brown Library; and the New York Public Library System. All calculate the date of publication as 1956, probably on the basis of the year of receipt.

we know, Yockey was commissioned by Weiss to write his material. There are Yockeyan peculiarities such as the references to 'our toynbees' in lower-case. We also know from Gannon, as previously stated, that Yockey was 'derisive' of Toynbee, who was being touted as the pre-eminent philosopher-historian of the post-war era. H Keith Thompson, who printed and edited the manuscript of *Hang on and Pray*, related that:

> I am sure that some of the contribution to that stemmed from the pen of Yockey, because Weiss was really quite incapable of handling the English language, and had difficulty gathering his thoughts. I did much of that for him. But I'm not a scholar of the Toynbee school or stamp, and that came from somewhere. But I would have guessed that Yockey in some way contributed to it, and I'm sure that he would have influenced Weiss to the extent that his own views would have been expressed there.[57]

The work was published under the La Blanc imprint as a Spenglerian evaluation of the post-war US ideology that was touting 'world peace' through a world state.

The Zionist policymakers in Washington were split between a hawkish attitude towards the USSR and one of co-existence. World racial conflicts would emerge, with China as a new factor in leading the coloured world rebellion. Spengler had referred to this coloured world revolt under the auspices of communism in *The Hour of Decision*. Weiss and Yockey (we may assume) were developing this theme using Toynbee to establish a dialectic for analysis. So far from being a disaster for the West, war with the USSR might serve as a catalyst for renewal. What was not required was either victory or defeat but 'stalemate' which would eventually see the disintegration of both the USA and the USSR. This would leave room for the reinvigoration of Western civilization, if there was 'a National revival in America, in union with a revival of the European Elite', which could create a 'regenerative outcome of a series of catastrophes'. 'An enraged white race, decimated by perhaps two-thirds of its numbers after prolonged wars, might rise in blind fury against its tormentors.'

57 Thompson interview with Keith Stimely, op. cit.

> Without such a stalemate the Western World is doomed to perpetual slaughter in stupid wars and to inevitable miscegenation with colored races. Civilization will crumble, music will even more revert to that of the jungle, literature will be cast aside, history will be unread, and our cities will decompose as the dark inhabitants stalk the decaying streets.[58]

A choice was proffered: Prophets of Western demise, or 'our toynbees' with their advice to the West to 'hang on and pray'. 'Let us instead cut through the mighty Rockefeller-Financed propaganda machine which is promoting and deifying this little gnat of an Englishman.'[59]

Toynbee's entire system was considered to be derived from Spengler but is 'a pastiche, a massive plagiarism, a caricature, and a distortion of Spengler'. Toynbee acknowledges his debt, writing that he had been handed a copy of Spengler's *Decline* in 1920 and wondered whether his 'inquiry' into history had been already undertaken before he had even shaped the question in his mind? However, Toynbee saw a work that still needed to be undertaken: how civilizations originate, or their 'genesis'. To 'X.Y.Z.' such a question was 'of no particular importance'. Perhaps this was being a little shortsighted, as was Toynbee's claim that Spengler had not dealt with the issue. In the first volume of *Decline,* there are ample studies on the genesis of civilizations, especially in regard to the formation of 'peoples' and 'races'.

However, to 'X.Y.Z.' the 'entire purpose of Spengler's work was to arrive at the form of our future', to adjust to the possibilities of what might be done and what cannot be done.[60] It was Spengler who discovered that 'a high culture is an organic unity' whose destiny can be discovered by studying the analogous epochs of other high cultures. 'To life belongs death, and to each living stage belongs its appropriate tasks and events.'

We might appreciate easily enough that whereas Spengler issued a challenge for Western resurgence amidst an epoch of decline in the closing pages of *The Decline of the West*, this became a strident clarion call in his last book *The Hour of Decision*. However, Toynbee's purpose was quite different: his clarion call was for a 'World Civilization' of Afro-Asiatic conglomeration

58 X.Y.Z., *Hang on and Pray*, (New York: La Blanc Publishers, [1956?]), 'Foreword'.

59 Ibid.

60 Ibid., 'Pilfered from Oswald Spengler'.

on the ruins of the West. It can be understood why in the post-1945 world, Toynbee was feted as the philosopher of the new era.

Toynbee also rejects Spengler's organic cycles of history in favour of what becomes the orthodox linear view. Hence, he refers to the 'Christian era' (which is really the Western), which is 'no more than the twinkling of an eye'. As 'X.Y.Z.' points out, this 'comparison of physical time with organic time' is 'meaningless'. However, it is a primary Toynbee theme.[61]

Toynbee presents himself as a pacifist and an opponent of Western imperialism, save as it served British imperialism, as in the wars against the Boers, which he regarded as a necessity in crushing 'Dutch nationalism'. He is however avidly Germanophobic to the point of considering the permanent suppression of Germany as a post-war necessity. On the other hand he exalts India, China, Islam and 'the savages of Africa' while disapproving of everything Western other than its technics. This is because Western technics will be harnessed by the coming world state with Afro-Asia in the ascent. His detestation of the White race is patent; he is quoted as writing that 'the triumph of the White Race may be judged to have been a misfortune' because of its being 'race-conscious'. He sees Islam as having a special mission in eliminating 'race-consciousness' in the world state.[62]

What 'X.Y.Z.' sees in Toynbee behind the millions of words of pseudo-scholarship is a 'propagandist'. Politicians have always been glad to have priests, philosophers and scientists to purify their motives. 'Vulgar lust for power is dignified and disguised by these propagandists' and 'every word he writes is in support of Zionism[63] and the Washington regime'. His magum opus, *A Study of History*, had provided 'a library of material' to justify all the long-range policies of Zionism the Washington regime and the United Nations. He was a zealous advocate for the transfer of technology to Africa, saying it was immoral for the West to have 'more than our backward brothers'; that Europeans had 'cold-bloodedly' despoiled the Africans. The major

---

61 Ibid., 'Toynbee Logic Everything both Ways'.

62 Ibid., 'Toynbee, the Historical Geo-Politician'.

63 Toynbee's comment on Judaism being part of a 'fossil' Civilization (the equivalent to Spengler's *Fellaheen*) did however somewhat blot his copybook.

problem of the post-war world for Toynbee was that an atomic war might eliminate Africans, whose lofty conception of God was without equal.[64]

Toynbee was a type of Marxist. While Marx directed his 'resentment-feeling' against the 'upper stratum' of each country, Toynbee 'applies it to World culture collectively'. Marx used the proletariat for this purpose, Toynbee uses the 'savage, the barbarian, the fellah'. Toynbee referred to the coloured races as 'the outer proletariat'[65] and it is a theme that was adopted a few decades later, with calls via the United Nations for a 'new international economic order' and a 'North-South Dialogue' that would have seen the transfer of technology and credit to the Third World and even a world tax, to try to address world economic imbalance. Like most such humanitarian crusades, it was the plutocracy that stood to gain in terms of the expansion of cheap labour, mass markets, Western de-industrialisation and the Western guarantee of Third World debts. While the slogans change, the aims remain the same. Toynbee's rhetoric was even regurgitated during the 1970s and 1980s in regard to a 'new international economic order' and claims that the unequal distribution of the world's goods between and privileged minority and an underprivileged majority had become an 'intolerable injustice' in view of 'the latest technological inventions of Western man'. The unequal distribution of the world goods had become 'a moral enormity' and both 'Class and War' had to be 'abolished'.[66]

As for Europe, 'it would better for there to be no Europe whatever' than for the supposed inevitability coming to pass, of Germany eventually becoming 'the mistress of Europe', when they would 'ply the whip' and 'dig in the spurs'. 'This German crux would appear to be an insurmountable obstacle to the construction of a European Third Great Power'.

However, it is the coloured races that are the key to the future: it is historical 'Necessity' that they provide the catalyst for a World State where there no longer exists 'race-consciousness', which is in the sole possession of the Whites. Toynbee sees a universal human destiny in the 'center-point of all human affairs' being 'in the neighbourhood of Babylon, on the ancient portage across the isthmus between the Continent and its peninsulas [sic] of Arabia

64 X.Y.Z., op. cit., 'Toynbee the Political Propagandist — A Second Face'.

65 Ibid., 'Toynbee, The World Marxist'.

66 Ibid., 'Toynbee, The World Marxist'.

and Africa'. The world centre might travel further to 'some locus between China and Russia'. X.Y.Z. regarded Toynbee as advocating, despite the 'fog of words', Israel as the world centre.

For Toynbee, in contrast to Spengler, the whole purpose towards which Western culture has been leading has been to unite the world then self-destruct. It is Western technics that have made this united humanity possible. Toynbee sees, like Spengler, a coloured-world revolt but, unlike Spengler, sees the victory of the coloured world as a positive historical development, or what today is termed 'the end of history' by protagonists for American world hegemony. The world amalgamates and that is History's finale. Toynbee put the coloured-world revolt in terms of a world rebellion of 'peasants' that included not only Africans and Asians but the peasants of Eastern Europe. They would revolt to seize what they regarded as theirs from the West, and all of humanity, including the majority of whites, will be happier for it. 'The technological scaffolding' will fall away and mankind 'will be untied at last', based on a synthetic new religion. It is only Westerners who are narrow in outlook while all the coloured races have this world-outlook.

In his essay 'The Dwarfing of Europe', Toynbee states that this is an accomplished fact and the Marshall Plan gives Western Europe 'at least the solace of seeing her dead supremacy given Christian burial'. 'Europe's will no longer decides Europe's destiny. Her future lies on the knees of the giants who now overshadow her.' 'Toynbee tells us this!' Of Westerners and Europeans, there will be nothing left. There will be an amalgam of all races founded upon an amalgam of all religions.[67]

Russia presented a questionable factor for the internationalists and the Zionists. They still hoped to integrate Russia into their world system.[68] 'The idea is impossible', stated X.Y.Z., but 'it is the only policy the Zionists have'. They are not empire builders but 'the sons of fish-peddlers and coin-clippers'. Their policy is 'schizophrenic', their ascent to world power is accentual and transitory: 'The mighty evolution of Western culture is not to be suddenly nullified by a gang of rootless *Fellaheen*, however sly, however stupid their

67 Ibid., 'The Latest Toynbee Line'.

68 Ibid., 'What Toynbee's Mother Didn't Tell Him'.

dupes.' The peaceful coexistence with the USSR that was being pursued at the time, and of which Toynbee was a proponent, rested on the belief that a war with the Soviets would include a resurgence of Germany. Toynbee, as a primary intellectual spokesman for the internationalist agenda, expressed this view. Another Zionist faction was willing to pursue war using Germans as cannon fodder. However, while peace persisted, or at least the Cold War, the Zionists and the Washington regime would pursue a policy of industrialising the coloured world, and 'united humanity', as Toynbee explained, would eventuate. While peaceful co-existence continued the possibility existed that the Soviet Russian bloc could be subverted culturally and financially. Zionists in the USA and Russia might then join in unison to establish a United Nations and Toynbee's projected world centre would be located in what suspiciously seemed like Israel.

How far-fetched was this analysis by X.Y.Z. in circa 1956? Today, with hindsight, we can see that the Zionists and plutocrats achieved their objective of subverting the Soviet bloc. Soviet presses were warning at the time, especially during the 1968 revolt in Czechoslovakia, that the world Zionist apparatus in tandem with the USA was trying to destabilise the Soviet bloc. Soviet bloc literature on Zionism was far more instructive than much of the Western right-wing 'anti-Semitic' literature that insisted the USSR was still secretly run by Jews. As we can now appreciate, Zionist Culture-distortion did enter the Soviet bloc and culminated over several decades in the 'colour revolutions' that caused the Soviet edifice to implode as a Eurasian geopolitical entity.

In *Hang on and Pray*, all the themes of Yockeyan thought are evident. He had expressed the geopolitical themes in 'America's two ways of waging war' and the themes were reiterated in his final essay, 'The World in Flames'. The finale of *Hang on and Pray* offered a clarion call:

> Against Toynbee's mountains of words, which speak to prove the inevitability and the desirability of Europe's complete destruction in permanent petition between Zionism and Russia, we say quite simply this:

> *The future belongs to Europe, the home-soil of the Western Culture, to its colonies, its Christendom, and to its white race; and not to Zionism, nor to the black-yellow-brown masses which it seeks to mobilise against us.*
>
> Let history decide.[69]

## Ullstein and Einstein

A treatise from La Blanc preceding *Hang on and Pray* seems to offer a contrast in style, although not in ideology. Its date of publication is circa 1954–1955. The pamphlet *Without Ullstein — No Einstein* is likely to be Weiss's creation without Yockey, presumably with editing by H Keith Thompson. While both Weiss and Yockey were thoroughly imbued with Spengler, *Without Ullstein* focuses on physics — a particular interest of Weiss, who had studied physics at the Sorbonne. On the other hand, Einstein is not mentioned, so far as can be determined, in anything Yockey wrote, despite Einstein's influence on the world intelligentsia being as profound as Marx, Freud and Darwin, who each receive treatment from Yockey. Moreover, Yockey could have cited Marx, Freud and Einstein as the dominating Jewish triumvirate of our era.

Weiss's essay on Einstein might then give us the opportunity to consider Weiss's writing style as distinct from Yockey's. Unlike Weiss, Yockey coined his own neo-Spenglerian terms, while Weiss used Spenglerian terms, referring here for example to the 'springtime' of a culture, whereas Yockey — strangely — did not. When considering this essay alongside other essays by 'X.Y.Z.', and in particular *Hang on and Pray*, perhaps we can discern what publications are mainly written by Weiss, or by Yockey, or as a collaboration of both, probably with Thompson's editing input.

Weiss considers Einstein as having become a primary part of Jewish intellectual hegemony over the West, through a publicity campaign by the leading German Jewish publishing house of Ullstien. While Weiss does not attempt to disparage Einstein's contribution to science, he does state that Einstein has eclipsed a long line of Western scientists, without which there would be no physics. In particular Weiss compares what we might now call the celebrity

69 Ibid.

status of Einstein with that of Max Planck. For Weiss, modern Western physics starts in 1901 with Planck's *quanta* theory, proceeding only then to Einstein's theory in 1905, among the many others such as Rutherford, Bohr, de Broglie, Heisenberg, Hahn and Meson, who in turn built on the work of Western science, which dates back centuries.[70]

Weiss states that Ullstein launched Einstein's celebrity career in 1918, giving the Special Theory of Relativity as the foundation of the new worldview of the modern era. He became a god of the city-dwelling intelligentsia, which becomes the dominant class of a civilization in its twilight years, when everything is reduced to a matter of weights and measures. Western science and mathematics was a reflection of the Western world-feeling, unique to this culture, of 'infinite SPACE'.[71] This was what Spengler defined as the West's unique *Faustian* soul, although oddly neither Yockey nor Weiss used the term *Faustian*. In thoroughly Spenglerian mode, this passage might be compared with that of Yockey's writing style and with other 'X.Y.Z.' essays such as *Hang on and Pray*:

> And so, more than the work of any other scientist, has Einstein's General theory of relativity destroyed the faith-forms of our cultural springtime. Now suddenly we are overcome by an annihilating doubt about things that just yesterday were the unchallenged foundations of physical theorem about the meaning of the energy-principle, the concept of Mass, space, Absolute time, and, above all about causality laws generally. This is not the fruitful doubt of yesterday, which brought the knower and the object together. It is a doubt affecting the very fundamentals of our Nature-Science. This doubt destroys our Soul![72]
>
> The Western form-feeling is that of unrestrained, strong-willed, far-ranging soul, and its symbol pure, imperceptible, unlimited SPACE. Our universe of infinite space, whose existence for us is accepted without doubt or challenge, simply does not exist for any other Culture! Infinite space of our physics is a form of

---

70 F. C. F. Weiss, *Without Ullstein—No Einstein: The Story of the Press and the Professor* (New York: La Blanc Publications, ca. 1955), pp. 5–7.

71 Weiss, ibid., p. 11.

72 Weiss, ibid., pp. 11–12.

> very numerous and extremely complicated elements tacitly assumed, which have come into being only as an expression of our Soul.[73]

The Western soul intuits this physics and symbolises it in the word 'space'. The whole of Western mathematics from Descartes onwards 'is devoted to the theoretical interpretation of this great and wholly religious symbol': 'The aim of all pure physics since Galileo is identical. *Destroy this specifically Western intuition of space and you destroy our soul.*'[74]

How perceptive was Weiss? The name Einstein is identified as the archetype of genius. It is even 'hip' for an adolescent's bedroom wall to be adorned with a poster of Einstein or for him to wear a T-shirt with Einstein's face — but one is unlikely to see the face of Max Planck anywhere. Perhaps for the same reason, one will see Marx treated the same way rather than, say, Werner Sombart, or Freud rather than Jung. Although Yockey strangely does not address the influence of Einstein, Marx, Freud and Einstein have dominated the present era's intellectual hegemony.

***

Clearly, Weiss was as anathema to many on the radical right as Yockey and for the same reasons. Rockwell regarded Yockey as a traitor to the USA vis-à-vis the Cold War. He described Yockey as a 'Strasserite', a reference to Otto and Gregor Strasser, leaders of a 'Left-wing' faction of National Socialism critical of Hitler.[75] There seems no basis for the claim that Yockey was a 'Strasserite', a designation also mentioned in an FBI report on the founding of the ELF. However, to Hitlerites, 'Strasserite' is a term for traitor.

In 1953, Arnold Leese wrote with concern to James Madole, leader of the National Renaissance Party in the USA, about Yockey's heretical views on race. Madole replied, assuring Leese that the NRP had not abandoned its orthodox-Hitlerian 'racial or political principles',[76] despite having published in the December 1952 'special edition' of *National Renaissance Bulletin*

---

73 Weiss, ibid., p. 14.

74 Ibid.

75 See Troy Southgate, *Otto Strasser: The Life and Times of a German Socialist* (London: Black Front Press, 2010).

76 Madole to Leese, February 28, 1953.

an anonymous article introduced as being a report paid for by 'a group of important gentlemen recently arrived from Germany'. It was Yockey's seminal essay, 'What is Behind the Hanging of Eleven Jews in Prague?', which aimed at a fundamental reorientation of the right.[77]

Yockey had returned to the USA under the alias 'Frank Healy', the name by which Madole knew him, and met Weiss and H Keith Thompson at this time with a close collaboration ensuing. Madole, in introducing the essay, stated that he had been provided with a mailing list of 'nearly every' important 'Fascist leader' in Europe, Africa and South America, and that the *Bulletin* was being sent to an exceptionally large number of people because the cost had been underwritten. Weiss funded the printing and mailing, and was the primary financial backer of Madole for several years, also setting the policy for the NRP.[78]

Yockey's essay contended that the trial in Prague of top Communist Party functionaries, most of whom were Jewish, was evidence that the Jews had lost control of the Soviet bloc to the resurgent forces of Slavism. These functionaries had not merely been tried for 'treason' but for being part of a Zionist plot with connections to Zionists in the USA. Yockey held that until 1952, the USA and USSR had worked in accord with Jewish interests as indicated by the support of both for the creation of the state of Israel in 1948.

Yockey did in fact recognise in the essay that there had been a breach between the USSR and the USA since late 1946, when Moscow rejected the Washington regime's plan to offer Stalin junior partnership in a world state via the United Nations organisation. The basis of this, as Yockey pointed out, was the so-called 'internationalisation' of atomic energy, which would mean *de facto* control of atomic energy by the USA. This was the so-called 'Baruch Plan' because it was offered up for public consumption by the so-called 'elder statesman' of the USA, the perennial adviser to US presidents Bernard M Baruch, banker and Zionist. These points show the breadth and depth of Yockey's knowledge of what was taking place. The result of the Soviet rejection 'that stymied the plans of the Jewish leadership' was the encirclement of

77 'What is Behind the Hanging of Eleven Jews in Prague?', *National Renaissance Bulletin*, Special edition, December 1952.

78 'Special announcement', *National Renaissance Bulletin*, ibid., p. 1.

Russia and the 'Cold War'. The Prague trials were 'an unmistakable turning point' in an historical process. 'Henceforth, all must *perforce* reorient their policy in view of the undeniable reshaping of the world-situation.' Talk of 'defense against Bolshevism' 'and the defense of Europe' at a time when 'every inch of European soil is dominated by the enemies of Europe,' belongs now to yesterday.[79] Now the Soviet bloc is the only obstacle to the domination of the entire earth by the 'united nations'.[80] Russia, under Stalin, was run by a 'pan-Slav nationalist-religious entourage',[81] which had been armed against Germany by the 'Jewish-American leadership' because of their obsessive hatred of Europe-Germany and by so doing sought to prevent peace between the two blocs. Yockey also stated that the aim of the American-Jewish leadership in Russia was to replace Stalinism with a return of Trotskyism. This would eliminate the religious impulse of Russia, which indeed had been attempted in the early years of the Bolshevik regime,[82] and return Russia to the path of internationalism. Yockey hoped that the events that forced Stalin to reshape his policy would likewise force the European elite to end American-Jewish hegemony over Europe. Explicitly stating the implications of Weiss's *Germania Delenda Est?,* Yockey wrote that if the 'American-Jewish leadership' refuses to concede the demands of Europe then 'the new leaders of Europe will threaten them with the Russian bogey' and bring about the liberation of Europe. Yockey also foresaw that Russia would ally with Islam and that Japan would increasingly assert its independence. The Prague trials had delineated enemies, 'cleared the air' and made it plain that Europe must not fight for any interest other than Europe, which included the supposed 'defense of Europe' against Russia at the behest of Morgenthau and others who wished to annihilate Europe.

What Yockey and Weiss offered the radical Right was unadulterated *realism*.

---

79 'What is Behind the Hanging of Eleven Jews in Prague', op. cit.

80 Yockey did not generally capitalise the names of individuals and institutions for which he had no respect.

81 For an assessment of Stalin, including his rejection of US overtures towards a post-war world state via the UNO, see Bolton, *Stalin: The Enduring Legacy*, op. cit.

82 Ibid.

Madole stated that someone had given him the essay under Yockey's *nom de plume* Ulick Varange. The individual in question was presumably Weiss, who informed Madole that Varange had gone to Lebanon. Madole replied to Leese that he had not previously heard of *Imperium* or the European Liberation Front. Madole noted to Leese that 'several other complaints' about the ELF had come from England and Spain.[83]

Despite Madole's assurances to Leese regarding his commitment to Nazi orthodoxy vis-à-vis the USSR and race, Madole did indeed maintain the Yockeyan position even after his break with Weiss. DTK states that 'Mr Madole, under the aegis of Weiss, fell in line'.[84] Moreover, until his death in 1979, and with it the demise of the NRP, Madole continued to make *Imperium* available.[85]

The next issue of *National Renaissance Bulletin* ran a front-page article by Weiss, which dealt with the Russia issue by analysing President Dwight Eisenhower's Inaugural Address and State of the Nation speech. Weiss pointed out what the Socialist Reich Party in Germany had also been contending — that during World War II, Russia had quickly gone from a noble, freedom-loving nation fighting for world democracy to a purveyor of tyranny and corruption. Weiss argued that the USSR was the same now as it had been during World War II. What had changed was that she had rejected US overtures to become junior partner in a world state and Eisenhower was now using warmongering rhetoric against the Soviet leadership of the same type that had preceded the USA's entry into two world wars. The USSR had also started to pursue an anti-Zionist line coupled with a resurgent nationalism. Weiss noted that there was also much talk about the benefits of free trade from Eisenhower, indicating one of the real motives for war. Germany, while remaining occupied, was expected to conscript troops for possible use on the front line of any confrontation between the USA and the USSR. Eisenhower was even urging Europe to unite to defend her culture and spirituality. Yet a few years previously, he had been in the forefront of allowing the Red Army to

83 Madole to Leese, February 28, 1953.

84 DTK to Bolton, April 20, 2014.

85 *NR Bulletin*, (probably the last before Madole's death) Vol. 30, No's 4 and 5, April–May 1979, p. 9, listed *Imperium*.

overrun Europe and had received the Order of Suvorov from Stalin for a war that had devastated Europe and razed the ancient culture capital of Dresden. At a time when much of the American Right was calling the United Nations Organisation part of the 'international Communist conspiracy', Eisenhower was stating that actions against the USSR must be undertaken under the auspices of the United Nations — what Weiss in 1953 called a 'United Nations Imperium'.[86] The analogies between this period and the new 'Cold War' against Putin's Russia are more than curious.

George Lincoln Rockwell, who founded the American Nazi Party in 1959, wrote four years after Yockey's death and three years before his own at the gun of a former ANP member,

> There is rising all over the world, among hard-core National Socialists, a new cult of what I call Yockeyism. I found much of interest in Yockey's book *IMPERIUM* and actually helped promote it. But the cult founded on this man is dangerous and, I believe, in some ways downright evil.[87]

Rockwell and Madole were rivals, although the American Nazi Party could upstage the National Renaissance Party through its flamboyant stunts, comparative professionalism and the charisma of Rockwell, a naval veteran of World War II and Korea. While the ANP followed a standardised Right-wing line of supporting the Establishment during the Cold War era, the NRP, influenced from its early days by Weiss and by Yockey, adopted an increasingly pro-Soviet approach up to the point that Madole even began stocking material from the Soviet embassy. The NRP also pursued a pro-Third World course to the extent of praising Castro and Nasser in particular. Madole's distribution of pro-Arab literature was of particular concern to the FBI, judging from the number of times this is referred to in the FBI files on Madole and the NRP. One such FBI report in 1956 refers to Madole having obtained a large quantity

86 Frederick Chas. F. Weiss, 'An Analysis of Eisenhower's Inaugural Address', *National Renaissance Bulletin*, New York, January 1953, pp. 1–8.

87 G. L. Rockwell, *Rockwell Report*, Arlington, Virginia, July of 1964.

of 'pro-Arab and pro-Egyptian' literature for distribution.[88] Madole compared Nasser, Sukarno, Kassem and Castro to Hitler in pointing the way to a 'renaissance... among the peoples of Africa, Asia and Latin America'.[89]

In 1961, the FBI noted that the American Jewish Committee reported Madole was 'now espousing Fidel Castro' and mentioned Madole organising a Cuba-American Friendship Rally in March. Madole wrote in an invitation to the rally: 'The sinister campaign of hatred and vilification directed against the government of President Gamal Nasser of the United Arab Republic and Premier Fidel Castro of Cuba by America's Zionist-dominated press, radio and TV is turning the peoples of the Middle East and Latin America into bitter foes of the United states. We urge our Cuban and Arab friends to join with members of the National Renaissance party in a mass unity rally to oppose this Zionist-sponsored campaign of hate.'[90]

All this is Yockeyan in character and particularly evident in Yockey's last essay, 'The World in Flames', co-written and posthumously published by H Keith Thomson, which sees encouraging signs in anything of an anti-American, anti-Zionist nature.[91] The NRP rally for Arabia and Cuba against Zionism came one month after the limited publication of 'The World in Flames', in February 1961.[92]

Yockey considered that the USA/Zionist combine was losing ground throughout the world, as Latin America and the Arab states and Asia increasingly became 'neutral'. Yockey saw the spread of revolt among both Arabs and Latin Americans as rolling America back. Because Russia remained

88 'James H Madole', FBI New York office, July 1, 1957, NY 105–6129, p. 3.
Such seems to have been the concern about Madole's distribution of Egyptian government and other Arab literature that the FBI enquired as to whether Madole was registered as a 'foreign agent' with the Justice Department. 'James H Madole', 'Egypt', 'Registration Act', January 29, 1957, New York 105–6129.

89 Madole, 'Race and Religion, The Keys to Historical Understanding', *National Renaissance Bulletin*, Feb-March 1961, Vol. 12, Nos. 2 and 3, p. 4.

90 'James H Madole. Correlation Summary', January 31, 1964, FBI main file 105–52256, p. 44.

91 Yockey, 'The World in Flames: An Estimate of the World Situation', was published in February 1961 and republished in 1971 by DTK in *Yockey: Four Essays* (New Jersey: Nordland Press).

92 The date is given by DTK in the introduction to *Yockey: Four Essays*, op. cit.

committed to the destruction of the West, the Jewish-American leadership was torn between its own anti-Western tendencies and its loss of control over Russia. Therefore, the Jewish-American leadership was not committed to total war against Russia as it had been against Germany. Germans have been too 'denationalized' and 'brainwashed' to be of any real use to the USA in a war against Russia. Yockey saw Nasser, whom he had met, as 'great and vigorous' and referred to neutralist leaders such as Sukarno as 'brilliant statesmen'. Each led great masses and thereby diminished 'Jewish-American power' without augmenting Russia's. Castro's Cuba was a sign of the 'restive mass of some 180,000,000 Latin Americans'. 'The growing tide of neutralism in the world is due to the political incapacity of the leadership corps of American-Jewry.' Something similar might arise in Europe, and de Gaulle, although an 'idiot' and a 'cretin', could yet save Europe because he wished to 'be equal to the masters who created him'. 'An idiot might save Europe. History has seen things as strange.'

Neither America nor Russia could win this 'Third World War'. However, Yockey was confident that the peace would be established on Russian terms, not because of Russian cleverness but because of American stupidity. America denied arms to Batista and allowed Castro to win (as it did with Chiang kai-Shek), then opposed Castro. Yockey pointed to many other such anomalies in US foreign policy and explained this by 'two minds' of Zionism 'which function independently'. 'As Zionists they are committed to the destruction of Western civilization' and hence in this they sympathise with any anti-Western state or movement including Russia, although as the leaders of the USA they must maintain Western technics and wealth: 'In a word they are working simultaneously for and against the Western civilization.' Russia represents 'Stupidity'; the Zionist-run West, 'Malice'. The play on the world stage is entitled 'Where Ignorant Armies Clash by Night': 'The producer is Destruction, and the company is called The Forces of Darkness.'[93]

Yockey's premise might seem odd: that the Jewish-American leadership strata can be both pro- and anti-Western simultaneously; both pro- and anti-Russia. However, it is well known that many parasites have an innate

93 Yockey, 'The World in Flames', op., cit., VII.

tendency to destroy their own host and hence themselves. While Yockey does not use this precise analogy it does accord with his idea of Culture-pathology.

## National Renaissance Party

Despite their eccentric character, even by radical Right standards, Madole and the National Renaissance Party were of much interest to the FBI and heavily infiltrated by the Anti-Defamation League and the Non-Sectarian Anti-Nazi League. The NRP and *Common Sense* were the primary targets of the Congressional investigation into 'neo-Fascist and hate groups' in 1954.[94] The NRP was one of the first neo-Fascist groups formed in the USA after World War II; it was also the most enduring, lasting from 1949 until Madole's death in 1979, and many 'fascist' luminaries served an apprenticeship there. These included Matt Koehl, an officer of the NRP's 'Elite Guard' in 1953 who became organiser of the segregationist National States Rights Party[95] and was also Rockwell's heir as leader of American Nazism; and Eustace Mullins, artist, photographer, racial agitator and protégé and biographer of Ezra Pound.[96] For our purposes, the significance of the NRP was that it was funded and influenced by Weiss, and that Madole provided a platform for the writings of Weiss and Yockey. From the mid-1950s, the FBI began to take a particular interest in Madole's contact with Egyptian, Syrian, Saudi and Algerian sources. In 1957, it noted that Madole praised Nasser and other Arab leaders, saying that there would be no peace in the Middle East until Israel was 'obliterated'. Madole 'obtained a large quantity of Egyptian and Arab literature', which he distributed through the NRP,[97] and the sale of the literature, which Madole had acquired gratis, augmented party funds.[98] These activities on behalf of the Arabs raised the question as to whether Madole should be registered as an

94 House Committee on Un-American Activities, *Preliminary Report on Neo-Fascist and Hate Group Activities*, December 17, 1954.

95 'James H Madole. Correlation summary', January 31, 1964, FBI main file 105–52256, p. 35.

96 Eustace Mullins, *This Difficult Individual Ezra Pound* (Hollywood: Angriff Press, 1961).

97 'James H Madole, Internal Security', ibid., January 7, 1957, inter alia.

98 'James H Madole, Internal Security', ibid., p. 6.

agent of a foreign government.[99] Some of Madole's *NRP Bulletin* articles were previewed by the Egyptian embassy and were reported to have been accepted for reprinting in the Egyptian press.[100]

The roots of the NRP go back to 1947, when Madole founded the Animist Party, which described itself as a 'New Nationalist Third Party Movement'. The slogan of the party was 'The Ultimate Destiny of Man Lies in the Stars'.[101] This reflects Madole's lifelong interest in science, including science fiction. The programme of the Animist Party included 'protection of the Christian faith against enemies within and without',[102] a contrast to Madole's later interests in witchcraft, theosophy and paganism. Madole was soon in contact with veteran Nationalists, including W Henry MacFarland, director of the Nationalist Action League (NAL) and editor of *National Progress.*

Already in 1947, while still under the name of the Animist Party, also ineptly referred to by the FBI as 'Animalism', Madole ('Maddle' in the FBI report) was in contact with Weiss, who was named as 'Fred Wise'. The comment was that 'little is known of Fred Wise', although 'considerable correspondence has flown between Wise and Maddle'.[103] Perhaps a lot more would have been known of Wise (sic) had FBI files for *Frederick Weiss* been consulted. These files are substantial, given that Weiss was on the Security Index until 1955 as a significant potential threat to national security. Madole contacted Weiss after reading his booklet *Quo Vadis America?,* asking Weiss to be the Animist Party's New York organiser. Weiss declined, one reason for his caution being that he was not an American citizen. However, Madole and Weiss maintained weekly written communication during 1947. Weiss was impressed by Madole's knowledge of philosophy.[104] They first met in mid-1947 at Weiss's home, thereafter meeting frequently at a café to discuss politics. He was however

99 'James H Madole, Egypt, Registration Act', FBI New York file no. 105–6129, January 29, 1957. FBI Office Memorandum 105–52256, March 5, 1957.

100 'James H Madole, Egypt, Registration Act', ibid., December 27, 1957, p. 5.

101 FBI Memorandum, 'Re. Animist Party', April 25, 1947.

102 Point 4 of the Animist Party program, ibid.

103 FBI Memorandum, 'Re. Animist Party', ibid.

104 'Animist Party', FBI New York office, 'Frederick Charles Ferdinand Weiss', op. cit., p. 4.

under no illusion that Madole's organisation would ever amount to anything substantial.[105]

In mid-1949, unity talks led to close co-operation between the NAL, what was by then being called the National Renaissance Party, and the newspaper *Common Sense.* There was also a carry-over of the remnants of the pre-war Christian Front, the Coughlinite organisation. It is significant that Madole always focused his activities in Yorkville, the German area of New York, which had prior to the war been a centre of activities for the Christian Front and the German-American Bund. Also from that era was prominent German-American spokesman Kurt Mertig of the Citizens Protective League,[106] who served as New York chairman of the NRP.

In 1950, the NRP was also associating with lawyer Edward A Fleckenstein's Voters Alliance for Americans of German Ancestry.[107] This organisation, which was active in opposing post-war US genocidal policies against Germany, was part of the network around Thompson and Weiss.

The FBI named Weiss as Madole's 'principal financial contributor'[108] and stated that Weiss had directed the 'functions of the party' and the content of Madole's speeches.[109] Another contributor and adviser to Madole was Benjamin H Freedman, a millionaire manufacturer and Jewish convert to Catholicism, who was also a major backer of *Common Sense*, writing much on Zionism, Khazar origins of the Jews and the anti-Christian teachings of the *Talmud*, the Jewish religious code.[110] Freedman wrote material for Madole's *Bulletin*, according to a 1956 report.[111] In 1957, the FBI noted that Freedman advised Madole on articles for the *National Renaissance Bulletin*, gave him money and was anxious to maintain contact with Madole as 'a vehicle for his views and propaganda.'[112] When Weiss and Madole seem to have stopped

---

105 'Animist Party', ibid., p. 7.

106 'James H Madole. Correlation summary', op., cit., pp. 1–9,

107 'James H Madole. Correlation summary', ibid., p. 10.

108 'James H Madole,' FBI New York office, August 31, 1956, NY 105–6129, p. 2.

109 'James H Madole,' FBI New York office, ibid., p. 5.

110 See Freedman, *Facts Are Facts* (New York, 1954).

111 'James H Madole. Correlation summary', op. cit., p. 26.

112 James H Madole, FBI New York, January 7, 1957, NY 105–6129, p. 5.

communication, Freedman supplanted Weiss as Madole's financial backer and geopolitical expert.

However, in early 1954 the Weiss-Madole alliance still existed and Yockey, under the name 'Frank Healy', was writing material for pamphlets published by Weiss and distributed by Madole.[113] Although Yockey had been known in the NRP as 'Frank Healy' in 1952, when the *National Renaissance Bulletin* had published his seminal essay on the 'Prague Treason Trial', it does not seem to be until late 1954 that the FBI started hearing from an informant about Yockey (called 'Yacci') as a colleague of Weiss. He had recently returned from Germany and had a girlfriend named Virginia[114] but nothing more was known.[115]

William Goring, one of many 'anti-Nazi' infiltrators of the NRP, albeit reporting objectively, wrote that Yockey and the European Liberation Front played 'an important part in the formation of the ideology of the NRP'. Goring had a good understanding of *Imperium*, which he summarised in his report in a few paragraphs. Goring states that Madole thought *Imperium* was 'the greatest book on racial nationalism since *Mein Kampf*' and stated that 'Frank Healy' joined the NRP in 1954 'but stayed only long enough to publish an article entitled "The Destiny of America" in the *National Renaissance Bulletin* under the name of James H Madole, the Party leader'. He adds: 'Then he told

113 'James H Madole. Correlation summary', op. cit., p. 18.

114 This was Virginia Allen, a physician's assistant, who decades later had bitter memories of Yockey and H Keith Thompson. According to someone who knew Allen in the 1970s and telephoned her in 1988: 'Alas, our phone conversation was a disaster. It went really well as we exchanged pleasantries and she remember me, or pretended to. She'd had a few drinks that day, I could tell. When I brought up the name of Francis Yockey she went stark barking-mad. Obviously there was something there, a secret long buried. She demanded to know where I got this information. I said it came from H Keith Thompson. "Well he was a Nazi too! Yockey was a Nazi and so was Keith Thompson! And you must be a Nazi too if you know these people!" It was very intense. But as I say, she did have a load on.' Margot Metroland, personal communication, November 23, 2014.

115 'Frederick C. F. Weiss — Internal Security', New York, 105–6112, September 7, 1954.

the astonished Madole, who had been unaware of his identity, that he was leaving for East Germany.'[116]

Similarly, 'The Destiny of America' appeared in one of the more amateurishly produced, mimeographed issues of the *National Renaissance Bulletin*, and comprised the entire issue of nine pages.[117]

'The Destiny of America' is a eulogy to the America of the pioneer who ploughed the land with rifle at the ready, whether to fight off Indian savagery against his family and land, or as a 'Minute Man' to respond to a call to mobilise against British troops at a moment's instant. Yockey alluded to the excellence of both American soldiers and statesmen at its founding as being motivated by the heroic spirit of the white race, which will last as long as the race endures. Yockey appealed to this heritage for another revolution that would secure the USA 'independence and the liberation of the pristine American colonial spirit', which will show the world 'that Americans are not the weak-willed, self-interested, pleasure-mad morons that Hollywood has tried so desperately to make them'. Yockey refers to the opening of the American continent by the 'individual imperialism' of the frontiersman with 'slung rifle, wife and children'. The American Civil War was a tragedy showing how 'vicious agitators' are capable of 'consigning nations to the flames in order to actualise their fantastic equalitarian theories'. Those of influence who condemned and ridiculed the idea of American expansion while wanting to keep fellow-American in the southern states suppressed still exist to constrict American greatness and heroism with liberalism, pacifism and internationalism. These are 'sub-Americans' in 'the service of America's inner enemy'. The true and great Americans of yesteryear have been replaced by the likes of the Morgenthaus, Baruchs, Lehmans, Goldmans and Mayers.

In tracing the history of the Jews among the early European nations of Goths, Lombards, Franks and Anglo-Saxons, Yockey states they were intuited

116 William Goring, 'The National Renaissance Party: History and Analysis of an American Neo-Nazi Political Party', National Information Center Newsletter, December 1969-January 1970, pp. 2–4.

117 Yockey under the by-line of James H Madole, 'The Destiny of America', *National Renaissance Bulletin*, January 1955. Republished by DTK in 1971 as part of his compilation, *Yockey: Four Essays* (Nordland Press, New Jersey).

as aliens. They were killed by Crusaders on the way to the Holy Land, despised as usurers and excluded form England for 400 years. The Industrial Revolution brought the Jews from despised usurer to the top of a money-orientated society.

Zionism was established to maintain Jewish identity and solidarity worldwide, behind the façade of the simple desire for nothing more than a Jewish homeland. Hence, while few Zionists have actually gone to Palestine, it is the USA that remains 'their land of promise, the last base for their power, the last place for their revenge'. Liberalism opens the way for alien rule. Liberalism 'is the enemy of national greatness, the virus that eats up national feelings'. The second factor is the aggressive unity and cohesiveness of Jews, whose mission is that of destruction. Jews insinuated themselves into every institution and 'thus America was given a semitic countenance': 'The white American listens to the music the Jew has chosen for him. He reads the books the Jew allows him to and sees the plays edited for him.' The American sees things as the Jew wants him to see them. Occasionally, the Jew drops his disguise. 'His press has referred to Hollywood as "the glittering ghetto".'[118] 'The Jew teaches he is mentally superior and with this myth he awes Americans.'[119]

'America must disassociate her future foreign policy for the diabolic machinations of World Jewry and become again a functioning part of the White European family of nations. [...] America's destiny lies in her racial unity with a white Christian Europe' and the basis for that unity remains Germany.[120]

Yockey's essay was a rare appeal from him to American patriotism. The closing words that a strong America and a united Europe could withstand communism, and that Jews constituted a pro-communist fifth column.[121] This should probably be viewed dialectically, as Yockey then departed to the Soviet bloc for several years. An anti-communist crusade such as that instigated by Senator Joseph McCarthy would have the effect of galvanising an American

118 For a more recent example see: Neal Gabler, *An Empire of Their Own: How the Jews Invented Hollywood* (Crown, 1988).

119 'The Destiny of America', op. cit.

120 'The Destiny of America', ibid.

121 'The Destiny of America', ibid.

nationalist movement; anti-communism was merely the simplest of means. The US ruling coteries feared that American nationalism might arise out of anti-communistm and the Cold War. The US ruling coteries required opposition to the USSR to be based on liberalism, not Nationalism. The USSR was not being opposed because it was communist but because it was pan-Slavic authoritarianism. That is why many of those recruited by the CIA during the Cold War were notable Marxists and especially Trotskyites, such as Professor Sidney Hook, who hated Stalinism more than capitalism. Hence, those anti-communists promoting nationalism, such as Senator Joseph McCarthy, General Douglas MacArthur[122] and military personnel such as Major Arch E Roberts and General Edwin Walker, were purged. Theirs was the type of 'anti-communism' that might become a mass nationalist movement capable of overthrowing the Liberal system.

Goring states that after Yockey travelled to East Germany, 'he travelled through Russia'. He added that those comrades of Yockey's who occasionally show up in fascist circles 'sometimes show passports indicating a lot of travel in communist countries.'[123] Goring suspects that Yockey was funded by the Eastern bloc, adding: 'There is no way to explain the fact that the Russians let these people travel in their country. They must have known sometimes that there was something suspicious about these travellers. There is also the problem of getting passports; someone was furnishing these fascists with forged passports and papers.'[124] Goring recalls: 'Yockey even showed James Madole his passport with the various stamps once he let on as to who he was. (He had joined the NRP initially under a pseudonym). I remember Jim talking about the subject with me and others.'[125]

Goring's suspicions have some backing. That year (1954), the FBI received communications from a former intelligence agent of the post-war Germany Federal Republic. He had discovered that the Soviets were using National

---

122 See: K. R. Bolton, 'Joe McCarthy's Real Enemies', *The Occidental Quarterly*, Vol. 10, No. 4, Winter 2010–2011, https://www.toqonline.com/archives/v10n4/TOQv10n4Bolton.pdf.

123 William Goring, ibid., p. 4.

124 William Goring, ibid., p. 19, note 17 to chapter I.

125 Goring to Bolton, November 18, 2014.

Socialists and 'Rightists' to assist them against the USA and considered that Fred Weiss was one of these agents.[126] This was around the time when the US authorities feared the 'neutralist' line being advocated for Germany by the Socialist Reich Party and other 'neo-Nazis' with whom Weiss, Thompson and Yockey were associating.

Much of the literature prepared by Weiss was for distribution in Germany and the NRP was utilised for preparing and mailing bundles of material from Madole's New York apartment. At this time, in 1954, a primary contact was the Hamburg-based organisation *Gemeinschaft Schwarz-Weiss-Rot* (Black-White-Red, a reference to the German imperial colours), run by SS veterans. Another important contact was Einar Åberg of Norrviken, Sweden,[127] whose torrent of 'anti-Semitic' tracts distributed throughout the world caused such consternation that Sweden passed 'Lex Åberg', a law intended to prohibit racial literature. The NRP redistributed large quantities of Åberg's tracts to Europe. Weiss also received 'advice' from Buenos Aires,[128] that is, among others, from Dr Johannes von Leers, who published *Der Weg*, and whom H. K. Thomson was to refer to as 'the higher authority'. They seem to have facilitated contact with important individuals in Cairo, including the Grand Mufti of Jerusalem,[129] an ally of Germany during World War II. A worldwide network was in place, the hub of which seems to have been von Leers, when Yockey embarked on his world odyssey.

However, by 1957 Weiss had fallen out with Madole.[130] It seems that was also the year Madole took an anti-Christian turn, first manifesting as anti-Catholicism, when he devoted an issue of the *NR Bulletin* to 'The Catholic Church Versus Racial Nationalism'.[131]

---

126 'James H Madole. Correlation summary', op. cit., p. 19.

127 FBI Office Memorandum, 'National Renaissance Party', May 4, 1954, NY 105–6112, p. 2.

128 FBI Office Memorandum, May 4, 1954, ibid., p. 3.

129 FBI Office Memorandum, May 4, 1954, ibid., p. 3.

130 'James H Madole', 'Internal Security—Egypt—Registration Act', July 3, 1957, FBI New York office, NY 105–6129, p. 3.

131 'James H Madole', 'Internal Security—Egypt—Registration Act', December 27, 1957, ibid., p. 4.
Madole, 'The Catholic Church Versus Racial Nationalism', *NR Bulletin*, Vol. 8, Nos., 10 & 11, October & November 1957, pp. 1–6.

The FBI noted that Madole seemed to have now come under the influence of Charles Smith,[132] editor of *Truth Seeker*, the oldest atheist publication in the USA. What is of interest about Smith is that he was noted as a vehement opponent of Jews and egalitarianism, and combined atheism with 'racism'. He was a prominent figure among an intellectual racist circle in New York, hosting the 'New York Racist Forum'. As such, it was Smith, with the imprint of *Truth Seeker*, who published the first edition of *Imperium* since the Westropa Press edition of 1948, through his association with Willis Carto.

In late 1957 and early 1958, Madole was speaking at Smith's meetings[133] and by the early 1960s he was holding his NRP meetings at Smith's office.[134] Goring states that the NRP's 'closest ties' were with *Truth Seeker*, in whose offices fascists and racists from sundry factions congregated. Goring also states that *Truth Seeker* was one of the main sources of funds for these groups.[135] However, Madole also maintained his relationship with the Catholic oriented *Common Sense*. Madole's appeal, however, was not for the Catholic supporters of the NRP to repudiate their Church but for them to counter the 'Jewish and anti-racial influences now prevalent in the Roman hierarchy'.[136] An article shortly afterwards attacked both Catholicism and Protestantism for their anti-racialism, while condemning Zionism and Judaism and applauding the anti-Zionism of the USSR and the rise of Islam and leaders such as Nasser and Sukarno of Indonesia,[137] a theme that would be articulated in Yockey's final essay, 'The World in Flames'. But by 1971, Madole had specifically rejected Christianity per se, writing of it in Nietzschean terms as a 'Semitic spiritual creed and a morality of slaves which subjugated the minds of our healthy pagan ancestors'.[138] Nevertheless, co-operation with Klan factions continued

---

132 Ibid.

133 Madole, 'The Catholic Church Versus Racial Nationalism', op. cit., p. 5.

134 'James H Madole. Correlation summary', op. cit., p. 47.

135 William Goring, op. cit., p. 11.

136 Madole, 'The Catholic Church Versus Racial Nationalism', op. cit., p. 6.

137 Madole, 'Is Anti-Semitism Justified by History?', *NR Bulletin*, Vol. 9, No. 2, February 1958, pp. 1–5.

138 James H Madole, 'A Stern Rebuke to the Critics of the National Renaissance Party', *NR Bulletin*, Vol. 22, nos. 9 & 10, September & October 1971, pp. 6–7.

stronger than ever. The NRP and several Klans formed an alliance with ex-American Nazi Party officer Frank Drager's White Action Movement.[139] Yockey's *Four Essays* and *The Proclamation of London* continued to be sold, as did Spengler's *Hour of Decision* and *Decline of The West*.[140]

Such was Madole's orientation by this time, along with *Common Sense*, in regard to the Weiss-Thompson-Yockey line, that General Albert C Wedemeyer, one of a coterie of distinguished military men supporting 'extreme Right' causes, sent the FBI the May 1958 issue of the *National Renaissance Bulletin*. This featured the article 'J Edgar Hoover, America's Foremost Master of Deceit', a condemnation of the FBI director's anti-communist magnum opus, *Masters of Deceit*. The book was held by sections of the right to have been influenced by the ADL in an effort to repudiate the widespread perception of the Jewishness of communism, given the number of Jews that came up in Senate and Congressional investigations on communism and in espionage trials. Wedemeyer assumed, for reasons unclear, that pro-Soviet industrialist Cyrus Eaton was funding Madole,[141] a fairly unlikely scenario. Wedemeyer asked the FBI for information on Madole that he could use to expose the NRP as a Soviet tool. It was not Hoover's policy, however, to 'dignify' attacks from the radical right with a response. Such was the anti-Russian obsession among most of the right that even American Nazi Party commander, George Lincoln Rockwell, turned copies of all ANP membership applications over to the FBI to show his good faith as a fellow anti-communist. Although Rockwell knew of the FBI's surveillance 'he had had fanatical devotion to Hoover's Bureau [and] saw Hoover as a strident anti-communist, practically the only government official doing anything to thwart communism'. FBI memos in turn referred to Rockwell as 'very co-operative with Agents'. However, FBI reports did not offer any positive portrait of Rockwell. Additionally, Southern segregationists such as Dr E. R. Fields of the National States Rights Party had no illusions about the FBI and were suspicious of Rockwell's stance.[142]

139 'Frank Drager, a former Rockwell Lieutenant, Joins with NRP and its Klan allies to form the White Action Movement', *NR Bulletin*, ibid, pp. 1–4.

140 *NR Bulletin*, ibid, p. 10.

141 'James H Madole. Correlation summary', op. cit., p. 32.

142 William H Schmaltz, *Hate: George Lincoln Rockwell and the American Nazi Party* (Washington: Brassey's, 1999), p. 153.

It is noted at the conclusion of the FBI's 'Correlation Summary' on Madole that a request by the FBI to have him named on the Security Index as a possible national security threat was declined. However, Weiss had been placed on the Index for 'pro-German and neo-Nazi organizational activities'. He was deleted from the Index on September 26, 1955. He was also erroneously named as the author of Yockey's book *The Enemy of Europe*, 'which was distributed in Germany by the outlawed Socialist Reich Party and which stated Russia will be the only salvation of Western Europe'.[143]

By the late 1950s, Madole was augmenting his stock of Arab literature with literature from the Soviet Consulate. An FBI informant mentioned that Madole had been given a recommendation to the Soviet Consulate by 'Iraqi officials'.[144]

---

143 'James H Madole. Correlation summary', op. cit., 'Letter to SAC New York Re: James H Madole 105–52256', September 28, 1972.

144 'Confidential Source', FBI New York, 105–6112-721, January 8, 1959, p. 2.

# H Keith Thompson Jr

Harold Keith Thompson Jr, more familiarly known as Keith Thompson, was Yockey's closest American collaborator. Thompson worked with Frederick Weiss on writing and printing, was an early speaker at NRP meetings and was the registered US agent for both the Socialist Reich Party and the German-Argentine émigré periodical *Der Weg*.

The European Liberation Front was particularly close to the Socialist Reich Party, again through the efforts of Gannon, who introduced Yockey to the party. The Luftwaffe air ace Heinz Knöke met Gannon and L. F. Simmons twice at Cambridge circa 1952, where they 'discussed full co-operation'.[1]

Therefore, the paths of Thompson and Yockey intersected on several major levels and they were bound to meet.

Born in Orange, New Jersey, on September 17, 1922,[2] of Anglo-Saxon, German and Scottish descent, he was the son of a printer-publisher widely respected as being a local Post Commander of the American Legion and active in civic affairs. Scientist and inventor George K Thompson was his grandfather.[3] The German branch of the family is called Thomsen. Dr Hans Thomsen, Keith's cousin, was the last German *chargé d'affaires* in Washington prior to World War II. They worked closely together to keep the USA out of the war.[4]

---

1 Gannon to Stimely, November 24, 1981.

2 FBI documents on Thompson, April 5, 1984, in regard to passport enquiries.

3 FBI report on Thompson and 'Committee for Freedom of Major General Remer', July 21, 1952 105-919, p. 4.

4 David McCalden, *Revisionist Newsletter*, Manhattan Beach, California, no. 21, June, 1983. Although McCalden was here being strongly critical of Thompson and criticized the Institute for Historical Review for featuring him as a special guest speaker, Thompson commented on the McCalden article that although 'this was an attack on me

Indeed, it seems likely that at this time Thompson would have been introduced to his lifelong mentor, George Sylvester Viereck (1884–1962), a major figure in the American literati who had worked closely with Hans Thomsen in campaigning to keep the USA out of the conflict. Viereck, a poet, novelist and playwright, had worked for German interests in the USA during World War I, publishing *The International*[5] and *The Fatherland*. Viereck had interviewed Hitler in 1923 and had evoked particularly informative answers on the essential points of National Socialism.[6] During the 1930s, he took up the cause of Hitler's Germany, addressing a rally of the Friends of New Germany, precursor of the German-American Bund, in 1934. After establishing Flanders Hall as a publishing outlet for pro-German literature, Viereck was prosecuted for failing to register as a foreign agent and was jailed from 1942 to 1947. A key state witness against him had been ADL agent Sandy Griffith, who during the 1950s was ensconced by the ADL across from the remote Weiss farm to try to keep tabs on the elderly German hub of neo-Nazi activities.

Part of Thompson's anti-war campaign involved the Friends of New Germany and the German-American Bund.[7] As a result, Thompson, presumably helped by his connections with Viereck and with Dr Hans Thomsen, was appointed special agent with the rank of SS Sturmbandführer, in the SD/Overseas Intelligence Unit, on July 27, 1941.[8]

After the war, Thompson explained his views as deriving in part from his descent 'from a long line of Prussian field marshals', the Keith family, of Scottish descent, who had emigrated to Prussia and one of whose members had served as a General under Frederick the Great. From this he had the

---

(there have been many) … it is an interesting one as it came right out of US intelligence files and is unusually accurate'. Thompson to Bolton, February 20, 1995.

5 Because British occultist Aleister Crowley became an editor of *The International* on the pretext of being an Irish republican, while working for the British secret service, many of the issues seem inordinately concerned with occultism rather than German interests. See *The International* at http://hermetic.com/crowley/international/.

6 'No room for the alien, no use for the wastrel', Veireck interview with Hitler, Bavaria, 1923, published in *Liberty*, USA, July 1932; *The Guardian*, September 17, 2007, http://www.theguardian.com/theguardian/2007/sep/17/greatinterviews1.

7 McCalden, no. 21, op. cit.

8 David McCalden, *Revisionist Newsletter*, no. 22, July 1983.

feeling of 'pride of race', of the 'Prussian spirit' and of Germany. At the age of 14, he became interested in politics and German history and with the rise of Hitler, he was enthused by the new regime's 'socialism'[9] and the overthrow of the Versailles *diktat*. The German-American Bund was particularly active around New York and New Jersey and Thompson joined.[10]

Thompson toured Germany as a child and got to know Prince August Wilhelm,[11] Brigadier General in Hitler's SA stormtroopers. Thompson also maintained contact with Kaiser Wilhelm II, exiled in the Netherlands,[12] and remained in contact with Prince August Wilhelm until 1949, when the prince died prematurely as the result of imprisonment by the Allies.

At Drew College and Yale University, Thompson expressed his opposition to the USA having fought in World War I and becoming involved in another war against Germany. His views were already 'well known'.[13]

Having studied naval law at Yale, Thompson held posts in the Navy associated with legal matters. He served as an administration officer of the USS Franklin D Roosevelt in 1946, then on the USS Mount Olympus as part of the Antarctic expedition of Admiral Byrd, in 1947, after which he lectured to civilian groups on the Antarctic. That year he resigned from the Navy to accept a Marine Corps appointment. In 1948 he attended the founding meeting

9 What this 'socialism' was had been cogently explained by Hitler to Viereck in 1923. It is an indication also of what Yockey meant by 'ethical socialism': '"Why," I asked Hitler, "do you call yourself a National Socialist, since your party programme is the very antithesis of that commonly accredited to socialism?" "Socialism," he retorted, putting down his cup of tea, pugnaciously, "is the science of dealing with the common weal. Communism is not Socialism. Marxism is not Socialism. The Marxians have stolen the term and confused its meaning. I shall take Socialism away from the Socialists. Socialism is an ancient Aryan, Germanic institution. Our German ancestors held certain lands in common. They cultivated the idea of the common weal. Marxism has no right to disguise itself as socialism. Socialism, unlike Marxism, does not repudiate private property. Unlike Marxism, it involves no negation of personality, and unlike Marxism, it is patriotic."'

10 Thompson, 'I am an American Fascist', *Expose*, New York, Part 2, October 21, 1954.

11 'Nazis' US boy tells his goal', *The New York Compass*, October 26, 1952.

12 Thompson, 'American Fascist', op. cit., part 2.

13 'Nazis' US boy…', op. cit.

of Roosevelt's former Vice President Henry Wallace's Progressive Party.[14] This was one of Thompson's several enigmatic associations with Leftists.

Thompson alludes to his joining groups of both the 'extreme Right and the moderate Left' at this time but his 'dedication to the principles of practical National Socialism' was only strengthened.[15] He was appalled by the 'war crimes' trials of 'honorable soldiers', 'mock trials', 'the first in history', 'cold bloodedly vicious', instigated primarily by communist and Jewish interests, Thompson began to work on individual cases from 1945, when he was on active service. These included those of Baron Alexander von Falkenhausen, Reich Governor of Belgium; Grand Admiral Dönitz, Hitler's designated successor; Mannstein; Kesselring, and the 1945–1947 Dachau 'Flyers Case'.[16]

Something of Thompson's thinking is shown by his remark to *The New York Compass* that 'everyone should be free to express political views, no matter what their variety'. When asked by the reporter how he squared his civil libertarianism with his support for the 'resurgence of authority', he replied:

> When in Rome, do as the Romans do. [US Secretary of State] Acheson and the rest claim they are for democracy. Let them then be democratic. Let them stop trying to impose themselves on the German people. If the so-called war criminals had been shot by the US it might have been justifiable under the slogan, To the victor belong spoils, but to imprison them and deny them dignity is criminal.
>
> Understand, I am not fighting for any particular philosophy. I'm fighting for certain people, for justice. We contend that the interests of the US vis-à-vis the international communist movement are best served by a strong Germany. We've alienated Germany with the war trials. Now we ask the Germans to build an army to fight for us at the same time that we have under confinement thousands

14 FBI report July 21, 1952, (105-919), p. 5.

15 Thompson, 'American Fascist', part 2.

16 Ibid.

The 'Flyers Cases', tried at Dachau, included the infamous trials of the Malmedy defendants, the trial being condemned by Senator Joseph McCarthy and the US Army's van Roden Commission for the widespread use of torture. Additional allegations were made against Otto Skorzeny, the commando who led the rescue of Mussolini from Communist partisans, and nine officers of Panzer Brigade 150, who were found not guilty.

> of their soldiers, including the legal Head of the German State, Grand Admiral Dönitz. It was a foul and unspeakable process.[17]

After the war, Thompson had been shocked by the treatment of German former dignitaries and 'dedicated himself to the salvation of their civil liberties'. He mentioned the case of Mrs Himmler, who had only been a loyal wife yet had her property confiscated and was impoverished, saying: 'It is an outrage.' He had studied the transcripts and records of the 'war crimes trials' and the de-nazification trials and found that they 'were uniformly trumped up railroad jobs', adding: 'I deny that any Germans were war criminals.'[18]

While Thompson was engaged in these activities, he was also helping ex-Congressman Vito Marcantonio of the American Labor Party and there was an expectation that Thompson would run for the Labor Party in Marcantonio's former New York constituency.[19] Thompson wrote 'many' of Marcantonio's speeches[20] and had remarked at the time to Karl Hess, press editor of *Newsweek*, that Germans felt they could negotiate better with the USSR than the USA for their future.

He also maintained a friendship with left-wing Mexican muralist David Alfiero Siquieros. Thompson wrote an article on the case in leftist publisher Lyle Stuart's magazine, *The Independent*, when Siquieros was jailed in Mexico.[21] Thompson also represented pro-Soviet artist Rockwell Kent and broke the blacklist of Kent among publishers, arranging for the publishing of Kent's *Greenland Journal* by Ivan Obolensky in New York. How this dialectic worked is shown by what McCalden calls the USSR's release of a 'Nazi war criminal' of Thompson's choice.[22] Thompson told Coogan that his assistance for Siquieros was the return of a favour for the Mexican artist having recommended a safe house to Yockey in the USA, when he was sought by the FBI.[23] Thompson's

17 'Nazis' US boy…', *New York Compass*, op. cit.

18 Ibid.

19 FBI report, May 19, 1953, 105–919.

20 FBI report, October 29, 1953, 105–919, p. 8.

21 McCalden, no. 22, op. cit.

22 Ibid.

23 Kevin Coogan, *Dreamer of the Day* (New York: Automedia, 1999), p. 456.

assistance to Rockwell Kent opened the way for contacts with Soviet diplomat Valerian Zorin in 1961 and with the Soviet Ministry of Culture.[24]

In 1952, Thompson registered under US law as a foreign agent for the Socialist Reich Party. He began a campaign to support the SRP, which was being suppressed because of its growing electoral popularity and its 'neutralist' position vis-à-vis the Cold War. For this purpose, the Committee for International Justice and the Committee for the Freedom of Major General Remer were formed. Remer, hated for his role in suppressing the July 1944 plot to overthrow Hitler, was a particular target of the Bonn authorities and of organized Jewry, and remained so for the rest of his long life. Thompson wrote to *Time* magazine on June 23, 1952 protesting an article on those imprisoned at Spandau, which also attacked Remer and other German veterans.[25] Counsel for the committees was Edward Fleckenstein, president of the Voters' Alliance for Americans of German Ancestry.[26] According to a report in the *Newark Star-Ledger*, cited by the FBI, the purpose of the Committee for International Justice was to secure the release of all German military personnel jailed for 'war crimes' who were convicted on 'fraudulent evidence'. Thompson spent all of his spare time soliciting American support for the Socialist Reich Party. 'Thompson is quoted as saying that he has appealed to the State Department, the United Nations, and, in fact, to about everybody.' The committees also aimed to provide humanitarian relief 'to the families of the 1,045 German soldiers held as war criminals, to work for the overturning of the indictment against Remer, and to pressure the Bonn regime into halting the persecution of minority political parties'. Thompson was quoted as stating that he communicated with Inga Dönitz, the wife of the interned Grand Admiral and last president of united Germany, and a recipient of committee aid. The FBI file states that the *Newark Star-Ledger* article described Thompson as 'a mild mannered friendly young man who will patiently explain the ideology of his cause and who does not let himself be provoked into heated discussions'.[27]

---

24 Coogan, Ibid., pp. 441–442.

25 FBI report July 21, 1952, op. cit., p. 8.

26 FBI report, October 9, 1952, (105–919), p. 1.

27 FBI report, October 9, 1952, 105–919, p. 2.

The American Jewish Committee, reporting on the 'neo-nazi revival' in Germany, stated in a special section on Thompson that he had also registered as an American agent for the Munich-based publication *Die Andere Seite* (The Other Side), edited by Dr Rudolf Aschenauer.[28] The latter was instrumental in getting Senator Joseph McCarthy to investigate American use of torture on the defendants of the Malmedy trials of former SS personnel.[29] The American Jewish Committee commented on how gratified they were at the banning of the SRP. The AJC alluded to the alleged association between the 'neo-Nazis' and Soviet agents in eastern and western Germany, urging the Bonn government to be vigilant given the likelihood of the SRP re-forming in another guise.[30]

Thompson's brief registration as a foreign agent ended on October 31, 1952, due to the state prohibition of the SRP.[31] However, his committee for justice had made some significant contributions. While the regime at Spandau prison had been harsh for the first several years, it had relented and this was partly thanks to Thompson's efforts, according to Field Marshal Kesselring.[32]

According to the FBI, Fleckenstein stated that both the Committee for International Justice and the Remer committee were 'sub-committees' of his voters' alliance.[33] The committees had been formed in answer to the many requests to the voters' association to offer material assistance to impoverished Germans. Fleckenstein had turned the responsibility over to Thompson.[34] The two had been introduced in November 1952 by their mutual friend, Viereck.[35] Fleckenstein's voters' association had been denied application to incorporate in 1946 by Supreme Court Justice Hammer, who considered an association

---

28 American Jewish Committee, Germany File, Foreign Affairs Department Collection FAD — 1, August–December 1952, p. 5.

29 Edmond Taylor, 'Germany: Where Fascism and Communism Meet', *The Reporter*, April 13, 1954, p. 12.

30 American Jewish Committee, op. cit., p. 6.

31 FBI file, January 5, 1953, 105–919, p. 1.

32 Thompson, 'American Fascist', op. cit., part 2.

33 FBI report, December 16, 1952, 105–919, p. 1.

34 FBI report, December 16, 1952, ibid., p. 4.

35 FBI report, December 16, 1952, ibid., p. 4

referring to Americans of 'German ancestry' to be 'inadvisable', given that Germany was still an occupied country with its leaders being tried as 'war criminals' and a peace treaty yet to be negotiated.[36]

The American Jewish Committee sought to publicly expose Thompson as a registered agent for the SRP, which they claimed 'constituted another threat to the free world'.[37] Thompson, for his part, believed the American Jewish Committee, Anti-Defamation League, Society for the Prevention of World War III[38] and other groups friendly to Israel and antagonistic towards Germany should be required to register as foreign agents.[39]

Fleckenstein had intended to sue the US Government via the Committee for International Justice, on behalf of Americans who had sent several million dollars worth of humanitarian aid to Germans, his view being that a conquering nation has a duty towards the vanquished.[40] This was the era when the Morgenthau Plan for the genocidal starvation of Germans had been put into effect as a *de facto* policy.[41] It was Fleckenstein's efforts that 'paved the way' for the delivery of food parcels to Germany.[42]

Fleckenstein also stated that he intended forming a youth division of the voters' association with Thompson as leader.[43] In 1953 Fleckenstein visited Germany and spoke out against US policy. He was arrested, jailed, had his passport seized by US authorities and was deported, without being charged.[44]

Thompson praised Senators Joseph McCarthy and Robert Taft to *The New York Compass* as two statesmen who had opposed the post-war trials against

---

36 FBI report, December 16, 1952, ibid., p. 2.

37 FBI report, December 16, 1952, ibid., p. 2.

38 Not to be confused with the National Council for the Prevention of War, a Quaker sponsored organisation, which the FBI cites in its files on Thompson, describing the council as being critical of the Nuremberg trials, and post-war policy towards Germany. FBI report, September 17, 1952, 105–919.

39 'Nazis' US boy tell his goal', *The New York Compass*, op. cit.

40 FBI report , December 16, 1952, op. cit., p. 5.

41 James Bacque, *Crimes and Mercies*, op. cit.

42 Thompson, 'American Fascist', op. cit., part 2.

43 FBI file, December 16, 1952, op. cit., 5.

44 H. K. Thompson, 'I am an American Fascist', *Expose*, part 4, New York, December 1954.

the German leadership.[45] He had formed the American Voters' Union in 1952 for the purpose of campaigning for the presidential nomination of Robert Taft by the Republican Party.

The Voters' Union distributed provocative handbills praising General Douglas MacArthur and Senator Taft, headed 'if you enjoy having part of your weekly paycheck withheld to buy some Washington whore a mink coat, don't bother reading this'. The union announced its fight for the 'principles of Taft and MacArthur' against the creeping Marxism of 'New Deal' type programmes, which had infiltrated the Republican Party and was backing General Eisenhower's candidacy. The handbill ended 'Fight the Raw Deal and Fumigate the Ikeroaches,' in reference to 'Ike' (Eisenhower). Young Americans were urged to enrol in a support committee for Senator McCarthy for a planned speech at Yorkeville, New York, a mainstay of the German community, stronghold for the pre-war Christian Front and focus of National Renaissance Party activities.

Senator Joseph McCarthy had agreed to speak at a Voters' Union public meeting, called a 'German-American Friendship Rally', but cancelled because of an engagement with the young Republicans in Wisconsin.[46] However, other notables spoke, including Henry C Furstenwalde, formerly of the US Embassy in Berlin; Professor Austin J App, from LaSalle College, whose efforts as a writer against anti-German defamation endured for decades;[47] Dr Ludwig A Fritsch, Lutheran Minister and author of the hard-hitting *Crime of Our Age*;[48] and Father Emmanuel J Reichenberger, expert on the East German expellee problem.[49] Thompson served as floor manager of the meeting.

---

45 'Nazis' US boy…', *New York Compass*, op. cit.

46 Thompson, 'I am an American Fascist', *Expose*, part 2, October 21, 1954.

47 App's works include: *Ravishing the Women of Conquered Europe* (1946), *History's Most Terrifying Peace* (1946), *Morgenthau Era Letters* (1966), *A Straight Look at the Third Reich* (1974), *The Sudenten German Tragedy* (1979), *Power and Propaganda in American Politics and Foreign Policy* (1984).

48 Dr Ludwig A Fritsch, *Crime of Our Age* (Illinois, 1947).

49 Several million German ethnics died en route to Germany, 17,000,000 having been 'ethnically cleansed' from their ancestral homes in the East after the war. *Statistical Pocket Book on Expellees* (Wiesbaden: Federal Statistical

Thompson, Fleckenstein, and Arthur Koegel, head of the Steuben Society attended the Republican convention in Chicago to lobby for Taft.[50] They endeavoured to promote friendship with Germany among the delegates and met senators McCarthy and Dirksen, Congressman Hamilton Fish, (who had been an opponent of US entry into the world war), and conservative columnist Westbrook Pegler. 'All were very cordial and made a good impression on us', wrote Thompson.[51] The leaflets against the 'fumigation of Ikeroaches' were so effective that police searched for one of the distributors throughout the convention hall to eject him.

Returning from Chicago, Thompson became the subject of a widespread smear campaign, started by *Time*, and was wiretapped by a 'Jewish defense group'. Thompson obliged by feeding misinformation. Part of Thompson's reason for writing the 'Fascist' series for *Expose* and for feeding the FBI information was to thwart the activities of Sanford Griffith, the ADL spy. Thompson often pointed out to the FBI their dealings with dubious individuals, such as Griffith, and showed in the *Expose* series that Griffith and other 'anti-Nazi' and ADL agents were funding and encouraging Weiss and Madole, while these two were willing to play along. Indeed, Griffith even gave Thompson money for printing, claiming to be a 'friendly journalist' who intended to give Thompson some good publicity via the *Newark Star-Ledger*. Thompson stated that he gave Griffith a 'completely inaccurate picture' but apparently sufficiently convincing to warrant further funds from the ADL. Griffith would give Thompson ideas and money when publicity flagged. Thompson then discovered how the ADL operated as *agents provocateur* among the Right and why they are often 'the most dependable source of funds'.[52]

In 1953, Thompson began organizing the American Committee for the Advancement of Western Culture (ACAWC). Thompson stated that the aims

---

Office 1953), available online at http://www.balderexlibris.com/index.php?post/Federal-statistical-office-Wiesbaden-Statistical-Pocket-Book-on-Expellees.

50 FBI report, May 15, 1953, 105–6128, 15.

51 Thompson, 'I was an American Fascist', part 2.

52 Thompson, ibid., part 2. See K. R. Bolton, *Zionism, Islam and The West* (London: Black House Publishing (London: Black House Publishing, 2014), 'The Symbiosis Between Anti-Semitism and Zionism', 33–62,

were (1) as an advisory group for opposing internationalism and alien cultures and influences, (2) a political action group on US domestic and foreign policies, (3) a safeguard for the liberties of Americans regardless of their politics. 'Nationalists' would be recruited 'from Left, Right, and Center', including a 'high calibre European advisory staff'.[53] It is notable, given Thompson's seemingly perplexing association with Leftist causes, that he refers to working with the whole so-called political spectrum. The committee that Thompson put together included Dr A. O. Tittmann, ex-diplomat, author and opponent of the 'war crimes trials', who had founded the Voters Alliance of Americans of German Ancestry in 1947, as honorary chairman; James H Madole; Kurt Mertig, German-American activist who had helped found the National Renaissance Party and had established the pre-war Citizens' Protective League;[54] Eustace Mullins, regarded as an authority on the Federal Reserve Bank and on Jews but probably best remembered for the biography of his mentor Ezra Pound;[55] and Frederick Weiss. The overseas advisory committee included former SRP general secretary Dr Gerhardt Krueger; Alexander Raven Thomson, leading Mosleyite intellectual and editor of the Union Movement's newspaper *Union*; and Oswald Pirow, former South African minister of defence. Sundry others were drawn from the Right, the most prominent of whom was Keith Thompson's long-time friend King Carol II of Romania.

Thompson noted the rivalry that existed between individuals on the Right and indeed the committee was stillborn. By 1957 Thompson, Weiss and Madole were all in dispute. Jewish pressure had been intense, Thompson stating that blackmail, economic pressure and false scare stories were used to sow discord among members. Because of its size and dispersion, Thompson states that the committee was 'helpless' against infiltration from the ADL and Non-Sectarian Anti-Nazi League.[56] The latter organisation, led by Professor Sheldon, had thoroughly infiltrated the NRP to the extent of providing

53 H. K. Thompson, 'I am an American Fascist', part 4, *Expose*, New York, December 1954.

54 Originally formed as a type of anti-defamation league for Germans, to assist Bruno Hauptmann, defendant in the Lindbergh baby kidnapping case.

55 E. Mullins, *This Difficult Individual: Ezra Pound* (Hollywood: Angriff Press, 1961).

56 H. K. Thompson, 'I am an American Fascist.', op. cit., part 4.

Madole a significant proportion of the party's funding and personnel—a matter brought up by Thompson in his *Expose* series.

The 'committee' obviously had the potential to become something other than a think-tank or a purely cultural association. When the German concert pianist Walter Gieseking was being picketed at Carnegie Hall because, although not a Hitlerite, he had never repudiated his people or the Reich, Thompson and some friends confronted the picketers and attempted to get police to ensure the orderly entrance of patrons. He was 'promptly identified' by angry Zionists whispering his name, who surrounded Thompson's group while a Jew threw a German naval flag at Thompson's feet and 'screamed', 'Is this your flag?'[57] With cameramen swarming in, Thompson 'reacted explosively'. The media, including television, made the most of the fracas to smear the committee and Thompson's colleagues, including Viereck and others not involved with the committee. Thompson stated that he was 'hemmed in' by the number of agents from various organisations keeping him under surveillance. Merely being a social acquaintance would bring harassment.

One such target was a college student, Donald A Swan, who was to become an anthropologist and co-founder of the International Association for the Advancement of Ethnology and Eugenics (IAAEE),[58] an association of prominent social and physical scientists including C. D. Darlington and John R Baker of Oxford University, American psychologist Professor Henry E Garrett, et al. Swan was suspended from Queens College, supposedly for 'neo-Nazi', 'anti-Semitic' activities but in particular for having associated with Thompson. The 'authorities' had described Thompson as a 'subversive'

---

57 Presumably the Zionist groups had been tipped off to Thompson's plans, otherwise it seems unlikely one of their number would happen to have shown up with a German naval flag. Thompson himself states in the *Expose* articles that the NRP, for example, was infiltrated and that Sandy Griffith, the ADL and ANL agent, had paid agents in the group.

58 Swan was noted as having been a mainstay of the IAAEE, which was active in trying to resist desegregation of schools in the South through the courts. Swan became assistant editor of the anthropological journal *Mankind Quarterly*, which continues to function. His suspension from Queens College did not prevent him from receiving a New York State Regents Scholarship after graduation and he became a professor at the University of Southern Mississippi.

to Margaret V Kiely, a Dean of Queens College, who stated she had heard Thompson's telephone conversations — that is, the FBI had played taped phone calls to her. This controversy happened at a time when faculty at Queens College were themselves under investigation for Communist affiliations.

The 'youth group' that Fleckenstein aimed to create under Thompson's leadership is likely to have been the group formed by Swan at Queens College, the German-American Youth Cultural Society, which he founded in October 1953.[59] The name suggests influence from Fleckenstein's German-American organisation. Thompson had advised Swan to stay clear of radical Rightist groups, so that he could proceed with activities without being harassed by the FBI, ADL, American Jewish Committee and the like. Swan seems to have followed Thompson's counsel, as the FBI informant stated that the youth group was non-political, although the *National Renaissance Bulletin* was available at its social gatherings.[60]

Another factor that caused fluster among the FBI was Thompson's allegations about collusion between the Justice Department and disreputable agents of the ANL and ADL, a matter that Thompson continued to raise with the FBI, despite its indignant denial of such associations. As will be seen in a chapter on the FBI and ADL, the association between the two has been extensive. Thompson remarked that being on the payroll of the State, ADL and ANL simultaneously, and 'selling "secrets"', 'accounts for much of the baloney which ends up in various files, private and governmental'.[61] Thompson provided the FBI with such 'baloney'.

In August 1954, Thompson issued a press release stating that he had dissolved the ACAWC, dissociating himself from those who had been implicated. He had done so primarily to take the attention away from his 'foreign friends', who had been implicated in an organisation that was soon infiltrated and victimized. One of those who had targeted Thompson was the Armenian-born 'John Roy Carlson', notorious author of the wartime best-seller *Under Cover*, which had smeared America First isolationists as German

59 FBI report, April 25, 1954, 105–6128.

60 FBI report, April 25, 1954, ibid.

61 H. K. Thompson, 'I am an American Fascist…', op. cit., part 4.

agents and 'Nazis'.[62] In subsequent legal hearings Judge John P Barnes described Carlson as 'someone who would write anything for a dollar'. Carlson had posed as 'George Pagnanelli', Italo-American, during the 1940s. Now he was posing as 'Yusef Nadir', writing from Germany and wanting to know about Thompson's contact with the Grand Mufti of Jerusalem. Carlson and the ADL described Thompson as the leader of an international Nazi organisation. Thompson stated that although there are 'nationalist' organisations throughout the world, any type of internationalism is inherently impossible. He was particularly encouraged by developments in Germany, although contacts such as Colonel Hans Rudel and Wolfgang Sarg of 'Natinform Germany' were being harassed. Thompson singled out the post-war Union Movement of Sir Oswald Mosley for particular praise. Thompson commented that 'even behind the Iron Curtain… we see evidence of resurgent nationalism within a framework of practical socialism'.[63]

In concluding his series for *Expose,* Thompson outlined his 'world-outlook'. It is classically Spenglerian, referring to Bolshevik Russia as the leader of a world race war, augmenting the Marxist class war.[64] However, this was a strategy by the Kremlin for world power, as 'old Bolshevism' had been re-

---

62 John Roy Carlson, *Under Cover: My four years in the Nazi underworld of America — The amazing revelation of how Axis agents and our enemies within are now plotting to destroy the United States* (New York: E. P. Dutton, 1943). The book had smeared some good friends of Thompson's including Viereck, and Lawrence Dennis, the part-Negro, Harvard educated intellectual exponent of 'American Fascism'. See Lawrence Dennis, *The Coming American Fascism* ([1936] republished 1993 by Noontide Press, USA); and *The Dynamics of War and Revolution* ([1940] Noontide, 1993). Dennis had worked for Seligman bank and the US State Department but was a defendant in the abortive Sedition Trial, having come to oppose both capitalism and US intervention. After the war he continued publishing *The Weekly Foreign Letter*, analysing world affairs, among whose readers were Joseph P Kennedy. On Dennis' view of the Sedition Trial see Dennis and Maximillian St George, *A Trial on Trial: The Great Sedition Trial of 1944* ([1945] Torrance, Ca.: Institute for Historical Review, 1984).

63 H. K. Thompson, 'I am an American Fascist…', op. cit., part 4.

64 See Oswald Spengler, *The Hour of Decision* (New York: Alfred A Knopf, 1933), chapters on 'The White World Revolution', referring to class struggle within the white nations, and 'The Colored World Revolution', referring to the anti-colonial revolts under Bolshevik direction.

placed by 'an ultra-nationalistic military junta, motivated by Pan-Slavism, and recognizing the Jew, with his "foreign" loyalty, as an internal enemy', what the *New York Times* was calling 'Russian Imperialism'. The USSR had, according to Jewish media such as *Commentary* and *The New Leader*, become 'a greater horror than Fascism'. 'The Prague trial of the eleven Jewish leaders in 1953 and similar actions in other satellite countries confirmed to the world the fact, long apparent to my friends', that the Jewish element had lost power. Public opinion, moulded by the press, had gone from being anti-German and pro-Russian to anti-German and anti-Russian. However, it was the regime that ran Washington that had delivered half of Europe to the USSR and it was late for purging the Western World of the 'power force' that was responsible. What is required is the renewal of the *spirit* of the West:

> This Spirit must be opposed to Finance-Liberalism, to any weakening of the State, and to the desecrating misuse of the State for private economic interest; this Spirit must grow out of any fundamental life-forces that still exist in the Western Peoples, that instinct for power and possessions, for possessions as power, for honor, for order, for tradition, for inheritance, fecundity and family.[65]

ACAWC had attempted to arouse that Western spirit to a 'Common Destiny', not a mere common set of interests, 'in this Hour of Decision' (citing the title of Spengler's book). The Committee was 'savagely attacked' for lamenting that the 'great Western Culture' that had been welded into a 'spiritual unit by a thousand years of struggle' faced death by Western Europe being 'overwhelmed by the hordes from the Asian Steppes...' However, given that Russia had become the main enemy of Jewish interests, Thompson et al were smeared as 'Commu-Nazis' for pointing out that Western Europe would now prefer Russian occupation 'because it could be more quickly thrown off' than the moral, spiritual and cultural rot under US occupation. Despite the smears that had been faced, the struggle continued to 'sweep the slate clean and prepare to meet our Destiny—or perish in the struggle'.[66]

In 1954, Thompson was appointed US correspondent for *Der Weg* (The Way), published by German émigrés in Perón's Argentina. This gave

65 H. K. Thompson, 'I am an American Fascist...', op. cit., part 4.

66 H. K. Thompson, 'I am an American Fascist...', cit.

Thompson press accreditation to the United Nations.[67] Thompson wrote to FBI director Hoover, offering to make information about communism and associated 'jewish [sic] pressure groups' available personally to him in the course of Thompson's work as a journalist.[68] Thompson, like Weiss, kept his enemies close to him and offered the FBI a mixture of accurate and inaccurate information, often criticizing the FBI's willingness to associate with the Anti-Defamation League and the disreputable actions of FBI agents. FBI agents were cautioned to be circumspect about Thompson and to seek advice when dealing with him.[69] Thompson's aim vis-à-vis the FBI seems to have been to undermine the ADL and particularly its unscrupulous agent Sanford Griffith, and others of the type, in exchange for information on communists, about whom Thompson had supplied the FBI 200 documents. Thompson castigated the FBI for discourtesy in not acknowledging this information and for its association with Jewish groups.[70]

Of particular concern to the FBI was Thompson's series of articles in *Expose*, detailing not only his life as an 'American Fascist' but also what he knew of FBI, ADL and Non-Sectarian Anti-Nazi League activities and the role of the ADL in funding 'anti-Semitic' and 'neo-nazi' groups such as the National Renaissance Party.[71] Thompson used the series of articles as an opportunity to show that 'anti-Semitism in the United States is in no small measure directed and financed' by the Anti-Defamation League and the Non-Sectarian Anti-Nazi League. In particular, a paid ADL and ANL agent, Mana Truhill, a petty criminal, had attained a leading position in the NRP. Truhill was a communist who had been instructed at the Communist Party's Jefferson School of Social Science. Thompson regarded the NRP as thoroughly compromised and used by the ADL and others.[72] He made it clear to the FBI that he had a collection

67 *Der Weg* accreditation, August 27, 1954.

68 Thompson to Hoover, September 30, 1954, cited by FBI report, October 7, 1954, 105–6128.

69 FBI office memo, October 21, 1954, 105–6128.

70 Thompson to FBI New York Bureau, October 16, 1954. The FBI decided soon after to accept information from Thompson but was dubious about contact in person. FBI memo to Department of Justice, October 20, 1954, 105–6128.

71 William P Rogers, Deputy Attorney General to FBI director J Edgar Hoover, October 22, 1954, 105–6128.

72 Thompson, 'American Fascist', op. cit., part 3, October 1954.

of affidavits, obtained for legal purposes in connection with the *Expose* series, showing the reprehensible actions of certain FBI agents.[73]

Thompson met Madole in 1952. He did so at the request of Colonel Hans Rudel and Dr Johannes von Leers, both then working in Perón's Argentina. Thompson stated that at the time he was not only the 'official US representative of the SRP, [but] also represented the leadership cadre of the "survivors" of the Third Reich, scattered throughout the world'. Rudel and von Leers asked Thompson to 'evaluate the NRP frankly to see if contact with it was "safe" and to see if it could organizationally contribute to the higher authority',[74] Remer, Rudel, Skorzeny, von Leers, et al., at times referred to by journalists as ODESSA and 'Die Spinne'.[75]

Thompson stated that he met Madole at the latter's New York apartment and about a dozen times thereafter. Thompson considered Madole as lacking charisma and leadership qualities, although he was a skilful orator and a man of 'courage'. He had a tendency to speak in monologue rather than exchange ideas. Despite these shortcomings, Thompson considered it 'vital to keep Madole afloat since he was certainly in one sense an irritant to the Jews and other non-whites but, more important, he naturally "drew fire", taking some of the pressure off other persons and operations which were deemed by my associates as more important to their interests, which were my principal concern'.[76]

## Meeting Yockey

Thompson was a literary agent of note and acted for some extraordinary characters. One notable was Viereck, 'one of the highest German agents in the US up to World War II'.[77] He arranged for Viereck's books to be published by the US publisher Lyle Stuart and for Viereck to go to Germany in 1955 to meet Dr

73 FBI Teletype message, 'urgent', October 19, 1954, 905–6128.

74 H. K. Thompson, 'Some recollections on James Madole prepared for Kerry Bolton 8/95'.

75 Paul Meskil, *Hitler's Heirs* (New York: Pyramid Books, 1961). 'Die Spinne', 'The Spider', a coterie of Nazis especially in South America and the Middle East,who were supposedly spinning their web over the world.

76 H. K. Thompson, 'Some recollections…', op. cit.

77 H. K. Thompson, 'Some recollections…', ibid.

Werner Naumann, designated propaganda minister in Hitler's will, and Inga Dönitz, wife of the jailed Grand Admiral, Thompson's main hero, who had been named by Hitler as his successor.[78]

Viereck and Thompson were the focus of an intellectual circle that included Lawrence Dennis,[79] Dr Charles Callan Tansill of Georgetown University,[80] Dr Harry Elmer Barnes,[81] and other historians, 'when they were passing through town', and literati, including novelist Charles Jackson.[82] Thompson had a particular regard for Dennis, and dined frequently with him at the Harvard Club.[83]

Thompson met Yockey at an expensive Jewish-owned luncheonette in New York, in the company of Weiss. Thompson was delighted to find that Yockey was as 'anti-American' as himself.[84] Yockey became what Thompson called his 'dearest political friend and companion in many great ventures'.[85] From then, Thompson provided 'a steady outflow of money' for Yockey's 'various projects'.[86]

One of the first and most significant of these various projects was *Der Feind Europas* ('The Enemy of Europe'), published in German in 1953 as a manual of *realpolitik* for the Socialist Reich Party (SRP) but originally written in 1948 as a sequel to *Imperium*. When the SRP was founded in 1952, Yockey

78 David McCalden, op. cit.

79 Dennis, the chief ideologue of 'American Fascism', was of Negro descent. Harvard educated, he had worked for Seligman bank and for the US State Department. He wrote *The Coming American Fascism* (1936), *The Dynamics of War and Revolution* (1940) and was co-author with Maximillian St George of *A Trial on Trial: The Great Sedition Trial of 1944* (1945), detailing the abortive attempt by the Roosevelt Administration to jail Dennis and dozens of other critics during World War II.

80 Tansill was an historian and opponent of America's entry into World War II, regarding Roosevelt as having pushed Britain into war.

81 Barnes was professor of history at Columbia University. He repudiated the accusation that Germany was responsible for World War I and opposed US entry into World War II. After the war he questioned whether 6,000,000 Jews had been exterminated.

82 Thompson interview with Stimely.

83 Thompson to Bolton, October 22, 1996.

84 Thompson interview with Stimely.

85 Thompson to Bolton, April 16, 1995.

86 Thompson interview with Stimely.

sought the leadership and became a political adviser. *Der Feind Europas* was funded by Thompson.[87] Two-hundred copies were printed, intended for the leadership of the SRP, but they were seized and destroyed — as were the printer's plates — by K-16, the German secret service.

Despite the poor translation that had been made in Germany by a Dr Malz, in January 1954 Weiss received a letter from Fritsch of Dürer Verlag, the Buenos Aires publisher of *Der Weg*, stating that *Der Feind* had been 'well received' and that he was interested in arranging a good translation.[88]

An English translation was serialised in the Yockeyan journal *TRUD* in 1969 and was published as a single volume with a long critique by Dr Revilo P Oliver by *Liberty Bell* in 1981.

DTK states of this time:

> Yockey often would visit Keith at one of K's offices and use a vacant typewriter. When the "heat was on" from the Feddies (always), Y would flop in one of Keith's offices overnight. Then, there was a shabby apartment in the city of Elizabeth, New Jersey owned by Weiss. FPY would sometimes stay there. In the early 1950s there was regular train service to Middletown, NY, which was very close to the Mt Hope sub-district, location of the Weiss farm. Y would use the train and never ride in cars driven by others at certain times and in most areas, especially in the New York metro area... too many spies, loose lips, and innocent but blundering types. Y's travels and bold operations would have put James Bond to shame. Then, back in the 40's and 50's things were much looser than today.[89]

## Dönitz

In 1957, Thompson again became of particular interest to the FBI, which closely monitored his whereabouts and his correspondence. Local postal authorities were asked to relay information on Thompson's mail to the FBI and his contacts were checked as to their affiliations. At this time Thompson was soliciting views on the 'war crimes trials' and on the fate of Dönitz in particular from military, legal and other eminent people, with a view to publishing a book on the trials. The FBI was investigating Thompson for violation of the

87 Thompson interview with Stimely, op. cit.

88 Edward A Brandt, FBI file no. 105–23413–9; March 29, 1954.

89 DTK to Bolton, May 8, 2015.

Foreign Agents Registration Act,[90] beginning on November 21, 1956,[91] in regard to his letters on behalf of Dönitz and on the 'war crimes trials', although the grounds are not cited in FBI reports and it was concluded that there had been no violation. Some of the recipients of Thompson's form letters asking for testimonials on Dönitz forwarded the letters to the FBI. This would not have perturbed Thompson, as he had sent such a letter to FBI director J Edgar Hoover asking for his input. To one recipient, Judge Clark, Thompson wrote:

> Instead of writing silly letters to the *New York Times* protesting perhaps the first sensible act of a US dominated "allied parole commission" why don't you participate in the testimonial album described in the enclosure, as many really prominent Americans are doing? I have never understood how a man of your education could fall for such jewish [sic] traps and mouth such fiction as "3,000,000 jews [sic]" (murdered). The jews [sic] claim that it was 6,000,000. Were there really any murdered? I think they are all here in New York City. Perhaps we should send some down to Princeton?[92]

When Dönitz was released from Spandau in 1956, Thompson organised an international campaign that succeeded in getting him his full pension rights. On Dönitz's release from Spandau, Thompson and Viereck sent him a telegram dated October 1, 1956:

> Telegram to the legitimate president of Germany, Grand admiral Karl Doenitz, on the occasion of his release from eleven years of illegal confinement by the "allies" for "war crimes":
>
> On the day of the triumph of your steeled will over the plans of your vengeful persecutors, your American friends congratulate you and wish you a long, healthy life. Throughout the entire despicable Nuremberg proceedings — brought about by the criminal co-guilt of the USA and world jewry [sic], your soldierly honor shone forth as the sole hope of those who wished to rebuild the collapsing Western World.

90 FBI report, May 3, 1957, 105–6128.

91 FBI report, June 27, 1957, 105–6128.

92 Thompson to Clark, December 29, 1956, cited in FBI report May 22, 1957, 105–6128, p. 3.

> Through your personal courage, you have triumphed over the calculated plans of the destroyers of Western Culture, and you stand today as the personification of Honor, Loyalty and Faith. Let no considerations dissuade you from this position. You are unique in History! Today we also greet your courageous wife who has fought for you so valiantly through these difficult years.[93]

The Society for the Prevention of World War III (SPWWIII) asked Senator Jacob Javitz of New York whether there were any laws that could be used to prosecute Thompson and Viereck for having sent their greetings to Dönitz.[94] What concerned the Society was the possibility of an alliance between a revived Germany and the Soviet bloc. The democracies had fallen out with their wartime ally, Stalin, soon after the end of hostilities, when Stalin rebuked the generous offer to become junior partner in a new world order.[95] Even the 'pacificist' guru Lord Bertrand Russell, of 'nuclear disarmament' fame, was calling for the A-bombing of the USSR before she became a 'threat to world peace'.

The possibility of a united Germany under Soviet auspices, while palatable to sections of the right in Germany and the USA, was a nightmare scenario. However, most of the radical Right in the USA zealously signed up to propagate the Cold War against the USSR, while the Stalinists called the 'Washington regime' (in Yockey's parlance) 'rootless cosmopolitans'[96] in the same sense that Yockey called them 'Culture-distorters' and both terms were synonymous with being Jewish.

The SPWWIII stated to Javits that while they did not know Dönitz's attitude on being referred to by Viereck and Thompson as 'the legitimate president of Germany', they claimed that shortly before Germany's surrender Dönitz had signed a memorandum in April 1945 stating that Germany's revival could only be achieved in collaboration with the USSR. The memorandum advocated an alliance to dominate the Eurasian landmass and to 'confront the old rotten entrenched power of the West'. Simard and Lipshutz referred

---

93 Thompson and Viereck to Dönitz, October 1, 1956.

94 Albert Simard and Isadore Lipschutz to Javitz, October 18, 1956.

95 K. R. Bolton, *Stalin — The Enduring Legacy*, op. cit.

96 F Chernov, 'Bourgeois Cosmopolitanism and its Reactionary Role', *Bolshevik*, no. 5, March 15, 1949, pp. 30–41. See Bolton, *Stalin…*, ibid., pp. 38–46.

Javitz to an article from the magazine[97] of the SPWWIII that had been written by Congressman Arthur G Klein of New York and introduced into the Congressional Record.[98] Here, Klein discussed a pro-Russia orientation among German policymakers since Frederick the Great, through to Bismarck and the Weimar era Treaty of Rapallo. The Hitler-Stalin Pact, regardless of whether Hitler or Stalin were sincere in their intentions, was part of this Eastern-oriented tradition of German *realpolitik*. From this and the Dönitz memorandum we can appreciate that Yockey, Remer, Thompson and Weiss, so far from representing a heretical strand within the Right, were continuing the tradition that saw a Russo-German alliance as an organic historical development, and never more so than in confronting the victors after two world wars.

The success of the campaign for Dönitz reflected Thompson's wide contacts with influential people. The correspondence connected with the campaign was published as a book in 1976, *Dönitz at Nuremberg: A Reappraisal*.[99] The letters had been presented as an album to Dönitz on his release.

The hundreds of letters Thompson had sent to eminent people throughout the world asked for their opinions of the 'war crimes trials' to form 'a better historical perspective'. Describing himself on his letterhead as a 'journalist and public relations counsel' and as a literary agent and news analyst, he referred to Dönitz as having been jailed for performing the duty that any military man would be sworn to uphold. Thompson pointed out that the Nuremberg Military Tribunal did not have any legal precedent or authorisation, that it was not a genuine 'military tribunal' and that it was in violation of 'Anglo-American constitutional principles'. Thompson cited Rear Admiral Daniel V Gallery, who wrote in *Twenty Million Tons Under the Sea* that the 'war crimes trials' were 'a libel on the military profession' and that the trial of

97 Arthur G Klein, 'Germany looks East… "An alliance between the young socialist forces against the old rotten entrenched forces of the West"', *Prevent World War III*, no. 31, September–October 1956.

98 Arthur G Klein, US Congressional Record, September 14, 1956.

99 H. K. Thompson and Henry Strutz (editors) *Dönitz at Nuremberg: A Reappraisal, War Crimes and the Military Professional* (New York City: Amber Publishing Corp., 1976).

Dönitz was 'barefaced hypocrisy'. He referred to Admiral Nimitz,[100] who testified for the defence at the trial of Dönitz, that unrestricted submarine warfare, for which Dönitz had been tried, had also been undertaken by US submarines in the Pacific. Thompson stated in his appeal letter that he had been collecting opinions for more than a year and that 'this collection of opinions will represent a milestone in the historical reappraisal of the dangerous precedent set at Nuremberg'. Thompson then provided a three-page list of hundreds of eminent persons who had already contributed their opinions.[101]

The preface of *Dönitz at Nuremberg* was written by William L Hart, Justice of the Supreme Court of Ohio, who concluded by stating: 'There was no legal justification for the trial, conviction or sentence of the so-called "war criminals" by the Nuremberg Tribunal. We have set a bad precedent. It should not be followed in the future.'[102] There follow opinions against the Nuremberg Trials by hundreds of legal, diplomatic, political and military authorities throughout the world, such as Dwight Eisenhower's lawyer brother, Edgar, and in particular by many naval commanders from the Allied states. Hence, the book remains a valuable source of authoritative opinions against the mentality of revenge that has informed the victors after an increasing number of globalist wars, resulting in the barbaric treatment of the defeated leaders of Serbia, Iraq, Libya. Nor should one forget, as this is written, the eye to vengeance turning against Syria's Assad.

When Grand Admiral Dönitz was released from Spandau in 1957, Thompson initiated a campaign in defense of his reputation. The campaign was successful in that it forced the West German government to pay Dönitz his full pension rights.[103] After Dönitz was released from Spandau, he thanked Thompson for his support.[104]

As a literary agent, Thompson's clients included General Fulgencio Batista, president of Cuba. Thompson also represented an Argentine-Bolivian combine selling arms to Batista when he was fighting Castro's hill guerrillas.[105]

---

100 Nimitz contributed an opinion to the Dönitz book (p. 44).

101 FBI report, October 2, 1958, 105–6128.

102 William L Hart, *Dönitz at Nuremberg*, xx.

103 D McCalden, op. cit.

104 Martin Lee, *The Beast Reawakens* (London: Little Brown & Co., 1997), p. 88.

105 McCalden, no. 21, op. cit.

The USA had placed an arms embargo on Batista at a crucial time.[106] This was a long-standing US measure that had been enacted against supposed 'allies' against communism, such as Chiang Kai-shek, and against Somoza, president of Nicaragua, when fighting the Sandinistas.[107] Thompson is acknowledged in Batista's book *Respuesta*, in regard to the Nuremberg trials.[108]

The Left-liberal publisher Lyle Stuart was Thompson's neighbour. In 1962-63, King Farouk of Egypt threatened Stuart with a slander suit because of the publication of a book alleging sexual improprieties with prostitutes in Miami. Through Thompson's well-placed contacts in Egypt, he handed Stuart a dossier on Farouk and the suit was promptly dropped.[109] In return, Stuart opened columns of his magazine, *Expose*, to Thompson, where the series 'I am an American Fascist' was run, the primary purpose being to explain the way the ADL and others, working with the FBI, infiltrated and often manipulated 'neo-Nazi' organisations such as the NRP. Thompson was threatened by a Mossad agent around this time, who soon after disappeared.[110] In the 1970s Thompson served in Rhodesia under the alias Brigadier Paul D North, travelling on a fake Canadian passport, which brought him to the attention of a Black militant group called Black Avengers.[111]

After a long period behind the scenes, in September 1982 Thompson addressed a convention of the Institute for Historical Review. This raised former IHR director David McCalden's ire; he demanded to know whether this was the direction in which the 'Revisionist movement' should proceed, despite McCalden's conceding that the speech would certainly be 'intelligent and pithy'.[112]

---

106 Mario Lazo, *Dagger in the Heart: American Policy Failures in Cuba* (New York: Twin Circle Publishing, 1968), 160–161.

107 Anastasio Somoza (with Jack Cox) *Nicaragua Betrayed* (Boston: Western Islands, 1980). The National Guard, courtesy of US policy, were left firing their last bullet.

108 F. Batista, *Respuesta* (Mexico City: Manuel Leon Sanchez, 1960), 213; http://www.cubarepublicana.org/books/respuesta/c27.pdf.

109 McCalden, no. 21, op. cit.

110 McCalden, 'Revisionist Newsletter' no. 22, July 1983.

111 McCalden, no. 21, op. cit.

112 McCalden, no. 21, op. cit.

The FBI took a renewed interest in Thompson in 1984, in regard to his passport status.[113]

Thompson's opinion of the 'American Right' was not high. However, it never had been and nor had Yockey's. Thompson said to Stimely:

> As to the American "right-wing", I had no respect for it from my earlier experience, and I have even less today. I don't think anything constructive will ever appear from the *political* right-wing. It is not inconceivable that some day a group of well-intentioned military men may reach a point of frustration, and take this thing over. The military are basically conservative, and I think that they *used to*, at any rate, possess a realistic view of the forces that work internationally. Now that has been eroded, to some extent by, I'm sure, mis-education in the service academies, along the lines of Holocaust propaganda, anti-German propaganda, racial tolerance nonsense and the like. But from the military generation that I knew, and these were the people who were in World War I — those senior officers pretty well knew where things were at. They knew that the Nigras were by and large worthless as soldiers unless you had three White men standing behind the back of each Black, to make sure that he conducted himself in a reasonably productive fashion. And they were aware of the Jews, later aware of the American subservience to Israel, etc. General George S Brown was probably one of the last martyrs to American interests, when he very forcefully pointed out while Chairman of the Joint Chiefs of Staff that Israel was absolutely not only worthless as a military ally, but a great disadvantage to the United States, and he was quickly, of course, shut up and forced out, as was General Singlaub shut up and forced out by Jimmeh [sic] Carter in quite recent years.
>
> It's not impossible that ultimately a coup will come from the right, and salvage this shit-barge of a country. I don't think it's worthy of salvage. I would much prefer it ruled, perhaps, by a Red Chinese field marshal. But what will happen in the future — I don't know.[114]

Stimely opined that a coup might only eventuate if there was a major military reversal overseas. Certainly, we now know, from occasional leaks and quips, that the Pentagon still includes personnel who are not happy with the USA's subservience to Israeli interests in the Middle East and other globetrotting

113 Department of Justice to Office of Passport Services, May 7, 1984.

114 Thompson interview with Stimely.

expeditions on behalf of US commerce. However, in Thompson's heyday there were many military luminaries militantly active in the Right and contemptuous of Zionism, such as Lieutenant General P. A. del Valle, USMC; Lt. Gen. George Stratemeyer, USAF; Lt. Gen. Edward M Almond; and Vice Admiral T. G. W. Settle, to cite four military men who not only contributed to Thompson's book on Dönitz but who endorsed Colonel John Beatty's anti-Zionist book *The Iron Curtain Over America.*[115] A decade later (1962), General Edwin Walker was leading what the Kennedy Administration feared was an incipient revolt at the University of Mississippi against desegregation, imposed by Federal Troops at bayonet point.

Under Keith Stimely's editorship, Thompson contributed book reviews to the *Journal of Historical Review* (JHR), journal of the Institute for Historical Review, and in particular articles on the two men he esteemed most, Grand Admiral Dönitz and Major General Remer.

Writing of Dönitz as the 'last president of a united Germany', Thompson's opening lines were that the Third Reich was 'the last heroic stand of Western civilization' and Hitler was 'the last natural leader of Europe'. The Allied victory was a triumph for 'the forces of Asiatic Communism and Russian Nationalism on the one hand, and Jewish Bolshevism (as exemplified by the United States, England, France and their multitude of last-minute vassals and hangers-on) on the other'. In the few weeks of April and May 1945, Dönitz unexpectedly became head of state and set up a Cabinet of military and technocratic personnel. He refused to denigrate Hitler, although it would have been opportune to do so, and sought to surrender to the Western Allies, a primary concern being the fate of refugees fleeing from the East — a concern not shared by Eisenhower, et al, who refused the offer of a separate surrender without the USSR. The Nuremberg Tribunal sentenced Dönitz to ten years' imprisonment, much to the outrage of many Allied military leaders.

115 When Lt. Gen. Stratemeyer received a letter form Henry Schultz of the Anti-Defamation League of B'nai B'rith, warning him not to be associated with an 'anti-Semite' such as Professor Beatty, Stratemyer replied: 'Who are you and your organization to tell me what I should read and what I should recommend other loyal American citizens to read? And, by the way, just what is the purpose of your organization?' He stated that he 'resented' the letter as 'a veiled threat', the 'most outrageous letter' he had ever received and that he would widely publicise it. Stratemeyer to Schultz, October 12, 1955.

Although apolitical, Dönitz never forsook his oath to Hitler, noted co-defendant Albert Speer. During 1952–1953 a commando operation was planned to rescue the internees at Spandau and reconstitute a Government-in-exile. Thompson states that those involved included residents of Spain, Portugal and the USA. However, security was compromised and the plan was discarded. Thompson wrote that in the early 1980s he burned a file on the matter that had long been sought 'by at least four intelligence agencies'. When Dönitz was released in 1956 the press noted that his wife, Inga, had maintained contact with German nationalists and Thompson had kept in communication with her. Dönitz always kept the many letters that Thompson had solicited from eminent figures in support of him. Although he never became involved in politics, Dönitz readily spoke before conventions of veterans. In 1980, just a few months before his death, Dönitz wrote to Thompson expressing the hope that they would meet again.[116]

Thompson's review for the *Journal of Historical Review* of a book by Remer relates the circumstances of the 1944 plot against Hitler, which was stymied by Remer's decisiveness. Thompson wrote that if there is any one word that describes Remer it is 'courage'. Remer, Thompson wrote in 1988, was head of another organization, the German Freedom Movement. Remer's outlook had not changed since the days of the SRP. He advocated total European union, with Russia included, but excluding Britain and the USA. Even in 1988, Thompson still saw Remer as the leader of a new Europe and continued to express this in a Yockeyan manner:

> The historical reasons for such a program are eminently understandable. Many geopolitical thinkers, for instance Francis Parker Yockey, were early supporters of this viewpoint. In 1988, few can fail to respect Remer's courage and honesty in advancing it. It is possible that he can become the inspiring, visionary leader needed by Europe to effect its liberation from the counter-cultural forces which now infest and occupy it, and guide it toward a future free of economic and armed conflicts.[117]

---

116 Thompson, 'Grand Admiral Karl Dönitz: Last President of a United Germany', *Journal for Historical Review*, vol. 4, no. 3, Fall 1983, http://www.ihr.org/jhr/v04/v04p305_Thompson.html.

117 Thompson, 'Conspiracy and Betrayal', JHR, vol. 8, no. 1, Spring 1988, http://www.ihr.org/jhr/v08/v08p100_Thompson.html.

Thompson wrote other reviews for the JHR during the 1980s and he arranged the appearance of Remer at the Eighth International Revisionist Conference in 1987. When Remer died 10 years later, Thompson wrote on 'the loss of this old friend, with whom I had so many shared experiences', writing further that 'we cannot permit either Remer or Yockey to become forgotten as long as we can do something about it'.[118]

In the few years before his death on March 3, 2002, Thompson became a notable donor to conservative elements of the Republican Party, including Oliver North, Jesse Helms, David Duke and Patrick Buchanan. He was awarded membership of the party's Presidential Legion of Merit.

Why the Republican Party? At the time of the Reagan administration, there seems to have been an in-house conflict for supremacy between what became known as neoconservatives and palaeoconservatives. The 'neocons', as we might call them, are neither 'new' nor 'conservative'. They were in fact Wilsonian-type liberal-Democrats and internationalists, or ex-Trotskyites who came over to the US side during the Cold War in their hatred of Stalinism.[119] The palaeoconservatives, a term coined by Professor Paul Gottfried, were traditionalist Republicans of the Taft, America First variety, including President Reagan's treasury secretary, Paul Craig Roberts, and White House communications adviser Patrick Buchanan. At the time an 'ethnic outreach' programme by the Republican Party also recruited from among East European anti-Communist émigrés, who had fascist associations. The programme was headed by Laszlo Pasztor, founding chairman of the Republican Heritage Groups Council, who had been a member of the Arrow Cross Party-Hungarist Movement — or *Hungarists*, during the war. The heritage council included Radi Slavoff, a Bulgarian supporter of German-American campaigner Dr Austin J App; Florian Galdau, a veteran of Romania's Iron Guard; Nicholas Nazarenko, a Cossack Waffen SS veteran; et al.[120] This organization

---

118 Thompson to Bolton, December 29, 1998.

119 K R Bolton, *Stalin*… op. cit., pp. 109–124.

120 For a critical summary see: Carla Binion, 'Nazis and the Republican Party', http://www.theforbiddenknowledge.com/hardtruth/nazis_republican_party.htm.
We might now say 'Trotskyites and the Republican Party', as the faction that triumphed, setting up globalist subversive organizations such as the National Endowment for

campaigned against the Office of Special Investigations (OSI), established to hound European émigrés who had fought against the Soviet invasion during World War II.

***

When Yockey returned to the USA and met Thompson courtesy of Weiss, they began their closest collaboration in a campaign to support Major General Otto Remer, who had been jailed for his politics, and the Socialist Reich Party, which had been banned after its rapid success. Thompson stated of Remer that not only was he leader of the SRP but that he 'also represented the leadership cadres of "survivors" of the Third Reich scattered throughout the world… a great deal of that data will die with me…'[121]

In 1952, Thompson, Yockey and Viereck founded the Committee for International Justice, and with the jailing of Otto Remer, the Committee for the Freedom of Major General Remer, to campaign for the legal and civic rights of Germans prosecuted under the Nuremberg regime and for political prisoners such as Remer.

As early as 1947, Thompson and his 'friends in the [Mosley] Union Movement in England' were working for the release of Field Marshal Albert Kesselring, top German commander in Italy during World War II, who had been arrested in 1945 as a 'war criminal' and held in Werl Prison, Germany, 'on vague charges'. Thompson's Committee for International Justice established contact with Kesselring in 1952 while he was a patient at a private hospital in Bochum, Germany. Kesselring 'warmly' endorsed Thompson's Committee.[122] After Kesselring's release he was pressured into repudiating Thompson. The Bonn Government sent Baron von Lilienfeld of the West German Foreign Office to New York to lobby the press into not publicising the Committee's work.[123]

---

Democracy to continue the 'world revolution' under US auspices. Again, the primary target remains Russia.

121 H. K. Thompson to K. R. Bolton, August 1995.

122 H. K. Thompson, 'American Fascist', *Independent*, August 1962, p. 9.

123 Ibid.

A particular worry for the US authorities was the 'neutralist' and anti-American line being pursued by many on the German Right, whose anti-Communism would have superficially demanded a different course. The writings of Yockey and Weiss encouraged this neutrality and even support for the USSR against the USA. Even traditional German conservatives, let alone National Socialists, did not see the USA as a paragon of Western Civilization. American conservative scholar Professor Paul Gottfried points out that 'Anti-Americanism has had a long-standing tradition in European society and has appealed to the traditional Right even before it became a staple of far leftist propaganda'. Gottfried states that in Germany, while the Christian Democrats based their ideology on a rejection of Communism and Nazism as 'twin totalitarian movements' and were committed to the US cause during the Cold War, 'this however was not a rightwing or nationalist argument'. The 'real German Right', represented by figures such as Carl Schmitt and Hans Zehrer, hated the Americans for imposing their will upon a prostrate Europe and vulgarising German society. Many German nationalists were calling for 'a less pro-American foreign policy and for playing off the Americans against the Soviets'. The famous German legal theorist Carl Schmitt stressed the advantage of playing the USA and USSR off against each other.[124]

Apologists and collaborators for the Occupation attempted to portray the 'neutralist' line of the German Right as serving the interests of 'communism'. However, an anti-communist campaign had certain inherent dangers for the Washington regime lest it encourage the re-emergence of American nationalism and isolationism. That is why there was a focus on opposing the USSR and Stalinism but not on opposing communism *per se*. When Senator Joseph McCarthy undertook a more pointed crusade against communism he found himself, to his eventual ruin, not so much against communists as

124 Paul Gottfried to K. R. Bolton, January 16, 2013. Gottfried cites these sources: For Zeher see: Hans B. von Sothen, 'Hans Zehrer als politischer Publizist nach 1945' in *Die Kupierte Alternative: Konservatismus in Deutschland nach 1945*, edited by Frank-Lothar Kroll (Berlin: Duncker & Humblot, 2005), 125-80; and Kroll's introduction to this anthology, 3-24. For Schmitt see: *L'Unità del mondo*, ed. Alessandro Campi (Rome: Antonio Pellicani Editore, 1994).

against the Washington regime and global corporations.[125] Hence when the pro-McCarthy publicist Freda Utley went to Germany in 1954, warning that the Occupation was infested with Reds and that most of the 'Red Morgenthau boys' who had been fired by General Lucius Clay had been reinstated, her anti-communist rhetoric was condemned together with the 'neutralist' position of the German right.[126] Only certain types of 'anti-communism' were acceptable to the Washington regime during the Cold War, specifically anti-Stalinism, while the USA cultivated the support of Trotskyites and other Leftists.[127]

An influential circle of German conservatives formed around Miss Utley's friend, the lawyer Dr Ernst Achenbach, a leader of the Free Democratic Party (FDP) who, according to *Reporter* columnist Edmond Taylor, had contact with Senator McCarthy via Miss Utley.[128] Achenbach was associated with former Goebbels functionary Dr Werner Naumann, head of the so-called 'Naumann Circle' which was accused of having conspired to overthrow to the Adenauer Government.[129] Naumann and others were arrested in the British Zone and alleged to have planned to take over the FDP, of which Naumann had been foreign policy spokesman, with the aim of establishing a liberated Western Germany 'oriented toward the Soviet Union'.[130] In a new slant on conspiracy theories, Taylor described influential contacts cultivated by Achenbach as a leading corporate lawyer, in what was called 'a world-wide fascist-communist conspiracy', which was in the USA centred on Frederick Weiss.[131] Taylor commented that the Bonn authorities kept close tabs on Weiss's publications and Weiss adopted a vigorous line against anti-Soviet propaganda in the USA,

125 K. R. Bolton, *Revolution from Above* (London: Arktos Media Ltd., 2012), 'McCarthy's Threat to the Globalist Establishment', pp. 40–41.

126 Edmond Taylor, 'Germany: Where Fascism and Communism Meet', *The Reporter*, op. cit., p. 10.

127 K. R. Bolton, *Stalin: The Enduring Legacy*, op. cit., and *Revolution from Above*, op. cit. The Trotskyites and other anti-Stalin Leftists flocked to the CIA-sponsored Congress for Cultural Freedom, and ended up as zealous exponents of US Cold War policy.

128 Edmond Taylor, op. cit., p. 11.

129 Edmond Taylor, ibid.

130 Edmond Taylor, ibid., p. 12.

131 Edmond Taylor, ibid., p. 13.

while also supporting Senator McCarthy.[132] Like Yockey, Weiss saw the 1952 Prague treason trial against mainly Jewish functionaries of the Communist Party, who were hanged for being agents of Zionism and Israel, as a declaration of war by the USSR against Jewish-run America, and predicted that anti-Soviet propaganda would intensify.[133]

Within this worldwide conspiracy, as explained by Taylor, Yockey was an important figure in 'international fascism'. Taylor pointed out that Yockey was advocating 'anti-Americanism' and 'the avoidance of any anti-Soviet policy'.[134]

What Taylor neglected to state in his 1954 article was that in 1953 Dr Naumann had been released by a Federal Court on the grounds that 'no suspicion of criminal intent' had been proven against him. This despite British High Commissioner Sir Ivone Kirkpatrick's comment to the *New York Herald Tribune* that British agents had found evidence that the 'Naumann Circle' were 'plotting to seize power', although he was 'not completely certain what they were up to'.[135] However, the proceedings did prevent Naumann from entering the Bundestag and he lost his position in the FDP.

Taylor stated that the 'neutralist' position among the radical Right was represented in the Socialist Reich Party, for which Thompson acted as the registered American agent, at the same time registering with the US State Department as personal agent for party leader Dr Rudolf Aschenauer.[136] Despite the close association of the SRP with National Socialism, the fact that the party gained two seats in the Bundestag indicated that 're-education' had a long way to go and where persuasion was ineffective more forceful means would have to be continued. This resulted in the banning of the SRP and the jailing of its most widely known figure, Major General Remer.

---

132 Edmond Taylor, ibid.

133 Edmond Taylor, ibid.

134 Edmond Taylor, ibid., p. 14.

135 Oswald Mosley, *The European*, March 1953; *Mosley Policy & Debate* (Euphorion Books, 1954), p. 128.

136 Edmond Taylor, op. cit., p. 14.

## Thompson-Yockey Correspondence with US State Department

Thompson had founded two committees in regard to the prosecution of Germans, one of which dealt specifically with the Remer case. There followed an exchange of letters with the US State Department on the trials of 'war criminals' and on the imprisonment of Remer. For four months during 1951–1952 Remer had been jailed for his criticism of the Bonn regime and for insulting Chancellor Adenauer. While in jail, Remer was also tried and convicted for making 'defamatory remarks about the Twentieth of July Conspirators'[137] whose coup against Hitler in 1944 had been stymied due to the actions of Remer and the Berlin garrison under his command. On October 23, 1952, the SRP was outlawed and Remer was denied the right to vote and hold public office.[138]

In his interview with Keith Stimely, Thompson spoke of the circumstances of the correspondence with the State Department:

> Well, at the time I was a registered foreign agent, representing Generalmajor Otto-Ernst Remer and his party, the Sozialistische Reichspartei (SRP), a very strong post-war German political party. And as a registered agent I was at the time drafting a letter to Acheson on behalf of the prisoners incarcerated at Spandau, and I was in Yockey's presence at the time as I recall, and he made some amends and suggestions as to wording, and things that might be added, all of which I incorporated into the final draft. Yockey knew that I was required by law to mention anyone who assisted me in the furtherance of my activities as a registered foreign agent. So I did so in my foreign agent's registration reports: reported that I had been assisted by one "Frank Healy", which was the name that Yockey was using in New York at the time.[139]

Thompson and Yockey wrote to Dean Acheson, US Secretary of State, in regard to Remer's arrest, in a letter dated June 16, 1952. Henry B Cox, Officer-in-Charge, Division of German Information, Office of German Public Affairs, wrote back briefly stating that this was a German domestic matter outside

137 Martin Lee, op. cit., pp. 82–83.

138 Martin Lee, ibid., p. 84.

139 H Keith Thompson to Keith Stimely, March 13, 1986.

the jurisdiction of both the USA and the UNO.[140] Given that West Germany was overseen by an Allied High Commission until 1955 and did not achieve full sovereignty until 1991, the State Department reply to Thompson was disingenuous.

Thompson and Yockey again addressed themselves to Acheson, Thompson this time appealing to him as a fellow Yale graduate, who was therefore presumably well-versed in international affairs and history, commenting that an honest exchange between Yale alumni is 'never out of order'. At the time, there were 1,045 Germans held as 'war criminals', not only in Germany but elsewhere in Europe. In addition the seven highest-ranking officials were being held at Spandau and 'countless German "prisoners of war" held by the Soviet Union'. Thompson and Yockey stated that German soldiers cannot be expected to support a Western alliance when their officers and fellow soldiers are being incarcerated for 'war crimes'. It was a move designed to play on the fears of the USA that Germany would not be a reliable ally in the Cold War. They wrote:

> I respectively submit to you, Mr Secretary, the following considerations: that the position of the future German military officer is made exceptionally difficult by the war crimes convictions; that a German cannot justifiably be asked to fight for or with an alliance of which other members are holding Germans as prisoners for war-time acts (World War II) which the Germans believe the Allies also have committed; that the presence of Soviet "judges" at the Nuremberg proceedings tend to render such proceedings invalid in view of subsequent disclosure concerning the Soviets [particular reference is made to the matter of the Katyn Forest Massacre]; that when men act as agents of a Government representing the collective will of a nation, there is a definite incongruity involved in later convicting such men as individual "war criminals".[141]

Thompson and Yockey stated that many young people in both Germany and the USA had no confidence 'in the humbug formulae which have served as the basic orientations of official thought and propaganda lines in the matter of "war criminals"'. To most Germans the 'war criminals' remained the leaders

140 Henry B Cox to H. K. Thompson, June 20, 1952.

141 Thompson to Acheson, July 30, 1952.

of a great 'national effort'. It was therefore urgent that the US release all 'war criminals', including the Spandau inmates, as a matter of 'good faith'.[142] They then introduced the issue of the suppression of the SRP:

> I have viewed with growing concern the matter of the apparent persecution of minority political parties, of the anti-communist Right, by the Government of Federal Republic of Germany. The particular, but not the exclusive, target has been the Socialist Reich Party of which Major General Remer is an official. The history of the actions of the Bonn Government, and local administrators, and the SRP is too lengthy to set forth in this letter. I take the liberty of enclosing a partial history of such actions. This has been followed in recent weeks by an injunction prohibiting the SRP from conducting public meetings, distributing its publications or otherwise bringing its case to the people. As a climax, the Bonn government is placing a legal ban against this party, contrary to the interests of the United States in that it (1) is indicative of an attempt within Germany to restrain free speech and freedom of political expression and (2) tends to destroy unity amongst the conservative political parties which will be our strongest sources of strength in any anti-Communist endeavor. I submit that the United States has responsibilities in Germany in view of the presence of our troops there and in view of the extent of United States influence, direct and indirect, in German affairs.[143]

Thompson then addressed the contention raised by Henry B Cox of the State Department, who claimed that the US had no jurisdiction over German affairs. Thompson referred to the Austrian parliament having just passed a law restoring property and civil rights to 34,000 'former Nazis'. He directed Acheson's attention to a telegram that had been sent to the Secretary of State by the President of the American Jewish Committee, Jacob Blaustein, in which Blaustein states that the USA still had 'responsibility in Austria' and should apply pressure to have the new law repealed. In response to the Jewish demand, on July 26, 1952, Thompson wrote:

> The United States State Department made public its disapproval of the Austrian laws in question. Mr Lincoln Waite, a State Department spokesman said that the

142 Thompson to Acheson, ibid.

143 Thompson to Acheson, ibid.

> State Department has communicated "its fairly strong" views on the subject to the Acting High Commissioner for Austria.[144]

Thompson and Yockey contended that if this action could be taken in response to a demand by the American Jewish Committee, why couldn't the State Department make such a protest, conversely, to restore the rights of German politicians and veterans?

> Apparently the United States State Department is willing to intervene in the affairs of another country when urged to do so by the "American Jewish Committee", but will not intervene in the interests of justice in the case of General Remer, the persecuted rightist political parties of Germany, and the 1,045 "war criminals". The United States has far more at stake in intervening in the aforementioned cases than in serving the cause of international Jewry by adversely interfering in a small administrative matter restoring rights to persons plainly entitled to hold such rights.[145]

Perry Laukhuff, Acting Deputy Director, Bureau of German Affairs, replied to Thompson that his views were so much at variance with the policy of the USA towards Germany that there was no point in replying in detail. Laukhuff contended that the US attitude to the prisoners was based on judicial principles of Anglo-Saxon law and that it has the support of 'important elements of the new Germany',[146] which of course it did since the law was designed to protect the collaborationist Bonn regime. In regard to the issue of Remer and the SRP, Laukhuff responded:

> … Here again it is obvious that there is little or no common ground for a discussion of the issue. You apparently feel that Herr Remer leads a worthy cause and is being persecuted for it. You also consider that support for him and his party would greatly advance the cause of anti-communism and United States policy in Europe. You are well aware, however, that the State Department holds entirely different views. From Remer's speeches, from the known views held by him and the other leaders of the SRP, and from other information available to the Department, there seems to be every indication that this man and his movement

144 Thompson to Acheson, ibid.

145 Thompson to Acheson, ibid.

146 Laukhuff to Thompson, September 2, 1952.

> are neo-Nazi in character. You make the common mistake of considering that because a man is not a communist he is a good democrat. Far from being in league with anti-Communist parties, Remer and his partners are bitterly hostile to the moderate democratic forces in Germany. Under these circumstances, the Department can scarcely be expected to intervene with the German Government on Remer's behalf, even if it has the technical right to do so. It is no part of American policy to assist Nazism to arise once more in Germany.[147]

It might be noted that Laukhuff is less obfuscationist than Cox: that it is not so much a matter of the US being unable to intervene than that the US supports the measures taken against Remer and the SRP — which of course would not come as a surprise to Thompson or Yockey. Laukhuff was after all merely outlining the *raison d'être* of the Occupation. Finally, Laukhuff rejected Thompson's reference to US attempts at intervention in the Austrian matter to appease Jewish interests, claiming that it was simply a matter of justice and restitution for 'the victims of National Socialism'.

The apparently final letter sent to the State Department over Thompson's name, as Executive Secretary of The Committee for International Justice and The Committee for the Freedom of Major General Remer, is the lengthiest of the correspondence and includes a great deal of Yockey's ideology. The letter begins by stating that the campaign for the release of Remer was not based on a personal commitment but a 'superpersonal Idea' in support of what Remer represents. The letter was written to explain the Committee's worldview and was presumably written with the view to reaching a wider audience, rather than merely trying to convert functionaries of the State Department. Turning first to the matter of 'war crimes', Thompson/Yockey write:

> In the democratic Germany you mention, the authoritarian Adenauer regime has found it necessary to make it a criminal offense for anyone publicly to write the word "war criminal" in quotation marks. This was necessary because, generally speaking, all Germans regard the use of the word "criminal" in connection with their political and military heroes of the War as a cowardly and vile slander by a dishonorable victor, and because the Adenauer regime, supported only by American bayonets, is necessarily obliged to enforce, by all possible means, the internal policy relayed to it through you. Until the forces you represent are able

147 Laukhuff to Thompson, ibid.

> to pass similar legislation here, we shall continue at all times to write this phrase in the manner which is forbidden in democratic Germany.[148]

The concept of 'war crimes' is explained as an illicit manoeuvre by the victors who contrived a law that did not exist at the time of the alleged 'crimes'. On the other hand, the code of conduct of soldiers is already set forth and known by them. This code was not, and is not now, the basis of 'war crimes' charges. In the case of the 'war-crimes terror' in Germany, no such laws had existed and the defendants were not being tried under American or German laws, nor under the terms of the Geneva Convention for Prisoners of War. The 'international law' that was contrived for the purpose of prosecuting the German leadership was at variance with the traditional concepts of 'international law' that had hitherto been practiced on the basis of ethics rather than 'mock trials'.

Yockey and Thompson referred specifically to the Malmedy Trial as an example of the nature of the post-war prosecutions. This is a matter in which they had first-hand knowledge. They referred to the 1946 trial of Waffen-SS men and officers accused of killing American soldiers who had surrendered in 1944 at Malmedy during the 'Battle of the Bulge', describing the trial as 'a foul process … a hideous caricature of the American constitutional principle of separation of powers… a satanic debauch'.[149] Thompson and Yockey referred to the Congressional investigation of the trial methodology undertaken by Texas Supreme Court Judge Gordon Simpson. Additional to Yockey's personal experiences with the post-war Occupation, Thompson knew Judge Leroy van Roden, who was instrumental in having Senator Joseph McCarthy examine the Malmedy case.[150]

Yockey and Thompson stated that the jailing of Remer, the banning of the SRP and the prosecution of numerous others, including Frau Heinrich Himmler, was proof that the Bonn regime was imposed and maintained by American bayonets, only allowing an 'opposition' that substantially agreed with the regime. It was now disingenuous for the USA to mention

148 Thompson/Yockey to Acheson, October 15, 1952.

149 Thompson/Yockey to Acheson, ibid.

150 Refer to the previous chapter 'War Crimes Investigator'.

anti-communism and state that Remer et al are not 'genuine anti-communists' when Remer and others who were being prosecuted had fought the USSR while the Allies were backing the Soviet invasion of Europe.[151]

Yockey and Thompson conclude with philosophical themes that are fundamental to *Imperium*, namely that:

> The German National Socialist Movement was only one form, and a provisional form at that, of the great irresistible movement which expresses the spirit of the Age, the Resurgence of Authority. This movement is the affirmation of all the cultural drives and human instincts which liberalism, democracy, and communism deny. General Remer's movement is a current expression of the irresistible Resurgence of Authority in the Western Civilization.[152]

It seems unlikely that such sentiments would have been understood by Acheson, or more specifically the desk jockey who was allotted the task of reading the letter, which does not seem to have been answered. The conclusion is a clarion call for European unity and destiny:

> The Resurgence of Authority has both its inner and outer aspect. The inner has been touched upon in the preceding paragraph. Its outer aspect is the creation of the European-Imperium-State-Nation, and therewith the reassertion of Europe's historically ordained role, that of the colonizing and organizing force in the entire world.[153]

Thompson and Yockey reiterated that the USA is dominated by Jewish interests. They outlined the beliefs of the committees, which go beyond freeing and rehabilitating German 'war criminals'. Remer and the SRP were seen as the most promising symbols of a renascent Europe.

151 Yockey and Thompson to Acheson, October 15, 1952.

152 Thompson/Yockey to Acheson, ibid.

153 Thompson/Yockey to Acheson, ibid.

# 11 Hanged Jews

I see how in the East, in Russia, fascism is rising — a fascism borderless and red.

— Robert Brasillach[1]

The hanging of 11 Communist Party functionaries in 1952 was an epochal event for Yockey and Weiss. The nature of the proceedings against the Jewish communists showed that the Kremlin was warring against Zionism and Organised Jewry. According to Weiss, Yockey observed the trial proceedings, which were held in a theatre, from a balcony.[2]

In 1951, Rudolf Slansky, Secretary General of the Communist Party in Czechoslovakia, was arrested for 'antistate activities'. A year later he and 13 co-defendants went on trial as 'Trotskyite-Titoist-Zionist traitors'. It is interesting that Trotskyite and Zionist were used in conjunction. They were accused of espionage and economic sabotage, working on behalf of Yugoslavia, Israel and the West. Eleven of the 14 were sentenced to death, the other three to life imprisonment. Slansky and the 11 others were hanged on December 3, 1952. Of the 14 defendants, 11 were Jews and were identified as such in the indictment. Many other Jews were mentioned as co-conspirators, implicated in a cabal that included US Supreme Court Justice Felix Frankfurter, described as a 'Jewish nationalist', and Mosha Pijade, the 'Titoist Jewish ideologist' in Yugoslavia. The conspiracy against the Czechoslovak state had been

1 Stated shortly before Brasillach's execution as a 'collaborator' during World War II. Brasillach, one of many of the French literati who supported a 'national-socialist' France in a united Europe, was the brother-in-law of post-war French Fascist luminary and Yockey admirer Maurice Bardèche.

2 DTK to Bolton, April 25, 2014.

hatched at a secret meeting in Washington in 1947, between President Harry Truman, Secretary of State Dean Acheson, former Treasury Secretary Henry Morgenthau and Ben-Gurion and Moshe Sharett, who soon assumed leadership of the State of Israel. In the indictment, Slansky was described as 'by his very nature a Zionist' who had in exchange for American support for Israel agreed to place 'Zionists in important sectors of Government, economy, and Party apparatus'. The plan included the assassination of President Gottwald by a 'freemason' doctor.[3]

As we have seen, Weiss had previously written several articles on the nature of Russia for the *National Renaissance Bulletin*, such as 'Oswald Spengler, The American Jewish Committee and Russia', which the FBI reported had a 'pro-Russian slant'.[4] From 1948, there had been claims from Union Movement and elsewhere that Yockey preferred a Russian military occupation of Europe to the Americans. Be that as it may, as we know, in 1952 Yockey stated unequivocally in his seminal essay, 'What is Behind the Hanging of Eleven Jews in Prague?' (also known as 'Prague Treason Trial'), first published unsigned in the *National Renaissance Bulletin*, that the Prague trial represented a declaration of war by the Soviet bloc against World Jewry and the 'Right' must realign its thinking accordingly.

While Yockey had adopted a fairly orthodox Hitlerite view of the Slav as incapable of a nation-building idea and Russia as only having a mission of destruction, which had been perfected by Bolshevism and its strongly Jewish element, he had also foreseen Russia's future direction. Even in 1948, in *The Proclamation*, he wrote of this dichotomy and the way that it might serve Western Civilization:

> Before the First World War, Russia had figured as a Western state. Its ruling strata, its ruling outlook, were Western. The tension which existed between the Western elements of Russia and the Asiatic will-to-destruction underneath was however strained to the breaking point by the First World War, and the Asiatic elements, in conjunction with and assisted by the Culture-State-Nation-Race-People-Society of the Jews over the world, gained the upper hand and

3 Paul Lendvai, *Anti-Semitism in Eastern Europe* (London: Macdonald & Co., 1972), pp. 243–245.

4 FBI report, August 4, 1954, file no. 105–8229 — 2, p. 3.

> re-oriented Russia against Europe. From then onward, and also today, 1950, Russia figures as one of the leaders of the coloured revolt against the European race. But European possibilities still exist within Russia, because in certain strata of the population adherence to the great organism of the Western Culture is an instinct, an Idea, and no material force can ever wipe it out, even though it may be temporarily repressed and driven under.[5]

Already, Yockey had discarded the idea of a 'Russian threat' to Europe as being a bogeyman used by the real subjugators of Europe. He stated that Russia is a threat only so long as Europe is divided. He stated that it is a 'crass lie' to say that Europe cannot defend herself against Russia; a united Europe can 'destroy the power of Russia at the moment of its choosing'.[6] Yockey however was soon to state that any such war would serve anti-Western interests. To the contrary, concessions could be wrung from the occupying powers, Russia and the USA, by remaining neutral. It was a position held by the Socialist Reich Party and other German Rightists, although the US Right was, at best, slow on the uptake, if not vehemently antagonistic. This was also a decisive argument that Yockey already had with Mosley.

## Yockey, Spengler and Russia

The attitude of Weiss and Yockey towards Russia, as in other issues, is Spenglerian.

It would be easy to regard Spengler, like Yockey, as a Russophobe. The role of Russia in the unfolding of History from this era onward could be dismissed, opposed or ridiculed by proponents of Spengler and Yockey, while the value of these historian-philosophers might receive a similar negative treatment from those who desire a Russian resurgence. However, while Yockey and Spengler regarded Russia as part of 'Asia' and a threat to Western civilization, they also foresaw other possibilities.

While Spengler wrote to Germany, and the broader West, in 1936 of the 'hour of decision' with the rise of Fascism and of National Socialism on the one hand and that of the 'coloured world', led by the USSR, on the other,

5 Yockey, *The Proclamation*, op. cit., II: C, p. 51.

6 Yockey, *The Proclamation*, ibid., p. 66.

these concerns were a reflection of the epochal aftermath of World War I.[7] The aftermath of World War II unfolded another 'hour of decision'; the one addressed by Yockey.

## The Character of Russia

Spengler regarded Russians as formed by the steppes, as innately antagonistic to the Machine and the dominance of money, as rooted in the soil, irrepressibly peasant, religious and 'primitive'. Yockey provided the same description. While Peter the Great attempted to bring Russia into the West, the great mass of Russians remained 'primitive and religious', detesting the alienness of Western cities, arts, technics, religions. The 'true Russia' is that of the 'Third Rome', 'the mystical successor to Rome and Byzantium', despising the 'rotten West'. 'Russia's spiritual gravity is in instinct.' This instinct is antithetical to the Jews.[8] Hence, the revolt against the Romanovs, a Western-oriented dynasty, was two-fold: that of the primitive Russian soul and that of Jewish intellectualism. Russian and Jewish aims coincided insofar as they both have a hatred of the West. Hence, the often dual — fragmented — character of Jewish policy, since its power rests with its control of Western technics and money, yet it is self-destructive in its hatred of Western culture.[9] An analogy is the role of the parasite in destroying its own host. This explains why so many Jews remained Communist Party functionaries in the West and especially Soviet spies, even when Soviet policy was at odds with Jewish interests and had eliminated Marxism as all but propaganda rhetoric. They were blinded by the ages-old pull of hatred for Western civilization and for Christianity. Many of the anti-Semites and 'neo-Nazis' cannot see this fragmented character of the Jewish psyche and could only conclude that 'anti-Semitism' in the USSR was part of a hoax guided by Jewish commissars.

Far from Bolshevism sweeping away the materialism of the West, the Jewish element reinforced it and American mass-production methods and industrialisation became the aim of Soviet policy.[10]

7 Oswald Spengler, *The Hour of Decision*, pp. 81–230.

8 Yockey, *Imperium* (Wermod ed.), op. cit., pp. 723–724.

9 Yockey, *Imperium*, ibid., p. 725.

10 Yockey, *Imperium*, ibid., p. 725.

After World War II, Bolshevism remained as nothing other than a means of warring against the West.[11] However, as Yockey pointed out, the USA itself was thoroughly Bolshevik in ideology and remains so. He called both Moscow and Washington during the 1930s the 'Concert of Bolshevism', that waged war against a resurgent Europe. Yockey's perception of the USA as 'Bolshevik' insofar as it fulfils the will-to-destruction of Western civilization by the Culture-distorter can be clearly perceived in this consideration: while the USA was establishing the Congress of Cultural Freedom with Trotskyite and other anti-Stalinist Marxists to export 'abstract expressionism' and jazz to the world, the Stalinists were warring against 'rootless cosmopolitanism' in the arts as being 'anti-national' and 'anti-Russian'.[12]

Without a wider understanding of Spengler's philosophy, it appears that he was — like Hitler — a Slavophobe. Likewise with Yockey, accused of being both a Russophobe and a Russophile.

When Yockey and Spengler wrote of the great mass of Russian people as being 'primitive', 'religious', 'peasants', these are not derogatory expressions. Moreover, in organic history, the society that is still based on a religious outlook and a peasant population remains within the 'Spring' epoch of its culture, the healthy cycle pregnant with potential. It contrasts with the 'Winter' epoch, dominated by commerce and the City-man — the last man — as a spent force about to leave the stage of world history and become *Fellaheen* like Egypt. Our sophisticated West, depraved and ego-driven, assumes that the superstition-ridden, mystical peasant is an inferior that perhaps might be educated up to the depravity of the modern Westerner. 'Peasant' here *is* used in a derogatory or demeaning sense.

The USA has been assiduously propagating across the globe what Yockey called the 'ethical syphilis of Hollywood'. US strategists such as Colonel Ralph Peters laud America's culturally and spiritually destructive role, describing it in *messianic* terms. Yockey referred to the American strategy for world conquest, in contrast to the military means of the USSR, as 'degenerative

11 Yockey, *Imperium*, ibid., p. 728.

12 A Zdanov, speech at the discussion on music at the Central Committee of the Communist Party SU (Bolshevik), February 1948. See Bolton, *Stalin: The Enduring Legacy*, op. cit., pp. 21–54.

propaganda, puppet regimes which conduct their own terror, and financial conquest'. Yockey stated that of these the military means is superior.[13] As events have unfolded over the last several decades, Yockey seems to have *underestimated* the corrosive efficacy of Culture-distortion and the influence of Culture-retarders and traitors that emerged even within the Soviet bloc. Yet one of his most significant points was that Culture-distortion was more lethal than military occupation and hence the American occupation of Europe was more destructive than the Russian. Yockey did on the other hand consider that European liberators could use the internal split between the true Russians and those obsessed with Western technics to undermine and overthrow the regime. While Russia remained a political unit it would be an 'enemy of the West'.[14] This certainly does not accord with the allegation by Yockey's detractors that *Imperium* was sympathetic towards the USSR.

Spengler and Yockey unequivocally stated that the Russian soul is not the same as the Western Gothic, the Classical of the Hellenes and Romans, or the 'Magian' of the Levant. Each is unique. The Western culture imposed on Russia by Peter the Great and continued under the tsars until Nicholas II, with a strong culture stratum from the Germans, is a veneer. The basis of the Russian soul is not infinite space, as in the West's *Faustian* imperative, but is 'the plane without limit'.[15] Russian Orthodox Church architecture, originating in Byzantium, therefore does not represent the upward infinity of the Gothic Cathedral spire, nor the enclosed space of the Mosque of the Magian culture, but gives rather the impression of sitting upon a horizon. Spengler considered that this Russian architecture is 'not yet a style, only the promise of a style that will awaken when the real Russian religion awakens'. Hence, Spengler stated that Russia, unlike The West, is still youthful and far from entering a cycle of cultural etiolation. Here we see then, from a Spenglerian perspective, indications of Russia's potential, while Spengler writes of Western civilization's finale.[16] We can surmise from Spengler that after the West had fulfilled its destiny and departed the world stage, like others before it, the next world civilization would be Russian.

---

13 Yockey, *Imperium*, op. cit., p. 730.

14 Yockey, *Imperium*, ibid., p. 732.

15 Spengler, *The Decline of The West*, Vol. I, p. 201.

16 Spengler, *The Decline of The West*, ibid.

Spengler was altogether more generous towards Russia vis-à-vis the West than Yockey, although even Yockey's outlook quickly adapted, especially after 1952. Spengler wrote that while Tolstoi, the *Petrinist*, whose doctrine was a precursor of Bolshevism based on Late Western ideas, was 'the former Russia', Dostoyevsky was 'the coming Russia'. Dostoyevsky 'does not know' the hatred of Russia for the West. His passionate power of living is comprehensive enough to embrace all things Western as well. Spengler quotes Dostoyevsky: 'I have two fatherlands, Russia and Europe.' He states that Dostoyevsky as the harbinger of a Russian High Culture 'has passed beyond both *Petrinism* and revolution and from his future he looks back over them as from afar'. 'His soul is apocalyptic, yearning, desperate, but of this future he is *certain*.'[17] Spengler cites Dostoyevsky's *The Brothers Karamazov*, where Ivan Karamazov says to his mother:[18]

> I want to travel in Europe… I know well enough that I shall be going only to a churchyard, but I know too that that churchyard is dear, very dear to me. Beloved dead lie buried there, every stone over them tells of a life so ardently lived, so passionately a belief in its own achievements, its own truth, its own battle, its own knowledge, that I know—even now I know—I shall fall down and kiss these stones and weep over them.[19]

Tolstoi, on the other hand, as the product of the Late West, is 'enlightened' and 'socially minded' and sees only a problem, whereas Dostoyevsky 'does not even know what a problem is'.[20] Spengler stated that the problematic nature of life is a question that arises in Late civilizations and is a symptom of an epoch where life itself has become questionable. As such, Tolstoi and his like

> … stands midway between Peter and Bolshevism, and neither he nor they managed to get within sight of Russian earth. Their kind of opposition is not apocalyptic but intellectual. Tolstoi's hatred of property is an economist's, his hatred of society a social reformer's, his hatred of the State a political theorist's. Hence his

17 Spengler, *The Decline of the West*, op. cit., Vol. II, p. 194.

18 Fyodor Dostoyevski, *The Brothers Karamazov* (1880), Part II, Book V: Pro and Contra, Chapter 3.

19 Spengler, *The Decline of the West*, op. cit., p. 195.

20 Spengler, ibid.

> immense effect upon the West — he belongs, in one respect as in another, to the band of Marx, Ibsen, and Zola.[21]

Tolstoi's Christianity was a misunderstanding. He spoke of Christ and he meant Marx. But to Dostoyevsky's Christianity, the next thousand years will belong.[22]

Where Yockey saw the true Russian soul as intrinsically detesting Western Culture,[23] despising the 'rotten West',[24] Spengler saw the true Russian as having an admiration for Western culture prior to its epoch of decadence. Yockey stated that 'Russia is the bearer of no Utopian hopes for the West, and anyone who believes it is a Cultural idiot'.[25] Obviously, Yockey did not believe Spengler to be a 'Cultural idiot'. Certainly, while Russia does not provide a 'Utopian hope' for the West, past, present or future, relations between Russia and the West are not necessarily those of eternal conflict. Yockey and Spengler saw Bolshevik Russia as an enemy of the West but they both also saw other possibilities. Even when Trotsky and Lenin were still in power, Spengler foresaw Russia changing to the extent that a Russo-German alliance against the plutocracies would be possible.

In an early essay, Spengler referred to 'the two faces of Russia'[26] when considering options for German foreign policy. Spengler, and hence Yockey, insisted that Russia is not a part of 'Europe', let alone Western civilisation. She is a culture of a quite different type than any other, whose own restless spirit is imbued with the infinity of the landscape as distinct from the 'Faustian' Western 'infinity of space'. A mystical religion had yet to blossom from the Orthodox Church, as the Russian people are still 'immature'. So far from that being a racial slur, in cultural morphology this means that the Russian has the vital forces of a young people-culture-nation-state in the process of forma-

21 Spengler, ibid.

22 Spengler, ibid.

23 Yockey, *Imperium*, op.cit, p. 722.

24 Yockey, *Imperium*, ibid., p. 724.

25 Yockey, *Imperium*, ibid., p. 731.

26 Spengler, 'The Two Faces of Russia and Germany's Eastern Problems', address to the Rhenish-Westphalian Business Convention, Essen, February 14, 1922. First published in Spengler, *Politische Schriften* (Munich, 1932).

tion, as distinct from the culturally spent (the *Fellaheen*, the Orient, Islam) and the culturally aged (West). The 'two faces of Russia' were — and are — (1) the Western veneer that was introduced by Peter the Great (*Petrinism*), when the leadership stratum adopted the Western culture, and (2) the great mass of Russians who remained rustic and mystical, possessing what Spengler calls a 'genuine crusading spirit' looking to its mystical origins in Constantinople and Jerusalem, and analogous to the Gothic crusader epoch of the Western 'Spring'. Yet even the Westernised *Petrine* ruling strata looked on the Western states only so as to see how Russian interests could be served. Russia played a prominent role in European affairs, such as in the Holy Alliance and the Congress of Vienna, and alliances with Russia became primary aims of the diplomacy of the Western states.

The Leninist imposition was *Petrinist*, insofar as it was derived from Western economic thinking. Spengler called Marxism nothing but the capitalism of the lower classes rather than a revolt against capitalism *per se*. Money-based thinking is alien to the Russian soul in the same way that Arab-Jewish money trading was alien to the Gothic Westerner. Spengler predicted that this alien veneer, then called Bolshevism, would 'perish'. Although it is a revolt against the West, it is derived from economic ideas percolated in the West. (Marx formulated *Das Kapital* in the reading room of the British Museum, perusing English economists.) It was an imposition by a small group of revolutionaries, 'almost without exception dunces and cowards', upon the Russian soul. However — and here we might think in terms of a *dialectical* historical process — Bolshevism had cleared the way 'for a new culture that will some day awaken between "Europe" and East Asia'. The peasantry, repressed by Bolshevism, 'will some day become conscious of its own will, which points in a wholly different direction'. The peasantry would gradually 'replace, transform, control, or annihilate Bolshevism in its present form'. This would depend on the emergence of 'decisive personalities who… can seize Destiny by their iron hand'. The awakened Russian peasantry will be like the Gothic epoch of Western civilization, young and vigorous and 'will not count the victims who die for an idea'. Spengler saw the possibility of Bolshevism itself being changed. Russia would look east and south for expansion, not towards Europe, unless it made serious errors in foreign policy. There were such 'serious errors' in foreign policy during and after World War II, which brought Russia West.

With all these possibilities, Spengler, the anti-Marxist, ultra-conservative, insisted that Germany and Russia are not necessarily enemies but that great skill would be required to effect a realistic foreign policy. 'The financial interest-groups of the Allied nations' aimed to make Russia a 'colony'. This was in 1922, when there was indeed a rush by international capitalism to get into Russia.[27] German business would first have to assist in getting the German house in order, to subordinate money to politics, from which opportunities in Russia could then proceed.

Bolshevism itself did indeed undergo great changes in Spengler's lifetime. In 1928, Stalin eliminated Trotsky and Russia was set on a different path to that envisaged by the Culture-distorters, whom Stalin would purge as 'rootless cosmopolitans' two decades hence.

While *Imperium* cast Russia as a barbarian threat to Western civilization, the 1952 Prague trial demanded a fundamental realignment in thinking. Yet even prior to this, Yockey and his associates had been accused of pro-Russian sentiments, albeit by 'right-wing' rivals whose anti-Sovietism was paramount.[28]

---

27 This was condemned at the time by the American anti-Bolshevik labour leader Samuel Gompers in regard to negotiations in Genoa between international bankers and the USSR. 'Soviet bribe fund here says Gompers. Charges strong group of bankers with readiness to accept Lenin's betrayal of Russia.' *New York Times*, May 1, 1922; in Bolton, *Revolution from Above*, op. cit., p. 60.

28 The organisation Natinform issued smears against Yockey as a Soviet agent. Any opposition to the US occupation of Europe was regarded as 'Red'. This is considered in the chapter 'Whited Sepulchres'.

# *Der Feind Europas*

Yockey had written *Der Feind Europas* ('The Enemy of Europe') in 1948, as volume three of *Imperium*. While *Imperium* was meant to explain the organic laws of history, *Der Feind* explained the forces that were working against the West's organic destiny. Material on Russia was revised in 1952, in light of the Prague trials. Yockey stated that it was pointless for Europeans to hope that the Culture-distorting regime in Washington would be overthrown; a 'Nationalist Revolution' cannot even be envisaged in the USA. Only a 'heroic ethic' by Europeans can fulfil Europe's 'mighty destiny'.[1]

It is notable that in 1951, even prior to the Prague trial, Yockey had exhorted the 'European elite' that America alone was the enemy of Europe. He stated 'let us not attack phantoms, let us attack the real enemy of Europe: America.'[2]

Two-hundred copies of a German edition of *Der Feind* were printed for the leaders of the Socialist Reich Party and others of the 'elite' but the German secret service, K-16, seized them. Some had already been sent to the USA.[3] The American journal *TRUD* serialised *Der Feind* from a copy given to DTK by Mrs Weiss and translated by Thomas Francis. There seems to be some uncertainty as to what edition this was. It has been assumed that DTK was given one of the few surviving editions that had been sent to Weiss from Germany. However, Weiss had published his own German edition in the USA, under his Le Blanc Publishers, New York, imprint.[4]

---

1 Varange, 'Introductory Note', *The Enemy of Europe* (Reedy, West Virginia: Liberty Bell, 1981), pp. 1–3.

2 Varange, 'The Death of England', Part 2, *Frontfighter*, No. 13, June 1951, p. 3.

3 Thomas Francis, 'A Note on Yockey's Career', ibid., p. 135.

4 One of these editions came on the market in 2015 from Biffer Books; http://www.blograrebooks.co.uk/bookstore/description.php?id=3144.

Liberty Bell Press published *Der Feind* as a book, *The Enemy of Europe/The Enemy of Our Enemies*, in 1981 with a lengthy critical analysis by Professor Revilo P Oliver forming the second part. *Der Feind* and Oliver's critique had previously been published as a series in George Dietz's magazine *The Liberty Bell*.[5]

Yockey's position on Russia was guided by the interests of Western civilization. He saw the Asian horde from the eastern steppes as having occupied half of Germany through American contrivance and Russia as lacking any positive sense of world-mission — as being wholly destructive. On the other hand, the US as the carrier of a contagious Culture-distortion was immensely more harmful insofar as it imposed a spiritual, moral and cultural disease on the Western culture organism, whereas Russian domination was only material and could be overthrown or subverted. Yockey's Russia outlook was pragmatic and in keeping with the tradition of *realpolitik* of the German elite for the past several hundred years. Moreover, as we have seen, it was in keeping even with conservatives such as Oswald Spengler, who had foreseen other possibilities for Russia beyond Marxism.

## Conflict Between American-Jewish and Russian Bolshevisms

Like Spengler, Yockey saw the Russian as a 'barbarian' without intending this as a derogatory term. He meant that the Russian race is still tough and uncontaminated by the diseases of advanced civilization. 'The barbarian is rough and tough', not 'legalistic or intellectualised. He is the opposite of decadent. He is ruthless and does not shrink back from destroying what others may prize highly.' Bolshevism, imported from the West largely by Jews, had been modified by the Russian steppes.[6] (Indeed, Trotsky lamented this 'Betrayal of the Revolution' in his book attacking Stalinism[7]). The American, on the other

5 Yockey, 'The Enemy of Europe', *The Liberty Bell*, Reedy, West Virginia, Vol. 8, No. 10, June 1981. Oliver, 'The Enemy of Our Enemies', three parts, Vol. 8, No. 11, July 1981; 8/12, August 1981; 9/1, September 1981.

6 Yockey, *The Enemy of Europe*, op. cit., p. 75.

7 Leon Trotsky, *The Revolution Betrayed* (1937); see Bolton, *Stalin...*, op. cit., particularly chapter 7.

hand, had become culturally primitive in his detachment from Europe, while also being 'over-civilised' because of his preoccupation with 'peace, comfort and security'.[8] American and Russian Bolshevik ideologies still possessed in common the obsession with technics and production. However, for Europe 'the following distinction is important: American-Jewish Bolshevism is the instinctive destruction of the West through primitive, anti-cultural ideas… through the imposition of Culture-distortion and Culture-retardation'. 'Russian Bolshevism seeks to attain the destruction of the West in the spirit of pan-Slavic religiosity, i.e., the Russification of all humanity.'[9]

This is the crux of the differences between Yockey towards Russia and the views of a range of other thinkers, whether anti-Semites such as Gittens, Hitlerites such as Arnold Leese, Rockwell and Jordan, or other pan-Europeanists such as Mosley. Yockey stated in *Der Feind*: 'Thus American-Jewish Bolshevism poses a real spiritual threat to Europe. In its every aspect, American-Jewish Bolshevism strikes a weak spot in the European organism.' The 'Michel-stratum', that is, the inner enemy, comprises much of the leadership stratum of post-war Europe, representing 'the inner-America', motivated by 'the purely animal American ideal' of comfort, security and conformity.[10] If this serenity is upset, bayonets can reimpose it. What Yockey described in 1952 is now boasted of as the lethality of 'American culture' by the spokesmen of the 'American millennium'. 'Russian Bolshevism is therefore less dangerous to Europe than American-Jewish Bolshevism.' There is in Europe an 'inner-America' that appeals to the decadent elements of the West but there is no 'inner-Russia'. The communist parties had already stopped serving any Russian interest and it was 'political stupidity' if Moscow kept using Marxism as an export-article, as it had lost its value. When Russia turned against Jewry after World War II, the fate of every communist party in the West was sealed.[11] Indeed, the Communist International was eliminated by Stalin in 1943 and

8 Yockey, *The Enemy of Europe*, op. cit., p. 76.

9 Yockey, *The Enemy of Europe*, ibid., p. 78.

10 Yockey, *The Enemy of Europe*, ibid.

11 Yockey, *The Enemy of Europe*, ibid., p. 80.

the foreign leaders of the Communist parties in exile in the USSR, especially those from Germany, were decimated.[12]

The 'American-Jewish Symbiosis' in its occupation of Europe is entirely 'anti-Cultural'. (That is the meaning of what Yockey refers to as the USA's 'Bolshevism'.) Its effects were immediately known. If Russia occupied Europe, by which Yockey means the non-Slavic lands, her effect could be surmised by looking at the 'barbarian' invasions of other civilizations, such as the Northern invasion of the Egyptian, the Kassite conquest of Babylonia, the Aryan conquest of the Indus and the Germanic invasions of Rome. In no case were those cultures destroyed. Rather, the barbarians were absorbed into the culture-body or they were expelled.[13] Indeed, the barbarian is prone to become the custodian of the best values of the host culture. In comparison to a fossilised culture such as the Jewish, or *Fellaheen* (i.e., *passé*) cultures such as the Chinese or the Muslim/Magian, the barbarian brings uncontaminated vigour and the prospect of cultural renewal rather than destruction, distortion, retardation or parasitism. The other possibility for a late civilization threatened by a barbarian invasion is that the outer enemy impels the civilization to unite around its traditional ethos, thus in that way also reinvigorating it.

## 'A New Symbiosis: Europe-Russia'

Yockey contended that Russia only occupied one-tenth of (non-Slavic) Europe after World War II and that was only made possible due to the contrivance of the 'Washington regime', motivated by a pathological hatred of Europe. In the event of a Russian occupation of Europe, Yockey saw two possibilities: (1) endless uprisings until Russia tired and left; (2) a relatively lenient regime that would be infiltrated, causing within a few decades the 'Europeanisation' of Russia to a more meaningful extent than the *Petrinism* of prior centuries. This would 'eventually result in the rise of a new Symbiosis: Europe-Russia'. 'Its final form would be that of a European Imperium.'[14]

12 Bolton, *Stalin…*, op. cit., p. 8.

13 Yockey, *The Enemy of Europe*, op., cit., pp. 80–81.

14 Yockey, *The Enemy of Europe*, ibid., p. 82.

Here, we read the most unequivocal statement of what Yockey saw for Russia, different to his Slavophobic sentiments: the prospect of a 'Europe-Russia Symbiosis' that would be the foundation of imperium from the Atlantic to the Urals, by force of Historical necessity rather than European *Lebensraum*. It was a vision that was revived by the pan-European thinker and activist Jean Thiriart.[15]

Yockey stated that in the event of a Russian occupation of Europe, the first victims would be the local communist parties, as the types attracted to these could not be trusted. They were Marxist theorists, whereas Russia's true religion was not Marxism but *Russia*.[16] That is at any rate what Stalin had been doing in the USSR since 1928 and after World War II in Poland, Czechoslovakia, Hungary and elsewhere, with his elimination of the Comintern.

Hence, the Russian occupation of Western Europe would eliminate the 'inner enemy', 'the Michel-stratum' and 'thus liberate all creative forces within Europe from the tyranny of the Past'. Petty-statism would go with the traitors, kept in power by American bayonets. 'The barbarian, whether he wished it or not, would complete the spiritual unification of Europe by removing the only inner-European obstacle to that unity'. 'From the Spiritual to the Political is but one step.' Should Russia try to incorporate Europe into its empire, it could do so only by according Europe 'significant concessions', including autonomy as a unit. Should brute force be used, that would provoke a united and revived barbarian reaction.[17]

While American-Jewish Bolshevism and Russian Bolshevism do not stand for anything creative from the Western perspective, there were major differences. Because of the presence of an 'inner America' in Europe, US occupation and influence are deeper and more dangerous to Europe's soul than Russia ever could be. Barbarian Russia could only awaken Europe's own barbarian inner instincts to resist, or concede much that would liberate rather than enslave Europe. On the other hand, 'the American-Jewish Symbiosis'

15 On Thiriart and Yockey see the chapter, 'Resurrection'.

16 Yockey, *The Enemy of Europe*, op. cit., p. 82.

17 Yockey, *The Enemy of Europe*, ibid., p. 84.

appeals to the worst of Europe.[18] Russian occupation would even eliminate the inner enemies of Europe.[19]

To Yockey, real enslavement comes from the USA. It is the Huxleyan 'soft' slavery.[20] As for mass murder, that came with the USA's Morgenthau Plan and the war crimes trials. Hence, to the question 'Who is the Enemy?' Yockey replied: 'America-Jewry.' Europe will not fight for its enemy in a conflict with Russia. Should the USA be expelled before war with Russia, then Europe would fight to oust Russia[21] (although Yockey is only referring to the need to oust Russia from a portion of Germany). However, Yockey held that only Europe would fulfil a destiny in creating *Imperium Mundi.*[22] He was writing for a political elite, to inspire them to keep struggling at a time when Europe was in ruins and many of the political, military and cultural leaders who survived were dispossessed and persecuted.[23] The immediate message was — do not fight for the enemy of Europe, the American-Jewish Symbiosis, even if this means collaboration with a Russian occupation that at least would eliminate the traitors and might itself become Europeanised.

---

18 Yockey, *The Enemy of Europe*, ibid., p. 85.

19 Yockey, *The Enemy of Europe*, ibid., p. 86.

20 See Aldous Huxley, *Brave New World* (London: Chatto and Windus, 1969 [1932]). Also, the discussion in Bolton, *Revolution from Above*, op. cit., pp. 48–54.

21 Yockey, *The Enemy of Europe*, op. cit., p. 91.

22 Yockey, *The Enemy of Europe*, ibid., p. 92.

23 A significant example is the intervention of the USSR in favour of the Norwegian novelist Knut Hamsun (always popular in the Soviet Union). Hamsun supported Hitler and Quisling during the war. 'At the end of 1945, the Soviet Minister for foreign affairs, Molotov, informed his Norwegian colleague, Trygve Lie, that it "would be regrettable to see Norway condemning this great writer to the gallows". Molotov had taken this step with the agreement of Stalin. It was after this intervention that the Norwegian government abandoned plans to try Hamsun and contented itself with levying a large fine that almost bankrupted him. The question remains open: would Norway have condemned the old man Hamsun to capital punishment? The Norwegian collaborators were all condemned to heavy punishments. But the Soviet Union could exert a strong and dreaded influence in Scandinavia in the immediate post-war period.' 'Knut Hamsun: Saved by Stalin?', *Counter-Currents*, July 6, 2010, http://www.counter-currents.com/2010/07/knut-hamsun-saved-by-stalin/.

# *Kto Kovo*

Frederick Weiss and H Keith Thompson developed the theme regarding Russia from mid-1955 to 1956. Signed 'X.Y.Z.', Weiss's Le Blanc Publishers released a series of articles entitled 'Russia', distributed via the National Renaissance Party with Weiss's funding. It is plausible that the essays had major input from Yockey. Thompson stated that he 'believed' Yockey had been writing Weiss's articles since December 1952[1] and one can discern Yockey's style. Thompson printed the series, intended as a book, at his father's enterprise, Cooper Forms, of which he was manager. While the initial response seems to have been slow, Thompson printed 3,500 copies of the second part, *Kto Kovo* ('Who Kills Whom') in November 1955. Although four parts were intended, the third seems to end on a final note that the future belonged to a Russian Imperium.[2] In December, Weiss had a further 5,000 copies of part two printed because of the high demand.[3] He had said of part three when he was preparing it that this would be 'plenty hot' and that it 'would contain the advice that Germany and all of Europe must depend on Russia for their salvation and survival'.[4] In was reported in 1956 that Weiss had stated that every

1 FBI interview with Thompson, October 19, 1953. In this report Thompson claims to have dissociated from his former colleagues, especially Weiss and Fleckenstein, and stated that individuals had attempted to turn his American Committee for the Advancement of Western Civilization into an 'anti-Semitic pressure group'. However, it is evident this was a ruse, at least in part, in regard to Weiss, as they were soon co-operating again, one such project being the series on 'Russia', distributed by Madole, from mid 1955.

2 'Frederick Charles Weiss', FBI report, NY 100–111893, November 21, 1955.

3 'National Renaissance Party', FBI office memorandum, February 1, 1956.

4 'National Renaissance Party', February 1, 1956, ibid.

National Socialist 'is secretly working for a united Germany under Soviet domination. Only through a union with the Soviets can Germany be saved'.[5]

The FBI regarded the articles as pro-Soviet, despite their references to the Russian-Mongolian hordes threatening the West. While the West was portrayed as weak and collapsing, the USSR was portrayed as being a country of invincible and united Will, where questions of 'democracy' are irrelevant. The Russians had overthrown the Bolshevism that had been imported by Jewry and had restored the Russian soul that sees man's meaning as part of a collectivity and not as an individual whose government is only concerned with contractual rights. For comprehension of the Russian soul that had been reasserted in the USSR, one would look to Dostoyevsky rather than to Lenin or Trotsky. The Western analysts should look beyond superficial questions about repression and slave labour, and ask rather whether 250,000,000 Russians were working in 'syntony' with the State in a common 'rhythm' that was also attracting German genius. The purpose was to understand the 'Russian soul', for in another 25 years of 'co-existence' there would remain only a soulless Western mass, subservient to a 'tremendously powerful array of Eastern forces, advanced in scientific, military and industrial development, and imbued with unshakeable Unity of Purpose'.[6]

The Russian soul is shaped by the vastness of the plains. This description is Spenglerian, as we have seen.[7] A strong will was developed by 'willingness to suffer' and a tendency to fatalism forged by centuries of conflict and iron rule. An inherent nomadism results in a restlessness and a wandering that has been transformed into 'unceasing expansion'. It was under Stalin that the Russian peasantry awoke from centuries of slumber, after rulers from Peter the Great to Lenin and Trotsky had tried to impose foreign thinking. The Russian peasantry had become 'the folk of the future' with a destiny 'not unlike that dreamed of by Dostoyevsky'. Despite the atheistic propaganda of the early Soviet regime, the Russian remained profoundly religious. *The New York Times* pointed out that 20 Orthodox Churches 'were flourishing in Kiev

---

5 FBI office memorandum, February 29, 1956, NRP NY 105–6112.

6 X.Y.Z., 'Russia', Part I, Foreword, (New York: Le Blanc Publications, Summer 1955).

7 Oswald Spengler, *The Decline of The West*, op. cit., Vol. 1, p. 201.

alone'. However, because of the Westernization begun under Peter (*Petrinism*)[8] there existed 'two Russias' fighting for supremacy. A nihilistic tendency in Bolshevism sought to annihilate *Petrinism* (although the importation of Marxism is a symptom of the *Petrine*). This type of 'Bolshevism' is the mortal enemy of Lenin and Trotsky, which would evolve into 'an outspoken, revitalized nationalist movement', even if it is still meaninglessly called 'communist'. 'What's in a name?' Under the mantle of Communism, the Russian people had resumed their messianic world mission to replace a decadent civilization, as foreseen by Dostoyevsky. Weiss (or X.Y.Z.) saw a great technical and scientific state arising, and the creation of a Eurasian empire. The question was whether a leader of a united West would arise to confront these challenges?

Part three of 'Russia' appeared in summer 1956, dedicated by the 'authors' to Mrs Weiss, 'a veteran of 30 years' fight for the survival of Western culture'. The pamphlet opens with a condemnation of the 'American Way of Life' that has been made synonymous with the 'Western', with historically meaningless concepts such as 'universal happiness', 'economic progress' and democracy. This is the USA's world mission to the 'under-privileged',[9] a mission that infects much more of the world today than in Yockey's time. The historically flawed thinking is in not recognising that history is cyclical, with a rise and fall of civilizations in succession, and that there is no 'finality' about the present. Such anti-historical thinking is very much in evidence again today as part of the 'American ideology', with theorists referring to 'the end of history' once the 'American way of life' dominates the world. The point Weiss introduced is that 'the new culture' now springing from the 'mother region of the Eurasian Plains' will not be 'brought in line' by a revival of Trotskyism. His comment at this early stage of the Cold War was perceptive. The US began to avidly use Trotskyites in its propaganda against the USSR and Sedova Trotsky, Sidney Hook, Max Shachtman and other Trotskyite luminaries entered the ranks of the 'Cold Warriors'. Many became founders of the oddly named

8 Again the influence of Spengler is apparent, and it was a theme that had been considered by Yockey. See Yockey, *Imperium* (Abergele: Wermod & Wermod, 2013), pp. 721–732.

9 X.Y.Z., 'Russia', Part III, 'The Impact of Ancient Religious and Racial Antagonisms Upon World Events', Foreword (New York: Le Blanc Publications, Summer 1956).

'neo-conservative' ('neo-con') movement that continues to play a major role in US foreign and military policy.[10]

Weiss ('X.Y.Z.') used an article by Jewish historian Dr Franz Borkenau, published in the American Jewish Committee's influential journal *Commentary*, as a basis to examine the role of Russia, the USA and Israel in world historical developments. Borkenau believed that Israel's 'mission' was to act as a nexus between 'East and West', with Israel as the only entity 'within the orbit of Western civilization' where both worlds could meet.[11] The outlook is in keeping with Israeli strategy at the time, which sought to remain neutral during the Cold War while posturing as an outpost of Western democracy when the occasion suited. We might recall here the messianic vision that Prime Minister David Ben-Gurion had for Israel as the 'supreme court of mankind', adjudicating between East and West: 'In Jerusalem, the United Nations (a truly *United* Nations) will build a Shrine of the Prophets to serve the federated union of all continents; this will be the seat of the Supreme Court of Mankind, to settle all controversies among the federated continents, as prophesied by Isaiah.' The USSR would become increasingly democratized and Western and Eastern Europe would become a socialist federation.[12]

While Israel, New York and Washington hoped for a merger between East and West, the aim of their ill-fated United Nations and 'Baruch Plan', both unequivocally rejected by Stalin — for *nationalistic* reasons — immediately after World War II, much of the 'Right' feared that such a merger was imminent. The USA's 'anti-Semitic crackpots', as 'X.Y.Z.' called them, believed that the USSR was still run by Jews and the Jews in Washington and Moscow were in cahoots to bring about a communistic Jewish world state. They pointed to the continuing influence of Lazar Kaganovich, one of the few Jews to survive the Stalin purges, as the real power in the USSR. 'X.Y.Z.' addressed themselves to Rightist circles that insisted on these fantasies.[13] Kaganovich and other remaining Jews in the Soviet bureaucracy had long since been de-Judaised and

10 Kevin MacDonald, 'Neoconservatism as a Jewish Movement', http://www.kevinmacdonald.net/understandji-3.htm.

11 Borkenau cited by X.Y.Z.,op. cit., III, 'Explanation'.

12 David Ben-Gurion, *Look*, January 16, 1962.

13 X.Y.Z., op. cit., III, 'Explanation'.

the Jewish nation within the USSR had been finished since 1937-38 (that is, the era of the Great Purges). The Jewish culture, the binding element of Jewry, had been eliminated.[14] Much of the 'Right' and Jewish zealots both saw the role of Israel as unassailable, as a nexus around which the world revolves, and assumed that the 'Russianized' Jews of the USSR acted and thought in the same ways as the Jews in the West and in Israel.[15] The impress of the Russian Plains, Russian mysticism and fatefulness, impacted on Russian Jewry as it did on the Russian masses. The development of Jewry in Russia was quite different from that of Jewry in the West. The Russian Jew was 'under the spell' of the 'mysterious power of the land'.[16] Where the West had lost its unifying power of Church and State, Jewry was able to maintain its 'Consensus' as a separate people-race-nation-church-state and impose itself upon the West. In Russia the religious impulse was maintained. The Jews could not break through even with the Bolshevik interregnum of Lenin and Trotsky, which was eliminated by 1937-38.[17] Not least, this was because capitalist (money-thinking) economics (as Spengler had pointed out) had never assumed predominance in Russia other than during the first years of Bolshevism. Stalin finished whatever Jewish influence remained.[18]

The Jewish influx into New York City was seen as establishing it as the centre of the '*city* economy' of the entire Western world. Here, money ruled. The Jewish 'Consensus' knew how to use it and made the industrialist, engineer and labourer subjects of their will. The capture of Jerusalem was required to provide a metaphysical centre around which East and West would revolve. To believe that the USSR remained part of a 'Jewish Consensus' was to believe 'in the present existence of a politically powerful and metaphysically unspoiled Jewish upper-stratum in Russia in closest contact with the Consensus in the West… it presupposes belief in the willingness of Great Russiandom… to have

---

14 X.Y.Z., ibid., III: I.

15 X.Y.Z., ibid., III: II.

16 X.Y.Z., ibid., III: III.

17 Yockey traced the eclipse of Jewish power in the USSR earlier still: 'The expulsion of Trotsky in 1928 marks the downward turning point of Jewry in Russia.' *The Enemy of Europe*, op. cit., p. 59.

18 X.Y.Z., op. cit., III: IV.

its inspired mass-unit shaken and loosened to its depths; to willingly commit suicide at a time when it is about to waken in a great spiritual upheaval'. And now that Russia has thrown off alien Petrinism and 'short-lived Trotzkyism' 'new the Jews — yet our crackpots who want us — expect the lord of Asia to modestly revolve about their pole in "Jerusalem!" There, these cosmopolitan sorcerers would indoctrinate the Russian Giant with their 'American Way of Life' serum, thus making him a worthy member of the human family under the all-protecting roof of the United Nations!'[19]

Yockey had astutely observed in his 1952 essay on the Prague treason trials that Stalin had rejected the prospect of subordination to the United Nations Organisation and the control of atomic energy under the Baruch Plan.[20] This rejection, if not the purge of Slansky and other Jews from the Communist Party, should have alerted the anti-communist Right to changes in the USSR, yet even up to the implosion of the USSR they still prattled about the United Nations being a 'communist plot'.

What 'X.Y.Z.' foretold was that the Russian World-Mission, which for a short while took on a 'Marxist' veneer, was 'to establish on the Eurasian continent the Imperium of Great-Russiandom'.

> Yet our crackpots want us to believe that the actual masters of this inspired Asiatic Mass-unit were and are the "invisible government" of the Kaganovichs and the Borkenau Jews, together with our "Statesmen" in Washington, want us to believe that in the near future the Jews over there — in unison with their co-believers over here — are to bring about a peaceful "interpenetration" between East and West. And this process would first materialise on the Eleusian Fields of Palestine! Whereupon the cherished dream (and in the case of our crackpots, the frightful nightmare) of a Jewish World Government would finally become a reality and, whereupon the bright, imaginative Western man, together with the equally bright, imaginative Great-Russian of today, are to submerge themselves into the silent service of being the two pillars of an eternal Pax Judea![21]

For the assorted 'crackpots', the 'soul and spirit' of 'a thousand different other nations, peoples, races, clans and tribes on the globe — now in the status of a

19 X.Y.Z., ibid., III: V.

20 Yockey, 'What is Behind the Hanging the Eleven Jews in Prague,' 1952, op. cit.

21 X.Y.Z., op. cit., III: VI.

rude awakening — *mean nothing*'. 'They mean nothing, because these crackpots cannot comprehend that (in Goethe's words): 'what is important in life is *life*, and not the result of it!'[22]

***

In 1955, Yockey returned to Germany using the name Edward Max Price on his passport and was 'believed to be "flirting with the Communists"'. The FBI noted that Yockey reportedly aimed to become 'the Lord Haw Haw of Russia and to attack the USA' and was informed that he had 'been in touch with the Soviet authorities and has been exploring matters connected with the cobalt bomb'. 'Yockey is believed to have "a complete loathing for the US"'. Frederick Weiss was continuing to financially support Yockey.[23]

For Thompson, Yockey, Weiss and their contacts in Germany, Soviet affiliations were part of Cold War intrigue between the superpowers. Thompson stated that the party he represented as a registered agent in the USA, the Socialist Reich Party, 'had communist affiliations'.

> Almost any right-wing entity in Germany, to get any power and money, had to reach to the East Germans to some extent or other, and there existed funds available to finance right-wing activities in West Germany. The motive of the East Germans being to embarrass and cause difficulties for the west Germans exclusively; they were naturally not interested in promoting fascism in any form — although the East Germany secret police consisted in part measure of many former members of the SS and SD who'd gone to the East Zone and were living there, some of whom I knew. So the idea of taking support where you can find it is one which is very practical. Even today, if the Soviet Union would care to finance any activities of mine, I would rush to the bank with the check and the hope that it was good.[24]

This association with the Soviet bloc went as far as Yockey serving as a paid courier for Czech intelligence, taking documents between Czechoslovakia

---

22 X.Y.Z., ibid.

23 FBI report, July 2, 1955, 105–8229 — 2, p. 1.

24 Thompson interview with Stimely.

and the USA, as Yockey mentioned to Thompson.[25] Thompson's ongoing interest in the USSR was a matter of concern for the FBI, which noted in 1960 that according to a highly confidential source, Thompson had requested to be put on the mailing list of the Soviet Embassy to receive reports and other information about the USSR.[26] The FBI also cited the artist Rockwell Kent, whom Thompson represented when Kent, as chairman of the National Council of American-Soviet Friendship, became the subject of a boycott.[27]

## Realignments

The realignment of Rightist thinking vis-à-vis Russia, accepted by Madole and sections of the 'German 'Right', had not fallen altogether on deaf ears in the USA. The monthly *Political Reporter*, roughly produced even by mimeographed standards, was published in Memphis by Harry William Pyle, a retired house painter who had campaigned for the unemployed during the 1930s.[28] What is significant was that his writers included some of the most prominent on the 'radical Right', such as Marilyn R Allen,[29] Charles B Hudson,[30] Henry H Klein,[31] and Edward J Smythe.[32]

---

25 Thompson interview with Stimely, ibid.

26 FBI report, October 20, 1960

27 FBI report, October 10, 1962. Most of this page is blacked out.

28 FBI report, Memphis, August 22 1955, ME 100–3412, p. 2.

29 FBI report, Memphis, ME # 100–3214, April 4, 1955, pp. 44–46. Organiser of the 'Pro-American Vigilantes' in 1946, according to FBI report, Salt Lake City, SU 105–266, July 6 1955.

30 FBI report, Memphis, ME # 100–3214, ibid., p. 57, citing *The Political Reporter*, January 1954. Hudson published *America in Danger* during 1936–1948, and had been a defendant in the abortive Sedition Trials due to his anti-war campaigning.

31 FBI report, Memphis, ME # 100–2314, ibid., p. 61. Klein was a prominent investigative journalist during the 1920s, famously exposing New York City corruption. As an attorney he represented Colonel Eugene Nelson Sanctuary, a defendant at the Sedition Trials. Klein was a New York Jew who avidly opposed Judaism, Zionism and communism. His pamphlets included *A Jew Exposes the Jewish World Conspiracy*.

32 FBI report, ibid., p. 74, citing *The Political Reporter*, February 1955. Smythe was associated with the German-American Bund and the Klan, and was a defendant at the Sedition Trials. After the war he was editor of the Protestant Press Association.

Despite the makeshift character of *The Political Reporter*, Pyle was of sufficient note to feed the paranoia of the Anti-Defamation League. Melwyn Dan, investment banker and ADL operative, stated to the FBI's Memphis office that the southern regional director of the ADL wanted to know about Pyle. The ADL noted that Pyle was getting material from an unidentified New York City organisation and had recently been visited by a representative of the organisation. Dan went to the FBI to advise that the ADL would be investigating Pyle.[33] Specifically, the influence on Pyle was plausibly Weiss, whom the FBI and ADL had regarded as the real head of the NRP. The FBI noted that Le Blanc Publications was on the Pyle mailing list[34] and that the NRP had been written of favourably in *The Political Reporter*.[35] In 1955, in regard to the investigation of Pyle and his contacts, the Pittsburgh office asked for information on Weiss.[36]

Pyle was primarily a segregationist and was director of the Pro-Southerners. He was also Grand Wizard of the Knights of the Kuklos[37] Klan and a director of the long-running National Citizens Protective Association (publishers of *The White Sentinel*), besides being associated with the White Circle League, the National Patrick Henry Organization and various Klan factions.[38]

In June 1953 Pyle wrote in *The Political Reporter*:

> The American public has been conditioned to howl [...] against Communism but as Mr Monk[39] has asked "which Communism?" So the public, being condi-

33 FBI office memorandum, SAC Memphis 105-0-97, 'The Political Reporter, Harry W Pyle, Internal Security', November 2, 1953.

34 FBI office memorandum, Memphis, SAC 100-3214, February 25, 1955.

35 FBI report, Memphis, ME # 100-2314, April 4, op. cit., 1955, p. 4.

36 FBI report, Pittsburgh, PG 105-952, June 30 1955, p. 6.

37 *Kuklos*, meaning 'circle' in Greek, was the origin of *Ku Klux* when the KKK was founded in 1865.

38 FBI office memorandum, Memphis, SAC 100-3214, ibid.

39 John Henry Monk seems to have been the first among the newsletter's writers to focus on Trotskyism, and the loss of Jewish control in the Soviet bloc. FBI report, ME 100-3214, op. cit., p. 66. Monk published his own newsletter, *Grass Roots*, described by an FBI informant as 'devoted to the exposure of Trotskyite-Communist-Jews'. FBI report, Norfolk, NF 105-229, July 29, 1955, p. 3.

> tioned, they howl about "Russian Communism" yet, the press and pulpit, either ignorant or being paid off, never mention "Trotsky Communism" [...] "Russian Communism", now controlled by Gentiles, is bad, but, "Tito's Communism, Israel's Communism, and England's Socialism" [are] Kosher. Now the Trotskyites are out "Russian Communism" is bad, nasty and should be fought.
>
> [...] Why do we howl "Russian Communism", and ignore Trotskyism? [...] The answer is simple. It is, who controls the Communist State. A Gentile-ruled Communist State is wrong. A Trotsky-Communist ruled State is Kosher. When you see all of this, you can begin to understand why our press, pulpit and politicians accept Tito's Communism and try to jerk and rug from under Gentile ruled Russian Communism.[40]

Pyle maintained this position on Russia in *The Political Reporter* until the final year of publication in 1955:

> Most everybody is against Communism in America [...] That Jew-Russian-Communism. That Zionist-Jew-Russian-Communism. Just put anything with Jew and tag Russia onto it, and Communism as an after thought and you're in tune with the PEDDLERS OF HATE RUSSIA. The tacking of Jew is a must, just so long as you don't say Jew-Trotksy-Communism. [...]
>
> While we refuse to accept any Communism [...] I do think we should recognize facts and tell the truth so that an unnecessary war with Russia, as planned by these Trotskyites, won't ruin us.[41]

This is the stance that had first been advocated by Weiss and Yockey, and does not seem to have antagonised the Rightist luminaries and segregationists that backed Pyle. Many such as Mrs Lucille Miller, the editor of the *Green Mountain Rifleman* who was committed to Saint Elizabeth's asylum by court order because of her criticism of conscription, opposed the war in Korea for the same reasons that America Firsters had opposed US involvement in European wars: they were wars that spilled the best American blood for no American interest. Pyle and John Monk of the long-running Grass Roots

---

40 H. W. Pyle, 'It's Time for Some Sound Thinking', *The Political Reporter*, Vol. 2, No. 10, June 1953; cited in FBI office memorandum, SAC 100–3214, ibid., pp. 22–23.

41 H. W. Pyle, 'Let's Tell the Truth for a While', *The Political Reporter*, Vol. 4, No. 5, February 1955; cited in FBI office memorandum, SAC 100–3214, ibid., p. 25.

League had written heretical views on the Trotsky-Stalin breach shortly after the 1952 publication of Yockey's essay on the Prague trials and about a decade before *Common Sense* started featuring the same theme. Despite outrage from quarters both in the USA and outside, the ideas had fallen on fallow ground, waiting as long as two decades to sprout and bloom.

## Common Sense

In 1954, the House Committee on Un-American Activities (Velde Committee) deemed both *Common Sense* and the National Renaissance Party to be sufficiently important to merit the focus of their investigation and 'preliminary report'. The committee expressed concern that neo-fascists were exploiting the menace of Communism in pursuit of their own anti-democratic aims.[42]

*Common Sense* was founded in 1947 by Conde McGinley and published by the Christian Educational Association, Union, New Jersey. McGinley had been a member of Father Charles Coughlin's pre-war Christian Front, for whose magazine, *Social Justice*, Yockey had written his first published article, 'The Tragedy of Youth'. McGinley began publishing a paper in 1946 called *Think*. The following year, McGinley's paper became a tabloid and the name was changed to *Common Sense*. *Common Sense* began as a comparatively mainstream anti-communist conservative newspaper for those times and billed itself as 'leader in the nation's fight against communism'. The Velde Committee report even mentions that: 'At the outset, its columns carried a certain amount of factual information on communism.'[43] The report states that *Common Sense* changed direction in 1948 and became explicitly fascistic and anti-Semitic: 'Beginning in 1948, however, *Common Sense* became increasingly outspoken in its statements of a pro-Nazi and anti-Semitic nature.'[44]

*Common Sense* first published articles opposing the US Cold War policy against the USSR as early as 1952, the year of Yockey's article 'Prague Treason Trial'. The Velde report notes that 1952 was the year the National Renaissance

42 Harold Velde *et al.*, *Preliminary Report on Neo-Fascist and Hate Groups, House Committee on Un-American Activities* (Washington, D.C.: US House of Representatives, December 17, 1954).

43 Velde, ibid., p. 12.

44 Velde, ibid.

Party adopted the *Common Sense* 'line' on the USSR. *Common Sense* editorialised that the German army, which had been prevented from destroying communism during World War II, was now expected to do so at the behest of the USA. 'This is to be a war against the Russian people — not against communism.' The Velde report comments: 'In this statement, McGinley's "anti-Communist" and "patriotic" publication apparently is not averse to serving the Communist propaganda cause.'[45]

There can be little doubt that the catalyst for this outlook was Yockey's 1952 article on the Czech trials of Slansky, et al. The perspective was repeated by a 'European' correspondent to *Common Sense*, whose warnings were cited by the Velde report:

> If your paper is to continue its excellent work of opposing the policy of the Jew, please do not fight Russia also, for we in Europe look upon it as the only hope to prevent Jewish world domination by means of its stupid, willing, technically clever American slaves, the destroyers of Europe's cities, the hate-mongers of the vile occupation and the hangmen of Nuremberg.[46]

However, this pro-Soviet orientation does not seem to have been pursued and was not resumed until 1966. At least from 1954[47] until 1966, *Common Sense* expressed a standard American Right-wing line that 'Communism is Jewish' and that the USSR remained under Jewish control. DTK, publisher of the journal *TRUD*, *The Proclamation of London* and *Yockey: Four Essays*, who worked on *Common Sense*, states:

> Yockey admired Conde McGinley for his courageous stand and the very substantial risks he took. Mr McGinley thought that "Francis should be a better Catholic", I was told. Please recall that the 1950s was an age of Cold War jumping and screaming. Commies under the bed, hiding behind trees, injecting fluoride into our water supplies. Russia was digging a tunnel under the Atlantic and would soon send an invasion force through this tunnel to emerge through the Statue of Liberty's arm and send a death-ray to destroy Wall Street. Yockey's

45 Velde, ibid.

46 Velde, ibid.

47 *Common Sense*, 'The World Dictatorship: Christianity Losing Fight for Survival', No. 220, December 15, 1954.

> thoughts were not well received, especially after he wrote of Stalin hanging Jew communists in Bohemia.[48]

But Yockey's ideas *were* well received at *Common Sense*. In 1966, *Common Sense* published an article that was to be of seminal influence on the direction of the paper from then until it closed in 1972. The article is entitled 'New York—Capitol of Marxism'.[49] While the article was written anonymously, the author can be confidently identified as Fred Farrell. *Common Sense* cautiously prefaced the article by stating: 'Time alone will reveal the truth.'[50] Not surprisingly, *Common Sense* quickly lost a third of its subscribers and outraged patrons such as Lt. General P. A. del Valle. DTK comments: 'The change in direction came ca. 1966. The paper "lost" a third of their subscribers (good riddance). Gen Del Valle (a C.S. board member) and many in his circle, all basically country club conservatives, threw a fit.'[51, 52] *Common Sense* was an important newspaper with 30,000 readers. Published by the Christian Educational Association, McGinley and his staff had worked closely with James Madole in assisting him with printing[53] and providing a common platform at meetings.

The primary instigator for the change of the long-running, Catholic-orientated newspaper that was billed 'leader in the nation's fights against communism' was Morris Horton (known to *Common Sense* readers as Fred Farrell). Farrell was a ship radio officer, author of erotic dime novels and possibly a veteran journalist for the Communist Party USA newspaper *The Daily Worker* prior to the war. DTK had met Horton in Europe in 1966, when he was already writing anonymous articles for *Common Sense*. A Texan 'with a deep, harsh vocal delivery, which was pleasant enough', he was 'an old Stalinist

48 DTK to Bolton, April 13, 2014.

49 Fred Farrell, 'New York—Capitol of Marxism', *Common Sense*, No. 473, March 15, 1966.

50 *Common Sense*, No. 473, ibid., p. 1.

51 DTK to Bolton, April 13, 2014.

52 DTK to Bolton, April 20, 2014.

53 See for example reference to 500 copies of *National Renaissance Bulletin* printed by *Common Sense* in December 1956. 'James H Madole', FBI New York office, April 2, 1957, NY 105–6129, p. 4.

loyalist'.[54] To Farrell and others, nobody had done a more thorough job of ridding Russia of Marxism and fighting Jewish influence than Stalin.[55] At a time when there was a vitriolic dispute between Lt. General del Valle and Farrell, DTK wrote of the latter that 'his articles are like firecrackers tossed under the seats of the mighty slobs of the Right-wing'. DTK appreciated his 'latent Stalinism and Spenglerian approach'.[56]

Farrell begins: 'I am tired of Anti-communists who talk about "Moscow, Center of the World Communist conspiracy". Moscow is NOT and never has been the real center of communism.'[57] Farrell explained that the real centre of Marxism 'is always located at the centre of Jewish Power and that centre today is not Moscow but New York'.[58] The rivalry between Trotsky and Stalin was not merely one of personal power but was a fundamental power struggle between 'Jewish Bolshevism' and Russian Nationalism. Anti-communism in the USA was a racket. That theme gained momentum in *Common Sense.*

Farrell ended by praising Stalin as 'fighting a lonely battle against the Jews'. American anti-communists, on the other hand, 'could not make a patch on Stalin's pants'.[59]

It is Farrell who seems to have referred to Yockey most extensively. Ken Hoop, a Yockeyan who wrote for *Common Sense*, knew Horton/Farrell and describes him as 'a hard-core Yockeyite who was pro-Russian'.[60]

Farrell also acknowledged when writing to Dr Revilo Oliver that Frederick Weiss had 'attempted to tell the facts of life about Russia in his brilliant pamphlets many years ago'.[61] In a 1970 issue of *Common Sense*, while castigating the American Right and rejecting the Left-Right political dichotomy, Farrell

54 DTK to Bolton, April 19, 2014.

55 For background see Bolton, *Stalin...*, op. cit.

56 DTK to Oliver, November 29, 1971.

57 Farrel, 'New York — Capitol of Marxism', op. cit.

58 Farrel, 'New York — Capitol of Marxism', ibid.

59 Farrel, 'New York — Capitol of Marxism', ibid.

60 Ken Hoop to Bolton, October 6, 2014. Hoop was a Yockeyan who is cited extensively in the chapter 'Resurrection' ('National Youth Alliance').

61 Morris Horton (Farrel) to Oliver, June 23, 1972.

referred to Yockey as an example of the way the majority of the Right will deal with somebody of real ability:

> The Right Wing is firmly in the grip of a DEATH WISH. Time and again, I have seen idealistic young Americans get into these phony Right Wing movements, hoping to accomplish something solid and real. They learn quickly that the Lord High Nabobs of the Right quickly extinguish any spark of any real intelligence or effectiveness which flares in their ranks. They see that the Right, far from actually fighting Communism, secretly collaborates with Communism.
>
> Typical is the way in which the Right Wing gasbags dealt with Francis Parker Yockey. Yockey never had an American supporter during his lifetime. The great Conservative gasbags of the American Right Wing want nothing to do with any living writer. They weren't there when Yockey was murdered in his jail cell. Can you imagine Norman Mailer dying in jail? There would be a thousand Jews rattling the bars to bail him out. The young Gentile writer dies alone in a cell.
>
> We think that it is a wonderful thing for Yockey's books to be circulated and read. He had something extremely important to say and the American people ought to hear it. What they really need is an American publishing industry which will give adequate recognition to the young Yockeys who are alive today![62]

The Christian Educational Association sold Yockey's *Imperium*, *Proclamation of London* and *Yockey: Four Essays*.[63] Yockey's first published essay, 'The Tragedy of Youth', was reprinted in a 1970 issue of *Common Sense*.[64]

In a 1971 article, Farrell quoted Yockey from the *Proclamation of London* when comparing democratic politicians with Russia's Marshal Zhukov who, Farrell relates, staged a coup against 'the notorious Chief of Police, Lavrenti Beria', in 1953 by bringing two divisions of troops into Moscow. Farrell considered 'military power' the only remaining means of dislodging Jewish power.[65]

---

62 Farrell, 'The Third Man Emerges', *Common Sense*, No. 565, August 1970, p. 2.

63 *Patriotic Reading* (New Jersey: Christian Educational Association, c. 1970), p. 1.

64 Yockey, 'Tragedy of Youth', *Common Sense*, No. 552, January 1, 1970, pp. 1, 4.

65 Farrell, 'Calley Thrown to the Wolves', *Common Sense*, No. 581, April 15, 1971, p. 2. Farrell was making the point that the 'American Jewish Establishment' was trying to destroy the American military class because of its instinctive distrust of the military. For the details on the army coup against Beria who, after his role in Stalin's death, tried to

He quoted from Yockey's *Proclamation* to illustrate his repugnance of the parliamentary politicians:

> These deputies are mere things, replaceable units desirable only mathematically, in aggregates. Among them there is not, and cannot be, a strong individuality, for a man, a whole and entire man, does not sell himself like these parliamentary whores.

That year also, Farrell quoted Yockey from *Four Essays*. Farrell's theme was that the USSR was outmanoeuvring the USA in the Middle East and that the USA was cultivating the support of China, the USSR having always opposed the communization of China, while the USA had backed the ouster of Chiang by Mao. His assessment of Stalin's opposition to the Maoization of China is certainly correct and was a matter that outraged Trotsky. Farrell assured his readers:

> Disaster will not be long in coming. Today the Soviet Union is implacably hostile towards American Zionism. No better description of this hostility exists than that found in Francis Parker Yockey's *Four Essays*. Yockey observed the decline of American Jewish power and the rise of Russian power in the world: "The basic reason for the diminution of power is spiritual-organic. Power will never stay in the hands of him who does not want power and has no plan for its use."[66]

A few months later, Farrell cited Yockey's final essay, 'The World in Flames', which Farrell described as 'brilliant'. In this a World War III is forecast in which Third World dictatorships will line up with the USSR to defeat the USA and Israel. Farrell believed that the nuclear destruction of the USA was imminent. In Yockeyesque terms, Farrell concluded by stating that Russia, having recovered from Jewish Marxism, 'narrowly watches the follies of the funny little men who cavort in New York and Washington, not to mention Tel Aviv and Jerusalem. Russia will exploit these follies to the hilt'. He predicted

---

reintegrate the USSR into the global economic system (subsequently reattempted by Gorbachev and Yeltsin but now blocked by Putin) see Bolton, *Stalin...*, op. cit., pp. 147–148. The coup was a move by the Russian Army under Zhukov against the Jewish-dominated Secret police under Beria, as Farrell indicated.

66 Farrell, 'USA Sold Out China, End of Line for Zionism', *Common Sense*, No. 587, August, 1971, p. 4.

that the future of the Jews would be nuclear annihilation in New York and Jerusalem and disappearance through assimilation in Russia. The West was finished and anti-communist crusades were futile, as were political and economic arguments. The future would be based on military power.[67]

The final issue of *Common Sense* was intensely pessimistic. The writers had done all they could to warn the USA of impending disaster, namely nuclear devastation at the hands of the USSR, and that the only option left was faith in Christ. The final word was left to Farrell, whose opening statement was that 'the American civilization is beyond the point of no return'. America would be destroyed along with the Jews.[68] *Common Sense* ended when the successor to Conde McGinley, Katherine Littig, called it quits after 26 years and went to live with the Catholic community at Saint Jovite, Quebec. The newspaper retained many readers and Horton would have liked to have kept it going but was feuding with sundry luminaries such as Lt. General del Valle and Willis Carto. He retained communication with Oliver, although the two disagreed fundamentally, in particular over the position of Jews in the USSR.

DTK attempted without success to have *Common Sense*, which had been running for 26 years, handed over to a younger generation rather than see it closed in 1972.[69]

Horton maintained a commitment to 'the utter and total destruction of the Left-Right polarity, which is the Jewish control mechanism'. Horton was as enigmatic as Yockey. He claimed to have established a Wieland Naval Academy, to be involved with ship brokering on behalf of the Arabs, and to have during the 1930s acted as an agent for Krupp in buying up French newspapers.[70]

---

67 Farrell, 'USA Sold Out China', ibid.

68 Farrell, 'Looking Ahead', *Common Sense*, final issue, May 15, 1972, p. 4.

69 DTK to Oliver, May 11, 1972. DTK believed that the closure of *Common Sense* was caused by the FBI's COINTELPRO (Counter Intelligence Program) of the time 'which aimed at disrupting the "Right" by rumour-mongering, threats and agents provocateur'. The editor, Katherine Littig, was 'visited' several times by the FBI. The newspaper, which still retained many readers, believes that Littig's withdrawal to Canada to peel potatoes and carrots in the St. Jovite kitchen was a 'face-saving'. DTK to Oliver, November 1, 1976.

70 Farrell (Horton) to Oliver, ca. 1974.

# 'Whited Sepulchres'

Those whom Weiss called the 'crackpots' in the 'Right' continued to see the conflict between the USSR and Zionism as a 'family quarrel' between Jews, or as a trick to fool the *goyim*, including the Arabs, into believing that communism was no longer Jewish. What Yockey reportedly observed first-hand at the Prague trial was something of historical importance, but it was over the heads of most of the 'Right'.

Seven years after Yockey's death the Arab-Israeli war provided a new impetus for Soviet anti-Zionism. By this time, in Paul Lendvai's opinion, Moscow had become the 'Center and Exporter of Anti-Semitism'.[1] The liberal uprisings of 1968 in Czechoslovakia and Poland, hurrahed by the 'Right', served as the impetus for an increase in the anti-Zionist, and arguably 'anti-Semitic, 'propaganda output from the USSR'. Lendvai writes of the 'Zionist plot' against Poland, in which the State accused Zionists of 'an open attack on the political system and its leaders' in the form of intellectual dissent and student demonstrations, which had been prompted by the State suppression of a student theatrical production. This State repression was undertaken in the name of anti-Zionism. Factory and political meetings organised by the Communist Party functionaries were held under the slogan 'Purge the Party of Zionists'.[2] Lendvai states that since 1966 there had been a 'Jewish department' in the Ministry of Interior, led by Colonel Walichnowski, 'author of the anti-Zionist best-seller, *Israel and the Federal Republic of Germany*'.[3]

---

1 Paul Lendvai, op. cit., pp. 10–20.

2 Paul Lendvai, ibid., pp. 113–125.

3 Paul Lendvai, ibid., p. 126.

In Czechoslovakia, the 1967 Arab-Israeli war instigated a new campaign of anti-Zionism. Dissidents criticised the anti-Israel policy of the regime. The Czechoslovak Writers' Congress of June 26-29, 1967, addressed itself to the Party leadership. The Congress' pro-Israel position was also aligned with demands for liberalisation. During the May Day demonstration of 1967, students carried the Israeli flag and placards demanding: 'Let Israel Live.' The philosophy faculty at Prague's Charles University issued a petition demanding the resumption of diplomatic relations with Israel.[4]

To the Right in the USA, the prospect of 'Moscow as the centre of anti-Semitism' was a theoretical impossibility. The Right, from Southern segregationists to self-declared 'Nazis', saw Soviet anti-Zionism as a Jewish plot to fool Gentiles and the Arabic bloc. The theory was that anti-Zionist posturing by the (Jewish-controlled) USSR would beguile the Arabs into being aligned with the Soviet bloc and that the Jewish cabal that controls both the Eastern and Western blocs would have driven the Arabs into the arms of Jewish communism. King Faisal of Saudi Arabia, who was then the senior statesman of the Arab world, held this conspiratorial view. In 1970, *Newsweek* quoted Faisal as stating in reply to a question on the Arab-Israeli conflict:

> If the crisis is tackled as we suggest, Soviet influence and penetration will cease. But Zionism and communism are working hand in glove to block any settlement to restore peace. It's all part of a great plot, a grand conspiracy. Communism is a Zionist creation designed to fulfil the aims of Zionism. They are only pretending to work against each other in the Middle East. The Zionists are deceiving the US into believing they are on their side. The communists, on the other hand, are cheating the Arabs, making them believe that they are on their side. But actually they are in league with the Zionists.[5]

Most of the 'Right' had not budged from its dogma since The Britons had condemned 'Ulick Varange'.

---

4 Paul Lendvai, ibid., p. 263.

5 King Faisal, 'A Grand Conspiracy', *Newsweek*, December 21, 1970.

## Natinform

Among those most vehemently opposed to Yockey was 'Natinform' (Nationalist Information), intended as the opposite number to the USSR's 'Cominform'. Founded by Wolfgang Sarg, a contact of H Keith Thompson's, Imperial Fascist veteran A. F. X. Baron[6] and ELF veteran Peter J Huxley-Blythe,[7] Natinform issued a 'confidential' bulletin on Yockey in 1953, augmented in 1954. Signed by Sarg, a Wehrmacht veteran who had been a member of the advisory committee of Thompson's abortive Committee of the Advancement of Civlization,[8] it was written by Baron, according to H Keith Thompson.[9]

Later that year (October), Sarg was raided by the police and investigations were initiated against him as head of Natinform in West Germany.[10] Sarg was sentenced to eight months' jail in 1956 for 'conspiracy, libel and fraud'. According to Jewish sources: 'Sarg, who is only 30, admitted during the two-week trial that, together with other leading neo-Nazis in Northwest Germany, he had signed a manifesto pledging "unconditional loyalty to National Socialism"'.[11]

---

6 Around the same time as the founding of the ELF and UM Baron and Anthony Gittens of The Britons, both Imperial Fascist League members, founded the Nationalist Workers Movement but a few years later had fallen out and the NWM vanished.

7 As will be seen, Huxley-Blythe (1925–2013) in later years wrote of Yockey with esteem and came to regard Yockey as correct in regard to the USA. Huxley-Blythe published *Natinform World Survey* and worked with the Northern League, a worldwide pan-Nordic association based in Britain, which published *Northern World*. He was particularly remembered in Rightist circles for his book *The East Came West*, describing the forcible return by the British, under the Yalta Agreement, of thousands of anti-Soviet Cossacks and Russians, including their families, after World War II to the USSR for immediate execution. He later became a noted psychotherapist. See obituary, *The Telegraph*, October 15, 2013, http://www.telegraph.co.uk/news/obituaries/10380814/Peter-Huxley-Blythe.html. He returned to politics as a contributing editor for Willis Carto's journal *The Barnes Review*.

8 H Keith Thompson, 'I am an American Fascist', Part IV, op. cit.

9 Thompson interview with Stimely, op. cit.

10 'German Authorities Start Investigation of Anti-Semitic Editor', Jewish Telegraphic Agency, October 6, 1953.

11 'Anti-Semites in Germany Fined for Insulting Chancellor Adenauer', Jewish Telegraphic Agency, May 18, 1956.

Supposedly an intelligence backgrounder, littered with errors and vitriol, some of the information from this bulletin found its way into FBI files.

## Bruderschaft — The Secret Brotherhood

The primary allegation was that Yockey was a Soviet agent. Sarg/Baron began by claiming that the European Liberation Front (ELF) developed into activities promoting collaboration with the USSR and the East German State. Yockey supposedly joined the US Army Psychological Warfare branch and the War Crimes Commission at Nuremberg. 'According to his account, upon arrival in Europe he became converted to the cause of "Authoritarian European Nationalism".'[12] None of this information was correct. Sarg continues: 'Cultivating contacts within Mosley's Union Movement, the breakaway ELF primarily included Guy Chesham, Baroness Alice von Pflugel [sic], and Anthony Gannon'. They were of an 'Eastern orientation, advocating neutralism and extreme anti-American activity'. ELF linked with Alfred Francke Kriesche, UM legal advisor and German war veteran, through whom contact was established with the *Bruderschaft* veterans' association in Germany. Sarg/Baron claimed that Karl Kaufmann and Beck-Broichsitter of the *Bruderschaft* had also been contacted by Yockey with the prospect of anti-US and pro-Soviet underground actions in Germany but that they had rejected the plan. *Imperium* was supposedly written with the assistance of Guy Chesham, Yockey's Oxford-educated colleague in the overseas liaison office of the UM. It is claimed that Yockey 'likes to be considered a disciple not only of Spengler but of Moeller van den Bruck'[13] and 'completely rejected the ideas' of Nazi ideologue Alfred Rosenberg. 'The style of *Imperium* is a crude imitation of Spengler's, similar to a Hollywood film production.' It is claimed that

---

12 Wolfgang Sarg, A. F. X. Baron, 'Francis Parker Yockey and the European Liberation Front', Natinform, Germany January 28, 1953; Papers of Sir Oswald Mosley, OMD/7/1/6, Special Collections, Cadbury Research Library, University of Birmingham.

13 Moeller van den Bruck was a Weimar-era 'National Bolshevik', who like certain other German nationalists supported a pro-Russia policy to counter the victor's policies after World War I. While Yockey's stand vis-à-vis Russia and Western Europe after World War II is analogous, there is no reason to believe that Yockey was an adherent of Moeller van den Bruck.

*The Proclamation of London* was jointly authored by Yockey, Gannon and Chesham.[14]

Yockey supposedly had a meeting with an 'agent' of Natinform in England, where, speaking in Germany, he attacked Union Movement as pro-US and praised Soviet policy, and in particular the German POWs under Sedlitz and Paulus who went over to the Soviet side in World War II. Yockey is then supposed to have asked whether the Natinform contact could organise partisans in Western Germany to collaborate with the USSR. Baroness von Pflügl allegedly spoke about the soul of Germany and its eastward orientation. If Yockey's proposals were accepted those present would be 'initiated into a vast worldwide secret organization'. Guy Chesham allegedly had two meetings with a Natinform agent, outlining a plan to infiltrate nationalist groups, to promote an anti-US policy and to obtain funding from the Soviet Embassy. There would be a focus on contacting 'ex-soldier organisations'[15] and *Bruderschaft* is inferred.

Yockey is described as 'small, dark, of unknown mixed races, pale and intense'.[16]

There is a touch of plausibility mixed with much nonsense in the Natinform report.

Yockey replied from Beirut, Lebanon, stating that the slanders had not caused any breach between himself and his 'personal and political friend Keith Thompson', to whom Sarg had sent the memo. Yockey affirms his authorship of the article on the Prague treason trial that had been published in the *National Renaissance Bulletin*, reiterating his stand that Russia had broken with Jewry. This break would assist Europe's liberation from its 'outer enemies', both America-Jewry and Russia. This 'did not reach your limited comprehension because you, like a true Freudian, wish, not to understand, but only to besmirch anything superior to you'. Yockey counters the claim that he had been 'converted' to 'Authoritarian European Nationalism' in Europe after the war by pointing out that he had held these principles, which he was

14 Sarg/Baron, op. cit.

15 Sarg/Baron, ibid.

16 Sarg/Baron, ibid.

calling 'Imperialism', since 1936.[17] Yockey states that he left UM when he found that Mosley was 'pro-American and anti-Russian' to the 'extent of mobilizing Europe to fight for American-Jewish victory over Russia…'. 'Mosley is an effective American agent, just as Adenauer [West German Chancellor] is, just as you are. It is entirely unimportant whether or not you and Mosley are paid as well as Adenauer.'[18] Yockey points out that he had never read or quoted Moeller van den Bruck and indeed there is no reason for believing otherwise. Perhaps Sarg wanted to put Yockey in the pre-war German 'National Bolshevik' camp that had rivalled the Hitlerites. Yockey charges that Sarg/Baron lied about the writing of *Imperium* and *The Proclamation*. Indeed, there is no substance to the claim that Chesham helped with writing *Imperium*. As we know from Anthony Gannon, the only ELF publication that was co-authored was the 12-point programme, by Yockey, Chesham and Gannon. As Yockey said, 'only an idiot' would believe in the possibility of multi-authorship for such works.

Yockey was particularly affronted by being associated with Chesham, whom Yockey claimed had been expelled from the ELF in 1949 'for intrigue with stupid and vicious elements'. Actually, according to Gannon, Yockey and Chesham had quarrelled about what Yockey regarded as interference from Chesham's wife and Chesham had left.[19] Also questionable is why Yockey denied any association with Alice von Pflügl,[20] at whose mansion he had lived.

What incensed Yockey most, however, was the suggestion that the ELF pursued a pro-Russian policy and that he was a Soviet agent. He demanded a retraction. To the Russophobes of Natinform and much of the rest of the 'Right', we can by now readily appreciate why Yockey and his followers might be regarded as pro-Russian and worse. Yockey's friends in Germany were indeed pursuing a line that was 'neutralist' at least. This made them suspect to the intelligence services of the USA and Germany. This dispute in regard to

17 Yockey to Wolfgang Sarg, Beirut, January 24, 1953. Yockey is referring to 'The Philosophy of Constitutional Law', written as a student paper while at Georgetown University School of Foreign Service in 1936. His 1940 essay, 'Life as Art', develops his philosophy.

18 Yockey to Wolfgang Sarg, op. cit.

19 Gannon, 'A Remembrance of the Author of Imperium', op. cit.

20 Yockey to Sarg, op. cit.

the Russian question might explain the exception Yockey took to the Sarg/Baron claim that he had met Beck-Broichsitter and Karl Kaufmann. These two *Bruderschaft* officials were the least likely to be approached with any anti-US plan and Yockey would have been fully appraised of factions within the *Bruderschaft*.

The *Bruderschaft* (Brotherhood) was formed in 1949 in the British occupation zone by former SS officers, NSDAP officials and POWs. They advocated a united Europe independent of both the USA and the USSR.[21] Hence, the policy was in line with that of the ELF and the Socialist Reich Party. However, it is also the policy that caused a rift and the ending of the *Bruderschaft* in 1951, two years after the Sarg/Baron memo on Yockey. From the start the organisation was under the surveillance of US Army Counterintelligence Corps (CIC).[22] The *Bruderschaft* was founded by SS Major Alfred Franke-Gricksch and Major Helmut Beck-Broichsitter. *Bruderschaft* official Karl Kaufmann was a veteran of the NSDAP since 1922, and governor of Hamburg during the war.[23]

Yockey's contact, Franke-Gricksch, advocated an anti-US orientation for Germany. However, Beck-Broichsitter pitched by Germany to the USA as an anti-communist ally, spoke to Allied authorities and the press, and told US High Commission members that the USSR aimed at 'Bolshevizing' Germany through 'phoney peace initiatives' and 'the offer of German unity'. He stated that Germany's historic mission was to defend the West against Russia and that German honour had been besmirched by the war crimes trials. However, the CIA noted that the *Bruderschaft* ideology remained National Socialist. The *Bruderschaft* aimed to infiltrate and to form alliances among right-wing parties, from the moderate Christian Democrats to the 'neo-Nazi' Socialist Reich Party, and to forge a 'state within a state'.[24] The whole political life of Franke-Gricksch is problematic. Despite leaving the Hitlerite NSDAP in 1930

---

21 Richard Breitman and Norman J. W. Goda, *Hitler's Shadow: Nazi War Criminals, US Intelligence and the Cold War* (DIANE Publishing, 2011), p. 53. The book is a review of the US National Archives.

22 Richard Breitman, ibid., p. 54.

23 Richard Breitman, ibid.

24 Richard Breitman, ibid. p. 56.

to join Otto Strasser's rival Black Front and to briefly go into exile to Prague with Strasser, he was able to return to Hitler's Germany and assume a high-ranking position in the SS Personnel Office. He had disputed Strasser's repudiation of Germany's claim on Saar and Memel and became part of Himmler's 'inner circle' under the name of Alfred Franke; and with the personal support of Himmler, his Strasserite background seems to have been overlooked.[25]

While Beck-Broichsitter tried to align with the USA, that was not the policy of the *Bruderschaft*, which rejected NATO. A CIC agent noted that the Brotherhood was 'not pro-Allied' and opposed 'protection' from both East and West. The 'covert program' of the *Bruderschaft* was described by the CIA as a 'united Europe,' that would 'withdraw from close political and military cooperation with the US, and although opposing international Bolshevism and Soviet interference in European affairs, could take a neutral position between the US and USSR or even enter as an equal partner into an alliance with the USSR'. The Fascist form of government would presumably be enacted in other European states where the *Bruderschaft* had contact with neo-fascist organisations.[26] The line taken by the dominant faction in the *Bruderschaft* was in accord with that of Yockey.

The *Bruderschaft* established contact with the Soviet-sponsored 'National Front', the alliance of parties in the DDR that included the NDPD. It was reported in 1950 by the Munich press that the *Bruderschaft* even offered to amalgamate with the Soviet Army.[27] Franke-Gricksch maintained contact with East Germany and had set up 'courier nets' with members of the *Bruderschaft*. Contacts included officials of the Socialist Unity Party and the Soviet military administration. Both Kaufmann and Franke-Gricksch agreed that Germany should play the USA and USSR off against each other in securing concessions and unity for Germany.[28]

In 1951, Beck-Broichsitter and other members in the *Bruderschaft* advocated co-operation with the USA. Franke-Gricksch and his supporters

25 Brian A Renk, 'The Franke-Gricksch "Resettlement Action Report": Anatomy of a Fabrication', *The Journal of Historical Review*, Vol. 11, No. 3, Fall 1991, pp. 261–279.

26 Richard Breitman, op. cit., p. 57.

27 Brian A Renk, op. cit.

28 Richard Breitman, op. cit., p. 58.

maintained that NATO could not be trusted and that NATO commander Dwight Eisenhower 'remains a German hater'. At a 'bitter meeting' in February 1951, Franke-Gricksch accused Beck-Broichsitter of spying for the West German intelligence agency, BfV. Beck-Broichsitter resigned from the *Bruderschaft* rather than be investigated by a *Bruderschaft* court of honour. The CIC later established that Beck-Broichsitter was an informant for the BfV, which wanted to know of Franke-Gricksch's connections with the Soviets. Beck-Broichsitter split and took factions from the French and US occupation zones, forming the *Bruderschaft Deutschland* as a paramilitary formation, presumably intended to align with NATO in a confrontation with the USSR.

For reasons unknown, Franke-Gricksch was arrested in East Germany in 1951 as a 'war criminal' and reportedly died in a Soviet concentration camp in 1953.[29] Why Franke-Gricksch would be jailed by the Soviets is problematic. Certainly, the USSR and East German authorities co-operated often with German veterans and Rightists, and established a political party in the DDR on that basis, the National Democratic Party of Germany (NDPD), which remained part of the Soviet regime until the very end of the East German state. High-ranking officials of the Third Reich were well-placed in the military and police of the DDR.[30] Is it possible that Franke-Gricksch was set up by Western intelligence services, or alternatively that the USSR considered he had become a liability? Renk, who had contact with Franke-Gricksch's son, speculates:

> Could Franke-Gricksch have been playing some complicated intelligence game between East and West, Britain's SIS and its Soviet counterpart, while all the while striving to resurrect a neutral Germany following a "third way" beyond capitalism and communism?[31]

It is little wonder that Yockey was incensed at any exposure by Sarg/Baron of communications with the *Bruderschaft*, which involved espionage and

29 Richard Breitman, ibid. p. 59.

30 K. R. Bolton, 'Stalin's German-Nationalist Party', *Inconvenient History*, Vol. 6, No. 1, 2014, http://inconvenienthistory.com/archive/2014/volume_6/number_1/stalins_german_nationalist_party.php.

31 Renk, op. cit.

Cold War intrigue. Further, it is not likely Yockey would have communicated with Franke-Gricksch's rival, Beck-Broichsitter, given the latter's pro-American orientation. On the other hand, he was in contact with Franke-Gricksch, whose orientation was pro-Soviet. Moreover, the line of most of the *Bruderschaft*, like that of the Socialist Reich Party, was the same as Yockey's: to play the USSR and USA off against each other to secure concessions for Germany and Europe, with a preference for the Russians. If Yockey did talk at a meeting of the ELF of a secret order with worldwide contacts, pursuing an anti-US strategy, he was probably alluding to the *Bruderschaft*. For Sarg/Baron to blurt out such matters to all and sundry would have been a serious matter for Yockey and others.

Yockey explained in his open letter to Sarg his policy vis-à-vis Russia and the USA, which paralleled that of the *Bruderschaft*:

> You and your kind—I refer to the European *Michel* stratum, and in particular to its leaders the churchills[32]—are Europe's most dangerous enemies. You and your kind would make Europe into a Sarg. You are a whited sepulchre, uncreative, uncomprehending and full of malice and crooked jealousy of those with life in them, those who would lead the West forward on its great mission. You and your kind alone make possible the looting and despoiling of Europe by the American-Jewish forces. You and your kind alone made possible the victory of the Jewish-American-Russian coalition over Europe. With your talk of petty-nationalism, you are helping to perpetuate the conditions in Europe which make possible the continued Jewish-American domination.

> I now state—not confidentially[33]—that you are an agent of American-Jewry charged, on a lower plane, with the same mission as Gasperi, Gaulle, Adenauer, Zeeland, Mayer, Churchill et al. namely, the maintenance of the Jewish-American hegemony over Europe. Your method is the same as theirs: the attempt to identify American-Jewish interests with Europe's interests. Your propaganda is the same: you label all European Imperialists as Russian agents.

32 Yockey often used lower case for names of the leading figures of the *Michel* stratum of 'inner traitors'.

33 The Sarg/Baron memo against Yockey was apparently intended to be confidential among Rightist contacts.

> My policy, and the policy of the European Liberation Front aims at the unconditional Liberation of Europe's soul and Europe's soil from America-Jewry and from Russia. America-Jewry controls 90% of Europe's soil; Russia controls 10% of Europe's soil. Elementary political tactics reveal from whom Europe can gain power over its own Destiny once more. Publish this if you dare, you vile coward. I give you my permission. My policy is not "Confidential"![34]

## Ami Go Home

Sometime in 1954, Sarg added to his Yockey memo. He claimed that Yockey's ideas had split the Mouvement Social Européen (MSE), the breakaway movement being the National Forces of Europe (NFE).[35]

The MSE had been formed in Malmö, Sweden, in September 1951, at the instigation of Swedish fascist Per Engdahl. Delegates from 20 organisations attended a congress in May 1951, including representatives from the Socialist Reich Party and the Movimento Sociale Italiano, with support from Hans Rudel, Oswald Mosley, Bardèche, et al. There was a general move to distance the new organisation from the old Hitlerian racialism and there was a focus on corporatism.

The actual breakaway was the Nouvel Ordre Européen (NOE), which continues to exist. Founding members included Gaston-Armand Amaudruz of Switzerland, who continues to publish the NOE bulletin *Courrier du Continent*, secretary general of the movement, and René Binet. Other NOE leaders included Pierre Clementi, co-founder in 1942 of the Legion of French Volunteers against Bolshevism that fought on the Eastern Front. NOE, through its affiliate, Editions Celtic, Montreal, published Binet's books, *Contribution to a Racist Ethics* (1975) and *National Socialism Against Marxism* (1978).[36] So far from the breakaway from the MSE being influenced by Yockey, it was committed more than the MSE to what Yockey discounted as the 'materialistic' and 'Darwinian' idea of 'vertical race'.

---

34 Yockey to Sarg, op. cit.

35 Sarg, 'Francis Parker Yockey and the European Liberation Front', op. cit., 1954 addition.

36 R.-L. Berclaz, NOE, to Bolton, August 31, 2014.

Sarg claimed that 'one of the leading [sic] of the NFE is one René Binet, who was a close collaborator with Gannon-Yockey-ELF'. According to what Maurice Bardèche recalled, Yockey had met Binet once, via Bardèche, had argued and there had been no collaboration between them. On the other hand, in 1950 Gannon had written to Arcand, who was interested in a French translation of *The Proclamation*, that this had been delayed because of the arrest of Binet 'and other French comrades, and their impending appeal against sentences ranging from 2 years to 6 months'.[37] Yockey's influence on NOE might have percolated through to the MSE through individual delegates. The 'Malmö Manifesto', adopted at the May 1951 congress, accords much with Yockey's ELF programme:

1. Defence of Western culture against communism;
2. Creation of the European Empire;
3. Prices and salaries controlled throughout the European Empire;
4. The armed forces of all countries under the control of the central government of the Empire;
5. The right for colonial peoples to enter the Empire once they have attained a certain educational and economic level;
6. The election of heads of government through plebiscite;
7. Regulation of social and economic life through the organs of a corporate state;
8. The aim of education will be to produce men and women who are *strong*;
9. The co-operation of idealists who found themselves on either side of the lines during the last war will be sought;

37 Gannon to Arcand, March 30, 1950, Arcand collection, Archives Canada, vol. 1, file no. 1, p. 2.

10. The aim of this European Revolution will be the spiritual regeneration of man, society, and the State.[38]

The reference to a 'European Empire' is more suggestive of Yockey than Mosley, whose preferred term was 'Europe-a-Nation', although certain of Mosley's themes are evident, such as what he called the 'wage-price mechanism'. The convenor of the conference, Per Engdahl, had a programme since before the war based on the corporatist state, which finds its expression in point 7.

Yockey's real influence was via the Belgian activist and theorist Jean Thiriart, who advocated a 'European Empire'.

Sarg equated any opposition by the Right to American occupation and Culture-distortion as pro-Soviet and in particular as indicating Yockey's influence. Hence, Sarg comments that 'at a recent NFE congress in Brussels, Belgium, Binet made a typical Yockey speech violently attacking the USA and giving his own rendering of the communist slogan, "Ami Go Home"'. 'This pro-Red outburst caused a visiting émigré Russian Nationalist representative (present as an observer for RONDD[39] of Munich) to expose such propaganda.'[40] Opposition to Americanisation was, however, far from a fringe current among the radical Right. As we have seen, the argument split the *Bruderschaft* in Germany. There were also pro- and anti-NATO factions in the Movimento Sociale Italiano and although the pro-American faction briefly won in 1950 when G Almirante was replaced as MSI leader,[41] he subsequently remained leader for most of the MSI's history.

Sarg and other such 'nationalists' had completely thrown in their lot with the USA in the cause of Russophobia and 'anti-communism', and missed the historical boat, ignoring the epochal events that had been taking place in

---

38 'Malmö Manifesto', Mouvement Social Européen, May 1951; Roger Griffin, *Fascism* (Oxford University Press, 1995), p. 342.

39 Russian All National Popular State Movement, based in West Germany, included remnants of Vlassov's Russian liberation army that fought with the Germans during World War II, and Czarist émigrés. Ironically, RONDD's founder, E. P. Artsyuk, went to the USSR during the Kruschev era, and was won over to 'Soviet patriotism'.

40 Sarg, op. cit., 1954.

41 Roger Eatwell, *Fascism: A History* (London: Vintage Books, 1996), p. 199.

the USSR since Trotsky was purged in 1928.[42] Any opposition to 'America-Jewry' and the 'cleansing of the soul of Europe from the ethical syphilis of Hollywood'[43] was condemned as 'pro-Red'. It was this 'ethical syphilis' that Moscow had been condemning as 'rootless cosmopolitanism' and purging from the Soviet Motherland while the USA was spreading its contagion over the world via the Congress for Cultural Freedom.[44]

Sarg stated that 'Yockey is known to have started the current propaganda line that Bolshevism is no longer communism — the tool of American high finance which originally financed Lenin — and the Russian rulers had become National Socialists'. On the other hand, given his comment that Bolshevism had been funded by 'American high finance' did he suppose, with his pro-US outlook vis-à-vis the Cold War, that it was the USA that had divested itself of rule by 'high finance'? Had the USA at some unknown stage been transformed into a nationalist state, while the USSR remained a Jewish-plutocratic satrap? This paradox was one that has yet to be explained by the Birchers and Nazis who maintained a pro-US position during the Cold War.

While Yockey might indeed have been the first in the post-war era to promote the idea for an understanding of *realpolitical* strategy, it seems likely that Frederick Weiss, if not others, had reached the same conclusions independently after 1945. Why did this line have such a ready reception among German veterans, particularly in the Socialist Reich Party and *Bruderschaft*? The answer is the pro-Russian orientation among conservative Rightists dating from the Weimar era. These rightists, and not only the National Bolsheviks, saw an alliance even with 'communists' as preferable to the decay and serfdom of liberal-democracy and its plutocratic masters. 'National Bolshevism' was marked by its pro-Russian orientation, while remaining part of the radical right, and included seminal literary figures such as Moeller van den Bruck and Ernst Jünger; the leader of the paramilitary anti-communist *Freikorps*, Ernst von Salomon; and Ernst Niekisch and Karl O Paetel, publishers of *Widerstand*. Moreover, the USSR had sought out German nationalists

42 Bolton, *Stalin…*, op. cit.

43 Point 5 of the ELF programme, op cit.

44 F Chernov, 'Bourgeois Cosmopolitanism and its Reactionary Role', *Bolshevik*, no. 5, March 15, 1949. See Bolton, *Stalin…*, op. cit., pp. 28–54.

via the Association for the Study of the Planned Economy of Soviet Russia (Arplan), which included as chairman Lenz, a National Bolshevik; Count Ernst Graf zu Reventlow, a foreign policy adviser for the NSDAP; and Captain Römer, an officer of the Right-wing militia, *Bund Oberland*. The League of Professional Intellectuals (BGB) was of particular interest to the USSR for gaining the support of 'highly placed Rightist intellectuals'. Niekisch, Jünger and Lenz were members.[45] When the Hitler-Stalin Pact was signed it was not such an anomaly and could have endured as an alliance against plutocracy and liberalism.

Sarg claimed that Yockey's outlook was that 'communism was now "National Communism" and "anti-Semitic", [and that] it should be supported in its fight against Jewish high finance in the USA, today's sponsor of Trotskyism'.[46] From what is now known of the CIA sponsorship of Trotskyites, art-Bolsheviks and other anti-Soviet Leftists,[47] Yockey's realisation of this dichotomy at such an early stage of the Cold War reveals a keen perception. Likewise, his recognition in his essay on the Prague trial[48] that Stalin had stymied a world state by rejecting US plans for the UNO and the 'Baruch Plan' for the 'internationalisation of atomic energy'. If Sarg and the bulk of the Russophobic Right could not by then understand the difference between Stalinism and Trotskyism-Leninism, they should have read Trotsky's *The Revolution Betrayed*—although they might have insisted it was all a cunning plan between Trotsky, Stalin and the Jews to fool the *goyim*.

Sarg claimed that Yockey's supposedly pro-Russia line 'has met with considerable success in the United States, as can be seen from articles and letters in the American Nationalist press'.[49] This is difficult to quantify and does not seem evident in 1954. Despite a line on Russia in the US national-

---

45 Bolton, 'Jünger and National Bolshevism', in Troy Southgate (editor) *Jünger: Thoughts & Perspectives*, Vol. 11, (London: Black Front Press, 2012), pp. 14–20.

46 Sarg, op. cit., 1954.

47 On the American sponsorship of Trotskyites and other anti-Soviet Marxists during the Cold War see: Frances Stonor Saunders, *The Cultural Cold War: The CIA and the World of Arts and Letters* (New York: The New Press, 1999).

48 Yockey, 'Prague Treason Trial', 1952, op. cit.

49 Sarg, op. cit., 1954.

ist press claiming that Stalinism was 'national communism' in conflict with America-Jewry, which was using Trotskyism, the same idea introduced by Yockey and Weiss in the *National Renaissance Bulletin* in 1952[50] did not become a notable theme until 1966, when a self-declared 'Stalinist', Fred Farrell, joined the staff of *Common Sense.*

Sarg concluded his 1954 addendum to the Natinform memo by claiming that Yockeyism had influenced the British Right through Guy Chesham, Yockey's Union Movement and ELF colleague with whom he had soon rowed. Sarg alleged that it was through Chesham, who was regarded by Natinform as particularly pro-Soviet, that a strident and lasting anti-US outlook was injected into the British Right. Sarg or possibly his British colleague, A. F. X. Baron, claimed that 'Chesham wrote the original manifesto for the National Front and indoctrinated Andrew Fountaine with virulent anti-Americanism'.[51] The National Front here referred to is an early, abortive precursor of the National Front that was founded in 1967 with the merger of the British National Party of John Bean and Andrew Fountaine and A. K. Chesterton's League of Empire Loyalists. Fountaine had founded the 'National Front Movement' in 1950 after being expelled by the Conservative Party,[52] despite his popularity as an election candidate.[53] Chesham seems to have been running the National Front Movement for Fountaine and included extracts from *Imperium* and other Yockey quotes in the NFM's newspaper, *Outrider*. Despite Chesham having broken with Yockey under bitter personal circumstances, he apparently remained loyal to Yockey's ideas. Fountaine's NFM, like the later NF, was committed to the unity and development of the British Empire. This contrasted with the European unity of Mosley and Yockey. John Bean notes that Chesham's influence over the NFM was evident in the *Outrider*'s references to a 'new Europe', which 'contrasted strongly with Fountaine's views'. The first policy point of the 4-point NFM programme did however include 'all out opposition to UNO, NATO, Strasbourg and other international tie-ups'. Nothing

50 Yockey, 'Prague Treason Trial', op. cit.

51 Sarg, op. cit., 1954.

52 John Bean, *Many Shades of Black* (London: New Millennium, 1999), p. 187.

53 John Bean, ibid., p. 93.

came of the NFM and Chesham urged 'infiltration' as 'the new policy'.[54] Sarg continues that:

> Chesham also contacted A. K. Chesterton while the latter was Assistant Editor of the magazine *Truth* and gave him all this Yockey-information. He wrote a carefully guarded article extolling this, which Chesterton published in *Truth*. Chesterton having had this talk with Chesham re "the new political developments in the East", went to see [Anthony] Gittens of the Britons Publishing Company and urged him to support this "line".
>
> When Hilary Cotter, a member of Natinform, wrote *World Dictatorship by 1955*, he was invited to visit Chesterton to get his opinion. There, Chesterton suggested that Cotter should delete all attacks on communism, stating that this "line" was now out of date. It is known that Chesterton and Cotter have collaborated in the past, and the Chesterton-sponsored League of Empire Loyalists took up the Chesham programme, later written for the National Front, with a few alterations of their own. An appraisal of Chesterton's *Candour* shows virulent anti-Americanism, or Yockeyism.[55]

These final paragraphs of the Sarg memo are particularly ill-informed at best. Here, we see something that Yockey and his followers encountered on both sides of the Atlantic: that opposition to US occupation and the 'spiritual syphilis of Hollywood' was regarded as serving 'communism' and the USSR.

A. K. Chesterton, a literary critic of note, had joined Mosley's British Union of Fascists but had left in 1937. Invalided from the army in 1943 due to malaria, he became chief leader writer and deputy editor of *Truth* in 1944, literary adviser to Lord Beaverbrook and special writer with the Daily Express Group. Displeased with the compromising policy of *Truth*, Chesterton founded his own journal, *Candour*, which still exists, and the flamboyant movement, the League of Empire Loyalists, which had branches throughout the Empire, protesting against the post-war scuttle of British world interests. Chesterton edited *Candour* until his death in 1973. In 1967, he was elected first chairman

54 John Bean, ibid., pp. 93–95.

55 Sarg, op., cit., 1954.

of the National Front.[56] His book *The New Unhappy Lords*, published in 1965, has remained a seminal statement on power-politics and money-power for the Anglophone 'Right'.[57]

As should be apparent, Chesterton did not need to be instructed on any new 'line' by Chesham, Yockey, Mosley or anyone else. He was a well-connected journalist, lecturer and author. Yockey's enemies merely made opposition to US global machinations synonymous with 'Yockeyism' and a Soviet agenda. Hence, Binet and Chesterton were assumed to be under Yockey's spell. It was the USA, not the USSR that was behind the scuttling of not only Britain's Empire but of all European empires after World War II. The 'Atlantic Charter' signed between Winston Churchill and President Franklin D Roosevelt in 1941 stated, with Churchill too impotent to object, that free trade and the abolition of imperial preferences were major Allied aims and would be imposed over the world after the war. Churchill, speaking with 'despair', stated: 'Mr President, I believe you are trying to do away with the British Empire…' Imperial trade blocs were obstacles to the free trade that Wall Street aimed to foist upon the world.[58] Chesterton specialised in exposing the 'money power' in *Candour* and *The New Unhappy Lords*. Yockey saw the USA, not the USSR, as the main enemy for similar reasons but focused on Europe and the entire Western Civilization. Chesterton, far from adopting a pro-Soviet line, saw the USSR as a bogeyman useful to the USA for scaring the world into embracing American 'protection', which would include detaching Britain's colonies and dominions and pushing them into US-run institutions such as SEATO. He held that there was covert cooperation between the USSR and the USA to push out the former colonial powers. For example, Chesterton wrote of 'the hypothesis that the Power Elite in New York and the masters of the Kremlin work to an agreed schedule…'[59] For Yockey, the equivalent of Europe's subordination, under the same anti-Soviet pretext, was NATO. Although there

---

56 Aidan Mackey, 'Farewell to A. K. Chesterton', *Candour*, http://www.candour.org.uk/#/1-farewell-to-ak-chesterton/4541686669.

57 A. K. Chesterton, *The New Unhappy Lords*, 1965; online at https://archive.org/stream/TheNewUnhappyLords#page/no/mode/2up.

58 K. R. Bolton, 'The Geopolitics of White Dispossession', *Radix*, Washington Summit Publishers, Vol. 1, 2012, p. 114.

59 A. K. Chesterton, 'The Decisive Decade', *Candour*, Vol. 21, No. 495, January 1970, p. 2.

were fundamental differences between Yockeyism and Chestertonian post-war British nationalism, both saw the USA as the primary enemy.

## Fraudulent Conversion?

While Yockey was presumed in some quarters to have not gone beyond Hitlerism, for orthodox Hitlerites such as George Lincoln Rockwell and Colin Jordan, he was a heretic. Colin Jordan, protégé and heir of Arnold Leese as leader of British National Socialism, responded to the issue of Jews and the Soviet bloc with *Fraudulent Conversion: The Myth of Moscow's Change of Heart*. Although Jordan does not mention Yockey, Weiss or the 'X.Y.Z.' series on Russia, it is notable that his tract was published in 1955; the same year as the first two parts of 'Russia'. Jordan also starts with reference to the Slansky trial in 1952, stating that it was this year (that is, the year of Yockey's essay on the trial) in which claims were made on the fall of the Jews in the Soviet bloc. Jordan explains actions against Zionism in the Soviet bloc as a 'family feud' among Jews. 'Communism, under its Jewish leadership, has been conducting a drive against the rival Jewish movement of Zionism, particularly since the creation of the state of Israel in 1948.'[60]

Jordan's views on the Jews and the Soviet bloc were standard 'neo-Nazi' opinion. In *Fraudulent Conversion,* Jordan saw any and every Jew with a position in the Soviet bloc as evidence that everything was still Kosher. Conservatives such as Gerald L. K. Smith and Lt. General P. A. del Valle held the same views. As Weiss's series on Russia contended, Russian Jewry had been obliged to become Russified or be classed as enemies of the state. This Russification was not based on 'social anti-Semitism', which Yockey alluded to as serving Jewish interests (e.g. by affirming Zionist separatist ideology), but on 'cultural anti-Semitism', which routed Culture-distortion and retardation from the Culture-organism. Writing of this in regard to Germany, Yockey stated: 'For the first time, anti-Semitism was as total as semitism. Mere social anti-Semitism was welcome to the Culture-distorter, for it unified his

60 Colin Jordan, *Fraudulent Conversion: The Myth of Moscow's Change of Heart*, 1955; http://greatwhitedesert.org/dir/index.php?title=Fraudulent_Conversion.

followers. But cultural anti-Semitism meant the end of the sway of power within the West of the distorter.'[61]

In the USSR, this meant a State campaign as far-reaching on the Russian culture-organism as that of Germany's measures vis-à-vis the Western culture-organism. This campaign was something more far-reaching than a family squabble between Jewish-communists and Zionists, or a clever trick to fool the *goyim*. Cultural-Bolshevism was rejected in favour of a Soviet culture founded on the 'Great Russians', laid out by Andrei Zdanov in 1948.[62] In 1949, F Chernov launched the Soviet campaign against 'rootless cosmopolitanism'.[63] Meanwhile, the USA was promoting throughout the world abstract expressionism and jazz to show how free artists were in the West, compared with the repressive USSR. Trotskyites[64] were heavily involved in this campaign, which was primarily sponsored by the CIA, US State Department and Rockefeller Foundation.[65]

'Rootless cosmopolitans' were widely regarded as synonymous with 'Jews'. One of the first and most famous to be arrested in what would the following year become the campaign against 'rootless cosmopolitanism' was Solomon Mikhoels, director of the Moscow State Jewish Theatre. His body was dumped outside Minsk and the Soviet authorities claimed that he had been the victim of a hit-and-run road accident. Mikhoels was regarded as the leader of Soviet-Jewish culture and was feted throughout the world. His death has been lamented as an 'anti-Semitic' Stalinist outrage ever since.[66] However, recently declassified CIA documents show that there was a Zionist network within the

---

61 Yockey, *Imperium*, Wermod ed., op, cit., p. 716.

62 A Zdanov, Speech at a discussion on music to the Central Committee of the Communist Party SU, February 1948.

63 F Chernov, 'Bourgeois Cosmopolitanism and its Reactionary Role', *Bolshevik*, (Theoretical and political magazine of the Central Committee), No. 5, March 1949, pp. 30–41.

64 Trotsky had co-authored an arts manifesto in 1938, 'Towards a Free Revolutionary Art', with Andre Breton and the Mexican communist muralist Rivera, defending modernism.

65 See Frances Stonor Saunders, *Cultural Cold War*, op. cit., inter alia. Also, Bolton, *Stalin...*, op. cit., pp. 28–54.

66 Arkady Vaksberg, *Stalin Against the Jews* (New York: Alfred A Knoppf, 1994), pp. 159–182.

Soviet bloc working with the CIA.[67] The CIA documents state that 'Mikhoels, a prominent Jewish leader who maintained contact with the West', died in 1948, the same year in which the Israeli legation was established in Moscow. Mikhoels maintained contact with Israeli diplomats in Moscow. Soviet authorities found that the Israeli Legation in Moscow immediately established links with Soviet Jews. The CIA worked through *Hashomer Hatzair* (Young Guard), which the CIA describes as an 'international Zionist radical-socialist political party'. In 1948, the *Hashomer Hatzair* central branch in Palestine joined with *Abdut Avodah* (United Labour Zionist Party) to form *MAPAM*, the second largest party in Israel. *MAPAM's* pro-Soviet stance was shaken by the Prague trials. *MAPAM* leader Mordechai Oren, noted for his pro-Soviet stance, was arrested when staying in Prague and obliged to testify at the trial of Slansky et al. He was sentenced to 15 years imprisonment, was released in 1956 and returned to Israel. The pro-Soviet stance maintained by some important Zionist elements increasingly evaporated. The CIA documents state that Zionist organisations worked closely with the CIA, as alleged by the Soviet authorities. An article in the Russian Soviet journal *New Times*,[68] included in the CIA file, states the CIA's European Division director, Schwartz, was the main link between Zionists in New York and in the Soviet bloc. He worked with the 'Joint Zionist Organization'[69] director in Budapest named I Jakobson, who was later expelled from Hungary for 'spying and subversive activities'.

Another more recent declassified CIA document comments on the operations of the Israeli secret service, *Mossad*, in the Soviet bloc, which included subverting the Soviet bureaucracies:

> Intelligence objectives to the USSR and East Europe consist of determining governmental policy toward Israel and the problem of Jewish emigration; recruiting persons strategically located in Soviet and East European bureaucracies who,

---

67 CIA memo, undated, Assistant Director, Special Operations to Assistant Director, Reports and Estimates; http://milfuegos.blogspot.co.nz/2014/08/the-cias-cold-war-allies-included.html.

68 *New Times*, January 21, 1953.

69 The organisation is likely to have been the American Jewish Joint Distribution Committee.

> motivated either by conviction or corruption, are willing to assist Zionist action in those countries.[70]

In 1989 Václav Havel, first post-Soviet Czech President, named Slansky's son, Rudolf Slansky Jr, as the Czech ambassador to Moscow. Havel was what Yockey referred to as the 'inner enemy' and what Stalinists referred to as a 'rootless cosmopolitan'. He had been a significant agent in subverting the Soviet bloc as a founder of 'Charter 77' in 1977. Hungarian-Jewish currency speculator and globalist luminary George Soros stated that he had funded the organisation since 1981. When Havel died in 2011, Israeli President Shimon Peres and other Zionist leaders eulogised Havel as a 'friend of Israel'.[71] Czechoslovakia, whose 1952-53 purge of Zionism was regarded by Yockey as an epochal event, ended with Havel, according to leading Jewish newspaper *Forward*, making the Czech Republic Israel's firmest friend in Europe:

> In April of that year, Havel became the first leader of a free former Soviet bloc country to visit Israel. As president, Havel opposed the sale of weapons to regimes hostile to Israel. Today, according to Israeli Ambassador Yaakov Levy, "the Czech Republic is considered by Israel to be its best friend in Europe and the European Union".[72]

It is notable that Slansky's son was a leader of the 1968 Prague revolt in which support for Israel was a catalyst. Slansky junior remained a leader of anti-Soviet dissent and was involved with Havel's Charter 77.[73]

---

70 'Israel: Foreign Intelligence and Security Services', CIA Directorate of Operations Counterintelligence Staff, March 1979, p. 16.

71 Bolton, 'Václav Havel: "The Inner Enemy"', *Counter-Currents*, http://www.counter-currents.com/2011/12/vaclav-havel-the-inner-enemy/.

72 J Kirchick, 'Havel was Friend of Israel and Jews: Czech Playwright-Turned-President Led Region to Right Path', *The Jewish Daily Forward*, December 20, 2011, http://www.forward.com/articles/148247/.

73 'Former Czech diplomat and communist era dissident dies at 71', Radio Praha, April 18, 2006, available online at http://www.radio.cz/en/section/curraffrs/rudolf-slansky-former-czech-diplomat-and-communist-era-dissident-dies-aged-71.

# Capture

Using the aliases Edward Max Price and Edward Max Briceman, Yockey had visited Germany, France, England, Belgium and Austria during 1954-56. The US State Department was having trouble keeping track.[1]

It is likely that Yockey was in the Soviet bloc circa 1955–1957, perhaps working for an anti-Zionist department, as he had in Egypt.

1955-57 were years during which the Jewish question in the USSR was taking other avenues. When Stalin died in 1953, his secret police chief, Lavrenti Beria, whose star had been in decline for several years, and who probably had a role in Stalin's death,[2] was looked upon with hope by Soviet Jews. His ascent was very short-lived and he and his subordinates were tried and executed by the end of the year.[3] Questions again began to be asked about the future of Soviet Jews under Khruschev. Interestingly, among the most persistent challengers were the Western-based Communist parties, whose many Jewish leaders and cadres had found the situation of Jews under Stalin unsettling. At the end of 1955, the USSR adopted a flagrantly pro-Arab position. Many Jewish communist leaders in the West felt embittered towards Khruschev's lack of acknowledgement regarding the Jews as victims of Stalin's purges or the anti-Jewish basis of the 'Doctors' Plot'. In April 1956, the Polish Jewish newspaper *Volksstimme* published an article listing the names of Jewish social

---

1 FBI memorandum, September 8, 1960, p. 2, 105–8229 — 3.

2 According to V. M. Molotov, Minister of Foreign Affairs, Beria boasted to him on May 1 1953 of Stalin's death: 'I did him in. I saved you all!' *Molotov Remembers*, p. 237, cited by J Brent and V. P. Naumov, *Stalin's Last Crime: the Doctors' Plot* (London: John Murray, 2004), p. 320.

3 *On the Crimes and Anti-Party, Anti-Government Activities of Beria*, Plenum of the Central Committee of the Communist Party of the Soviet Union, 2-7 July 1953.

and cultural leaders executed during the 1937-38 purges and during 1948-52. The gauntlet was thrown down and Jews, including visiting communist delegations from the West, tried to put the USSR on the defensive. To questions posed by a delegation from the French Socialist Party in Moscow in 1956, Khruschev made it clear that the USSR would not reopen Jewish schools and cultural centres. In 1957 the last Jew of note, Lazar Kaganovich, around whom the 'Right' had woven such myths about Jewish power in the USSR, was removed. With the Suez Crisis of 1956 the USSR embarked on anti-Zionist propaganda which often included condemnation of Judaism. Communist Party leaders in the West were critical of the Soviet stance. The Suez Crisis also saw the formation of Zionist organisations in the USSR.[4]

If Yockey was in the Soviet bloc at this time, he witnessed a most significant era in regard to Soviet anti-Zionism. However, he was back in the USA in 1958.

While travelling as 'Richard Hatch', Yockey was arrested in the USA on June 6, 1960. On June 8, 1960 an 'Airtel' report from San Francisco to FBI director J Edgar Hoover stated:

> Francis Parker Yockey was apprehended on a violation of the Selective Services Act on June 6 1960. He came to the attention of this office as the result of a call from American Airlines when his bag was left at the airline without identification. American Airlines opened the bag to determine if there would be any data contained therein which bore the photograph of subject YOCKEY. One was an American passport; one was a Canadian passport; one was a British passport, and one was a German passport. [...]
>
> Upon interview HATCH declined to identify himself or to give any explanation as to the possession of these passports. In view of the similarity of the name on the German passport of FRANZ YORK, it was thought that he might be identical with Subject YOCKEY.
>
> At the time of his apprehension, HATCH had in his possession $2,276.90. [...].

---

4 See Alexander Solzhenitsyn, *Two Hundred Years Together* (2001, 2002), 'Before the Six Day War', Vol. 2, Chapter 23, https://wikispooks.com/iframeDocs/200yt/Chapter23.html.

> As far as can be determined, HATCH has no visible means of support, in that he does not state any given employment, and refused to give any explanation as to the source of this money.[5]

Yockey had not had time to collect his bag when his flight from Washington to San Francisco was re-routed due to mechanical troubles. At Fort Worth, Texas, American Airlines had searched the unclaimed bag, which contained a large amount of documentation for the procurement of false passports.[6]

An early account of the happening states that the FBI's San Francisco Office was notified and the baggage was held at San Francisco, with FBI agents awaiting Yockey to claim it. Yockey gave the name of Hatch and refused to talk about the contents of the baggage. He proceeded to leave the interview room at the airport. FBI Special Agent Robert Leonard attempted to stop Yockey 'by placing his hand on the subject, and the subject continued to walk through the door with the Agent pursuing'.[7]

The now accepted version of Yockey's capture states that the bag was delivered to the Oakland address of Alex B Scharf, where Yockey was staying. Scharf invited the FBI agents Robert Leonard, Keith Teeter and Alfred Miller into his apartment. Yockey started to walk away from the 'living room' toward the kitchen door.[8] Yockey then rushed to the kitchen door. Leonard grabbed Yockey's sleeve and wrist. Yockey opened the back door of the kitchen leading to the porch and managed to get outside, slamming the door on Leonard's hand.[9] This required 'extensive medical and hospital care and, accordingly, such an offence is regarded as most serious'. The injury required 28 stitches and hospitalisation for five days.[10] However, Leonard maintained his hold of Yockey's wrist. Yockey used his free hand to pry Leonard's fingers away and ran down the back stairs with Leonard in pursuit. Yockey started towards the street and was intercepted by Special Agent Miller, who came out of the front

5 San Francisco FBI to Hoover, Airtel, June 8, 1960; 105–8229—3.

6 FBI report June 5, 1960; 105–8229—3.

7 FBI office memorandum , June 8, 1960, p. 1; 105–8229—3.

8 FBI report, September 6, 1960, p. 23; 105–8229—3.

9 FBI report, September 6, 1960, p. 23; 105–8229—3.

10 Assistant Attorney General Yeagley to Assistant Attorney General Malcolm Wilkey and FBI director Hoover, June 13, 1960; FBI file no. 105–8229—3.

door of the building. On noticing that Leonard's hand was bleeding, Yockey apologised.[11]

Yockey was booked at Oakland City Jail, San Francisco, the original charge being failure to register under the Selective Service Act.[12] That charge was dropped and proceedings were initiated for passport violations. The charges of Selective Service Act violation and even of assaulting a Federal Officer were considered to be of a technical nature that would be difficult to pursue. Assistant US Attorney Clancy determined that Yockey was not required to register under the Selective Service Act[13] and that the State Department should proceed on passport violations.[14]

Yockey was arraigned before US Commissioner Joseph Karesh on June 8. The State Department asked bail to be set at $50,000, one reason offered for such a high bail being the injury to Special Agent Leonard's hand.[15] *The San Francisco Examiner* commented that Yockey was of 'great interest' to executive branches of the Federal government. This was indicated by bail having been set at $50,000 instead of the 'usual bail' of 'around $3000 for passport fraud.' A government source stated of Yockey that 'this is not a small fish. This is a man that we are very, very interested in.'[16] *The Oakland Tribune* referred to a source saying that Yockey's arrest was 'definitely a security matter.'[17] The office of Assistant US Attorney Clancy later told press that orders had come from Washington 'not to discuss the case further.'[18]

On June 9, Yockey was again brought before Commissioner Karesh. A new attorney, Carl Hoppe, a patent lawyer, and patently out of his depth,

---

11 FBI report, September 6, 1960, op. cit., p. 24; 105–8229 — 3.

12 FBI report June 6, 1960; FBI file no. 105–8229 — 3.
US Military Selective Service Act, Section 426A, Title 50.

13 FBI report, September 6, 1960, p. 30; 105–8229 — 3.

14 FBI office memorandum, June 8, 1960, pp. 2–3; FBI file no. 105–8229 — 3.

15 FBI Communications Section, June 9, 1960; FBI file no. 105–8229 — 3.

16 '3 Passports Jail Mystery Visitor Here, Secrecy in Arrest, High Bail on US Fraud Charge', *San Francisco Examiner*, June 9, 1960, FBI file no. 105–8229 — A.

17 'Mystery Surrounds Man Seized with Fake Passports', *Oakland Tribune*, June 9, 1960, FBI file no. 105–8229 — A.

18 'Mystery Man seized with 3 Passports', *San Francisco Chronicle*, June 9, 1960; FBI file no. 105–8229 — A.

asked that Yockey be examined by a court-appointed psychiatrist. Yockey reacted with a 'sibilant, resounding whisper, "That's a dirty trick"', then stated that he had not been advised of this and that he would have to dismiss his lawyer.[19] Karesh adjourned to discuss the matter with Yockey and the attorney and on continuation of the hearing the motion for a psychiatric examination was dismissed and the hearing continued to June 9 and to June 10, in regard to lowering the bail. Press and television interest in the hearing was high.[20] Yockey's attorney requested it resume on June 13, as one of Yockey's sisters, Vinette Coyne, had supposedly been persuaded to commit him to a mental institution.[21] As we know, Yockey faced the prospect with dread and, as will be seen, with good reason. Yet when Mrs Coyne arrived she was combative, interrupting court proceedings, waving a copy of the US Constitution, and declaring: 'According to the Constitution no one shall be held upon excessive bail. And there is nothing in the Constitution about a mental examination.'[22] It seems that the authorities were playing mind games with Yockey and lied in claiming that Vinette had agreed to a mental examination for her bother.

## 'The Rabbi' on the Bench

Jospeh Karesh had been a rabbi. It might be wondered whether he was chosen for the purpose of feeding Yockey's supposed paranoia? Can it really be a coincidence that Yockey was arraigned before a former rabbi? Was this more a matter of *Talmudic* vengeance, like the war crimes trials in Germany, which Yockey had witnessed first-hand, riddled as they were with Jewish interrogators and torturers in Allied uniforms? Karesh had served as a rabbi at San Jose's Congregation Bikkur Cholim and as an interim rabbi for San Francisco's Congregation Sherith Israel during the 1930s. His father was Rabbi David Karesh, from whom he received his rabbinic training while a student of law, and as a chaplain as Travis Air Force Base. In 1960, presumably just after

19 'Insanity Plea in Passport Case Hinted', *San Francisco Chronicle*, June 10, 1960; FBI file no. SF105–1769.

20 FBI Communications Section, June 9, 1960; p. 2; FBI file no. 105–8229 — 3

21 FBI Communications Section, June 10, 1960; FBI file no. 105–8229 — 3

22 'Both Sides Favour Yockey Mind Test', *San Francisco Examiner*, June 14, 1960, FBI file no. 105–8229 — A.

Yockey's suicide, Karesh was elected a Superior Court judge. According to his son Jonathon, his father would quote from the *Torah* and the *Talmud* in court and in chambers, and would bring his 'rabbinical sensibilities into the legal arena'. His nickname was 'the rabbi'.[23]

What the Jewish tributes do not mention is that in 1966 there was suspicion of Judge Karesh being involved in a pay-off and being removed from the Superior Court to a lower court.[24]

A particularly absurd ploy by the authorities was to claim that because Yockey was such a fanatical anti-Semite and pro-Nazi, high bail was required to ensure that he would not be released, as the subject 'might intend to bomb a synagogue'. An FBI report states that in an interview with the press Assistant US Attorney William P Clancy 'brought forth the anti-Semitic angle' with a 'specific reference' to Yockey's 'dismissal from the Nuremberg war trials'.[25]

The *Oakland Tribune* reported of the hearing before Karesh on June 10 that 'scholarly appearing Yockey' had 'snapped' at Karesh when he was called 'a young man' and demanded that news photographers and cameramen stop taking pictures, calling it 'practically assault and battery'; a request that was granted by Karesh. He also reacted to reporters, saying 'you guys never get anything right' in regard to the press articles about him.[26]

The hearing resumed on June 13 with a new attorney, Emmet Hagerty, and both of Yockey's sisters had arrived. However, it was the State's attorney who stated that he intended to ask for a psychiatric examination of Yockey.[27] Hagerty opposed the motion, insisting that his client was sane, stating of Yockey: 'He is a competent man even though a lot of people differ from his ideas and beliefs.'[28]

---

23 Leslie Katz, 'Joseph Karesh, a rabbi turned judge, dies at 88', *Jweekly.com*, June 28, 1996, available online at http://www.jweekly.com/article/full/3565/joseph-karesh-a-rabbi-turned-judge-dies-at-age.

24 June Naugle, *The Great American Swindle* (Author House, 2010), p. 491.

25 FBI Communications Section, June 10, 1960; FBI file no. 105–8229 — 3. As we have seen, Yockey was at Wiesbaden, not Nuremberg.

26 'Passport Suspect Angry at Hearing', *Oakland Tribune*, June 10, 1960; FBI file no. SF105–1769.

27 FBI Communications Section, June 13, 1960; FBI file no. 105–8229 — 3

28 'Yockey "Pal" Spills Plan to FBI Agent', *Oakland Tribune*, June 14, 1960; FBI file no. SF105–1769.

The FBI attempted to collate information on Yockey's 'mental condition or suicidal tendencies', as 'the data was necessary to obtain psychiatric exam'.[29] Assistant US Attorney William P Clancy asked for an adjournment on June 14, so that he could present a motion to the US District Court, San Francisco, for Yockey to be psychiatrically examined. US District Court Judge William T Sweigert took the matter on advisement and held the decision over until June 15. The proceedings then resumed before Karesh on June 14 regarding a defence motion for bail reduction. Clancy argued that Yockey had suicidal tendencies and had plotted to escape.[30]

Clancy advised Karesh that he intended to present the matters of passport violation and assaulting a Federal agent before a Grand Jury following Yockey's psychiatric examination, should it be granted, and expected the date would be July 22.[31]

Karesh, responding to the issue of a psychiatric examination had stated: 'The merits of the case have nothing to do with it. This man needs a mental examination.' Karesh further advised that Yockey's '"actions, conduct and outbursts" made a sanity check very advisable'.[32] Judge Sweigert ordered a psychiatric examination.[33]

Assistant US Attorney General Malcolm Wilkey expressed concern to the FBI that there would be an effort to reduce Yockey's bail. He asked whether the Bureau would 'authorize a disclosure of the facts respecting the alleged Silver Shirt activities of this subject'.[34] Karesh quipped that he wished the bail

29 FBI Communications Section, June 14, 1960; FBI file no. 105–8229—3

30 FBI Communications Section, June 14, 1960; FBI file no. 105–8229—3.
Jack Fambrough, a prisoner at San Francisco County Jail, informed police that Yockey had planned to escape with his cellmate Phillip Galati and Fambrough and that Yockey would have Galati's $1,000 bail posted, and Galati would effect the escape plan, obtaining guns and an automobile. (FBI Airtel, June 13, 1960, FBI file no. 105–8229—3).

31 FBI Communications Section, June 14, 1960; ibid., p. 2.

32 'Sanity Tests Ordered for Yockey', *San Francisco Chronicle*, June 16, 1960; FBI file no. SF1-5-1769.

33 FBI teletype, June 15, 1960; FBI file no. 105–8229—3.

34 Malcolm Richard Wilkey to J Edgar Hoover, US Government office memorandum, June 10, 1960; FBI file no. 105–8229—3.

could be set at $150,000.[35] Judge Sweigert set July 11 for a report by a psychiatrist and Karesh set the same day for a further bail hearing.

On June 15, Yockey was able to cross-examine Commissioner Karesh before Judge Sweigert. The supposedly 'mentally unstable' Yockey was sharp. He asked whether Karesh was an ordained rabbi. 'Karesh, the son of a rabbi, answered that he was not.' As we have seen Karesh had served as rabbi, his nickname was 'the rabbi' and according to his son he would bring his *Talmudic* sensibilities to the court. Yockey asked:

> "Have you read anywhere that anti-Semitism is comparable to mental disorder?" Karesh, speaking to Judge Sweigert and not Yockey, answered: "If the defendant is trying to say that I am speaking on religious conviction, it is not true. I stand here as an arm of the court. What I say has nothing to do with my religious beliefs."
>
> Karesh was referring to the fact that he urged a mental examination of Yockey. It was shortly after that that Judge Sweigert agreed it was necessary.
>
> Yockey claimed that "it is a tradition in our jurisprudence that insanity is something to be raised by the defendants. If the government can take away that defense and use it in the attack, no matter if it is the statute books, it is an injustice."[36]

FBI Agent Edward M Cunningham testified that Yockey had been discharged from the US Army in 1943, diagnosed with 'demential praecox, paranoid type'.

Several salient points arise from this court appearance on June 15:

1. Yockey was mentally astute, despite being confined with rapists and robbers in the San Francisco jail, and enduring the glare of media publicity.
2. Yockey realistically assessed the forces arraigned against him; this assessment was not the product of paranoia.

---

35 Willis Carto, 'ADL Closes its File on Yockey, Creative Genius Driven to Suicide', *Right*, no. 99, August 1960, p. 2.

36 'Mental Exam for Yockey Ordered', *Oakland Tribune*, June 15, 1960; FBI file no. SF105-1769.

3. Karesh was dishonest in saying that he was 'not a rabbi'. He had served as a rabbi for several congregations.

4. Karesh was being dishonest in stating that he was not motivated by Judaism in his judicial outlook; his son noted that he brought a *Talmudic* sensibility to the courtroom.

5. As Carto claimed in his obituary for Yockey, it was Karesh who pushed for a psychiatric examination of Yockey, in tandem with the State.[37]

6. Yockey's discharge from the Army in 1943 through his feigned mental illness came back to haunt him. However, the State does not seem to have mentioned that the initial diagnosis of 'demential praecox' was discounted on detailed examination. Yockey was considered to be suffering from anxiety caused by the treatment he was receiving as a private in the Army (perhaps motivated by Yockey's having been a supporter of the America First movement, Pelley and Father Coughlin before World War II) — an absurd position in which to place an honours law graduate with a genius IQ.

7. Yockey well knew that Leftist and Jewish psychiatrists and sociologists had for decades made opposition to Jewish agendas synonymous with insanity.[38] The USA confined dissidents to mental institutions.

---

37 Willis Carto, 'ADL Closes its File on Yockey, Creative Genius Driven to Suicide', *Right*, No. 99, August 1960.

38 See for example the seminal study, T. W. Adorno et al, *The Authoritarian Personality* (New York: Harper and Row, 1950). This survey established an 'F' (for 'Fascism') scale that diagnosed traditional conservative values such as respect for parents as a symptom of mental illness, along with any signs of (white) loyalty to one's own race or negative thoughts about Jews. The family per se is regarded as the seedbed of 'Fascism'. The study was funded by the American Jewish Committee.

# 'Dementia Praecox, Paranoid Type'

> ...[T]he system of Freudianism. The soul of Culture-man is attacked by it, not from an oblique direction of economics[1] or biology[2], but from the front. The "science" of psychology is chosen as the vehicle to deny all higher impulses of the soul.
>
> — Yockey, *Imperium*[3]

> For the anti-Semite has no morality, and he has no conscience. He understands but one language, and he must be dealt with on his own level. The Purim Jews stood up for their lives. American Jews too must come to grips with our contemporary anti-Semites. We must fill our jails with anti-Semitic gangsters, we must fill our insane asylums with anti-Semitic lunatics, we must combat every alien Jew-hater, we must harass and prosecute our Jew baiters to the extreme limits of the laws, we must humble and shame our anti-Semitic hoodlums to such an extent that none will wish to dare to become "fellow-travelers".
>
> — Rabbi Leon Spitz[4]

The FBI noted, according to an informant, that:

> Yockey _____ is more interested in avoiding psychiatric treatment than he is in avoiding criminal charges of passport fraud, judging from his conversation.

---

1 Marxism.

2 Darwinism.

3 Yockey, *Imperium*, Wermod edition, op. cit., p. 128.

4 Rabbi Leon Spitz, 'Glamorous Purim Formula', *The Amercian Hebrew*, March 1, 1946. Spitz's profile at: http://www.zoominfo.com/p/Leon-Spitz/70657817.

> Yockey has expressed a fear of being placed under a Jewish psychiatrist. _____ was discharged from the US Army in 1943 as a result of his efforts in "snowing" an Army psychiatrist into believing he was a psychopath. Yockey indicated he maintained contact with this Army psychiatrist, whose name he did not mention.[5]

Captain Schnap of the US Army Medical Corps had diagnosed Yockey with dementia praecox by at the US Army Hospital, Fort Gordon. He had been sent to a private sanatorium, Allen Hospital, in Georgia, on January 15, 1943[6] and he was released on January 25. The diagnosis of dementia praecox was not upheld. The conclusion from Allen Hospital was that Yockey was most likely to have been traumatised by his experiences in the Army at having to take orders from people of lesser intelligence.[7] Nonetheless, this was sufficient in assisting the US State Department in trying to railroad Yockey into an insane asylum for an indefinite period.

Yockey's closest friend and colleague in England, Gannon, remarks of this episode:

> FPY was as sane as the next man. As the paranoia issue seems to be established by US Army records, it seems to me that FPY was intelligent enough, and skilled enough to seek this route out of what he often referred to as the "Coca Cola Army". This route is well trodden in all countries, and has long been a favoured exit from the armed forces by those who know that feigning of mental illness is hard to challenge and to disprove. Thus I think that F "worked-his-ticket" out of the US Army by pretending to be neurotic.[8]

Five years before his death, when the FBI and US State Department were unsuccessfully hunting him, an FBI report summarised Yockey as 'having an IQ of around 170'. By temperament he was 'erratic', 'high-strung', 'unpredictable', 'dictatorial', with an 'air of superiority'. 'His mind is a veritable storehouse of information, and he retains most of what he reads.' He had a tendency to

5 FBI memo, file no. SF 105–1769, June 13 1960.

6 FBI report, July 7, 1960, p. 40, FBI file no. 105–8229—3.

7 FBI report, July 7, 1960, p. 40, FBI file no. 105–8229—3.

8 Gannon to Stimely, September 7, 1980. Stimely Archives.

alienate men but attract women.[9] In assessing Yockey's psychological state the Army psychiatrist in 1943 had mentioned his feeling of 'superiority' towards others and his displeasure at being forced to scrub floors as a private rather than being an officer. However, the FBI summary of Yockey's character in 1956 described a person who is a certifiable genius rather than a certifiable lunatic, a person with character traits that can reasonably be expected to go along with an IQ of 170. One's awareness of being a 'genius' is apparently the trait that at least partially determines whether one is unbalanced. Another — Jewish — branch of psychology might call such a recognition 'self-actualisation' and the highest point of human striving. It all depends upon one's political orientation: the same traits might be regarded as 'healthy' (left-wing) or 'psychotic' (fascist).

The mind games that the authorities played on Yockey are evidenced by the claim that his sister Vinette Coyne was arriving in San Francisco to sign documents to have him committed.[10] In fact, when both sisters, Alice and Vinette, arrived, they were as supportive of Yockey as ever and during court proceedings waved copies of the US Constitution, demanding Yockey's constitutional rights. As we have seen, they also spoke out in court against attempts to have Yockey psychiatrically examined. After his death, Vinette told the press that her brother was 'a true philosopher'.[11]

Yockey was correct in his concern that there would be efforts to railroad him into a mental asylum and that he would be tortured by psychiatrists in the name of 'treatment', to extract information on his contacts and to turn him into a vegetative state. Soon after he had been caught, the FBI was discussing such matters, noting that in 1952 a psychiatrist in Baltimore, Maryland, had stated that Yockey was a 'paranoid psychopath'.[12]

A press report after Yockey's death stated that:

> Francis Parker Yockey may have been driven to suicide by a tormenting fear of being certified as insane by psychiatrists. This was revealed today by probing

9 FBI report, February 20, 1956, p. 4; file no. 105–8229 — 2.

10 FBI communications section, teletype, June 23, 1960, p. 2, file no. 105–8229 — 3.

11 'Both Sides Favour Yockey Mind Test', *San Francisco Examiner*, June 14, 1960, FBI file no. 105–8229 — A.

12 FBI Teletype, June 15, 1960; FBI file no., 105–8229 — 3.

> the mysterious life and death of the alleged associate of Nazi and anti-Semitic organizations.
>
> "A psychiatric examination ordered by Federal Dist. Judge Sweigert may have been the factor that 'pushed him over the brink,'" they said.
>
> Judge Sweigert ordered the examination last Friday. Yockey, 47,[13] took poison on Saturday in his San Francisco County jail cell.
>
> Emmet Hagerty, Yockey's second attorney, said at the court hearing before Sweigert that Yockey feared the results of a psychiatric examination would be that he would be certified as insane and committed to an institution. The theory that he particularly feared examination by Jewish psychiatrists was developed later by government.[14]

How 'paranoid' was this? The FBI reported, shortly after his capture, that on September 24, 1954, the Bureau issued the following instructions:

> If the subject [is] located, interview should be conducted by two experienced agents who are thoroughly familiar with prior investigation in this case. Interview should be aimed at developing pertinent information concerning subject's activities and contacts in Fascist movement in both the United States and abroad, as well as details concerning Yockey's travel during recent years to include an exact description of travel documents held by subject.[15]

The report further commented that Yockey had been discharged from the Army in 1943 'by reason of dementia praecox, paranoid type with delusions of persecution.'[16] A week later, it was stated that the interrogation of Yockey concerning his worldwide fascist activities should be deferred until the charges of assault and passport violation were dealt with.[17]

Yockey had joked to Elsa Dewette about how he had tricked the Army in 1943 into thinking he was psychotic and discharging him. There also seems

13 Actually, 43.

14 'Fear Blamed for Suicide of Mystery Man', *Oakland Tribune*, June 20, 1960.

15 FBI Refairtel, San Francisco, June 9, 1960; FBI file no., 105–8229—3.

16 Ibid., p. 2.

17 FBI, San Francisco, June 16, 1960; FBI file no., 105–8229—3.

to have been a question of espionage for Germany that took him to Mexico, Yockey diverting attention from his reasons for being AWOL by feigning mental illness. However, the diagnosis of the Army psychiatrist came back to haunt Yockey 17 years later and the FBI had long mentioned in its reports that he was mentally unstable. When Yockey came to trial the motions for a psychiatric examination came from both defence and prosecution. This is what concerned Yockey most, for several reasons: (1) Yockey feared that he would be lobotomised or otherwise reduced to a vegetative condition by state psychiatrists; (2) he feared that he would be induced to betray his friends and comrades; (3) being diagnosed and confined as a lunatic would destroy the gravitas of the mission for which he had worked and sacrificed for so long.

Were Yockey's concerns themselves a product of a paranoid state? There is by now enough publicly available information exposing the horrendous experiments undertaken by CIA and other state-sponsored programmes in mental institutions.[18]

This was a time when there was a Government offensive against the 'Right'. This was the aftermath of the McCarthy era, when Senator Joseph McCarthy had attempted to purge communists from the state apparatus. After McCarthy's destruction primarily at the hands of Wall Street political fixers and their friends in the press,[19] there was a vicious reaction that saw a far more vigorous, Administration-supported programme to purge patriotic Americans from the state apparatus.

In 1961 the 'Reuther Memorandum'[20] was adopted by the Kennedy Administration as a formal guideline in purging nationalists from positions of

18 See Gordon Thomas, *Journey in Madness: Medical Torture and the Mind Controllers* (London: Corgi Books, 1989). This focuses on CIA-funded mind-destruction experiments at the Allan Memorial Institute, Montreal, Canada, during the 1950s and 1960s, under the direction of Leonard Rubenstein, an electronics technician. What was achieved was the zombification of patients, reduced to expressing themselves after 'treatment' with 'slobbering and choking sounds'. Administered by a Scot, Dr Ewen Cameron, others had names such as Zielinski and Gotlieb.

19 Bolton, 'Joe McCarthy's Real Enemies', *The Occidental Observer*, Vol. 10, No. 4, Winter 2010–2011, pp. 75–76.

20 Walter and Victor Reuther, 'The Reuther Memorandum to the Attorney General of the United States', December 19, 1961, http://www.scribd.com/doc/31124491/

influence, particularly from the military, where it was feared that nationalist officers might organise a coup. There was also a similar 'memorandum' issued by Senator William Fulbright of the Senate Foreign Relations Committee.[21] The primary target at this stage was Major General Edwin Walker, who had initiated a 'citizenship program' in the US Army in Germany, which explained communism and 'Americanism'. While the USA sought to contain the USSR, the ideology for doing so had to be liberalism, not nationalism, which, if spread among the military ranks, would pose a bigger threat than the Soviet Union. The Establishment in Washington and New York had made that clear already, when eliminating McCarthy and General Douglas MacArthur.

After Walker's anti-communist, nationalist programme in the army had been shut down, the General, retired from the army, led a virtual revolt in Mississippi in 1962, when Federal troops were sent to enforce at bayonet point the desegregation of the University of Mississippi. Walker stood beside Governor Ross Barnett, who was resisting the Federal Government. What is of particular relevance here is that Walker, despite his public recognition and popularity, was arrested for inciting sedition and insurrection. While awaiting the posting of a $100,000 bond, military aircraft took him to the US medical center for prisoners at Springfield, Missouri, for psychiatric assessment. This was the hell-hole to which investigative journalist Frederick Seelig had been consigned after exposing a network of homosexual child abusers within state social services. Seelig after several years was still at Springfield when Walker arrived. The pretext for confining Walker, like that used against Seelig and intended for Yockey, was that he was mentally unfit to stand trial. However, unlike Seelig and Yockey, Walker had a defence team and public recognition. The charges were heard before a jury and dropped.

Dr Thomas Szasz, professor emeritus of psychiatry at the University of Syracuse, New York Upstate Medical University, who was called on to advise Walker's defence counsel, wrote:

The-Reuther-Memorandum-Precusor-to-the-Ideological-Organizations-Audit-Project-Created-by-President-John-F-Kennedy-and-Attorney-General-Robert-Kenn.

21 J. W. Fulbright, 'Propaganda Activities of Military Personnel Directed at the Public', *Congressional Record*, August 2, 1961, 14433–14439 (Senate).

> I summarized the evidence for my view that psychiatry is a threat to civil liberties, especially to the liberties of individuals stigmatized as "right-wingers", illustrated by the famous case of Ezra Pound, who was locked up for 13 years while the government ostensibly waited for his "doctors" to restore his competence to stand trial. Now the Kennedys and their psychiatrists were in the process of doing the same thing to Walker.[22]

## 'Siberia Bill'

At the time, there was a major effort to establish a large state mental institution in Alaska, promoted by Senator Jacob Javits and by the Anti-Defamation League of B'nai B'rith. The American 'Right' was suspicious about what they were calling the 'Siberia Bill', contending that the Alaska Mental Health Act would be used to kidnap, incarcerate and mentally destroy dissident Americans, in a scenario similar to that existing in the USSR. DTK recalled the situation:

> In the early 1950s there was a large-scale campaign by the Jews and their helpers to declare politically active Aryans "dangerous" and outside the bounds of normal society. The Feds were about to build a huge "mental health" asylum in the Alaskan wilderness which would be outside the operational jurisdiction of any state government. Note Alaska was a territory, not a state of the Union. Jacob ("Jake the Snake") Javits, a good conservative Republican and Senator from New York, was behind the plan, encouraged greatly by the Anti-Defamation League and American Jewish Congress. The scheme was exposed by *Common Sense* and many others, and never went anywhere. The Jews are still pushing in this direction, however.[23]

As DTK mentions, the American 'Right' was very active in opposing the Alaska Mental Health Enabling Bill, which they characterised as the 'Siberia Bill'. Jewish columnist Milton Friedman, writing in *The Canadian Jewish Chronicle*, described the temper of the times:

---

22 Thomas Szasz, 'The Shame of Medicine: The Case of General Edwin Walker', *The Freeman*, Vol. 59, no. 8, October 2009, http://www.thefreemanonline.org/columns/the-therapeutic-state/the-shame-of-medicine-the-case-of-general-edwin-walker/.

23 DTK to Bolton, April 13, 2014.

> An assault on "Jewish quacks" in President Kennedy's new mental health program has emerged from the extreme Right-wing. The rightists are now seeking to brand psychiatry as subversive.
>
> Attacks on the mental health movement are jeopardizing gains made in public understanding in recent years according to a survey on anti-psychiatric activities throughout the country. The survey was made by Dr Alfred Auerbach for the American Psychiatric Association. APA's concern at the growing denunciations of mental health as "atheistic" or "communistic" was confirmed by the Association's president Dr C. H. C. Hardin Branch.
>
> **Main Targets**
>
> The Main targets have been the psychiatrists, psychologists and mental health leaders of the Jewish faith. Note was taken of the recent popularity of a play and film about the life of Dr Sigmund Freud.
>
> A recent Alaska Mental Health Act established mental hospitals in Alaska. It was previously necessary to send Alaskan patients to Portland, Ore., for treatment. Right-wingers charged that Christian anti-Communists were to be shipped off to Alaska for brainwashing by "Jew psychiatrists". They portrayed a sort of American Siberia.[24]

Friedman quoted Senator Thomas H Kuchel (Republican, California) about an upsurge in anti-Semitism among the extreme right, tying in the anti-communist John Birch Society which, although eschewing anti-Semitism and racism, was a major bugbear of the US Administration due to its success with grass-roots organizing. Javits commended Kuchel 'for rallying the Senate against resurgent Birchism.'[25] It is evident from the Friedman article that the liberal and Zionist partisans were themselves eager to link opposition to the Mental Health Bill to a wider condemnation on the American 'Right', including comparatively mainline conservatives such as the John Birch Society. Much of this is confirmed even from a liberal academic source of the period. Ralph E Ellsworth and Sarah M Harris in a paper on the 'American Right-Wing', which they define as anything that is 'not left-wing', just a few months

24 Milton Friedman, 'Washington Spotlight', *The Canadian Jewish Chronicle*, May 31, 1963, p. 6.

25 Milton Friedman, ibid.

after Yockey's death, stated in a section on the Rightist response to 'mental health':

> The mental health program is also interpreted as a conspiracy, and often as one aimed directly at the Right Wing. This interpretation is found in the articles by George Todt, which were read into the Congressional Record by Senator Barry Goldwater. The Alaskan Mental Hospital Law which was passed in 1956 distressed many conservatives because it appeared to them to create a kind of Siberia to which political prisoners might be sent against their will, and it seemed clear to them that these prisoners would be right wingers. There had already been the classic cases of Lucille Miller, the Finn twins, A. R. Fitzpatrick, Anthony Marino, Kathryn Deats, and, of course, most famous of all, Ezra Pound—all right wingers whose political views unquestionably figured in determining their assignment to mental hospitals. Lucille Miller, in her paper *The Green Mountain Rifleman*, first called the Right's attention to the incarceration in 1945 of Ezra Pound as a political prisoner at St Elizabeth's Hospital in Washington, D. C.
>
> John Kasper, of the Clinton, Tennessee, litigations, testified before a Senate Committee in 1956 that Pound was not insane, as certified, but was being punished for treason, for which he had never been tried in any court. Psychiatry, Kasper added, was a Jewish invention, and thoroughly un-American. Both Pound and Kasper himself have been defended by the American Civil Liberties Committee, on the ground that their civil liberties have been invaded, and it appears that in Pound's case the indignation of the Right, if sometimes a little histrionic, is certainly entirely reasonable.[26]

The case of Ezra Pound, the poet, who found himself and his wife trapped in fascist Italy when the USA declared war, and broadcast for Italian radio, was one of particular awkwardness for the American authorities, because of his worldwide fame. The embarrassment of a trial for treason was avoided by confining him to St Elisabeth's lunatic asylum for 13 years. Something similar had been attempted with Knut Hamsun in Norway.[27] After much behind-the-

26 Ralph E Ellsworth and Sarah M Harris, *The American Right-Wing, a Report to the Fund for the Republic Inc.* (University of Illinois Graduate School of Library Science Occasional Papers, No. 59, November 1960), pp. 14–15.

27 See Knut Hamsun, *On Overgrown Pathways* ([1949] London: MacGibbon and Kee, 1968); also Bolton, *Artists of the Right* (San Francisco: Counter-Currents publishing, 2012), p. 94.

scenes pressure from his (mostly liberal) literary friends, Pound was released, without ever being diagnosed. Pound returned to Italy, which he greeted with a fascist salute as the ship approached harbour.[28]

Even the American Legion expressed concern that normative American values were being redefined as symptoms of mental illness, and cited a leftist front on the subject:

> Characteristic of this reaction is the comment of the American Legion writer who quotes the following passage from an *American Friends Service Committee Bulletin* (May, 1952, p. 7): "What makes a super-patriot a super-patriot? The following paragraphs speculate on the forces within, which drive such men and women. It is an expression of a belief that understanding may enable us to help them. The superpatriots are clearly afraid. Being adults, they must rationalize their fears. They may call it 'concern for country'. They see a threat to the nation in the UN and UNESCO (or whatever) because these groups include strangers—people of different culture, language, religion and race. But their fears, to cause such hysteria, must be related to something far more basic than 'flag' or 'country'... This is the purest paranoid delusion: 'I have hundreds of lurking, secret enemies!' Explaining away the fancied enemies one by one forever will never relieve the condition for the person who is deluded. A friendly and loving attitude toward each mentally ill person is basic to being helpful. He feels the enemies and invents and seizes upon the person or group to be the enemy, to explain the feeling to himself..."

Ellsworth and Harris state of the American Friends Service Committee comments:

> The AFSC implies that "super-patriots" who refuse to be conditioned (to world understanding) are mentally ill. Presumably such mentally ill people should have the benefit of medical treatment as prescribed by world-minded individuals who are not afflicted with the "disease" of patriotism.[29]
>
> Compare this to Harry A Overstreet's statement in *The Great Enterprise* (1952): "A man, for example, may be angrily against race equality, public housing, the TVA, financial and technical aid to backward countries, organized labor, and the

28 See photograph of Pound, July 9, 1958 in E Fuller Torrey, *The Roots of Treason: Ezra Pound and the Secrets of St. Elizabeth's* (London: Sigwick and Jackson, 1984).

29 Ralph E Ellsworth and Sarah M Harris, op. cit., p. 15.

> preaching of social rather than salvational religion... Such people may appear normal in the sense that they're able to hold a job and otherwise maintain their status as members of society; but they are, we now realize, well along the road toward mental illness." This passage is quoted by Edith K Roosevelt in her article, "Bats in the UN Belfry?". "What Dr Overstreet describes, of course," she says, "is the prototype of millions of conservative people everywhere." Even more disturbing is her report that Povl Bang-Jensen, who served as Deputy Secretary to the UN Special Committee on the Problem of Hungary, and who refused to deliver to the United Nations a list of Hungarian witnesses against communism, was suspended as an officer of the UN and is now spoken of as not "rational" but as "aberrant", "odd", hence inevitably unreliable and incapable of telling the truth and exercising good judgment. Or as Mrs Alice Widener puts it, Povl Bang-Jensen stands officially accused, by a UN Committee, of conduct that departed markedly from normal and rational standards of behavior.[30]

Ellsworth and Harris refer to Walter Reuther, co-author of the 'memorandum' on how the state could eliminate the 'Right', as stating that Senator Barry Goldwater, a senior political figure, part-Jewish and moderately conservative, was in need of psychiatric examination. Reuther, a labour union leader, was influential in the Kennedy Administration.

> One learns, too, that Walter Reuther has stated that Senator Barry Goldwater needs a psychiatrist. This, of course, is exactly what Senator Goldwater would expect him to say. It appears that the Alaska Mental Hospital may eventually need its entire land grant after all.[31]

## Lucille Miller

The case of the above-mentioned Lucille Miller had attracted comment from the 'Right'. Frank L Britton, segregationist editor of *The American Nationalist*, and author of the enduring Right-wing bestseller *Behind Communism*, wrote of Lucille Miller's husband, Manuel, holding off Federal authorities for 12 hours when they attempted to take his wife to a mental asylum. Few

30 Ralph E Ellsworth and Sarah M Harris, *The American Right-Wing, a Report to the Fund for the Republic Inc.*, p. 15.

31 Ralph E Ellsworth and Sarah M Harris, ibid.

newspapers reported the facts behind the story, which occurred in 1955. In the small Vermont town of Bethel, Manuel Miller was a Justice of the Peace and had been elected to the school board and the local council. The Millers were parents of three pre-teen children. Their 'crime' was producing a mimeographed anti-communist newsletter, *The Green Mountain Rifleman*. They had focused over several years on a colony of mostly Jewish communists near the township. This had drawn the attention of conservative syndicated columnist Westbrook Pegler and of Senator Joseph McCarthy. The 'colony' included major names that had been exposed by McCarthy's Senate investigations, including Lee Pressman, John Abt, Owen Lattimore, et al. In February 1955, Mrs Miller had been arrested on the pretext of 'obstructing the Selective Services Act'. This odd accusation, without foundation, was the original pretext for wanting to detain Yockey but was immediately dropped once he was arrested. When Mrs Miller stated that she wanted a prompt trial and would defend herself, Judge Ernest Gibson instead ordered her committed to St Elizabeth's mental institution in Washington, until 'cured'[32] — the institution that held Ezra Pound for 13 years. Frank Britton writes:

> There she was confined in the institution's violent ward, where she was thrown into intimate proximity with violently insane Negro prostitutes, deranged criminals, perverts and other individuals of like description; conditions which would make imprisonment in a penitentiary system seem infinitely mild and preferable by comparison; conditions so horrible as to test the sanity of a normal person unfortunate enough to be detained there.[33]

Mrs Miller was suddenly released after 16 days and ordered by Gibson to stand trial on the Selective Services charge. Because Westbrook Pegler was able to draw attention to the case in *The Chicago Tribune* and some other major newspapers, Mrs Miller's confinement at St Elizabeth's attracted wide protest. Britton comments that she would have stayed there had it not been for this attention.[34] What assistance would Yockey have received if he had been

---

32 Frank L Britton, 'Denied Jury Trial by Federal Court as Protest Grows', *The American Nationalist*, Vol. 3, No. 35, July 1955, p. 1.

33 Frank L Britton, ibid., p. 3.

34 Frank L Britton, ibid.

committed? Willis Carto seems to have been the only person to have taken up Yockey's cause. Even Ezra Pound, despite his fame and the friendship of leftist literati, was buried away at St Elizabeth's for 13 years. There is no doubt that Yockey had assessed his situation rationally.

The American Jewish Committee, the financial patron of *The Authoritarian Personality*, in its 1955 'yearbook' reported that Mrs Miller was given concurrent suspended sentences and her husband was fined and given a suspended sentence. The Jewish Committee commented that the case had inspired 'anti-Semitic' agitation on 'mental health' programmes as part of a 'Jewish conspiracy' against opponents.[35] The report also discusses opposition to UNESCO, the United Nations Organisation, fluoridation of water, and other often conservative issues as being part of an 'anti-Semitic' agenda.[36]

The predicament of Frederick Seelig is an example of how this pathologising of traditional moral values was used to eliminate dissidents. In the case of Lucille Miller, opposition to the US draft by the Left would normally be heralded as heroic and moral but becomes psychopathic if raised as a 'conservative' issue.

## The Psycho-Hell of Frederick Seelig

At the time when Yockey was being threatened with mental house railroading by the State, long-time journalist Frederick Seelig had discovered a nexus between the Communist Party and homosexual child molesters at State and Federal levels. Seelig had his 11-year-old daughter and 10-year-old son taken from him and handed over to the custody of proven child abusers. He had brought down the ire of the Kennedy Administration for his investigative journalism. His children had been threatened with death should Seelig report what he had found out about corruption in California's social services and he was warned that he would be locked away as criminally insane. During court hearings throughout 1958–1959, Seelig was accused of being 'psychiatrically ill' for opposing the homosexual network in child services. He had shown with medical reports that his children had been abused.

35 George Kellman, *American Jewish Yearbook*, Vol. 56, 'Anti-Jewish Agitation', (American Jewish Committee, 1955), p. 185.

36 George Kellman, ibid., p. 182.

This was happening in the same state and at the same time, indeed the very month, that Yockey was being set up for enforced psychiatric examination.

Seelig, with the help of several other veteran reporters, worked to uncover a subversive network involved with child abuse, some of whose communist connections had been exposed by Senator Joseph McCarthy. This homosexual-communist network had set up a slush fund for political candidates at local and national levels. FBI agents warned Seelig that the information he had put him in danger.[37]

Seelig was arraigned on the pretext of libel. The Justice Department confiscated his files and property worth $60,000. However, instead of being tried for libel, Seelig was confined to a prison hospital in Texas, without a doctor's examination, court hearing or counsel, from December 1960 until November 1962. Seelig had been found by a state medical board to be of sound mind and with a high IQ but the Justice Department refused to allow Seelig's release on bail. It had taken seven separate proceedings to have Seelig committed. Seelig writes: 'Three times I was transported across the country shackled in chains, leg-irons and handcuffs; starved, degraded, demoralised and humiliated. Clothing rotted off my body; maltreatment caused toenails to curl into the flesh. For weeks my toes were caked with blood.'[38]

The Los Angeles sheriff's department stated that it would not release Seelig unless he was arraigned for trial. He was brought before a Los Angeles court not on a charge of libel but to have him committed as insane. He was not permitted his own witnesses nor evidence as to his mental health and was denied the return of confiscated evidence. Thomas Gore was the 'mental health director' for California, whose claims to being a doctor and a psychiatrist were fraudulent and who had himself been diagnosed as insane. Gore had been a loan shark when coming out of an administration role in the Army and had been dismissed from hospital service for mishandling funds and other criminal activities.[39] He had met Seelig once, for an hour, and testified that Seelig had been insane for 'five years' — the period during which he had been

---

37 F Seelig, *Destroy the Accuser*, (Miami: Freedom Press Publishing Co.), pp. 9–11.

38 F Seelig, ibid., p. 12.

39 F Seelig, ibid., p. 66.

investigating corruption.[40] The five-man psychiatric board that had examined Seelig for a month and determined that he was normal was disregarded.

In January 1962 Dr Richard Stamm, senior surgeon with the US Health Service, attempted to have Seelig's sister sign permission for her brother to be given electro-shock treatment, claiming that Seelig was incurably insane and dangerous. Seelig's older son from a prior marriage was threatened with psychiatric incarceration if he persisted into looking into his father's predicament.

Seelig was told that there was 'no escaping the new social order' and that he would never see his children again. Disagreement with this 'new social order' is diagnosed as 'rigidity of mind'.[41] This means that anyone with conservative or 'right-wing' opinions and with moral values that were until recently regarded as 'normal' has symptoms of 'mental illness'. Indeed, the seminal study, *The Authoritarian Personality*, funded by the American Jewish Congress, established an entire school of thought that has remained dominant and basically states: 'Left is normal, Right is sick.'[42]

Seelig's court-appointed Attorney, Gilbert Seton, warned him:

> There will never be a trial or a hearing allowed you on your charges. Nor will you get your property or files back. Refuse to plead guilty and you will be found insane, imprisoned for the rest of your life. You will never see your children again or know what became of them. That attitude will destroy you. You can't fight the new society. After two years, nothing has been gained except your arrest and indictment.[43]

It was with Seelig's refusal to plead guilty for sending 'libellous' materials in the mail that the bogus 'doctor' Gore sat in the corridor of a prison with Seelig for an hour. On that basis he determined that Seelig was insane, regardless of the previous month-long examination by a panel of five to the contrary. Seelig was not permitted by Judge Leon R Yankwich (of Romanian-Jewish descent)

---

40 F Seelig, ibid., p. 12.

41 F Seelig, ibid., p. 23.

42 For an examination of the mentalities of Left-wing luminaries such as Rousseau, Marat, de Sade, Marx, Lenin, Trotsky, Mao, Abbie Hoffmann, Jerry Rubin, Jim Jones, et al, see Bolton, *The Psychotic Left* (London: Black House Publishing, 2013).

43 F Seelig, *Destroy the Accuser*, op. cit., p. 59.

to dismiss his lawyer. Yankwich had a typically antagonistic attitude toward Seelig because he was a conservative, and referred to Seelig as a 'witch-hunter, Red-baiter and lunatic', making comparisons to the late Senator McCarthy.[44] Both Yankwich and Gore had concluded that Seelig was 'insane' on the basis of his opinions. These opinions were formed both by his work as a well-experienced journalist and his own observations of the social services in a custody dispute.

Yockey had faced the same predicament, in the same state, with the same types of threat, during the same era. Yockey appeared before a rabbi, Karesh. Seelig appeared before a Jewish judge, Yankwich, who, like Karesh, cared nothing for the defendant's Constitutional rights, which could be denied by the expedient of 'mental health'. Seelig pointed out that in a 'psychiatric prosecution' the defendant is not allowed his own witnesses, medical experts or evidence. This is what Yockey would have faced. Like Seelig, Yockey would have received nothing but ridicule and degradation — assuming that his plight would even be publicised, as such a hearing is not open to public or media. Indeed, Seelig, a veteran investigative journalist, was given the silent treatment by the Los Angeles press.[45] He was not permitted to contact anyone and his clothes were literally rotting on him after months of confinement in jail cells.

Seelig was taken to the Medical Center for Federal Prisoners at Forth Worth, Texas. He was given sweat-soaked shoes that were too tight for his feet, known as the 'shoe torture.' This was the first part of a routine for his 'psychiatric treatment'.

Seelig states of his time in the Federal 'drain hole' that:

> Prisoners stripped nude in the drain-holes are denied medication for injuries, illness, or infections. In the Kremlin manual it is called "punishment therapy". Cuts and wounds fester until scabs form and harden. The shoe torture was "therapy" for rejecting obedience on prescribed thinking. Nights I often heard the cries and moans of prisoners begging for water. Many times they were not cries but screams from unmerciful beatings. That was more "therapy".[46]

---

44 F Seelig, ibid., p. 61.

45 F Seelig, ibid., p. 74.

46 F Seelig, ibid., p. 24.

> Any prisoner who objects to prison conditions is given "insanity status" and this status is permanently on his record and might be used at any time in his life.[47]

Among the inmates that Seelig met was 80-year-old Richard Pavlic, committed as insane because of his intense dislike of the Kennedys.[48]

Seelig was told by the ward psychiatrist that he was in need of a lot of treatment and he would be put in a ward where the 'animals' were kept — that is, those in a zombified and vegetative state.[49] When four inmates crapped on the floor, squatted in it and ate it, Seelig was forced to mop it up as punishment for not giving the ward guard due respect. Seelig's refusal brought forth a psychiatrist and Seelig was sent to 'building 10', which housed the 'strip nude drain holes and nerve breaking cells'. In the centre of the cell was a stinking drain hole used as a toilet. There was nothing for a bed. The inmates had to lay naked on the cement floor. High-pitched, shrill music was played into the cell day and night. The ward psychiatrist was Dr Charles Keith, notorious for his experiments.[50] 'Therapy beatings' for disobedience were conducted in the showers and included stomping and kicking the inmates. Electric shock 'therapy' was another punishment. Seelig was on three occasions surrounded by staff and doctors and a light focused on his eyes, while they tried to prompt him into saying he 'felt persecuted'. When Seelig commented on the treatment at the institution he was sent to the 'hole' with the diagnosis that his comments were 'insane'.[51] Infected sores on Seelig's feet and legs compelled him to crawl for food like an animal. Judge Yankwich and others actively sought to prevent Seelig from filing affidavits on conditions at the institution and he was not permitted to communicate with attorneys.

Dr Keith told Seelig that he would break his nerves and he was sent to the tiny cells at 10-D. Seelig's oldest son was also threatened that he also would be declared insane and institutionalised if he continued making allegations about his father's situation.

---

47 F Seelig, ibid., p. 23.

48 F Seelig, ibid.

49 F Seelig, ibid., p. 80.

50 F Seelig, ibid., pp. 96–97.

51 F Seelig, ibid., p. 105.

In October 1962, Seelig was transferred to a Los Angeles jail to stand again before Judge Yankwich. A psychiatrist examined him for less than 10 minutes and considered Seelig sane. US Attorney David Smith moved for the dismissal of the libel and other indictments and in less than 10 minutes Seelig was free on $100 bail.[52] In less than 10 minutes — but after nearly two years in a hell-hole — the case was closed. Seelig was suddenly sane and free. It was made clear that Seelig could be recommitted if he ever caused further trouble.

Seelig, over the course of several more years, attempted to raise the issues with the courts but was met with silence. He had the support of Westbrook Pegler, who wrote the introduction to *Destroy the Accuser*, and radio commentator Richard Cotten also attempted to highlight these issues.

In his 'commentary' to Seelig's book, Dr Revilo P Oliver, at the time Classics professor at the University of Illinois, a luminary of the right and an avid promoter of *Imperium*, alluded to a similar case. Fletcher Bartholomew, temporarily working for Radio Free Europe, reported to the CIA, which ran the radio station, that homosexuals were working there. At the time, homosexuals were regarded as security risks. On July 28, 1956, an Army chaplain lured him into an Army hospital, where he was forcibly strapped to a bed and drugged. He was flown back to the USA to be placed in a mental ward. His wife alerted some prominent individuals in Washington and he was released. In late 1958, conservative commentator Fulton Lewis Jr published the incident.[53]

Seelig's book was endorsed by Westbrook Pegler, Congressman William Dorn of South Carolina, Congressman John Dowdy of Texas and Congressman John Rarick of Louisiana. Seelig, as predicted by his tormentors, died of a heart attack because of his ordeals, in September 1967. He did not finish a sequel to *Destroy the Accuser*.

## Eustace Mullins

Mullins was a veteran 'anti-Semite' of a particularly vociferous type. He had an early association with the National Renaissance Party and others such as

52 F Seelig, ibid., p. 123.

53 Revilo P Oliver, 'Commentary', in Seelig, ibid., p. 143.

the National States Rights Party. He worked with many veteran radicals such as National Socialist Matt Koehl, segregationist Admiral John Crommelin and Frederick Weiss. He was under constant FBI surveillance and was regarded with vindictiveness by the FBI because of his criticism of the Bureau's association with Zionists. Mullins was also noted as a confidante of Ezra Pound and was the poet's biographer.[54]

J Edgar Hoover was determined to put Mullins out of circulation and one suggestion was to have him committed to a mental asylum. A year prior to Yockey's capture, A Rosen of the FBI wrote a memorandum on Mullins in which he refers to information obtained by an informant of the Anti-Defamation League given to the FBI Chicago Office. The memo notes that Mullins is alleged to have been associated with the famous case in which a synagogue was bombed in Atlanta, Georgia; that Mullins writes 'extremely vicious anti-Semitic propaganda' and that he has written to and about the FBI in regard to what he considered the Bureau's methods. Rosen then opines: 'Mullins is a warped degenerate and a depraved individual.' Under the sub-heading 'action to be taken', Rosen writes: 'The Chicago Office has been instructed to immediately interview Mullins to demand that he put up or shut up.' This was in regard to accusations involving the FBI. The fact that Rosen referred in that memo to co-operation between the FBI and ADL would tend to confirm that Mullins was correct in his criticisms. Rosen continues:

> Mullins will be forcefully admonished to refrain from making such reckless and baseless charges in the future. Chicago was also instructed to determine whether there is any basis upon which the local authorities could arrange for the commitment of Mullins to an institution.[55]

The last sentence was underlined. A hand-written comment below states: 'We should give this job priority and see that some action is taken.'[56]

***

54 Eustace C Mullins, *This Difficult Individual Ezra Pound* (Hollywood: Angriff Press, 1961).

55 A Rosen to J Edgar Hoover, FBI Office Memorandum: 'Eustace Clarence Mullins Jr, Racial Matters,' June 2, 1959, FBI file no. 62–80382-116.

56 A Rosen to J Edgar Hoover, ibid.

This detour is relevant to Yockey's situation. These actions against American nationalists took place under the same regime in which Yockey was held captive. As these cases show, he had rational reasons for believing he would be institutionalised for the rest of his life, as 'right-wing' opinions were sufficient to have one committed and subjected to the 'therapy' of mind and body-crippling drugs, electrodes, beatings and other hellish 'treatments'. This genius, this philosopher, virtuoso, a person called 'artist' by those who knew him, faced the prospect of being reduced to squatting in his excrement on a concrete floor for the rest of his days, without recourse to legal representation or contact with the outside world. For a man such as Yockey, death was preferable.

DTK states that when he spoke with Yockey's daughter 'Brunni' (Brunhilde), she was staying with her aunt and uncle, the Coynes, both of whom had been so supportive of Yockey. Brunni stated to DTK that 'there was absolutely no doubt that her father would have received a frontal lobotomy and would have been tossed into a mental ward hell-hole for the rest of his life'.[57] The Coynes had been intimately connected with Yockey's arrest and imprisonment and Vinette had visited him in jail. It can be assumed that Brunni was repeating what she had been told by her aunt and uncle.

57 DTK to Bolton, May 29, 2014.

# Martyrdom

> It is therefore not surprising when the materialists persecute, by maligning, by conspiracy of silence, cutting off from access to publicity, or by driving to suicide ... those who think in twentieth century terms and specifically reject the methods and conclusions of nineteenth century materialism.
>
> — Yockey, *Imperium*[1]

Yockey feared being reduced to a vegetative state by the State psychiatric system. He also feared that he would be 'forced to reveal' knowledge 'about people he loved', according to a cellmate.[2] As we have seen, his fear was something more than paranoia. His cleverness in having fooled the psychiatrist in 1943 into believing that he was mentally unstable did not help his case in 1960, although it seems unlikely that it was crucial in the State's determination to railroad Yockey into a mental institution. As stated throughout the FBI files for years, the FBI's primary interest in Yockey was to interview him in regard to his worldwide fascist activities and contacts. That was also a major concern of Yockey's. Moreover, the FBI cryptically alluded in the press to Yockey's capture being a major security issue. The exact nature of this can still only be guessed. His answer was suicide.

An FBI Teletype dated June 17, 1960, from San Francisco, advised J Edgar Hoover that Yockey had been found dead in his jail cell. Yockey's cellmate had tried to awaken Yockey when the coffee wagon was being taken around the

1 Wermod edition, op. cit., p. 48.

2 Dave Braaten, 'Man of Many Names: Nazi Prophet?', *New York Post*, June 19, 1960, FBI file no. 105-8229 — A.

cells[3] at 7:25 a.m.[4] The FBI office advised that Yockey had left a note in pencil and found in a fold of blanket under Yockey's head:

> I shall write no messages which I know will never be delivered, only this which will be. You will never discover who helped me for he is to be found in your multitudinous ranks at least outwardly.[5]

How Yockey obtained cyanide remains another of the great mysteries. However, an unknown person contacted the FBI on June 30, claiming she overheard someone stating he knew the individual who had given Yockey a potassium cyanide pill when Yockey was at court. The woman was of unknown reliability and FBI agent A Rosen commented that often such information comes 'through Ouija boards or other sources which are obviously not reliable'.[6]

Yockey had been given a complete body search after his arrest and all of his belongings had been searched. He was transferred from Oakland Police Department Jail to San Francisco on June 8 and went from the County Jail for hearings to the Commissioner's Office on eight occasions, during which he was interviewed by media, family 'and miscellaneous persons'.[7]

Yockey had prepared two copies of a will and had given them to an inmate at Oakland City Jail, asking that a copy be given to 'any lawyer' and the other to his brother-in-law, Lieutenant Commander Coyne. The inmate had left the copies under a mattress at the jail and had forgotten them. However, when the inmate was moved to another jail, remaining contents were removed and destroyed and here the copies of the will had presumably also been destroyed. Among Yockey's possessions that another inmate, who had witnessed the will, stated had been willed to the Coynes was one of the Boschi painted pins.[8] What happened to this valuable pin does not seem to have been recorded.

3 FBI Teletype, San Francisco to J Edgar Hoover, June 17, 1960; file no. 105–8229 — 3.

4 A Rosen, FBI memorandum, June 25, 1960, 105–8229 — 3.

5 Yockey suicide note, FBI Teletype, San Francisco to J Edgar Hoover, June 17, 1960; file no. 105–8229 — 3. p. 2.

6 A Rosen, FBI memorandum, July 1, 1960; 105–8229 — 3.

7 A Rosen, FBI memorandum, June 25, 1960, p. 2, 105–8229 — 3.

8 FBI report, June 14, 1960, 105–8229 — 3.

It is clear that Yockey was accorded no respect or dignity while in custody, despite the charges being of mere passport fraud. Bail had been set at a preposterous $50,000 and the authorities raised a ludicrous claim that he might bomb synagogues because he is an 'anti-Semite'. Yockey was taunted with the certainty that he would be confined to a lunatic asylum, which would deny him a trial, during which he had entertained thoughts of publicising his views.

Willis Carto, one of the last to talk with Yockey, wrote after his death:

> As Yockey lay on his cot in jail, he must have considered his predicament as objectively as he could. The pattern had now become clear; his fate was planned. No jury trial was to be allowed. He had counted on a jury trial. Instead, he was to be declared insane and indefinitely held. He could expect unending grilling — mental torture and perhaps physical torture too, and finally … a frontal lobotomy, his mind sterilized. Worst of all, he thought, there was the public scorn. For a man like Yockey, ridicule was unbearable.[9]

The prison authorities had been fully appraised of Yockey's intention to commit suicide if he could not escape, the information having been furnished on June 13 in statements from prison inmates Fambrough and Galati, with whom Yockey was planning an escape. James Eagan, Deputy US Marshall; Captain Frank Heugle of San Francisco City Jail; Daniel Quinlin, Captain of Inspectors, San Francisco Police Department; and Lieutenant Donald Scott, General Works Detail, San Francisco Police Department, had all been advised of Yockey's intentions by FBI Special Agent Willard Ruch. The same day, Special Agent Wayne Welch had also advised Assistant US Attorney William Clancy Jr.[10] Hence, the authorities were fully aware that Yockey intended to either escape or to kill himself. The authorities did nothing to thwart that intention. Yockey would be railroaded into an asylum, would commit suicide or would be shot in the course of his escape. Did an obliging Federal agent slip the cyanide pill to Yockey at the Commissioner's court? Certainly, the FBI were most adamant that further investigations into Yockey should not

---

9 Willis Carto, 'ADL Closes its File on Yockey, Creative Genius Driven to Suicide', *Right*, No. 99, August 1960, p. 2

10 FBI report, July 7 p. 50, 105–8229 — 3.

proceed, and FBI memoranda make it clear that the FBI was aggravated that the case was being pursued by the US State Department after Yockey's death.

On being told of her brother's death, Vinette Coyne murmured: 'He felt that he was not going to get a fair trial… and he was right. Now—all that talent and brilliance—*gone*.'[11]

Carto concluded:

> The world already owes a great debt to Francis Parker Yockey. Let his noble life be an example to inspire our own nobility and his tragic death be a rebuke to our own cowardice and guilt. And let his watching spirit witness our perpetual and increased hostility towards the "inner enemy" which, by killing Yockey, gives birth to a brighter fire of self-sacrifice for ourselves.
>
> *Oh God, may his great, troubled soul purged now of the self-assumed burden of responsibility he bore, at last find the peace and rest he never thought of seeking in life.*[12]

The day before Yockey's reported suicide, Assistant US Attorney Clancy commented 'on the evening of June 16, 1960, that he had come into the possession of a "super-secret" file regarding YOCKEY, which was "dynamite"'. The FBI was intending to send two agents to speak with Clancy on this file on the afternoon of June 17.[13] What this 'dynamite' in a 'super-secret' file is does not seem to have been revealed. Yockey died that very night. What was this dynamite that had not already been pursued by the FBI over the course of nearly a decade, in regard to Yockey's fascist connections across the world, or his adept use of passports? Clancy stated that the Yockey case was one of 'national security' which they would continue pursuing and that others might be involved.[14]

---

11 Willis Carto, 'ADL Closes its File on Yockey, Creative Genius Driven to Suicide', *Right*, no. 99, August 1960, p. 2

12 Willis Carto, 'ADL Closes its File on Yockey, Creative Genius Driven to Suicide', *Right*, no. 99, August 1960, p. 2

13 FBI office memorandum, June 19, 1960, FBI file no. SF105–1769.

14 'Yockey's Death Hints Spy Work', *San Francisco Examiner*, June 19, 1960; FBI file no. SF105–1769.

# The Enigma of Alexander Benjamin Scharf

Almost as enigmatic as the secret Yockey file was Yockey's so-called 'friend', Alexander Benjamin Scharf, a Jewish teacher in whose apartment in Oakland, California, Yockey had been staying when he was cornered by the FBI. Questions remain as to why Yockey was staying with Scharf, and of the ex-Auschwitz inmate's own shady life. Scharf skipped town after Yockey's arrest and the FBI sought him for questioning.

Before Yockey's arrest, Scharf had told the two FBI agents that he was Educational Director of Temple Beth Abraham, in Oakland. He claimed that he had met Yockey a year previously in Nevada, where he had been gambling. Scharf, who had a girlfriend working at a casino, had lost his money gambling and Yockey had given him $20 to get him back to Oakland. Since then he had seen Yockey intermittently, claiming to have known him only as 'Hatch'. Yockey had telephoned him on June 4 to ask if he could stay at Scharf's apartment.[1] Scharf had witnessed a false passport application for 'Hatch' under the name 'Michael Joseph Taylor', dated June 26, 1959.[2]

While Scharf was being interviewed, Yockey telephoned him to ask whether his bag had arrived from the airport. Scharf said that it had and Yockey was thereby entrapped.

After the dramatic encounter and capture, the interview with Scharf was resumed. Scharf stated that he was born in Walfratshausen, Bavaria, Germany, on December 12, 1923. When he was nine, the family settled in Argentina and

---

1 FBI report, August 6, 1960, p. 12, 105–8229 — 3.

2 FBI interview report, June 14, 1960, p. 6, 105–8229 — 3.

after the death of his father he settled with his mother in Paraguay. With the death of his mother when he was 15, he moved back to Argentina, then in 1954 he moved to New York. He attended Columbia University and the Jewish Theological Seminary, until June 1957. He then went to France on a scholarship that was supposed to take him to Israel. However, he stayed in Paris instead, then returned to the USA. After working in Alaska, he arrived in San Francisco and became an instructor for the Bureau of Jewish Education.[3] Since August 1959, Scharf had been employed by Temple Beth Abraham, under Rabbi Harold Schulweis, and remained an alien resident.

Scharf was described by an ex-girlfriend, Mrs Ezra Cohen-Sitt, as 'very sad and very serious' and 'distant'. Her husband had been a roommate with Scharf when they worked at Temple Beth Abraham. Mrs Cohen-Sitt said Scharf had 'a deep feeling for Orthodox Jewry' and kept himself 'remote' as a result of his experiences during World War II. Scharf had never mentioned Yockey, Mrs Cohen-Sitt stated.[4]

Assistant US Attorney William P Clancy Jr told the press that Scharf was 'the key man in the case at this point'. What 'case' Clancy meant was presumably Yockey's suicide, although there might have been wider implications that remain hidden. Clancy stated that Scharf had left in such haste after Yockey's arrest that most of his possessions remained in his apartment. 'There are a lot of questions we want to ask Scharf,' Clancy told the press. Scharf had lied when he claimed that he had only known Yockey since June 5—he had known Yockey for more than a year.[5]

After Yockey's death, to the aggravation of the FBI, the press and the US Attorney's Office would not let the matter rest and both insisted on pursuing Alex Scharf. The US Attorney's Office had issued a 'material witness warrant' for his arrest. The FBI declined to get involved further and responded that it was a matter for the US Attorney's Office and the State Department. Scharf was front-page news. The FBI was not interested in pursuing him, however, to the point of refusing to hand the FBI's files on Yockey and Scharf over

3 FBI interview report, June 14, 1960, p. 13, 105–8229—3.

4 'Fascist and Victim, Puzzling Trial of Yockey's Friend', *San Francisco Chronicle*, June 20, 1960.

5 'Fear Blames for Suicide of Mystery Man', *Oakland Tribune*, June 20, 1960.

to Assistant US Attorney Clancy. Assistant US Attorney James Schnake was determined to bring Scharf before a Grand Jury in the hope of uncovering his background[6] and the US Attorney's Office had leaked material to the press, alleging that the files given to the State Department contained 'dynamite'. The FBI virtually threatened Schnake that 'it would be to his peril' should the press receive anything of substance. Schnake had the idea that Scharf was really a 'neo-Nazi' who had been 'flim-flamming' Jews.[7]

On a press enquiry to the Jewish Theological Seminary (JTS), New York, it was found Scharf had also lied about being a graduate, although he had attended Columbia for 'two or three years'. Scharf had applied for a position at the Plantel del Central Israelite de Cuba, a theological school, claiming to be a graduate of the JTS. The application was dated June 21, 1960, meaning that Scharf planned to flee to Cuba.[8]

Indeed, Scharf had fled to Havana and from there sought to sell his story about Yockey to a US newspaper for $800 but feared returning to the USA. The US Attorney's Office intended to have Scharf extradited to charge him with immigration or passport charges.[9] The FBI reported that Scharf was also adept at the use of aliases, including Britt Phillips, David Chappelle and Benjamin Younger.[10] Yet he is also described by those who knew him as 'a decent man', 'scared as a rabbit', always looking over his shoulder, not readily trusting people and difficult to get to know. He went to Reno every three months not because he was a serious gambler but to see his girlfriend, Hildegard King, who said of Scharf that 'he wasn't the type you'd meet today and become buddy-buddy with tomorrow'. He 'would never become friendly with a person until he was sure he could trust them'. She also stated that Scharf often talked of his years at Auschwitz. The *Oakland Tribune* asked: 'Was Yockey one of the people Scharf could trust? Authorities say the

6 W. B. Welte, FBI Airtel, June 20,1960, pp. 1–2; 105–8229—3.

7 J Edgar Hoover, FBI Airtel, June 20,1960, ibid., p. 3.

8 'Benjamin Scharf, Information concerning', FBI New York Office to Los Angeles Office, July 6, 1960, 105–8229—3.

9 FBI Airtel report, August 4, 1960, 105–8229—3.

10 FBI Airtel report, August 5, 1960, 105–8229—3.

Oaklander knew the mystery man under three names: Yockey, Richard Hatch and Michael Taylor. Would this fact encourage trust?'[11]

A sidelight was the departure of William Slomovich, a court reporter from San Jose, and a 'close associate' of Scharf's, who had boarded a ship from New York bound for Haifa, Israel. Assistant US Attorney Clancy had asked State Department representatives to 'be on hand when the ship docks to seek an "interview" with Slomovich.'[12]

From Havana, Scharf said that he 'could and would explain' the 'mystery' of Yockey, 'at the right time'. He did not, however, indicate when the right time was, or when he would return from Cuba.[13] Scharf returned to the USA in August 1960, claiming that he had run in fear after the FBI arrested Yockey, as it had brought back wartime memories. He appeared before a U.S Commissioner on August 22 to answer routine questions and was freed on his own cognizance.[14] Scharf claimed that he was naïve in thinking Yockey was his friend; that Yockey was only using him.[15] He stated that he had only known Yockey as 'Mike Taylor', whom he had met at the dice tables at the Nevada Club in Reno. 'He was a friendly fellow. He loaned me money and we got along well,' Scharf said. Scharf claimed Yockey wanted to set him up in business but he was an educator, not a businessman, and declined. Scharf believed the business offer was intended to provide Yockey with a front, with 'a respectable business address'. He claimed that he had never heard the name Yockey until reading 'newspaper clippings' on Yockey's suicide while in Cuba. Scharf had been impressed by Yockey's intelligence and Yockey would often quote from the Old Testament but referred to himself as a 'pagan'. He claimed that he had been 'terrified' after the FBI had arrested Yockey then brought up

11 'Where is Alex Scharf Hiding? And why did he Vanish?', *Oakland Tribune*, June 26, 1960; FBI file no. SF105–1769.

12 'New Link to Yockey Sought in Israel', *San Francisco News-Call Bulletin*, June 21, 1960, FBI file no. 105–8229 — A.

13 'Yockey's Pal Says He'll Talk — Later', *San Francisco Chronicle*, August 11, 1960, FBI file no. 105–8229 –A.

14 'Scharf's mystery life to get full US Probe', *San Francisco Examiner*, August 23, 1960; FBI file no. SF105–1769.

15 '"Pal" Says Yockey Exploited Him', San Francisco Chronicle, August 23, 1960; FBI file no. SF105–1769.

the canard of standing in line at Auschwitz waiting to be sent to the left or the right and that he feared being 'liquidated' by Yockey's colleagues. He did not know whether Yockey was perhaps a gangster, or a 'communist spy'. He was 'overwhelmed with fear'. He claimed that it was 'an ironic coincidence' that he fled to Cuba, where Yockey had spread 'anti-American propaganda', but he had been offered a job in 1957, saying Hebrew teachers were badly needed there. He had come back to the USA as soon as he had read the accounts of Yockey, to straighten things out, and was incredulous that anyone could believe he was a spy or the knowing associate of a 'Nazi'. He claimed that the Nazis had killed one of his brothers, two of his sisters, his parents and his parents' whole family.[16]

How Scharf's account of his Auschwitz experiences and the lifelong trauma that resulted in his flight squares with his statement to the FBI that he and his mother left Germany in 1933 and settled in South America is perhaps one of those anomalies that often appear in 'Holocaust survivor testimony'. It was also known that Scharf was willing to be guarantor for two of Yockey's fraudulent passport applications and that Scharf himself had several aliases. There was something dubious about Scharf, who gave the outward appearance of being a neurotic Holocaust survivor while using aliases, making false claims about his background and association with Yockey and lying about his educational qualifications to secure positions at Jewish establishments.

Scharf appeared before Commissioner rabbi Karesh and would appear before a Grand Jury to testify about his relationship with Yockey. The theory of Assistant US Attorney James Schnake, who was determined to expose Scharf's background, that he was a 'Nazi' who was 'flim-flamming' Jews seems untenable. Scharf's countenance is distinctly Jewish; additionally, the rewards relative to the efforts of posing as a Jewish scholar seem minimal. However, it is also notable that an Assistant US Attorney Schnake was threatened by the FBI to keep his mouth shut about Scharf.

Scharf flew from Havana to Miami under another assumed name, 'Ronald Davis', posing the question as to why he felt uneasy about Yockey's use of the

---

16 '"Pal" Says Yockey Exploited Him', *San Francisco Chronicle*, August 23, 1960, FBI file no. SF105-1769.

name 'Hatch'. He arrived with only 95 cents and was 'slapped' with a subpoena to appear before Federal Grand Jury.[17]

However, Scharf was actually Benjamin Junger and despite claiming to have been born in Germany he was born in Czechoslovakia.[18] He had claimed that his parents died at Auschwitz but also stated that he had lived with his mother in South America. He had falsely claimed to be a graduate of the Jewish Theological Seminary in securing teaching positions, although he had failed to graduate. He had used a scholarship to stay in France rather than further his education in Israel. He had claimed to have been morally offended by Yockey using pseudonyms but had himself used aliases. A 'close associate' of Scharf's, William Slomovich, a court reporter at San Jose, suddenly took off to Israel.

In 1991, there was a 'Professor Alex Scharf', formerly of Czechoslovakia, who scripted an Auschwitz survivor story, 'The Holocaust: When God Looked Down and Wept'.[19] This Professor Alex Scharf was resident at Lexington, Massachusetts; so is an 'Alex B Scharf'. 'When God Looked Down and Wept', in two videocassettes, is described thus:

> Professor Scharf discusses the ordinary details of his boyhood and youth in Europe, sketching in the historical background of the time. He covers the Holocaust as it unfolds, beginning in the year 1933 when the Nazis came to power and culminating with his miraculous survival at the end of World War II.[20]

It seems likely that Professor Alex Scharf of Lexington is the same as Alex B Scharf of Lexington,[21] who is the same as 'Yockey's Pal', the timid 'Jewish scholar' with several aliases, who never finished Seminary, who claimed to be

---

17 'Yockey's Pal back for Quiz', *San Francisco Examiner*, August 21, 1960; FBI file no. SF105–1769.

18 'Check Swindles by Yockey Hinted', *San Francisco Chronicle*, October 13, 1960, FBI file no. SF105–1769.

19 Alex Scharf, 'The Holocaust, When God Looked Down and Wept', Pentangle Productions, Boston, 1991.

20 http://www.worldcat.org/title/holocaust-when-god-looked-down-and-wept/oclc/25344561?referer=di&ht=edition.

21 'Alex B Scharf', Lexington, MA., http://www.lookupanyone.com/results.php?ReportType=8&qs=MA&qc=Lexington&qf=Alex&qn=Scharf&recordid=06NK3A6MPN3.

born in Germany and to have been born in Czechoslovakia; who claimed to have survived Auschwitz but also migrated with his mother to South America in 1933; whose parents both died at Auschwitz but whose mother took him to Paraguay when he was a lad. No doubt his 'miraculous survival at the end of World War II' was precisely that — 'miraculous'.

The FBI file of the San Francisco office stops at the arraignment of Benjamin Junger/Scharf but proceeds four years later with one small clipping from the column of Herb Caen, mentioning that a private detective, Al Gilstein, 'hired by a private group', 'is almost ready to close in on the man who smuggled in the cyanide' for Yockey.[22] One can confidently assume that this 'private group' that hired Gilstein was the Anti-Defamation League. Gilstein, according to Coogan, was an Israeli war veteran often used by the Israeli Embassy for the security of visiting dignitaries and was closely associated with Mossad.[23] Coogan renders Gilstein as 'H Allen Gilstein' but he was also known as Alain Gilstein, head of 'Gilstein Investigations'.[24] In addition to work for Israel and the ADL, Gilstein was a sponsor of the Chile Emergency Committee, established to protest the coup against the Marxist Allende regime. This communist front included many Jews.[25] Gilstein was not only an 'Israeli war veteran', but he had been a member of the *Irgun* Zionist terror gang fighting the British during 1946 and 1947. When Barclay's Bank of London announced that it would be opening a branch in the USA, Gilstein reportedly quipped that he would open an account for sentimental reasons: 'Barclay's practically financed our operations against the British. We held up one of their branches practically every night!'[26]

What happened to Gilstein's impending identification of the individual who gave Yockey cyanide remains unknown, like much else.

---

22 Herb Caen, *San Francisco Chronicle,* July 21, 1964; FBI file no. SF105–1769.

23 Kevin Coogan, *Dreamer of the Day*, op. it., p. 43.

24 San Francisco Directory, 1969.

25 Chile Emergency Committee, advertisement , *New York Times*, September 23, 1973, p. 9, http://keywiki.org/Chile_Emergency_Committee.

26 Herb Caen, 'New To Me', *Advocate*, Victoria, Texas, April 25, 1965, p. 33.

# FBI and ADL

In 1962, *Imperium* was republished for the first time since Yockey's own Westropa, London, two-volume edition of 1948. Although it is generally thought that the new one-volume edition was first brought out by Noontide Press, veteran nationalist Willis Carto's publishing house, Carto having visited Yockey in jail shortly before his suicide, the edition was in fact published as a cloth-bound single volume by Charles Smith of *Truth Seeker*.

The promotion of the new edition of *Imperium* was accompanied by allegations that Yockey had been a martyr hounded to death by State and Jewish agencies for writing it. This was a theme developed by Carto in his magazine *Right*, in one of the few obituaries on Yockey from the US 'Right'. Carto wrote:

> Frustrated and driven to despair, hounded and persecuted like a wild beast, deserted and ignored by easy-living cowards for whom he had fought so hard, a great creative genius committed suicide in the San Francisco County Jail on Thursday night, June 16. … The man was Francis Parker Yockey. … He was a talented pianist. He was a gifted writer. But most of all, Yockey was a philosopher.[1]

That Carto's obituary for Yockey is entitled 'ADL Closes its File on Yockey' is apt given that several press sources alluded to the ADL commenting on Yockey as 'a leading fascist of the day'.[2] The ADL later stated that Yockey had returned to the USA 'to contact ultra-right-wing and anti-Semitic elements'.[3]

---

1 Willis A Carto, 'ADL Closes its File on Yockey, Creative Genius Driven to Suicide', *Right*, no. 99, August 1960, p. 1.

2 'New Charges Fly in Passport Probe', *San Francisco Examiner*, June 15, 1960, FBI file no 105–8229 — A.

3 'Passport Mystery Man kills Himself', *San Francisco News-Call Bulletin*, June 17, 1960, FBI file no 105–8229 — A.

Carto alludes to Yockey's opposition to the procedures used by the war crimes team at Wiesbaden and the report made on the matter by Chief Justice Jackson, the head of the US prosecuting team against the German political and military leadership, as the start of the interest in Yockey's views and activities:

> This was the turning point in his life, for Jackson immediately reported Yockey's attitude to his superiors. Back in New York's bustling offices of the Anti-Defamation League, a new file was opened. The name on it was, "Yockey, Francis Parker".[4]

Carto wrote that after Yockey's contact with European nationalist groups, he secluded himself at Brittas Bay, Ireland, to write *Imperium* in six months and without references, continuing:

> *Imperium* is a book which will live a thousand years. It is a deeply spiritual study of the organic culture, viewed from the standpoint of Western survival. From the moment of the publication of this book, his doom was sealed. For it must have become apparent to international Jewry at that time that Yockey had to be destroyed and his book suppressed at all costs. The file in the ADL labelled "Yockey" was stamped "Priority".[5]

After a 'disappointing' trip to the US, Yockey returned to Europe in 1951, writing to an American of his lack of confidence in the 'Right' in the USA: 'I can't take it any longer. People are so dumb and our own patriots are so divided and can't grasp the danger we are in.'[6] Carto continued:

> By now the federal agreement had been pressed into the service of the ADL and it began systematic, worldwide persecution of Yockey. This finally became unbearable; Yockey dropped completely out of sight. Back in the US the FBI questioned hundreds of people at a cost of an unknown thousands of dollars. A few people asked the FBI why they were so interested in this anti-communist, whose only crime had been to write a book. The FBI would sometimes answer that Yockey was suspected of heading an "international conspiracy" against the government. This stupid excuse was the best the ADL could devise to justify their inhuman

4 Willis A Carto, 'ADL Closes its File on Yockey…', op. cit.

5 Willis A Carto, ibid.

6 Willis A Carto, ibid.

> treatment of Yockey. In the meantime, Yockey apparently resorted to the use of fake names and passports — anything to escape the mad dogs on his trail.[7]

As several thousand pages of FBI files show, the Bureau was specifically interested in interrogating Yockey in regard to his 'fascist' activities. The passport and visa violations were entirely matters for the US State Department. When Yockey was caught it was the State Department that filed criminal charges, not the FBI, which attempted to keep out of the public spotlight and have the Yockey matter dropped once he was dead. DTK, writing on Alex Scharf and why the FBI was so reluctant, even threatening in regard to the State Department continuing the matter, opines that: 'Once Yockey was "contained" and dead, the US Government probably didn't want to carry things further. J Edgar Hoover had a rule: "Never embarrass the Bureau." Better still, the maxim: "Never embarrass the Jews." A hot potato drops.'[8]

Are these references to FBI connections with the ADL by both Carto and DTK merely a stereotypical example of 'Right-wing paranoia' of the type that supposedly afflicted Yockey himself? Throughout the FBI files on Yockey and others there are frequent anonymous reports and leads provided by 'informants'. Thanks to the Freedom of Information Act, a large corpus of material is now available on the links between the FBI and the ADL that were encouraged by J Edgar Hoover. In 1940, the ADL offered its confidential list of 1,600 operatives to the FBI so that they could be utilised as informants and undercover agents.[9] Although some of the ADL leaders were implicated in illegal Zionist underground activities, from the 1940s on ADL operatives were utilised as FBI informants.[10]

While many FBI agents were circumspect about associating with the ADL, a private Zionist information-gathering apparatus specialising in smearing anyone in the way of their interests, Hoover zealously cultivated a connection with it. In 1951, the US State Department asked the FBI to investigate Arab

7 Willis A Carto, ibid.

8 DTK to Bolton, April 25, 2014.

9 FBI file 1199215-00 — 100-HQ-530 — Sections 1, 2,3.

10 For the links between the FBI and ADL obtained under the Freedom of Information Act see 'The FBI and the Anti-Defamation League', http://www.irmep.org/ila/adl/.

League representatives in New York at the urging of the ADL. This happens to be the time when the FBI started its files on Yockey.

Moreover, ADL operatives were stalking Nationalists and conveying information to the FBI. A 1955 FBI memorandum reports that Chicago ADL operative William Pinsley advised Special Agent Lloyd O Bogstad that Maynard Nelsen of the Realpolitical Institute and William Wernecke[11] of the Nationalist Conservative Party were visiting each other, Nelsen having gone horseback riding at Wernecke's farm. Clearly, the ADL's surveillance was close. 'Wernecke had recently purchased a printing press, which is kept at his residence, and used for both organisations,' the ADL operative advised. 'Pinsley had learned that Nelsen may go to Japan on business for the company he is employed [sic]. Nelsen's wife has recently returned from visiting relatives in Germany.' Pinsley also informed the FBI that Yockey's sister, Vinette Coyne, had moved from California to Massachusetts.[12] (Wernecke had known Yockey's sister Alice during the 1940s, via social contacts with German-American saboteur Hans Haupt).[13]

Pinsley was also keeping a close watch on Eustace Mullins and informed the FBI that Mullins was living at Wernecke's farm and assisting with printing.[14]

The information from ADL operative Pinsley to the FBI on Nelsen, Wernecke, Mullins and Vinette Coyne indicates the character of the ADL's scrutiny of those on its blacklist, including relatives. As we have seen, it was the ADL in Chicago that informed the FBI of the move of Vinette and William Coyne. It seems likely that the ADL, and the Jewish apparatus

---

11 Before the war Wernecke was a member of the German-American Bund, Knights of the White Camelia, etc. FBI office memorandum, September 14, 1955, Lloyd O Bogstad, 'Nationalist Conservative Party, Internal Security—X'.

12 Lloyd O Bogstad, FBI office memorandum, October 17, 1955; Lloyd O Bogstad, 'Nationalist Conservative Party, Internal Security—X'.

13 FBI office memorandum, October 17, 1955; Lloyd O Bogstad, 'Nationalist Conservative Party, Internal Security—X'.

14 FBI office memorandum, December 21, 1955; Lloyd O Bogstad, 'Nationalist Conservative Party, Internal Security—X', Mullins had been a researcher at the Library of Congress, until he was removed through pressure from the arch-Zionist politician and banker, Senator Herbert H Lehman, of Lehman Bros. See FBI memorandum December 27, 1955.

around the world, would have kept better track of Yockey than the FBI, US State Department and Military Intelligence. Was Alex Scharf part of this?

The FBI was now in a flap over advertisements for *Imperium* which alluded to him being hounded by the FBI. 'Discrete' enquiries of those involved with the republication of *Imperium* proceeded. An FBI memorandum notes that an advertisement appeared in *The Nation*, January 19, 1963, stating that *Imperium* was sold by Carto's Noontide Press, Sausalito, California. The FBI notes that the advertisement states: 'As a result of this book, the author was hunted for years by the FBI. He was finally captured and thrown into the San Francisco Jail, where, on June 17, 1960, he committed suicide.' The memo writer, M. A. Jones, comments that the only reference to the Noontide Press the FBI held was as the publisher of the 1962 edition *The First National Directory of Rightist Groups, Publications and Some Individuals in the United States and Some Foreign Countries.* It was noted that many of the organisations listed had been 'subject of Bureau investigations'.[15] Regarding Carto:

> In view of the reference contained in the advertisement to the FBI and the fact that W. A. Carto has prepared an "Introduction" for *Imperium*, it is felt that it would be well to have the San Francisco Office obtain a copy of this book discreetly to determine if there are any references in the introduction to the FBI. Further, it is felt that it would be well to have the San Francisco Office discreetly obtain information regarding Noontide Press.[16]

On the FBI files that Stimely had sent to Gannon, the latter commented: 'The standard of the records is so appalling that I can only wonder at the status of the FBI as a serious security organisation; the style and format is more suitable for a lower school pupil doing a first run on an exercise of little value. […] Much of the information is NOT correct and I do not pretend to conjecture as to the sources.'[17]

---

15 M. A. Jones, FBI memorandum to Mr DeLoach, January 30, 1963, FBI Airtel report, August 5, 1960, 105–8229 — 3.

16 M. A. Jones, FBI memorandum to Mr DeLoach, p. 2.

17 Gannon to Stimely, November 8, 1981.

# Ecce Homo

DTK, who knew some of Yockey's closest friends, such as the Weisses and H Keith Thompson, remembered that Yockey 'loved his children deeply, and when visiting but for a limited time he would spend every available moment playing with them'.[1] His playfulness and affection for children accords with the memories of Anthony Gannon, while Johnny von Pflügl does not recall Yockey having any interaction with his brother or himself when he stayed at the Baroness' home in London. Gannon recalls:

> I would say that Yockey liked children and he had a very happy relationship with my son and daughter, often taking them — and the family dog — for a walk and sometimes being left in charge of them so that my wife and I could have an evening out.

Gannon states that his children considered Yockey 'a sort of 'uncle', amusing, friendly, good for physical games and walks but, most of all, for his 'funny' American way of speaking. For instance, he always called them 'smalls', rather than children, which was unheard of in England.[2]

DTK states of Yockey's appearance:

> This may be a minor point, but two sources suggest that FPY dressed in a rather downscale way. (1) The transcript of an interview of HK Thompson by Keith Stimely has HKT stating that Yockey wore clothing suggesting "Kleins" in NY City, which was a Jew dump with cheap "merch" about one step up from the pushcart. (2) Anthony Gannon remarked that when first meeting him, FPY appeared in a rather casual manner, not well dressed. Hmmmm. I was told by two

1 DTK to Bolton, May 19, 2014.

2 Gannon to Stimely, March 1, 1981.

> sources that Y always considered clothes to be of great importance, and that he bought and wore traditional styles of high quality. Well... time and circumstance dictate these things. On the lam means instability in all matters. … Y must have been a genius at improvisation in all things while on the lam. Napoleon, on the lam, used a flag as a sail.[3]

Gannon confirms certain points made by DTK about Yockey. His memoir of Yockey for Keith Stimely refers to his personal traits:

> In the seven years or so that I worked with Yockey, I came to know him well, as well, I believe, as anyone could know him. He frequently stayed with me in my home for prolonged periods and we did a fair amount of travelling together within Britain. In the process of all this, he met many people in my company. In almost every case, such people were visibly impressed by his intellect and power of expression and, certainly, they had never met anyone like him before. He was a talented pianist who could play the works of Chopin and Liszt in concert hall style and with a fire and expression that was remarkable. Ladies liked Yockey and he liked the ladies; they felt his magnetism and intensity and responded readily to both. Some of the people we met were German-born and with them Yockey would converse in German, without difficulty, most of them congratulating him on his grasp of the language and on his accent.
>
> In spite of first impressions, if Yockey met some people frequently and for long periods, there was always the chance of a quarrel. He did not suffer fools gladly and could become quite insulting and contemptuous to those he believed were being unduly obstinate or slow in conceding a point in dispute. Of course, this kind of behaviour is fatal if one is seeking to make converts and obtain their support. In moments of personal tension, Yockey would often engage others in staring-out contests, prosecuted to the point where the other party should avert his gaze. Such contests could arise anywhere, even on an Underground train with a complete stranger, and Guy Chesham and I often had to intervene and hurry Yockey away before the engagement ended in possible violence.

3 DTK to Bolton, August 13, 2014.

> From all of this, it is plain that one either liked Yockey—with all of his gifts and foibles—or, one did not; there was no halfway house, no one could be, or ever was indifferent to Yockey, and those who met him would never forget him.[4]

Gannon refers to Yockey's appearance at their first meeting:

> In appearance he was somewhat bohemian, wearing a dark green jacket, navy blue roll-top sweater, and corduroy trousers. Some five feet seven inches tall, of slim but wiry build, dark brown hair and eyes, and pale complexion. One noticed those deep-set eyes, and the intensity of their expression combining both intelligence and authority.[5]

Gannon doubted whether he ever saw Yockey in a suit. 'His dress was bohemian and casual. Odd trousers (often corduroy), ex-Army jacket or sports coat, plus a rolled up jersey were his usual uniform. In dress, FPY was the arch anti-type of the Prussian.'[6]

On the other hand, in regard to his attire, in 1960 Yockey, going by the name of Richard Hatch, living with Patricia Jane Lagerstrom at hotels in New Orleans, spending every day in his room typing, was described as a 'very neat dresser and always wore a gray Homburg hat when going outside'.[7]

Yockey followed the nutritional advice of Adelle Davis,[8] an advocate of unprocessed food and vitamin supplements. A bestselling author in her time, with a conventional academic background in science and dietetics, she stated that many social ills are the result of poor nutrition. Gannon states that: 'Yockey had an informed approach to food, vitaminology, etc., BEFORE the Health Food revolution became popular in Europe.' He did not smoke and occasionally took wine with food when it was provided. He had a daily brisk

4 Anthony Gannon, 'Francis Parker Yockey 1916–1960: A Remembrance of the Author of *Imperium*', from the Keith Stimely collection, op. cit.

5 Anthony Gannon, 'Francis Parker Yockey 1916–1960: A Remembrance of the Author of *Imperium*', from the Keith Stimely collection, ibid.

6 Gannon to Stimely, September 7, 1980, Stimely collection.

7 Wayne K Welch, Special Agent, FBI file SF 105–1769, July 7, 1960, p. 56.

8 DTK to Bolton, May 19, 2014.

walking regimen and no chronic ailments 'but he looked a migraine-type, pale and nervy, yet never complained of such an affliction'.[9]

Yockey 'never suffered fools gladly. In fact, he never suffered them, period. Zero tolerance for stupid people of all social strata'. On the other hand, with great powers of persuasion, he could 'introduce himself into just about any situation, roll along, gain confidence of an individual or group, and prevail'.[10] Gannon recalled:

> FPY inspired in most persons he met a feeling of intellectual inferiority, and this did not seem to bother him. In fact, he likes to establish the "relationship" quickly with most people he met, and even indulged in the "hard-staring" technique to underpin his attack. The more vain the person, the more hostile was the counter-reaction to FPY. Those who could not withstand this experience — and see beyond it — were few. For this reason, and many others, FPY proved that he could NEVER be a Leader of a mass-movement or a serious organisational figure. FPY was by nature an artist, a romantic forced by his own mind to play the role of a realist — and failing in the result. He was a thinker and writer and God knows, both to a degree that few could ever equal! Many of the cheap attacks made upon FPY by vertical "comrades" on grounds of race, sexual attitudes et al were made because such persons could not even begin intellectual exchange with FPY. Such conduct is beneath contempt.[11]

Yockey's movements have been described as 'quick and cat-like'. One envisages a grace of movement opposite to that of the jerky or the shambling movements that often mark mental illness. James Madole of the National Renaissance Party, who only knew him as Frank Healy, recalled that 'Yockey could leap from a sofa and be on his feet within a split second'.[12] Whether he undertook this in the Madole apartment is not known. 'His body language indicated that he was always at the ready and had muscle tone that

9 Gannon to Stimely, November 24, 1981.

10 DTK to Bolton, May 19, 2014.

11 Gannon to Stimely, September 7, 1980, Keith Stimely collection.

12 DTK to Bolton, May 19, 2014.

was spring-loaded.'[13] Gannon's recollections concur, describing Yockey as 'of strong, wiry build, tense, staccato, active and quick in movement'.[14]

Maurice Bardèche recalled Yockey as 'a man of striking courage' but 'too bluff and absolute to obtain the cooperation he was seeking at the time'.[15] In his 'Note' on Yockey, Bardèche regarded him as unrealistic in his expectations on the liberation of Europe and not open to compromise. Bardèche also described him as 'a handsome young man'. 'Physically vigorous and well-built with an Anglo-Saxon and not particularly American personality, appearing to have absolutely no sense of humour. Your [Stimely's] questionnaire indicates to me that he was a musician: I would never have suspected that.'[16] His persona in France seems in several major aspects to be totally different to that given to others. Piano playing was one of the great features of his life, for which he was exceptionally gifted, as noted by both Gannon and Arcand. Bardèche quipped that Yockey drank large amounts of coffee and seemed to have a bladder or prostrate problem. However, one gets the impression from the account that Yockey, when visiting Bardèche and arguing with Binet, was unwell, trying to keep warm, perhaps suffering from a chill. His life was one of constant activity; he seems to have lived off nervous energy.

While Bardèche saw Yockey as 'humourless', Gannon saw someone very different:

> Yockey could be, and usually was, a charming companion, with an unsuspected sense of humour and a great gift for mimicking others. W. C. Fields had always been one of his favourites, and Yockey could do a very acceptable imitation of Fields in some of his most famous roles. As a result of this little-known side of his nature, Yockey was always a welcome visitor to our home, and my wife, Marjorie, and children greatly enjoyed his visits and were always sorry when the time came for him to leave.[17]

---

13 DTK to Bolton, May 19, 2014.

14 Gannon to Stimely, September 7, 1980, Stimely collection, op. cit.

15 Bardèche to Stimely, March 9, 1982.

16 Bardèche to Stimely, 'Note sur F. P. Yockey', op. cit., 1982.

17 Anthony Gannon, 'Francis Parker Yockey 1916–1960: A Remembrance of the Author of *Imperium*', op. cit.

Writing to Stimely, Gannon also stated: 'Certainly, he had a great sense of humour, sometimes of the barrack-room American type, sometimes sophisticated. He was often somber, but could also be very entertaining and amusing.'[18] He was also 'likeable and generous, within his enforced limitations, a good comrade and friend'. 'This was not a general reaction, however, and he proved incapable of supporting long term relationships with many — perhaps this is also an aspect of genius, inescapably! He was also fond of the ladies, and treated them rather badly; in this I neither liked his attitude nor condoned it. These aspects, with an uncontrollable impatience when things got rough or difficult, were his faults. There have been others, and worse in the ranks of genius — and the World has, in time, overlooked them.'[19]

When Yockey met Bardèche and Binet, he seems to have been ill. Moreover, the circumstances probably did not call for an impersonation of W. C. Fields.

Bardèche saw in Yockey an English rather than an American character. Perhaps this, and the sensitivity of an artist, accounts for Yockey's taking exception at slights against his character, which he responded to in an Old World manner where honour was foremost. Wolfgang Sarg, one of those willing to place Germany in the service of the USA, was challenged to a duel for his slur on Yockey's 'race', which was a 'stupid attempt at personal slander'. If Sarg would not give satisfaction he would be flogged before witnesses. To Yockey, DNA did not count as much as character and 'vertical race' did not interest him:

> I merely know from your name that your ancestors practiced a particularly loathsome and disgusting trade, and that from your letter you continue in their tradition. I attack you because of your political orientation: I repeat: you are an agent of America-Jewry; you are a miserable spy, a professional liar, a traitor to Europe, a Culturally-retarded idiot, an agent of Culture-distortion, a wretched Michel, a foul conniver, a crooked, effeminate gossip.
>
> Copies of this letter are going to those members of my race who should be warned of your hateful mission and your vile character.

18 Gannon to Stimely, September 7, 1980, op. cit.

19 Gannon to Stimely, July 13, 1980.

> Meantime, swine Wolfgang Coffin, retract all your lies about me and about the Front. I shall be kept informed as to your poisonous letter-writing activities. You have been warned.[20]

On the other hand, Gannon saw certain very American traits in Yockey:

> Yockey had a colorful and highly descriptive vocabulary, and two good examples of how effective this could be is manifested by his terms "ethical-syphilis" and "spiritual-leprosy" to describe the condition of certain Inner Traitors. When he wished to, he could be very North American, with that directness of speech less usual in polite circles in Europe, and most of those he encountered found this very amusing.[21]

Gannon assumed that Yockey was not a platform speaker in England because his speaking style would be ineffectual, writing:

> I have never heard FPY speak in public, but I did hear that in his early days in London he had spoken for UM. He never spoke in public meetings for the ELF, and I do not believe that FPY was gifted as a moving, exciting public speaker and knew it himself. His was flat, staccato in style, and very American.[22]

Conversely, as we have seen, before the war, the youthful Yockey was noted as a speaker by significant American nationalist movements, such as the Silver Legion. Mrs Lois de Lafayette Washburn of the National Liberty Party suggested Yockey for leadership, impressed by his oratory. After the war, he spoke before a large congress of Gerald L. K. Smith's Christian Nationalist party in Saint Louis. It seems most likely that it was because of his 'very American' style that Yockey thought it best to confine his public speaking to the USA, given that the primary aim was to get the American monkey off Europe's back. As a highly capable lawyer, one suspects that Yockey's public speaking style was very persuasive.

One American trait Yockey did not possess was an interest in cars. Gannon commented: 'One final observation. Most Americans can drive a motor car,

---

20 Yockey to Sarg, 1953, op. cit.

21 Anthony Gannon, 'Francis Parker Yockey 1916–1960: A Remembrance of the Author of *Imperium*', op. cit.

22 Gannon to Stimely, September 7, 1980.

and I always had a motor car, but FPY never showed any inclination to drive, or to refer to driving.'[23] It seems plausible that this was at least partly because of the automobile accident Yockey had as a youth, which damaged the nerves in a hand and destroyed his opportunities to be a concert pianist.

The question of whether Yockey was bisexual has been raised, not least by Keith Stimely, who was homosexual and asked H Keith Thompson, who had the same proclivities. He also asked Gannon.[24] Additionally, the FBI at the time constantly spread rumours about 'sexual deviance', particular targets being the longtime conspiratologist and Ezra Pound confidante Eustace Mullins and the elderly, wealthy Jewish convert to Catholicism, Benjamin H Freedman, a patron of the National Renaissance Party and *Common Sense*. Thompson rejected any such suggestions to Stimely.[25] Gannon states:

> Yockey was NOT homosexual. He lived with my family for long periods, and I am quite sure that if any such propensities had existed, these would have been apparent to myself, my wife, and even to my children. I would say that Yockey had a dual attitude to homosexuals, public and private; his public position would have been one of disapproval, for the usual reasons that such persons can become security risks, and engage in seduction and corruption of others to the general detriment; his private position would have been one of tolerance, so long as the fore-stated situations did not arise, this being the expression of his *civilis* approach to the problems of others. I have heard Yockey joke in the crudest American terms about homosexuals in general…[26]

When Gannon raised the question with Elsa Dewette 'her laughter at this suggestion was long, loud and entirely healthy': 'As Y was the only man she ever loved, and has ever remained true to in total terms since their meeting, I think she is a good judge of the subject.'[27]

Gannon felt that Yockey was inclined to 'use women' and was not faithful to any of them: 'I cannot explain his attitude to women, of which he knew that I disapproved, but it could be likened to that of a sailor who felt the need for a

---

23 Gannon to Stimely, ibid.

24 Stimely to Gannon, 'Questions on Francis Parker Yockey', #4, n.d.

25 Thompson interview with Stimely, op. cit.

26 Gannon to Stimely, September 7, 1980, op. cit.

27 Gannon to Stimely, March 1, 1981.

girl in every port.'[28] What seems to emerge is a persona conflicted by an urge for a family and love of his children, with an overriding sense of supra-personal duty that meant no stable family attachments were possible. His great love was Elsa Darciel/Dewette. Gannon, who knew her, stated that Yockey was the only man by which she ever wanted children. Yockey 'wished to father a family' with Darciel 'but under conditions which she was wise enough to reject at her age and in her position of great insecurity'.[29]

Dewette was offended by Gannon's depiction of Yockey's relations with women, commenting that his judgements were the product of what he had described to her as having been 'all his life a stern, rigidly practicing Catholic', although 'extremely honest'. Dewette insisted that Yockey did not treat women 'rather badly': 'I knew exactly what Francis' attitude towards women was and how he had treated some of them and why. (He even wrote a text about it). He was certainly no angel, but he was also certainly not like other men … To portray him like a third-rate little Don Juan and a Bluebeard! … Poor F! What a way to strut down the path of history!' She thinks also that Yockey's manner in England was something of a pose in regard to his shabby dress, coarse language and bragging of female conquests. She stated that he was not a 'He figure' type. 'To a sharp observer, he might have been in rags, but still always looked aristocratic!'[30]

## Catholic

When Yockey stayed with Adrian Arcand, the Canadian fascist leader reminisced a decade later that this man who 'certainly was (as he boasted) *un grand artiste* at making mashed potatoes, as he taught my wife when he was here', also had the blueprint for the victory of the West. Arcand remarked: 'How he could play a Bach prelude on my miserable piano is beyond words!' Arcand, whose politics were motivated by his Catholicism, saw Yockey not only as 'a hero in the true sense of the word, but also a saint'. While staying with the Arcands at the little village of Lanorai, he accompanied Arcand to Mass

28 Gannon to Stimely, September 7, 1980, ibid.

29 Gannon to Stimely, February 15, 1981, Stimely collection.

30 Dewette to Stimely, January 1981, quoted by Stimely to Gannon, November 17, 1981.

and to Arcand, 'he made very intimate religious confidences' which Arcand never revealed. He wrote of their meeting: 'His "appearance" in my life was a most potent injection of Hope for the future. My wife considered him a "man perfect" and was most perturbed at the news of his "disappearance".'[31] Yockey had said to Arcand that 'the West would be CAPITAL ZERO without what Christianity gave it'. He added in regard to Yockey's religiosity:

> I have had day-long talks with Yockey, a Catholic as I am—and who insisted on attending Mass in my parish church pew—and he confided many profound views which he could not write about because they were controversial (for the average) and were not of the political domain.[32]

Gannon, also a Catholic, confirms that Yockey maintained at least a high regard for Catholicism and even what seems to be a belief:

> He was a religious man, born, raised, and educated in a strong Roman Catholic environment, an expert in Scholastic Philosophy but, at the same time, not a practicing Catholic by observance. Nevertheless, he always spoke of Holy Mother (sic) with respect, and never sought to hide his origins in this respect, nor to underestimate the influence they had brought to bear in the making of his character. One could describe Yockey as a Gothic Catholic, a term he accepted to describe himself and others of like opinion. Some who knew him a little dispute this contention, and usually cite Yockey's admiration of Nietzsche's writings in support of this. I concede this admiration on Yockey's part, but do not change my position, having known many others who could—without too much intellectual indigestion—accept the same stance as did Yockey.
>
> In support of my contention, I quote Yockey on racial decadence: "The message of Hollywood is the *total* significance of sexual love as an end in itself — the erotic without consequence. The sexual love of two grains of sand, two rootless individuals, not the primeval sexual love looking to the continuity of Life, the family of many children… The instinct of decadence takes many forms in this realm; dissolution of Marriage by divorce laws, attempts to discard, through repeal or non-enforcement, the laws against abortion, preaching in the form of novel, drama, journalism, the identification of 'happiness' with sexual love, holding it up as *the* great value before which all honor, duty, patriotism, consecration

31 Arcand to H Keith Thompson, July 16, 1961.

32 Arcand, ibid.

> of Life to a higher aim, must give way." I doubt if any member of the Curia could have put it better![33]

Gannon, a Catholic, educated by the Brothers of St Francis Xavier and of the Jesuits, was taught how to think critically and 'emerged as a Catholic fascist'. Figures such as Hitler, Goebbels and Mussolini remained fundamentally Catholic, 'for better or for worse'. Fascism was most successful in nations that were Catholic and in Protestant Germany's case, the center of the NSDAP was Catholic Bavaria. Gannon states that he often discussed such Catholic issues with Yockey 'without much discord, if any'. Gannon sates that he never heard Yockey speak with disrespect of the Catholic faith, 'which, for FPY, was something of a record — for he had little respect for most things established!' and again, Gannon states that Yockey 'designated himself as a Gothic Catholic'. Gannon also surmises that the reason for the special bond between Yockey and Elsa Darciel was that they shared Catholicism, 'which gave their relationship a special quality'.[34]

> Thus, in my experience, FPY was a deeply religious man, at heart, and the contradictions in his lifestyle were just a part of his tortured soul's agony, its sorrow and tragedy. Why did he attach the name "St Ignatius" to his most trusted and valued friend in America?[35] Why did he often assume the name "Torquemada"[36] when writing anonymously? That is something which comes back to me now, and of which I have not spoken before to you. Of course, his attitude to Torquemada was NOT that of Protestant vilifiers masquerading as historians.[37]

Yockey had stated in *Imperium* and *The Proclamation* that Gothic Christianity had been the Faith and the unifying factor of the West during its Spring epoch. He termed himself a 'pagan', believing in 'many gods', according to his

---

33 Anthony Gannon, 'Francis Parker Yockey 1916–1960: A Remembrance of the Author of *Imperium*', op. cit.

34 Gannon to Stimely, February 15, 1981, Stimely collection.

35 St Ignatius Loyola was founder of the Jesuit Order. The identity of Yockey's most trusted American friend, whom he nicknamed St Ignatius, remains unknown.

36 The Grand Inquisitor of the Inquisition who sought to purge the Church of bogus Jewish converts to Catholicism (the *Marranos*) in Spain, who continued to secretly practise Judaism.

37 Gannon to Stimely, February 15, 1981, ibid.

Jewish associate Scharf.[38] Perhaps this was one of Yockey's infamous wind-up lines for the benefit of his Orthodox Jewish companion, intended as an affront to Scharf's religious sensibilities? Among the notes of random thoughts Yockey typed up are references to the new religion of the resurgent West being *skepsis*. However, he was clear that this is not the anti-religious scepticism of the rationalists and materialists; to the contrary, it is skepticism towards those doctrines that insisted they had all the answers to life through scientism, by weighing and measuring everything until metaphysics no longer exists.

DTK states:

> I had heard from a person lately close to Y that Y had the amazing ability to "compartmentalize" his life. Had I mentioned this before? He could close off one "room" and step into another room, scenario, relationship, antic, adventure with aplomb. So could Wagner.[39]

We are here dealing with artistic genius. Such compartmentalism explains why Yockey could appear 'humourless' to those who did not know him well, such as Bardèche, while being recalled by Gannon as witty, with a particular appreciation for W. C. Fields; depressed and ill to some, vibrant and optimistic to others; aloof and quickly irritating to some, able to fit into any social situation to others. It explains how a man who wrote of coming 'total wars' yet apologised to an FBI agent for slamming his hand in a door. Yockey had a multi-faceted character but without displaying the characteristics of a fragmented personality. Compartmentalisation can be a defence mechanism of dissociation but it is also a coping mechanism for the creative to provide efficient organisation to a life that would otherwise become contradictory and frenetic.[40]

## Artist

To Gannon, Yockey was firstly an 'artist' and Arcand made a similar comment. Yockey's ability as a pianist is also recalled by Gannon:

---

38 '"Pal" Says Yockey Exploited Him', *San Francisco Chronicle*, August 23, 1960, op. cit. For Yockey's posthumous influence on Norse neo-paganism see below.

39 DTK to Bolton, July 24, 2014.

40 See Ryan Blair, '5 Steps of Compartmentalization: The Secret Behind Successful Entrepreneurs', *Forbes*, June 26, 2012, http://www.forbes.com/sites/ryanblair/2012/06/26/5-steps-of-compartmentalization/.

> FPY was a wonderful pianist, excelling in Chopin, Lizst and Beethoven. I never saw him play by manuscript, then neither do the great concert pianists. His playing was accepted as brilliant by all who heard him, and all were moved by it. Here, again, the Artist rather than the Politician. One could be both, agreed, but FPY was the former, not the latter.[41]

We might see Yockey's temperament as being that of an 'artist', which included a sensitivity to slights from what he would have regarded as his inferiors. Yockey wrote of Sarg being incapable of comprehending his ideas and therefore 'besmirching anything superior'. Additionally, Sarg had 'insulted' Yockey's race, having called him 'small, dark, of unknown mixed races...'. Yockey responded: 'My height is that of Adolf Hitler, my complexion is white, my race is exclusively European.' What Yockey demanded was that his honour be satisfied, in the 'Old World' manner that shows Yockey's temperament to be more aristocrat than lawyer, writing: 'For this stupid attempt at a personal slander, you will give me satisfaction if I am ever in your vicinity. If you refuse out of cowardice, I shall flog you before witnesses.'[42] This was not idle talk, threats at a safe distance. Yockey concluded his mortal life for the sake of honour. Of Yockey's use of words, Gannon wrote:

> He regarded terminology as of tremendous importance in the arsenal of those fighting to liberate Europe, and devised a most effective system of his own. His designation of America and Russia as the Extra-European forces occupying Europe—the Outer-Enemies using their Inner-Traitor puppet-regimes to administer Europe under such as "Governor" Churchill, "Governor" Adenauer, "Governor" Spaak, "Governor" De Gasperi, etc. The people of the *real* America were governed by Culture Aliens/Culture Parasites (the Jew, a surviving remnant from the Arabian Culture) posing as an "American" government and creating conditions of Culture-Pathology/Culture Distortion. Readers of *Imperium* will discover a host of other examples of Yockey's terminology—all highly effective in pinpointing the Enemies of Europe and their "Michel" agents of control and division. I commend this terminology to those fighting for the liberation of Europe.[43]

---

41 Gannon to Stimely, September 7, 1980, op. cit.

42 Yockey to Sarg, op. cit., 1953.

43 Gannon memoir op. cit.

Yockey was a devotee of Shakespeare. In writing of Elsa Dewette's relationship with Yockey, he states that 'as a token of her exceptional relationship with Y she holds his beloved copy of Shakespeare, well-thumbed, read and re-read, cherished almost beyond any other item of property: I know of Y's attachment to this volume and would not have believed that he would ever have parted with it to anyone'. Gannon further stated that while Yockey did not have a library on tour, 'I never saw him without his Shakespeare and Spengler collection'.[44]

Gannon concluded his memoir of Yockey:

> Apart from the jealousy and enmity which Yockey's intellectual brilliance evoked in others, there were those who went even further and sought to betray him to his pursuers. Ever since his angry farewell to Mr Justice Jackson and the American "war crimes" industry Yockey had been a marked man. The FBI were always interested in his movements and sought to entrap him. That is why he trusted so few people, never announced his travel plans until the last moment, and never stayed too long in one place. In this respect, I have had the opportunity to read the FBI material on Yockey, which has been declassified and is available for public scrutiny under the American freedom of information legislation. Much of it is quite comical in retrospect, both in the views ascribed to Yockey and the nature of his activities, and he must have had a great time "pulling-the-leg" of the FBI agent on his trail. The FBI material also reveals the approach made to the FBI by one of Yockey's former supporters in England, seeking to collaborate with them in the frustration of his activity. I found this treachery nauseating on the part of one who should have known better, and never would have been suspected of being so base.
>
> I last saw Yockey in the summer of 1954, having told him that I intended to move to South America in the October of that year, where I had a business interest and many personal and political contacts. He was very upset by my news, and warned me that I was entering one of the graveyard areas of former European colonial activity. It never crossed my mind that I would never see Yockey again, and I heard nothing more from him, or of him, until I learned of his death in the late summer of 1960.

44 Gannon to Stimely, March 1, 1981.

> Francis Parker Yockey died in a prison cell in the San Francisco Jail on the night of June 16, 1960, in mysterious circumstances. Suicide is alleged, but I am not convinced of it. Yockey had been detained in Oakland, California on June 6 and charged with having three passports in his possession. Bail was set at 50,000 dollars by Judge Joseph Karesh (an ordained rabbi), whereas the usual sum on such a charge is 5,000 dollars. It was suggested that Yockey needed a "mental examination" and the San Francisco official of the Anti-Defamation League publicly accused Yockey of being a top fascist, pro-Russian, and anti-American. There is a great deal more to be said of Yockey's capture by the FBI, his imprisonment and death, but I will say nothing further here.[45]

What Gannon had in mind in his final remark on Yockey's death will probably never be known, as he does not appear to have elaborated elsewhere. In a quip to Stimely, Gannon remarked of Yockey being found dead in his cell, in bed, with his sheet pulled up to his face, wearing his underwear and boots: 'You know, I just cannot stop laughing at the idea of FPY dying in his boots and his underwear! It may be irreverent and I do not mean to be, but he was a bohemian to the last!'[46]

Gannon recalls: 'FPY was a strange man [...] he was also a genius, which made things more complicated; add to this sincerity and dedication to the Idea [...]' Gannon states that Yockey would not have sought martyrdom but he was often 'needlessly aggressive and troublesome, even to the point of making loud, provocative remarks upon the London Underground when we travelled together'. Describing another odd foible, he said he would 'fix people with a penetrating stare until they either dropped their gaze or commented upon his behaviour, or he would engage them in argument and rapidly reduce them to pulp by virtue of his own brilliance'. He added: 'These were perversions on his part, and I often told him so. However, he never did this to me, and I came to accept that in this sort of thing he was a little childish, not to say eccentric. [...] Still, you must understand that FPY was not a crackpot, in spite of his tiresome enfant terrible displays on occasion. He could also be charming, witty, do impersonations, and when he played the piano...!'[47]

---

45 Gannon memoir, op. cit.

46 Gannon to Stimely, September 7, 1980, op. cit.

47 Gannon to Stimely, February 15, 1981.

On first encounters, most were 'charmed and greatly impressed' by Yockey. 'On further encounters he would do his *infant terrible* act for reasons of pure devilment with the result that he was shown the door by those too superficial to appreciate his enormous potential and true nature.'[48]

When Gannon writes of one of Yockey's former comrades treacherously seeking to collaborate with the FBI, he is referring to Peter J Huxley-Blythe, who had gone over to the Natinform organisation of Wolfgang Sarg and A. F. X. Baron at any early stage. However, Huxley-Blythe did not give the FBI anything other than what they already had in his attempt to find out what they had on Yockey.

Huxley-Blythe had written to the 'Press Officer' of the FBI more than a year after Yockey's death describing himself as 'a journalist interested in political affairs'. He referred to reports at the time of Yockey's arrest stating that Yockey had been of interest to the State Department and the Justice Department, citing a government spokesman that 'this was definitely a security matter'. As an anti-communist who had established a reputation as author of *The East Came West*,[49] Huxley-Blythe's main interest at this time seems to have been the rumour that Yockey was a Soviet agent. He recounted information to the FBI that they had received long ago, apparently originating with Huxley-Blythe himself. It is here that the allegation, repeated by Wolfgang Sarg and Baron in their Natinform smear against Yockey, that he and Guy Chesham advocated collaboration with the Soviet military seems to have originated. At any rate, Huxley-Blythe recited the claims that Sarg had circulated against Yockey in the Natinform memo. In fact, Huxley-Blythe was merely quoting the Natinform memo verbatim. He stated that he was seeking information from the FBI because he believed Yockey was about to be promoted as a martyr in the USA and he wanted to expose his background, stating: 'It is rumoured in Europe, and in the United States, that Yockey visited the Soviet Union in the mid-1950s and I wonder if you would care to comment on this? I would also be extremely grateful if you would comment on the points I have taken from

48 Gannon to Stimely, December 27, 1985.

49 Peter J Huxley-Blythe, *The East Came West*.

my file on Yockey and whether behind Yockey's arrest both the FBI and State knew Yockey was working for the USSR?'[50]

Gannon regarded the Huxley-Blythe material given to the FBI as rubbish, along with much of the other material in FBI files. He wondered whether Huxley-Blythe had naively fed nonsense to the FBI — indeed, as we have seen, material that the FBI long held — to gain the Bureau's confidence. Gannon, as 'Frontleader' of the ELF in England, had appointed Huxley-Bythe as *Frontfighter* editor. Yockey was not involved in such matters and Gannon doubts whether Huxley-Blythe had met Yockey more than once; he probably had never met Guy Chesham. He also doubts whether there was any meeting at which Guy Chesham advocated collaboration with the USSR in opposing US occupation in Europe.[51]

Hoover replied to Huxley-Blythe that information is only provided to government departments.[52] An addendum to the Hoover letter mentioned Huxley-Blythe was associated with *The Northland*, published by the North League (sic). It is another example of FBI sloppiness. The actual names were *The Northlander* and the Northern League, promoting pan-Nordic unity.[53] The

50 Peter J Huxley-Blythe to FBI, October 2, 1961, FBI file 105–8229-288.

51 Gannon to Stimely, November 8, 1981.

52 Hoover to Huxley-Blythe, ibid., October 12, 1961.

53 Appended to Hoover letter, ibid. *The Northlander* was established in Britain in 1958 as a 'pan-Nordic cultural association'. The first issue referred to Negro troops having been brought to Germany by the USA and Moorish troops by France during the post-war Occupation as a deliberate policy, the result being rampages of rape and a large number of children fathered by them. *The Northlander*, Vol. 1, No. 1, April 1958, p. 1. *The Northlander* was edited by Roger Pearson, then in India, who became an eminent physical anthropologist. Huxley-Blythe incorporated his anti-communist newsletter, *World Review*, with *The Northlander*. *The Northlander*, Vol. 1, No. 3, June 1958, p. 1. Colin Jordan, later Arnold Leese's heir as the leader of British Hitlerism, affiliated his White Defence League with the Northern League as did John Bean with his National Labour Party (later British National Party, one of the major constituents of the National Front when formed in 1967). *The Northlander*, Vol. 1, No. 8, January–February 1959, p. 4. In 1959 Charles Smith of *The Truth Seeker*, who several years later was to publish *Imperium*, was billed as a speaker for Northern League conferences in Britain and Germany in July–August 1959 Willis Carto at the time was an organiser for the Northern League in California. *The Northlander*, Vol. 2, No. 3, June–July 1959, p. 2.

Northern League parted from Yockey in major ways: they were devoted to a biological, Darwinian basis of 'race' and specifically to the unity of the Nordic race, although League supporters Carto and Charles Smith in the USA would be instrumental in promoting *Imperium* several years hence. Intriguingly, with Huxley-Blythe as editor of *The Northlander* in 1958, one detects a hint of Yockeyan influence, with the lead article on 'cultural decay' referring to 'Hollywood culture destroyers' and the 'cultural leadership' of Britain being subverted by 'aliens'.[54] It seems that Huxley-Blythe, like Mosleyite philosopher Alexander Raven Thomson, despite their disagreements with Yockey (in both instances over the Russian question among others), did not repudiate the value of Yockey's Cultural Vitalism.

---

54 Huxley-Blythe, 'Cultural Decay Spreads: Entertainment Media Heavily Infected', *The Northlander*, Vol. 1, No. 7, November–December 1958, p. 1.

# Resurrection

## The World in Flames

In 1960, Thompson had collaborated with Yockey on what would be the latter's final essay, as Yockey was to die in a prison cell in San Francisco that year after finally being caught by the FBI. 'The World in Flames: An Estimate of the World Situation' analysed the Cold War era and the role of the 'Third World'. The original Yockey title was 'An Estimate of the World Situation'. It was Thompson who gave the MS the 'lurid title intended as an eye-catcher', 'The World in Flames'.[1] Thompson commented that he had persuaded Yockey to add commentary on the 'neutralist regimes as well as Nasser to enforce the point' that the world is turning against the USA. The essay appeared posthumously in 1961, Thompson having seen 'that work through from his [Yockey's] rough manuscript to the printed production'.[2] Gannon heard of Yockey's death from Peter Huxley-Blythe, who gave him a copy of 'The World in Flames' and perceptively commented several decades later that he found the essay 'rather strange reading in parts, as if added to by another'.[3]

While Gannon's suspicions were correct, he had not heard anything of Yockey for a decade and remained disinclined to believe that Yockey could have been associated with the Soviet bloc, and would not have known that Yockey had worked with the Egyptian government. Gannon regarded Huxley-Blythe as 'an excellent chap', although 'a little theatrical'. He told Gannon that the FBI, CIA and British Intelligence had been trying to 'intercept' Yockey

---

1 Thompson to Timothy FitzGerald, March 7, 2000.

2 Thompson to Bolton, April 16, 1995.

3 Gannon to Stimely, September 7, 1980, op. cit.

for years. Huxley-Blythe told Gannon that these agencies believed Yockey to have 'been in and out of Cuba, and that he was being financed by the Kremlin via Castro'.

> I rejected such accusations then, and I have never had any reason to reconsider the matter since. [...] Peter was also giving me the impression that he was being constantly pestered by the British security people about FPY, and sounded rather conspiratorial to the point where, if I had been impressed — which I wasn't — he seemed to be inviting me to cross-examine him. He claimed that FPY had ample funds available when he died, and that these were very likely from behind the [Iron] Curtain. Further, he asked if I had received any of these monies! At which I laughed so derisively that he changed the subject.[4]

Perhaps it was in an effort to distract attention from himself that Huxley-Blythe had written to the FBI shortly after Yockey's death? An attempt to provide redundant and inaccurate information on Yockey from the old Natinform memo in exchange for information from the FBI, while alluding to his credentials as an anti-communist researcher and writer? Yet Gannon also thought it strange that he had never been questioned, despite his well-known public association with Yockey. Perhaps the answer lies in ineptitude, or even in whether Soviet moles in the higher echelons of MI5 at the time ensured a hands-off or blind-eye attitude?

In 1961, Thompson wrote to General Friedrich Foertsch, who had been appointed Commander of the Bundeswehr. The letter, in German, was in response to a widely publicised press release from the Embassy of the USSR in Washington, condemning Foertsch as 'the former Hitler general and war criminal'. As a commander at the siege of Leningrad, after the war Foertsch had been sentenced to 25 years' internment by the Soviets but had been released in 1955. Given the Soviet government's allegation that he had presided over the murder of Russian POWs and committed 'capital crimes', one might wonder whether the Soviet treatment of German 'war criminals' was more lenient than that of the West? The Soviet statement, originating with Soviet Deputy Minister of Foreign Affairs V. S. Semyonov, condemned the German Federal Government for appointing 'German war criminals' who

---

4 Gannon to Stimely, September 7, 1980, ibid.

had undertaken actions in the USSR as a 'direct unfriendly act towards the Soviet Union' and other victims of German aggression.[5]

The USSR sought to embarrass the Bonn regime by highlighting any Hitler-era official who was appointed to a position of influence under the Federal government, attempting to indicate the resurgence of groups such as the Socialist Reich Party and even to promote anti-Semitic incidents in the West,[6] thus giving the impression of a revival of Nazism in Germany and the role of the USSR as the only bulwark against new Prussian aggression. Sections of the German Right did not mind playing their part in the Soviet strategy. The German Democratic Republic (DDR) did not have any scruples, under Stalin's direct prompting, in appointing Hitler-era officials to the highest positions in the DDR, nor in reconstituting a nationalist political party that served a prominent role in DDR administrations.[7]

In writing to Foertsch, Thompson condemned the 'spirit of July 20th' (a reference to the abortive coup against Hitler, scotched by Otto Remer) prevalent in the German Federal military. He mentioned to Foertsch the 'imperative' need to organise groups in the army that can maintain an independent attitude toward 'world developments and to act accordingly'. Thompson was presumably advocating clandestine preparations in the military for mounting a coup in the case of an emergency. Thompson mentioned to Foertsch the 'ineptitude' of US espionage that had 'been placed in the hands of leftist stargazers whom even the Russians regard as ridiculous'. He stated that 'these people have the power and the stupidity to start a war' but not the military and scientific knowhow to win one. 'The days of the uninvited American meddler are about over.' Thompson asked whether the power vacuum would be filled by the Russians, the Afro-Asians or if there were still representatives of the 'Prussian spirit' that could assume the role?[8]

Madole put Yockey's final ideas on the 'estimate of the world-situation' on to the street. Always sympathetic to Nasser's Egypt and Arab causes, he went

---

5 Press release, no. 85, April 10, 1961, Embassy of the USSR, Washington DC.

6 See *The Anti-Semitic and Nazi Incidents*, from 25 December 1950 until 28 January 1960, White Paper of the Government of the Federal Republic of Germany (Bonn, 1960).

7 K. R. Bolton, 'Stalin's German-nationalist party', Inconvenient History,

8 Thompson to Foertsch, May 10, 1961.

further with his support for Fidel Castro's Cuba, holding a Cuban-American Friendship Rally on March 11, 1961. The American Jewish Committee Institute of Human Relations noted that 'Madole is now espousing Fidel Castro'. Madole saw the vilification of both Nasser and Castro as coming from the Zionist-controlled news media, which would 'turn the peoples of the Middle East and Latin American into bitter foes of the United States'. 'We urge our Cuban and Arab friends to join with members of the National Renaissance Party in a mass unity rally to oppose this Zionist-sponsored campaign of hate.'[9]

## Re-Publication of *Imperium*

Gannon recalled Yockey's attitude toward the impact of *Imperium*:

> FPY KNEW that FEW people would READ *Imperium* — even FEWER really FEEL it — but contented himself with the belief that of the Few who did READ and FEEL it, just a FEW of these would be enough to transmit his message and situation-estimation to the Culture-bearing stratum in whose hands the future of the Western Imperium would rest. Notice I say FEEL rather than UNDERSTAND or COMPREHEND. FPY had a greater regard for INSTINCTIVE acceptance than for mere intellectual comprehension [...] FPY was RIGHT in his own intention and estimation, was witness to your own involvement and that of other members of the FEW throughout the Western Imperium: We all FELT *Imperium*, as well as experiencing the more usual reactions to it of those of lesser metal.[10]

The first American edition of *Imperium* was published by Charles Smith, who combined atheism with racialism and was equally well-known for both. The involvement of Smith of *Truth Seeker* and an organisation with the unlikely name National Liberal League was duly noted by the FBI, after an advertisement for *Imperium* was anonymously sent in with ordering details to be directed to Smith. *Truth Seeker* was the USA's most notable atheist publication.

---

9 Cited by the FBI, 'James H Madole, Correlation Summary', Main File No. 105–52256, January 31, 1964, p. 44.

10 Gannon to Stimely, February 15, 1981, Stimely collection, op. cit.

Smith had long been closely associated with James H Madole and other 'racists', including Roger Pearson's Northern League and *Northern World* in Britain. In 1959 Smith lectured before the Northern League in England and Scotland and proceeded to the League's 'Teutoberger Moot' celebration in Germany.[11] He hosted meetings at the *Truth Seeker* office under the name of the 'New York Racist Forum', where Madole and others spoke. An FBI memorandum mentions that Smith was a 'notorious anti-Semite'.[12] A Bureau report noted in 1957 that Madole had long adopted an anti-Christian position and had increasingly come under the influence of Smith, 'who is presently on an all-out campaign against equality and [is] spreading anti-Semitism'.[13]

Hence, *Truth Seeker* published the first edition of *Imperium* since 1948 as a hardcover edition with Carto writing the introduction. In regard to claims that most of the introduction was written by Dr Revilo P Oliver, Mrs Elizabeth Carto relates:

> I was there when my husband wrote the introduction. We were living in San Francisco near our office. My husband worked at the introduction diligently; he was on a mission you might say. He literally worked day and night on it. I went with him to New York to meet with Charles Smith, who was quite a character. My husband still thinks fondly of him. Willis then arranged for Mr Smith to publish the book.[14]

The reference to Oliver and Smith as the primary writers of the 'Introduction' to *Imperium* is found in the last lines:

> And lastly — now you must accept this is my word and question me no further — it is most strange that two men — neither of whom can bring themselves to believe in either "Destiny" nor "Eternal Justice" — that these two heathens and bitter realists — these two rationalists, if you will — were the only ones with faith

---

11 *The Northlander*, Vol. 2, No. 3, June–July 1959.

12 'Attacks Against the FBI', March 14, 1963, p. 2, 105–8229 — 3.

13 'James H Madole, Internal Security, Egypt, Registration Act', FBI NY 105–6129, December 27, 1957, p. 4.

14 Elizabeth Carto to Bolton, June 4, 2014.

> enough to take it upon themselves to see to it that *Imperium* is not forgotten but is made available for you, dear reader.[15]

Mrs Carto states:

> As to your understanding that the Intro to IMP. was written by three people, perhaps you have never seen the original one. Willis Carto wrote it and referred at the end that two people made the publication possible without giving names. One was Charles Smith who published it and the other one a good friend who financed it, A. T. Swisher. Both long-dead. This must have been the misunderstanding you had.[16]

It is notable that Mrs Carto does not mention Oliver as being the second person involved but A. T. Swisher, who does not seem to have been known to Coogan, Stimely or other researchers of Yockey.

Willis Carto wrote to Oliver's literary executor, Kevin Alfred Strom, in this regard:

> I appreciate this opportunity to clarify the misunderstanding that I did not personally write the Introduction to IMPERIUM in 1960 and that I forged my name, the real author being the late Dr Revilo P Oliver.
>
> I have great respect for the memory and the work of Dr Oliver but in 1960 I believe I knew him only by reputation. I doubt if Revilo knew Yockey even by reputation then and am even more sure that Yockey did not know him. I strongly believe that Revilo was not in San Francisco when Yockey was captured, and am positive that he did not visit him in jail, as I did.
>
> The confusion may have something to do with the article Revilo wrote for THE AMERICAN MERCURY June 1966 issue. I enclose a copy which, as you see, could have been used as an introduction to IMPERIUM.

---

15 'Introduction', *Imperium* (1969), xxliii.

16 Elizabeth Carto to Bolton, August 21, 2014. 'The misunderstanding was not mine, but a belief among many students of Yockey that Smith and Oliver had written most of the introduction.'

> Anything you can do to straighten out the situation will be appreciated.[17]

However, Oliver had written to Keith Stimely in 1984:

> You have asked me a direct question, and I shall answer it in strict confidence for the reason that I shall state. When Carto thought of having *Imperium* reprinted—and the idea was entirely his and he deserves great credit for it—I wrote a lengthy and signed memorandum on Yockey's importance as a philosopher of history and a nationalist, hoping to enlist the support of persons who would subsidise a new edition of *Imperium*. Charles Smith later told me that the memorandum convinced him of the need for such an edition, which, as you know, was published by the *Truth Seeker*. The memorandum does reappear as a large part of the present introduction, but must not be identified as mine, because at the time I felt that I was so prominently associated with the Birch Society that if I wrote an introduction to the published volume it would be assumed that the Society was sponsoring Yockey, and that would have been distinctly disadvantageous to the Society. I accordingly told Carto to make whatever use he wished of what I had written for an introduction by him or anyone he chose to introduce the new edition. I therefore gave him the material, and it would be dishonourable of me to try to reclaim it. [...] I must therefore disavow the authorship of any part of the introduction, and the fact that Carto now has fits when he hears my name[18] does not alter the fact that I am obligated morally to disavow the connection.[19]

What seems plausible, stylistically and philosophically, is that Carto wrote the first biographical half of the 'Introduction' and Oliver wrote the second half, commenting on the Yockeyan doctrine of Culture-pathology.

Carto's recollections of his prison meeting with Yockey begins the 'Introduction':

> Dimly, I could make out the form of this man—this strange and lonely man—through the thick wire netting. Inwardly I cursed these heavy screens that prevented our confrontation. For even though our mutual host was the San

17 Willis Carto to Strom, March 10, 2005, http://www.revilo-oliver.com/news/1962/01/introduction-to-imperium/.

18 The feeling was at least mutual, as Oliver habitually referred to Carto as 'Wiley Willy', just as he referred to John Birch Society founder Robert Welch as 'The Welcher'.

19 Oliver to Stimely, January 17, 1984; http://www.revilo-oliver.com/news/1962/01/introduction-to-imperium/.

> Francisco City Jail, and even though the man upon whom I was calling was locked in equality with petty thieves and criminals, I knew I was in the presence of a great force, and I could feel History standing aside me.[20]

The day previously, Carto had read the headlines in the San Francisco newspapers. He then wrote the words that were to become bylines for the advertising of *Imperium*: 'I know now that the only real crime of Francis Parker Yockey was to write a book, and for this he had to die.'[21]

The *Truth Seeker* edition had a plain brown paper dust cover with simple black type. That edition was followed by Carto's Noontide Press edition in 1962. The cover design that readers of *Imperium* became familiar with over several decades, the red, white and black imperial background with sword, was designed by Hugo Fonck.[22]

In 1964, Yockey's first wife, Alice M Yockey, contacted Noontide Press in regard to royalty payments from the sale of *Imperium* for her daughters. She refers to the aid given by Yockey's sister, Vinette Coyne, in the publication. Mrs Yockey wrote:

> I am sure you are aware that Mr Yockey has two daughters, Isolde and Brunhilde, who are now nineteen and eighteen years old respectively. I am writing on their behalf to ask what arrangements have been made in regard to the rights of my former husband's children to receive royalties which may accrue from the sale of the book.[23]

The letter from Mrs Yockey did not reach Carto until May 1965. He replied with publishing history of *Imperium*:

> The first American printing was done by the *Truth Seeker* company at New York, and consisted, if I recall right, of 2,000 copies, and sold for $5 retail. The second was published by Noontide Press and is still in print. We have been unable to get any worthwhile book reviews at all except in the John Birch Society's *American*

20 Willis A Carto, 'Introduction', *Imperium* (Sausalito, California: The Noontide Press, 1969), ix. This 1969 edition was the first paperback edition, the other American editions having been published in 1962 and 1963.

21 Willis A Carto, 'Introduction', *Imperium*, 1969, x.

22 DTK to Bolton, July 24, 2014.

23 Alice M Yockey to Jason Matthews, January 31, 1964.

> *Opinion* magazine, and this was accomplished only by some diligent efforts. It resulted in only a few sales. All sales have been made due to direct mail advertising and advertising and review in the new magazine, *Western Destiny*, published by Noontide. There is no hope for any surplus until some outside reviews are made, or until the book becomes controversial — something which those who control such things do not seem likely to allow. So, at this time at least, the whole matter of royalties is only of academic interest. Vinette has received none; in fact she helped underwrite the first printing, as did some of my friends.[24]

Other than from a monetary viewpoint, *Imperium* had, however, made 'notable effect upon the thinking of a great many people, and we have put forth the new magazine [*Western Destiny*] on the philosophical basis of the book'.[25]

Alice Yockey had another try for Isolde and Brunhilde — who had since changed her name to Fredericka — four years later, having heard that a new paperback edition of *Imperium* had been published.[26]

Carto, in his reply, referred to the two hardback editions by *Truth Seeker* and Noontide, having been printed in 5,000 copies. He stated that *Imperium* 'started to catch on'. A paperback edition was necessary when the National Youth Alliance was established and 25,000 copies were printed. Carto stated that after two months on the market, about 3,500 had been sold. The printing costs ran to $16,000, funded with a loan obtained by Carto, and the book was selling for $2.50. Once costs had been met, the plan was to turn copyright over to the National Youth Alliance,[27] which of course did not happen due to the disputes that soon ensued. Carto closed with a pitch for the NYA, hoping to recruit Isolde (whom he had met) and Brunhilde/Fredericka.[28]

Smith's publication of the first edition of *Imperium* since the Westropa edition drew him to the attention of the FBI. Advertisements for *Imperium* appeared in *The Nation* and other mainstream journals, naming Smith as the distributor. The main concern seems to have been that the advertisement mentions the FBI as having hounded Yockey. The FBI noted that Smith was

---

24 Carto to Alice M Yockey, May 21, 1965.

25 Carto to Alice M Yockey, ibid.

26 Alice M Yockey to Carto, July 8, 1969.

27 Carto to Alice M Yockey, July 19, 1969.

28 Carto to Alice M Yockey, ibid.

president of the Truth Seeker National Liberal League and editor of *Truth Seeker* magazine. He had been charged with disorderly conduct in Newburgh, New York, on August 4, 1961 for distributing 'hate literature', accompanied by the shouting of slogans. Smith was noted as a 'notorious anti-Semite' and *Truth Seeker* as including anti-Semitic and anti-Negro material.[29]

Something of Charles Smith's racial doctrine can be deduced from a 1965 article written by him and republished as a leaflet by the NRP. Smith introduced a critique of Christianity and the churches into the issue of opposing the Rumford Act, which prohibited racial discrimination in the sale or renting of houses and apartments in California. Smith contended that the 'social program' of the National Council of Churches and the Communist Party were the same. It was an observation common among conservatives and rightists of all shades at the time that wherever the World Council of Churches operated, it guaranteed to support any anti-White cause going.[30] What was different about Smith's position was that he was not only against the liberals in the churches but, like Nietzsche, he saw Christianity *per se* as at fault. He regarded Christian support for racial integration as doctrinally the same as the communist theory of 'Lysenkoism', which claims people can be permanently modified intellectually and culturally by changing their environment. The result was proliferation of low-grade people, particularly Negro welfarites. 'Christian preachers and communist agents' were inducing a guilt complex in whites for the slave trade but civilised countries do not support 'hereditary guilt'.[31] Madole added to the leaflet an advertisement for *Imperium*, subheaded 'Who are the Culture Distorters?' Paradoxically, at the same time the Smith leaflet was being distributed by the NRP, Madole was issuing a leaflet aimed at creating a 'Christian Youth Corps', appealing to White Christian youths as the only potential saviours of the USA against 'Satan's children', the Jews.[32]

29 FBI SAC New York 66-7398, 'Attacks Against FBI', March 14, 1963.

30 See for example Henry R Pike, *Religion Red and Rotten* (Johannesburg: The Christian Mission to Europe, 1974); Pike, *Why?* (Johannesburg: Christian Mission to the Communist World, 1975).

31 Charles Smith, 'Christian Preachers and Communist Agents Oppose the Repeal of the Rumford Act', NRP, New York, 1965.

32 'Christian Youth Corps', NRP, New York, 1965.

The NRP was always full of paradoxes or contradictions. Madole appealed to Christian whites, yet was a card-carrying member of the Church of Satan and the *NR Bulletin* sold LaVey's *Satanic Bible* and books on witchcraft. Madole praised Castro as a nationalist while also aligning with the anti-Castro, pro-Fascist 'Cuban Commandos'. The NRP picketed the US Friends of the Soviet Union, although Madole had long accepted the Weiss-Yockey-*Common Sense* contention that the USSR had purged herself of Jewish rule.

In 1965, Madole revised the NRP programme, making Yockeyan influences more visible than hitherto. Jews are described as 'an alien virus within our national blood stream' who must be purged from 'cultural, economic and political life'.[33] This is suggestive of the concept of Culture-pathology and the nation state as an organism. In particular, the foreign policy included: 'Unity of all European peoples, including the Slavic elements of the Soviet Union, within the framework of a united Europe to act as a mighty bulwark against the colored hordes of Asia.'[34] Madole envisaged the USSR becoming conscious of its existence as a white nation vis-à-vis Asia, and we might conclude in particular China, with which the Russians were then engaged in armed conflict over disputed border areas.[35]

There were also individuals promoting *Imperium* on their own initiative. The FBI noted an Illinois attorney, Oscar Wyclif Harmal, as having sent out mimeographed circulars promoting *Imperium* as being available from Carto's magazine *Western Destiny*. In commemoration of Yockey's death, Harmal dated his flyer June 17, 1965, writing:

> Five years ago Francis Parker Yockey was murdered by the Marxist enemies of our country and the distorters of our Western Civilization. This brilliant philosopher gave the answer to the case of his murder "My Enemies Have Evaluated Me Better Than My Friends".

---

33 James H Madole, *NRP Program*, New York, 1965, 'Racial Program', point 3.

34 Ibid., 'Foreign Policy', point 2.

35 See K. R. Bolton, *Geopolitics of the Indo-Pacific* (London: Black House Publishing, 2013) for a history on the enmity between Russia and China, and scenarios for future conflicts despite the present pragmatic rapport.

Having served in the armed Services of our country during the Second World War (to make the world safe for communism, distortion and destruction of the culture of the West) Mr Yockey was with the "War Crimes Tribunal". He agreed with the late Senator Taft that the lynching bee at Nuernberg was serving the interests and "was meant to serve the interests of international communism". A few sane men like Yockey, Senator Taft and the one honest judge who was taken in custody and sent home prevented a false finding by our Marxist lynchers that the West (the Germans) were guilty of the Katyn Massacre of over 100,000 leaders of Poland.

Yockey knew that murder and assassination such as that used at Nuemberg, and on our late President, require a high level policy decision of the distorters (not Mr Warren's "right wingers")[36] and that the distorters' criteria for such a murder is (1) it must be highly effective, and (2) must serve as some sort of an example.

In his book *Imperium* which the distorters have been able to burn and ban from our shelves, he proceeded to expand on Spengler's method of showing the behavior of a cultural organism, as a spiritual force. He showed up the hypocrisy of the culture distorters who have such tremendous race pride and nationalism, but have been able to make race pride and nationalism a cardinal sin and taboo for the peoples of the West. He exposed the criminal propaganda of those who would unite Europe in one money economy but destroy it as a "people, race, nation, state, society" with a will to live, as such, and resist the distorters whether form Asia, or existing in our own territory as parasites. He exposed the inorganic thinking of the distorters who would destroy our High culture by dealing with it as an inorganic problem. Spengler, the pessimist, believed that our world cities of London, New York and Berlin would disappear under jungle vegetation as did the Sumerian and other High Culture cities. Yockey exposed the capitalistic mentality (engaged in competition to get rich) who would picture the spirit of the West as an animal world.[37] The time is past when men will die to help the distorters "improve the world". Sane men will only die in order to "be themselves" and not to follow the dictates of the Marxist hired men, who cannot understand the Spirit of the West and who win by inciting class hate as though it were the inevitable instinct of man. Their cult of co-existence and brotherhoods

---

36 A reference to Supreme Court Justice Earl Warren's implicating the 'Right' in the assassination of President John F Kennedy.

37 Yockey, like Nietzsche, contended that Darwinism was used to reduce man to the animal level, as did Freudianism and Marxism. See Yockey, *Imperium*,

of man has convinced the hired men of the West that hate has been eliminated from all human activities and that we must surrender our Western civilization to the distorter, the Marxist and the barbarian of the East. On the other hand, the distorter lives on hate and uses communism as an Eastern barbarian weapon of foreign policy. Marxism has been able to prove that hate is effective as a political weapon to create losing wars, between the estates of the West.

*Imperium* exposes the Marxist Old Testament ideas that work is a curse laid upon men as a sin, all of which is contrary to the belief of the High Culture of the West that "to work is to pray". Our distorters can only win by convincing the world that work is to be despised and that the masses, if they can control them, should steal the products of those who work. Communists, their hired men and distorters, cannot understand anyone who sees otherwise. They cannot understand work, labor, achievement, accomplishment, greatness and a high culture destiny for the human race, never having experienced any of these fine emotions. This explains their criminal Freudian attempts to animalize, sexualize, mechanize and destroy the great men and the Spirit of Western High Culture. *Imperium* exposes the internationalist of the 30s and 40s who in the name of a crusade for humanity and democracy as an ally of Russia shared and still share the occupation of Europe.

Contrary to Spengler, Yockey was an optimist.[38] He believed that the High culture of the West will unite. That occupied Europe, the suits of the High Culture of the West, will drive out the occupation forces, the Asiatic horde and the hired men from Colonial America.[39]

Attorney Harmal's 'memorial' to Yockey and sales pitch for *Imperium* is an interesting example of how Yockeyanism, despite the depth of the philosophy,

38 Yockey in fact rejected notions of 'pessimism' applied to Spengler, as to Spengler in regard it his critics. Both stated that it was not a matter of 'pessimism' or 'optimism' but a matter of destiny—that like any organism, a culture lives and dies, and by the organic laws of history, none are eternal. See Yockey, *Imperium* (Wermod ed.) pp. 95–110. For Nietzsche as a critique of Darwinism, see Bolton, "Nietzsche Contra Darwin" in T Southgate (ed.) Nietzsche: Thoughts & Perspectives Vol. 3 (London: Black Front Press, 2011).

39 Oscar Wyclif Harmal, 'Memorial to Francis Parker Yockey', Chicago Illinois, June 17, 1965, FBI file, 105-8229—3.

was amenable to being presented concisely and to appealing to some of the major preoccupations of the time among the American 'Right'.

In 1966, syndicated columnist Drew Pearson, a well-known muckraker, wrote another of his sensationalistic exposes of the American 'Right', focusing on Carto and a newly formed Francis Parker Yockey Movement. His column had 'penetrated the Mafia-like secrecy of a sinister, neo-Nazi movement that seeks to overthrow the US government'. This was Carto's Liberty Lobby, which Pearson stated had expended a budget of $850,000 a year to influence Capitol Hill, 'publishes one of America's famous old magazines' (*American Mercury*), 'controls a dozen front organizations' and in 1968 handed out $90,000 to candidates for Congress. Pearson claimed that Carto furnished speeches and research for a dozen Congressmen and had the entire Southern delegation 'eating out of his hand', including Strom Thurmond; while others were 'patsies', such as Rep. Otto Passman and Rep. John Rarick[40] — although given Rarick's uncompromising Nationalism, including his spirited condemnation of the Anti-Defamation League in Congress, it is more likely he consciously endorsed the work of Liberty Lobby. Others, such as Congressman James Utt, had accepted Liberty Lobby awards. Pearson stated that it is doubtful any knew of Carto's 'neo-Nazi' background.

Specifically, Carto's most singular thought-crime was his publication of *Imperium* and his promotion of a new Yockeyan group, The Francis Parker Yockey Movement, which planned, on April 20, to celebrate Hitler's birthday and sing the old songs. Pearson warned that these were not unformed 'misfits' but 'lawyers, writers and businessmen form America's upper middle class' who had organized into 'secret cells' where they were only known by code names.[41]

What Pearson did not mention was that he himself and a gaggle of other muckraking 'champions of democracy' in the press, posing as crusaders for the 'common man', were hack writers for the Central Intelligence Agency, as part of a CIA project to manipulate the news media, called Operation Mockingbird. Perhaps their proudest moment was when these hack writers

40 Drew Pearson, 'Thriving Neo-Nazi Group Seeks Overthrow of US', Los Angeles Times, April 8, 1969.

41 Drew Pearson, 'Thriving Neo-Nazi Group...'

were unleashed upon Senator Joseph R McCarthy, whose investigations into communist subversion were starting to get close to Establishment-controlled Leftists, including CIA operatives.[42] So far from all being 'Soviet agents', much of the Left was manipulated and funded by the CIA as part of a counter-offensive against the USSR. McCarthy was about to go after top CIA operatives such as Cord Meyer, in the naïve belief that he was just exposing Soviet agents. Of this CIA-managed coterie in the press, John Simpkin writes, naming Drew Pearson among other notable pressmen:

> Wisner [head of Operation Mockingbird] unleashed Mockingbird on McCarthy. Drew Pearson, Joe Alsop, Jack Anderson, Walter Lippmann and Ed Murrow all went into attack mode and McCarthy was permanently damaged by the press coverage orchestrated by Wisner.[43]

## German Edition

An abridged German translation of *Imperium* was made during 1973 and 1974 by a South Africa resident, Mrs Ursula von Gordon. She read *Imperium* in 1972 and contacted Noontide Press for translation rights and authorisation to have the work published in Germany. Mrs von Gordon stated that she believed 'Yockey is the only writer who ... fully grasps the meaning of the present world-situation'.[44] The reply came from David McCalden, an Anglo-Irishman working for The Noontide Press, granting Mrs von Gordon permission.[45]

An abridged translation was undertaken on the advice of Germans publishers, also suggesting, for marketing reasons, that another title be used, with *Imperium* as a subtitle.[46] Von Gordon worked diligently on the translation at an isolated farm, using a 'very old' Langenscheidts dictionary. The translation was in longhand, then typed on an antiquated portable typewriter. DTK

42 K. R. Bolton, 'Joe McCarthy's Real Enemies', *The Occidental Quarterly*, Winter 2010–2011, Vol. 10, No. 4; online: http://www.toqonline.com/archive/2010-2/winter-10-11/.

43 John Simpkin, 'Operation Mockingbird', *The Journal of History*, Vol. 9, No. 1, Spring, 2009, http://www.truedemocracy.net/hj31/38.html.

44 Ursula von Gordon to The Noontide Press, April 2, 1972; Stimely collection.

45 Lewis Brandon to von Gordon, May 22, 1972.

46 Von Gordon to Brandon, August 8, 1972.

writes that von Gordon did this work 'with absolute dedication and with an obsession to be precise'.[47]

In late 1973 or early 1974, von Gordon had found a publisher, Dr Herbert Grabert. He published *Imperium* in 1976 under the title *Das Abendland zwischen Untergang und Neubeginn* ('Chaos or Imperium? The Occident Between Downfall and Rebirth'), under the name Yockey rather than Varange, as volume 8 of the Publications of the Institute of Postwar History.[48] However, von Gordon was upset with the publisher's changing some of the translation, 'especially some parts that were dear and important' to her. 'There was a disastrous mistake in the first edition that was a bitter pill for her to swallow'.[49]

DTK states that Mrs von Gordon had undertaken this great task of translation because of her 'immense admiration and respect for Yockey'. 'It fascinated her that an American could think so "European". She saw *Imperium* as one of the most important books of modern times.'[50]

Grabert had an interesting background. Born in 1901, he had fought with distinction in the *Freikorps*, who battled the communists in chaos-racked post-World War I Germany. During the Weimar era, having gained a doctorate, he was involved in theological and psychological issues. However, Grabert was an opponent of National Socialism, seeing it as ethnically divisive for Germany and un-Christian. This changed with Grabert's prominent role in the German Faith Movement, a pro-National Socialist movement that aimed to weld Christianity into an especially Germanic creed, founded in 1934. He then rejected Christianity as intrinsically Jewish and concluded that National Socialism as a civic religion was sufficient to fulfil all religions within Germany. In 1939, he joined the NSDAP and was an official in Alfred Rosenberg's Reich Ministry for the Occupied Eastern Territories. Subjected to 'denazification' proceedings, he was barred from teaching, and decided to focus on publishing. In 1950, he founded an association to campaign

47 DTK to Bolton, February 6, 2015.

48 Yockey, Francis Parker. *Chaos or Imperium? The Occident Between Downfall and Rebirth*. Publications of the Institute of Postwar History, Vol. 8, ed. (Tübingen: Grabert-Verlag), 1976.

49 DTK to Bolton, February 6, 2015.

50 DTK to Bolton, February 6, 2015.

for the reinstatement of teachers who had been subjected to 'denazification'. In 1953, Grabert established a revisionist publication, *Der Deutschen Hochschullehrer-Zeitung*, defending Hitler-era teachers, which became the Grabert-Verlag in 1973.[51] Among the revisionist titles that Grabert published, in 1961, one of the most successful was a German edition of Professor David L Hoggan's *The Forced War*,[52] based on his 1948 Harvard doctoral dissertation, 'The Breakdown of German-Polish Relations in 1939'. In 1960, Grabert was sentenced to probation for writing in 1955 *Volk ohne Führung*. During the Third Reich, he had written titles such as: *The Protestant Mission of the German People: Broad German religious History from Luther to Hauer* (1936); *Crisis and Task of the Nationalist Faith* (1937); *The Nationalist Task of Religious Studies. One Objective* (1938), and *The Faith of the German Peasantry* (1939). Grabert-Verlag continues and was recently described by the Office for State Protection Baden-Württemberg as 'one the most important independent extreme right-wing publishing houses in Germany'.[53] The present head of Grabert-Verlag, Wigberg Grabert, grandson of the founder, continues to be harassed and prosecuted by the German authorities and was even sentenced to eight months' jail in 2009 for 'sedition'.[54]

In 1977, *Imperium* received a notable review in *Das Ostpreussenblatt*. This was a self-styled 'Prussian conservative' weekly newspaper founded in 1950, directed toward post-war expellees from central and Eastern Europe. To broaden its appeal it was renamed *Preußische Allgemeine Zeitung* in 2003.[55] The review was by Paul Brock (1900–1986), born in Memel, who had become a noted novelist in 1937 with the publication of *Der Strom fließt*. With a long experience in seafaring, Brock served in the navy during World War II and also worked as a speaker and writer for the Reich Propaganda Ministry. In

51 For a general but critical report on Grabert see 'Blick nach rechts: Der Grabert-Verlag im Vortrags-Visier', *Tagblatt*, 29. April 2010.

52 David L Hoggan, *The Forced War: When Peaceful Revision Failed* (Costa Mesa, California: Institute for Historical Review, 1989).

53 Office for State Protection Baden-Württemberg, *Constitutional Protection Report 2011*.

54 'Landgericht macht Tübinger Rechtsaußen-Verleger für zwei Hetz-Artikel verantwortlich', *Schwäbisches Tagblatt*, December 23 2009.

55 *Preußische Allgemeine Zeitung*, http://www.preussische-allgemeine.de/.

1944, he received the Johann Gottfried von Herder Prize from the University of Königsberg for *The Wait for the Morning* (1939). He was an early contributor to *Das Ostpreussenblatt* and remained an honoured writer after the war. His review of *Imperium* is significant:

> Will it ever happen that the countries of Western Europe will join together to form a state, Europe, with a central government chosen by the people of those countries, that is, join together in a manner representing something more than the utilitarian purpose of an economic community and that they will do this with all the consequences that would flow from such an act? If so, it would constitute the saving of a West now in the process of decline. In the opinion of those cultured Westerners with awareness and insight, there is no surpassing the reality of this question.[56]

Brock, as part of the West's culture-bearing stratum, considers the question of a united Europe as being in the forefront of the thinking of this stratum. This is moreover the very stratum to which *Imperium* is addressed, and its members recognised Yockey primarily as a fellow 'artist'. Brock also mentions the realisation among this stratum that the Common Market, as the European Union was once called, was not the united Europe of their vision but a 'utilitarian' entity based on trade. Economics and trade as the foundations of such a union does not 'save' a culture from decline; it accelerates the process of what Spengler called the triumph of money in the closing stages of a civilization. The West of Spengler, Yockey and Brock subordinates economics to politics; hence Spengler's 'Prussian socialism' and Yockey's 'ethical socialism'. Brock sought the origins of a united Europe in Napoleon's vision:

> This question is not new. Napoleon concerned himself with the necessity of such a fusion. There is a saying attributed to him: "I know of two nations, the occident and the orient." After he had fallen from power and looked back he sought to justify his thoughts and plans: "I wanted to prepare the merging of the major interests of Europe just as I had achieved the merging of all parties. The passing resentment of the peoples concerned me but little for I knew that the final outcome would without fail bring them around to me. In this manner Europe would have

---

56 Peter Brock, 'Stirbt das Abendland? Mysteriöser Tod eines jungen Autors nach Kritik an Amerika', *Das Ostpreussenblatt*, February 5, 1977, No., 6, p. 14. ('Is the West Dying? Mysterious Death of a young Author following his Critique of America').

> truly become a united nation and everyone no matter wherever he happened to be would have been in his own country. Sooner or later the facts will force this merger; the impulse was given and now after I have been overthrown and my system no longer exists the arrangement in Europe will come about through the consolidation of the great nations."
>
> Here Napoleon is holding himself out as a prophet. Meanwhile, more than a century-and-a-half have passed and two fearful wars have almost changed fundamentally the point of departure aimed at a definitive solution to this problem. Serious scholars doubt that a Europe as patterned by Napoleon will ever come into being. Every program, no matter how well and intelligently it may have been thought out, shatters on the general sense of helplessness.[57]

The aim of a truly European nation had been militarily defeated twice. Perhaps just as bad, the imperative of European unity has been taken over by the West's inner and outer enemies and its life-course redirected by Culture-retardation on a mass scale, in the service of both Culture-distortion and parasitism — that is to say, in the service of money. Brock commended *Imperium* as the answer of the culture-bearing stratum to the Western malady:

> What is to be done or what can be done? This twofold question has been taken up by a young American, Francis Parker Yockey, in a book that recently appeared in German. (The English-American edition has already gone through several printings.) In his book he comes to the alternative *Chaos or Imperium* which is at the same time the title of this book.[58]

Brock proceeds with a commentary on Spengler. This is of particular interest insofar as the opinion of a German cultural figure who had lived through Spengler's own era and into our time offers a more useful insight than some of the criticisms of *The Decline of the West* that continue even among advanced elements of the 'Right':

> In the presentation of his ideas which are partly cultural-philosophic and partly historical in nature, he refers frequently to another, older work which appeared shortly after the First World War, a book which at the time of its appearance

57 Peter Brock, ibid.

58 Peter Brock, ibid.

> attracted attention and aroused anxiety but which soon fell into the background and finally in view of the more current problems became all but forgotten — the book: Oswald Spengler's *Decline of The West.*
>
> For a better understanding of our later presentation it might be helpful to know something of Spengler's view regarding the course of history and of the phenomenon that accompanies it.
>
> Based upon the theory of cultural cycles, he developed a general morphology (study of forms) of world history in which he describes the changes in form of cultures, viewed as higher organisms, and of their styles of living, the course of which, according to this view, is determined by the organism's pattern of the three stages of initial unfolding, maturity and decline, a development which cannot be changed by anything; not even by resolution of human will. Thus every rising culture develops its own style which is neither interchangeable or reproducible.
>
> Spengler recognises eight cultures which by their respective courses attest to the validity of his interpretation: the Egyptian, the Babylonian, the Indian, the Chinese, the Classical, the Arabian, the Western and the Mexican. He conceived the attainments of each of these cultures as symbols of the state of their souls and of their respective epochs. The present (1920) situation of the West he described by analogy to the corresponding phases of other cultures as a stage of decline which however is not to be understood as a collapse of catastrophic proportions but rather as a dying out of cultural creativity. As such it is characterised by a lowering of philosophic and artistic force to professorial philosophy and industrial art and to a technical mass existence. As regards politics, he predicted wars of annihilation, imperialism, Caesarism and ever more primitive political forms.[59]

This is where so many get confused with Spengler, and consequently Yockey, as 'pessimists'. Spengler was making an objective observation, not a value judgement, on how the last stages of the West would unfold. His point was that the epoch — high culture ('*Spring*') of great art and philosophy was gone and could not, or even should not, return. A revival would be pointless. Consequently, this was not the termination of Western civilization but a new

59 Peter Brock, ibid.

epoch in which the focus would be on great political and martial events backed up by the *Faustian* urge for conquest and *Faustian* technics, in which the roles of technicians and engineers would assume a martial meaning.[60] In the final pages of his last work, *The Hour of Decision*, Spengler commented that fascism might be the herald of this new great epoch[61] and Yockey saw National Socialism and fascism as the 'provisional forms' of this epoch. Spengler saw the duty of those in the service of Western-destiny as being to overthrow the rule of money and establish this new epoch. The battle between 'money and blood'[62] that Spengler predicted was fought shortly after his death and money won. Yockey of course wrote and organised with the aim of resuming the battle between 'money and blood' in the hope that 'blood' would win and the West would resume its organic lifecycle. So far it has been the USA that has arrogated the leadership of the West to itself and assumed a course that is remote from anything 'Western' — again, what Yockey called Culture-distortion and Culture-retardation. 'Wars of annihilation' and 'imperialism' are undertaken in the name of 'democracy' to assure the extension of trade, 'Caesarism' has been assumed in a grotesque caricature by the American Presidency and indeed 'political forms' are 'evermore primitive' as America assumes the mantle of a world-clown with weapons of mass destruction.

Brock argues of Spengler that 'in one of his forecasts he erred: he foresaw in Russia the ascending culture of the future which would save that of the West'. He adds: 'It would be mistaken to ascribe this to him as an error. When Spengler wrote his book, he could not have known what a disastrous course Russia would take.'[63] Whether Brock would have changed his mind about Russia were he alive today, as did Huxley-Blythe, is a moot question. Brock resumes his appreciation of Yockey:

> A Solemn Appeal.
> As to the final result, it is probably immaterial whether he has borrowed Spengler's thesis for his book or whether he has arrived at the same views

---

60 Spengler, 'The Machine', *The Decline of The West*, op. cit., Vol. II, pp. 499–507.

61 Spengler, *The Hour of Decision*, op. cit., p. 230.

62 Spengler, *The Decline of The West*, op. cit., Vol. II, p. 507. 'Blood' in the symbolic sense of the organic rhythm of a Culture, distinct from the artificial character of money-thinking.

63 Peter Brock, op. cit.

> through his own creative initiative—he has done more! He has illuminated the meaning and content of every sentence, every perception, every conclusion and has ordered the facts as formulated like building stones both horizontally and vertically and erected a structure of thought of truly enormous magnitude that will endure as if it either were an arch of triumph or as a monument of death, and at the same time, based upon historical data, he has set forth the present European situation in a reliable manner not subject to being misunderstood. He almost writes in a manner and in accordance with the rules of inventory taking as to what yet remains of the one-time cultural and religious substance of the West. Culture-pathology, culture-parasitism, culture-distortion have clearly increased and deepened many times over the harm which has already been indicated by Spengler; manipulated ideology and terror deliberately and purposely introduced from outside are suitable for hastening the slide into chaos.
>
> "The present chaos," writes the author in an epilogue, "can be traced back directly to the attempt to block the uniting of Europe. In consequence, Europe finds itself in a morass and the onetime European nations have sunk to colonies of extra-European powers. Either Europe unites or it disappears from history and the vigour of its leadership and its achievements will forever serve extra-European powers."
>
> Yockey, who belonged to America's younger generation, wrote this work while under the impression of his activity with the trials of "war criminals" during which he uncovered serious errors and false explanations. Thus he warns of the danger of liberal, democratic and communistic views and with hard standards he examines the political situation of the world powers and unsparingly takes America to task. Whether his arrest and his mysterious death in prison are connected with this criticism cannot be excluded.
>
> The appearance of this book could not be blocked by these events, the effect upon the public at large could not be lessened.[64]

Paul Brock's review is one of the most significant for *Imperium*. Brock was still prominent in the German *literati*, despite his role in the Third Reich and his continuing Rightist views. He was precisely the type of individual to whom Yockey had addressed *Imperium* and he appreciated Yockey better than most, perhaps better than Yockey himself. For he saw *Imperium* as much more than

64 Peter Brock, ibid.

a re-writing of Spengler, but as a work which has 'illuminated the meaning and content of every sentence, every perception, every conclusion' and 'erected a structure of thought of truly enormous magnitude'.[65]

## Mosley & Ivor Benson

> I found him personally an interesting and engaging mind.
>
> — Mosley, 1965

Despite the vehement condemnation of Sir Oswald Mosley by Chesham, and the Yockeyan split from UM, which seems to have cost the UM 10% of its core membership, Mosley, perhaps afforded clarity by the distance of years, did not reciprocate the bitterness.

A rather surprising letter written to Dr Oliver by a Mosley confidante in the post-war years, a letter accompanying a copy of Mosley's book *The Alternative*, states that the 'Englishman knew and admired Yockey'. He added that reading *The Alternative* would show 'a number of resemblances to the philosophy of history' developed by Yockey. *Imperium* was regarded by this Mosleyite, who must presently remain anonymous, 'as a very practical complementary volume' to *The Alternative*. It seems that this Mosley confidante knew something more of Sir Oswald's opinions on Yockey than the dismissive attitude that Mosley supposedly had toward him.[66]

Writing to an ex-BUF member, journalist Ivor Benson, who became the information adviser to Rhodesian Prime Minister Ian Smith after UDI, and a seminal conservative author throughout the Anglophone world, Mosley stated of Yockey:

> … I have intended to write to you for some time concerning a discussion I had in Rome, which threw some further light on the subject of Varanage [sic] and may interest you. I met among other university people a man who had been approached by Yockey concerning the possible publication of his book in Italy and who had become very interested in him. He complained to the young man that I regarded him purely as a disciple of Spengler. I asked this man whether

65 Peter Brock, ibid.

66 Letter to Oliver, February 2, 1972.

> he considered Varanage [sic] had added anything to Spengler. He replied: no, because Yockey was convinced that Spengler had said everything that could be said and nothing could be added to his thesis; the rest was commentary. He then went on to say something which interested me extremely and reminded me of the point at which Yockey fell out with the Secretary of our party Raven Thomson, who was also an ardent neo-Spenglerian; Raven Thomson was much more concerned with Varanage [sic] in the last stage than I was.
>
> It appeared that Yockey became so convinced of the Spenglerian thesis that our civilization was exhausted and that a renewal of life and the cycle must come from elsewhere that he turned toward Russia and consequently communism as the successor of our failing civilization. I would myself be reasonably sure that that view rested purely in the sphere of theory and that the American treatment of him was unjustified, but it accounts in some degree for their action if they regarded him as a communist agent. He was in my recollection a man who talked most openly and without regard for discretion and the last type to be a secret agent for anyone. But all of this accounts to some extent both for the tragedy and for our differences with him.
>
> In my all too cursory writing on the subject of Spengler before the war I had always taken the line that his premise was correct but his conclusion avoidable by the will of man exerted in European renaissance. This more than ever is my own opinion. This civilization will fail as others have, if the European will fails. But it is not inevitable, as we are aided in the struggle with Destiny by what we have learnt from Spengler in his massive premise of doom.[67]

Sir Oswald raised some interesting points with Benson. The contention that Yockey provided nothing more than a postscript for Spengler is perhaps partly accountable by Yockey's own reluctance to compare himself to 'The Philosopher' in greatness. That he was not ego-driven is indicated by his offer to even have Mosley put his name to *Imperium* for the sake of getting it into print and distribution. Yockey was much more than an appendix to Spengler. In particular, Yockey's doctrine of 'Cultural Vitalism' stands alone in its enduring validity. That was also recognised by Raven Thomson, as one readily sees the influence in Thomson's mostly unpublished doctrine of 'social

67 Mosley to Ivor Benson, July 4, 1964, University of Birmingham Mosley archive, MS124/1/2/36.

pathology'. As we have seen, the main bugbear in both Spengler and Yockey is their supposed 'pessimism'. This is something that Spengler and Yockey faced in their own times. Most people have a vague sense of immortality, which diminishes with age, or illness, and this too is unavoidable in civilizations. To point out the inevitable can readily be seen as undermining the morale of a civilization well into decline among those who wish to see its revival, and who are already too few in number — a revival for which Spengler and Yockey were among the foremost champions. One can appreciate the concern at the negative impact of such ideas by men like Mosley who were attempting to motivate the masses. But neither *Imperium* nor *The Decline of The West* are intended for the masses. They are intended for the small culture and leadership strata as tools for a realistic assessment of the Western predicament.

Despite Yockey's success in illuding the US State Department, Military Intelligence and the FBI for over a decade, and his reputation as a 'conspiratorial' figure, he was not particularly discrete and would have made a poor secret agent, as Mosley and others who knew him noted. One is reminded of the Nazi anthems he would knock out on a piano while in military service. It could be that his sense of humour sometimes got the better of his discretion. Nonetheless, he seems to have spent several years in the Soviet bloc and to have had some contact with the Castro regime. He might well have undertaken some work as a courier for the Czech Soviet regime and it seems plausible that, as in Egypt, he might have served as an anti-Zionist propagandist in the Soviet bloc. He could never have been a 'communist' but he could have served as a 'Stalinist'. There is a difference.[68] As we have seen, the Catholic anti-communist newspaper *Common Sense* had a 'Stalinist' orientation for the last decade of its life, while for the most part continuing to bill itself 'leader in the nation's fight against communism'. Yockey was possibly the first to see that the 'Washington regime' was in essence 'Bolshevik', doctrinally more so than the USSR, and remains so to this day.

Ivor Benson became a well-known name among the Nationalist Right in Southern Africa and the British Commonwealth. He wrote numerous small books of a 'conspiracist' nature, explaining the links between capitalism and Left-wing revolution, including the 'Black revolution'. *Imperium* was included

68 Bolton, *Stalin: The Enduring Legacy*, op. cit.

in the recommended reading lists of most of these books.[69] Benson replied to Mosley mentioning his new task of reorganisation of the Rhodesian government information service and hoped that Rhodesia would be the place to undertake 'some interesting and exciting experiments' perhaps 'unique in the Western world'.

> Your remarks about Yockey and Spengler were interesting. If there is anything depressing in Spengler and Yockey, it has passed over me like water off a duck's back. In any case, I believe that those who read pessimism into Spengler have failed to get the real message of *Decline*. And even if it were found that Spengler's conclusions are pessimistic I should still remain unaffected because I am not in the habit of attaching much importance to any philosopher's conclusions. There is a tendency to-day for those who fight against the prevailing sickness of rationalism to insist on confronting it with another rationalism of reversed polarity—a watertight answer to the rationalism of the Left. For me the value of Spengler and of his disciple Yockey is not their "arguments" or "reasoning" as such but the luminous insights which they both communicate and which have helped me to see and understand many things more clearly. By stimulating my mind they have produced a good deal of light which is not theirs but my own. Nietzsche can be criticised on the same grounds that his conclusions are not sound. While his influence for good has been prodigious, his arguments and conclusions have made more cranks and crackpots than any other philosopher I know.
>
> I hope that in a way I have become pessimism-proof. For me any ideas which inhibit, except temporally and for obviously sound purposes, are anti-life and wrong. Or, to put it differently, no opinions are sound except those which

69 *Imperium* is listed in: Ivor Benson, *This Worldwide Conspiracy* (Melbourne: New Times Ltd., 1972), *The Struggle for South Africa* (Perth: The Australian League of Rights, 1978), *Behind Communism in Africa* (Durban: Dolphin Press, 1975), *Truth Out of Africa* (Bullsbrook, Western Australia: Veritas Publishing Co., 1982). Born in South Africa, Benson served at Fleet Street for several years, and later as Chief Assistant Editor for *The Rand Daily Mail*, and news analyst for the South African Broadcasting Corporation, and as advisor to the Rhodesian government. He drafted Prime Minister Ian Smith's speeches. Benson resigned as advisor to Smith due to the latter's compromises. (See: Stephen Mitford Goodson, *Rhodesian Prime Minister Ian Smith: The Debunking of a Myth* (South Africa, 2017)). He moved back to South Africa, established the National Forum, and published a newsletter, *Behind the News*.

> prompt us to fight with the utmost eagerness. There are those who will condemn this attitude as being purely subjective but again I reply that in contests of strength and will the unconquerable subjective is what must prevail in the end. The secret of victory is not the discovery of sound reasons for victory but only the clean, liberated will to victory. No one has expressed that feeling better than you have, so you will know what I mean.
>
> The story of what really happened to Yockey at San Francisco must dispel any suggestion that he had any communist inclinations. We cannot always know a man by his friends because not all friends are genuine. But we can know a man by his enemies and we know that Yockey's enemies were no anti-communists. The latest edition of his book, published by the Noontide Press, contains a good account of his last days written as a preface by Willis A Carto, now a key figure in Liberty Lobby, one of the more influential Conservative pressure groups operating in Washington. *Imperium* has also given rise in recent months to a new serious magazine dealing mainly with cultural subjects, entitled *Western Destiny*.[70]

Benson understood Yockey and Spengler better than many. Even thinkers of the stature of Raven Thomson, Britain's leading 'neo-Spenglerian', sought to overcome what he thought was Spengler's pessimism with his doctrine of 'civilization as divine superman', which contends that cultural vitality can be focused on not only heroic and exceptional individuals, Nietzschean style, or what Spengler called the 'return of Caesars', but on the entirety of the cultural organism if this is of heroic mould. Certainly, there is no contradiction between both ideas and it is surely what fascism, and what Mosley, pre-war and post-war, sought in a revitalised, heroic European civilization — as did Yockey. Benson saw nothing 'pessimistic' in Spengler or Yockey. Rather, both called for a new heroism to revive Western Civilization. Spengler

70 Benson to Mosley, July 16, 1964. University of Birmingham Mosley papers, MS124/1/2/37. *Western Destiny*, mentioned by Benson to Mosley as being inspired by *Imperium*, was established a Willis Carto in 1964. Dr Roger Pearson, editor of the British-based magazine *Northern World*, assumed editorship in 1965. *Western Destiny*, which had incorporated Carto's journal *Right*, was closed in 1966 when Carto took over the prestigious literary magazine *The American Mercury*. Pearson, a physical anthropologist of note, who continues to edit the peer-reviewed *Journal of Social, Political and Economic Studies* from Washington, was never a Yockeyan. However, *Western Destiny* included Yockeyan concepts, with references to 'Culture distorters'.

referred to the triumph of cultural vitality over money-rule (the 'conflict between money and blood'). Yockey called for renewal by the 'liberation' of the Western cultural organism. Spengler's final book, *The Hour of Decision*, was a clarion call for action, not an invitation to go into Oriental worldly detachment and navel-gazing. Moreover, we might add today that what happens to Western civilization determines the type of civilization that comes after it. Spengler saw quite specifically that a post-Western civilization would arise. Yockey alluded to a symbiosis with Russia.

Again, Benson also never appreciated the changes that had taken place in Russia with the rise of Stalin. Like many conservative nationalist writers, he regarded Washington and Moscow as operating in conjunction to rule the world between them, with the Jews standing at the back of both. While Yockey referred to the 'Concert of Bolshevism' between both the USA and USSR, this 'concert' did not hold together after World War II and both represented antithetical forms of 'Bolshevism'. Benson did not recognise this, hence his reference to Yockey not possibly being a 'communist' agent because of the enemies he had in the USA. Again, this is the failure to recognise the essential Trotskyism of the USA and the Stalinism of Russia, neither of whose situations has changed radically. Nonetheless, Benson has shown in his letter to Mosley his calibre as a thinker and his commitment to Yockey.

## Robert D Kephart — Would-Be Biographer

Further interest in Yockey directed to Mosley came from Robert D Kephart, then working with, and later publisher of, *Human Events*, which Kephart described to Mosley as 'America's largest right-wing periodical'. Kephart diverted to libertarianism but in 1965 wrote to Mosley 'as a disciple of Francis Parker Yockey'. Kephart's knowledge of the meanderings of European rightist politics seems to have been sketchy, for he addressed Sir Oswald as 'Mr Mosley' and apparently assumed Mosley to have been a close Yockey associate. He asked Mosley for the addresses of Yockey associates such as Huxley-Blythe, Baroness von Pflügl and Anthony Gannon, and asked whether Mosley had set down his ideas on European unification in book form? Kephart wrote of Yockey:

> For some time I have felt that a study of Yockey's life and cryptic circumstances surrounding his death, should be compiled in the form of a biography or a series of essays, always depending on the amount of information available. I am certain that it is no secret to you that *Imperium* has gained rather a wide circulation in this country following its republication by Willis Carto. Impressed by the great genius implicit in it, readers are quite naturally curious to know more about its author.
>
> The force of his ideas, of course should stand alone. But the Culture Distorter in this country has so successfully captured the instrument of mass communication that they can, without great difficulty, badly damage the book by exploiting the absence of information about Yockey.
>
> Toward the end of eventually attempting to publish whatever material I could gather about Yockey, I have undertaken to research public documents and periodicals dealing with the curious circumstances surrounding his death. In addition, I have endeavoured to develop from private sources certain other information about his life prior to 1948.
>
> Of primary concern at the moment is to frame some outline of his activities between 1946 and 1960. It has been suggested to me you could provide information about Yockey during these years. It would be helpful to learn something about the European Liberation Front, and the *Proclamation of London*. I would like to know whether *Imperium* has ever been reviewed in the European press, where, and by whom.[71]

Again, Mosley refrained from resorting to the type of vitriol that had been heaped upon him by some Yockeyans:

> Yockey came to see me after the war [...] and we had some interesting discussions. To summarise them would take more than the space of one short letter. In brief his writings seemed to me to a very large extent to be a reproduction of

71 Robert D Kephart to Mosley, April 26, 1965. University of Birmingham Mosley papers, MS124/1/11/13.

> Spengler's thought. When this was pointed out to him he used to say in effect that nothing could be added to Spengler's thinking.
>
> I was, of course, familiar with Spengler and wrote before the war something on the subject. We accepted many of Spengler's premises, but differed from the pessimistic fatality of his conclusions. This is a very brief and crude summary of our differences. I found him personally an interesting and engaging mind.
>
> His book was advertised I think in the Times during this period, but the sale was practically nil. I remain of the view that it is an interesting statement of the Spenglerian position.
>
> I know nothing but hearsay of his actions after my brief meeting with him soon after the war. It is understandable that his near-Spenglerian pessimism leading him to the conclusion that European civilization was finished, might cause him certain difficulties.
>
> I enclose details of my book *Europe Faith and Plan* and another book in the form of question and answer called [*Mosley*] *Right or Wrong?* An earlier book called *The Alternative* was published at about the same time as Yockey's and illustrates the differences in our thinking. Details of these publications will be sent to you under separate cover.
>
> I shall always be glad to hear from you.[72]

Noteworthy again is the generosity of Mosley's remembrances about Yockey, the description of Yockey as 'an interesting and engaging mind', and *Imperium* as 'an interesting statement of the Spenglerian position'. Clearly, Mosley's real opinions towards Yockey were not as dismissive as they are usually portrayed. No references to Yockey being 'cold shouldered',[73] of considering Yockey 'a bit mad', as Diana Mosley claimed her husband believed. Mosley supposedly even punched Yockey on the nose during a dispute at Hyde Park.[74] A confidante of Mosley dismisses the latter claim, which has entered Yockey/Mosley myth, as 'improbable', adding: 'I once met someone who "swore blind" that

72 Mosley to Kephart, May 7, 1965, ibid., MS124/1/11/14.

73 Robert Skidelsky, *Mosley* (London: Macmillan, 1975), p. 491.

74 Stephen Dorrill, *Black Shirt: Sir Oswald Mosley & British Fascism* (London: Penguin Books, 2007), p. 576.

he saw Mosley personally administer castor oil to a (predictably) helpless Jew—in 1929!'[75]

Kephart does not appear to have written anything on Yockey. Instead, he became one of the USA's foremost libertarians, and *Human Events* a leading exponent of American libertarianism. His father, Dr Calvin I Kephart, a race theorist, was a contributing editor of Carto and Pearson's *Western Destiny*, along with Ivor Benson and many other rightist luminaries.[76]

That *Western Destiny* maintained a Yockeyan influence is indicated by an article, 'America's Duty to the West', by Alan L Benjamin. Benjamin argued that 'US national policy seems to be directed [...] to the unhappy goal of national and Western annihilation. [...] [I]ts policy is to extirpate Western civilization and replace it with the "new culture" descended from savagery and cultural primitivism.' As examples, Benjamin points to the US policy of installing in South America 'democrats of the left' as the best defence against communism, US opposition to France's colonial policies in Indochina and North Africa, opposition to Portugal's imperial possessions, the Morgenthau Plan in Germany, the betrayal of England as an imperial power. 'There hardly now exists in Europe a nation which has not seen its interests trampled upon by the purportedly pro-Western State Department.' The current US offensive was against Rhodesia as one of the last bastions of Western civilization. Benjamin concluded:

> It is not America's duty to protect the East. It is not her duty to advance cultural decay. Her duty is to stand firm against cultural and physical destruction. Yet, this it does not do. That the most powerful nation in the West is one of its weakest defenders is undeniable.
>
> What is the problem? It is that the forces of international culture-distortion control the lifeblood of America. They pay their respects to our Civilization in the

---

75 Personal communication to the author, April 29, 2014.

76 *Western Destiny*, Vol. XI, No. 2, February 1966, p. 2. Among the others were German-American scholar Dr Austin J App; British 'Empire Loyalist' leader and writer A. K. Chesterton; Colonel Ernest S Cox, a veteran white race activist and author of the classic *White America*; noted psychologist Dr Henry E Garrett; anthropologist Dr Robert Kuttner; former Senator Jack B Tenney; et al.

> same manner that Chicago mobsters paid their respects to those whom they had executed. They pontificate in our colleges, they babble forth from the pages of books and magazines; they shout at us form the radio and television: Give up! Abandon the West. And as Pavlov's dogs responded, so do we respond. But America's inexorable duty is to the West and to no other. To abandon our kinsmen to the forces of evil is cultural treason. And is it folly to think that it would also be suicide.[77]

Although Yockey is not cited, Benjamin's article is an excellent example of how Yockeyan thought had permeated the 'Right' by the mid-1960s. The themes are thoroughly Yockeyan, including the references to 'culture-distortion' and 'culture treason'. Benjamin's analysis is moreover one that holds just as true today in regard to the USA's world position.

## Belated Union Movement Appraisal

Many years after the Yockeyan split from Union Movement, Mosley stalwart Robert Row felt obliged to write a Mosleyite repudiation of *Imperium*; perhaps the first. Stimely mentioned Row's authorship of this piece to Gannon, after having received a copy from Jeffrey Hamm,[78] who had assumed administration of Union Movement, *Action*, and the later Action Society. Robert Row was not suitable for the task and should not have attempted it. Those with far more background for such a task also failed. It is doubtful that the Row critique did anything other than sit among the Mosley, wherein it was found with a UM file that includes the Wolfgang Sarg handout against Yockey. Row stated that: 'We can ignore old feuds of long ago, the sarcasm of Sarg at Yockey's expense and Yockey's attacks in reply. Yockey is dead. A serious study of his ideas compared with those of Mosley is needed instead.'[79] Why such a 'serious study' — although 'serious' it is not — was 'needed' is not explained.

---

77 Alan L Benjamin, 'America's Duty to the West', *Western Destiny*, Vol. XI, No. 2, February 1966, p. 6.

78 Gannon to Stimely, April 8, 1982.

79 Robert Row, 'The Ideas of Oswald Mosley and those of F. P. Yockey', n.d.; Mosley papers, op. cit., OMD/7/1/6.

Row refers to an open letter from Yockey to Mosley in 1953, in which Yockey refers to Mosley as 'Hitler's voice on the island'. Naturally, this is repudiated by Row, as Mosley's Fascism had been 'a natural British idea' before the war. Since 1918, a veteran of the World War I, Mosley entered politics as an adherent of 'socialist imperialism', derived from Joseph Chamberlain, and of Keynesian economics. Mosley's 'pro-Churchill' stance, which Yockey 'discovered', was predicated on the real possibility of war with the USSR and in such a case Mosley would have felt duty-bound to support Churchill. That, of course, was a primary difference between the men, as Yockey thought a Soviet military occupation of Europe was preferable to the 'ethical syphilis' bought by US occupation. Row contended that Mosley was a practical politician, Yockey a theorist.[80] But Yockey was a theorist of rare clarity, given the higher perspective of Cultural Vitalism. Russia might tyrannise over Europe, but America would rot its soul until resistance to any inner or outer force was impossible.

Row affirmed that Yockey's claim that Mosley was 'pro-American' was true, recalling that it was only due to Marshall Aid that Western European was saved form communism. Row asked: 'Would Yockey have preferred no American aid to Europe and Red governments in Rome and Paris?'[81] The answer is 'yes', because the Washington regime was far redder than Moscow. Even some of Mosley's key German contacts, war veterans — at the coalface — accepted Yockey's analysis.

Row states that the 'accusation that Mosley wanted to "mobilise Europe to fight for an American-Jewish victory over Russia" is ludicrous'. Ironically, Mosley had of course, throughout much of his political life, been accused of 'anti-Semitism' but again Yockey was the 'blinkered theorist' in seeing all political events 'in terms of the Jewish question to the exclusion of all else'. 'Mosley saw them in terms of whole nations. Whether Jews would gain if Russia did not over-run Western Europe was beside the point. Mosley's point was that communism should not triumph over the nations of Western

80 Row, ibid.

81 Row, ibid.

Europe.'[82] This was the pretext used for America's post-war hegemony, similar to the present scaremongering regarding Russia, as well as the 'war on terror'. The psychology, tactics and aims are the same.

Row's greatest misunderstanding was in thinking that 'Yockey was a theorist who fell under the spell of nationalism, or national-socialism, and did not advance beyond it.' Mosley, on the other hand, had discarded first democracy and then his pre-war fascism, the latter because of the post-war erosion of Britain's imperial role, and then had moved towards 'Europeanism'. While Row states that the Empire had been 'destroyed by the war', he did not appreciate that it was the USA that gave the British Empire the final push into the abyss. All such empires were obstacles to the USA's post-war vision, set out — to Churchill's dismay — in the Atlantic Charter, and similarly in President Woodrow Wilson's Fourteen Points after World War I.[83] Row misunderstood Yockey to the extent that it must be wondered whether he had read *Imperium* or *The Proclamation of London*. Row continues: 'Yockey's tragedy was that he embraced national-socialism or what he called "Authoritarian European Nationalism" when it was too late. The war had made all nationalism obsolete in Europe. The future lay, in the field of power, with super-states such as the USA, the USSR and communist China; in the economic field with continental economics; and in the world of ideas with concepts such as Mosley's "Europe-a-Nation".'[84] But Yockey only accepted the third Reich as a 'provisional form' of the 'Imperium'. He had rejected nationalism since his student days; when Mosley's slogan was still 'Britain First', Yockey was already describing himself as a 'European imperialist'. Indeed, Yockey's thinking is evident in the idea of 'Authoritarian European Nationalism', a supra-national European bloc and indeed more than that, the total union of the Western culture.

Stimely referred to Row's article as 'claptrap'.[85] Unlike Gannon's particular contempt for Jeffrey Hamm, Gannon allowed that Row was 'a decent

82 Row, ibid.

83 For the USA's role in destroying the European empires see: K. R. Bolton, *Babel Inc.* (London: Black House Publishing, 2014), pp. 41–77.

84 Row, op. cit.

85 Gannon to Stimely, April 8, 1982.

farm-labourer type from Lancaster, gawky, unkempt [...] a more likeable human being'. 'A country boy who never did overcome the impact of London living upon his simple soul.' What Gannon objected to, whether in his contempt for Hamm or his more charitable attitude towards Row, was what he regarded as 'dog-like devotion'[86] to Mosley. At times it seems as if Gannon — and Chesham — were overcompensating for their loss of faith. Row had joined the British Union of Fascists at 17, in 1934, and was a Blackshirt in the Lancaster branch. He was one of the 1,000 imprisoned under Regulation 18B during the war but later saw service in Palestine. He became deputy editor of Union, under the editorship of Raven Thomson, and took over after Thomson's death in 1955.[87] In 1963, thugs from the *Yellow Star* group attacked him. They broke into Action offices, bound him hand and foot and repeatedly kicked him in the face and body.[88] He became a founder member of the Friends of Oswald Mosley, writing for their journal, *Comrade*;[89] a brave, sincere and dedicated man, regardless of factional disagreements.

## *TRUD*

During the late 1960s nationalist youth, in a challenge to the New Left era, established a magazine. DTK observed of this: 'A Polish comrade, a man working for a large private security guard firm, who was capable of ripping the neck and head from any sub-human creature, suggested the Polish word for work, *truda*.' The nationalist youths 'wanted a labor slant to the periodical, à la Huey Long, Pope Leo XIII, Robert Ley, some of the early British socialists, the social legislation of Bismarck, et al.' *TRUD* was printed on the small offset press at *Common Sense*.[90]

---

86 Gannon to Stimely, April 20, 1982.

87 'Robert Row', Friends of Oswald Mosley, http://www.oswaldmosley.com/robert-row/.

88 Jeffrey Hamm, *Action Replay* (London: Howard Baker, 1983), p. 199.

89 'Robert Row', Friends of Oswald Mosley, op. cit.

90 DTK to Bolton, June 11, 2014.

*TRUD* propagated the position that *Common Sense* had been counselling, much to the chagrin of many on the 'Right'. *Common Sense* lambasted 'conservatives' and the 'Left-Right' dichotomy as a fraud. DTK writes of the founders of *TRUD* that their 'first thought of a title was *The Winslow Sludge Report*; "Winslow", the name of any generic conservative moneybags faker, and sludge, of course, descriptive of the myth-peddling promoted endlessly by conservative fakers'. *TRUD* could not endure beyond 1972. It was 'blasted from one conservative outfit to another for being "pro-Russkie" and pro-socialist. Well, that's America.'[91] They underwent the same rejection as Yockey and *Common Sense* for attempting to inject realism into the 'Right'.

The character of *TRUD* was defined in a letter of intent:

> Whiteman!
> This letter is your passport to the world of TRUD. TRUD? What is that? Well, TRUD is from the White Underground, and is one of the most startling adventures in rightist journalism ever seen.
>
> TRUD! TRUD! TRUD! What kind of word is that? What does it mean? It means that finally there is an independent periodical that says out loud what many people only whisper to themselves and to each other. In other words TRUD does not pussyfoot around like the usual conservative journal....
>
> TRUD! Listen to that word! Listen to the sound of TRUD. It is the crack of a police club smashing the skull of a ghetto rioter or student anarchist. TRUD! It's the sound of a paratrooper's boot kicking the backside of a pinko college professor. TRUD! The sound of a peacenik being strangled to death. TRUD! The sound of marching feet stamping leftism, old and new, into the mire. TRUD is the angry sound of White American working people fed up with the humanitarian crap that picks their pockets and uses their kids as pawns in crack-brained, race-mixing social experiments. ...
>
> TRUD: A bullet in the heart of a social worker, a nail on a bureaucrat's seat, a hornets' nest in a hippie's hairdo. TRUD sears like napalm and pops like a grenade in a Vietcong tunnel complex. TRUD is hell on humanitarians, anarchists, peace creeps, one-worlders, social gospel clergy, panty-waist conservatives,

---

91 DTK to Bolton, June 11, 2014.

> money-crazed Establishment slobs, race-mixers, social parasites, Zionists and similar outpourings from the cesspool they call democracy.
>
> TRUD is a coat of tar and feathers on the anti-White Supreme Court... a big gob of spit on Allen Ginsberg's face... a chamber pot dumped over the head of Golda Meir.
>
> TRUD is deadly serious and uproariously funny. TRUD has something to say about everything: current events and personalities, art, music, drama, literature, science, religion, and... RACE. TRUD approaches all liberal-moron ideals with a spirit of cynicism, sarcasm and ridicule.[92]

*TRUD*'s analysis of the decline of America and the West showed the vibrancy of Yockeyan thought. Founded in 1968, it was edited by John S Sullivan, a *Common Sense* columnist. Sullivan, commenting on a papal statement on birth control, offered a classic Spenglerian and Yockeyan approach by stating that birth control is a sign of moral decay and life negation: 'A race that practises sterility as a social virtue is, for all higher purposes, washed up. The desire for children is an affirmation of life itself. The sterility-wish — the triumph of the grave over the cradle — is a denial of the creative force of the universe. It is a mark of senescence and death.' It is the solution of the 'rootless urban intelligentsia' to the population crisis. American capitalism does not regard the family as the 'germ cell of the future' but as the source of moronic consumers. A strong, spiritually healthy race 'would crack the two-headed monster of capitalism-Marxism like an eggshell'.[93]

*TRUD* regularly featured newspaper cuttings of 'Culture-distortion' in the movies, publishing, music and stage; headlined 'More from the Yiddlefag Machine' and 'Democracy Titbits'. A newly formed rock group called MC 5 were described as 'this quintet of freaks, resplendent in love beads and pimples' and to look at their countenance was to understand the 'inner essence of the so-called "youth revolt"'. Rock music was a contrivance of the 'ever-present distorter of culture and poisoner of youth'. However, it is a stupidity of the conservatives to ascribe the 'youth revolt' to a 'communist conspiracy':

---

92 'TRUD! From the White Underground', n.d.

93 John S Sullivan, 'Breed, Whiteman — Breed!', *TRUD*, New Jersey, No. 6, 1969.

it was a symptom of Culture-pathology. In contrast, Russian youth 'concern themselves with the pulse-beat of their father-culture and mother-soil'.[94]

Quoting H. L. Mencken that 'democracy would go stark raving mad', *TRUD* goes on to say that democracy is a political sacred cow and 'nothing more than a glorified sucker-trade system, a system for laughs, a system deserving nothing other than ridicule and abuse'; 'a flea-bag Gypsy circus that provides a stage for all the stunted morons of the world, the overeducated nincompoops, the prancing and powdered court jesters with little bells on their caps, whose sole aim in life is to slap and slap again the face of decent humanity whenever and wherever the opportunity presents itself'.[95]

A front-page editorial on the American Space Program described the Faustian Soul that Spengler had said was the unique imperative of Western civilization: 'limitless Space [as] the prime symbol of Western culture', the 'Will to conquer the Universe and contest Nature for her secrets'. This imperative now expressed in space exploration had in prior epochs of the West manifested, for example, from Gothic architecture 'pointing its spires to a point in infinity' to a Bach organ composition. With such profound achievements, the West nonetheless remained committed to such superstitions as democracy and equality, based on 'putrid Jewish ideals of universal messianic democratism' where the culture of Bach and Raphael had been overthrown by 'the art-Bolshevism of Picasso and the hideous clangor of acid rock'. 'Family, Authority, a sense of moral worth and the aristocratic ideal of a sharply honed State as the instrument of Destiny have given way to the sterile dreams of the literary sodomites.'[96]

In May 1969, at DTK's prompting, *TRUD* began the (incomplete) serialisation of *The Enemy of Europe*, translated by Walther von der Vogelweide and edited by Sullivan. The manuscript had been given to *TRUD* by Maria Weiss[97] and it was the first English translation. In that issue, another feature was inaugurated, 'Most Horrid Culture Distorter of the Month'. The first honour went

94 'Demo-Decadence in Review', *TRUD*, No. 6, 1969.

95 'Open up those Padded Cells', *TRUD*, No, 6, op, cit.

96 John S Sullivan, 'Editorial', *TRUD*, No. 7, February 1969.

97 Preamble to 'The Enemy of Europe', *TRUD*, No. 11, June 1969.

to Leonard Bernstein, former music director of the New York Philharmonic Orchestra. He is described as a 'prime example of how the Jews who control our nation's cultural life are able to foist talentless kosher charlatans off on the credulous public as "geniuses"'. Bernstein had wrecked the orchestra with 'his bizarre and neurotic interpretations of the classic repertory' and 'lethal doses of degenerate, clangorous modern music'. 'Bernstein succeeded in creating an atmosphere wherein the sublime aesthetic of Western music was stifled by the poisonous miasma of extreme Jewish intellectualism.'[98]

Were such criticisms mindless anti-Semitism, heedless of real ability? Yehudi Menuhin showed that Jews can be genuinely immersed in and contribute to Western high culture and his son and father showed that Jews can be active champions of that Culture to the point of enduring persecution from the worldwide Jewish establishment. What of Bernstein? Musical director and producer Rodney Greenberg, with Bernstein in Vienna in 1978, stated that the 'maestro' quipped to Greenberg: 'To write a great Broadway musical, you have to be either Jewish or gay. And I'm both.'[99]

> He rubs his hands, sits at the keyboard, and — to a gathering of mostly non-Jews — tinkles the ivories with the repetitive little falling motif that dominates the first movement of Beethoven's Pastoral Symphony. Then he sings along: "Now I'm barmitzvah'd, now I'm barmitzvah'd..." It is incongruous, wacky and will colour my hearing of that music ever after.
>
> Perhaps it was Bernstein's wry sense of humour that led him to flaunt his Jewishness in the Austrian capital. The tenor Jerry Hadley, asked how he thought an American Jew could enjoy such adulation in notoriously anti-Semitic Vienna, replied: "He flung it in their faces. And they loved him for it."
>
> Bernstein's excessive podium style (perhaps "athletic" is a better word) was as natural to him as it was anathema to others. The pianist and film star Oscar Levant turned his barbed wit on Lenny in full flow: "His conducting has a masturbatory, oppressive and febrile zeal, even for the most tranquil passages. He

98 'Most Horrid Culture Distorter of the Month', *TRUD*, No. 11, June 1969.

99 Rodney Greenberg, 'The Jewish Leonard Bernstein', *Jewish Quarterly*, Winter 2007, No. 208, http://www.jewishquarterly.org/issuearchive/article1756.html?articleid=327.

uses music as an accompaniment to his conducting." In other words, there was too much *schmaltz*.[100]

Greenberg described Bernstein's music as expressing the American ideal of the 'Melting Pot', a term coined by playwright Israel Zangwill in his 1909 play by that name.[101]

Bernstein said that his 'urge to teach' was 'Talmudic'. Greenberg writes: 'No one except the Swiss composer Ernest Bloch has devoted as much energy to bringing Jewish music into the concert hall.' Of Bernstein's loyalties, 'above all, in terms of his Jewish background, stands his loyalty to the state of Israel. ... He never failed to proclaim his Jewishness'.[102]

Stravinsky coined the 'mischievous phrase' a 'department store of music', in describing Bernstein's style.

Despite the satirical style of *TRUD*, *Trudnik* commentary on Culture-pathology was undertaken with surgical precision, albeit often following the old axiom 'laughter is the best medicine'.

Part two of a series on 'World Plutocracy' focused on the nature of usury or 'Shylocracy' and the need for 'white socialism', or what Spengler called 'Prussian Socialism' and Yockey called 'Ethical socialism'. Under this, American banks would be nationalised and the state would create credit. American currency would be freed from 'the world spider-web of international finance'. 'The demise of international finance-capitalism would break down the barriers that separate white nations,' allowing for worldwide Caucasian unity. Domestically, debts to the usurers would be annulled and a new state bank would provide loans at 3% interest. Freedom from the pervasive influences of usury would allow for the creation of an organic life. This would be the manifestation of what Spengler in *The Decline of The West* called the last battle between blood and money,[103] ushering a revived West under an authoritarian form of socialism based on duty.

---

100 Ibid.

101 See: K. R. Bolton, *Babel Inc.*, (London: Black House Publishing, 2013), pp. 140–147.

102 Rodney Greenberg, op. cit.

103 'World Plutocracy', Part II: 'Blood Sucking Gold Bugs of American', *TRUD*, No. 11, June 1969.

A Euro-Russian orientation was reflected in Sullivan's editorial condemning the Zionist-orientation of US foreign policy, which had pushed the Mediterranean basin into the Kremlin orbit and would make Europe turn to the USSR. It was a familiar theme from Yockey and Weiss, and by then from Fred Farrell, lead columnist for *Common Sense*. Sullivan wrote that Europe was 'sick of dollar imperialism', of 'degenerate American "culture"' and sickest of all of 'negroid occupation troops', and would welcome the Russian military. 'Marshall Gretchko's troops are not black—they are blonde and barbarian. They will not march into Vienna and Paris and Rome and Athens at the behest of a "victorious communist revolution" but rather as allies of a "conservative, traditional", "nationalistic" Europe, whose brains, resources, culture they shall weld into a ferocious war machine, an Imperium of Blood, against which the "product"-satiated, mongrelized rabble of the North American continent will be as dust before the wind. ... Among racial nationalist circles in Europe it is becoming almost a platitude that Bolshevist Russia is becoming Imperial Russia and has metamorphosed, ironically, into the sort of state into which European nationalism in the 20s and 30s was moving; i.e. pan-Caucasian racial nationalism.' Writing at a time when the Nixon-Kissinger regime was courting China in an anti-Russia partnership, Sullivan believed that the only salvation for the USA was to jettison its support for Zionism, dispose of dollar imperialism and enter into a 'hands-off' alliance with Russia to stem the 'rising tide of colored world revolt'. However, US policy was based on Jewish Russophobia and the capitalist thirst for a market of 800,000,000 Chinese. American conservatives, led by the 'racketeers of patriotism', would support this anti-Russian offensive, in the name of anti-communism, even though it would bring victory to the coloured world.[104]

Winslow Sludge had the hippie/New Left pegged as a plaything of the Establishment, a 'gruesome combination of Jewish ideology and American Big Money'. Understanding the 'alliance between coins and culture-distortion' was a prerequisite for American and Western rebirth. This was not a 'communist conspiracy' but a 'sweetheart contract between dollars and decadence, that is, between international Big Money (the filthy rich) and the

104 John S Sullivan, 'Page One', *TRUD*, No. 33, February 1970.

international Jewish nihilism (the just plain filthy)'. Sludge gave some salient examples: Michael Brovsky, folksinger turned millionaire promoter of campus rock concerts; Frank Rowena, a Puerto Rican who had made a fortune catering to hippie clothes and hair fashions, and as publisher of *Head East Magazine*; Jann Wenner, owner of *Rolling Stone*; the millionaire fraudster and Woodstock promoter Bernie Kornfield, and others who had made a fortune out of the 'counter-culture' and 'youth rebellion'. All the while the conservative loudmouths 'bleat out … the same old crap about "Communism destroying our children" and the "international conspiracy against free enterprise"'. Mr Sludge ended by stating that it is conservatism that allows this to happen, that it is conservatism that stands in the way of 'those who can straighten out the mess'.[105]

Now it is known how the CIA set up the 'New Left' and the tax-exempt foundations provided the funding. The 'New Left', including feminism and the CIA backing for Gloria Steinem, was and remains a controlled opposition and was also part of a Cold War operation to run an anti-Russian Left.[106] As such, a multitude of Trotskyite-communists jumped aboard and many, such as Sidney Hook, Max Shachtman and Trotsky's widow Sedova, became the staunchest champions of the USA against the USSR.[107] The same scenario has been played out for the past few decades by a post-New Left, bought and paid for by George Soros, the National Endowment for Democracy and many other NGOs, think-tanks and tax-exempt foundations, starting with the collapse of the Soviet Bloc, 'the colour revolutions' and most recently the 'Arab Spring'. How Culture-distortion continues to be used has recently been publicised by the blasphemous 'Pussy Riot' performance and the kudos they received from the worldwide media and entertainment industry for their insult to Russian tradition. Another recent example is the horror at the Muslim attack on *Charlie Hebdo*, a convergence of Grand Orient Freemasons, communists,

105 'The Hippie Proletarians', The Winslow Sludge Report, *TRUD*, No. 37, n.d.

106 K. R. Bolton, *Revolution from Above*, op. cit., pp. 110–200;

107 Bolton, *Stalin…* op. cit., pp. 93–124.

and Zionist neo-cons who delight in heaping bile upon the traditions of the West, and the Catholic Church in particular.[108]

*TRUD* came to a thud after issue 39. In a 'Fact sheet', the *Trudniks* pointed out the difficulties they had with launching a journal to counter the hippie outpourings. There had been complaints because *TRUD* was a name similar to several Soviet journals. Conservative backers were soon pressuring the *Trudniks* to 'tone down'. The desertions led to a more modest format than the mass-distributed colour tabloid that had been intended.[109] A separate letter advised that *TRUD* would be replaced by *Third Force*. A letter a 'few months' later advised supporters that *Third Force* would not be forthcoming due to lack of support. The *Trudniks* had encountered the same mentality from the right that Yockey had often encountered and that had resulted in a drastic drop in the circulation of *Common Sense* for its insistence on offering the Right unpalatable realism. The *Trudniks* were concerned about how to develop a mass movement and opted to support *White Power*, a tabloid newspaper published by the National Socialist White People's Party, the name given by Rockwell to the American Nazi Party shortly before his assassination in 1967. It might have been a surprising choice, given that Rockwell had rejected Yockey for his heresies, but *White Power* was probably the type of mass distribution tabloid that *TRUD* was supposed to be, although not specifically directed, in satirical style, towards youth. The *Trudniks* were however impressed by the efficient 'young people' with 'honesty and guts' working on *White Power* 'without compromise'.

## Rockwell

Despite Rockwell's denunciation of Yockey, Yockeyan thought had influenced Rockwell, as it had the Mosleyite philosopher Raven Thomson. Apart from the tabloid, *White Power* was also the name of Rockwell's primary philosophical work. Whatever one thinks of Rockwell's swastika waving, which was motivated by his frustration with the timidity of the 'Right', the book *White*

108 Bolton, 'Charlie Hebdo: All Idiots Now', *Counter-Currents*, http://www.counter-currents.com/2015/01/charlie-hebdo-all-idiots-now/.

109 *TRUD* 'Fact Sheet', n.d., 1970.

*Power* is mainly a sober analysis of America's decline from the viewpoint of a conservative Naval Commander and war veteran. Like many such Americans, Rockwell had pinned his hopes on General Douglas MacArthur and Senator Joseph McCarthy, only to see them scuttled by the 'Establishment' that was supposedly 'fighting communism'.[110] Rockwell's basically conservative nature can be seen from the initial name of his organisation, the World Union of *Free Enterprise* National Socialists (WUFENS), albeit later shortened to WUNS. The first chapter of *White Power*, 'Death Rattle', comprises examples of Culture-distortion, presented *TRUD*-style with news cuttings: Negro Le Roi Jones' acclaimed play 'The Toilet', unisex fashion, inane pop music and adolescent dancing in the aisles of a church in Boston during Sunday service, the portrayal of Sir Lancelot in a High School play by a Negro footballer, public displays of trash art, etc.[111] Significantly, the second chapter is named 'spiritual syphilis', analogous to Yockey's phrase 'ethical syphilis'. Rockwell even alluded to Spengler and diagnosed America's problem as a culture-pathogen:

> It is not physical lack of hardship that bears down on our people and drives them unconsciously toward national and racial suicide. It is a SPIRITUAL failing, a DISEASE of the spirit which has our people down and beaten. Our people are rotting from the inside, no matter how the outside gives the appearance of prosperity and happiness ... unless something changes mighty quickly, America — and all of Western civilization with us — will fold up with a whimper and die. No spiritually healthy people would ever tolerate the sort of horrors catalogued in Chapter I. Western civilization as Spengler predicted long ago, and America in particular, are far gone down the road towards decay and death.[112]

---

110 See Rockwell's autobiography, *This Time the World* (New York: Parliament House, 1963). Rockwell acknowledged General Douglas MacArthur, Senator Joseph McCarthy and trans-Atlantic aviation hero Colonel Charles Lindbergh (who had led the American First movement in opposing Roosevelt's pro-war policies) as the seminal influences on his political thinking.

111 G. L. Rockwell, *White Power* ([1967] Hollywood, Ca.: New Christian Crusade Church, 1972), pp. 9–50.

112 Ibid., pp. 57–58.

Rockwell then asked, 'where is all this spiritual syphilis coming from?'[113] He spends several chapters considering the activities of those whom Yockey called Culture-distorters.

With Chapter XIII, Rockwell returns with another Yockeyan phrase, entitling the chapter 'White Imperium'. Drawing on the spectre of the 'colored world revolt' headed by China, Rockwell refers to the antagonism between Russia and China as racial. 'Russians are "White" and the Chinamen hate and attack them as imperialists and exploiters — just the same as they attack us "dirty American fascists"'. What Rockwell saw coming, like Spengler in the final chapter of *The Hour of Decision*, was 'not a war between communism and capitalism' but a world race war. Rockwell said that communism was a 'colored world mutiny',[114] precisely as Spengler had stated it in 1934,[115] and what Yockey called the 'outer revolt', accelerating since the World War I.[116] Rockwell explained his version of Western Imperium in calling for 'a united White race, supremely conscious of its natural destiny … a noble race able to create the wonders of Western culture — only such a united race can muster the will and the strength to restore order to a world in the process of suicide and disintegration'.[117] Drawing on the Spenglerian and Yockeyan concepts of cultural 'destiny', Rockwell said that 'it is not yet our "time" to die'. 'Destiny' had 'brought forth the greatness of Rome' and then the cleansing sweep of northern barbarians 'when it was time' for Rome to make room for a new civilization. 'Destiny had brought forth the British Empire' then 'withdrew her blessing' when it was time for that empire to leave the world stage. Now 'destiny' is 'conceiving the new Imperium of our time, the White Imperium — the unification of the White race and its conscious racial mastery of the Globe'. 'In spite of all the signs of death and disease … the embryo of that that unity and that White Imperium is growing' and will destroy all that stands in its way.[118]

113 Ibid., p. 58.

114 Ibid., pp. 422–423.

115 Spengler, *The Hour of Decision*, op. cit., pp. 204–230.

116 Yockey, *Imperium* (Wermod ed.), op. cit., p. 716.

117 Rockwell, *White Power*, op. cit., p. 426.

118 Ibid., p. 427.

Clearly, despite Rockwell's rejection of Yockey on the issues of 'horizontal and vertical race' and the USSR, Yockey's ideas nonetheless had an influence on Rockwell. Indeed, *Imperium* is still sold by Rockwell's successor, Matt Koehl.[119]

The move of *TRUD* to the NSWPP was motivated by frustration with the shilly-shallying and inner-squabbles of the 'Right'. DTK's Nordland Press continued and a circular announced the publication of *Yockey: Four Essays*, while Nordland and subsequently Atlantis Archives distributed a large number of books.

Bylined 'A fortnightly of fact and abuse',[120] *TRUD* fulfilled its promise to be both outrageously funny and deadly serious. The *Trudniks* showed how the philosophical complexities of Spengler and Yockey could be creatively rendered with satire, showing up the absurdity of modern-day political, social and cultural pathogenic icons. *TRUD* was a valiant, unique effort. There was a failing within the 'Right' and not with the *Trudniks*. Over four decades later, *TRUD* continues to stand unmatched. Had it appeared as intended, as a mass distribution tabloid, history might have been made. The *Trudniks* had the wit and the wisdom. Additionally, *TRUD* was the first to publish, at least in part, *The Enemy of Europe* outside of the quickly suppressed German edition.

## Louis T Byers and the National Youth Alliance

The name Louis T Byers only seems to have been maintained among Rightist circles by Dr Revilo P Oliver's dedication to him of *The Enemy of Our Enemies*, Oliver's critique of Francis Parker Yockey's *The Enemy of Europe*.

Dr Oliver's dedication reads:

To the Memory of
The Founder of the Francis Parker Yockey Society[121]
Louis T Byers

---

119 NS Publications, http://nspublications.com/philosophy/imperiumbk.htm. Koehl died in October 2014. However *Imperium* is still sold by Koeh's successor, Martin Kerr.

120 *TRUD*, No. 33, February 1970.

121 The correct title was in fact The Francis Parker Yockey Movement. DTK to Bolton, April 13, 2014.

Aryan of the Aryans
Who Fought a Good Fight to its Tragic End
22 October 1981

Yet, although apparently little known today, Byers played a seminal role in the establishing of a doctrinal foundation for the Right above and beyond the common run. In his day, he drew significant smears from hacks such as Jack Anderson and Drew Pearson.

Byers, like many others of the radical Right, including Dr Oliver, started his political sojourn in the John Birch Society as the area co-coordinator for western Pennsylvania and New York but was, like many other stalwarts, expelled from the JBS in 1968 for radical views. Also in 1968, Byers was the Pennsylvania organiser of the presidential campaign of segregationist Alabama Governor George C Wallace. Byers was instrumental in transforming the Youth for Wallace, which had been founded by Carto,[122] into the National Youth Alliance (NYA). Under Byers' direction, the NYA intended to establish its presence on the streets and on the campuses by physically confronting the New Left, which was then running rampant under the covert auspices of the Establishment it claimed to be fighting.[123]

Byers, described as 'a fast-talking, articulate Philadelphian',[124] was head of the Francis Parker Yockey Movement, a type of Rightist version of the Fabian Society, designed to infiltrate and redirect the Right. NYA was to effect street organisation based on the philosophy of *Imperium*. A *Washington Post* photograph shows the NYA office adorned with a large picture of Yockey handcuffed and flanked by police.[125] The NYA symbol was the mathematical sign for 'not equal' and its axiom was: 'Free Men Are Not Equal; Equal Men Are Not Free.'

With factionalism rife, an attempt to elect Dennis McMahn chairman had failed in favour of Patrick Tifer. Carto declared the election invalid but

122 Robert S Griffin, *The Fame of a Dead Man's Deeds: An Up-Close Portrait of White Nationalist William Pierce* (1st Books, 2001), p. 118.

123 Cf. Bolton, *Revolution from Above*, op. cit., 'New Left from Old'.

124 Paul W Valentine, 'The Student Right: Racist, Martial, Insular', *Washington Post*, May 15, 1969.

125 Paul W Valentine, 'NYA: Alive & Well Here', *Washington Post*, December 22, 1969.

said he would support Tifer if Carey Winters was elected as Secretary and James Ferris as treasurer. Carey Winters stated that *Imperium* should form the ideological basis of the NYA and Byers stated that only those who had read *Imperium* should be able to vote in the NYA election.[126]

A coup had taken place at the founding meeting, under the auspices of Byers' Francis Parker Yockey Movement (FPYM) and Willis Carto. The FPYM that evening held a dinner at which Carto was guest of honour and the evening started with a reading from *Imperium*. The second speaker was Byers, followed by Mike Russell, who spoke on 'Plato the Fascist'. Carto concluded with a talk on his visit to Yockey and on *Imperium*. The FBI and the hack Drew Pearson claimed that the Horst Wessell song and other German National Socialist anthems were played throughout the evening.[127]

Tifer moved to expel Carto, remove Winters and Ferris, ban the sale of *Imperium* and turn all moneys over to his faction. Carey Winters responded by telegramming to Tifer that the Board of Directors had expelled him.[128]

The supposedly moderate John Acord and Dennis McMahon left to form their own organisation[129] and the dispute between two NYAs became vitriolic. Acord et al were outraged that the Youth for Wallace, turned NYA, had been placed under the jurisdiction of Carto's Action Associates and Liberty Lobby, although Carto provided the funds for everything.

The first issue of the Byers/NYA tabloid *Attack!* was issued in Fall 1969, listing Byers as publisher and Carey Winters as editor. It announced a campus programme called 'Right Power' with the byline 'Stop Riot Power with Right Power', featuring films and speakers but with the advice that hippies would not be admitted. The programme was launched at UCLA, hot-bed of New Left militancy. The front page of *Attack!* depicts Byers addressing a student audience of 2,000, while another picture shows 'a spellbound hippie' reading *Imperium*. Following the rally, the students presented their demands to the Dean: Restore law and order to the campus; continue to give credit for ROTC; rename Ralph Bunche Hall as Douglas MacArthur Hall; add eugenics,

126 FBI New York, 'National Youth Alliance', May 20, 1969, 157–12589, p. 6.

127 FBI New York, 'National Youth Alliance', May 20, 1969, 157–12589, p. 4.

128 FBI New York, 'National Youth Alliance', May 20, 1969, 157–12589, p. 6.

129 Drew Pearson, Jack Anderson, 'Our Hitler Youth', *New York Post*, April 21, 1969.

genetics and ethology to the curriculum; fire teachers who encourage anarchy; dissolve the Students for a Democratic Society. If demands were not met, Rightist counteraction was threatened. Page 3 of *Attack!* carried a large advertisement for *Imperium*.[130]

The mainstay for establishing *Attack!* was Carey Winters, a Dean's list graduate of Carnegie-Mellon University.[131] DTK states that Winters did most of the work and drafted the cartoons. Byers was most adept at organising and dealing with the news media.[132] However, by issue 2, while Byers was still listed as publisher, William Pierce, under the name Luther Williams, had assumed editorship. *Imperium* was still being advertised.[133] From issue 7, Fall 1971, Byers no longer appeared as the publisher. From issue 5, April 1971, Pierce had dropped the nom de plume. While an article on modernist art was termed 'culture distortion', from issue 6 (Summer 1971, and Byers was still there), references to Yockey had gone. While at this stage the absence of *Imperium* might have been a reflection of it no longer being supplied by Carto, Spengler's *Hour of Decision* and *The Decline of the West* were being advertised by the NYA-affiliated Western Destiny books,[134] run by Robert Lloyd, who had left the NSWPP at the same time as Pierce. Issue 6 was also describing Willis Carto as 'probably the slipperiest snake-oil salesman in the conservative sucker business'.[135]

In July 1969, Byers appeared with another NYA officer, Mike Russell, on the Barry Farber New York radio talkback, opposing two attorneys for the Jewish Defense League who were as much violently obsessed with Soviet diplomats as with 'neo-Nazis'. Byers stated his sole purpose for participating was to promote *Imperium*. Two former NYA officials were present — John Acord, who had run 'Youth for Wallace', and Dennis McMahon, claiming that the NYA was 'neo-Nazi', indicating that a schism had already been attempted.

---

130 *Attack!*, National Youth Alliance, Vol. 1, No. 1, Fall 1969.

131 *Attack!*, No. 1, ibid., p. 2.

132 DTK to Bolton, October 4, 2014.

133 *Attack!* Vol. 2, No. 2, p. 6; issue 3, p. 6 (as was Spengler's Hour of Decision, p. 4); no. 4, p. 7.

134 *Attack!*, No. 6, Summer 1971, p. 7.

135 'Conservative Swindler Thriving', *Attack!*, No. 6, Summer 1971, p. 2.

Acord and McMahon stated that they had resigned due to the takeover of the NYA by Carto and the Francis Parker Yockey Movement.[136]

The FBI was concerned from the start that the NYA would use violence to counteract the New Left on campus. Their aims were cited by the FBI from a New York meeting, as being 'the opposing of the use of drugs on college campuses, the neutralization of black power, the preserving of Western civilization and the expulsion of communists from college campuses'.[137] J Edgar Hoover felt that a congressional investigation was 'imperative', given recent revelations from Drew Pearson.[138] As Senator McCarthy and anti-communists in the military such as Major Arch Roberts and General Edwin Walker discovered, one could oppose the Soviet threat abroad but an anti-communist movement at home that might develop into militant nationalism was regarded with horror by the 'Establishment' and suppressed.[139] In particular, there was concern that the Students for a Democratic Society, the Establishment's New Left controlled-opposition group,[140] might be run off campus.

While the NYA was attacked by the mass media it also received condemnation from those 'Patriotic Americans' who believed capitalism to be a God-given doctrine. Zygmond Dobbs, 'research director' of the Veritas Foundation, circulated a smear-sheet against Oliver, Carto and the NYA at the 'American Council of Christian Church Convention' in Pasadena in 1970. The 'Neo-Nazi Menace' was threatening 'our freedoms' and 'undermining the Bible-believing churches'. The axis for this plot centered on Willis Carto and Liberty Lobby. The real concern might have been that many Christians were giving money to this 'neo-Nazi' network. Mentioned were *Statecraft*, *The Washington Observer* and *American Mercury*, the latter two periodicals owned by Carto. The organisation responsible for duping youth was the

136 FBI memorandum, New York, July 28, 1969, NY 157–3447.

137 G. C. Moore, FBI memo, April 3, 1969, 157–12589–2, p. 1.

138 Hoover, FBI communications section, April 22, 1969.

139 See for example: Walter and Victor Reuther, 'The Reuther Memorandum to the Attorney General of the United States', December 19, 1961, http://www.scribd.com/doc/31124491/The-Reuther-Memorandum-Precusor-to-the-Ideological-Organizations-Audit-Project-Created-by-President-John-F-Kennedy-and-Attorney-General-Robert-Kenn.

140 K. R. Bolton, *Revolution from Above*, (London: Arktos Media Ltd. 2011), pp. 151–160.

National Youth Alliance, which had emerged from a neo-Nazi takeover of the Wallace for President campaign 'and has Prof Revilo P Oliver as it's [sic] theoretical spokesman'. Richard Cotten of *Conservative Voice* was also singled out.[141] Dobbs continued:

> The common denominator and programmatic guide to all of these groups is the book *Imperium* authored by a pro-Nazi, the late Francis Parker Yockey (alias Varange) who committed suicide in jail in 1960. [...] The book stands for "Ethical Socialism" which is a semantic synonym for Nazi National Socialism. It is anti-Semitic, anti-Christian and attacks our Constitutional Republic. It calls for a "World Authoritarian rule" of the entire human race by white Caucasians minus the Jews.[142]

Richard Cotten's National Documentation Institute was supposed to be the 'cover group' representing the leadership of all the groups of this network.[143] Others included Oliver; the German-American scholar and academic Dr Austin J App; Lt. General P. A. del Valle; the eminent psychologist Dr Henry E Garrett; and Lt. Colonel Arch Roberts, among several others.

Dobbs, returning to *Imperium*, states most oddly of all that it was based on 'the atheistic French *Encyclopedists*, such as Diderot and Voltaire and their historical mentors'. There is perhaps no philosophy that is more antithetical to the doctrines of the *Encyclopedists* than that of *Imperium*. Dobbs called on Christians to 'take an open and public opposition to this growing anti-Christian menace'.[144]

The Dobbs circular is cited here because it is such a fine example of the ignorance that caused Dr Oliver to finally give up on 'American conservatism' and refer to 'fifty years of failure'. Despite Dobbs being one of the more capable American conservatives, his circular was bereft of philosophical and historical understanding. Given that 'American conservatism' revolves around the Constitution and the Founding Fathers, it possesses inherent flaws, as the American Revolutionary ideal shares its origin with French Revolutionary

---

141 Z Dobbs, 'Neo-Nazi Menace', two-page, mimeographed circular, Pasadena, 1970.

142 Z Dobbs, ibid.

143 Z Dobbs, ibid.

144 Z Dobbs, ibid.

Jacobinism, Illuminism and other Deistic, Masonic, secular and humanist currents of which the *Encyclopedists* were the philosophical heralds. Two separate branches sprang from a common root: Liberalism and Marxism. What Americans call 'conservatism' and the 'Right' is this Liberalism. It continues to inform the ideological motivation of US foreign policy in what remains a Jacobin aim of 'world democratic revolution' in the name of what the Jacobins were calling *le droit humain* within the shadow of the guillotine and what the US Establishment today calls 'human rights' in the shadow of its bombers. Ironic, given that Dobbs claims this is the current from which Yockey and *Imperium* emerged. Yockey is as far removed from Diderot as it is possible to imagine. The whole doctrine is a complete repudiation of Jacobinism, including rationalism and atheism. That Yockey was so misunderstood by Dobbs is indicative of the ignorance with which *Imperium* was met even among the better minds of American conservatism.[145]

During 1971, Byers had fallen out with Willis Carto. Byers kept NYA assets and mailing lists and established 'Power Products'. Kirkpatrick W Dilling,[146] in his capacity as a partner in his father Albert's law firm, represented Carto. He wrote to Dr Revilo P Oliver advising that Byers was a man of unscrupulous character.[147] Oliver, a founding patron of the NYA, giving respects to the contribution of Dilling's mother to the Nationalist movement, responded that he would consider the matter with objectivity but had observed that Byers had always acted in a 'manly and honorable fashion'.[148] One of the differences that provoked a sympathetic response for Byers was that he was a 'panthe-

---

145 Dobbs was author of *The Great Deceit: Social Pseudo-Sciences* (New York: Veritas Foundation, 1964). The book is an interesting study on the Marxian-type foundations of sociology and anthropology but is marred by Dobbs' obsession with everything associated with 'socialism'. Hence, Hitler's National Socialism is seen as having commonality with Marxism, as is the Christian guild social ethos of Medieval Europe. While Dobbs deplores the suppression of scientific studies on racial differences between Blacks and Whites he deplores as 'socialistic' any critique of Jews.

146 Son of Elizabeth Dilling, the famous 'anti-Semite', organiser of We the Mothers Mobilize, that opposed the USA's entry into World War II, and one of the Sedition trial defendants.

147 Kirkpatrick Dilling to Oliver, April 9, 1971.

148 Oliver to Dilling, April 15, p. 1, 1971.

ist', according to Dilling, and not being a Christian was therefore 'amoral'. However, Oliver himself was critical of Christianity within a milieu that was largely Christian. Indeed, Oliver had been persuaded to support the NYA when it was formed in 1969 largely because of the confidence he had in Byers as its leader.[149]

By the fifth issue of *Attack!* Dr William Pierce had become the editor, succeeding two prior editors, while Byers remained the publisher. Dr Pierce, who had been a physics lecturer, had edited *National Socialist World*,[150] the NSWPP's ideological journal, since meeting Rockwell in 1964.[151] It was *Attack!* and NYA that provided him with his springboard after falling out with the NSWPP's Matt Koehl in 1970.[152] With the seventh issue (Fall 1971), Byers' name no longer appeared. By the time Pierce had met Byers in 1970, Byers said that he intended closing down NYA, as it was in debt to half-a-million dollars since losing the support of Carto. Pierce was interested in continuing the organisation.[153] His NYA was reincorporated as a manoeuver to avoid bankruptcy. Byers was retained as chairman of an advisory committee that included veteran segregationist Admiral John G Crommelin, Lt. General Pedro del Valle (USMC), German-American author Professor Austin J App, news analyst Richard Cotten, and Professor Oliver. In 1974, the NYA was changed into the National Alliance, which Pierce led until his death in 2002. Byers became a well-known jazz critic for the mainstream media but maintained contact with Oliver until Byer's death from cancer in 1981. Having established Power Products, Byers published Dr Oliver's lecture, 'Conspiracy or Degeneracy?'[154] Under Dr Pierce's direction, Yockey was no longer a focus of NYA or NA ideology. Indeed, from what he told his biographer, Pierce did not even read *Imperium*.[155]

---

149 Oliver to Dilling, ibid., p. 2

150 Robert S Griffin, ibid., p. 109.

151 Robert S Griffin, op. cit., p. 87.

152 Robert S Griffin, ibid., p. 115.

153 Robert S Griffin, ibid., p. 117.

154 Dr Oliver to Mrs Edith L Fox, January 23, 1970.

155 Robert S Griffin, op. cit., p. 117,

Although the obvious choice of alignment for *TRUD* would seem to have been the NYA and *Attack!*, the *Trudniks* chose the NSWPP at a time when there were bitter disputes between Carto, Byers, Oliver, et al. and the NSWPP seemed more vibrant.[156] These disputes resulted in the complication of there being two organisations named National Youth Alliance. The alternative version had already started in 1968, with its own tabloid newspaper, *Statecraft*. The vice-chairman and assistant editor was Dennis McMahon; the chairman and publisher, Daniel Paulson. Like *Attack!* and *TRUD* it was a combination of intellect and guts. Oddly, however, this NYA chose as its symbol an American eagle holding a US dollar sign in its talons. The eagle looked menacingly leftward against any attack. The dollar sign was explained as a 'symbol of American productivity'.[157] The byline of *Statecraft* was: 'For the Productive, Against the Destructive.' Like the Byers' NYA, it aimed to physically resist the New Left. The primary enemy was the 'cancer' of 'liberalism'. *Statecraft*/NYA was particularly conscious of eschewing 'neo-Nazism' and maintaining adherence to George C Wallace. They mentioned support for Wallace in their statement of policy. However, their approach was hardly moderate and did not eschew the label of 'racist'. *Statecraft* supported Wallace's American Independence Party and[158] C. B. Baker editorialised that 'racism is a preference for one's own group and one's own kind',[159] that 'all normal people are racists'. The article ended with a still from the early cinematic classic *The Birth of a Nation*, depicting Klansmen holding a wide-eyed Negro captioned: 'Is you sure dis hear is de Black power meeting? Them sheets shar don't look like no African clothes to me.'[160] A cartoon on the same page depicts suited figures labeled 'YAF' (Young Americans for Freedom) looking nervous as they are

---

156 DTK to Bolton, October 4 2014.

157 The oddity of the dollar sign as an emblem was remarked upon by a student from the University of Ohio in a letter in *Statecraft*, Vol. 2, No. 2, February–March 1969, p. 3. He suggested instead a lightning bolt. By at least 1972 the lightning bolt had replaced the dollar sign. *Statecraft*, Vol. 4, No. 1, January 1972.

158 'American Independence Party News', *Statecraft*, Vol. 2, No. 2, February–March 1969, p. 6.

159 C. B. Baker, 'Who is a Racist?', *Statecraft*, ibid., p. 1.

160 C. B. Baker, 'Who is a Racist?', ibid., p. 5.

approached by armed Black Power Negroes. The YAF characters ask whether they should stay and 'debate' or run away lest they be called 'racists'. *Statecraft*/NYA upheld 'revolution'[161] as much as the Byers/Pierce NYA.

In October 1971, in an effort toward clarity and a change of direction, *Statecraft*/NYA became Youth Action. In a dramatic shift, YA found itself with the support of Carto, who had fallen out with Pierce and Byers. A new board of directors had been elected in September. The prime enemy was now the 'Materialistic System' and the aim was to 'smash the Establishment'. Paulson and McMahon were out. The Chairman was Luke Herda; vice chairman, Ken Hoop. C. B. Baker remained editor of *Statecraft*[162] and the new emblem was the lightning bolt.[163] Of particular significance here is the Yockeyan direction that was taken up, with its chief spokesman being YA vice Chairman Ken Hoop. The advertisement for *Imperium* in Statecraft ran:

> Condemned by Jews and Nazis alike. The late George Lincoln Rockwell (commander of the American Nazi Party) called IMPERIUM "Jewish". The ADL Jewish thought Police—called IMPERIUM "NAZI". Liberals and "responsible conservatives" alike become hysterical over the mere mention of IMPERIUM. What kind of book can generate such violent emotions? Marxists fear IMPERIUM'S revelation of the hidden laws of history, which forecast their doom. Who was the HERO OF THE SECOND WORLD WAR? Who are the CULTURE DISTORTERS? What is the FUTURE OF AMERICA? You'll discover the answer to these and many other VITAL QUESTIONS of the day when you read IMPERIUM. The Mystery Book of our Time by Ulick Varange (Francis Parker Yockey).[164]

The Yockey influence now became apparent, with references for the first time to 'Khazarish[165] culture distorters'. Ken Hoop was named as representative of

---

161 K. R. Valhal, 'The American Revolutionary', ibid., p. 7.

162 'Youth Leaders Elected', *Statecraft*, Vol. 4, No. 1, January 1972, p. 3.

163 Peter C Reynolds, 'NYA is Youth Action', *Statecraft*, Vol. 4, no. 1, January 1972, p. 2.

164 *Statecraft*, ibid., p. 8.

165 The reference is to the theory that most of today's Jews are descended from Khazars, when Khazaria, a large empire stretching from the Black Sea, converted to Judaism in the eighth century AD. The theory was popularised by the Jewish novelist Arthur Koestler, in his book *The Thirteenth Tribe* (London: Pan Books, 1977); and among

the Yockeyan current within Youth Action and 'all Yockey fans' were urged to contact him. In perhaps the first article on Yockey in *Statecraft*, Hoop described Yockey's term 'Culture distorter', from his 'masterpiece *Imperium*', as 'probably the most all-inclusive accurate term for the enemy'. Hoop included not only the Jewish culture-alien but liberals, communists and all others working against Western civilization, whom Yockey would designate as the 'inner enemy' and the 'Culture-retarder' rather than as Culture-distorter.[166]

Friedrich Wolf also addressed Yockeyanism in a discussion on National Socialism. Wolf stated that American patriots would reject any reference to 'socialism', no matter how it was explained. He cited both Hitler and Goebbels as stating that National Socialism was a German phenomenon and not for export. Wolf pointed out that Rockwell became an overt 'Nazi' because he was fed up with the inaction of the conservatives and wanted to attract fighters with daring methods; but still he retained 'American values' and did not try to become a synthetic 'German', as some of the Hitler cultists attempted. Wolf honoured Rockwell's memory for his guts and honesty. He contended that it is as foolish for such Nazi cultists to claim to be followers of Yockey, as it is for the liberal press to call *Imperium* a 'Nazi book'. He thought it 'totally impossible for a thinking person to follow both Hitler and Yockey'. As we have seen, Yockey regarded German National Socialism as an epochal historical movement in ushering the imperial cycle of Western civilization. However, he stated that it was 'provisional', not the final answer. While following both Hitler and Yockey is far form 'totally impossible', Wolf's contention that Yockey's Western 'Imperialism' and Hitlerism diverged ideologically is a legitimate comment; indeed, this divergence outraged orthodox Hitlerites such as Rockwell, Leese and Jordan. Wolf argued, citing the NSDAP's 25-point programme and the Nuremberg Laws, that the Hitlerite definition of a Jew, and his place in society, was based on blood; Yockey's definition was based on 'culture'. Wolf cited Yockey's contention that Jews can assimilate and be thoroughly imbued with Western culture. Indeed, Yockey wrote that just as

Rightist circles by Benjamin H Freedman, a retired millionaire manufacturer, Jewish convert to Catholicism, and major sponsor of *Common Sense*, in his pamphlet *Facts Are Facts* (New York City, 1954).

166 Ken Hoop, 'The Enemy—An Interpretation', *Statecraft*, ibid., p. 8.

someone who has imbued himself with all things Jewish can become a 'Jew' in the fullest sense of the word, regardless of blood, so have Jews 'acquired Western race'. This process of what the Zionists contemptuously call 'assimilation' was the *raison d'être* for the birth of modern Zionism, and while being 'social, anti-Semitism' is welcomed by them (as the distinct form 'cultural anti-Semitism').[167] Wolf quotes Rockwell as writing that Yockeyanism was a perversion of everything for which Hitler had died and that it 'smacks of a Jewish scheme to emasculate National Socialism'.[168] The conclusion for Wolf was that the orthodox Hitlerites, who preferred wearing their armband to fighting effectively, were a hindrance and would have been eschewed by Hitler for their lack of adjustment to reality.

*Statecraft* was changed into *Youth Action News*[169] but Youth Action seems to have slowly withered to non-existence. Louis Byers, whom Oliver held in unique esteem, became a well-known journalist on the jazz scene. When he was struck by cancer in 1978 and undertook treatment in the Bahamas, Wild Bill Davison, an icon of 'traditional Dixieland jazz', returned from Europe in January 1980 to hold a benefit-concert for Byers, with the participation of other notable jazz musicians.[170] Though the treatment seemed to be working, Byers succumbed to liver damage. An obituary notes that he served in the Army in Korea, became a newspaper columnist of 'rare ability' and supported the campaign of conservative Senator Barry Goldwater for the presidency. He was influenced by Nietzschean thought, and was a coordinator of The John Birch Society in Pittsburgh, in New York in the mid 1960s, and in Pennsylvania with the 1968 George Wallace presidential campaign. In 1969 he was appointed chief lobbyist for Carto's Liberty Lobby in Washington and

167 Wolf was citing the Noontide Press ed. of *Imperium*, p. 296, (Wermod ed.: p. 379).

168 Wolf, ibid., p. 10, citing *The Rockwell Report*, September 15, 1964. As we have seen, Rockwell borrowed several major principles from Yockey: Culture pathology in what Rockwell called 'spiritual syphilis' and Yockey called 'ethical syphilis', and the concept of a 'White Imperium'.

169 Ken Hoop to Bolton, October 8, 2014. After Youth Action Hoop worked with Carto's relatively influential Liberty Lobby, then with the Populist Party founded by Carto and Don Wassall. They later had a falling out.

170 'Internationally famed Cornetist to give Benefit Concert here', *The Journal Messenger Manses*, Virginia, January 1, 1980, pp. 1 and 3.

after the NYA episode he worked on radio commentator Richard Cotten's *Conservative Viewpoint* magazine during 1971-72. When *The Enemy of Europe* was published in 1981, Oliver gave the first copy to Byers' widow, Ruth.[171]

## Professor Revilo P Oliver

Dr Revilo P Oliver was one of the first to recognize Yockey's brilliance soon after his death in 1960. Despite his disagreement with two fundamental premises — that the Jews had lost power in the USSR and that race as a biological construct was of lesser importance than race as a spiritual and cultural identity — Oliver never repudiated Yockey's significance. Oliver, Professor of Classics at the University of Urbana, Illinois, for 32 years, had learned Sanskrit by the time he finished High School and had mastered 11 languages. As a scholar of international repute who directed a branch of military intelligence during World War II, for which he received commendation for his innovative methods, Oliver had a particularly caustic, no-nonsense manner. Nevertheless, he seems to have cordially replied to every individual who sent him even a scribbled note making some enquiry about a book, person or group. He was generous with both his time and his money but scathing and unforgiving towards those he viewed as duplicitous.

Oliver had been a co-founder with Robert Welch of The John Birch Society and contributing editor of the JBS magazine *American Opinion.* He was a member of the National Council until 1966, when, as he states it, he 'discovered that the supposed head of the organisation, Robert Welch, was then operating under the supervision of four Jews'. He goes on: 'Of course, I then severed my connection with what had become a pseudo-patriotic hoax.'[172] That year, Oliver was targeted by the Anti-Defamation League and attacked in the news media as an 'anti-Semite' when he spoke at the JBS-sponsored 'New England Rally for God, Family and Country' in Boston.[173] Veteran 'anti-

171 Oliver to Ruth Byers, November 17, 1981.

172 Oliver to Katherine Baker, July 20, 1989.

173 'Openly Anti-Semitic Rally in Boston Features key Birch Society Spokesman', *The California Jewish Voice*, July 15, 1955. 'Robert Welch, Founder and Head of the Birch Organization, is Prominent at Meeting where Dr Oliver Delivers Vile Anti-Semitic Speech', *American Examiner*, July 14, 1966.

Semite' Joseph P Kamp was also present. The press exposure of Oliver, who often referred to Jews as 'sheenies', in connection with the JBS, sent Birchite founder Robert Welch into a panic. The mere fact that the JBS was conservative and anti-communist was enough to have brought criticism from Jewish organisations against them from the start. Welch was always at pains to describe 'anti-Semites' and segregationists as 'neutralisers', serving the 'international Communist conspiracy' by undermining the efforts of responsible 'Americanists'. Oliver's address was entitled 'Conspiracy or Degeneracy' and became a classic among the more forthright sectors of the 'Right'. While the Jewish and other press claimed that Oliver blamed Jews for a pervasive conspiracy, the speech, which drew enthusiastic applause form the large audience, stated that the real problems were ultimately caused not by 'conspiracy' but by the genetic degeneration of the population. Oliver's statements were not reported in context.[174] However, Oliver had found that the JBS was supervised by a 'secret committee' comprising four Jews whom he named: Sam Blumenfeld, Kogan, Greene and Solomon. At the Boston rally he had sought to provoke them by stating that LSD was imported to the USA from Israel. His letter of resignation from the JBS cited this 'secret committee' and Oliver was offered $5,000 to withdraw his resignation letter during a conversation with Welch, which Oliver insisted on openly taping. It was Blumenfeld, promoted as an expert on communism in Europe, who 'tried to plant all sorts of canards' as 'inside information' with Oliver, including 'a "documented" story that Yockey was a communist agent in the service of Castro.'[175]

Welch was aware of Zionism, although seemingly naïve on Judaism. In 1962 he even stated to a supporter of the JBS, Verne P Kaub, president of the American Council of Christian Laymen, that he was 'probably as anti-Zionist' as Kaub but considered Zionism to be of lesser importance than communism. Welch wrote to Kaub that Zionism had been 'practically the father of the International Communist Conspiracy' for two decades from 1905 but that communism had 'far outgrown the parent' and Zionism was in a 'comparatively minor position'. Welch even stated that Gordon Winrod,

---

174 Revilo P Oliver's forthright speech, 'Conspiracy or Degeneracy?', can be read or heard here: http://www.revilo-oliver.com/news/1966/07/conspiracy-or-degeneracy/.

175 Oliver to Joseph P Kamp, June 12, 1982; private archives.

successor to his father Gerald Winrod, who was regarded as one of the USA's most avid supporters of the Third Reich prior to World War II and who had built up a large 'anti-Semitic' following, was 'on our side' insofar as he was an anti-communist Christian.[176] It is doubtful whether the JBS could have been founded without the backing of those who opposed Jewish agendas. Certainly, it had been widely perceived since the Bolshevik Revolution that communism and the left were intimately connected with Jews, a link which became most conspicuous when most of those uncovered by Senate and Congressional hearings into espionage or subversion were found to be Jewish. By 1966, however, those critical of Jews or supportive of segregation were being purged or pushed out of the JBS and Dr Oliver was among these. Welch had already alluded in 1961 to being threatened twice by the Anti-Defamation League on account of Welch's association with Merwin K Hart, a JBS officer and veteran 'anti-Semite' whose activities predated World War II. Welch had even acknowledged being a long-time subscriber to *Common Sense* and other papers critical of Jewish activities.[177]

Interestingly, Welch concurred with the contention of Yockey, *Common Sense* and Weiss that the 'Zionists had lost power in the USSR by 1937 or 1938, when Stalin had finally succeeded in taking into his own hands all of the reins of communist power stretching out all over the world'. Welch saw Zionism as being subordinated to the communist conspiracy and contended that 'blaming Jews' for the communist conspiracy was playing into the hands of the communists.[178] Welch had come to certain similar conclusions to those of Yockey in regard to the USSR but reached a different perspective on their basis. Communism, with or without Zionist/Jewish dominance, remained the primary enemy for Welch and most other American conservatives; they lacked the higher perspective that Yockey had provided with his concept of Culture-pathology.

Just three years after Yockey's death and a year after the publication of *Imperium* in the USA for the first time since 1948, Oliver wrote an appraisal of Yockey in the magazine of the John Birch Society (JBS), *American Opinion*.

---

176 Robert Welch to Vernon P Kaub, April 4, 1962.

177 Robert Welch, ibid.

178 Welch to Dr Lawrence A Lacey, February 10, 1961.

That Oliver could get his discussion of racial matters, the four-part series, 'History and the Historians', published in *American Opinion* is remarkable given that the JBS, established in 1958 as an anti-communist organization, was always anxious to purge itself of 'fascists', 'anti-Semites' and 'racists'. As Oliver explained, he wrote the series to raise the intellectual tone of the JBS and get readers thinking about ethnology and history, rather than the monotony of the 'International Communist Conspiracy'.[179] Among the historians Oliver discussed was Oswald Spengler, whose 'morphology of history was the great intellectual achievement of our century', the 'Copernicus of historionomy', regardless of whether one agrees with his conclusions.[180] Oliver objected to Spengler's subjective meaning of 'race', as he did Yockey's. However, Spengler should always be honoured because he has 'forced us to inquire into the nature of civilization and to ask ourselves by what means — if any — we can repair and preserve the long and narrow dykes that alone protect us from the vast and turbulent ocean of eternal barbarism.'[181]

After discussing Arnold Toynbee's historical method, based on the concept of civilization being shaped by the challenges a people faces in shaping its environment, Oliver introduced Yockey, among Voegelin and others, under the sub-heading 'The Mood of Empire' in part III of the series.

> About a decade ago students of history began to hear of a great new formulation of historical perspectives, admittedly based on Spengler, but extending and revising the Spenglerian analysis. It was the work of an unknown American, rumored to have been an officer of our diplomatic service, who wrote in Ireland under the strange pseudonym of Ulick Varange. It had been published by an obscure house in London in 1948. But it was virtually unprocurable. Book dealers despaired of finding a copy. When I finally obtained one, it cost me (unbound!) well over one hundred dollars, and I have been told of a man who paid three hundred for his. The book was at last reprinted in New York in 1962 in an edition that was

179 Oliver, 'History for Conservatives', *America's Decline: The Education of a Conservative* (London: Londonium Press, 1982), p. 182. Originally published in *American Opinion*, Belmont, Mass., Spring 1963.

180 Oliver, 'History and Historians', Part I, *America's Decline…*, ibid., p. 193.

181 Oliver, ibid., p. 200.

> quickly sold out.[182] A new edition, handsomely printed from the same plates, is now available: *Imperium — The Philosophy of History and Politics* (Sausalito, California, the Noontide Press). It is now known that Ulick Varange was not, as first rumored, a diplomat. His real name was Francis Parker Yockey, and he was an American lawyer, author of a still unpublished work on Constitutional law.[183]

Oliver outlined what little was then known of Yockey's life. He comments that when Yockey joined the war crimes commission in Germany, he 'appears to have entertained some illusions when he accepted the position'. He sought the position and joined in order to get to Germany to (1) try to assist the defendants where he could and (2) make contacts. Oliver also writes that the State Department confiscated Yockey's passport and that he had to go 'underground' to avoid 'assassination'. For this there now seems to be no documentation; either Oliver was in error or had learned something through his own sources.

Oliver points to some small historical oversights in *Imperium* (in particular Yockey's stating that Germany had long disappeared from the scene of European history, which overlooked the Thirty Years' War of 1618–1648). But of course Oliver's primary objection is that like Spengler, Yockey discounts the biology of race, while describing culture in 'quasibiological' terms as an organism subjected to 'quasibiological' laws.

> [...] But Yockey's major conclusion is substantially that which emerges from every honest and discerning attempt to construct a philosophy of history, although it is sometimes stated less clearly or with more reservations. And that conclusion is the fundamental unity of the West today. As against the rest of the world, the West is a political unity, since the differences between Germany, Italy, France, Britain and ourselves are, like the differences between Maine, Virginia, Wyoming, and California, relatively negligible — and necessarily negligible when the survival of the whole is at stake. Furthermore, the culture of the West, like every viable civilization, is a unity in the sense that its parts are organically interdependent. Although architecture, music, literature, the mimetic arts,

182 This was the edition published by the racist and atheist Charles Smith, through his atheist publication, *Truth Seeker*. Smith was the organiser of the 'Racist Forum', where academics such as Donald Swan met with activists such as James Madole. Oliver thought highly of him.

183 Oliver, 'History for Conservatives', *America's Decline*, ibid., p. 217.

> science, economics and religion may seem at first glance more or less unrelated, they are all constituent parts of the cultural whole and the disease of any one will sooner or later affect all the others. Your hands will not long retain their strength, if there is gangrene in the foot or cancer in the stomach.
>
> Now, unless history has been written in vain and the human mind is impotent, that proposition is a fundamental truth. And Yockey expresses it so persuasively and even eloquently that it lends cogency to the whole of his argument. His book, therefore, can be dangerous, if you accept it without a full awareness of its implications.[184]

Oliver recommended Yockey in conjunction with Spengler and Lawrence R Brown's *Might of The West*,[185] considering the latter better than *The Decline of the West* because Brown's theory is not reliant on the notion of civilization as an organism that necessarily declines and dies. Oliver does say, however, that Brown reached similar conclusions to Yockey:

> The most recent formulation of a philosophy of history is a brilliant book by Lawrence R Brown, *The Might of the West* (Ivan Obolensky, New York; 562 pages). The author is an American engineer and mathematician who evidently undertook a study of history to ascertain why the United States and the West are committing suicide. So far as I can tell from a careful reading of the text, there is no indication that Mr Brown has read Yockey or even heard of him. It is significant, therefore, that he has reached, by an entirely different route, what are substantially the same conclusions.[186]

In 1966, Oliver wrote in *The American Mercury*:

> For us, the problem became urgent in the early decades of the twentieth century, when thoughtful men began to suspect or foresee that the world's mightiest civilization was moving rapidly toward a climax that might be catastrophe. There have been many attempts to ascertain and formulate laws of history that would enable us to predict — or, perchance, to control — our future. This study, both analytic and synthetic, of the historical process is often called historionomy, and by now it has produced thousands of books and articles — but the powerful and

---

184 Oliver, 'History for Conservatives', pp. 218–219.

185 Lawrence R Brown, *The Might of The West* (Washington: Joseph J Binns, 1963).

186 Oliver, 'History for Conservatives', op. cit., p. 221.

original minds that have been engaged in this inquiry do not number more than a score. As a kind of introduction to them (including Francis Parker Yockey), I undertook a survey of which the first four instalments appeared in *American Opinion* for May, June, November, and December, 1963.

The great modern philosopher of history is, of course, Oswald Spengler, whose *Decline of the West* formulated the problem in terms so clear and universal that everything written on the subject since 1918 has perforce had to be a commentary on Spengler — an attempt to extend, modify, or refute his magisterial synthesis. That great work, which has certainly been read and pondered by all who are interested in a philosophy of history, is not the clearest and most immediate proof of Spengler's genius. That is to be found in a shorter and later book that comparatively few seem to have read, *Die Jahre der Ent-scheidung*, of which the first volume was published in Germany (Munich, 1933) and felicitously translated into English by Charles Francis Atkinson as *The Hour of Decision* (New York, Knopf, 1934). [...]

Francis Parker Yockey proudly proclaimed himself the disciple of the man to whom he often refers as simply The Philosopher and it is true that at least a general understanding of Spengler's historionomy is taken for granted in the pages of Yockey's major work. But the young American had his own method and reached conclusions of his own. We must recognise in him a powerful and original mind. And we must be grateful that his *Imperium*, which a few years ago was one of the rarest of rare books, is now available in a handsome and beautifully printed edition from The Noontide Press.

This is not a book for "liberal intellectuals" or other children. No man can study history until he has learned that he must study it objectively and dispassionately, without reference to his emotions or predilections. Whether you view Caesar with admiration or horror, whether you love or hate him, has nothing whatever to do with the fact that he was victorious at Pharsalus.

No man should consider problems in historionomy if he does not realize that the only question before him will be the accuracy of the diagnosis or prognosis. The validity of the analysis does not in the least depend on the reader's emotional reaction to the future that it portends. When a physician diagnoses diabetes or arteriosclerosis or cancer, the only question is whether he has observed the symptoms accurately and reasoned from them correctly. Our wish that the patient did not have the disease is utterly irrelevant.

> Infantile minds, accustomed to living almost entirely in the vaporous realm of their own imagination, are incapable of distinguishing between reality and their own fancies. That is why I counsel "liberal intellectuals" not to read *Imperium*. If they are able to understand it, the book will certainly send them into a tantrum and may induce a paroxysmic fit. They had better stay in their academic lecture-halls or other playpens, where they can be happy making mud-pies, which they can call "world peace" and about which they can dance in a circle, chanting:
>
> *Higgledy-piggledy, my fat hen,*
> *Now we've got a big UN*[187]

Oliver also counselled that American Conservatives would find *Imperium* disturbing to their cherished faith in the rationalistic foundations of the American Republic, with its fetish for free enterprise and personal liberty. 'I also hope that *Imperium* will not fall into the hands of tenderhearted Conservatives who want to Love Everybody. Those dear ladies have noble souls but they are much too good for this world'.[188]

Yockey saw the necessity of discipline and authority, the antithesis of those values which are today more than ever being promoted as 'Western' and led by the USA. Oliver continued with a cogent description of what amounts to 'Ethical Socialism', as Yockey called it, or Spengler's 'Prussian Socialism'. He hoped that American conservatives would be capable of abandoning their ideological junk for the realities confronting the modern age:

> The future prefigured by Yockey is an almost complete antithesis to what American conservatives want and hope to attain. The one point of agreement is that the Bolsheviks and their feral conspiracy must be defeated and destroyed. What Yockey offers us, apart from that, is shocking: an authoritarian and absolute government under a new line of Caesars, personal liberty restricted by the need for solidarity, discipline in all matters of political importance, an economy controlled and regulated by the Caesars and a society that coheres by virtue of an ethos that will, if necessary, be ruthlessly enforced. And such domestic peace as we may know can be attained only by recognizing the West's "Inner Imperative of Absolute Imperialism".

---

187 Revilo P Oliver, 'The Shadow of Empire: Francis Parker Yockey After Twenty Years', *The American Mercury*, June 1966.

188 Oliver, 'The Shadow of Empire', ibid.

> That is why a reading of *Imperium* is a salutary experience for thoughtful American conservatives today. It forces us to reexamine the realities of the situation before us and to decide to what extent our objectives are still possible. For most of us, I am certain, there will be no question of changing in any way our conception of what is desirable. The problem will be that of deciding which, if any, of our specific objectives we should abandon because they can no longer be attained. If we abandon any, we shall do so in the spirit of men who, on a crippled ship, jettison some or all of the cargo because otherwise they would have no chance of bringing the ship and themselves to port. We shall do so for the reasons that impel a man to abandon his most valuable possessions in a burning house in order to save his wife and children.[189]

Oliver saw the situation now faced as one of bare survival for the West. All other 'issues' were diversions. That year, 1966, he quit The John Birch Society. His falling out with Robert Welch, founder of the JBS, was bitter. Welch had got the hard word from what Oliver states were his shadowy sponsors,[190] after Oliver had delivered his enthusiastically received lecture, 'Conspiracy or Degeneracy?' While Welch himself had thought the speech was great, Oliver had stated that the 'communist conspiracy' was a rebellion of the genetically inferior or unbalanced and that a major racial factor involved.[191] While this had been a conservative axiom before 1945, as demonstrated by such bestsellers as Lothrop Stoddard's *Revolt Against Civilization*,[192] it no longer featured in American conservative opinion of the Birchite type.

Oliver was enthused by the founding of *TRUD* in 1969, writing of it as 'a really brilliant little journal' and hoping that it would be 'a harbinger of the

---

189 Oliver, 'The Shadow of Empire'. ibid.

190 Oliver, *America's Decline…*, op. cit., p. 330.

191 Oliver, 'Conspiracy or Degeneracy?', speech to the New England Rally for God, Family, and Country; July 2, 1966, Boston, Massachusetts. This can be heard at: http://www.revilo-oliver.com/news/1966/07/conspiracy-or-degeneracy/.

192 Lothrop Stoddard, *The Revolt Against Civilization: The Menace of the Under-Man* (London: Chapman and Hall, 1922). A new edition is available from Wermod & Wermod, http://shop.wermodandwermod.com/books/all-non-fiction/the-revolt-against-civilization-the-menace-of-the-under-man.html. See also: Bolton, *The Psychotic Left: From Jacobin France to the Occupy Movement* (London: Black House Publishing, 2014).

future'. He noted the serialisation of *Der Feind Europas*, writing of his hope that *Der Feind* would be published as a book.[193]

Oliver continued to zealously promote *Imperium*, writing to an enquirer:

> Our chance to survive as a nation and a race depends on the formulation of a new doctrine that can be promoted and disseminated on all levels simultaneously—that will appeal to and inspire especially (a) the most intelligent among the best educated, and (b) the working masses. It will have to be expressed in different terms, of course, but the intellectual analysis for *a* must be strictly compatible with the simple and more emotional appeal to *b*. So far as I can see, *Imperium* provides the only available basis for a movement that has any chance of success.
>
> Francis Parker Yockey was a brilliant young man, as you will see from the enclosed reprint of an article that he wrote 32 years ago when he was 21. His book, *Imperium*, has, as I pointed out in two reviews of it, one in *American Opinion* and the other in the *American Mercury*, defects that were inevitable at the time and in the place where it was written, but, as I have said, it is the only work now available.[194]

When the National Youth Alliance was formed in 1969 to recruit youth, with *Imperium* as the ideological foundation, Oliver saw one last glimmer of hope for America. He enthusiastically joined the board of directors with other notables, Admiral Crommelin, Lt. General del Valle, Richard Cotten and Dr App. Oliver prepared a talk which was filmed for showing at NYA meetings, entitled 'After Fifty Years'. The text was printed in the first issue of *Attack!* and he stated that since the 1920s, American conservatives have failed despite some strenuous and sincere efforts. He regarded the NYA as the first effort to organise the elite of American youth, and described Louis Byers as 'a young man of undoubted integrity'. The NYA was speaking to youth not about 'free enterprise' and the wonders of consumerism but about 'honour, loyalty, race' and Western man's will to conquer or die. 'I do not venture to predict the future of the National Youth Alliance. It has great potentiality but it will therefore be the target of open and stealthy assaults delivered with a fury and

193 Oliver to *Trudniks*, November 28, 1969.

194 Oliver to Mrs Fox, January 23 1970.

cunning surpassing all that we have seen so far. And the time in which any action is possible will be perilously short. I merely say that American youth is our last hope, and that at long last an effort is being made to rally it.' Oliver stated that the fight will be for the young and doubted that the older generation had a right to tell them how to fight or introduce the 'sentimentality and squeamishness that was fatal to us and to our successors'. The future if there is one, is theirs.'[195]

In the filmed version of 'After Fifty Years', Oliver introduced *Imperium* as the fundamental text of the NYA, also recommending Brown's *Might of the West* and Spengler's *Decline of The West*. With such hopes, when NYA was quickly factionalised and Byers was pushed out, Oliver's disappointment was particularly bitter and his condemnation of those at *Statecraft*/NYA, with its initial dollar sign emblem and absence of Yockey, was scathing. Even though direction changed, as we have seen, when Carto redirected his support to *Statecraft*, Oliver never reconciled with Carto.

The venerable cultural magazine *The American Mercury*, founded in 1924 by the Nietzschean literary critic and author H. L. Mencken, had published some of America's most eminent literary figures, and had gone through a series of owners, all of the 'Right' to some extent, ending with Willis Carto. A 1971 edition of *The American Mercury* editorialised that Yockey was 'without doubt one of the greatest minds of the twentieth century, the towering genius whose most notable achievement was *Imperium*'. The article advertised Kaye's Nordland Press collection *Yockey: Four Essays*, giving particular attention to Yockey's final essay 'The World in Flames'. This described US foreign policy as being subjected to Jewish interests and hence outmanoeuvred across the world by the USSR as the result of American short-sightedness in its own interests, rather than as the result of Soviet cleverness.[196]

## *The Enemy of Europe*

One of the ventures with which Dr Oliver became involved, indicating his drift from conservatism, was *The Liberty Bell*, a magazine published by

195 Oliver, 'After Fifty Years', *Attack!*, Vol. 1, No. 1, Fall 1969. The film of the talk can be viewed at: http://www.youtube.com/watch?v=oQoH6KOvBGA.

196 'The Nameless Tyrant', *The American Mercury*, Summer 1971, pp. 3–4.

George Dietz. Dietz had been in the Hitler Jugend during the war. He was a realtor with the money to fund numerous projects, which included *White Power Report*, the White Power Movement (whose emblem was a swastika and star in red-white-and-blue) and a large array of reprints of pamphlets, books and articles, ranging from conservative to National Socialist — all from his vigorous printing enterprise in Reedy, West Virginia.

*The Enemy of Europe* had been published in Germany shortly after the war as *Der Feind Europas*. Yockey intended it as the third volume of *Imperium*, for the instruction of Socialist Reich Party leaders. But German authorities had quickly seized *Der Feind* and destroyed the printing plates.

However, several were sent to Britain and to Frederick Weiss, a copy being given to the US Library of Congress and one to Professor Daams.[197] Yockey had translated *Der Feind* into German himself because he had lacked the funds in Germany to have it done and according to DTK several German native-speakers of his acquaintance remarked that there were faults. Marie Weiss gave DTK her late husband's copy. This was translated back into English and was serialised in DTK's journal, *TRUD*. Despite the clearly Yockeyan orientation of *TRUD*, the series of *Der Feind* attracted little interest. 'Most readers were still under the ether of the System's smear against "Yockeyism" as a "Leftist" plot to steer "patriots" from the pursuit of Commies.'[198]

The *TRUD* translation had been undertaken by a '*German* nationalist' who was neither a Spenglerian nor on the 'Yockeyan Wavelength', according to DTK. Yockey had rendered the German edition in a poor translation himself after his translator quit due to doctrinal disagreements. Likewise, *TRUD's* German nationalist translator quit after DTK had given him the fourth Xeroxed instalment and he realised that Yockey 'was a pan-European

197 Dr Gerrit Daams, assistant professor of philosophy at Kent State University, who was appointed to the advisory board of *Mankind Quarterly*, when still under the editorship of Dr Robert Gayre, in Scotland. Kent State University reported that Professor Daams had written articles on the race problem. Others named by Kent State as being appointed to the Board of *Mankind Quarterly* included the psychologist Henry E Garrett and the revisionist historian Charles C Tansill. It is surprising that Kent State University, paragon of liberalism, reported this with apparent pride. See 'Gerrit Daams Honored by Scott Journal', *Kent State University Summer News*, Vol. 12, No. 1, June 23, 1966, p. 3.

198 DTK to Bolton, April 21, 2014.

and did not promote the idea of the Prussian generals and the faggy, lace-cuffed aristo-craps — in league with their Chinese buddies — initiating a war in Eastern Europe for the purpose of regaining the potato fields and sandy plains of East Prussia'.[199]

Thomas Francis undertook the definitive English translation of *Der Feind*. The manuscript was given to DTK with the intention of publishing hard and soft cover editions and he asked Oliver to write an introduction.[200] Francis discovered Yockey on reading Oliver's review of *Imperium* in *American Opinion* in 1964.[201] Given the anathema directed towards anything or anyone of an 'anti-Semitic' character by The John Birch Society, that magazine was indeed an extraordinary place to discover Yockey.

Finding a printer became problematic but Oliver had worked with George Dietz. Therefore, it was in Dietz's *Liberty Bell* that Thomas Francis' translation of *The Enemy of Europe* was serialised in 1981.[202] Thomas Francis was very eccentric and very brilliant, being able to converse with Dr Oliver in Attic Greek and Sanskrit, and was also a talented artist.[203] Oliver regarded the Thomas translation of *Der Feind* as exemplary, insofar as it was a 'retroversion' from Yockey's German to English and Francis had stayed true to Yockey's *style*.[204]

DTK noted that Yockey's original German edition, undertaken hurriedly, had resulted in the printer being 'hauled before the Office for the Protection of the (Western German) Constitution and being given a few new gray hairs by our Democratic Inquisitors of 1953'. 'I also learned that the print shop was raided, the plates destroyed and most copies confiscated. Yockey managed to mail out a few copies to the US and elsewhere before NATO's goonsquad got busy with their sledgehammers.'[205] Thomas Francis asked Oliver to write the introduction. Oliver was impressed with his translation and the feeling that

199 DTK to Oliver, March 15, 1978.

200 DTK to Oliver, March 15, 1978.

201 Francis to Oliver, February 22, 1985.

202 Yockey, 'The Enemy of Europe', *The Liberty Bell*, Reedy, West Virginia, Vol. 8, No. 9, May 1981 to Vol. 8, No. 10, June 1981.

203 A personal communication to Bolton, November 23, 2014.

204 Oliver to Francis, November 3, 1984.

205 DTK to Oliver, March 15, 1978.

Francis had for Yockey's ideas. He thought that 20 pages would serve[206] but his critique was to become lengthier than *Der Feind*. Working on the introduction in 1979, and commenting on the length, Oliver stated:

> I think some systematic, objective and scholarly critique of Yockey is necessary to counteract the disparaging estimates of him now prevalent in some quarters … I want to establish Yockey's position in contemporary thought quite definitely.[207]

The two parts were followed by Dr Oliver's critique, *The Enemy of Our Enemies*.[208] Oliver maintained his position that

> As an exegesis of historical causality, *Imperium*, and of course its sequel are radically defective, even in terms of their own premises. They have other values. I have always believed that *Imperium* was enlightening and even inspiring for young men and women whose minds have not been irredeemably blighted by the denaturing superstitions inculcated in the public schools. And both books are studies in politics […] in the original and proper sense of the word, not as it is used in our great ochlocracy in reference to the periodic popularity contests between Tweedledum and Tweedledee which many Americans find as exciting a baseball games.[209]

Oliver was a rationalist and materialist who believed genes determine history,[210] not spirit. Given the differences in worldview that existed between Oliver and Yockey, it must have been a rare detachment that enabled Oliver to persistently promote Yockey and Spengler. The series was published as a book

206 Oliver to DTK, June 10, 1978.

207 Oliver to DTK, August 13, 1979.

208 Revilo P Oliver, 'The Enemy of Our Enemies: A Critique of Francis Parker Yockey's The Enemy of Europe', *The Liberty Bell*, Vol. 8, No. 11, July 1981 to Vol. 9, No. 1, September 1981.

209 Oliver, ibid., Vol. 8, No. 12, August 1981, p. 50.

210 Oliver, 'History and Biology', Part IV of 'History and Historians', *American Opinion*, December 1963.

in November the same year[211] with a tribute to Louis Byers who had died in October and has since been kept in print by others.[212]

However, by 1985 there was much friction among the luminaries of the 'revisionist movement' and Francis thought of withdrawing permission for Dietz to continue publishing *The Enemy of Europe*. He held that Dietz had failed to give *The Enemy* adequate promotion and that the effort had been tantamount to not having been published at all.[213] Nonetheless, he felt honour-bound to allow *The Enemy* to continue for the sake of Oliver's work on the introduction.[214] In 1985, Francis and Oliver were still collaborating on refining the translation.[215]

The 1981 publication of *The Enemy* revived interest in Yockey. In 1982 John Tyndall, leader of the British National Party, reviewed *The Enemy of Europe* in his magazine *Spearhead*. Tyndall, because of his own ideological dispositions, actually regarded Revilo P Oliver as the 'superior political and historical philosopher'. Writing of Spengler's *The Decline of the West* and Yockey's *Imperium*, Oliver maintained his position for the union of Europe, which Tyndall opposed for the same reason that he opposed Mosley's post-war policy. Tyndall advocated the union of the British race and the restoration of the greatness not just of Britain but of the British race across the world. That was his *raison d'être*. He was therefore disappointed that Oliver had not critiqued Yockey's European idea. Tyndall thought the European Union would result in a melting pot, albeit a white one, of the sundry European subgroups. Yockey, he argued, was not able to write with the hindsight of the Common Market imbroglio, although Yockey's concept of Europe was the antithesis of the Masonic-US-Bilderberg plan for Europe.[216]

---

211 Yockey/Oliver, *The Enemy of Europe/The Enemy of Our Enemies* (Reedy: Liberty Bell Publications, 1981).

212 See Wermod & Wermod: http://shop.wermodandwermod.com/the-enemy-of-europe-the-enemy-of-our-enemies.html.

213 Francis to Oliver, January 16, 1985.

214 Francis to Oliver, February 22, 1985.

215 Oliver to Francis, March 11, 1985.

216 John Tyndall, 'Spengler Updated', *Spearhead*, Hove, Sussex, No. 166, August 1982, pp. 13–15.

What Tyndall did appreciate about Yockey, however, was that he 'formulated a philosophy of history which perhaps more devastatingly demolishes the orthodox "liberal" doctrine than any written in the English language in his time or since'.[217] Unfortunately, Tyndall's British loyalty obliged him to describe Yockey's view of Western unity and regeneration as 'simplistic generalisations'. Tyndall stated that all the things that Yockey hated about the USA were now 'prevalent in Europe' and no more so than in Germany. However, that was precisely Yockey's point, his warning to the Western Civilization to fight US-imposed Culture-distortion. The point was that the USA is the standard bearer of Culture-distortion.

Tyndall agreed that the 'old nationalism' that caused fratricidal wars between European states was outmoded and dangerous. He argued that it would therefore be better to be loyal to the entire 'white Race' than to a geographic location (Europe). 'Europeans, and not Europe, are our most important treasure and the entity whose welfare we should regard with the greatest concern, 'including those in North American and Australasia'.[218] Tyndall particularly objected to the portrayal of the USA and Russia as enemies of the White race. He also thought it ridiculous to regard the USA as 'The Enemy' when the power establishments of Europe are just as anti-White. Tyndall had misunderstood or perhaps overlooked the character of Yockey's concept of Cultural Vitalism but it is difficult to say why he stated he did not accept that the USA was the seat of the Culture-distorter. Certainly, Tyndall's ideological mentor, A. K. Chesterton, had identified the USA as the enemy. The question of the Jewish role in the USSR remained a quandary for Tyndall, as it did for much of the 'Right', and he leaves the possibilities open. However, Tyndall ends on a positive note in stating that while the focus has been to critique *The Enemy of Europe*, 'there is a vast amount in the Yockey text that cannot be faulted'.[219]

---

217 John Tyndall, 'Spengler Updated', ibid., p. 13.

218 John Tyndall, 'Spengler Updated', ibid., p. 14.

219 John Tyndall, 'Spengler Updated', ibid., p. 15.

## Wilmot Robertson and *Instauration*

In 1982 the American magazine *Instauration*, founded in 1972 by Wilmot Robertson, author of the bestselling *The Dispossessed Majority*,[220] also ran its first article on Yockey. Given that *Instauration* and *The Dispossessed Majority* focused on what was called Culture-distortion in Yockeyan parlance, and given that Robertson controversially argued that the USSR was no longer *Kosher*,[221] his review was a long time coming. Again, however, there is the old bugbear that caused Yockey to be rejected by much of the 'Right' — his Spenglerian and essential Germanic Idealist conception of 'race' rather than the zoological conception of skeletal indices. Moreover, Instaurationists were Nordicists, their primary concern being the decline of the Nordics, rather than 'Europeans' or 'Whites', such as in particular Mediterraneans.[222] There was no basis for Western unity, for a union of Spaniards, Italians, Britons, Swedes, French, Germans, Flemings, Portuguese. Too many Europeans were dark-eyed, short and olive, and would swamp the blond, blue-eyed, tall Nordic. Disparagingly, Robertson concluded: 'A five-foot, olive-skinned, black-haired, black-eyed Sicilian, imbued with the wildest superstitions of the Catholic Church, is a member of the same race and culture as a six-foot, empirically minded, blue-eyed, blond Swedish agnostic.'[223] Rather, Robertson later developed the concept of the Ethno-state to preserve the sub-races (or to keep the non-Nordics at bay).[224]

---

220 Wilmot Robertson, *The Dispossessed Majority* (Cape Canaveral: Howard Allen Enterprises, 1973). *The Dispossessed Majority* was probably the first effort from the 'Right' to empirically document the impact of Jews and others on American culture.

221 Wilmot Robertson, *The Dispossessed Majority*, ibid., 'The United States and Russia', pp. 451–465.

222 Wilmot Robertson, ibid., 'Unassimilable white Minorities', pp. 141–148.

223 'Francis Parker Yockey and the Politics of Destiny', *Instauration*, Cape Canaveral, Vol. 7, No. 3, February 1982, p. 6.

224 Wilmot Robertson, *The Ethnostate* (Cape Canaveral: Howard Allen Enterprises), online at: https://archive.org/stream/TheEthnostate/EthnoState#page/n2/mode/1up. The idea of the 'ethno-state' has become increasingly popular among American racial-nationalists, as the USA is seen as unviable and subject to ethnic Balkanisation. It could be seen as the antithesis of Yockey's 'Imperium', although the breakup of the US entity would

The author of the *Instauration* article on Yockey was, according to Stimely, Wilmot Robertson.[225] Robertson began:

> In the six years of its existence, *Instauration* has not once touched upon the problem of Francis Parker Yockey. We say problem because it's hard to know exactly what to make of this mysterious character, who has become a cult figure of certain hermetic elements of the American right. His much touted and much thumbed-through *Imperium* (Noontide Press) is part twentieth-century *Book of Revelations*, part postscript to Oswald Spengler, part revised and updated edition of *Mein Kampf*. His suicide or murder in a San Francisco jail makes him a candidate for martyrdom in some future century, provided that in the meantime his writings and his tragic life story have not been scourged out of the West's consciousness.[226]

The writer — Robertson — has trouble accepting Spengler's concept of organic, self-contained civilizations that rise and fall — and hence his problem is also with Yockey and again the Spengerlian conception of 'race'.

> All high cultures more or less follow the same timetable. Like flowers and trees and *Homo sapiens*, they live and die, in their later stages turning into civilizations, in their last stages becoming empires (imperiums). Europe, in Yockey's eyes, reached the imperial stage in the 1930s, and Hitler's Germany was rigorously complying with Spengler's law by piecing together the prescribed Western empire. But it was not to be. A passel of culture distorters and barbarians in America and Russia choked off the normal flow of organic history and Europe, the heart and brain of the West, was all but destroyed. Instead of the Western imperium, there was chaos.[227]

Robertson also seems to have a fundamental misunderstanding of the Spenglerian principles. Hence, he assumes that Yockey is an Anglophobe, perhaps due to Yockey's Irish background, and his identifying England as

---

also accord with a Yockeyan aim for the dissolution of worldwide Jewish influence via US global hegemony.

225 Stimely to Gannon, February 28, 1982.

226 'Francis Parker Yockey and the Politics of Destiny'. *Instauration*, Cape Canaveral, Vol. 7, No. 3, February 1982, p. 5.

227 'Francis Parker Yockey and the Politics of Destiny', ibid.

the home of materialism.[228] Robertson seems to have failed to appreciate the German Idealist movement that posited a 'nationalism' and 'racism' beyond rationalism and materialism, detaching German patriotism from the Jacobinism of the French Revolution. In the German Idealist tradition, a state reflects a *Zeitgeist*, or a 'spirit of the age.' In this school of thought Spengler and Yockey following him identified 'Prussian' (Spengler) or 'Ethical' (Yockey) Socialism as arising in Germany against the capitalist, free trade *Zeitgeist* of Britain. Hence, anything that arose in England during that *Zeitgeist*, including Marxism, would be a reflection of the English *Zeitgeist*. Hence, Marxism, so far from being a rejection of British economics, was also a materialist ideology. The Economic School of List, on the other hand, was developed under the German *Zeitgeist* and is therefore something quite different from both Marxism and capitalism. However, as Yockey and Spengler argued, one's race soul is not necessarily dependent on the zoological category one is born into. Ironically, the Nazi regime was closer to English 'racism' than German.

The misunderstandings continue. Again, it is the inexorable laws of Spengler's culture morphology that pose a problem for Robertson:

> Yockey's works are overweighted and overpollinated with allusions to Destiny. What happened and will happen happens because of Destiny. Too many pages are burdened with "organic predispositions" and pedantic "laws" of political behavior which on closer examination are discovered to be little more than aphorisms and expanded cliches. It is all very rhetorical, occasionally even poetic, but not very enlightening. This defect, however, probably strengthens rather than weakens his message. Prophetical flourishes and rousing manifestos win over more minds than cool analysis and synthesis. Although Yockey accepts·Spengler's organic history with hardly a caveat, he does view the imperial stage, which the Philosopher described as a time of decline and decadence, as an Indian summer (to borrow a metaphor from Toynbee) of power and glory.[229]

A frequent criticism of *Imperium* is its length, Robertson stating that it is 'overweighted'. The edition then available from Noontide Press runs to some 600 pages. The chapters are all quite brief and the ideas are clearly explicated.

---

228 'Francis Parker Yockey and the Politics of Destiny', ibid., p. 6.

229 'Francis Parker Yockey and the Politics of Destiny', ibid., p. 6.

I suspect that the real reason is that *Imperium* rejects pet assumptions on race, Jews and the nation-state and like *The Decline of the West*, its theory of cycles is misconstrued as 'pessimism'. Robertson also erred in thinking that Spengler regarded the imperial epoch of a civilization as part of its decline and decadence. Rather, the imperial epoch arises when still healthy forces in a civilization reassert the founding values of the culture, against the forces of decay.

Yockey is faulted for not referring to what Robertson regards as the greatest example of Culture-distortion imposed on the Westerner: Christianity.

> As Revilo Oliver points out in his dismayingly discursive, yet devastatingly definitive critique of Yockey's long essay, *The Enemy of Europe* the supreme example of cultural distortion is unmentioned in *Imperium* or elsewhere. Oliver is referring to the transplant of a Magian or Levantine religion into the body spiritual of the West. If the Western soul has such a different tempo and resonates to such a different beat, then the adoption of an alien religion like Christianity should be lethal. On this crucial point, however, Yockey is most silent.[230]

As we have seen, Yockey regarded Gothic Christianity as the ethos during the high-mark of Western civilization. Perhaps the Instaurationists and rationalists would have preferred Yockey to make a pitch for a pagan or an atheist revival in post-war Europe? In fact, there was a stage in which Oliver appealed to Christianity on the grounds that it is synonymous with Western high culture, arguing that those who seek a Western resurgence cannot ignore that fact. Beginning with a quote from *Imperium* that the 'men of this generation must fight for the continued existence of the West',[231] Oliver pointed out that Christianity is 'the religion of the West'. Whether the reader is a Christian or an atheist, Oliver wrote,

> [I]t is a fact, which Christians will regard with satisfaction and some atheists may deplore, that Western civilization, for about half of its recorded history, has been a Christian civilization in a sense that the great majority of the people belonging to it (though never, at any time, *all* of them) believed implicitly in the

230 'Francis Parker Yockey and the Politics of Destiny', ibid., p. 7.

231 Revilo P Oliver, *Christianity and the Survival of the West* (Cape Canaveral: Howard Allen, 1973), vi.
Oliver's book was published by Howard Allen Enterprises, publisher of *Instauration*.

> truth of the Christian revelation. [...] [W]e of the West regarded our religion as the bond that united us and distinguished us from the rest of the human species.

Despite their differences and changing borders, Westerners recognised their unity and 'called themselves Christendom. [...] Christianity is a religion of the West and, for all practical purposes, *only* of the West.' Oliver wrote that

> [Christianity] is not, as its polemical adversaries so often charge, a Semitic cult, for it has never commanded the adhesion of any considerable number of Semites, and it is not, as Christians once generally believed, a universal religion, for experience has proved that it cannot be successfully exported to populations that are not Indo-European.[232]
>
> The loss of the Christian faith as the West's bond of union was a disaster; the spiritual vacuum this created was a catastrophe.

Oliver was writing as an 'atheist' but in a detached manner, looking at fact. He concluded that

> Christendom survived at Châlons, and at Tours, and at Vienna, and in many another crisis, not by book, bell, and candle, but by the grace of the shining sword in a mailed fist directed by a dauntless heart.[233]

Despite the major criticisms, Robertson, like Tyndall and Oliver, finds major premises with which to heartily agree. Robertson, in regard to Jews and the USSR, is placed in an altogether different position. He agrees with Yockey rather than Oliver that the Jews had lost control of the USSR.[234]

> [Yockey's] great selling point is that amid all the despondency of the present age he is one of the very few thinkers who offers us Balm in Gilead, some shreds of hope, some possibility of white resurgence. Expectedly, it is not the deep space of the cosmos that Yockey is interested in, but the equally deep and equally mysterious space of the inner man. This is all to the good because in these days anyone who writes seriously and earnestly about the soul, about the Western

232 Revilo P Oliver, *Christianity...*, ibid., p. 2.

233 Revilo P Oliver, *Christianity...*, ibid., p. 74.

234 'Francis Parker Yockey and the Politics of Destiny', op. cit., p. 7.

> soul, strikes a bell that reverberates most pleasantly up and down our increasingly spineless spines.
>
> So more power to Yockey! He is still alive and kicking in the hearts of a sizeable number of true believers. Despite his shortcomings, his life and his works are proof that no matter how far *they* get us down, we will never be out.
>
> We must never forget that at the nadir of European history, in the aftermath of World War II when Russian troops were barbarizing and looting their conquered territories and American troops were holding lynching bees in theirs, when hardly anyone dared raise his voice against the deliberate starvation, massive brainwashing and the official Allied policy of unlimited retribution and unmitigated vengeance, when it appeared the lights had gone out all over Europe — this time for good — a young American idealist named Francis Parker Yockey broke the general silence and pointed a long, menacing finger at those who were trying to erase the greatest continent on Earth from the map and reduce some of the greatest people on Earth to the status of zombies. As all the silent ones knew, it was an act of incredible courage to speak up at that time. In the end it cost Yockey his life.
>
> In regard to guts, Yockey certainly lives up to the example set by his Hero. In regard to loyalty, he spent the best part of his life faithfully elaborating on the theories of his beloved Philosopher. As a reward for those rare and now almost extinct virtues, Yockey himself may turn out to be the true philosopher and the true hero of his age. Destiny often plays strange tricks — even on those who claim to know most about Destiny.[235]

In the final analysis, it was the inspiration of Yockey's personality even after his death that won over even a sceptic, as it had the arch-rationalist and cynic, Revilo Oliver. However, the shortcomings of the *Instauration* review are particularly surprising given Robertson's erudition. Stimely, who held *Instauration* as 'the most intelligent forum on the American neo-fascist scene', points out to Gannon that Robertson is

> an archetypal Verticalist — and not just that: he has an absurd and infuriating (to me) "Nordic" fixation; constantly in the magazine will be found slighting references to Southern and Eastern Europeans.

235 'Francis Parker Yockey and the Politics of Destiny', ibid., pp. 7–8.

> This is uncalled for and actually quite self-defeating, for among America's White "ethnic" population (Italians, Poles, Russians, and assorted Balkan Slavs) are to be found the most ardent opponents of liberalism. For Robertson to "write-off" or, by his comments, to "turn off" these white Americans, in quest of some dreamy and elusive goal of making America once again "Nordic", is short-sighted in the extreme. It was not the "ethnic" Whites who sold America to the Jew, it was the WASP class of elegant blue-blood Nordics. So, yes, strict Verticalism is alive and well (even though dead) in the American "scene", unfortunately. Some of this approach is evident in the article on Yockey, although ultimately it is a quite favorable treatment.[236]

## Influence on *La Nouvelle Droite*

Although not so discernible now, *Imperium* had a seminal impact on the European New Right, or *La Nouvelle Droite*, as the French media christened a movement that emerged around Alain de Benoist during the late 1960s. *La Nouvelle Droite* is based around hierarchy, a rejection of individualism in favour of the organic state, and opposition to the Americanisation of European culture. It does not recognise the USA as the 'leader of the Western world' but rather as doctrinally inimical to the Western cultural organism. The flagship of *La Nouvelle Droite* has been GRECE, *Groupement de Recherche et d'Études pour la Civilisation Européenne*, founded by Alain de Benoist in 1968. With its seminars, journals and books directed to the intelligentsia, *La Nouvelle Droite* aimed to put into practice a 'Rightist' version of the Marxist 'march through the institutions' developed by the Italian communist ideologue Gramsci.[237]

Alain de Benoist's reaction to material from the National Youth Alliance and to *Imperium* was enthusiastic. He wrote to Dr Oliver:

> I am especially delighted to known the fine work you are doing to make more known the book written by Yockey, *Imperium*. I consider it as one of the most important works published since World War II. We have begun to speak out about it in France for some years already, and will continue.

---

236 Stimely to Gannon, February 28, 1982.

237 See Dr Michael O'Meara, *New Culture, New Right: Anti-Liberalism in Postmodern Europe* (London: Arktos, 2013).

Referring to his magazine *Nouvelle Ecole*, which continues to be the primary journal of the New Right in Europe, de Benoist stated that 'it is not very far' from what Yockey stated.[238] De Benoist expressed interest to Oliver in selling *Imperium* in France. By the time Oliver replied the NYA was already factionalised, financially bereft and the stock of *Imperium* at the NYA's Washington office had been stolen during a break-in. Oliver maintained a bitterness towards Carto for what he saw as the sabotaging of the NYA and the ouster of his friend Louis Byers.[239]

## Down Under and Above

The fact that *Imperium* found its way to the Antipodes can be seen as a symbolic manifestation of the far-flung organic unity of the Western cultural organism. Dr Jim Saleam, in his essay on the arrival of Yockeyan thought to Australia, states that *Imperium* reached there in the 1950s through a German war veteran, Klaus Nikolai, who had fought as an officer with the Waffen SS on the Eastern Front. Having joined the Socialist Reich Party in 1949, Nikolai came to regard the Russians as an essential element in Europe's resurgence. In 1975, he confided to Saleam that German Eastern policy had been 'colonialism against part of the white race'. Saleam writes of this:

> Nikolai said that Yockey had an influence on the SRP and advocated a unity of all the true nationalists. His book was a "new beginning" because it identified "American liberalism as a greater enemy of European culture than Soviet communism". Indeed, the SRP were officially "neutralist", a position many Germans favoured. It seems that Nikolai had acquired a copy in English (a major coup given that the book was published in so few copies) along with other materials published in German, and had brought these works to Australia.[240]

*Imperium* met with little understanding among Australian rightists and National Socialists but was taken up by Dr E. R. Cawthron, a young nuclear

238 Alain de Benoist to Oliver, June 15, 1970.

239 Oliver to de Benoist, September 29, 1970.

240 J Saleam, *Francis Parker Yockey's Thought in Australia*, 'A German Brings the Word', http://home.alphalink.com.au/~radnat/fpyockey/australia.html.

physicist, who read it circa 1965. This caused Cawthron to re-evaluate his views on National Socialism and the meaning of race.[241]

One enclave of Yockeyan thought in Australia was among the Hungarian émigrés. Here the Arrow Cross Party-Hungarist Movement from the pre- and wartime years provided counsel to Dr Cawthron which transcended the inanities of post-war Anglophone Hitler fetishism, according to Saleam.[242] For decades these Hungarian refugees, as an outpost of the World Association of National Socialist Hungarians, published editions of their monthly journal, *Perseverance*, in several languages. A 1975 issue of *Perseverance* reprinted an article that had been published by the Movimento Sociale Italiano, written by the notable Italian journalist, author, film critic and scholar, Maurizio Cabona, beginning:

> In the weighted atmosphere reigning after World War II it was not advisable to take the side of the vanquished and naturally very few persons did so. One could expect voices raised among the vanquished (we mention only Maurice Bardèche with his work *Nuremberg or the Promised Land* or the literary Nobel Prize winner Knut Hamsun); what was really surprising were similar reactions in the ranks of the victors. There were persons, in England and the USA, who brought up the fact that serious war crimes that were attributable to the Allies were ignored while much noise was being made over certain excesses imputable to the Axis. Among these discordant voices, there was one who dared to oppose openly the triumphant ideology and became thereby guilty of criticising Democracy; this man was situated in the best possible observation post…[243]

At a time when very little was known of Yockey's background, Cabona, like Bardèche, erred on several points, stating that Yockey was a 'judge' at the Nuremberg trials; perhaps a mistranslation. Noting that Yockey was marked for his thoughts and deeds, Cabona states that his death was 'part of a mysterious series of violent deaths whose victims were all the most illustrious heroes of American anti-communism', including the assassination in 1935

---

241 Cawthron's Yockeyan essay, 'The Culture as an Organism', is discussed below in the chapter 'Interpretations and Adaptations'.

242 J Saleam, *Francis Parker Yockey's Thought in Australia*, op. cit.

243 M Cabona (MSI) 'Francis Parker Yockey', *Perseverance*, Merredin, Western Australia, Vol. 15, No. 8, August 15 1975, pp. 15–16.

of 'the pro-fascist Governor of Louisiana, Huey P Long, who was a serious challenge to the presidency of Franklin D Roosevelt; the death of General George Patton in 1945 after two consecutive motor accidents; the 1948 alleged 'suicide' of James Forrestal, Secretary of Defense; the death of Senator Joseph McCarthy, regarded by Cabona as 'mysterious', and the attempted assassination of Alabama Governor George C Wallace, a presidential contender, which was 'still an unsolved mystery'.

Cabona mentions the philosophical debt Yockey owes to Spengler and the need to overcome 'racist nationalism' that has divided the West. He states: 'It is due to Yockey's book that the American Right has partially freed itself from some of its faults consisting of chauvinism bordering on illness, a blind conservatism and an anti-communism of often contradictory manifestation.'[244] Cabona concludes by noting the hope offered by the recruitment of youth by the National Youth Alliance, with *Imperium* as its doctrinal foundation.[245]

***

Following the obsolescence of Australian National Socialist parties, which largely copied the symbols and ideology of the 1930s, a new generation of advanced thinkers arose from the Australian Right that was able to appreciate Yockey. *Imperium* enjoyed readership around largely student-based cadres such as the Eureka Students' League (1975–1976) and the Sydney-based National Resistance/Australian National Alliance (1977–1981). *Imperium* also sold through the Australian League of Rights,[246] despite the latter's Anglophile base, while Dr Cawthron continued to promote Yockey.

Even the New Zealand backwater had a Yockeyan presence. In the 1970s a Chinese businessman, Ian Bing, New Zealand's first Chinese hotelier, thoroughly imbued with the philosophy of Spengler, imported cartons of *Imperium* from Noontide Press. It was distributed by a relatively successful conservative project, Essential Books (which later changed its name to Western Destiny publications, a one-man operation working out of Hamilton for many years) as well as by the New Zealand League of Rights. At that time

244 M Cabona, 'Francis Parker Yockey', ibid., p. 17.

245 M Cabona, 'Francis Parker Yockey', ibid.

246 J Saleam, op. cit., , 'Commonplace'.

the New Zealand Right, with its nucleus of war veterans, was much more advanced philosophically than it is today, with widespread sentiments among pro-British and pro-Southern African New Zealanders serving as a catalyst. During the mid-1980s this author obtained several cartons of the remaining copies of *Imperium* imported by Ian Bing, as well as the several remaining copies then held by the League of Rights. The 1949 edition of *The Proclamation of London* was reprinted during the 1990s, as well as DTK's publication *Four Essays*. While such Antipodean efforts were meagre, the spark was nonetheless ignited in these far-flung parts of the Western cultural organism.

## Impact on the Rebirth of Odinism

As mentioned previously, according to Alex Scharf, Yockey would often quote from the Old Testament but referred to himself as a 'pagan', saying that he believed in 'many gods'.[247] To his Catholic friends who knew him best, Gannon and Arcand, Yockey was a Catholic and intimated thoughts about his faith which will probably never be known. He described the faith of the new epoch of Western resurgence as *skepsis*, not in the secular-humanist sense but, on the contrary, a skepticism in regard to the atheism, scientism, rationalism and materialism of the current epoch of decay. At the very least, Yockey recognised the positive dialectical role of 'Gothic Christianity' in the shaping of Western high culture.

Nonetheless, Yockey has had an impact on the Northern pagan revival that regards Christianity as a Levantine intrusion that serves Culture-distortion. Known as Odinism, after the head of the Norse/German pantheon, Odin,[248] or Asatru, faith in the Norse gods, Odinism might be seen in its current popularity as riding the wagon of a revival of alternative spiritualities. Spengler predicted that there would be a second religiousness in the epoch of banality, materialism and faithlessness. The Odinist revival is largely thanks to the efforts of an Australian solicitor and later a Danish migrant to Canada.

Alexander Rudd Mills founded The First Anglecyn Church of Odin in circa 1929. Mills was part the 1942 round-up of Australians interned during

247 '"Pal" Says Yockey Exploited Him', *San Francisco Chronicle*, August 23, 1960, FBI file no. SF105–1769.

248 German = Wotan, English = Woden.

the war. These were mostly members of the Australia First Movement led by the literary figure Percy Stephensen.[249]

Mrs Else Christensen (1913–2005) is probably the individual most responsible for the revival of Odinism in the post-war world. Christensen, as editor *The Odinist* and founder of the Odinist Study Group in 1969, which became the Odinist Fellowship, sought to make Odinism philosophically relevant, rather than a mere re-enactment society or New Age escapism.

Christensen had remained 'neutral' during the German occupation of Denmark, although her husband Alex was interned for prior political activities. There was generally little resistance to the Germans. In reply to a question she stated that the Germans were disciplined and very well behaved: 'no problem'. Although she had not joined the Danish National Socialist Party out of dislike for its leader, Dr Fritz Clausen, she regarded the war as wrong and Hitler as the rightfully elected leader of Germany. The Christensens settled in Canada, where they became aware of revived Odinism during the early 1960s after reading Rudd Mills' *Call of Our Ancient Nordic Religion.*[250]

Their other primary inspiration was *Imperium. The Odinist* ran for 151 issues from 1971 until 1992.[251] Yockey was often discussed in its pages. Christensen's interpretation is close to that of Willis Carto's 'Cultural Dynamics', which accords 'rights' to all races and eschews notions of supremacy or superiority. To Christensen, Odinism is the native religion of the Northern Europeans who have as much right to their own ethnos as any other human group. Although she, like Carto, held to race-biology, her views on race were akin to Yockey's:

> The "racial purists" will eventually have to accept that some "beautiful blond people" are rotten on the inside and that brunettes may have a far more realistic understanding of our ancient beliefs and as such will be more valuable for the overall picture; All branches of our Folk are within the realm of our common moral and religious attitudes, so to speak. They were held over our territories; we refer to Northern Europe only because they survived there the longest and

249 Bruce Muirden, *The Puzzled Patriots: The Story of the Australia First Movement* (Melbourne University Press, 1968).

250 William B Fox (aka Thor Sannhet), 'An Interview with Else Christensen', *Vor Tru*, Winter (2243), 1993.

251 William B Fox, ibid.

> we know about them because historians have written down some of the concepts although much was destroyed. If we were able to research Russian folklore we would probably find concepts close to ours. Indo-Aryan ideologies are certainly similar in many essential areas. Greek mythology has been somewhat distorted but we find many philosophical concepts pretty close to the Nordic. I prefer a brunette with the right attitudes to a rotten person with a perfect "Nordic" appearance. Substance rather than an empty shell. Now that is controversial in some circles.[252]

In a letter in 1991, Christensen explained the potential of the Odinist revival to serve as the Faith of a post-Western high culture:

> From a historic viewpoint it seems that our Christian High culture is in its senility phase (Spengler/Yockey); and we have to get our act together, for the cultural seeds of the next High Culture must already be sown now. In view of the fact that this culture has been international in structure (Christianity, capitalism, labor unions, communism) and these ideologies have come to the end of their life-cycle, and looking at the present fighting going on along natural racial/national/religious lines, it doesn't take much vision to suggest that those spiritual/cultural sentiments might have a strong enough carrying force and become dominant in the future; especially if we can put them into a "pagan" form in which we follow the old dictum, "do what you will and harm none".[253]

Again the 'harm none' (the primary axiom of modern Witchcraft — *Wicca*) is more akin to Carto's 'Cultural Dynamics' than the total wars between blood and money envisaged by Spengler and Yockey, although it could be argued that World War II represented that final Western conflict of 'blood versus money' and 'money' won. The concept of the 'ethno-state' and the break-up of larger state edifices was becoming increasingly popular among American 'racial-nationalists' and remains so. The first advocate of the ethno-state was Wilmot Robertson, editor and publisher of *Instauration*. While the ethno-state is contrary to the world-conquering Western union envisaged by Yockey its intention, at least for some such as Christensen, is to bypass rather than to cure the sickness of 'The West'; to inaugurate a post-Western civilization that

252 Letter from Christensen to Fox, ibid.

253 Christensen to Fox, November 5 1991, *Vor Tru*, ibid.

contains elements of Europe's healthy past. Christensen cogently explained this to Ben Klassen, founder of the unapologetically White supremacist, anti-Christian 'Church of the Creator':

> It is our destiny to be born in a historic period where the present cultural period is dying; it will still take maybe a couple of more centuries before the final collapse. The new has not been born yet but I hope and believe that we are today doing the groundwork for the foundation upon which the new basis for the religious/philosophical moral concepts will be built. They will have to be racial, discriminatory, self-assertive, proud.[254]

Of the influence of Yockey, Fox comments:

> The enormous impact of Yockey on Else's thinking was explained in an early series of articles in *The Odinist* beginning with "Culture" (issue No. 6, Dec 1972) and continuing with "Destiny Thinking" (No.7), "The Relativity of History" (No. 8), "Historical Facts" (No. 9), "Our View of History" (No. 10), "The Structure of History" (No. 11), "More Yockey" (No. 12), and "Yockey" (No 14, Dec 1974).[255]

Christensen first used Yockey in *The Odinist* to define 'Culture'. According to Yockey and Spengler, there had been seven high cultures prior to the Western: Egyptian, Mesopotamian, Indian, Hwan-Ho Valley, Arabian, Classical (Greco-Roman) and Mexican-Peruvian.

> Each such organism has its own individual Culture-soul; it takes nothing from the other cultures and gives nothing to them. If an idea seems to be taken over by one culture from another, this is only apparently so; actually it is re-shaped and adapted to conform with the spirit of the proper culture-soul.[256] As far as that particular culture-soul is concerned, whatever is on its frontier is foreign, whoever is not absorbed into the culture is an enemy and a barbarian.[257]

Knowledge of the cyclic character of high culture gives us the ability to understand what is 'taking pace before our eyes'. Since Odinists are members of the

254 Christensen to Klassen, 1986, cited by Fox, ibid.

255 Fox, *Vor Tru*, ibid.

256 Examples of this include the Western reshaping of gunpowder and printing, invented by the Chinese, apparently, but shaped by the West in a uniquely dynamic manner.

257 E Christensen, 'Culture', *The Odinist*, December 1972, No. 6, p. 1.

culture organism, they must take part in the struggle for its destiny. The only choice is to 'participate as subjects or as objects', as Yockey put it.[258]

In defining 'destiny', Christensen stated that every organism has a set of predetermined possibilities laid out since birth; life is the unfolding of these possibilities. 'Fate' is not destiny, as it works through outside influences, as distinct from 'the inner necessity of the organism'.[259] History is the record of fulfilled destinies of cultures, nations, religions, ideas and so on.[260] Hence, each High Culture has its unique relationship to history, a relationship which develops according to the inner character of the culture. Within each high culture there are a series of Ages, reflecting the stage of the culture-soul.[261] 'Life-facts are the data of History' and are defined as 'something which has happened'. Life-facts need to be recognised as standing beyond moral judgement or preconceptions. However, the way these facts are interpreted or uncovered is subject to one's creative thinking. How they are creatively interpreted is determined by the culture-soul into which one is born. Thus 'life-facts' are 'subjective and objective'. 'What the facts are, depend on what man is experiencing them; whether he belongs to a High Culture, to which Culture, and to which Age thereof, to which nation, to which spiritual stratum, to which social stratum.'[262] The realisation of the cyclic character of History, which substituted the idea of history as a procession of events marching ever forward, was the insight given to the Westerner by Spengler and Yockey.[263]

In the following issue of *The Odinist*, Christensen considered the cyclic character of history according to Spengler and Yockey. She pointed out that the nineteenth century was one of Western egocentricity in seeing Western civilization as somehow unique, in whose garb all races must clothe themselves so as to represent the perfection of thought and deed.[264] The paradox maintained by the liberals, despite their supposed belief in universal human

---

258 E Christensen, 'Culture," ibid., p. 2.

259 E Christensen, 'Destiny-Thinking', *The Odinist*, Mach 1973, No. 7, p. 1.

260 E Christensen, 'Destiny-Thinking', ibid., p. 2.

261 E Christensen, 'The Relativity of History', June 1973, no. 8, p. 1.

262 E Christensen, 'Historical Facts', *The Odinist*, September 1973, no. 9, pp. 1–2.

263 E Christensen, 'Our View of History', *The Odinist*, December 1973, No. 10. p;. 1.

264 E Christensen, 'The Struggle of History', *The Odinist*, March 1974, No. 11, p. 1.

equality, insists that liberal politics, economics and ethics are the best ever seen in the world at any time and any place. Once liberal-democracy-economics-values are universally triumphant — globalism — there will be a messianic 'end of history'. 'Mankind' will have fulfilled all that there is to achieve. Marx had the same notion as the liberals and capitalists. All these nineteenth century ideologies see this increasing universalism as 'progress'. Spengler and Yockey rejected any such notions. Civilizations cannot be universal because they unfold from the soul and not from material forms, which are only the soul's outward projection. Art, religion, social structures, customs, are all reflective of the spirit of a culture.[265]

Whatever their difference with Yockey's ideas, these Odinists appreciated the enduring value of 'Cultural Vitalism':

> Odinists do not agree with all views expressed by Yockey in his book *IMPERIUM* but, to be sure, we concur with a substantial part of what he has written, particularly in the first part of the book, and although Yockey by no means can be called an Odinist, he in fact put into words many thoughts on which, in our opinion, the moral as well as the political ideology of the Future will have to be based.[266]

Christensen applauded Yockey's depreciation of materialism and its ideologies as merely the symptom of an epoch of decline, and not as some valuable attribute of 'progress'. The new epoch would emerge from the old not because one or other is 'true' but because of the unfolding of the historical cycle. While Odinism is a creed of decentralized ethnic tribalism for the North European, Christensen nonetheless recognised that Western culture is a single organism. She also addressed the bugbear of 'pessimism' that has caused rejection of both Spengler and Yockey, asking how it can be 'pessimism' to realise that all organisms are finite. This generation has its mission according to the *Zeitgeist* of the epoch, as did prior generations, and as will future generations. Great tasks remain for this generation, as Spengler wrote in *The Hour of Decision* and the closing pages of *The Decline of The West*, and as Yockey reiterated in *Imperium*, and *The Proclamation* and elsewhere:

---

265 E Christensen, 'The Struggle of History', *The Odinist*, March 1974, No. 11, pp. 1–2.

266 E Christensen, 'More Yockey', *The Odinist*, June 1974, No. 12, p. 1.

> Task after task remain for Western civilization. The entire spectrum from politics to archaeology, from philosophy to the legal system, the economy, all have to be imbued with the twentieth century spirit and above all an education must be created in the grand sense of consciously training the coming generations in the full light of the historic necessity of our future for the great life-task of the Civilization.[267]

Fear of death does not distract from heroic duty. Christensen alludes to the defenders of the Alamo fighting despite the hopelessness of their situation,[268] a deed which shaped history after their deaths. Despite notions elsewhere of 'live and let live', Christensen did not eschew the mission of the West to become an 'Empire': 'This Age and its Spirit would not shrink from entering upon its task of building the Empire of the West, even if it were told it would never succeed, because the outer forces were too strong. It prefers to die on its feet rather than live on its knees.'[269] However, its age and its spirit are those of the civilization stage of a culture-organism. To fulfil the destiny of Western civilization requires overcoming the money power that dominates in the civilization stage, and to reassert the inner character upon which the Western culture-organism was founded, albeit in new forms appropriate for the Age. Christensen ends on the same positive note as Yockey:

> When the spiritual division of Europe comes to an end, the extra-European powers will not be able to hold down the strong-willed population of the West. The first step of action is thus the liquidation of the spiritual division of Europe; there is only ONE FUTURE, the organic Future.[270]

Even in articles that do not allude to Yockey, one finds various Yockeyan themes. Hence, in an essay on 'Nationalism', Christensen points out, like Yockey, that with people in a state of flux across the world, the new meaning of nation is that of 'a people containing a Culture Idea'. While this idea is new to the people of the West, it can most readily be understood by looking at

---

267 E Christensen, 'More Yockey', ibid., p. 2.

268 E Christensen, 'More Yockey', ibid., p. 2.

269 E Christensen, 'More Yockey', ibid., p. 2.

270 E Christensen, 'Yockey', *The Odinist*, December 1974, No. 14, p. 10.

how Jews, despite spreading across the world, have nonetheless maintained a strong unity as a people. The old petty-nationalism is passé.

> The West allows itself to be divided and conquered. Never again will we let ourselves be goaded into civil wars. The West is partitioned into many sections of regional groupings; each section naturally and commendably takes pride in its specific achievements, its peculiar history and its distinctive characteristics which set each apart from kinsmen in other regions. But to us in this century a nation means a people expressing a Cultural Idea; the geographical location is of little significance; the West is where people adhere to the same Western intellectual culture, where they are part of the same ancestral heritage, where they share the same spiritual outlook. The West consists of many varied peoples and the creative and vital feeling of pride and attachment to the place of origin is fundamental, but taken as a whole the West is but one entity—the West is wherever Western man lives.[271]

Chistensen had a rare depth of understanding of Yockey. Her articles on him in *The Odinist* are particularly cogent and demonstrate that Yockey *can* be readily understood and explained, despite the objections of many critics.

---

271 E Christensen, 'Nationalism', *The Odinist*, June 1974, No. 4, p. 7.

# Interpretations and Adaptations

While the early 1970s marked the rise of interest in Yockey, especially with the formation of the National Youth Alliance under Byers, there were also efforts to reinterpret Yockey with a focus on reconciling biological views on race with Yockeyan-Spenglerian 'Cultural Vitalism'. We have previously seen how Yockey was rejected among the American and British 'Right' in particular because of his repudiation of 'race' as a biological fact. However, there were important figures on the Anglosphere 'Right' who, rather than reject Yockey out-of-hand, saw the over-riding importance of 'Cultural Vitalism'. Intriguingly, Robert Burros (not to be confused with his distant cousin, Dan Burros, who committed suicide when exposed as Jewish by *The New York Times*), an organiser of the National Renaissance Party, had in 1965 written *Tyrannium*, advertised by the NRP as a 'sequel' to *Imperium*.[1] *Tyrannium* does not appear to have been published.

Probably the earliest of the interpretators was the chief Mosleyite ideologue and organiser, Alexander Raven Thomson, who had been one of Yockey's first contacts in England. Already from 1954, Yockey's ideas were evident in Thomson's own formulation of an organic theory, 'social pathology', despite the quite bitter relations between Yockeyans and Mosleyites.

---

1 Robert Joseph Burros, 'The National Renaissance Party Presents an American Patriot's Program', leaflet, 1965.

## Raven Thomson's Theory of 'Social Pathology'

Despite Raven Thomson's criticism, Yockey significantly influenced him. Thomson was not induced to reject Mosley and join those who left Union Movement. He was to serve as *de facto* head of Union Movement and chief ideologue until his untimely death in 1955, editing *Union* and running the daily affairs of the Movement while Mosley consolidated his own doctrines. Thomson had been one of the first of Yockey's contacts in England and had been introduced by Anthony Gannon. As the most recognised intellectual of the Mosley movement, both before and after the war, Thomson had been the leading proponent of the Corporate State in Britain. He had studied economics at German and Scottish universities and developed a concept of the organic state,[2] his most notable book being *Civilization as Divine Superman.*[3] Starting in the Communist Party, he soon rejected Marxism because of its materialistic interpretation of history and its idea of man as the product of nothing other than economic forces. Since the British Union of Fascists, founded in 1932, was the most significant body campaigning for a Corporate State, Thomson had already joined in 1933 and became the BUF's director of policy. He saw the organic state as the means by which the Cultural-pathology described by Spengler could be diverted, and fascism as the means of putting this into effect, as he explained in *The Coming Corporate State*, a policy statement of Mosley's British Union of Fascists.[4]

Thomson developed his own theory of 'social pathology' in the pages of *Union* and in an unpublished manuscript called simply *World History*, which resides with a Mosleyite archivist but is no longer accessible.[5] Pugh remarks

---

2 Peter Richard Pugh, 'A Political Biography of Alexander Raven Thomson', Ph.D. thesis, University of Sheffield, June 2002.

3 Alexander Raven Thomson, *Civilization as Divine Superman* (London: Williams and Norgate, 1932). A new edition is due out from Black House Publishing, London.

4 Alexander Raven Thomson, *The Coming Coporate State* (British Union of Fascists, 1938).

5 Pugh was permitted to read the Thomson MS, *World History*, for his Ph.D. thesis on Raven Thomson and any information is reliant on this. However, I wish to thank Jeff Wallder of the Friends of Mosley for providing several of Thomson's articles on 'social pathology' published in *Union*.

that: 'The introduction of this concept of social pathology can be seen as the result of the influence on Raven Thomson of American fascist and early Union Movement member, Francis Parker Yockey.' Pugh remarks that historians had hitherto considered Yockey as 'making little impact on Mosleyism'.[6] He states of Yockey and Thomson that: 'The American thinker profoundly influenced the Secretary of Union Movement.'[7] As we have seen, Yockey developed a new theory of Cultural Vitalism, which diagnosed the Spenglerian morphology of a civilization as becoming pathogenic when forces of Culture-distortion, Culture-parasitism and Culture-retardation are allowed to infect the culture organism through laws of internal decay, a process analogous to cell destruction during old age. Despite his supposed 'Spenglerian pessimism', Yockey stated that cultural death proceeds when these cultural pathogens are *permitted* to destroy the cultural organism. They can be warded off and the organism returned to health by a regenerative movement among the Heroic vestiges of a civilization even in its epoch of decay. Spengler also alluded to these forces of regeneration as 'new Caesars' bringing a return to faith and authority by defeating the hegemony of money-thinking.

Raven Thomson had addressed the problems of cultural decay with his advocacy of the organic state. Corporatism was the means of bringing society back into organic integration. His organic approach to history is based on monist biology, which he developed in Germany, according to which life ascends by an increasing complexity of cell organisation, until reaching the 'superorganism' where the cells have 'integrated' into groups or societies. Civilizations are a cluster of such societies integrated at the highest level and therefore go through organic stages of life. Hence, the similarity between Thomson's view and Spengler's. From Nietzsche, who had also influenced Spengler, Thomson took the heroic will-to-power of the individual and transposed it onto the heroic qualities of society itself, writing: 'Civilization itself is the superhuman force that expresses and realises the ideal of the "superman".' He rejected Nietzsche's notion of a far-off evolution of superhuman individuals by force of heroic individual will in favour of a social will. This social will is realised by each individual being part of a social function, just as the individual cell

6 Pugh, op. cit., p. 239.

7 Pugh, ibid., p. 14.

operates in the service of the organism. Anything which divides the social organism is a pathogen and therefore a doctrine such as communism is analogous to a 'cellular rebellion' or cancer. It was the purpose of Fascism, in implementing the Corporate State, 'to give a new impetus to civilization through the regenerative force of youth in revolt against materialistic values'.[8]

We might then consider fascism as a collective or social will-to-power and 'overcoming' of decay, as distinct from Nietzsche's individual self-overcoming and will-to-power. In both instances it is a will-to-health and life. This collective will-to-power would be organised as the corporate state.

Yockey's Cultural Vitalism provided an added dimension to this thought. His concept of 'Culture-retardation', where inner forces strike at the unity of a cultural organism and cause social disintegration, prompted Thomson to develop a similar theory of 'social pathology'. The most apparent social pathogen is class war, engendered by the break-up of the organic societies by liberalism, free trade and labour-socialism.

Pugh observes:

> Raven Thomson's resulting philosophy returned to arguments about the underlying historical forces at work in society, though now Spenglerian morphology was replaced by the concept of cultural pathology... The antidote was a new society populated by *Homo Socialis*, the higher man, dedicated to service.[9]

This 'dedication to service', in contrast to the economic egotism of both liberal-capitalism and Marxism, was what Spengler had referred to as 'Prussian Socialism' and Yockey as 'Ethical Socialism'. It was a development of the thoughts Raven Thomson had already expressed in 1931 in *Civilization as Divine Superman*. Fascism itself had arisen as an answer to social decay, positing that through a heroic will-to-power the forces of social disintegration can be eliminated. Many 'socialists' turned to Fascism as the new dialectic.[10] Henri de Man was leader of the Socialist Party in Belgium; Mussolini had been a leader of the Socialist party; Mosley had been a Labour Member of

8 Thomson, 'Correspondence', *Fascist Quarterly*, Vol. 1, no. 4, p. 513, quoted by Pugh, op. cit., , p. 62.

9 Pugh, ibid.

10 See Zeev Sternhell, *The Birth of Fascist Ideology* (Princeton University Press, 1995).

Parliament; Raven Thomson had briefly joined the Communist Party; Jacques Doriot, the most successful of the French fascists, had started as a leader of the Communist Party. Fascism to these meant social cohesion and the regeneration of society and civilization; not its disintegration into warring factions, like the cells of an organism being at war among themselves: they wished to cure this cancer, not nurture it. All this is consistent with Yockey's views in *Imperium* on how the political laws of the organic state establish a polity resistant to Culture-pathology.[11]

It is apparent that Yockey's Spenglerian thinking had had an impression on Thomson's Spenglerian thinking, and Thomson started to reformulate the concept of Culture-pathology, using the term 'social pathology' in several articles in *Union* and in his unpublished manuscript written in 1955. Thomson saw value in Yockey's premises despite the disagreements between the American and Mosley. Thomson had written to H Keith Thompson of Yockey being a 'brilliant young intellectual American expatriate with a strong anti-American phobia… taking the view that the present American influence in Europe is more damaging to European culture than the alien threat of communism in the East'. Thomson stated that Yockey had joined Union Movement in the hope of getting funding for *Imperium*. This was rejected because of Yockey's 'Spenglerian pessimism' and his being 'quite unnecessarily offensive to America'.[12] Again, the old bugbear of 'Spenglerian pessimism' comes up, despite its absence in *Imperium*. Yockey aimed to solve the Spenglerian problem, as did Thomson. The reference to the USSR and 'anti-Americanism' reflects Mosley's belief that Soviet occupation of Europe was more harmful than American. Mosley still regarded Soviet occupation as a spectre of Asian hordes under the banner of the USSR, as did Thomson. Thomson also found Yockey to be 'conceited and unstable in personal relations', rendering him impossible to work with, even allowing for his 'extremist views, which are however stated in most brilliant terms'.[13] Mosley had seen no need to compromise or accommodate any more than Yockey.

---

11 Yockey, *Imperium*, Wermod ed., op. cit., 'The Laws of Totality and Sovereignty', pp. 197–198.

12 Raven Thomson to H. K. Thompson, March 27, 1953, cited by Pugh, op. cit., p. 240.

13 Raven Thomson to H. K. Thompson, ibid.

The concept of Culture-pathology or social pathology is straightforward but requires a vision of society as an organism rather than a collection of individuals or groups contending for their separate interests. It is intrinsically opposed to the ego-driven spirit of capitalism, communism and liberalism. A nation-people-state is an organism insofar as the state is the 'brain', groups or classes are organs, individuals are cells, and the institutions connecting them all are the nervous system and the arteries. If classes, individuals, even the rulers, of a state pursue self-centred interests that do not accord with the common interest, then they are acting as pathogens, like cancerous cells. One of the obvious manifestations of pathology is class conflict, which Marx made into a political creed in his role as a Culture-distorter. Another major sign of Culture-pathology is the rise of political parties as the main representational bodies of a state in place of the traditional guilds and corporations. That is why an organic state usually takes the form of a corporate state, where the trades and craft associations (guilds, corporate bodies) are revived as organs of the social polity in place of parties and trade unions. Another significant factor in causing social pathology is the presence of alien elements functioning as *Culture-distorters* if they attain power, or *Culture-parasites* if they merely live off the host culture. Those who have a selfish interest in maintaining this pathology, usually politicians and businessmen, are *Culture-retarders*, or simply traitors.

Raven Thomson rejected the view of Spengler that because civilizations are organic they must go through a process leading to death. As the Fascists had asserted prior to the world war, such decay and death can be averted and the organism can be restored to health by a willed regeneration. Yockey had argued that a culture organism need not succumb to decay and death if culture pathogens are prevented or eliminated. Likewise, in his unpublished manuscript, Thomson stated that a civilization only needs die if it is 'subject to some form of pathology'.[14] 'It is very evident that all Civilizations have declined and eventually collapsed, not because of the advent of natural senility but because they are all subject to a pathology of decline.'[15] Thomson's presumed departure from Spengler in rejecting the latter's 'morphology of

14 Thomson, unpublished Ms., 'World History', 1955, p. 21; cited by Pugh, op. cit., p. 237.

15 Thomson, ibid, 'World History', pp. 33–34, Pugh, ibid., p. 238.

Civilizations' is somewhat obscure, as Thomson seems only to substitute the word 'pathology' in the place of morphology. Yet a pathology enters into the social organism because of the weakening of the organism through the historical laws identified by Spengler. Spengler too stated that even in its maturity, approaching old age, a civilization can be regenerated for a final dramatic bow on the world stage by the resurgence of authority and the overthrow of money-thinking and money-power. The primary difference seems to be that Thomson believed such regeneration could last indefinitely, arguing that a civilization could become immortal if invading pathogens were continuously eliminated. As in 1932 with *Civilization as Divine Superman*, in 1955 Thomson had recourse to the example of the insect colony as the role model of a healthy organism. Once humans understand the organic character of a civilization they have the same opportunity to maintain its health as the social organisms of insect communities. Thomson used the analogy of insects; Spengler, plants subjected to seasons. However, one might recall that plants, if growing in sufficiently healthy soil, survive Winter and grow back stronger than ever during Spring.

Thomson argued that once a diagnosis of pathology has been made a cure could proceed. The main pathogen was individualism, introduced into the Western organism by liberalism, which we can identify as the preferred weapon of the merchant class for overthrowing the traditional culture-bearing strata of land, church and throne. The answer was a leadership stratum formed by *Homo Socialis*,[16] a higher type of human being who puts service to the community above self. *Homo Socialis* would be bound by a strict code of honour, making him akin to Plato's 'Guardians' in *The Republic* — the influence of which Thomson acknowledged.

Thomson began introducing his theory of 'social pathology' to Union Movement a year prior to his death. In 1954, he wrote that it was possible to transcend the historical determinism of Spengler and Marx. He saw a kinship between the two insofar as both posited a march of History to a definite end. While Marx applauded this trend as ending in communism, Spengler opposed its degenerative ethos — but both had arrived at the same conclusion.[17]

---

16 Thomson ibid., 'Homo Socialis', 33, Pugh, ibid., p. 242.

17 Raven Thomson, 'Spengler and Marx: A Study in Social Pathology', *The European*, No. 18, August 1954, pp. 20–21.

Thomson seems to be overlooking a salient point about Spengler, as many do who conclude that he was 'pessimistic' and even that he had a negative influence on the forces of regeneration:

1. Spengler states that, according to the past experiences of civilizations, Western civilization will transcend the epoch of decay and enter an epoch of renewal by reviving tradition;
2. Marx, in the *Messianic* tradition of Judaism, which he thought he was rejecting, prophesied the end of history, with world communism as the conclusion, beyond which there can be no further options for humanity. This 'end of history' is also a theme of the apostles of American globalism,[18] who see the American Idea as the ultimate goal of humanity.

While Marx thought that once Western civilization had passed away the world would enter into an eternity of communism, Spengler, to the contrary, stated that after Western civilization had fulfilled its possibilities, another civilization would unfold, as has always happened over millennia. He alluded to this next civilization coming from Russia but he did not see Bolshevism as part of this, considering it rather as a temporary and alien import into Russia.

Thomson called Spengler 'paradoxically… a much better socialist than Marx'. He said Marx was no real socialist at all, since after communism had been established across the world, the state would 'whither away' and there would not be any higher service to the social body to be performed; the social body would no longer exist.[19] The doctrine is ultimately anarchistic; where anarchists and Marxists differ is that Marxism insists that the State is a necessary transitional phase towards this anarchic communism.

Thomson differed from Spengler in regarding Spengler's culture-morphology as over-systemising in seeing death as the inevitable end of a civilization, as with any organism. Thomson pointed to organisms in nature dying out to make way for new growth of the same species. Those specimens that

18 For example Francis Fukuyama's book *The End of History and the Last Man* (1992) which sees Democracy as the final product.

19 Raven Thomson, ibid., 'Spengler and Marx', p. 21.

die are replaced by their replicas.[20] The implication is that it is not entire civilizations which must enter states of old age and death, but it is rather the cells of civilization that need eliminating from the culture-organism, to be replaced by new cells. Again, Thomson has recourse to the analogy of the insect world, rather than that of Spengler's plant world, stating that insect communities regenerate themselves by 'swarming' without requiring the death of the parent community.[21]

However, Thomson argued that civilizations have declined through social pathology rather than 'morphological decay'.[22] Recognising social pathology, it is therefore possible to provide a cure. Marxism is merely human greed transformed into a doctrine, from the worship of the Golden Calf among the Old Testament Hebrews to the doctrine of liberal economics of the nineteenth century. Marx merely made the greed of the few into the greed of the many, forming this into a doctrine of History.[23] Spengler and Yockey had indicated this in referring to Marxism as a product of capitalism, as we have seen previously. This greed, whether individual or collective, is a form of social pathology, manifesting itself as class struggle. Using the analogy of Thomson's social pathology and Yockey's culture-pathology, such disintegrative elements are literally cancers dividing the cells of the Culture-organism against itself. Thomson has a remedy:

> Is there, then, no hope for the maintenance of the social order which alone by its communion of the spirit of man can raise mankind above the level of the beasts? Is man so devoid of social instinct, which maintains the insect communities in perpetuity that every one of his civilizations… must perish from the Earth amid the plaudits of the greed-crazed masses and their misguided leaders, who misuse the noble description *socialist* to complete the destruction of society?
>
> By no means. If the elite of our European society can grasp the message of Spengler without succumbing to his pessimism regeneration of our society is

20 Raven Thomson, ibid., 'Spengler and Marx', p. 22.

21 Raven Thomson, ibid., 'Spengler and Marx', p. 22.

22 Raven Thomson, ibid., 'Spengler and Marx', p. 22.

23 Raven Thomson, ibid., 'Spengler and Marx', p. 23.

> eminently possible, once the disease from which it suffers is diagnosed, and the necessary treatment for its eradication has been undertaken.[24]

Yockey had undertaken to resolve the Spenglerian quandary in 1948 with the development of his theory of Cultural Vitalism. Thomson focused on an aspect of this, Culture-pathology, introducing this to Union Movement as 'social pathology'. He had been one of Yockey's first British contacts and recognised Yockey's genius. Yockey had stated precisely what Thomson was restating: that culture-morphology need not inevitably end in the death of a civilization if the social disease is recognised and removed.

## Dr E. R. Cawthron: 'The Culture as an Organism'

One of the first of the post-1960 interpreters of Yockey was from a far-flung 'cultural colony' — in Yockey's terms — of Western civilization, Australia. Dr Edward Robert Cawthron was a physicist, the leader of the National Socialist Party of Australia (NSPA) and editor of the party's ideological periodical, *Australian National Socialist Journal*, where his consideration of Yockey's 'Cultural Vitalism' was published in two parts. Considering that the NSPA was affiliated with the Rockwellite World Union of National Socialists, Cawthron's departure from Rockwellian orthodoxy in giving a positive review to Yockey indicates that there was a lot more to Cawthron that departed from the standard 'neo-Nazi' line.

Dr Jim Saleam, in writing of the influence of Yockeyanism on the Australian 'Right', states that Dr Cawthron was 'the main figure in the propagation of Yockey's thought in Australia in the period of the 1960s and 1970s'.[25] Cawthron, born in 1940, studied science at Adelaide University and then obtained his Doctorate in physics in 1970 from Australian National University, where he worked under the renowned Sir Mark Oliphant.[26] Dr Saleam, who knew him well, writes that Cawthron, although head of the NSPA, was

---

24 Raven Thomson, ibid., 'Spengler and Marx', p. 24.

25 J Saleam, 'Francis Parker Yockey's Thought in Australia', Sydney, June 11, 2003.

26 Such was Edward Cawthron's reputation as a scientist that in 1969 and 1970 he co-authored scholarly papers with Sir Mark. See 'Sir Marcus Laurence Oliphant papers', http://www.adelaide.edu.au/library/special/mss/oliphant/oliphant_series21.html.

widely suspected of aiming to rid the party of Hitlerism and Rockwellism and build a new movement. Cawthron had helped to found the NSPA during 1963–1964 but had two 'motivational ideas' in doing so: (1) He was a radical Australian nationalist outside the norms of the 'right-wing' and wanted to see the creation of an activist movement, focused on Australia not as an offshoot of Britain but more widely as an outpost of European civilization; (2) He considered World War II as European fratricide. 'Cawthron's "Nazism" was then at the start *highly conditional*.'[27]

Specifically, Cawthron saw merit in Yockey's rejection of 'vertical race' theory as outdated. At first, he only discussed these ideas with some of the émigrés in the Hungarist Movement in Australia, who encouraged Cawthron and whose own doctrine was that of 'co-nationalism' or co-operation rather than chauvinistic antagonism between European states. As early as 1970, Matt Koehl, who assumed leadership of the American 'Nazis' after Rockwell's assassination in 1967, admonished Cawthron for referring to *Imperium*, stating that it was 'not really a National Socialist text'. In 1970, Cawthron was deposed from leadership of the NSPA and the Yockeyan influence went with him, to be resumed under new and youth-based groups during the mid-1970s.[28]

Cawthron's primary treatise on Yockey, 'The Culture as an Organism: Cultural Vitalism as New Concept,' was among the first in the Yockey revival of the early 1970s. Indeed the first of two instalments appeared in late 1969. Cawthron recognised the seminal importance of Yockey's 'Cultural Vitalism' in bringing an added dimension to pro-European doctrine and analysis, thereby developing the insights provided by Spengler's cultural morphology.

Cawthron opens by stating that his essay is 'heavily indebted' to *Imperium* and explains that Yockey's definition of a culture is 'organic'. The concept is more straightforward than it at first appears, 'for nobody can deny a culture exhibits the organic regularities of birth, growth, maturity, fulfilment and will die if the proper life-sustaining measures are not taken to keep it healthy and productive'. The 'West' is a 'cultural UNIT' beyond the individuals who compose it. 'This concept of a High culture is relatively new' and although some nineteenth century scholars such as Nietzsche foresaw it, the concept was

27 J Saleam, 'Francis Parker Yockey's Thought in Australia', op. cit.

28 Ibid.

overwhelmed by the materialistic outlook of Marxism and capitalism, with what Nietzsche called its democratic 'counting mania', which asserts quantity over any elitist role of a 'culture-bearing stratum' in favour of nebulous voting majorities and parliaments. This 'culture-bearing stratum' is always small and gives shape and force to a culture; it does not seek permission to act via electoral majorities. It is most strongly focused on the birthplace of a culture and dissipates as the culture expands outwards. Hence, the USA, for example, lacks the 'depth of historical perspective possessed by the intellectual leaders of Europe'.[29] Again, the notion of a 'culture-bearing stratum' is an *organic* concept because such a directing elite is analogous with the brain or the central nervous system in a living organism. 'The stratum articulates the culture and imparts to it both drive and direction'. The 'culture-distorter', the alien element in a culture that, when achieving power, by its innate character redirects a culture from its natural life cycle, seeks to 'decimate' either financially (through taxes on inherited wealth and landed estates in particular) or physically (through Bolshevism and wars) the culture-bearing stratum.

To this nineteenth century creed was countered National Socialism, which recognised the concepts of high culture and race-soul. However, this resurgence of authority, which marks a certain cycle of a civilization reacting to internal crisis (such as Caesarism in the Roman civilization) was crushed by the enormity of the plutocracies in combination with the USSR and hence the Age of Authority for the West was prematurely ended. The US leadership went to war against the Western heartland because they were dominated by 'an alien anti-Western force', 'a parasitic minority which was bent on war for its own purposes', despite the reluctance of the American majority to interfere in a European war.

With the defeat of the new order for Europe, the culture-bearing stratum was eliminated, reduced to poverty and to unemployment, when not actually killed like Robert Brasillach in France. We might think here of the fate of Knut Hamsun, the Nobel Laureate, in Norway, or the French intelligentsia that became 'collaborators' and were subsequently made *personae non gratae*. Cawthron states that 'the Jewish Marxist distorters flooded back into

29 E. R. Cawthron, 'The Culture as an Organism: Cultural Vitalism as New Concept', part I, *Australian National Socialist Journal*, Volume I, no. 4, Summer 1968.

an impoverished Europe, which had expelled them during the short-lived Cultural Renaissance 1933–1945, and the decimated culture-bearing stratum remaining was helpless to resist them.'

Two of Yockey's most important posthumous advocates were Willis Carto and Revilo P Oliver, despite both being adherents of a primarily genetic conception of race. They were among those who could see the value of Cultural Vitalism within the context of their genetic determinism and they considered that the two concepts are not irreconcilable. Cawthron likewise stated, from a more orthodox National Socialist viewpoint, that a 'High Culture' is a 'consequence of racial-biological factors, not of circumstances or environment'. Cawthron stated that this is evidenced by the similar creativity of nations within the West, regardless of their geographic location. Spengler and Yockey contended, rather, that the Western peoples, impelled by a 'Faustian soul' whose definition is that of striving towards the Infinite, have been formed by land-space and moulded by history, not by genetics or biological evolution. Western man, therefore, is unique not only from other peoples such as the Oriental and Levantine but also from other 'white races' of the past such as the Roman and the Greek. Cawthron recognised this uniqueness with respect to that of other High Cultures in his reference to a distinctly Western 'world-view' (Faustian), reflected in every branch of its culture, whether in music, painting or mathematics. Here Cawthron defines the *Faustian*, writing that 'the Western mind reaches out to nearly infinite bounds of knowledge'.[30] In our time, the ultimate manifestation of this Western — *Faustian* — soul has been 'the understanding of time-space and the conquest of the heavens'.[31]

It is the Faustian uncovering of nature that has manifested in the Western arts and sciences. The Faustian reflection of nature in aesthetics is contrasted with that of the 'culture-distortion and culture-parasitism by non-Western minorities' who do not share 'our intrinsic spiritual values'. 'We cannot condemn the Jew or the Negro for failing to appreciate these deep spiritual values but we should condemn those Western traitors who insist that our race

30 Cawthron, part I, 'The Scope of a High Culture'.

31 Cawthron, Part II, 'The Western Concept of Beauty', *Australian National Socialist Journal*, Vol. II, No. 1, Winter 1969.

and culture must surrender to the alien by some obscure "liberal" line of reasoning.'

Returning to the Faustian soul, Cawthron states that the specific outlooks of Western nations are moulded by the interaction between the 'race soul' and the environment, such as the maritime-commercial spirit of the British or the 'rural-technical spirit' of the German. However, both are within the context of the *Faustian* soul whose prime symbol, to quote Spengler, 'is pure and limitless space'.[32] However, Spengler and Yockey saw a fundamental breach between the outlook of the British and that of the Germans, epitomised by the 'Prussian' spirit in the latter. Spengler, writing in his essay *Prussianism and Socialism,* saw Marxism as typically manifesting itself on British soil as a product, not an opponent, of English capitalism. If 'socialism' means being opposed to capitalism, then the true antithesis of capitalism was what Spengler called 'Prussian socialism' and Yockey called 'ethical socialism', Marxism being but the mirror image. For Spengler and Yockey, this 'Prussian' or 'ethical socialism' is defined as duty to one's nation, not towards an economic class interest, whether that of the merchant or the proletarian. However, according to the Yockeyan definition of 'race', this 'Prussian' socialism might be found in a Jew or an Englishmen and that of the Jewish and English commercial spirit in a German or even a Prussian. According to the cyclic character of Spengler and Yockey's cultural morphology, this 'socialism' and 'capitalism' had analogous counterparts in the prior civilizations.

Despite the differences that National Socialists and genetic determinists such as Oliver had with the historico-cultural determinism of Yockey and Spengler, they found of overriding value in Yockey's power to enable us to view the problems of the Western civilization 'in a new perspective', as Cawthron put it. This is the enduring value of Yockey's 'Cultural Vitalism':

> It has long been debated by the best Western minds, of all shades of philosophical opinion, why the Jew does not blend into the Western culture but clings stubbornly to his materialistic and, to us, spiritually void worldview. The explanation lies in the essentially alien nature of each cultural soul and not in some monstrous and conscious conspiracy by Jews to rule the world. Of course, leading Jews confer and plan how best to propagate their own worldview but there is

32 Cawthron, Part II, 'The Faustian Soul of Western Man'.

> probably no single conspiratorial apparatus which plans ALL Jewish activity on a co-ordinated global scale. How can the anarchist Jewish student of the "New Left", or the young Zionist constructing a kibbutz on some newly seized Arab land, or the Jewish financier waxing rich on the "no-win" Vietnam war and planning some new "anti-communist" venture elsewhere, be expected to think in terms of Western Destiny, when he does not share the Western Race-soul. His activities MUST lead to culture-distortion, whether he wills this or not.[33]

Cawthron states that the Blacks in the USA understand the meaning of 'race-soul' far better than white intellectuals, 'for they call each other "soul-brother" and patronise "soul-business", and demand to be taught their own "soul-culture"'. The 'Negro and Jewish problems' arise when these groups seek to impose their own interests 'within the cultural organism of the West'. Hence, what proceeds, according to Yockey, is 'culture distortion' and 'culture retardation'.

So influential have these alien interests become that Western youth in particular has succumbed to nihilism and the survival of Western culture is precarious. National Socialist Germany, Cawthron states, was an attempt at a 'national renaissance'. What is required now is a 'cultural renaissance' for the building of a

> Western *Imperium*, a new order of free, autonomous White Nations, bound together Spiritually by a common worldview or Culture, founded in a common blood. Free of alien distortion or parasitism, the rejuvenated Western cultural-organism will go forward to achieve as yet undreamed of feats and our youth will again be inspired by clean, wholesome spiritual values. True Western art will find new dimensions of expression to rival, if not surpass, the masterpieces of the past and our Race will surely fulfil the role destiny ordained for it.[34]

Cawthron's final call is somewhat more upbeat than the Spenglerian outlook. Spengler saw the civilization cycle as altogether different from the cycle of 'High Culture' that the West had concluded several centuries earlier. For Spengler, Western art would not find new and even higher forms of expression. That era of high aesthetics had gone. Spengler wrote in the final

33 Cawthron, Part II, 'The True Meaning of the Jewish and Negro Problems'.

34 Cawthron, Part II, 'National Socialism'.

chapter of *The Decline of The West*, and specifically in *The Hour of Decision*, that the new cycle facing the West was one of battle for survival and a martial — *Prussian* — spirit was required. Yockey addressed himself entirely to this question. Naturally, such a martial resurgence, however, does require that aesthetics is not permitted to degenerate; just how that degeneration proceeds was the question answered by Yockey's concept of 'Cultural Vitalism', which provides the diagnostic means of excising the pathogens from the Western cultural organism.

## Willis Carto (aka Dr E. L. Anderson): 'Cultural Dynamics'

Carto had read *Imperium* in 1955 and had committed himself to Yockey when meeting him just prior to his death in 1960. With Oliver, he was instrumental in having published the first readily accessible edition of *Imperium* in 1962. Carto has ensured that *Imperium* has stayed in print and other publishers, most notably Wermod & Wermod, have also more recently published their own editions.

Already in 1960 Carto, using the *nom de plume* E. L. Anderson, had published an essay entitled 'Cultural Dynamics: Why do Civilizations decline and what can be done about it?' The essay was primarily an adaptation of Yockey and Spengler, cogently simplified with the aim of formulating a new social science that would incorporate the aims of all social sciences. The task was undertaken two years prior to Carto's publication of *Imperium*. The essay was reprinted in *The American Mercury* magazine. *Mercury* was a venerable journal founded by H. L. Mencken in 1924 and it went through a series of changes in publisher and editor; sold to Rightist millionaire Russell Maguire in 1952, owner of the Thompson Submachine Gun Company; and in 1961 to Rev. Gerald Winrod, one of the 'sedition trial' defendants during World War II. Rev. Winrod's *Mercury* merged with Carto's *Western Destiny* in 1966.[35]

In this issue of *The American Mercury,* Carto editorialised that 'without doubt, one of the greatest minds of the twentieth century was Francis Parker Yockey, the towering genius whose most notable achievement was *Imperium*.'

35 See *American Mercury* Archive 1924–1960, http://www.unz.org/Pub/AmMercury.

Carto then referred to the four essays that had been reprinted in a single volume by DTK of Nordland Press. Carto credited Yockey with a prophetic foresight in writing 23 years previously (in *Imperium*) that 'the American Nation is not sovereign but is literally a Zionist dependency', making 'International Zionism' alongside the USSR and China, one of three 'superpowers' for which the American people were not even a factor other than as cannon fodder. The US Government has become 'by its inner nature alien and hostile to the majority of Americans'; American patriots blame their nation's plight on 'bureaucracy', 'creeping socialism', 'infiltration' or 'bad advice' but the real issue is that of the Zionist apparatus that runs the USA. The most effective way of determining if one's nation is truly sovereign is to consider how it is being served by its foreign policy. Readers were invited to name one decision by the State Department since 1930 that has served American interests. From the collection of four essays, Carto cited Yockey's last, 'The World in Flames'. Yockey had written that the key to understanding what could be said to be the schizophrenic, fractured policy of the 'Zionist Washington regime' is what we might also call the predicament of the parasite: the parasite must by its character simultaneously both use and destroy its host. Carto quoted Yockey's observation from the essay that this is a 'psychological riddle' insofar as the Zionists have 'two minds'. While they relied on the USA to keep their enemies at bay — namely at the time Germany, Arabia, and the USSR — their inner imperative was to destroy Western Civilization and therefore the traditional foundations that had built America. American patriots, however, were too fearful to name the real enemy, hence Carto called it the 'Nameless Terror'.[36] This editorial comment on US foreign policy under the control of Zionism was a sequel to an issue that had been raised by Carto in 1960, writing as E. L. Anderson, in his essay 'Cultural Dynamics': that of the destructive effects of imperialism upon the conquering state.

In introducing 'Cultural Dynamics', Carto emphasised that the only event of significance that had occurred since the first publication of the essays in 1960 was the republication of *Imperium* in 1962. Carto pointed out that the primary difference he had with Yockey was that the latter 'rather downgrades

36 Willis Carto, 'The Nameless Terror', 'In the *Mercury's* Opinion', *The American Mercury*, Summer 1971, pp. 3–4.

the importance of race, a factor which I feel is of primary importance'. In fact, 'race' is also of 'primary importance' to Yockey but 'race' in a different sense — as an idea which gives meaning to the European beyond the measuring of skulls. Race is rather a we-feeling between individuals of a specific historical-cultural unit. Carto continued: 'Nevertheless, I commend the study of this book as an important step in the understanding of the vital imperative of the West to comprehend the *pathology of culture*. There is nothing in this world so infinitely important as this.'[37]

Cultural dynamics is synonymous with cultural pathology, since Carto aimed to explain the answer to 'the mystifying problem of the loss of social unity in a civilization; to the problem of the disintegration of the arts; public and official corruption; loss of popular confidence in man as an individual; the decline of faith in a common religion and even the loss of pride in one's own race'. 'In short, why do civilizations decline and what can be done about it?'[38]

Carto turns first to Spengler's 'theory of the organic nature of civilization', that 'a cultural unit (composed always of more than one nation; for example, Europe) is an *organism* with a definite life cycle of gestation, birth, youth, maturity, old age and death'. 'Spengler taught that nothing can be done to interfere with this natural cycle.'[39]

To Carto and many others who have read Spengler, the inevitability of cultural decline and death is 'pessimistic'. However, as Yockey pointed out, to realise that all organisms have a limited life span is not 'pessimism' but reality.

The individual human is conscious of his own mortality but a mentally healthy person does not view this as 'pessimism'. In fact, consciousness of one's own mortality pushes the normal individual to fulfil his potential within that life span. Spengler and Yockey gave Western humanity that conciseness necessary to realise the course on which the Western cultural organism should proceed. Both stated that Western civilization must face its 'outer enemies', referring to the 'coloured world revolution' and its 'inner traitors' and

---

37 E. L. Anderson (Willis Carto), 'Cultural Dynamics: Why do Civilizations decline and what can be done about it?', 1960; *American Mercury*, Summer 1971, pp. 45–51.

38 E. L. Anderson, p. 45.

39 E. L. Anderson, p. 45.

'culture distorters'. Spengler wrote of this 'mission' in the closing pages of his magnum opus, *The Decline of The West*, and devoted his final published work, *The Hour of Decision*, to the tasks yet to be completed. Yockey was concerned primarily with the fulfilment of these tasks and expressed what they were in *Imperium*, 'The World in Flames', *The Enemy of Europe* and other essays.

Carto stated that Spengler merely chronicles the West's decline, whereas 'Cultural Dynamics' is intended to diagnose and then remedy the disease of the cultural organism. 'Cultural dynamics' holds that the diseases of a cultural unit are not inherent but are the result of conditions that have always prevailed in mature cultures and which are today 'festering as an open sore' in the West.[40] Though this may seem to be a matter of semantics, Carto's point is vital: when an alien people settles in a Civilization it might act as a pathogen upon the cultural organism. Alien religions, ideas and ideals kill the cultural organism. Alien pathogens are most influential during the empire stage of a civilization, when it confronts alien cultures. These 'alien microbes' consume and kill the 'conquering' civilization.[41] This is what Yockey called 'culture distortion'. For Carto and Yockey, the pathogens of 'culture distortion' were carried into the Western cultural organism by the Jewish culture.

The introduction of the 'strange and exotic' into a civilization undermines the finely tuned cultural balanced that has developed over centuries by the sudden presence of alien mores. To illustrate this, Carto quotes Richard LaPiere from *The Freudian Ethic*:

> A dynamically balanced social system is like a healthy organism in that it is composed of a great many interdependent "parts" — institutions, customs, values systems, etc. — comparable to the cells, organs, etc., in an organism and, like a healthy organism, it tends to correct for any disturbance to its balance by contemporary changes.[42]

In the West's present cycle, any attempt to 'correct for any disturbance to its balance' is condemned as 'anti-Semitism' and 'Right-wing extremism'.

---

40 E. L. Anderson, pp. 45–46.

41 E. L. Anderson, p. 46.

42 Cited by Anderson, p. 46.

In summing up what is meant by 'Cultural dynamics', Carto wrote that it is 'the study of cultural units as individual organisms'.[43] All cultural units have the *duty* 'to be true to themselves'. What this means for Carto, probably reflecting his commitment as a traditional American 'populist', who opposes the USA's role as a world policeman, is opposition to 'imperialism'. It means an end 'to the filthy and hypocritical fraud of Marxian and finance capital "internationalism", the conspiracy of an obscene alliance which daily becomes more oppressive to freedom-loving men, and which has wreaked already a far heavier toll to the honest and peaceable people of the world than they are willing to pay'. Hence, 'cultural dynamics' means the development of all peoples 'according to their own destiny and their own inner needs and drives; not according to the unknown or vaguely-defined plans of a greedy, powerful outsider'.

This anti-imperialist outlook can be seen as having been incorporated by Yockey himself in his support for the emerging Third World as a bulwark against world Zionism and the USA. Yockey's work with the Egyptian Ministry of Information and his contact with Cubans reflect this. His final essay, 'The World in Flames', addresses this very theme.

Where Carto, like others, differs from both Yockey and Spengler is in his drawing from the findings on race from the social and physical sciences; Carto names examples of scientists such as Sir Arthur Keith in physical anthropology, Wesley C George in biology, C. D. Darlington in botany, Carlton S Coon in anthropology, Ruggles Gates in genetics, Henry E Garrett in psychology, Robert Kuttner in zoology, et al. The findings of science on racial differentiation show the necessity, states Carto, of halting 'the present worldwide, disastrous trend towards cosmopolitan formlessness and disintegration of all different cultures, races and nations.'[44] While the philosophy of Spengler and Yockey are in accord with this sentiment, the reasons are those of Historical rather than biological imperatives. The destiny of Western man for Carto is, however, one of continuing biological ascent by ensuring that the races do not mingle. Drawing on both Darwin and Nietzsche, Carto holds that the latter's 'overman' is reached through an application of evolutionary principles — that

43 E. L. Anderson, p. 46.

44 E. L. Anderson, p. 47.

is, through 'eugenics' or human upbreeding.[45] Carto's 'cultural dynamics' therefore embraces 'evolutionary ethics' which are at odds with the outlook of Spengler and Yockey, and indeed of Nietzsche, all of whom eschewed the social application of Darwinism as reducing man to the level of the beasts.

Yockey would also not accept an 'anti-imperialist' adaptation of his philosophy, as he had since his university days described himself as a 'European imperialist'. Western Imperium would include the development, not the repudiation, of imperialism; it would mobilise the expansion of the West as a unified cultural organism, transcending the separate and rival imperial adventures of the colonial powers of prior centuries. It would be the advance across the world not of a Germanic *Lebensraum* but a Western *Lebensraum*.

Carto was writing as an American 'populist' and nationalist, which includes a strong anti-imperialist element inspired by the American Revolution. So far from aiming to secure American world supremacy, American populist nationalism advocates 'America First' isolationism; refraining from interference in foreign affairs, especially European ones, which lie outside of America's hemispheric interests. American populists opposed the USA's entry into the war against the Axis, establishing the America First movement not so much because they were 'pro-Nazi' but because they saw no benefit to the USA of getting involved in overseas wars. If today supposed 'rightists' or 'neo-conservatives' as they are now called, advocate the USA's role as a 'world policeman' it is not any doctrine deriving from American populism or nationalism but from Wilsonian liberal internationalism, in an attempt to create a 'new world order', as it is now called. Wilsonian internationalism took on an anti-Soviet orientation when Stalin purged the USSR of Trotskyites. Many went over to the US in the Cold War and some of the leading Trotskyites became leading Cold War ideologues. Even Trotsky's widow, Sedova, ended up supporting the war in Korea as a necessary counter to the USSR, which was regarded as worse than fascism or capitalism.

To that extent Yockey, and several factions such as *Common Sense*, the NRP, and Frederick Weiss, were also 'anti-imperialist'; they saw, like the prewar America First movement, US interventionism as serving non-American interests — or in Yockeyan terms, the interests of the Culture-distorter. The

45 E. L. Anderson, p. 49.

anti-imperialism of Willis Carto and today's paleo-conservatives is in agreement with Yockey insofar as 'American imperialism' does not serve any nativist American interest. Yockey — and his sister Vinette — had been actively involved in the America First movement. However, in direct opposition to US interventionism, which serves interests that are not even 'American' let alone 'Western', Yockey and the ELF advocated a unified 'Western' imperialism.

## Ronald Lee Slote: 'Cultural Relativity'

Similar to Carto's 'Cultural Dynamics' is Ronald Lee Slote's 'Cultural Relativity'. Slote was organiser of the Americans for Western Unity (AWU), which arose in the early 1970s. Like Carto, Slote held that Western interference in non-Western societies was a distortion of the Faustian soul, of Western man's innate drive to explore and conquer. The West's imperialism, like the imperialism of Rome, Greece and others, would come back to haunt us, bringing in cheap, coloured labour, analogous to the black slaves of antiquity, spilling European blood in foreign conflicts, arming and mechanising the coloured world with the technics that would eventually be turned against Western civilization.

Slote stated that Western civilization as no other has 'sought to make the entire world conform to Western ideals and traditions'. 'To a large degree this has been superficially done.' This 'Western universalism' was given impetus by the universalism of Christianity and the Faustian urge was also taken up under the mantle of the missionaries, who sought to save souls through what really had become a Western religion. However, the Western impress on an alien culture can only be an artificial construct.[46] This reflects Spengler's concept of *pseudomorphosis*, a term he borrowed from geology to describe how a new culture will only be superficially implanted on an older culture and its land, and will itself become distorted by the older established culture.

An example of this *pseudomorphosis*, although Slote does not use the term, is the way that Christianity in Africa has been fundamentally altered to suit the African psyche. Slote gives the very clear example of Catholic imagery employed by Haitian *voodoo*: 'The have taken something of ours and

---

46 Ronald Lee Slote, 'Cultural Relativity', Americans for Western Unity, Dearborn Heights, Mich., ca. 1972.

transformed it into a product of their culture, for nothing can be lifted from one culture and accepted into another without it being modified to fit the preconceived patterns of the recipient culture.'[47] This is very much analogous to Yockey's 'Cultural Vitalism' and appears as a symptom of 'cultural pathology'. It is what Yockey called Culture-retardation.

The imposition of alien cultural attributes on to another culture interacts negatively on both, and while the modern progressive liberal might call this 'cultural enrichment', 'Cultural pathology' points to the experiences of history and of present-day societies, showing that retardation, parasitism and distortion are the results. Hence, as Slote states, the moral outlooks are different, and because it is an innate survival trait for normal people to regard the culture into which they are born — whether Kalahari Bushman, Chinaman, Hopi, Russian or Westerner — as 'better' or 'superior', or just 'normal', even if that 'normal' involves the cannibalisation of maggot-ridden corpses, such as was the custom of prehistoric Polynesian society for example.

Slote's 'cultural relativity' argues that to expect the world to accept Western standards 'is asking them something that is impossible to do'. However, as Yockey showed, what have long been called 'Western standards' are generally the product of the distortion or retardation of those standards. Slote stated that 'a few long-sighted people were able long ago to overcome this basic drive of our culture and see that what is good for us is not necessarily what is good for the rest of the world'. This is now increasingly evident. The West, argues Slote, must awaken to the reality of the rest of the world 'and deal with people as they are rather than as one wishes them to be'; in doing so, 'many of the problems of the world would soon disappear'.[48]

While AWU adopted the quirk of 'Identity' religion, holding that the European races were the true lost tribes of Israel, the Yockeyan inspiration becomes more apparent when AWU explained 'the drive for Western unity', clearly an adaptation of Yockey's 'imperium'. The world struggle was one that would determine whether the 'Western Culture' would survive. While Eastern Europe was described as being under 'barbaric communists', the 'free' world is 'subjected to the distorting influence of the culture aliens', which through

47 Ronald Lee Slote, 'Cultural Relativity'.

48 Ronald Lee Slote, 'Cultural Relativity'.

their inner cohesion had virtually taken control. The West, from being master of the world shortly before, has come to find that its 'will-to-power is gone'. Americans are 'no longer in the service of a high culture but in the service of culture aliens'. 'Those aliens, which can never create but can only subvert and destroy, have now put us under their will.' Americans were called on to take back control of their own culture and throw off 'parasites like Kissinger and Burns', the US Secretary of State and Governor of the Federal Reserve Bank respectively, 'as one would a cancer'.

> We must create a new West that is again in the service of our High Culture. A pride in our heritage and our race again must be instilled in our integrated white youth. A unity of the Western nations must be formed and a new crusade against the infidels started. A free and united West is what we demand and shall fight to the death for... to instil the spirit of the West into the hearts of Americans. Your place it in the front! March with us![49]

Slote had revived the spirit of the old European Liberation Front founded by Yockey in London in 1948. Indeed, his concluding remark on the 'drive for Western Unity', 'Your place is in the front! March with us!', was the byline that concluded *Frontfighter*, the newsletter of Yockey's original Front.

## Gerhard Lauck: 'Blood and Soul'

While Anglophone National Socialist luminaries such as Lincoln Rockwell, Colin Jordan and Arnold Leese had offhandedly dismissed Yockey because of his views on race, others saw the overriding importance of Yockey's concept of 'Cultural Vitalism' as granting an added faculty of perception to the struggle for European survival. While not rejecting the biological determinism implicit in orthodox Hitlerian post-war National Socialism, particularly of the Anglophone variety, Gerhard Lauck, like Dr Edward Cawthron, saw the merits of adapting Yockeyan-Spenglerian ideas.

Lauck had written a Spenglerian thesis in 1972 entitled *Blood and Soul*, published by the Westropa Social Alliance, obviously named after that Westropa Press under which *Imperium* was first published in London in 1948.

---

49 Ronald Lee Slote, 'The Drive for Western Unity', Americans for Western Unity, Dearborn Heights, Mich., ca. 1972.

Lauck sent a copy of *Blood and Soul* to Oliver in 1974 after meeting him at a social function organised by Louis Byers[50] of the National Youth Alliance and Francis Parker Yockey Movement. Lauck wrote to Oliver:

> *Blood and Soul* deals with Spenglerian and racist (National Socialist) thought, and with the conflict between these two philosophies, both of which have something important to offer. In the belief that these two philosophies should not be held totally incompatible, but rather that both serve a function in that they show various aspects of the "problem", i.e. the decay of civilizations or "social entropy", and should indeed be complementary perspectives used in viewing this complicated problem, I felt compelled while still a student a few years ago to sort my thoughts on how at least a partial reconciliation could be attempted.
>
> In the Spring of 1972 I sent out a few dito-copies. One of them went to Helmut Suendermann, the former deputy press chief of the NSDAP, who wrote back that I had "hit the nail on the head" and invited me to visit him, although he unfortunately passed away unexpectedly just a few weeks before my arrival in Germany, in September 1972. It was Suendermann who first referred to *Blood and Soul* as a "study".[51]

When Lauck, the son of an engineering professor, had written *Blood and Soul* in 1972 he was a College student of 19. He would soon become known as the 'Farm Belt Fuhrer'. Lauck established a world headquarters in Nebraska, where he published a tabloid newspaper, *The New Order*, stickers, books, pamphlets, posters and videos in 10 languages for distribution around the world. This network was called the NSDAP — AO, taking its name from the original German National Socialist 'Ausland Organisation', or overseas organisation, that had been responsible for the promotion of the Third Reich around the world. Lauck founded the NSDAP — AO in 1972,[52] the year he published *Blood and Soul*.

Oliver and Lauck agreed that Yockey and Spengler were wrong to reject the biological basis of race as being a mere hangover of that nineteenth century materialism which sought to quantify and measure everything, including

50 Lauck to Oliver, July 25, 1974.

51 Lauck to Oliver, July 25, 1974.

52 'An Introduction to the NSDAP — AO', http://www.nazi-lauck-nsdapao.com/the-fight-goes-on.htm#An Introduction to the NSDAP/AO:.

man. Oliver replied to Lauck that he was correct in saying that Spengler, and therefore Yockey, had been misled on the 'biological basis of race' by the Left-wing anthropologist Franz Boas, who claimed that skull form is altered by environment after one generation among immigrants. Boas's theory therefore implies that landscape, as Yockey and Spengler would have it, forms 'race'. Secondly, they cited the capacity of *mimesis* 'among all anthropoids, which enables a person of any race to conform outwardly to the Civilization in which they live'. Oliver cited the capacity of an ape to learn to ride a bicycle, etc. The Hottentot was able to achieve something similar but the Jew, with his superior intelligence, could affect the mannerism far more successfully. Such an 'oversight' 'impairs' Spengler's cyclic theory, because no civilization has been able to assimilate alien races without collapsing from 'blood poisoning'.

However, Oliver goes on to state that if the Jews defeat the 'Aryans', they might lose in a struggle for supremacy against the Mongols and in particular the Japanese. This would depend on whether Jewish influence has been totally eradicated from Chinese and Japanese societies, as Jews have the ability, 'still unexplained by genetics, to remain Jews, even after they have, by interbreeding, taken on the physical characteristics of other races'.[53] This a concession by Oliver to the literally *meta-physical* aspects of race, beyond genetics or at least not currently explained by genetics, and returns us to the contention that the relevance of 'race' to history means something other than what is statistically quantifiable in it.

Lauck explained in the introduction to *Blood and Soul* that Yockey was a Spenglerian and that 'their names are often used interchangeably' and his opening words address Yockey's 'romantic Spenglerian concept of race'. For the relevance of history, one 'has race', that is to say 'character', and indeed Spengler defined 'race' as the endurance of character, rather than the endurance of a skull type. The ruling stratum of a 'healthy Culture', Lauck explains, epitomises 'race' in terms of character and the general population of that culture (or what is called a 'people' as an organised unit) possesses that character to varying degrees.[54]

---

53 Oliver to Lauck August 2, 1974.

54 G Lauck, *Blood and Soul* (New York: Westropa Social Alliance Publications, 1972), p. 5.

Lauck, however, maintains that race is biological and hence his aim is to reconcile biological determinism with Yockey and Spengler's cultural determinism. Lauck sought to understand why Spenglerían philosophy is 'anti-race' in terms of biology, 'which is what race means'.[55] Lauck also poses the question as to what motivated Yockey to 'deviate from biological race'. He maintained that every civilization has been created by the White race, and in particular the Nordic, and that a Civilization collapses due to 'mongrelisation'. Lauck, however, does allow for the Spenglerian cyclic waxing and waning of civilization, but only insofar as all High cultures proceed from Nordics. However, a large non-Nordic population, albeit part of the cultural stream, is required to sustain that high culture. Yockey took up the Spenglerian notion that race is formed by the 'rhythm' of 'landscape'. This is not the same as the Left-wing conception that a culture is the product of environment or of economic forces; it is a difference between the materialistic and the metaphysical conceptions of History. Lauck points out that it was the source of the conflict between Spengler and the National Socialists, and that Yockey believed the biological conception of race was an error of the Third Reich.[56] Lauck — conversely to Yockey — states that the West can unite in an Imperium without the mingling of the Nordic sub-stratum with non-Nordic elements, by maintaining the separate identities of the nation states of the White sub-races; he uses the wartime alliance between Germany and Italy as an example.[57] This is what Yockey opposed in his demand that we speak of 'Europe' and the 'we-feeling' of all Europeans.

A lot of confusion would have been eliminated if the German word *volk* were used, which implies the idea of 'race' as defined by Yockey. *Volk* implies something more than biology; it implies spirit, soul and culture. The German Idealists of prior centuries referred to 'Germany' as a nation possessing a *volk soul*. Hence, it can be contended that Spenglerian 'race' is a more specifically German concept than the race theory of Hitlerism. It is also a reflection of the difference between English materialism and German Idealism, insofar as Darwinism was used both to define 'race' and to define capitalism. German

---

55 G Lauck, *Blood and Soul*, p. 5.

56 G Lauck, *Blood and Soul*, p. 6.

57 G Lauck, *Blood and Soul*, p. 7.

Idealists opposed both as materialistic. What Spengler called 'Prussian socialism' and Yockey 'ethical socialism' was Germany's answer to English materialism.

Lauck agrees with Spenglerianism that when Civilizations reach a point where material existence replaces the founding spiritual ethos of a High Culture, then 'money thinking', as Spengler put it, becomes dominant, and social, cultural, moral and religious enervation result. Lauck explains that life 'becomes more artificial' and proceeds down the path of self-destruction.[58] As economic expansion becomes a dominant theme, the West has put its technology into the hands of what Yockey called the 'outer enemy'.

Lauck returns to 'the physical and the racial', pointing out Spengler and Yockey's rejection of Darwinism.[59] Spengler and Yockey refer to 'blood' in a spiritual sense; the descent of that 'character' which was long symbolised by the Aristocracy, whose wealth was based on land, rather than the 'aristocracy' of money — the plutocrat and oligarch who replaces the landed nobility in the downward cycle of a Civilization. 'Blood' in the Spenglerian sense is the symbolic transmitter of character down through generations — and that is what is called 'race'. This is also what is meant by Spengler's statement in the final pages of *The Decline of The West* on the 'final conflict between money and blood', which near the end of a civilization sees the resurgence of 'blood' — of aristocracy, hierarchy, authority, duty, martial ethos — when a civilization fulfils its destiny on the stage of world history with a last dramatic hurrah.

However, Lauck insisted that 'blood' — that is to say, 'race' — is both physical and spiritual. The physical is a manifestation of the spiritual. Spengler and Yockey stated that bodily structure is an anatomist's explanation and does not explain History. It is consideration of the inner life that is required to explain a culture.

What Lauck saw, like Oliver and others who maintained a biological worldview, was the undeniable reality of historico-cultural-spiritual cycles within a race or people. Lauck wrote:

> Who can deny the significance of spiritual differences between Western Man of the Middle Ages and Western Man of today, or between Nordic rulers of ancient

58 G Lauck, *Blood and Soul*, p. 10.

59 G Lauck, *Blood and Soul*, p. 14.

> India and those of Europe? Such differences cannot be explained in purely racial or folkish terms.

It is important even for biological determinists or racialists to recognise the importance of 'life style' and its connection with Spengler and Yockey's 'spirituality of action, of form, of "tactics of living"'.[60] Lauck sought to utilize Spenglerian cultural morphology within the context of biological races, in explaining why races, for example, 'mongrelize'. From this biological racist viewpoint, we might, using Spenglerianism, postulate that the Roman civilization collapsed through the mixing of Roman stock with non-white slaves and labourers, initiated by the need for cheap labour as economics came to dominate Roman thinking at a certain point of Roman civilization. We might say with this hypothesis that as Rome became 'sophisticated' and increasingly disregarded the martial and aristocratic ethics of its founders in favour of luxury and ease, the very idea of being 'Roman' slowly underwent a fundamental change; it came to be based on wealth — the rise of an oligarchy — rather than descent from patrician families. This change in ethos opens the way for a deluge of foreign ideas, religions and lifestyles until the original Roman ethos is barely perceptible. A reaction might occur — such as the rise of Caesar in the case of Rome, or Napoleon, Hitler and Mussolini in our own cultural epoch — to restore some of the original values. There is then a 'conflict between money and blood'. The West underwent this conflict with World War II, in which 'money' won over 'blood' through sheer force of numbers and the mobilisation of the 'outer barbarian', Russia, which was supplied with Western technics.

However, to return to our Roman example, by applying a racialist interpretation to Yockey and Spengler, as Lauck attempts, Spengler's 'cultural morphology' and Yockey's 'Cultural Vitalism' explain the *how and why* of 'mongrelization'. 'Cultural Vitalism' and Spenglerianism are not concerned with miscegenation as the cause of cultural collapse. These see the epochal cycles as proceeding regardless of miscegenation. What is important for a Spenglerian in terms of the presence of alien races in a cultural organism is not the co-mingling of 'blood' but the alien influences introduced into that culture by foreigners acting as pathogens. The epochal stages of a high culture

60 G Lauck, *Blood and Soul*, p. 14.

from birth to maturity, old age and death take place regardless of genetics. What matters for survival is the maintenance or restoration of the culture's founding *ethos*. A clear analogy might be found in considering the Jewish 'Nation-Race-People-Culture', as Yockey put it, whose character — and hence 'race' in the Spenglerian sense — has endured through millennia regardless of miscegenation or indwelling with alien tribes and nations, through the force of (1) a rigorously enforced ethos and (2) a powerful rabbinate. The duration of character of 'race' has been so paramount in shaping a Jewish identity that even so-called 'self-hating' Jews such as Karl Marx can only contrive a variation of Judaism when trying to de-judaise themselves. And of course, the race-character is so strong that it impacts wherever the Jews settle, which Yockey called the predominant example of 'Culture-distortion' in Western civilization. Again, this is explained in Spenglerian-Yockeyan terms as only being possible because the Western cultural organism has reached the epoch in which money rules above 'blood' and culture aliens can influence the cultural organism because there no longer exists the strength of the traditional ethos to act as antibodies against a cultural virus. This is an organic phenomenon that occurs whether by accident or design, just as a Missionary amid an African tribe becomes a 'Culture-distorter' who will aim to change the religion, dress, manners, customs of that tribe — if the tribe allows itself to be influenced through its own lack of will.

Unlike Yockey, who regarded the Soviet bloc as at least a necessary evil if not a bulwark against the 'Judaeo-American Establishment destroying Western civilization', to quote a headline from *Common Sense*, Lauck did not concede the possibility of the USSR opposing world Zionism. Nor did Lauck consider that Russia, even under the Soviet system, might contain the potentialities of a new Russian civilization, perhaps even as part of a Russo-Western synthesis — a possibility at times considered by Yockey, Spengler, Remer and Jean Thiriart. Lauck wrote, rather, that 'the Soviet Union is not at the stage of an infant Russian Culture'. Like Charlemagne, this empire came much too early and only oppresses other members of the same cultural entity more than it truly unites them. Lauck saw the USSR as the enemy of the West, one furnished with Western technics — a Slavic front against the West. Like Hitler, Lauck did not concede the civilization-building potentialities of the Slavs and accorded Russia's culture to a Germanic stratum: 'Asiatic Russia is a total enemy.' Under Nordic leadership, the 'Western Slavs' might be integrated into Europe and serve as a buffer zone against Asia. Lauck therefore departed from Yockey's view that a Russian occupation of Europe would not have the power to eliminate the Western race-soul and might even succumb to it.[61]

Lauck propounded an 'extension theory' for Western civilization. The 'cultural colonies' of the West, in Yockey's terms, represent the return of a spirit which has been exhausted in the European Homeland, through the renewal of the vigour of the race in that pioneer spirit they require. 'America is fresher for a regeneration attempt spiritually, than is Europe.'[62] One could say that these far-flung 'cultural colonies' of the old Western civilization — USA, Australia, Canada, New Zealand — are the newborn offspring and therefore restart from a position of youth. However, the West is threatened by Asia, including Russia, armed with Western technics.[63] This was also the thesis of Spengler's last book, *The Hour of Decision*, where he warns the West that it is faced by Asia led by Russia with the rallying cry of Bolshevism, and an internal class war engendered by Marxism and capitalism. Lauck's call was to break the cycle of decay. This was also Yockey and Spengler's view and they stated that in the declining years of a civilization there is a reaction and a resurgence. Lauck also questioned whether a post-Western civilization might arise if only the White race remains genetically intact. However, what is lacking now is a wellspring of uncontaminated White 'barbarians' to cleanse the decay of the old world and usher forth a new high culture. It is in search for such a repository of uncontaminated Whites that some rightists look to Russia as the source of this new culture.

Lauck closes by addressing the question of Western 'imperium'. He concludes that the imperialism of the European powers came close to achieving this, although it was based on nation states rather than a single empire under a single leader, as the imperiums of Greece and Rome had been.[64] However, Yockey pointed out that Europe had acted as a single culture-unit vis-à-vis the 'outer enemy' during the 'Spring' epoch of its high culture, under the impe-

---

61 G Lauck, *Blood and Soul*, pp. 17–18.

62 G Lauck, *Blood and Soul*, p. 19.

63 G Lauck, *Blood and Soul*, p. 22.

64 G Lauck, *Blood and Soul*, p. 23.

tus of a common religion and a common religious authority and a common 'Gothic' culture, which permitted it to act in the Crusades as a single military unit. As Lauck points out, Yockey stated that the Third Reich had been the embryonic Western Imperium but had been aborted by the combination of Western technics and Russian-led 'outer barbarians'. Spengler died just as the Third Reich was coming into existence but looked with optimism to the fascist legions of Italy as being the harbinger of a Western resurgence. He regarded the resurgence of authority ('Caesarism') as an inevitable part of the final cultural cycle. Yockey proceeded from the same premise and actively sought to make that resurgence a reality. His added faculty of perception — Cultural Vitalism — enables the Western thinker to diagnose the pathogens that have invaded the Western cultural organism and which accelerate the West's decline rather than permitting its final potential to unfold. Lauck states that Yockey — seeking to maintain the validity of Spenglerianism — held that 'imperium' might be an inner development rather than the emergence of a physical imperium. Lauck argues that this conception is vague.[65] Frankly, I am not familiar with this being a conception of Yockey's, although he does refer to the 'we-feeling' in the creation of a unified Western People-Race-Nation-State. However, this European consciousness is seen as a prelude to the territorial manifestation of a Western Imperium as real as the Roman Empire. As Lauck himself states, the physical and mental are part of an organic unity.

Lauck concluded by citing Hitler saying that the USA would play a leading role in the coming imperium, but he insists that Germany remains the 'mother and father of the Idea'. As a Hitlerite, Lauck also insists that understanding Hitlerism will always be a predicate on which to base any theory and action.[66]

In 1996, Thompson remarked on Russia, then under Yeltsin: 'Change must come in the form of a *coup d'etat* with the aid of the communist faction. The US regime would probably not dare to intervene… US capital is profiting there while it spreads its "democracy venom"'.[67] Change came in the form of Putin, who perhaps does not mark the final word on Russia, and the recon-

65 G Lauck, *Blood and Soul*, p. 23.

66 G Lauck, *Blood and Soul*, p. 24.

67 Thompson to Bolton, October 22, 1996.

stituted Communist Party under Zyuganov is of the nationalistic type that Thompson, Yockey and Weiss saw emerging.[68]

## 'Fascist', 'Imperialist'

### 1. Gannon's Critique

Anthony Gannon was scathing of such adaptations of Yockey. In particular, he continued to reject any notion of Darwinism and of 'vertical race' as remnants of nineteenth century thought that had had a negative impact on what Yockey called the 'provisional' manifestation of Imperium, the Third Reich. Gannon wrote to Stimely of this in 1981:

> FPY was an imperialist and certainly believed in the re-conquest of all of the IMPERIUM plus as much of anything else which would be required for its sustenance. He did not conceive of a truce with the Outer-enemies as a serious possibility and, thus, accepted the probability of a continuing war of survival. As for Willis Carto, I am sure he is sincere, devoted to FPY's memory, one of us, and your friend — it is necessary to say this in view of what must now follow. I do not believe that WC has read *Imperium* or understood it — even if his eyes followed every single line of print in the book. How is it possible for him to write such "crap"? as FPY would certainly have declaimed.
>
> It is all laughable — Cultural Dynamics, indeed! FPY would have rolled on the floor in agonies of laughter at that curious mixture of Imperialist terminology and philosopher's garbage. The man is simply a materialist, old-fashioned, VERTICAL racialist, Darwin-worshipper, Science-worshipper, Law-worshipper — I could go on! All of these types were DESPISED by FPY as having got in the way of everyone who ever wanted to do something for the Idea. Whatever excuse there may have been for such intellectual junk before *Imperium* was written, there never was such afterwards. You CANNOT accept

68 One Leftist lamented: 'The truth is though that it [Communist Party of the Russian Federation] … is no friend of anyone genuinely on the left. Their politics are poisonous mixture of extreme Russian nationalism, old-school Soviet era Stalin worship, overt racism, anti-Semitism and glorification of "the motherland" and Russian culture. One can genuinely compare their politics to the "left wing" of the German NSDAP in the 1920s and early 30s.' See https://shirazsocialist.wordpress.com/2011/12/15/the-truth-about-the-russian-communist-party/.

> *Imperium* and FEEL it or UNDERSTAND its analysis and continue to believe in that guff! To me it is nonsense to reject God but put in its place Nature or, on occasion, Destiny — all such conceptions being super-personal or supernatural in dimension. Worse if one could accept this rag-bag of worn-out nineteenth century nostrums, how did it all happen the way it did? In England, before the year 1950 there was no racially mongrelized population, and even today it is still not at the American level. If one could rely on the FACT that every blue-eyed, fair-haired human being was a FRIEND, and that the others were probably ENEMIES how simple and predictable life would be, and have been. Look at the degeneration of Scandinavia, where examples of non-Nordics are hard to come by. Believe me, I will go along the VERTICAL line for aesthetic reasons, and certainly exclude non-Europeans from our Imperium (our colonials excepted, of course), but for all the rest it is all quite absurd when taken to the lengths of determinism! FPY postulated that Race is what a man DOES. This means that someone who might appear to be a VERTICAL kangaroo might well be a HORIZONTAL Nordic, and vice versa. Willis Carto's ideas are a little nearer to Oswald Mosley's as expressed in *The Alternative*, but only a little, for O.M. was not a Verticalist either. I am afraid I cannot be kinder to WC than that.
>
> The plain fact is that what has happened is because of the supremacy of the Culture Distorters, a closed organism in the body of an open one, pursuing a parasitic policy with alarming success, proving that a determined minority can control a huge host-majority for long periods with complete success by adopting the method of an Order, secret and secure in its command positions, as FPY recognised and wished to emulate. It is nonsense to see conspiracies everywhere — it is even greater nonsense to pretend that none exist! Please do not show this letter to poor WC and do wrestle for his soul, if you agree with me — and FPY! Such a well-intentioned man deserved a better viewpoint.[69]

It is ironic that Yockey's primary heralds in the USA were atheists: Willis Carto, and most vehemently Revilo P Oliver, and the publisher of the first US edition of *Imperium*, Charles Smith, was a leading atheist. One can see the Catholicism inherent in Yockey's doctrine, whether it was intended consciously or not. The cause of Western illness is ascribed to morphological reasons as per Spengler and not to miscegenation. Hence, Yockey's thought to a significant extent will continue to be either rejected outright among the Right,

---

69 Gannon to Stimely, February 15, 1981.

or adapted in the fashion of Carto, while Darwinism remains, under whatever name, influential. The acceptance of cultural morphology and the rejection of miscegenation as the primary cause of cultural collapse would require a paradigm shift from much of the Right, which indulges what Yockey called 'vertical' racism as a defence mechanism for those who feel that their race is genetically endangered. This itself to the masses of rightists is a rationalisation of an instinctive dislike or suspicion of 'the other'. However, as Gannon stated, 'vertical race' does not explain the rise and fall of civilizations. That was explained more satisfactorily by Spengler and by Brooks Adams[70] rather than by race theorists such as Arthur de Gobineau. Western civilization is not in its final epoch of decay now due to miscegenation. Other reasons must be sought. Spengler and Yockey provided these reasons and they are of a spiritual character. The culture pathogens infecting the West were brought in by human agency — what Yockey called Culture-distortion. However, again, Culture-distortion is not a cause but a symptom, which cannot infect a healthy organism. The pathology itself is caused by the cycles of life of a culture organism, as in any other organism. Disease enters through old age. Their recognition of these life-facts has caused Spengler and Yockey to be dismissed as 'pessimists'.

## 2. Yockey

Yockey was clear. He was an 'Imperialist' in the sense of wanting to forge a unified Western imperialism, a Western world-empire as the organic destiny of Western civilization. He had described his philosophy as 'Imperialism' since his first essays on politics and philosophy as a college student. He preferred the term to that of 'Fascist', although that was the name most commonly applied by the ELF itself. Arcand had raised this question and Yockey replied in 1951:

---

70 Brooks Adams, *The Law of Civilization and Decay* (London: Macmillan, 1896). See also K. R. Bolton, 'Oswald Spengler and Brooks Adams: The Economics of Cultural Decline', in Troy Southgate (ed.) *Spengler: Thoughts and Perspectives Vol. Ten* (London: Black Front Press, 2012).
Brooks Adams' *Law of Civilization and Decay* was republished by Black House Publishing, London, 2017. It makes an essential companion to Yockey and Spengler.

> About the word "Fascism" I should like to say this: I, no more than you, am not particularly attached to the word. I prefer the word Imperialism. This word has the strongest possible organic roots, is a synonym for organic health, and describes alone the entire tendency of our Cultural stage, the stage of Imperium. Imperialism describes now not only the expansive tendency itself, which has been present ever since the rise of Spain, but also the feeling, the rationale, the philosophy and the doctrine of that great, wordless, undeniable instinct.
>
> I shall always devote my energy to trying to supplant the word fascism — during this fluid stage. I am no *Wortgläubiger*[71] but I do believe the word fascism is simply a tactical handicap for us. Imperialism is not: the Marxists have never been able to take the magic, the pride and the strength out of this fundamental word. Words too have a destiny and through the decades and centuries their meanings change. Compare the meaning of the word democracy in 1800 — everything bad — from its meaning in 1920 — everything good. The Marxists are losing out in the terminological struggle, and it is merely a coincidence that they have used some of the words we now use — with the opposite sign. This coincidence will be one day forgotten.
>
> However another problem arises: suppose at a public meeting, or in the press, or officially, we are asked: "Are you fascist?" What can we answer? Heroic is to say: "Yes, make the most of it." Clever is to say: "What do you mean by fascism? Tell that and then I shall answer." We cannot deny, without injuring ourselves, that we have the same fundamental doctrine as Mussolini and the Hero, that we stem from them and are loyal to their spirit.[72]

Yockey rejected the possibility that they could answer the 'fascist' and 'Nazi' smears by adopting Mosley's tactic of saying that they were 'beyond fascism'. The reaction, he had told Mosley, was 'pregnant with negative suggestion'. It was also unlikely that they could 'evade the question', given the 'recent past'. Yockey's attitude was that 'there comes a time in such circumstances when the object of the obloquy adopts the name and thus deprives the opponent of its

71 Dr Greg Johnson of North American New Right/Counter-Currents Publishing comments on this word: 'I guess it must mean "Wortgläubiger" — somebody who believes something literally/in a literal way (in the Bible, for example). It is usually not used as a noun, rather the adjective *wortgläubig*, so Yockey sort of made it up.'

72 Varange to Arcand, January 17, 1951, pp. 1–2. Arcand collection, Archives Canada, Vol. 1, file no. 1.

pejorative force'. Quoting Patrick Henry's response to accusations of 'treason', he said: 'If this be treason make the most of it!' Yockey contended that such a reply 'restores to the true issue to its place and necessitates a new term of abuse'. 'The term fascism [...] will have its own destiny. If history imposes it on us, we will accept it, even though at this moment we do not wish to tie ourselves to the word.'[73]

Yockey would have preferred his system to be called 'Imperialist' since college days.[74] He had urged Gerald L. K. Smith to assume the leadership of a trans-national movement to be referred to as 'white Imperialism'. On a more practical level, that was indeed a time when the European powers still had their empires, despite being worn out by the war.[75] However, while referring to Hitler as the 'Hero' of World War II, and to the National Socialist assumption to power in Germany as the 'European Revolution of 1933',[76] Yockey seems to have seldom, if ever, referred to himself as a 'National Socialist' while often referring to 'Fascism'. Indeed, in the letter to Arcand he refers to 'Fascism' having a destiny of which the ELF was of necessity a part. The word implies a generic reference beyond Hitlerism. Like Spengler, Yockey regarded fascism and National Socialism as provisional forms of the Western organic destiny, transient yet part of a dialectic. What Yockey and the ELF worked for was the historical configuration predicted by Spengler among the closing passages of his last book:

> The prefiguration of Caesarism will become clearer, more conscious and unconcealed. The masks will fall completely from the age of the parliamentary interlude. All attempts to gather up the content of the future into parties will soon be forgotten. The Fascist formations of this decade will pass into new, unforeseeable forms, and even present-day nationalism will disappear.[77]

---

73 Varange to Arcand, January 17, 1951, op. cit.

74 Yockey, 'Life as Art', 1940, op. cit.

75 On how the USA displaced the European imperialism see: Bolton, 'The Geopolitics of White Dispossession', *Radix*, Washington Summit Publishers, Vol. 1, 2012, pp. 105–130; Bolton, *Babel Inc.* (London: Black House Publishing, 2013), pp. 41–77.

76 Yockey, *Imperium*, Wermod ed., op. cit., inter alia.

77 Spengler, *The Hour of Decision*, op. cit., p. 230.

The outlook is most clearly defined by Yockey and H Keith Thompson in correspondence with US Secretary of State Dean Acheson: 'The German National Socialist Movement was only one form, and a provisional form at that, of the great irresistible movement which expresses the Spirit of the Age, the Resurgence of Authority.'[78] However, for the moment fascism was the most readily identifiable term. ELF correspondence used the Italian Fascist date of the 'Era Fascista', counted from Mussolini's 1922 'March on Rome', not the year of Hitler's assumption to power, 1933. An early circular for *Imperium* and *The Proclamation*, presumably written by Gannon as leader of the Front in England and proprietor of Westropa Press, is unequivocal about the 'Fascist' character:

> WESTROPA PRESS
> Proprietor: A. Gannon — BCM/Westropa Press, London
>
> The two fundamental works of post-war Fascism!
> The Bible and the Proclamation of the modern Fascist movement!
>
> IMPERIUM
> by Ulick Varange, 2 vol., 12/6
>
> A historico-cultural Weltanschauung of politics, outlining the foundations of the coming Fascist centuries, and the irresistible imperative of the Fascist state.
>
> THE PROCLAMATION OF LONDON
> by Ulick Varange 1/- per copy
>
> The official declaration of the European Liberation Front, setting forth the necessary Fascist thought and action in the conditions brought about by the catastrophe of the Second World War.
>
> Do not miss the opportunity to secure your 1st edition copies of these monumental fascist works.
>
> ORDER TODAY[79]

Replying to Arcand on Italian post-war fascism, Yockey described two schools of thought. One was the Imperialist, represented by the rightist critic

78 Yockey and Thompson to Acheson, October 15, 1952.

79 A Gannon, Westropa Press, mimeographed circular, 1949.

of fascism, Julius Evola, who attracted a post-war following among neo-fascist youth, and who saw Fascism as 'a means of conquering the world, as a spirituality, as Europe.' Although Evola had misgivings about *Imperium* and the centralised structure of the Europe that Yockey proposed,[80] Yockeyans regarded him as something of a kindred spirit, as evidenced by Gannon's favourable mention of him in *Frontfighter*. The other school is Gentilian, a reference to the pre-war fascist minister of education, Giovanni Gentile, generally regarded as the most eminent of the early fascist intellectuals.[81] Gentile's school regard fascism as 'a means of saving the world' and as 'universal', 'completely changing the meaning of Mussolini's famous dictum'. 'Mussolini meant universal-European, universal-Western, but never meant to include India, China, Russia, Islam, Indians and Negroes in one conception.' This 'stultifies' Mussolini, who was 'a realist, an artist of the possible', not a 'theological word-juggler'.[82]

Yockey, in unpublished typewritten notes, was clear that his 'Imperialism' was precisely that: territorial expansion in Africa and Slavia:

> Two other grand projects have less immediacy. As to which will, or can, be undertaken first, incident will decide. But both have the Destiny-quality. First, the Europeanization of North Africa. To effectuate this, the conversion of the Mediterranean into two lakes: causeways to Gibraltar, and from Italy to Tunisia, dams at Dardanelles and Bosphorous, closing of Suez. Irrigation of the African continent as far inland as possible with the power resources of the Gibraltar, Tunisian and Egyptian dams. Settlement of the new area with Europeans from

80 See Julius Evola's review of *Imperium*, 'On the Spiritual and Structural Prerequisites for European Unity', *Europa Nazione*, 1951; *Imperium*, Wermod ed., pp. 781–797.

81 Giovanni Gentile (1875–1944), Minister of Public Education in the first Mussolini cabinet, president of the Royal Academy (1943–1944), wrote *The Doctrine of Fascism* with Mussolini, first published in the philosophically seminal Italian Encyclopaedia in 1932, under Gentile's direction; he was also author of *The Manifesto of Fascist Intellectuals*, among many other books and treatises. He was killed by partisans, ironically after having just argued for the release of jailed anti-fascist intellectuals. His philosophy, 'Actual Idealism', was based on Hegelian dialectics and his conception of the Fascist State was one of incorporating opposites, such as that achieved in the economic realm by corporatism.

82 Varange to Arcand, January 18, 1950, p. 3, Arcand collection, Archives Canada, Vol. 1 File No. 1.

> the overcrowded petty-states of Europe. Total expulsion of all indigenous populations.
>
> Second, the Europeanization of the hither Slavic lands. This includes the Balkans, Bohemia, Poland, the Baltic, White Russia, Little Russia, Muscovy, the Ukraine and the Caucasus.
>
> To a certain extent, the two projects are substitutes for another. If either one could be completely accomplished, it would assure Imperium of security in one direction. Viewed however from the viewpoint of the next three centuries, both projects are necessary, if Imperium is to remain forever as the great monument of the West. From the standpoint of one century, one will suffice. Either one will take 50 years to actualize.[83]

The colonization of Slavia can be seen as a continuation of the Third Reich's *Lebensraum*, that of Africa of fascist Italy's new Roman empire. However, Yockey was a pragamatist and a realist, and adapted according to changes in the world-situation. One might readily see how Gannon could be so dismissive of those interpretations of Yockey which adapt his thinking to self-determination for all races, universal ethno-states, anti-imperialism, and the like. On the other hand, Gannon did not comprehend Yockey's ideas in his final essay, 'The World in Flames', mainly because of Yockey's endorsement of the new non-aligned states of the 'third world'. However, such a change of outlook is not surprising. The world enemy remained America-Jewry and if these non-aligned states that were emerging blocked the world hegemony of the former, then it might give respite for Europe, just as the 1952 Prague treason trial against a Jewish faction in the Communist Party symbolised a definitive change in the USSR. Yockey had worked for the Soviets, the Egyptians and the Cubans. It seems plausible that he would have supported the position of individuals such as Thiriart, who cultivates alliances with 'third world' liberation movements. What Yockey would have opposed, and what Gannon really meant, was opposition to European imperialism, including what remained of the colonial empires. America-Jewry, and even Israel in its early existence, presented themselves as champions of the 'third world' against the European empires, as they sought to displace Europeans in Africa, Asia and

83 Yockey, 'Thoughts Personal and Superpersonal', unpublished notes, n.d.

South America, in rivalry with the USSR.[84] After the European empires had been scuttled there was no realistic point in defending what no longer existed; and the way these newly independent states turned on their American and Israeli mentors was seen by Yockey, most explicitly in 'The World in Flames', as preferable to their exchanging colonial status to Europe for colonial status to plutocracy and Zionism.

84 K. R. Bolton, *Babel Inc.* (London: Black House Publishing, 2013), pp. 41–77. President Woodrow Wilson's 'Fourteen Points' and Franklin Roosevelt's 'Atlantic Charter' attempted to establish the USA as the leading opponent of European imperialism and demanded a new world order based on global free trade, that would replace the closed economic blocs of Empires.

# The Front Reborn

Yockey had hoped that *Imperium* and *The Proclamation of London* would be translated and inspire a new European elite. Yockey stated in the 'introduction' to the manifesto of the European Liberation Front: 'This Proclamation is published in the original in the German, English, Spanish, Italian, French and Flemish languages.'[1] Whether this widespread translation became a reality in his lifetime is unknown. It was a reality soon after his death and *Imperium* and *The Proclamation* continue to expand in translation. At the least, Yockey's writings received many adherents in these states, and even as far a field as South Africa and Argentina during his lifetime.

Although Yockey's meeting with Bardèche and René Binet had not achieved tangible results, France had a militant Euro-Right that had not been bowed by post-war persecutions. Youth-oriented movement such as *Occident* and *Ordre Nouveau* fought pitched battles with the Communists on the streets of France during the 1960s and 1970s.

Although Bardèche had translated *Imperium*, it had not been published in French. However, leading French rightists had soon after Yockey's death, with the publication of the *Truth Seeker* and Noontide Press editions, begun to study Yockey. Moreover, Bardèche had translated and published Yockey's final essay, 'The World in Flames', in his journal *Défense de l'Occident* in 1978.

One of the first Frenchmen to take up Yockey after his death was Alain de Benoist. He is considered a founder of today's European 'New Right' (*Nouvelle Droite*).[2] According to Dr Christian Bouchet, a leading French Euro-nationalist thinker, publisher and organiser, de Benoist, under the

1 Yockey, *The Proclamation of London*, Wermod ed., op. cit., p. 5.

2 James Shields, *The Extreme Right in France: From Petain to Le Pen* (New York: Routledge, 2007), p. 143.

pseudonym of Pietre Wilkinson, wrote a short introduction to Yockey, 'Un visionnaire: Francis Parker Yockey', published in *Europe-Action* in 1964.[3] Although de Benoist wrote that he no longer takes account of Yockey,[4] during the early 1970s, with the formation of the initially Yockeyan National Youth Alliance (NYA) in the USA, de Benoist had written with enthusiasm about Yockey to the NYA's patron, Professor Revilo P Oliver. De Benoist, already having published for several years the still seminal New Right journal *Nouvelle Ecole*, wrote to Oliver in 1970.[5]

De Benoist stated to Oliver that *Nouvelle Ecole* was similar to *Western Destiny*, a journal that had been founded by Willis Carto, and alluded to both as extensions of Yockeyan thought. Shortly after, de Benoist wrote to Oliver enquiring about the possibilities of distributing *Imperium* in France.[6]

By the time Oliver answered de Benoist in September 1970, there had been a bitter falling out between the NYA's patron Willis Carto, the NYA and Oliver, who accused Carto of reneging on funding the NYA and causing its bankruptcy. Oliver further stated that although NYA backers had assisted in funding the reprinting of the Noontide Press paperback edition of *Imperium*, no copies had been given to the NYA.[7]

---

3 Bouchet to Bolton, August 25, 2014. *Europe-Action* was founded in 1963 by Dominique Venner, who had led Jeune Nation, from which numerous other militant Euro-nationalist projects emerged. James Shields, ibid., p. 115. Venner, both a fighter and a philosopher, committed suicide at the altar of Notre Dame Cathedral in 2013 as a final act of protest against the degradation of France. De Benoist's 1964 essay, 'Une visionnaire: Francis Parker Yockey', under the initials 'P.W.', is online at http://www.voxnr.com/cc_arc/d_yockey/index-1.shtml. De Benoist states: 'Yockey was, perhaps, the first to fully perceive the need for the Union of Europe, the outdated aspect of political chauvinism, the arrival of the organic integration of the West.'

4 Communication with the author.

5 Alain de Benoist to Revilo P Oliver, June 15, 1970, The Revilo P Oliver Papers, http://www.revilo-oliver.com/papers/.

6 Alain de Benoist to Revilo P Oliver, ibid., September 25, 1970.

7 Oliver to de Benoist, September 29, 1970. Dr William Pierce, a physicist, took over the NYA in 1971 and broadened it into the National Alliance in 1974 leading NA until his death in 2002. Pierce was not a Yockeyan, however, and the NYA/NA dropped all mention of Yockey.

Although de Benoist states that he has moved on from Yockey, 'Cultural Vitalism' must have made an enduring impression. However, Christian Bouchet is the primary advocate of Yockeyan ideas in France. In 1981, he wrote 'Yockey le précurseur' for *Notre Europe*. In 1998, Gilbert Gendron wrote 'Yockey l'Européen' in the Rightist monthly *Ecrits de Paris*. In 2002, Jean Mabire[8] wrote 'Francis Parker Yockey, le mystérieux auteur d'un livre maudit' in *National-Hebdo*, the journal of the Front National,[9] now a major factor in French and European politics.

In particular, Bouchet has been the publisher of Yockeyan texts through his publishing house, Ars magna, and worked with Avatar, which published an anthology of Yockey in 2004, *Le Monde en flamme*. In 2009, Avatar published a French translation of *Imperium* and in 2011 Ars magna published *L'Ennemi de l'Europe*.[10] Many chapters from *Imperium* and several essays about Yockey have been published online at Ars magna. These include a French translation of the introduction to my 1998 compilation of Yockey material, *Varange: The Life and Thoughts of Francis Parker Yockey*;[11] articles on Yockey by ex-American Nazi party organiser Martin Kerr; Australian nationalist leader Dr Jim Saleam's essay on Yockey's influence on the Australian right; and American revisionist historian Theodore J O'Keefe.[12] In 2010, Ars magna published a French edition of *Francis Parker Yockey et la Russie*.[13]

Given the vibrancy of the French right, it is not surprising that the European Liberation Front should be reborn in France, despite Yockey's own failure to cultivate the movement in his lifetime. Although the reincarnated ELF is no longer extant it is an essential part of the chain that has kept the

---

8 A journalist and author of note, Mabire (1927–2006) was associated with Bardèche's *Défense de l'Occident*, *Europe-Action*, de Benoist's *Elements*, and had a regular column in the weekly *National Hebdo*. A pagan, Mabire wrote novels romanticising the Waffen SS, and with de Benoist was a founder of the French New Right. See: http://www.jean-mabire.com/Jean_Mabire/Jean_Mabire.html.

9 Bouchet to Bolton, August 25, 2014.

10 Bouchet to Bolton, ibid.

11 K. R. Bolton, 'Varange, la vie et la pensée de Yockey', http://www.voxnr.com/cc/d_yockey/EpZyElFZFVCMcMieBz.shtml.

12 Voxnr, http://www.voxnr.com/rubriques/dt_yockey.shtml.

13 K. R. Bolton, *Francis Parker Yockey et la Russie* (Nantes: Ars magna, 2010).

Yockeyan flame alive, especially via the continuing influence of the Belgian geopolitical theorist and activist, Jean Thiriart.

## Yockey and Thiriart

There is much in common in the outlooks of Yockey and Thiriart, not only in their common aim of European Empire but also in their ideas of how to achieve it. In particular, both regarded the expulsion of America — physically, culturally, spiritually — as a prerequisite, and went so far as advocating alliances with virtually anyone that would diminish the USA's world power. That is a point still lost on many — although today fewer — Euro-nationalists who see Islam or Russia as the foremost 'enemies of the West', rather than what Yockey called the 'American-Jewish symbiosis'. To this end Thiriart, like Yockey, sought out influential contacts in states and movements that were resisting America. Consequently, there has been much conjecture as to whether Yockey influenced Thiriart. Anthony Gannon wrote:

> Before concluding, I must refer to Jean Thiriart of "Jeune Europe", of whom I had never heard until I read the excellent memoir — "Jean Thiriart et le National Communautarisme Européen" — written by Yannick Sauveur. I am struck by the resemblance, in parts, of the positions of Yockey and Thiriart on Europe, and yet, so far as I can say, they never met, nor is there any reference to Yockey or his work in the memoir on Thiriart. Certainly, they were at one in the matter of a single European Imperium/Nation, rather than any narrow minded nationalism, or federalism. They agreed on the twentieth-century conception of horizontal (spiritual) race, and rejected the nineteenth-century conception of vertical (materialistic) race. Both saw the American occupation and division of Europe as being more dangerous than that of Russia — not that Russia's was acceptable, or benevolent — but because it was less visible and operated through former European nation-states and was, therefore, more difficult to identify in the public mind as an occupation regime.
>
> They would not have agreed on the possibility of the absorption of the Arabs by Europe, nor that of most of the Slavs, in general, exceptions confirming the rule in this matter. Yockey's objections would have been on Cultural grounds, not on those of vertical race. Their backgrounds were very different: Yockey's Catholic and fascist; Thiriart's communist, even Stalinist.

> Both envisaged a time when American occupation-forces might be attacked, and some of their members killed by European Imperialists. Thiriart in an interview in 1975 stated, *inter alia*: "European unity will come about more or less when 200 or 300 American occupiers will be killed in every corner of Europe just to prove our point. Then there will be no going back." Of course, Thiriart was not advocating such a policy, as he made plain to his interviewer.
>
> I am convinced that a detailed examination of the positions of Yockey and Thiriart will prove that they agreed to a great extent on the cause of Europe, one and free from occupation by the Extra-European forces of America and Russia. As Thiriart commenced in 1960 on the road leading to "Jeune Europe", the year in which Yockey died, it is unlikely that they ever met. Did Thiriart know of Yockey, or his *Imperium*? I would love to know the answer to that intriguing question![14]

The French pan-European theorist and activist Dr Christian Bouchet, a collaborator who was close to Thiriart, confirms that Yockey had an important influence on the Belgian's ideas. Bouchet writes:

> Thiriart read *Imperium* at the beginning of the 1960s in its English edition. When I meet Thiriart in 1990, he gave me a xerox of *Imperium* and when in September 1991 we created Nouvelle Resistance in France we created in the same time a European group called Front Européen de Libération which refers to Thiriart and Yockey. Yockey was, after 1991, and with Thiriart and Duprat,[15] one of the main influences of French nationalist-revolutionaries.[16]

Jean Thiriart (1922–1992) was 15 when he joined the Jeune Garde Socialiste and other socialist organisations.[17] When Belgium was occupied during the war, Thiriart joined a 'collaborationist' organisation, Amis du Grand Reich Allemand. Support for Germany from Francophone Socialists in both Belgium and France was not new and not a matter of opportunism. Many saw

---

14 Gannon, Yockey memoire, op. cit.

15 Francoise Duprat.

16 Bouchet to Bolton, August 25, 2014.

17 Dr Jaroslaw Tomasiewicz, 'The Idea of Europe in Terms of Jean Thiriart', European Centre for Geopolitical Analysis, http://www.geopolityka.org/analizy/jaroslaw-tomasiewicz-idea-europy-w-ujeciu-jeana-thiriarta.

the possibility of a united socialist Europe under the auspices of Germany. Moreover, there had been a crisis in defining socialism, particularly among the Francophone Left, many leading socialists seeing Fascism as 'ethical socialism' (as Yockey called it) and transcending the dialectical materialism of Marx. They had come to what Spengler called 'Prussian Socialism' through the crisis of socialist ideology that had largely been initiated by the French syndicalist philosopher Georges Sorel, who became a major influence on early fascist ideology in France and Italy.[18] Marcel Déat and Jacques Doriot, ex-Left leaders, the latter having been a leader of the French Communist Party, both formed large fascist parties that collaborated with the German occupation. In Belgium, Labour Party leader Henri de Man, 'one of the foremost theoreticians of European socialism', initiated what Sternhell calls the 'idealist revision of Marxism' into 'ethical socialism'. De Man had a major influence on Déat in France.[19] Already by the late 1920s, de Man was writing about the need to 'go beyond Marx' and even to 'liquidate Marxism'.[20] By the time Germany occupied Belgium, de Man was lauding the Third Reich as an exemplification of social unity. Hence, many French intellectuals such as the French writer Pierre Drieu La Rochelle, so far from lamenting the German occupation, as popular myths claim, saw the occupation as a chance for France to participate in the construction of a 'united and socialist Europe'. 'I am not just a Frenchman, I am a European,' Drieu La Rochelle explained. Moreover, even after the war, despite the horrendous terror that was unleashed against anyone suspected of any dealings with the Germans, there were serving 'collaborators' who remained unapologetic, one of these being René Binet.

After serving a prison term for 'collaboration', Thiriart returned to politics in the late 1950s. In 1960, he was co-creator of Comité d'Action et de Défense des Belges d'Afrique, meant to defend French interests in the Congo and supported the breakaway region of Katanga under Moise Tshombe, resisting

---

18 For a detailed discussion on this crisis in the Left and its contribution to the rise of Fascism see: Zeev Sternhell, *Neither Left nor Right: Fascist Ideology in France* (Princeton University Press, 1996).

19 Zeev Sternhell, ibid., pp. 119–120.

20 Zeev Sternhell, ibid., 125.

the pro-communist central government.[21] He promoted 'Euroafryki', the concept of an African empire of united Europe that was also promoted by Yockey and by Sir Oswald Mosley, along with South African Oswald Pirow, the former defence minister who had endorsed *Imperium*. Comité d'Action was renamed Mouvement Action Civique, and became publisher of *Nation Belgique* and *Jeune Nation*. Support was given to the French in Algeria, and the OAS (Secret Army Organisation) resisting President de Gaulle's betrayal of European interests. Thiriart, however, saw this as a foundation for a national revolution in France as the start of a new united Europe. By this time, he was calling his doctrine 'national-communitarianism'. With the scuttling of the empires, due to the devastation of World War II, Thiriart, like Yockey, saw the USA as the primary enemy of Europe and was willing to collaborate with the USSR and anyone else to eliminate American influence from Europe. In September 1961, Thiriart issued the *Manifeste à la Nation Européenne* and started forming a pan-European network. It was on the initiative of both Thiriart and Mosley that a congress was held in Venice in 1962 to form a national European movement, involving two major political parties, the NPD form Germany and the MSI from Italy, in the forming of the National Party of Europe. This did not proceed, however, due to disputes between the German and Italian parties. Thiriart instead created the Parti Revolutionaries Européen and Jeune Europe, with branches throughout Europe, and subsequently the Parti Communautaire Européen, which published the journal *La Nation Européenne*. Thiriart cultivated contacts in the Third World to develop a broad front against the USA and met with officials form Syria, Iraq, his former enemies of the Algerian FLN, Vietcong delegates, and the chairman of the Palestine Liberation Organisation. He met with Ceausescu of Romania, at the president's suggestion, Egypt's President Nasser, Chinese premier Chou En Lai.[22] This is a strategy that Yockey had recommended in 'The World in Flames' and for that purpose Yockey himself had sought out offi-

21 Among the advisers to Tshombe was the young French Rightist intellectual Francoise Duprat. United Nations troops went on a bloody rampage through Katanga. See G Edward Griffin, *The Fearful Master: A Second Look at the United Nations* (Boston: Western Islands, 1964).

22 Jaroslaw Tomasiewicz, op. cit.

cials of Castro's Cuba shortly before his death. Thiriart also intended creating Brigades Révolutionnaires Européennes as a pan-European liberation army that would throw the USA out of Europe in the event of a Cold War conflict. This did not get the backing from Third World and Eastern bloc states that he had hoped for, however, and he withdrew from politics in 1969.[23]

Thiriart, like Yockey, aimed to re-create Europe as a 'nation'. Also like Yockey, he rejected the zoological concept of 'race' in favour of a 'community of purpose', rather than a 'community of blood'. He thought that China might be Europe's ally against the USSR and USA. However, this position reversed when it was apparent that there was a Beijing-Washington axis against the USSR. Thiriart saw the possibilities of the Arab world being aligned with Europe.

Thiriart's ideas remained alive despite his own inactivity, especially among sections of the MSI in Italy, and among French 'European socialists', Spain, and Belgium where the Mouvement Socialiste Européen Occident was formed in 1981, and in 1984 Parti Populaire National Comunautaire-Européen, the latter attracting several prominent ex-communists. In France, alliances were formed with the Parti des Forces Nouvelles and Bouchet's Nouvelle Résistance.[24]

Thiriart re-emerged politically in 1991 and in March that year Front Européen de Libération (FEL) was formed by Marco Battara (Italy), Juan Antonio Llopart (Spain), Bouchet (France) and Thiriart. FEL had affiliates in Spain (Movimento Social Republicano), England (Third Way, renamed National Revolutionary Faction), RFA, Belgium, Italy (including the monthly *Orion*, Fronte Europeo di Liberazione, and Nuova Azione), Switzerland (Troisième Voie), Portugal (Jeune Révolution), USA (American Front), Argentina (radical Peronists) and France (Bouchet's Nouvelle Résistance and later Unité Radicale). Bouchet served as general secretary from 1991 until 1998, after which FEL stagnated and dissolved in 2002. Its work is continued by Unité Continentale.[25] This organisation sent volunteers to fight with

23 Jaroslaw Tomasiewicz, ibid.

24 Jaroslaw Tomasiewicz, ibid.

25 Bouchet to Bolton, September 11, 2014.

pro-Russian forces in the Ukraine and sees this as part of a wider struggle for the liberation and unity of Europe against American globalism.[26]

Front Européen de Libération combined the ideas of Yockey, Thiriart and Otto Strasser. Its symbol was the crossed sword and hammer of Strasser's 1930s anti-Hitler 'Black Front', League of Revolutionary National Socialists. Bouchet states: 'We developed a three-part strategy.'

> 1. The national liberation struggle against the American occupation was possible, as was possible the fight — inseparable in our eyes — for the unification of the European continent;
>
> 2. To do this, we need a European organization and either a Piedmont, i.e. a European country where we would have seized power and who had then played the role of Piedmont in the European unification or an external lung that is a European country or not that would bring us his support and serve our rear base;
>
> 3. It was necessary to act on the weak links of imperialism, which for us were the hot-spots of the former Soviet bloc and the areas affected by insurgent separatist movements, and we make allies among countries and liberation movements fighting against the Yankee empire.
>
> In the same vein ... on several occasions delegations FEL, sometimes accompanied by Jean Thiriart, travelled to Moscow where, thanks to our local correspondent, Alexander Dugin, we met a number of personalities including journalist Alexander Prokhanov, Gennady Zyuganov, the local leader of the Communist Party, and Viktor Anpilov, leader of the movement Labour Russia. But the crash of the attempted conservative and anti-Yeltsin coup in Moscow destroyed hopes

26 'Geopolitical Symbols from East to West', Unité Continentale communique, March 3, 2014, *Red & Black*, http://rougenoir76.over-blog.com/2014/03/geopolitique-des-symboles-d-est-en-ouest-par-unite-continentale.html.

that we could have "Russian aid".[27] Delegations of FEL also went at the time to Libya, Iran and North Korea.[28]

To show you the atmosphere in which we acted, I will cite two examples. Our German section was dissolved three times for "hostile attitudes toward the German state constitution". The first time as the Nationalist Front. It was reconstituted under the name of the Revolutionary Socialist Workers Front and was again dissolved. It then adopted the name of Direct Action and was dissolved immediately! Our Argentine correspondent was a Spanish immigrant. He had translated some of the works of Jean Thiriart into Spanish and broadcast them in Latin America. He was active in the Peronist Left and founded the "Right to Housing" association in Argentina. He died during a commando action of the Guerrilla Army of the people! The European Liberation Front was a precise historical continuity… Yockey, Strasser and Thiriart.

Francis Parker Yockey had founded the first European Liberation Front in the early fifties. Yockey was one of the first to advance the idea of a strategic alliance with the Soviet authorities and the Arab countries against the USA. Moreover, he himself worked for the Egyptian government in the wake of Nasser's revolution.

Otto Strasser, who was the leader of the "Left" of Hitler's NSDAP split from the party in the early thirties to create the Fighting League of Revolutionary National Socialists, known better as the Black Front. After the seizure of power by Hitler, he led an opposition. In exile, hunted by the Gestapo, he was under house arrest in Canada by the Allies and was allowed only very late to return to Germany. There he reconstructed a nationalist movement that took a neutralist position between East and West. He also founded a pan-European organisation, the European People's Movement. It had only a relatively short existence, but it is interesting to note that one of its respondents for France was our friend Henry Roques, well known for its historical research.

---

27 Anpilov is an example of the conjunction of hardline nationalism with the remaining communist factions, generally of Stalinist orientation. In 1993 he was a leader of the anti-Yeltsin coup. In 1999 his movement Labour Russia joined the electoral coalition, 'Stalin Bloc—for the USSR'. In 2012 Anpilov supported the presidential candidacy of 'ultra-nationalist' Vladimir Zhirinovsky.

28 The doctrine of North Korea is *Jucha*, meaning 'national self-sufficiency', which openly claims to have transcended Marxism.

Thiriart Jean, a former member of the Belgian collaborationist Left, created Young Europe during the Algeria War. This movement had branches in all the countries of Europe and multiplied contacts with anti-imperialist movements like Ceausescu's Romania, Nasser's Egypt, the PLO, etc. Two stories about Jeune Europe describe well the reality of the organisation. Jeune Europe provided the first Western volunteers for the Palestinians in their fight, and the first non-Arab who fell fighting the Zionist occupier, Roger Coudroy, was a member of Jeune Europe. Furthermore, Jeune Europe was the first political commitment of Renato Curcio, who later founded the Italian Red Brigades![29]

## Otto Strasser

Perhaps Yockey's position that Hitler ushered in the era of 'Authority against Money',[30] as the 'Hero of the Second World War,'[31] prevented his collaboration with Strasser. One of Yockey's leading German contacts, Franke-Gricksch, had been with Strasser before the war and his exact role — as Hitlerite agent or Strasserite agent — in returning to the Third Reich remains a mystery. Franke-Gricksch's cultivation of post-war German-nationalist contacts with the Soviet bloc adds to the perplexity. Another conjunction is that of Strasser's English advocate, Douglas Reed, former senior European correspondent for *The London Times*. Reed not only championed Strasser before, during and after the war[32] but as a 'conspiracist' critical of Jewish influence and the nexus between communism, capitalism and Zionism, recommended *Imperium* in the bibliographies of his books.[33]

Strasser had written in 1936 of European unity:

It is increasingly evident that the Federation of the Peoples of Europe is the vital precondition for the spiritual recovery of the European nations and for the

---

29 Bouchet to Bolton, September 11, 2014.

30 Although Yockey saw Mussolini as the leader of the 'first open revolt in Europe of Authority, Socialism and Faith'. See Yockey, *Der Feind Europas*, Liberty Bell edition, op. cit., p. 21.

31 To whom he dedicated *Imperium*.

32 Douglas Reed, *Nemesis? The Story of Otto Strasser* (London: Jonathan Cape, 1940). Reed upheld Strasser as Hitler's potential 'nemesis', a view not shared by the Allies.

33 Douglas Reed, *Behind the Scene* (Pinetown: Natal, 1976); *The Controversy of Zion* (Durban, Natal: Dolphin Press, 1978).

> preservation of the civilization and culture of the West… For this and nothing else is the meaning and content of the German Revolution: The resurrection of the West![34]

Strasser, like Yockey, contended with Mosley on the roles of the USA and USSR vis-à-vis Europe. Writing in Mosley's journal, *The European*, Strasser repudiated the 'ultimatum' to Europe by US Secretary of State John Foster Dulles that Europe must unite to serve US interests against Russia—a demand Dulles backed with the unveiled threat that if Europe does not proceed according to US plans then Europe would be left to her own devices. This is precisely the kind of thing that Yockey condemned and why he was condemned by Natinform and others whose interests were more anti-Soviet than pro-Europe.

Alluding to Dulles' statement at the 1953 NATO Conference in Paris, Strasser stated that the US plan for Europe was one that would eliminate the ancient peoples of the Continent and reduce them to a 'melting pot'. If Europe complied, however, the dollars would keep flowing and Europe could even have the blessing of US atomic bombs to face off against Russia.[35]

The primary demand was for the 'unification of France and Germany', in Dulles' words. Strasser's reply was that if it had not been for the 'interference of outside forces' in both world wars, particularly from the USA, the conflicts would not have spread. It was unfitting for the USA to lecture Europe on the requirements of peace while using the Russian threat as the means for imposing its agenda. To Strasser, Dulles' 'threat' that America would 'remain aloof from inter-European affairs' should Europe refuse to comply with US demands 'is ravishing music to the ears of every true European'.[36] This was also fundamentally the position of Yockey, the Socialist Reich Party and the faction of war veterans around Franke-Gricksch. 'The actual carrying out of such a welcome threat to leave [Europe] would do more to relieve the present world tension than the pumping of American atomic weapons into West

34 Otto Strasser, *The Establishment of Socialism* (Prague: Heinrich Grunov, 1936). Cited by Roger Griffin, *Fascism* (Oxford: Oxford University Press, 1995), pp. 114–115.

35 Otto Strasser, 'The Role of Europe', *Mosley: Policy and Debate* (London: Euphorion Books, 1954), p. 77.

36 Strasser, 'The Role of Europe', p. 79.

Germany and the indefinite retention of American air, land and sea forces strewn all over Europe,' wrote Strasser.[37]

Strasser also thought it an 'insult' to state that Europe needed American protection against Russia, when President Roosevelt had not long ago handed 'half the Continent' to the USSR; Strasser held that Europe was very capable of defending herself without the USA.[38] Again, this is a major theme of Yockey's *Der Feind Europas*. Strasser considered American 'lying chatter' about 'saving' Europe and her civilization as 'embarrassing to hear'. If Europe is really that 'decadent' then no amount of US money or weapons will save her: 'A tree drained of its inner vitality cannot be helped by propping up its dead branches.'[39] However, Strasser believed that Europe is still full of vitality and the basis of her health is her 'national and cultural differences', which America's demand for 'integration' would obliterate. Such diversity gives 'shape and colour... to the soul of Europe!!' and he regarded America's call for European unity on US terms as 'idiotic demagoguery'. Europe is what she is by virtue of the distinctiveness of Spaniards, Italians, Frenchmen, Germans, Poles, et al., and should resist becoming 'one great hodgepodge unit' for the sake of more efficient production or to become a more profitable enterprise for the World Bank.[40]

Mosley did not concur. In 'A Reply to Dr Strasser', he stated that while Strasser sought to maintain separate nations, he sought 'Europe-a-Nation'. Here, Yockey's European unity seems closer to that of Mosley than the federative Europe of Strasser. Sir Oswald regarded that as the main difference between Strasser and himself. However, another vital question lay in their divergent attitudes toward the role of the US in Europe. To Mosley, America had to remain the protector of Europe against Russia. Rather than an American withdrawal being, in Strasser's terms, 'ravishing music' to Europe, Mosley conjured up the image of a 'ravishing' Russia over the Continent.[41]

The crux of the issue for Mosley was that: 'At present we live under America; without America we should live under Russia. The difference is that

37 Strasser, ibid., p. 79.

38 Strasser, ibid., p. 79.

39 Strasser, ibid.

40 Strasser, ibid., p. 80.

41 Oswald Mosley, 'A Reply to Dr Strasser', ibid., p. 84.

under America Europe still lives, and under Russia Europe would be dead…' Mosley believed, contrary to Strasser and Yockey, that Europe could unite 'under cover' of the USA. While ridiculing Strasser's notion that Russia would permit Europe to regain her strength, Mosley believed that on the other hand the USA would permit Europe to unite on such a basis that she would become 'much too powerful to be governed from Wall Street'.[42]

42 Mosley, ibid., p. 85.

# Yockey — Today and Tomorrow

The West has not assumed its destiny of unity and empire. If the cyclic paradigm of history described by Spengler and elaborated by Yockey is trustworthy, why has this seemingly historic inevitably, apparently based on the iron laws of history, not eventuated? Was Spengler wrong, and Yockey? As wrong, perhaps, as Marx, who proposed the inevitability of world communism through the inexorable dialectic of class struggle? Spengler and Yockey were describing the organic character of history, taking cultures as analogous to living organisms with their own cycles of birth, adolescence, maturity, senility, decay and death, also analogous to the seasons of spring, summer, winter, autumn. Were they in error in applying such organic analogies to human cultures? While many, perhaps most, reading this will insist that it cannot yet be concluded that Western civilization is already passé, or *Fellaheen* in Spenglerian terms, let us for a moment assume that Western civilization has indeed entered an epoch of no return. Far from exiting the world stage with the last heroic and dramatic hurrah envisaged by Spengler and Yockey, what if Western civilization had its destiny aborted by the plutocratic-Bolshevist victory of 1945, a victory brought by the force of sheer numbers? Does Western civilization perhaps end, in T. S. Eliot's words, 'not with a bang, but with a whimper' — the whimper of pervasive decay and the emaciation of a pathogen? This possibility — or probability — does not repudiate Spengler or Yockey. It affirms in another manner the organic character of history and culture.

If cultures are analogous to living organisms, then they can be killed by a sudden external disaster, or an internal pathogen, like any organism. There is nothing inevitable about an organism living through its full life cycle. Its life might be cut short at any time. Cultural Vitalism can just as well assert that a cultural organism can be aborted, murdered or mortally diseased like any other organism, as it can optimistically assert that a culture can fulfil its entire natural life cycle. The Culture-distortion, Culture-parasitism and Culture-retardation described by Yockey are analogous to cancers in a biological organism. What both Spengler in the closing chapter of *The Decline of the West* and in *The Hour of Decision*, and Yockey in *Imperium*, *The Proclamation of London*, *The Enemy of Europe* and various essays, offered was the prescription to cultivate antibodies against cultural pathogens. However, as in a diseased organism, the antibodies that are released are not necessarily going to be sufficient to defeat the pathogens and antigens, and the organism might die. An individual organism can succumb at any age to a disease; so might a culture at any stage of its life cycle. When an individual organism is born we assume that, all things considered, it will live through all the cycles of life until dying of 'old age': likewise with a culture. However, neither assumption is etched in granite. There are variables.

Following from Spengler's diagnostic method for the life cycle of a high culture, Yockey offered a system for the cultivation of antibodies to protect and enhance the life cycle of the culture organism, so as to maximise the chances of its fulfilment. Such advice, for an individual organism or for our civilization, is not necessarily going to be heeded.

On the other hand, a dying organism will generally have left offspring to carry forward a life that, while different form the parent, nonetheless is founded upon that inheritance. Likewise, one option for a dying civilization is that a part of its culture-bearing stratum will somehow ensure the seeds of a new culture survive with the possibility of germinating on new, more fertile soil, to birth a new culture — in this instance, a post-Western culture.

There is a further possibility within the organic paradigm of cultures: symbiosis. Yockey referred to the possibility of a Russo-Western Symbiosis, contra the Jewish-American Symbiosis. In trying to herald the West's liberation, unity and destiny, in the midst of a tattered post-war Europe, Yockey said little about this possibility, though he clearly recognized it. A simple definition of an organic symbiosis is 'a close and usually obligatory association of two organisms of different species that live together, often to their mutual benefit'. Such Russo-Western symbiosis might develop through the recognition of a mutual enemy, as per the concept of 'the outer enemy' discussed by Carl Schmitt and Yockey — an enemy represented by the intransigence of China, or the messianic territorial incursion of Zionist-American-manipulated *Jihadists*.[1]

While there is today such a relationship between Russia and China, it is not historically sound. A Sino-American symbiosis is more plausible, despite rhetoric about the rivalry between the USA and China.[2] In 1950, Yockey had written to Arcand, who raised the idea of a 'world-front against Jewry', including those outside of Western civilization; Yockey responded that such an alliance could only exist on a Europe-wide level, and 'to a less intense degree [in] the colonies'. 'The world' could never be 'a political organism'. Alliances could come after the West had been re-created as a political organism. In this work, Africa, India and China did not figure at all and it could not be said that Islam had potential after the Arabs' 'miserable performance' against Israel.[3] In 1948, in *Imperium*, he had written,

> Politics is a struggle of will against will. India and China have, as such, no will. They are not organic units but mere collections of areas and populations brought under one name for convenience. Their negative will is diffused throughout all the individuals, distinct from the integrated unity and will of Japan. India and China would always remain mere spoils for powers from without.[4]

As his final essay, 'The World in Flames', shows, Yockey had revised his 'estimate of the world situation' by 1960 and had come to see in the non-aligned or 'third world' states a means of blocking the world hegemony of America-Jewry, just as he had from 1952 ceased to think of the USSR as an 'outer enemy' equally destructive to Western civilization as the USA. In 1953, when working

---

1 Ironically, that the worldwide *Jihadist* upheaval has its origins in the US creation of the anti-Russian *Mujahideen* in Afghanistan. See: K. R. Bolton, *Zionism, Islam and The West* (London: Black House Publishing, 2014).

2 Cf. Bolton, *Geopolitics of the Indo-Pacific: Emerging Conflicts, New Alliances* (London: Black House Publishing, 2013).

3 Varange to Arcand, January 17, 1950, op. cit., p. 2.

4 Yockey, *Imperium*, Wermod ed., op. cit., pp. 736–737.

in Egypt, he saw hope in Nasser and an Arab renaissance opposing America-Jewry. He made other covert contacts with Castro's Cuba and the Soviet bloc.

By 1959, Yockey's estimation of China had been revised. It was now an integrated unity with a destiny under Maoism, where 'mystical universalism' under Mao, a new 'god-king' is 'very much alive', and China is viewed by its people as the centre of the universe.

> Maoism has proceeded in a decade to force upon 680 million Chinese, as example and model for all, a way of life which had formerly existed only in limited communities, such as monastic orders: *the total collectivization and absolute subjugation of the human being.*
>
> Maoism proudly declares that in world history it is not technique but man, the masses of people — 680 million Chinese people — who shall determine the *fate* of mankind.[5]

China had made population a factor in world politics.

> Maoism incites millions of listeners by announcing that the basic problem of the future is *that of world population.* What will become of the earth when it is inhabited by *20 billion* persons, and what chance has China to impose its will upon those billions?[6]

Yockey concluded with reference to China's control of the headwaters of much of Asia:

---

5 Yockey, 'A Warning to America: an Estimate of China, a Warning to the West', 1959, unpublished MS, courtesy of DTK. The draft MS had been found among a file of unpublished articles by various authors, when the newspaper *Common Sense* was closed in 1972. DTK writes in a 'Foreword' with the intention of publishing the MS after finding it in 1972 that 'every indication points to assistance from close collaborators Frederick C. F. Weiss and H Keith Thompson'. We know that Thompson had co-written with Yockey the final essay 'The World in Flames'. The original draft segments were produced with a 'Royal Arrow' portable typewriter, the sort that always accompanied Yockey. Other material was disjointed and included paragraphs about physics, a characteristic of Weiss's writing, Weiss having studied physics at Sorbonne. Drafts were in both English and German.

6 Yockey, China, ibid.

> There is not one major river system in Asia whose headwaters are not found along the mountain ranges of China's borders: Mekong, Yellow, Yang-ze, Salveen, Bramaputra, Ganges, Indus. Any tampering by atomic bombardiers with these snow and ice-capped frontiers would have catastrophic effects not only in China but in every land bordering China.[7]

In only recent years, the crucial importance of water resources and references to 'water wars' is becoming more widely recognised.[8] However, since Yockey's time, when in 1959 he wrote of the stability of the Chinese landscape, this situation has become greatly volatile, causing serious problems of drought and flooding, loss of fertile soil and water pollution. There is an ongoing crisis in agriculture. To that extent, China has relied on Western technics and despite her growing status as a world economic power, she has set herself on a path of Western technical development which sows the seeds of decay, imported from the diseased Western organism. As American pundits such as Ralph Peters approvingly state, American culture is the USA's 'lethal' export and the means of assuring global hegemony — precisely what Yockey called Culture-retardation and Culture-distortion. This is coming to China as an unavoidable by-product of China's technical build-up. While Japan has not yet succumbed due to her continuing commitment to Shinto, China attempts to restrict the influence of Culture-distortion by the revival of Confucianism. Veteran Australian diplomat Reg Little, who approvingly sees China as the next dominant civilization, regards China as still guided by Confucianism and Mao as having retained a Confucian outlook.[9] As Yockey stated, China continues to see herself as the 'Middle Kingdom' around which the world revolves. Russia also has a world-mission, articulated by Dostoyevsky and others, to reshape humanity according to her own 'mystical universalism' shaped by Orthodox Christianity. The

---

7 Yockey, China, ibid.

8 K. R. Bolton, 'Water Wars: Rivalry over water resources', *World Affairs*, India, Spring 2010, Vol. 14, No. 1, pp. 52–83.
Bolton, 'Rivalry over water resources as a potential cause of conflict in Asia', *Journal of Social Political and Economic Studies*, Washington, Spring 2010, Vol. 35, No. 1.
Bolton, *Geopolitics of the Indo-Pacific: Emerging Conflicts, New Alliances* (London: Black House Publishing, 2013).

9 Reg Little, 'Mao's Communism', *New Dawn*, Melbourne, Special Issue, Vol. 9, No., 1, January–February 2015, pp. 58–59.

pragmatic alliance between Russia and China, where China has attained everything her own way, cannot endure. Russia and China represent conflicting worldviews: Russian, Christian and messianic; China, economically driven.

In light of changes in the world situation since Yockey's times, it is important to recall that Yockey remained a realist and adapted his thinking to new world developments. His attitude to China, Russia and the non-aligned states changed according to historical developments, as 'The World in Flames' shows. His most important contribution to philosophy, Cultural Vitalism, remains valid.

If the Western civilization becomes *Fellaheen*, like Egypt, there is not going to be a Historic void. While apologists for capitalism see the present Judaeo-American world dispensation as the millennial 'end of history', as Francis Fukuyama terms it, considering this as the final possibility of human endeavour is extreme *hubris*. A more likely scenario is that the ebbs and flows of History resume as they have with the destruction or decline of the Sumerian, Egyptian, Mayan, Indian, Etruscan, Greek, Roman, Chinese, Arabian, and perhaps also the Western civilizations. The one culture-race-people-nation-state that remains to fulfil her destiny is the Russian, awaiting to assume her world role on the ruins of the old. Spengler envisaged this and Yockey hinted at it, and Frederick Weiss expounded on it; all of these thinkers saw the 'primitive' Russian vigour waiting to assume the form of a new civilization of Faith that repudiates Money.

## Huxley-Blythe's 'Reappraisal'

Forty years after Yockey's death, Peter J Huxley-Blythe reappraised his old comrade and enemy. Huxley-Blythe had been named as the first editor of *Frontfighter* (although the actual editing was done by Gannon) and was a founder-member of the ELF. He had left for naval duties in 1951 but assured readers that he would continue to 'fight and spread the message of the coming Fascist European Imperium'.[10] Soon afterward, he fell out with Yockey. Huxley-Blythe at the time was a zealous opponent of the USSR, yet he was as aware as anyone else in the ELF of the character of the Washington regime and his lead article for the final issue of *Frontfighter* condemned the subservience of the Royal Navy to a US commander.[11] He became the British representative of Wolfgang Sarg's vehemently anti-Yockey Natinform and shortly after Yockey's death attempted to gain information on Yockey from the FBI by using his anti-communist credentials and by supplying the old smears against Natinform that had long existed in FBI files.

Huxley-Blythe became well known as the author of *The East Comes West* in 1955, exposing the callous forcible return to the USSR and to instant execution of anti-Soviet Cossack refugees who had sought refuge by surrendering to the British and American forces after World War II. He also wrote *Under the St Andrew's Cross: Russian and Cossack Volunteers in World War Two. 1941–1945*. Becoming a doctor of psychology and founding a psychotherapy institute, Huxley-Blythe continued to write on issues of interest to European nationalism.

In 1959, he was still regarded in the USA as the custodian of the 'Free World' against Soviet domination and favoured a strategy of supporting underground resistance in the Soviet bloc.[12] Not long after Yockey's death, after having sent shonky information to the FBI derived from Wolfgang Sarg's Natinform report of years earlier, Huxley-Blythe visited Gannon, acting 'ca-

---

10 P. J. Huxley-Blythe, '"Senator" Atlee Hands Over', *Frontfighter*, No. 10, February/March 1951, p. 1.

11 P. J. Huxley-Blythe, ibid.

12 P. J. Huxley-Blythe, 'We Can Have Victory Without War!', *American Mercury*, May 1958, pp. 111–115. This was at a time when the American Nationalist and industrialist Russell MaGuire owned *The American Mercury*.

gey and mysterious', implying that Yockey was a 'communist agent'. Gannon told Huxley-Blythe to 'cut the crap and come straight out with what he had to say'. Huxley-Blythe had been to the USA and was in contact with the John Birch Society, whose main focus was anti-communism. Huxley-Bythe claimed that Yockey had been 'in and out of Cuba and Iron Curtain countries' and was well paid by these sources. He gave Gannon a copy of Yockey's final essay, 'The World in flames', as evidence of Yockey's 'pro-communist nuances'. Gannon totally rejected these accusations. As Gannon looked fairly prosperous, Huxley-Blythe asked whether he had received money from Yockey or the Soviets; Gannon demanded a retraction, which was given. Huxley-Blythe finally stated that he was engaged in some international activity and was constantly watched by British Special Branch.[13] These worldwide activities involved work with an anti-Soviet underground of émigrés, namely an organisation called the Russian Revolutionary Forces, such associations having been evidenced by his early book *The East Came West*.

As we have seen, Huxley-Blythe was associated with publications that wound up in the publishing stable of Willis Carto, up to the point of his becoming a contributing editor to *The Barnes Review*. It was then that Huxley-Blythe composed his remembrance of Yockey in 2005. He wrote:

> As I had known Yockey in the very early days of the European Imperium Struggle, soon after the end of World War II, and that for a time I had opposed what he was doing, I knew that my reappraisal would be a very personalized one, but taking my personal involvement into account, I have tried to stick to the facts.[14]

Having traced Yockey's career and his experiences in devastated Europe, Huxley-Blythe explained the important ideological and tactical shift among sections of the Right after World War II. There were German nationalists who looked at the USSR as having changed direction and could assist in liberating Europe from the American 'stranglehold on Europe'. 'Yockey accepted this line', especially after the trial of mainly Jewish communist party leaders in Prague in 1952. Huxley-Blythe states he 'disagreed with Yockey in his belief';

13 Gannon to Stimely, April 20, 1982.

14 P. J. Huxley-Blythe, 'Inside the Mind of Ulick Varange', op. cit., p. 19.

he himself had believed that 'the patriots in America were stronger than they actually were, and that they would quite quickly oust the financial-Zionist octopus then in power in Washington D.C.' A patriotic government would then defeat communism throughout the world and stop pushing a US form of 'pseudo-International Socialism'.[15]

> In this respect I was totally and utterly wrong and Yockey was right. For the anti-Europe US Government and the culture-distorters pulling the governmental strings were far stronger and far more lethal than any plague or pestilence the world has ever experienced and the American patriots far weaker and divided than I could have ever imagined.[16]

Huxley-Blythe suggests that those who want to see 'where Yockey stood in the Stalin versus Washington conflict in 1955' should read *Kto Kovo*, published by Frederick Weiss and H Keith Thompson.[17] At the juncture of 2004, Huxley-Blythe argued that it was time to re-evaluate Yockey, which is no easy task because he was a 'far-sighted political philosopher' of a rare breed, feared by Washington bureaucrats and hunted by the FBI, CIA and others. Huxley-Blythe, who had worked closely with orthodox race theorists on the journal *Northern World*, now accepted Yockey's view that racial affiliation must be primarily 'spiritual-ethical'.[18] Huxley-Blythe 'initially found Yockey's advanced thinking on race difficult to accept'. However, when he saw the nominal 'British' and other politicians serving alien interests, he appreciated Yockey's description of the 'inner enemies' of Europe, whom Germans had long referred to as 'der Deutsche Michel', a term for those who are instinctively anti-social, traitorous, anti-national and cringe before alien interests — the 'Michel-stratum' who made Europe's subjugation to US occupation after the war possible. Huxley-Blythe commented: 'Nothing has changed.'[19]

---

15 P. J. Huxley-Blythe, 'Inside the Mind of Ulick Varange', ibid., p. 24.

16 P. J. Huxley-Blythe, 'Inside the Mind of Ulick Varange', ibid.

17 P. J. Huxley-Blythe, 'Inside the Mind of Ulick Varange', ibid. For details on *Kto Kovo* see the chapter on Russia.

18 P. J. Huxley-Blythe, 'Inside the Mind of Ulick Varange', ibid.

19 P. J. Huxley-Blythe, 'Inside the Mind of Ulick Varange', ibid. p. 26.

To the question that Yockey posed circa 1953 in *The Enemy of Europe* as to whether that enemy is the USA, Huxley-Blythe responded: 'The answer is a provable and resounding "yes".' However, the USA is not only the enemy of Europe but of the entire world. In other words it has become an uncontrollable rogue state, with 9/11 acting as the justification for the Washington regime's global adventures. However, the question is not posed by Washington as to why the USA is considered an enemy by so much of the world. For that answer, Huxley-Blythe turns to *The Enemy of Europe*, stating that if Yockey were alive today he would surely write a book called *The Enemy of the World*.[20] Indeed, it can be added, Yockey did write something of that nature — 'The World in Flames'. Huxley-Blythe observes that this widespread anti-Americanism is to a considerable extent based on the USA's uncritical support for Israel and, more widely, the USA's 'arrogance and failure to take into account other peoples' cultures and way of life'. What Yockey described as 'the ethical syphilis of Hollywood' in point five of the ELF's 12-point programme, Huxley-Blythe calls a 'plague' that is spreading throughout the world, 'coupled with US global and financial exploitation'.[21] This cultural 'plague' (what Yockey called Culture-distortion) is now openly considered by US strategists as the most potent weapon for maintaining US global hegemony.

In 'The World in Flames', Yockey saw neutrality and non-alignment working to the advantage of the Russia (then the USSR) in its conflict with the USA. The Cold War ended not with a bang but a whimper, as the USSR imploded with the help of internal treachery from its own 'Michel-stratum', but the push of Russia into the globalist fold was short-lived. The broad themes of Yockey's 'World in Flames' reasserted themselves with the rise of Putin, and with America's answer, of creating the 'Muslim terrorist' bogeyman.[22] He stated of the Cold War that 'Neutrality is the wish of all the peoples of Europe'[23] and we might contend today that it remains so — other than among the 'Michel-stratum.' Among the final observations of Yockey (with his co-

20 P. J. Huxley-Blythe, 'Inside the Mind of Ulick Varange', ibid. p. 27.

21 P. J. Huxley-Blythe, 'Inside the Mind of Ulick Varange', ibid.

22 See: Bolton, 'America's Jihad', *Foreign Policy Journal*, October 17, 2014, http://www.foreignpolicyjournal.com/2014/10/17/americas-jihad/.

23 Yockey, 'The World in Flames', February 1961; reprinted in *Yockey: Four Essays*, op. cit., VI.

author H Keith Thompson) was the rise of 'nationalist, neutralist regimes' led by 'brilliant statesmen' including in particular the 'Arab Revolt',[24] spear-headed by 'a great a vigorous man, Gamal Abdul Nasser'.[25] These final words by Yockey show a marked development of thinking away form a Eurocentric viewpoint towards an alliance with the 'Third World', perceiving in this latter a major obstacle to the hegemony of the Culture-distorters' regime. 'These personalities embody an Idea, none are out for money or publicity. They live simply, work for and live for their ideas. One such man, in a position of leadership, is a world-historical force.' Although all the leaders cited from the time — Tito, Sukarno, Nehru, and orthers — led 'weak political units', their significance was that 'in each case [....] they diminish the Jewish-American power' without augmenting the USSR or China. Yockey also saw the potential rise of Latin America as a bloc and pointed to Cuba as an encouraging sign. If neutralism were also to rise in Europe, 'America-Jewry would be defeated'. Despite his failings, de Gaulle had the most potential to become 'the spiritual leader of all Europe'.[26] Notably, de Gaulle pursued a sovereign course that was generally at loggerheads with the USA, did not join NATO and advocated a European union that embraced the USSR.

As we can now see, Yockey underestimated the pathology of Culture-distortion and Culture-retardation even in the Soviet bloc. Spiritual syphilis subverted the Soviet bloc, starting with Czechoslovakia;[27] US 'NGOs' such as the National Endowment for Democracy and Zionist agencies supported 'dissidents', Muslim militants were organised by the CIA so that Afghanistan would become 'Russia's Vietnam' and the Michel-stratum led by Gorbachev achieved the pinnacle of authority with its intention of dismantling the Soviet bloc.[28] However, Yockey might today describe Putin in similar terms to de

---

24 Not to be confused with the recent 'Arab Spring', a contrivance instigated, organised and funded by US-based globalists. See: Bolton, *Revolution from Above*, op. cit., "The Global Democratic Revolution," pp. 213–244.

25 Yockey, 'The World in Flames', op. cit.

26 Yockey, 'The World in Flames', ibid.

27 Bolton, 'Václav Havel: The "Inner Enemy"', *Counter-Currents Publishing*, http://www.counter-currents.com/2011/12/vaclav-havel-the-inner-enemy/.

28 Bolton, 'Mikhail Gorbachev: Globalist Superstar', *Foreign Policy Journal*, April 3, 2011, https://foreignpolicyjournal.com/2011/04/03/mikhail-gorbachev-globalist-super-star/view-all/.

Gaulle, as 'wanting to be equal to the masters who created him' and having 'accidentally alighted a spiritual force'.[29] Therefore, despite numerous changes on the political stage, which would appear to prove Yockey wrong in his final 'estimate of the world situation', in its broad vision his contention remains valid.

The final words… and critique… can go to Yockey's old comrade in his reassessment from the perspective of lapsed time:

> I have found in this reappraisal that time, and the passing of the years, have proved Yockey to be right and in conclusion I think the following is extremely apt. I was in Oxford, England, and as I walked through Christ Church College's War Memorial Garden, there was a tablet set in the ground. Upon it was an unsheathed sword in the same upright position as the "Sword of liberation" that formed the centrepiece of the flag of the "Europe Liberation Front". On the same tablet there were the words: "My sword I give to him that shall succeed me in my pilgrimage." Yockey could have written those words. And I can imagine him waiting for patriots to take up the sword and be proud of their spirit of the European Imperium.[30]

29 Yockey, 'The World in Flames', op. cit., VII.

30 P. J. Huxley-Blythe, 'Inside the Mind of Ulick Varange', op. cit., p. 27.

# Index

## D

## I

## O



## P

## X



## Y

## OTHER BOOKS PUBLISHED BY ARKTOS

| | |
|---|---|
| Sri Dharma Pravartaka Acharya | *The Dharma Manifesto* |
| Alain de Benoist | *Beyond Human Rights*<br>*Carl Schmitt Today*<br>*The Indo-Europeans*<br>*Manifesto for a European Renaissance*<br>*On the Brink of the Abyss*<br>*The Problem of Democracy*<br>*View from the Right* (vol. 1–3) |
| Arthur Moeller van den Bruck | *Germany's Third Empire* |
| Matt Battaglioli | *The Consequences of Equality* |
| Kerry Bolton | *Revolution from Above* |
| Isac Boman | *Money Power* |
| Ricardo Duchesne | *Faustian Man in a Multicultural Age* |
| Alexander Dugin | *Eurasian Mission: An Introduction to Neo-Eurasianism*<br>*The Fourth Political Theory*<br>*Last War of the World-Island*<br>*Putin vs Putin*<br>*The Rise of the Fourth Political Theory* |
| Koenraad Elst | *Return of the Swastika* |
| Julius Evola | *Fascism Viewed from the Right*<br>*A Handbook for Right-Wing Youth*<br>*Metaphysics of War*<br>*Notes on the Third Reich*<br>*The Path of Cinnabar*<br>*Recognitions*<br>*A Traditionalist Confronts Fascism* |
| Guillaume Faye | *Archeofuturism*<br>*Archeofuturism 2.0*<br>*The Colonisation of Europe*<br>*Convergence of Catastrophes*<br>*A Global Coup*<br>*Sex and Deviance*<br>*Understanding Islam*<br>*Why We Fight* |
| Daniel S. Forrest | *Suprahumanism* |

## OTHER BOOKS PUBLISHED BY ARKTOS

| | |
|---|---|
| Andrew Fraser | *Dissident Dispatches*<br>*The WASP Question* |
| Génération Identitaire | *We are Generation Identity* |
| Paul Gottfried | *War and Democracy* |
| Porus Homi Havewala | *The Saga of the Aryan Race* |
| Rachel Haywire | *The New Reaction* |
| Lars Holger Holm | *Hiding in Broad Daylight*<br>*Homo Maximus*<br>*Incidents of Travel in Latin America*<br>*The Owls of Afrasiab* |
| Alexander Jacob | *De Naturae Natura* |
| Jason Reza Jorjani | *Prometheus and Atlas*<br>*World State of Emergency* |
| Roderick Kaine | *Smart and SeXy* |
| Lance Kennedy | *Supranational Union and New Medievalism* |
| Peter King | *Here and Now*<br>*Keeping Things Close* |
| Ludwig Klages | *The Biocentric Worldview*<br>*Cosmogonic Reflections* |
| Pierre Krebs | *Fighting for the Essence* |
| Stephen Pax Leonard | *Travels in Cultural Nihilism* |
| Pentti Linkola | *Can Life Prevail?* |
| H. P. Lovecraft | *The Conservative* |
| Charles Maurras | *The Future of the Intelligentsia & For a French Awakening* |
| Michael O'Meara | *Guillaume Faye and the Battle of Europe*<br>*New Culture, New Right* |
| Brian Anse Patrick | *The NRA and the Media*<br>*Rise of the Anti-Media*<br>*The Ten Commandments of Propaganda*<br>*Zombology* |

## OTHER BOOKS PUBLISHED BY ARKTOS

| | |
|---|---|
| Tito Perdue | *Morning Crafts*<br>*Philip*<br>*William's House* (vol. 1–4) |
| Raido | *A Handbook of Traditional Living* |
| Steven J. Rosen | *The Agni and the Ecstasy*<br>*The Jedi in the Lotus* |
| Richard Rudgley | *Barbarians*<br>*Essential Substances*<br>*Wildest Dreams* |
| Ernst von Salomon | *It Cannot Be Stormed*<br>*The Outlaws* |
| Sri Sri Ravi Shankar | *Celebrating Silence*<br>*Know Your Child*<br>*Management Mantras*<br>*Patanjali Yoga Sutras*<br>*Secrets of Relationships* |
| Troy Southgate | *Tradition & Revolution* |
| Oswald Spengler | *Man and Technics* |
| Tomislav Sunic | *Against Democracy and Equality*<br>*Postmortem Report*<br>*Titans are in Town* |
| Hans-Jürgen Syberberg | *On the Fortunes and Misfortunes of Art in Post-War Germany* |
| Abir Taha | *Defining Terrorism: The End of Double Standards*<br>*The Epic of Arya* (2nd ed.)<br>*Nietzsche's Coming God, or the Redemption of the Divine*<br>*Verses of Light* |
| Bal Gangadhar Tilak | *The Arctic Home in the Vedas* |
| Dominique Venner | *For a Positive Critique*<br>*The Shock of History* |
| Markus Willinger | *A Europe of Nations*<br>*Generation Identity* |
| David J. Wingfield (ed.) | *The Initiate: Journal of Traditional Studies* |

Made in the USA
Columbia, SC
28 September 2023

23511888R00369